TRANSLATOR AND SENIOR EDITOR:
Rabbi Israel V. Berman

MANAGING EDITOR:
Baruch Goldberg

EDITOR:
Rabbi David Strauss

ASSOCIATE EDITOR:
Dr. Jeffrey M. Green

COPY EDITOR:
Alec Israel

BOOK DESIGNER:
Ben Gasner

GRAPHIC ARTIST:
Michael Etkin

TECHNICAL STAFF:
Moshe Greenvald
Inna Schwartzman

Random House Staff

PRODUCTION MANAGER:
Kathy Rosenbloom

ART DIRECTOR:
Bernard Klein

CHIEF COPY EDITOR:
Amy Edelman

THE TALMUD
THE STEINSALTZ EDITION

VOLUME XIV
TRACTATE TA'ANIT
PART II

VOLUME XIV
TRACTATE TA'ANIT
PART II

RANDOM HOUSE
NEW YORK

THE TALMUD

תלמוד בבלי

THE STEINSALTZ EDITION

Commentary by Rabbi Adin Steinsaltz (Even Yisrael)

Published in the United States by Random House, Inc., New York,
and simultaneously in Canada by Random House of Canada Limited, Toronto.

Originally published in Hebrew by the Israel Institute for Talmudic Publications, Jerusalem.

Library of Congress Cataloging-in-Publication Data
(Revised for volume XIV)
The Talmud.
English, Hebrew, and Aramaic.
Includes bibliographical references.
v.14. Tractate Ta'anit, pt. 2.
Accompanied by a reference guide.
1. Title.
BM499.5.E4 1989 89-842911
ISBN 0-679-44398-3

Manufactured in the United States of America on acid-free paper
9 8 7 6 5 4 3 2
First U.S. Edition

In loving memory

of

Edith Silberberg Guttman

and

Ida Guttman Berman

"וְהַחוּט הַמְשֻׁלָּשׁ לֹא בִמְהֵרָה יִנָּתֵק" (קהלת ד, יב).

"And a threefold cord is not quickly broken." (Ecclesiastes 4:12)

This volume is dedicated by

Carol Kaufman Newman

and

Melvin David Newman

with gratitude and love to our parents

for teaching us the love of learning

מִדּוֹר לְדוֹר

and to our children, who have enriched our lives.

May they continue to pass this tradition on to the next generation.

The Steinsaltz Talmud in English

The English edition of the Steinsaltz Talmud is a translation and adaptation of the Hebrew edition. It includes most of the additions and improvements that characterize the Hebrew version, but it has been adapted and expanded especially for the English reader. This edition has been designed to meet the needs of advanced students capable of studying from standard Talmud editions, as well as of beginners, who know little or no Hebrew and have had no prior training in studying the Talmud.

The overall structure of the page is similar to that of the traditional pages in the standard printed editions. The text is placed in the center of the page, and alongside it are the main auxiliary commentaries. At the bottom of the page and in the margins are additions and supplements.

The original Hebrew-Aramaic text, which is framed in the center of each page, is exactly the same as that in the traditional Talmud (although material that was removed by non-Jewish censors has been restored on the basis of manuscripts and old printed editions). The main innovation is that this Hebrew-Aramaic text has been completely vocalized and punctuated, and all the terms usually abbreviated have been fully spelled out. In order to retain the connection with the page numbers of the standard editions, these are indicated at the head of every page.

We have placed a *Literal Translation* on the right-hand side of the page, and its punctuation has been introduced into the Talmud text, further helping the student to orientate himself. The *Literal Translation* is intended to help the student to learn the meaning of specific Hebrew and Aramaic words. By comparing the original text with this translation, the reader develops an understanding of the Talmudic text and can follow the words and sentences in the original. Occasionally, however, it has not been possible to present an exact literal translation of the original text, because it is so different in structure from English. Therefore we have added certain auxiliary words, which are indicated in square brackets. In other cases it would make no sense to offer a literal translation of a Talmudic idiom, so we have provided a close English equivalent of the original meaning, while a note, marked "lit.," explaining the literal meaning of the words, appears in parentheses. Our purpose in presenting this literal translation was to give the student an appreciation of the terse and enigmatic nature of the Talmud itself, before the arguments are opened up by interpretation.

Nevertheless, no one can study the Talmud without the assistance of commentaries. The main aid to understanding the Talmud provided by this edition is the *Translation and Commentary,* appearing on the left side of the page. This is Rabbi Adin Steinsaltz's highly regarded Hebrew interpretation of the Talmud, translated into English, adapted and expanded.

This commentary is not merely an explanation of difficult passages. It is an integrated exposition of the entire text. It includes a full translation of the Talmud text, combined with explanatory remarks. Where the translation in the commentary reflects the literal translation, it has been set off in bold type. It has also been given the same reference numbers that are found both in the original text and in the literal translation. Moreover, each section of the commentary begins with a few words of the Hebrew-Aramaic text. These reference numbers and paragraph headings allow the reader to move from one part of the page to another with ease.

There are some slight variations between the literal translation and the words in bold face appearing in the *Translation and Commentary.* These variations are meant to enhance understanding, for a juxtaposition of the literal translation and the sometimes freer translation in the commentary will give the reader a firmer grasp of the meaning.

The expanded *Translation and Commentary* in the left-hand column is intended to provide a conceptual understanding of the arguments of the Talmud, their form, content, context, and significance. The commentary also brings out the logic of the questions asked by the Sages and the assumptions they made.

Rashi's traditional commentary has been included in the right-hand column, under the *Literal Translation*. We have left this commentary in the traditional "Rashi script," but all quotations of the Talmud text appear in standard square type, the abbreviated expressions have all been printed in full, and Rashi's commentary is fully punctuated.

Since the *Translation and Commentary* cannot remain cogent and still encompass all the complex issues that arise in the Talmudic discussion, we have included a number of other features, which are also found in Rabbi Steinsaltz's Hebrew edition.

At the bottom of the page, under the *Translation and Commentary*, is the *Notes* section, containing additional material on issues raised in the text. These notes deepen understanding of the Talmud in various ways. Some provide a deeper and more profound analysis of the issues discussed in the text, with regard to individual points and to the development of the entire discussion. Others explain Halakhic concepts and the terms of Talmudic discourse.

The *Notes* contain brief summaries of the opinions of many of the major commentators on the Talmud, from the period after the completion of the Talmud to the present. Frequently the *Notes* offer interpretations different from that presented in the commentary, illustrating the richness and depth of Rabbinic thought.

The *Halakhah* section appears below the *Notes.* This provides references to the authoritative legal decisions reached over the centuries by the Rabbis in their discussions of the matters dealt with in the Talmud. It explains what reasons led to these Halakhic decisions and the close connection between the Halakhah today and the Talmud and its various interpreters. It should be noted that the summary of the Halakhah presented here is not meant to serve as a reference source for actual religious practice but to introduce the reader to Halakhic conclusions drawn from the Talmudic text.

English commentary and expanded translation of the text, making it readable and comprehensible

Hebrew/Aramaic text of the Talmud, fully vocalized, and punctuated

Literal translation of the Talmud text into English

REALIA

קַלְתָּהּ **Her basket.** The source of this word is the Greek κάλαθος, kalathos, and it means a basket with a narrow base.

Illustration from a Greek drawing depicting such a basket of fruit.

CONCEPTS

פֵּאָה ***Pe'ah.* One of the presents left for the poor (מַתְּנוֹת עֲנִיִּים).** The Torah forbids harvesting "the corners of your field," so that the produce left standing may be harvested and kept by the poor (Leviticus 19:9).

The Torah did not specify a minimum amount of produce to be left as *pe'ah*. But the Sages stipulated that it must be at least one-sixtieth of the crop.

Pe'ah is set aside only from crops that ripen at one time and are harvested at one time. The poor are allowed to use their own initiative to reap the *pe'ah* left in the fields. But the owner of an orchard must see to it that each of the poor gets a fixed share of the *pe'ah* from places that are difficult to reach. The poor come to collect *pe'ah* three times a day. The laws of *pe'ah* are discussed in detail in tractate *Pe'ah*.

Marginal notes provide essential background information

TRANSLATION AND COMMENTARY

[1]**and her husband threw her a bill of divorce into her lap or into her basket,** which she was carrying on her head, [2]would you say **here, too,** that **she would not be divorced**? Surely we know that the law is that she *is* divorced in such a case, as the Mishnah (*Gittin* 77a) states explicitly!

אֲמַר לֵיהּ [3]Rav Ashi **said** in reply to Ravina: The woman's **basket is** considered to be **at rest, and it is she who walks beneath it.** Thus the basket is considered to be a "stationary courtyard," and the woman acquires whatever is thrown into it.

MISHNAH הָיָה רוֹכֵב [4]**If a person was riding on an animal and he saw an ownerless object** lying on the ground, **and he said to another person** standing nearby, **"Give that object to me,"** [5]if **the other person took** the ownerless object **and said, "I have acquired it for myself,"** [6]he has **acquired it** by lifting it up, even though he was not the first to see it, and the rider has no claim to it. [7]But **if, after he gave** the object **to** the rider, the person who picked it up **said, "I acquired** the object **first,"** [8]**he** in fact **said nothing.** His words are of no effect, and the rider may keep it. Since the person walking showed no intention of acquiring the object when he originally picked it up, he is not now believed when he claims that he acquired it first. Indeed, even if we maintain that when a person picks up an ownerless object on behalf of someone else, the latter does *not* acquire it automatically, here, by *giving* the object to the rider, he makes a gift of it to the rider.

GEMARA תְּנַן הָתָם [9]**We have learned elsewhere** in a Mishnah in tractate *Pe'ah* (4:9): **"Someone who gathered *pe'ah*** — produce which by Torah law [Leviticus 23:22] is left unharvested in the corner of a field by the owner of the field, to be gleaned by the poor — **and said, 'Behold, this *pe'ah*** which I have gleaned **is intended for so-and-so the poor man,'** [10]**Rabbi Eliezer says:** The person who gathered the *pe'ah* **has acquired it**

בִּרְשׁוּת הָרַבִּים [1]וְזָרַק לָהּ גֵּט לְתוֹךְ חֵיקָהּ אוֹ לְתוֹךְ קַלְתָּהּ — [2]הָכָא נַמִי דְּלָא מִגָּרְשָׁה? [3]אֲמַר לֵיהּ: קַלְתָּהּ מֵינָח נַיְיחָא, וְאִיהִי דְּקָא מְסַגְּיָא מִתּוּתָהּ.

משנה [4]הָיָה רוֹכֵב עַל גַּבֵּי בְהֵמָה וְרָאָה אֶת הַמְּצִיאָה, וְאָמַר לַחֲבֵירוֹ "תְּנָה לִי", [5]נְטָלָהּ וְאָמַר, "אֲנִי זָכִיתִי בָּהּ", [6]זָכָה בָהּ. [7]אִם, מִשֶּׁנְּתָנָהּ לוֹ, אָמַר, "אֲנִי זָכִיתִי בָּהּ תְּחִלָּה", [8]לֹא אָמַר כְּלוּם.

גמרא [9]תְּנַן הָתָם: "מִי שֶׁלִּיקֵּט אֶת הַפֵּאָה וְאָמַר, 'הֲרֵי זוֹ לִפְלוֹנִי עָנִי', [10]רַבִּי אֱלִיעֶזֶר

LITERAL TRANSLATION

in a public thoroughfare [1]and [her husband] threw her a bill of divorce into her lap or into her basket, [2]here, too, would she not be divorced? [3]He said to him: Her basket is at rest, and it is she who walks beneath it.

MISHNAH [4][If a person] was riding on an animal and he saw a found object, and he said to another person, "Give it to me," [5][and the other person] took it and said, "I have acquired it," [6]he has acquired it. [7]If, after he gave it to him, he said, "I acquired it first," [8]he said nothing.

GEMARA [9]We have learned there: "Someone who gathered *pe'ah* and said, 'Behold this is for so-and-so the poor man,' [10]Rabbi Eliezer says:

RASHI

קלתה – סל שעל ראשה, שנותנת בה כלי מלאכתה וטווי שלה. הכי נמי דלא הוי גיטא – והאנן תנן במסכת גיטין (עז,א): זרק לה גיטה לתוך חיקה או לתוך קלתה – הרי זו מגורשת!

משנה לא אמר כלום – דאפילו אמרינן המגביה מציאה לחבירו לא קנה חבירו, כיון דיהבה ליה – קנייה ממה נפשך. אי קנייה קמא דלא מתכוין להקנות לחבירו – הא יהבה ניהליה במתנה. ואי לא קנייה קמא משום דלא היה מתכוין לקנות – הויא ליה הפקר עד דמטא לידיה דהאי, וקנייה האי במאי דעקרה מידיה דקמא לשם קנייה.

גמרא מי שליקט את הפאה – אדם בעלמא שאינו בעל שדה. דאי בבעל שדה – לא אמר רבי אליעזר זכה. דליכא למימר "מגו דזכי לנפשיה", דאפילו הוא עני מוזהר הוא שלא ללקט פאה משדה שלו, כדאמר בשחיטת חולין (קלא,ב): "לא תלקט לעני" – להזהיר עני על שלו.

Hebrew commentary of Rashi, the classic explanation that accompanies all editions of the Talmud

Numbers link the three main sections of the page and allow readers to refer rapidly from one to the other

NOTES

מִי שֶׁלִּיקֵּט אֶת הַפֵּאָה **If a person gathered *pe'ah*.** According to *Rashi*, the Mishnah must be referring to someone other than the owner of the field. By Torah law the owner of a field is required to separate part of his field as *pe'ah*, even if he himself is poor, and he may not take the *pe'ah* for himself. Therefore the "since" (מִגּוֹ) argument

HALAKHAH

קַלְתָּהּ **A woman's basket.** "If a man throws a bill of divorce into a container that his wife is holding, she thereby acquires the bill of divorce and the divorce takes effect." (*Shulḥan Arukh, Even HaEzer* 139:10.)

הַמְלַקֵּט פֵּאָה עֲבוּר אַחֵר **A person who gathered *pe'ah* for someone else.** "If a poor person, who is himself entitled to collect *pe'ah*, gathered *pe'ah* for another poor person, and said, 'This *pe'ah* is for X, the poor person,' he acquires the *pe'ah* on behalf of that other poor person. But if the person who collected the *peah* was wealthy, he does not acquire the *pe'ah* on behalf of the poor person. He must give it instead to the first poor person who appears in the field," following the opinion of the Sages, as explained by Rabbi Yehoshua ben Levi. (*Rambam, Sefer Zeraim, Hilkhot Mattenot Aniyyim* 2:19.)

Notes highlight points of interest in the text and expand the discussion by quoting other classical commentaries

On the outer margin of the page, factual information clarifying the meaning of the Talmudic discussion is presented. Entries under the heading *Language* explain unusual terms, often borrowed from Greek, Latin, or Persian. *Sages* gives brief biographies of the major figures whose opinions are presented in the Talmud. *Terminology* explains the terms used in the Talmudic discussion. *Concepts* gives information about fundamental Halakhic principles. *Background* provides historical, geographical, and other information needed to understand the text. *Realia* explains the artifacts mentioned in the text. These notes are sometimes accompanied by illustrations.

The best way of studying the Talmud is the way in which the Talmud itself evolved - a combination of frontal teaching and continuous interaction between teacher and pupil, and between pupils themselves.

This edition is meant for a broad spectrum of users, from those who have considerable prior background and who know how to study the Talmud from any standard edition to those who have never studied the Talmud and do not even know Hebrew.

The division of the page into various sections is designed to enable students of every kind to derive the greatest possible benefit from it.

For those who know how to study the Talmud, the book is intended to be a written Gemara lesson, so that, either alone, with partners, or in groups, they can have the sense of studying with a teacher who explains the difficult passages and deepens their understanding both of the development of the dialectic and also of the various approaches that have been taken by the Rabbis over the centuries in interpreting the material. A student of this kind can start with the Hebrew-Aramaic text, examine Rashi's commentary, and pass on from there to the expanded commentary. Afterwards the student can turn to the Notes section. Study of the *Halakhah* section will clarify the conclusions reached in the course of establishing the Halakhah, and the other items in the margins will be helpful whenever the need arises to clarify a concept or a word or to understand the background of the discussion.

For those who do not possess sufficient knowledge to be able to use a standard edition of the Talmud, but who know how to read Hebrew, a different method is proposed. Such students can begin by reading the Hebrew-Aramaic text and comparing it immediately to the *Literal Translation*. They can then move over to the *Translation and Commentary*, which refers both to the original text and to the *Literal Translation*. Such students would also do well to read through the *Notes* and choose those that explain matters at greater length. They will benefit, too, from the terms explained in the side margins.

The beginner who does not know Hebrew well enough to grapple with the original can start with the *Translation and Commentary*. The inclusion of a translation within the commentary permits the student to ignore the *Literal Translation*, since the commentary includes both the Talmudic text and an interpretation of it. The beginner can also benefit from the *Notes*, and it is important for him to go over the marginal notes on the concepts to improve his awareness of the juridical background and the methods of study characteristic of this text.

Apart from its use as study material, this book can also be useful to those well versed in the Talmud, as a source of additional knowledge in various areas, both for understanding the historical and archeological background and also for an explanation of words and concepts. The general reader, too, who might not plan to study the book from beginning to end, can find a great deal of interesting material in it regarding both the spiritual world of Judaism, practical Jewish law, and the life and customs of the Jewish people during the thousand years (500 B.C.E.–500 C.E.) of the Talmudic period.

Contents

THE TALMUD

THE STEINSALTZ EDITION

VOLUME XIV

TRACTATE TA'ANIT

PART II

Introduction to Chapter Two

סֵדֶר תַּעֲנִיּוֹת כֵּיצַד

"When heaven is shut up, and there is no rain, because they have sinned against You, if they pray toward this place and confess Your name, and turn from their sin when You afflict them, then hear in heaven, and forgive the sin of Your servants and of Your people Israel, that You teach them the good way in which they should walk, and give rain upon Your land, which You have given to Your people as an inheritance." (I Kings 8:35-36.)

"Blow the shofar in Zion, sanctify a fast, call a solemn assembly. Gather the people, sanctify the congregation, assemble the elders, gather the children and those who suck the breasts, let the bridegroom go forth from his room, and the bride from her chamber. Let the priests, the ministers of the Lord, weep between the porch and the altar, and let them say, Spare Your people, O Lord, and give not Your heritage to reproach, that the nations should rule over them. Why should they say among the peoples, Where is their God? Then the Lord was zealous for his land, and pitied his people. And the Lord answered and said to His people, Behold, I will send you corn, and wine, and oil, and you shall be satisfied therewith, and I will no more make you a reproach among the nations." (Joel 2:15-19.)

Abstaining from food and drink on a public fast-day is not an end in itself, but the means by which the community is to arrive at a spiritual awakening and true repentance. To achieve these goals, the Rabbis enacted a fixed service to be observed on the public fasts. In addition to abstention from food and drink, special supplications were inserted into the regular prayer service, and numerous rituals were observed in order to emphasize the importance of the fast and to bring about improvements in the people's conduct and morality. These aspects of the fast took on special significance on the more stringent public fasts which were observed in times of drought or other impending danger, when there was particular need for sincere repentance.

In this chapter we find a description of the prayer service followed on the more stringent public fasts. The various rituals that accompanied the prayers and were supposed to lead the community to repentance are described in great detail. Emphasis is placed on the text of the special blessings that were inserted into the regular prayer service on these fasts, and on the manner in which these blessings were recited by the prayer leader.

This chapter also considers the days on which public fasts are not to be observed, and those individuals to whom the obligation to participate in the public fast does not apply. In addition to Shabbat and the major Festivals, on which fasting and any public demonstration of mourning or distress is forbidden by Torah law, there are other semi-festive days on which fasting is prohibited, whether by common custom or by Rabbinic enactment. There are also various categories of people who are exempt from participating in public fasts, whether on account of weakness or illness, or of their involvement in certain religious activities. The question of whether to give priority to the prohibition against fasting on certain days or to the obligation to observe a communal fast in times of impending calamity, as well as the issue of the relative importance of the religious activities in which certain people are engaged vis-à-vis their obligation to participate in the community's distress, are among the major topics of discussion in this chapter.

סֵדֶר

[1]תַּעֲנִיּוֹת כֵּיצַד? [2]מוֹצִיאִין אֶת הַתֵּיבָה לִרְחוֹבָהּ שֶׁל עִיר, [3]וְנוֹתְנִין אֵפֶר מִקְלֶה עַל גַּבֵּי הַתֵּיבָה, [4]וּבְרֹאשׁ הַנָּשִׂיא, וּבְרֹאשׁ אַב בֵּית דִּין, [5]וְכָל אֶחָד וְאֶחָד נוֹתֵן בְּרֹאשׁוֹ.

[6]הַזָּקֵן שֶׁבָּהֶן אוֹמֵר לִפְנֵיהֶן דִּבְרֵי כִבּוּשִׁין: [7]״אַחֵינוּ, לֹא נֶאֱמַר בְּאַנְשֵׁי נִינְוֵה: [8]׳וַיַּרְא אֱלֹהִים אֶת שַׂקָּם וְאֶת תַּעֲנִיתָם׳, [9]אֶלָּא: ׳וַיַּרְא הָאֱלֹהִים אֶת מַעֲשֵׂיהֶם, כִּי שָׁבוּ מִדַּרְכָּם הָרָעָה׳. [10]וּבַקַּבָּלָה הוּא

LITERAL TRANSLATION

MISHNAH [1]What (lit., "how") is the order [of service] on fasts? [2]They carry the ark out to the open area of the town, [3]and they place burnt ashes on the ark, [4]and on the head of the Nasi, and on the head of the president of the court, [5]and each and every one [else] places [ashes] on his head.

[6]The elder among them says before them words of admonition: [7]"Our brothers, it is not said about the people of Nineveh: [8]'And God saw their sackcloth and their fast,' [9]but rather: 'And God saw their deeds, that they had returned from their evil way.' [10]And in the Prophets (lit., 'the tradition')

TRANSLATION AND COMMENTARY

MISHNAH סֵדֶר תַּעֲנִיּוֹת We learned in the previous chapter (above, 10a) that if the beginning of the month of Kislev has arrived and it has not yet rained, the court decrees a series of three fasts to be observed by the entire community. If this first series of fasts has passed and it has still not rained, the court decrees a second series of three fasts upon the entire community. And if the second series of fasts has passed and it has still not rained, the court decrees upon the entire community an additional seven fasts (see above, 12b). On these last seven fasts there is a special order of prayer. Our Mishnah opens with a detailed description of the special prayers recited on these fasts, and of the various customs, intended to induce sincere repentance, which accompany the service. [1]**What is the order of** the **service on** these final seven **fasts?** In Mishnaic and Talmudic times the holy ark in which the Torah scroll was kept was not a fixed structure in the synagogue as it is today. Rather, it was a portable box which was kept in a locked room adjoining the synagogue and was brought into the synagogue during the prayer services. [2]On the final seven fasts, **the ark,** together with the Torah scroll that is kept inside it, **is carried out to the town square** where the special prayer service is conducted. [3]**Burnt ashes are placed on the ark** in order to invoke among the participants feelings of grief and humility. [4]Ashes are then placed **on the heads of** the most important members of the community, **the Nasi and the president of the court.** [5]**Each and every person** present then **places ashes on his** own **head.**

הַזָּקֵן [6]**The elder among** those assembled at the service stands up before the congregation and **rebukes them with words of admonition** in order to arouse sincere repentance. He speaks to them as follows: [7]**"Brothers,** wearing sackcloth and fasting is not an end in itself, but only a means by which a person can repent for his sins. True repentance manifests itself in a change in a person's deeds. For **it does not say concerning the people of Nineveh:** [8]**'And God saw their sackcloth and their fast,'** [9]**but rather** it says [Jonah 3:10]: **'And God saw their deeds, that they had returned from their evil way.'** [10]The same idea is also found **in** another passage

RASHI

משנה סדר תעניות כיצד כו׳. **אפר מקלה** — אפר ממש ולא עפר. ״אפר״ סתם הוא עפר, דכשם שאפר קרוי עפר, דכתיב (במדבר יט) ״מעפר שרפת החטאת״ כך עפר קרוי אפר סתם, והיינו דקתני ״אפר מקלה״ — אפר שריפה. אי הוה תני ״אפר״ סתם — הוה משמע עפר. ואפר מקלה גנאי יותר מעפר סתם, ובגמרא מפרש מאי טעמא נותנין אותו. **כבושין** — לשון עצירה, כמו מכבש, בלעז *פריש״א — שכובשין את הלבבות להחזירם למוטב, ואלו הן דברי כבושין: אחינו כו׳. **ובקבלה** — שהנביא מוכיח לישראל (עמדו בתפלה). והקשה תוספות מאן דהו: מאי שנא בהאי קרא דכתיב ביונה ״וירא האלהים את מעשיהם״ וגו׳ ולא קרי ליה ״דברי קבלה״, ובהאי קרא ד״וקרעו לבבכם״ קרי ליה ״קבלה״? ופריק איהו: כל מקום שהנביא מוכיח ומודיע ומזהיר את ישראל — קרי ליה ״קבלה,״ ובכל דוכתא דלא איתפקד נביא כי האי ״וירא האלהים״ שהוא כמספר והולך, דיליף מיניה אגב אורחיה מילתא — לא קרינן ליה ״קבלה״. **ברחובה של עיר** — בגלוי, וכי הך דאמרינן במסכת מגילה (כה,ב): בני העיר שמכרו רחובה של עיר, והתם מפרש בהדיא, אמר רבי זירא: הואיל והעם מתפללים בו בתעניות ובמעמדות.

CONCEPTS

קַבָּלָה **Prophets** (lit., "tradition"). This term is used in various places in the Talmud to designate the words of the Prophets. The term has several interpretations. Some authorities explain that it means that the words of the Prophets are not their own but received. In general terms Moses is regarded as the father of the Prophets, and all the subsequent Prophets are regarded as receiving the divine message by virtue of his illumination. Another interpretation understands *kabbalah* as being derived from the root קבל, meaning "to complain." Hence the words of the Prophets are *kabbalah* because they complain about the sins of the Jewish people.

LANGUAGE (RASHI)

פריש״א* From the Old French *presse*, meaning "a clothes press."

NOTES

אֵפֶר מִקְלֶה **Burnt ashes.** *Rashi* and others explain that the expression אֵפֶר מִקְלֶה ("burnt ashes") is used here because the unqualified term אֵפֶר can refer either to ashes or to ordinary earth, and the Mishnah wishes to inform us that

HALAKHAH

סֵדֶר תַּעֲנִיּוֹת **The order of service on fasts.** "On each of the last seven fasts decreed upon the community in times of drought, the ark is taken out into the open area of the town. All the people congregate and cover themselves

TRANSLATION AND COMMENTARY

in **the Prophets,** for **the verse says** [Joel 2:13]: **'And rend your heart, and not your garments,** and return to the Lord your God.'"

עָמְדוּ בִתְפִלָּה ¹When the elder has finished admonishing the assembled congregation, **they stand up** in their places in the town square and prepare themselves for **prayer.** Special care is taken in appointing a prayer leader to lead the service on these fast days. ²Thus, when **they appoint** a person **to come down before the ark** and lead the service, they choose **an elder, who is well versed in the prayers** and will be able to recite the special liturgy fluently.

³The prayer leader must also be a person **who has children** who are financially dependent upon him, **and** a person **whose house is empty** of riches, so that he has difficulty in supporting himself and his family. **⁴The heart** of such a person **will** surely **be perfectly** sincere **during the prayer** service, because he and his family are themselves in dire need of divine help.

וְאוֹמֵר לִפְנֵיהֶן ⁵The central feature of the prayer service is the Amidah (lit., "standing") prayer, also known as the *Shemoneh Esreh* (lit., "Eighteen"). The name derives from the number of blessings originally included in the prayer. (After the destruction of the Second Temple a nineteenth blessing was added.) The Amidah prayer is recited silently by the congregation, and is then repeated aloud by the prayer leader. When the prayer leader repeats the Amidah prayer on these last seven fast days, **he recites twenty-four blessings —** **⁶the eighteen** blessings that are recited **every day and another six** blessings **which he adds** between the seventh blessing, "Redeemer of Israel," and the eighth blessing, "Who heals the sick of His people Israel." **⁷**The six additional blessings that are inserted into the Amidah prayer **are as follows:** (1) *Zikhronot* (lit., "remembrances") — a blessing (also added to the musaf service on Rosh HaShanah) containing verses from the Pentateuch, the Prophets, and the Writings, praising God for remembering His people (for example, Noah during the flood, the Jewish people in Egypt, His covenant with Abraham, Isaac and Jacob, and the

LITERAL TRANSLATION

it says: 'And rend your heart, and not your garments.'"

¹They stand up in prayer. ²They send down before the ark an elder, who is well versed [in the prayers], ³and who has children, and whose house is empty, ⁴so that his heart will be perfect in the prayer.

⁵And he says before them twenty-four blessings, ⁶the eighteen of every day, and he adds to them another six. ⁷And these are they: Zikhronot;

אוֹמֵר: 'וְקִרְעוּ לְבַבְכֶם, וְאַל
בִּגְדֵיכֶם'״.
¹עָמְדוּ בִתְפִלָּה. ²מוֹרִידִין לִפְנֵי
הַתֵּיבָה זָקֵן, וְרָגִיל, ³וְיֵשׁ לוֹ
בָּנִים, וּבֵיתוֹ רֵיקָם, ⁴כְּדֵי שֶׁיְּהֵא
לִבּוֹ שָׁלֵם בִּתְפִלָּה.
⁵וְאוֹמֵר לִפְנֵיהֶן עֶשְׂרִים וְאַרְבַּע
בְּרָכוֹת, ⁶שְׁמוֹנֶה עֶשְׂרֵה שֶׁבְּכָל
יוֹם, וּמוֹסִיף עֲלֵיהֶן עוֹד
שֵׁשׁ. ⁷וְאֵלּוּ הֵן: זִכְרוֹנוֹת;

RASHI

וְרָגִיל — רגיל להתפלל, ותפלתו שגורה בפיו ולא יטעה, שכל חזן שטועה סימן רע לשולחיו. וביתו ריקם — משמע דהוא עני, ואין לו מחיה בביתו. ונגמרא מפרש טעמא אחרינא: וגופו נקי מעבירות, שלא חטא, ולא יצא עליו שום שם רע בשום עבירה כו'.

NOTES

ashes and not ordinary earth must be placed on the ark and on the heads of the people assembled for the special fast-day service. Ashes must be used rather than earth, because placing ashes on one's head is a more humbling act than placing ordinary earth. *Meiri* and *Rashbam* (*Bava Batra* 60b) explain that the term אֵפֶר מִקְלֶה refers to ordinary ashes — whatever remains of the coals used to fire a stove, to the exclusion of the ashes of the Red Heifer. *Tosafot* (below, 15b and 16a) maintains that the term "burnt ashes" refers to ashes of human bones.

וּבְקַבָּלָה הוּא אוֹמֵר **And in the Prophets it says.** The term קַבָּלָה usually denotes the words of the Prophets. Elsewhere (*Ḥullin* 137a), *Rashi* explains that the Five Books of Moses are called Torah, because they are the teachings given to

Israel for all generations, whereas the prophetic books are called "Kabbalah," because the prophecies contained in them were received by means of the divine spirit in accordance with the needs of the time, the generation, and the specific circumstances. An additional remark inserted here into *Rashi's* commentary notes that the Mishnah cites two verses, one from Jonah and one from Joel, but it is only the second verse that the Mishnah says is found in "the Kabbalah." That note explains that the term "Kabbalah" is used whenever the prophet issues a command or admonishes the people of Israel. Thus the verse, "And rend your heart, and not your garments," is described as being found in "the Kabbalah." But that term is not employed with respect to the verse, "And God saw their deeds," which merely tells a story.

HALAKHAH

with sackcloth. Ashes are placed on the ark, as well as on the Torah scroll contained in it. Ashes are placed on the heads of the Nasi and the president of the court on the spot where the tefillin are worn, after which each and every other person places ashes on his own head. An elder who is a

Sage is appointed to admonish the congregation, telling them that wearing sackcloth and fasting will not save them, but only repentance and good deeds. When the admonition has been completed, the people stand up and the prayer service begins." (*Shulḥan Arukh, Oraḥ Ḥayyim* 579:1.)

[1]וְשׁוֹפָרוֹת; [2]"אֶל ה' בַּצָּרָתָה לִּי קָרָאתִי, וַיַּעֲנֵנִי"; [3]"אֶשָּׂא עֵינַי אֶל הֶהָרִים, וגו'"; [4]"מִמַּעֲמַקִּים קְרָאתִיךָ, ה'"; [5]"תְּפִלָּה לְעָנִי, כִּי יַעֲטֹף". [6]רַבִּי יְהוּדָה אוֹמֵר: לֹא הָיָה צָרִיךְ לוֹמַר זִכְרוֹנוֹת וְשׁוֹפָרוֹת. [7]אֶלָּא אוֹמֵר תַּחְתֵּיהֶן: [8]"רָעָב כִּי יִהְיֶה בָאָרֶץ, דֶּבֶר כִּי יִהְיֶה", [9]"אֲשֶׁר הָיָה דְבַר ה' אֶל יִרְמְיָהוּ עַל דִּבְרֵי הַבַּצָּרוֹת".

[10]וְאוֹמֵר חוֹתְמֵיהֶן. [11]עַל הָרִאשׁוֹנָה הוּא אוֹמֵר: "מִי שֶׁעָנָה אֶת אַבְרָהָם בְּהַר הַמּוֹרִיָּה, הוּא יַעֲנֶה אֶתְכֶם וְיִשְׁמַע בְּקוֹל צַעֲקַתְכֶם הַיּוֹם

LITERAL TRANSLATION

[1]and *Shofarot*; [2]"In my distress, I cried to the Lord, and He answered me"; [3]"I will lift up my eyes to the hills, etc."; [4]"Out of the depths I have cried to You, O Lord"; [5]"A prayer of the afflicted, when he faints." [6]Rabbi Yehudah says: It is not necessary to say *Zikhronot* and *Shofarot*. [7]Rather, he says instead of them: [8]"If there be famine in the land, if there be pestilence," [and]: [9]"The word of the Lord that came to Jeremiah concerning the droughts."

[10]And he says their endings. [11]For the first he says: "He Who answered Abraham on Mount Moriah, He will answer you and will hearken unto the sound of your crying [on] this day.

TRANSLATION AND COMMENTARY

binding of Isaac). (2) [1]***Shofarot*** (lit., "shofars") — a blessing (also added to the Musaf service on Rosh HaShanah) containing Biblical verses that mention the shofar and express the hope of redemption to be heralded by the sound of the shofar. (3) [2]A blessing containing Psalm 120, **"In my distress, I cried to the Lord, and He answered me,"** and a concluding formula, as will be explained below. (4) [3]A blessing containing Psalm 121, **"I will lift up my eyes to the hills;** from whence does my help come," and a concluding formula. (5) [4]A blessing containing Psalm 130, **"Out of the depths I have cried to You, O Lord,"** and a concluding formula. (6) [5]A blessing containing Psalm 102, **"A prayer of the afflicted, when he faints,"** and a concluding formula. [6]**Rabbi Yehudah says:** The prayer leader **does not recite** the blessings of ***Zikhronot*** **and** ***Shofarot*** on the fast days decreed on account of drought, for these blessings are recited only on Rosh HaShanah, on Yom Kippur of the Jubilee Year, and during times of war. [7]**Rather, in their place** the prayer leader **says** the following blessings that relate directly to the calamity that is at present threatening the community: A blessing containing the Biblical portion beginning with the verse (I Kings 8:37): [8]**"If there be famine in the land, if there be pestilence,"** [9]**and** a blessing containing the Biblical passage beginning with the verse (Jeremiah 14:1): **"The word of the Lord that came to Jeremiah concerning the droughts."**

וְאוֹמֵר חוֹתְמֵיהֶן [10]When the prayer leader repeats the Amidah prayer, he recites an expanded version of the seventh blessing, "Redeemer of Israel," and then continues with the six additional blessings that are inserted into the service. At the conclusion of each of these seven blessings, the prayer leader **recites an** appropriate **concluding formula.** [11]**At** the end of **the first** of this series of blessings, the seventh blessing of the Amidah, the prayer leader **says: "He who answered Abraham on Mount Moriah, He will answer you and will hearken unto the sound of your crying on this day. Blessed are You, O Lord, the redeemer of Israel."**

RASHI

זכרונות ושופרות – כל הפסוקים שאומרים בראש השנה. **אל ה' בצרתה לי כו'** – כולן הן מזמורים. **ואומר חותמיהן** – על כל פרשה ופרשה, אחר זכרונות – חתימת זכרונות, ואחר שופרות – חתימת שופרות, וכן אחר כולם מעין הפרשה, כדמפרש ואזיל. **על הראשונה** – דהיינו ראשונה הוא אומר: מי שענה לאברהם כו', ב"גואל ישראל" היה מתחיל להאריך, והולך ואומר לכולן שש ברכות.

CONCEPTS

זִכְרוֹנוֹת וְשׁוֹפָרוֹת *Zikhronot* and *Shofarot*. *Zikhronot* and *Shofarot* are the names of two of the three long blessings recited during the musaf prayer on Rosh HaShanah. Both of these benedictions contain a series of ten Biblical quotations from the Torah, the Prophets, and the Writings. The *Zikhronot* blessing tells us that God remembers mankind and watches over us. The *Shofarot* blessing deals mainly with divine revelation in the world, and especially to the Jews, in the past and in the future.

NOTES

לֹא הָיָה צָרִיךְ לוֹמַר It is not necessary to say. *Ritva* suggests that Rabbi Yehudah's statement should not be understood according to its plain sense, that the prayer leader is not required to mention *Zikhronot* and *Shofarot,* but if he wishes to do so he may indeed recite them. Rather, this is what Rabbi Yehudah meant to say: The prayer leader does not recite the blessings of *Zikhronot* and *Shofarot* on the fast days decreed on account of drought. It is not necessary for him to recite those blessings to make the first two blessings as lengthy and full as the next four blessings, because instead of *Zikhronot* and *Shofarot* he can recite blessings containing Biblical passages more directly connected to the affliction on account of which the fast was decreed.

According to some versions of *Rambam's Commentary to the Mishnah,* the law is in accordance with the view of Rabbi Yehudah. (*Tosefot Yom Tov* and others argue that this reading is a scribal error.) But in his *Mishneh Torah* (*Hilkhot Ta'aniyyot* 4:5), *Rambam* writes that the prayer leader says *Zikhronot* and *Shofarot. Ritva* concludes from this that *Rambam* understood Rabbi Yehudah's statement literally: When the Mishnah said that the prayer leader recites the blessings of *Zikhronot* and *Shofarot,* it was reflecting the common practice, but it is not really necessary that these blessings be recited, for blessings consisting of Biblical passages more closely related to the calamity currently threatening the community may be said in their place.

הַזֶּה. בָּרוּךְ אַתָּה ה׳, גּוֹאֵל יִשְׂרָאֵל״. [1]עַל הַשְּׁנִיָּה הוּא אוֹמֵר: ״מִי שֶׁעָנָה אֶת אֲבוֹתֵינוּ עַל יַם סוּף, הוּא יַעֲנֶה אֶתְכֶם וְיִשְׁמַע קוֹל צַעֲקַתְכֶם הַיּוֹם הַזֶּה. בָּרוּךְ אַתָּה ה׳, זוֹכֵר הַנִּשְׁכָּחוֹת״. [2]עַל הַשְּׁלִישִׁית הוּא אוֹמֵר: ״מִי שֶׁעָנָה אֶת יְהוֹשֻׁעַ בַּגִּלְגָּל, הוּא יַעֲנֶה אֶתְכֶם וְיִשְׁמַע בְּקוֹל צַעֲקַתְכֶם הַיּוֹם הַזֶּה. בָּרוּךְ אַתָּה ה׳, שׁוֹמֵעַ תְּרוּעָה.״ [3]עַל הָרְבִיעִית הוּא אוֹמֵר: ״מִי שֶׁעָנָה אֶת שְׁמוּאֵל בַּמִּצְפָּה, הוּא יַעֲנֶה אֶתְכֶם וְיִשְׁמַע בְּקוֹל צַעֲקַתְכֶם הַיּוֹם הַזֶּה. בָּרוּךְ אַתָּה ה׳, שׁוֹמֵעַ צְעָקָה״. [4]עַל הַחֲמִישִׁית הוּא אוֹמֵר: ״מִי שֶׁעָנָה אֶת אֵלִיָּהוּ בְּהַר הַכַּרְמֶל, הוּא יַעֲנֶה אֶתְכֶם וְיִשְׁמַע בְּקוֹל צַעֲקַתְכֶם הַיּוֹם הַזֶּה. בָּרוּךְ אַתָּה ה׳, שׁוֹמֵעַ תְּפִלָּה״. [5]עַל הַשִּׁשִּׁית הוּא אוֹמֵר: ״מִי שֶׁעָנָה אֶת יוֹנָה מִמְּעֵי הַדָּגָה, הוּא יַעֲנֶה אֶתְכֶם וְיִשְׁמַע בְּקוֹל צַעֲקַתְכֶם הַיּוֹם הַזֶּה. בָּרוּךְ אַתָּה ה׳, הָעוֹנֶה בְּעֵת צָרָה״. [6]עַל הַשְּׁבִיעִית הוּא אוֹמֵר: ״מִי

LITERAL TRANSLATION

Blessed are You, O Lord, the redeemer of Israel." [1]For the second he says: "He who answered our forefathers at the Red Sea, He will answer you and will hearken unto the sound of your crying [on] this day. Blessed are You, O Lord, who remembers the forgotten." [2]For the third he says: "He who answered Joshua at Gilgal, He will answer you and will hearken unto the sound of your crying [on] this day. Blessed are You, O Lord, who hearkens unto an alarm." [3]For the fourth he says: "He who answered Samuel at Mitzpah, He will answer you and will hearken unto the sound of your crying [on] this day. Blessed are You, O Lord, who hearkens unto crying." [4]For the fifth he says: "He who answered Elijah on Mount Carmel, He will answer you and will hearken unto the sound of your crying [on] this day. Blessed are You, O Lord, who hearkens unto prayer." [5]For the sixth he says: "He who answered Jonah in the belly of the fish, He will answer you and will hearken unto the sound of your crying [on] this day. Blessed are You, O Lord, who answers in time of trouble." [6]For the seventh he says:

TRANSLATION AND COMMENTARY

[1]At the end of **the second** blessing relating to the special nature of the day — the first additional blessing inserted into the service, *Zikhronot* — the prayer leader **says: "He who answered our forefathers at the Red Sea, He will answer you and will hearken unto the sound of your crying on this day. Blessed are You, O Lord, who remembers the forgotten."** [2]At the end of **the third** blessing — the second additional blessing inserted into the service, *Shofarot* — the prayer leader **says: "He who answered Joshua** by causing the walls of Jericho to fall while the Israelites were encamped **at Gilgal** [Joshua 5:6], **He will answer you and will hearken unto the sound of your crying on this day. Blessed are You, O Lord, who hearkens unto an alarm."** [3]At the end of **the fourth** blessing — the third additional blessing inserted into the service, "In my distress, I cried to the Lord" — the prayer leader **says: "He who answered Samuel at Mitzpah** [I Samuel 7:9], **He will answer you and will hearken unto the sound of your crying on this day. Blessed are You, O Lord, who hearkens unto crying."** [4]At the end of **the fifth** blessing — the fourth additional blessing inserted into the service, "I will lift up my eyes to the hills" — the prayer leader **says: "He who answered Elijah on Mount Carmel** [I Kings 18:37], **He will answer you and will hearken unto the sound of your crying on this day. Blessed are You, O Lord, who hearkens unto prayer."** [5]At the end of **the sixth** blessing — the fifth additional blessing inserted into the service, "Out of the depths I have cried to You" — the prayer leader **says: "He who answered Jonah in the belly of the fish** [Jonah 2:3], **He will answer you and will hearken unto the sound of your crying on this day. Blessed are You, O Lord, who answers in time of trouble."** [6]At the end of **the seventh**

RASHI

על השניה — זו היא ברכה ראשונה של שש ברכות, כדאמרינן בגמרא. והיאך ד״גואל ישראל״ — זו היא ברכה עצמה של שמונה עשרה, ואינה מאותן שש, אלא שבה היה מתחיל להוסיף ולהאריך. על הזכרונות הוא אומר ״זוכר הנשכחות״ ועל השופרות ״שומע תרועה״ והיא שניה למנינה, ועל ״אל ה׳ בצרתה לי״ והיא שלישית למנין שש ״שומע צעקה״ (שלישית), וכן כולן. **ומי שענה את אבותינו על ים סוף** — לפיכך אומרה בזכרונות, לפי שהיו ישראל נשכחים במצרים כמה שנים, ונתייאשו מן הגאולה, וזכרם המקום וגאלם, דכתיב (שמות ו) ״ואזכור את בריתי״. **ובשופרות היה אומר מי שענה את יהושע בגלגל** — לפי שנענה בשופרות ביריחו, וזהו בעוד שהיו ישראל בגלגל. **ואליהו בהר הכרמל** — כנגד ״אשא עיני אל ההרים״ וכן כולן לפי ענין המזמורים, אליהו נענה בהר הכרמל מעין ״אשא עיני אל ההרים״, ושמואל במצפה דכתיבי קראי ומעין ״אל ה׳ בצרתה לי״. **ממעי הדגה** — מעין ״ממעמקים קראתיך ה׳״ ועונה בעת צרה, שכן כתיב ביונה ״קראתי מצרה לי״ (יונה ב), ובשמואל כתיב ״ויזעק אל ה׳״ (שמואל א׳ ו) ובאליהו כתיב (מלכים א׳ יח) ״ענני״ — זו תפלה. **ועל השביעית** — מפרש בגמרא מאי שביעית, מי שענה דוד ״ויהי רעב בימי דוד שלש שנים שנה אחר שנה״ (שמואל ב׳ כא).

TRANSLATION AND COMMENTARY

blessing — the sixth additional blessing inserted into the service, "A prayer of the afflicted, when he faints" — the prayer leader **says: "He who answered David** [I Samuel 21:1] **and Solomon his son in Jerusalem** [I Kings 8:35-36], **He will answer you and will hearken unto the sound of your crying on this day. Blessed are You, O Lord, who has mercy on the land."**

מַעֲשֶׂה [1]The Mishnah now relates that **an incident** once **occurred** [15B] **in the days of Rabbi Ḥalafta and Rabbi Ḥananya ben Teradyon, that someone took up his position before the ark** to lead the prayers on one of the last seven fasts decreed by the court during a time of drought [2]The prayer leader **finished the entire blessing,** "Redeemer of Israel," **but** those assembled for the service **did not answer "Amen,"** the congregation's usual response to a blessing, **after him.** Rather, they said: "Blessed is the name of His glorious majesty for ever and ever," the customary response to a blessing recited in the Temple. The synagogue attendant then proclaimed: [3]**"Sound a *tekiah*** [a long, uninterrupted blast], **priests, sound a *tekiah*."** [4]The prayer leader continued: **"He who answered Abraham on Mount Moriah,**

שֶׁעָנָה אֶת דָּוִד וְאֶת שְׁלֹמֹה בְּנוֹ בִּירוּשָׁלַיִם, הוּא יַעֲנֶה אֶתְכֶם וְיִשְׁמַע בְּקוֹל צַעֲקַתְכֶם הַיּוֹם הַזֶּה. בָּרוּךְ אַתָּה ה׳, הַמְרַחֵם עַל הָאָרֶץ.״

[1]מַעֲשֶׂה [15B] בִּימֵי רַבִּי חֲלַפְתָּא וְרַבִּי חֲנַנְיָא בֶּן תְּרַדְיוֹן, שֶׁעָבַר אֶחָד לִפְנֵי הַתֵּיבָה [2]וְגָמַר אֶת הַבְּרָכָה כּוּלָּהּ, וְלֹא עָנוּ אַחֲרָיו ״אָמֵן״. [3]״תִּקְעוּ, הַכֹּהֲנִים, תִּקְעוּ״. [4]״מִי שֶׁעָנָה אֶת אַבְרָהָם אָבִינוּ בְּהַר הַמּוֹרִיָּה, הוּא יַעֲנֶה אֶתְכֶם

LITERAL TRANSLATION

"He who answered David and Solomon his son in Jerusalem, He will answer you and will hearken unto the sound of your crying [on] this day. Blessed are You, O Lord, who has mercy on the land."

[1]An incident [occurred] [15B] in the days of Rabbi Ḥalafta and Rabbi Ḥananya ben Teradyon, that someone passed before the ark [2]and finished the entire blessing, and they did not answer after him "Amen." [3]"Sound a *tekiah*, priests, sound a *tekiah*." [4]"He who answered Abraham on Mount Moriah, He will answer you

RASHI

ושלמה — כשהכניס הארון לבית קדש הקדשים, אי נמי "רעב כי יהיה בארץ" וגו׳ (מלכים א ח) ולפיכך חותם "מרחם על הארץ", שהן התפללו על ארץ ישראל ו"תפלה לעני כי יעטוף" — על דוחק גשמים נופל, וכתיב ביה (שם) "בהעצר שמים". **בימי רבי חלפתא בצפורי** — אביו של רבי יוסי, דאמרינן בסנהדרין (לב, ב): אחר רבי יוסי בצפורי, [אחר רבי חנינא בן תרדיון] בסיכני. **וגומר כל הברכה** — כל אותה ברכה עצמה. הכי גרסינן: **ולא ענו אחריו אמן תקעו בני אהרן תקעו** — חזן הכנסת אומר להן על כל ברכה וברכה, והוא החזן, לא שליח צבור.

BACKGROUND

בִּימֵי רַבִּי חֲלַפְתָּא וְרַבִּי חֲנַנְיָא בֶּן תְּרַדְיוֹן In the days of Rabbi Ḥalafta and Rabbi Ḥananya ben Teradyon. These two Sages are mentioned together because they were both from Upper Galilee. Rabbi Ḥalafta came from Sepphoris and Rabbi Ḥananya ben Teradyon came from Sakhnin. Together they apparently convened a large prayer meeting for the people of their area.

It is known that Rabbi Ḥalafta was alive while the Temple still stood, so it is likely that he would have conducted the prayer meeting according to the custom he had seen on the Temple Mount. However, the meeting organized by the two Sages must have taken place long after the destruction of the Temple, for Rabbi Ḥananya ben Teradyon was killed during the anti-Jewish persecutions initiated by Hadrian after the failure of the Bar Kokhba revolt (132-135 C.E.).

NOTES

וְלֹא עָנוּ אַחֲרָיו ״אָמֵן״ And they did not answer after him "Amen." Our commentary follows the reading and interpretation of *Rashi*, according to which the Sages disapproved of the practice adopted by Rabbi Ḥalafta and Rabbi Ḥananya ben Teradyon, because those assembled for the special fast-day service did not answer "Amen" after the prayer leader, but rather: "Blessed is the name of His glorious majesty for ever and ever." Indeed, the Baraita cited below (16b) mentions that, in areas outside the Temple, the congregation respond to the prayer leader's blessings with "Amen," whereas in the Temple they answer "Blessed is the name of His glorious majesty for ever and ever." According to *Rashi*, Rabbi Ḥalafta and Rabbi Ḥananya ben Teradyon erred in that they applied the practice observed in the Temple to areas outside it as well. The primary difficulty with this explanation is that the texts of the Gemara in the hands of most of the Rishonim read: "וְעָנוּ אַחֲרָיו ׳אָמֵן׳" — "And they answered after him 'Amen,'" according to which it is clear that the problem with the practice adopted by Rabbi Ḥalafta and Rabbi Ḥananya ben Teradyon was not that the congregation failed to answer "Amen" after the prayer leader. Moreover, it is difficult to understand how Sages like Rabbi Ḥalafta and Rabbi Ḥananya ben Teradyon could have made such an error. The Rishonim suggest a number of ways of understanding the mistake that Rabbi Ḥalafta and Rabbi Ḥananya ben Teradyon made (see note below, 16b).

תִּקְעוּ, הַכֹּהֲנִים, תִּקְעוּ Sound a *tekiah,* priests, sound a *tekiah.* According to the reading found in the standard editions of the Talmud (תִּקְעוּ כֹּהֲנִים וְתָקְעוּ), the Mishnah states that the synagogue attendant said: "Sound a *tekiah*, priests," and the priests then sounded the trumpets. Our translation and commentary follows the reading of *Rashi* and others: תִּקְעוּ כֹּהֲנִים תִּקְעוּ, according to which these are all the words of the synagogue attendant. The synagogue attendant proclaimed: "Sound a *tekiah*, priests, sound a *tekiah*," and following the prayer leader's entreaty to God to answer His people's prayers as he did in Biblical days, the trumpets were sounded (though the actual sounding of the trumpets is not mentioned in the Mishnah). *Melekhet Shlomo* cites yet a third reading: תִּקְעוּ כֹּהֲנִים תִּקְעוּ וְתָקְעוּ, "'Sound a *tekiah*, priests, sound a *tekiah*,' and they sounded a *tekiah*."

HALAKHAH

וְלֹא עָנוּ אַחֲרָיו ״אָמֵן״ And they did not answer after him "Amen." "When the special fast-day service was conducted in Jerusalem, the people would assemble on the Temple Mount opposite the Eastern Gate. When the prayer leader reached the passage, 'He who answered Abraham,' he would say: 'Blessed is the Lord our God, the God of Israel, from everlasting to everlasting. Blessed are You, O Lord, redeemer of Israel.' And those assembled would answer after him: 'Blessed is the name of His glorious majesty for ever and ever.'" (*Rambam, Sefer Zemannim, Hilkhot Ta'aniyyot* 4:15,17.)

TRANSLATION AND COMMENTARY

He will answer you and will hearken unto the sound of your crying on this day," after which the priests sounded the trumpets. The prayer leader then recited the next blessing, *Zikhronot*, and when he finished, the synagogue attendant proclaimed: [1]**"Sound a *teruah*** [a series of very short blasts], **sons of Aaron, sound a *teruah*."** [2]The prayer leader continued: **"He who answered our forefathers at the Red Sea, He will answer you and will hearken unto the sound of your crying on this day,"** after which the trumpets were sounded. The same applied to each of the other special blessings recited on account of the fast — the prayer leader would complete the blessing, the synagogue attendant would announce that the priests were to sound the trumpets, the prayer leader would entreat God to answer His people's cries as He had done in Biblical times, and the trumpets would be sounded. [3]**When the matter** of the practices adopted by Rabbi Ḥalafta and Rabbi Ḥananya ben Teradyon **came before the Sages** for consideration, [4]**they said: We would not act this way except** in the days of the Temple, when we entered through **the Eastern Gate** to pray **on the Temple Mount** (see notes).

שָׁלֹשׁ תַּעֲנִיּוֹת הָרִאשׁוֹנוֹת As was explained above, in years of drought the court may impose on the community an initial series of three fasts, a second series of three fasts, and a final series of seven fasts. Our Mishnah now proceeds to discuss the differences between the three series of fasts as they affect the priests whose period of service in the Temple coincides with one of these fasts. The priests who served in the Temple were divided into twenty-four groups, called *mishmarot* ("watches"). Each *mishmar* served for one week at a time, so that each *mishmar* performed the Temple service for approximately two weeks every year. The *mishmarot* themselves were divided into six (or, according to another opinion, seven) *batei av* ("paternal families"). Each *bet av* served in the Temple for one day of the week. The Tannaim disagree about the obligation of the members of the *mishmar* and of the members of the *bet av* to observe the fasts decreed upon the community on account of the drought: [5]**On the first three fasts the members of the *mishmar*** whose week it is to serve in the Temple **fast, but** they **do not prolong their fast** until nightfall, for they must preserve their strength, lest the work to be done in the Temple prove too much for the members of the *bet av* whose day it is to serve, and the rest of the members of the *mishmar* be summoned to help them. [6]On these first three fasts, **the members of the *bet av*** whose day it is to serve in the Temple **do not fast at all,** for they will definitely serve that day. [7]**On the second three**

וְיִשְׁמַע בְּקוֹל צַעֲקַתְכֶם הַיּוֹם הַזֶּה". [1]"הָרִיעוּ, בְּנֵי אַהֲרֹן, הָרִיעוּ". [2]"מִי שֶׁעָנָה אֶת אֲבוֹתֵינוּ עַל יַם סוּף, הוּא יַעֲנֶה אֶתְכֶם וְיִשְׁמַע בְּקוֹל צַעֲקַתְכֶם הַיּוֹם הַזֶּה". [3]וּכְשֶׁבָּא דָּבָר אֵצֶל חֲכָמִים, [4]אָמְרוּ: לֹא הָיִינוּ נוֹהֲגִין כֵּן אֶלָּא בְּשַׁעַר מִזְרָח וּבְהַר הַבַּיִת.

[5]שָׁלֹשׁ תַּעֲנִיּוֹת הָרִאשׁוֹנוֹת, אַנְשֵׁי מִשְׁמָר מִתְעַנִּין וְלֹא מַשְׁלִימִין, [6]וְאַנְשֵׁי בֵּית אָב לֹא הָיוּ מִתְעַנִּין כְּלָל. [7]שָׁלֹשׁ

LITERAL TRANSLATION

and will hearken unto the sound of your crying [on] this day." [1]"Sound a *teruah*, sons of Aaron, sound a *teruah*." [2]"He who answered our forefathers at the Red Sea, He will answer you and will hearken unto the sound of your crying [on] this day." [3]And when the matter came before the Sages, [4]they said: We would not act this way except at the Eastern Gate and on the Temple Mount.

[5][On] the first three fasts, the members of the *mishmar* fast but do not complete [their fast], [6]and the members of the *bet av* do not fast at all. [7][On] the second three

RASHI

לא היינו נוהגין — שלא לענות אמן. **אלא בשער מזרח ובהר הבית** — כלומר, בזמן שבית המקדש קיים כשמתפללין בהר הבית נכנסין בדרך שער המזרח, לפי שלא היו עונין אמן במקדש, כדאמרינן בגמרא (טז,ב). ואין לומר לא היו נוהגין כן לתקוע אלא במקדש — דודאי תוקעין בגבולים. כדמוכח בכולה הך מסכת ומסכת ראש השנה (כו,ב. כז,א). **אנשי משמר** — של אותה שבת. **ולא משלימין** — שעדיין אינן חמורין כל כך. ובגמרא (יז,א) מפרש: שמא תכבד העבודה על אנשי בית אב, שהיו עובדין אותו היום, ובאים הן לסייעם. ואם היו מתענים — לא היה להם כח לעמוד בעבודה. **אנשי בית אב** — המשמרה מתחלקת לשבעה בתי אבות, כנגד שבעת ימי השבוע, בית אב ליום.

HALAKHAH

אַנְשֵׁי מִשְׁמָר וְאַנְשֵׁי בֵּית אָב The members of the *mishmar* and the members of the *bet av*. "On the first three fasts, the members of the *mishmar* whose week it was to serve in the Temple did not fast at all. On the second three fasts, the members of the *mishmar* whose week it was to serve in the Temple fasted part of the day but did not complete their fast, and the members of the *bet av* whose day it was to serve in the Temple did not fast at all. On the last seven fasts, the members of the *mishmar* whose week it was to serve in the Temple fasted the entire day, and the members of the *bet av* fasted part of the day but did not complete their fast," following the Sages against Rabbi Yehoshua. (*Rambam, Sefer Zemannim, Hilkhot Ta'aniyyot* 3:2,3,6.)

TRANSLATION AND COMMENTARY

fasts, which are more severe than the first three, **the members of the** *mishmar* whose week it is to serve in the Temple **fast and prolong their fast** until nightfall, just like the rest of the community. [1] **The members of the** *bet av* whose day it is to serve in the Temple **fast, but** they **do not prolong their fast** until nightfall, so that they will be strong enough to do the Temple service. [2] **On the last seven fasts,** which are the most severe of the fasts, **both** the members of the *mishmar* whose week it is to serve in the Temple, and the members of the *bet av* whose day it is to serve, **fast and complete their fast** at nightfall, just like everybody else. [3] **This is the viewpoint of Rabbi Yehoshua.** [4] **But the Sages say: On the first three fasts, both** the members of the *mishmar* and the members of the *bet av* **do not fast at all,** for the members of the *bet av* must serve in the Temple that day, and the members of the *mishmar* are on call should their assistance be necessary. [5] **On the second three fasts,** which are more severe than the first three, **the members of the** *mishmar* **fast, but** they **do not prolong their fast** until nightfall, lest they be summoned to help their colleagues. On these second three fasts, **the members of the** *bet av* whose day it is to serve in the Temple **do not fast at all,** for they will definitely serve in the Temple that day. [6] **On the last seven fasts,** which are the most severe, **the members of the** *mishmar* whose week it is to serve in the Temple **fast and prolong their fast** until nightfall, just like the rest of the community. [7] **On** these last seven fasts, **the members of the** *bet av*

whose day it is to serve in the Temple **fast, but** they **do not prolong their fast** until nightfall, for, even on the most severe of the fasts, they must preserve their strength in order to be able to serve in the Temple.

אַנְשֵׁי מִשְׁמָר [8] Having clarified the difference between the members of the *mishmar* and the members of the *bet av* regarding fasts decreed upon the community on account of drought, the Mishnah continues with another difference between the members of the *mishmar* and the members of the *bet av*. A priest is forbidden to enter the Temple Courtyard while intoxicated with wine. If a priest enters and serves in such a condition, his service is disqualified, and he is liable to death at the hand of Heaven. Priests whose turn it is to serve in the Temple must therefore refrain from drinking wine in order to be fit for the Temple service. **The members of the** *mishmar* whose week it is to serve in the Temple **are permitted to drink wine during the night,** for the work that must be done in the Temple at night is limited to burning portions of sacrifices that were offered the previous day, and it is unlikely that the members of the *bet av* whose day it is to serve will require the assistance of the rest of the members of the *mishmar* to complete this task. [9] **But the members of the** *mishmar* may **not** drink wine **during the day,** for they must be available to serve in the Temple if needed. [10] **The members of the** *bet av* whose day it is to serve in the Temple may drink wine **neither during**

LITERAL TRANSLATION

[fasts], the members of the *mishmar* fast and complete [their fast], [1] and the members of the *bet av* fast but do not complete [their fast]. [2] [On] the last seven [fasts], both these and those fast and complete [their fast]. [3] [These are] the words of Rabbi Yehoshua. [4] But the Sages say: [On] the first three fasts, both these and those do not fast at all. [5] [On] the second three [fasts], the members of the *mishmar* fast but do not complete [their fast], and the members of the *bet av* do not fast at all. [6] [On] the last seven fasts, the members of the *mishmar* fast and complete [their fast], [7] and the members of the *bet av* fast but do not complete [their fast].

[8] The members of the *mishmar* are permitted to drink wine in the nights, [9] but not in the days. [10] And the members of the *bet av* [drink] neither in the day nor in the night.

שְׁנִיּוֹת, אַנְשֵׁי מִשְׁמָר מִתְעַנִּין וּמַשְׁלִימִין, [1] וְאַנְשֵׁי בֵּית אָב מִתְעַנִּין וְלֹא מַשְׁלִימִין. [2] שֶׁבַע אַחֲרוֹנוֹת, אֵלּוּ וָאֵלּוּ מִתְעַנִּין וּמַשְׁלִימִין. [3] דִּבְרֵי רַבִּי יְהוֹשֻׁעַ. [4] וַחֲכָמִים אוֹמְרִים: שָׁלֹשׁ תַּעֲנִיּוֹת הָרִאשׁוֹנוֹת, אֵלּוּ וָאֵלּוּ לֹא הָיוּ מִתְעַנִּין כְּלָל. [5] שָׁלֹשׁ שְׁנִיּוֹת, אַנְשֵׁי מִשְׁמָר מִתְעַנִּין וְלֹא מַשְׁלִימִין, וְאַנְשֵׁי בֵּית אָב לֹא הָיוּ מִתְעַנִּין כְּלָל. [6] שֶׁבַע אַחֲרוֹנוֹת, אַנְשֵׁי מִשְׁמָר מִתְעַנִּין וּמַשְׁלִימִין, [7] וְאַנְשֵׁי בֵּית אָב מִתְעַנִּין וְלֹא מַשְׁלִימִין. [8] אַנְשֵׁי מִשְׁמָר מוּתָּרִין לִשְׁתּוֹת יַיִן בַּלֵּילוֹת, [9] אֲבָל לֹא בַּיָּמִים. [10] וְאַנְשֵׁי בֵּית אָב לֹא בַּיּוֹם וְלֹא בַּלַּיְלָה.

RASHI

אנשי [מעמד] — אֶחָד כֹּהֲנִים וּלְוִיִם וִישְׂרְאֵלִים הַקְּבוּעִים וְעוֹמְדִין וּמִתְפַּלְּלִין עַל קָרְבָּן אֲחֵיהֶם שֶׁיְּקַבֵּל לְרָצוֹן, וְעוֹמְדִים לְשֵׁם בִּשְׁעַת עֲבוֹדָה. דְּהֵיאַךְ קָרְבָּנוֹ שֶׁל אָדָם קָרֵב וְהוּא אֵינוֹ עוֹמֵד עַל גַּבָּיו? וְכוּלְּהוּ מְפָרֵשׁ בְּפֶרֶק אַחֲרוֹן (כו,א). מותרין לשתות יין — לֹאו גַּבֵּי תַּעֲנִית אִיתְּמַר, אֶלָּא אַגַּב דְּמַיְירֵי נַבֵּי מִשְׁמָר מַיְיתֵי לַהּ. בלילות — אֵין לָחוּשׁ שֶׁמָּא תִּכְבַּד הָעֲבוֹדָה, שֶׁהֲרֵי רֹאו מֵעֶרֶב שֶׁפָּסְקוּ הַקָּרְבָּנוֹת וְלֹא כָּבְדָה הָעֲבוֹדָה, שֶׁיָּמֵאוּ רוֹב קָרְבָּנוֹת וְלֹא יַסְפִּיקוּ בְּנֵי בֵּית אָב שֶׁל אוֹתוֹ הַיּוֹם, וּצְרִיכִין אֵלּוּ לְסַיֵּיעַ, וַהֲרֵי אֵין רָאוּיִין לַעֲבוֹדָה מִשּׁוּם שִׁכְרוּת. אַנְשֵׁי בֵּית אָב אֲסוּרִין בֵּין בַּיּוֹם וּבֵין בַּלַּיְלָה — לְפִי שֶׁהָיוּ מַעֲלִין כָּל הַלַּיְלָה אֵבָרִים וּפְדָרִים שֶׁפָּקְעוּ מֵעַל הַמִּזְבֵּחַ. אִי נַמֵי: לֹא גָּמְרוּ בַּיּוֹם — גּוֹמְרִים בַּלַּיְלָה. אֲבָל אַנְשֵׁי מִשְׁמָר אֵינָן צְרִיכִין לְסַיֵּיעַ בַּלַּיְלָה לַהֲפֹךְ בְּמִזְלָג, דְּבֵית אָב יָכוֹל לְהַסְפִּיק לְבַד הִיפּוּךְ הַמַּעֲרָכָה.

TRANSLATION AND COMMENTARY

the day nor during the night, for they will surely be needed to work both during the day and at night.

אַנְשֵׁי מִשְׁמָר [1]Corresponding to each of the *mishmarot* was a group of nonpriests, called a *ma'amad* ("a post" or "a division"). The entire Jewish people living in Eretz Israel was divided into twenty-four *ma'amadot*. Each time a *mishmar* went to Jerusalem to serve in the Temple, part of the corresponding *ma'amad* would go there as well, and would represent the entire people when the communal sacrifices were offered. The rest of the *ma'amad* would remain at home, and during that week would fast each day (from Monday to Thursday), read special portions from the Torah, and say special prayers. The Mishnah proceeds to discuss a regulation that applies both to the members of the *mishmar* and to the members of the *ma'amad* whose week it is to be present in the Temple. **The members of the *mishmar*** whose week it is to serve in the Temple **and the members of the *ma'amad*** whose week it is to stand in the Temple when the communal sacrifices are offered **are forbidden to cut their hair or wash their clothes** throughout the week of their service, so that they will cut their hair and launder their clothing before they begin their service, and not arrive for duty in soiled clothing and with untrimmed hair. [2]**But on the Thursday** of the week of their service, **they are permitted** to cut their hair and launder their clothing **in honor of Shabbat.**

כָּל הַכָּתוּב [3]The Mishnah now proceeds to discuss the regulations concerning the minor festivals recorded in *Megillat Ta'anit*, "The Scroll of Fasts." *Megillat Ta'anit* is a list of thirty-six minor festivals on which the Rabbis forbade fasting — and in some cases eulogizing as well — on account of happy events that occurred to the Jewish people during the Second Temple period. Our Mishnah discusses the differences between those days on which only fasting is forbidden and those days on which eulogizing is also forbidden: With regard to **all the days that are recorded in *Megillat Ta'anit*** when it is **not** permitted **to eulogize** the dead, [4]**it is** also **forbidden** to deliver a eulogy on **the day before** the date recorded in the scroll, lest one come to eulogize on the minor festival itself; [5]but on **the day after** the date recorded in the scroll, **it is permitted** to deliver a eulogy, for there is then no longer any concern that a eulogy will be delivered on the day of the minor festival itself. This is the opinion of the anonymous first Tanna of the Mishnah, [6]but **Rabbi Yose** disagrees and **says:** Both on **the day before** the date recorded in the scroll **as well as** on **the day after** the date recorded in the scroll **it is forbidden** to deliver a eulogy. [7]The Mishnah continues: The regulations applying to those days when *Megillat Ta'anit* states that one is **not** permitted **to fast** are less stringent. According to the anonymous first Tanna of the Mishnah, both on **the day before** the date recorded in the scroll **as well as** on **the day after** the date recorded in the scroll **it is permitted to fast.** [8]**Rabbi Yose** also disagrees with this

[1]אַנְשֵׁי מִשְׁמָר וְאַנְשֵׁי מַעֲמָד אֲסוּרִין מִלְּסַפֵּר וּמִלְּכַבֵּס. [2]וּבַחֲמִישִׁי מוּתָּרִין מִפְּנֵי כְּבוֹד הַשַּׁבָּת.

[3]כָּל הַכָּתוּב בִּמְגִלַּת תַּעֲנִית "דְּלָא לְמִסְפַּד", [4]לְפָנָיו אָסוּר, [5]לְאַחֲרָיו מוּתָּר. [6]רַבִּי יוֹסֵי אוֹמֵר: לְפָנָיו וּלְאַחֲרָיו אָסוּר. [7]"דְּלָא לְהִתְעַנָּאָה" — לְפָנָיו וּלְאַחֲרָיו מוּתָּר. [8]רַבִּי יוֹסֵי

LITERAL TRANSLATION

[1]The members of the *mishmar* and the members of the *ma'amad* are forbidden to cut their hair or wash their clothes. [2]But on Thursday they are permitted because of the honor of Shabbat.

[3][On] all [the days] that are written in *Megillat Ta'anit* "not to eulogize," [4]it is forbidden [the day] before, [5][but] it is permitted [the day] after. [6]Rabbi Yose says: It is forbidden [the day] before and [the day] after. [7]"Not to fast" — it is permitted [the day] before and [the day] after. [8]Rabbi Yose

RASHI

אסורים לספר ולכבס — משנכנסו למשמרתם, כל אותה שבת, אלא מסתפרין קודם לכן, וטעמא מפרש בגמרא. **ובחמישי** — של משמרתן מותרים. דרך רוב בני אדם להסתפר בחמישי, ולא בערב שבת, מפני הטורח. **כל הכתוב במגילת תענית דלא למיספד** — דאית יומיא דלא להתענאה, ומקצתהון דחמירי טפי דלא למיספד, ואותן שהן חמורים ואסורים בהספד — **לפניו** אסור בהספד, דילמא אתי למיעבד ביום טוב גופיה. **ולאחריו מותר** — דכיון שעבר יום לא חיישינן. ואותן שאינן חמורין ליאסר בהספד, אלא דלא להתענאה בין לפניו כו׳.

HALAKHAH

אַנְשֵׁי מִשְׁמָר וְאַנְשֵׁי מַעֲמָד אֲסוּרִין מִלְּסַפֵּר וּמִלְּכַבֵּס The members of the *mishmar* and the members of the *ma'amad* are forbidden to cut their hair or wash their clothes. "The members of the *mishmar* and the members of the *ma'amad* whose week it is to serve or to be present in the Temple are forbidden to cut their hair or to do their laundry throughout the week of their service, so that they will not begin their service in soiled clothing and with untrimmed hair." (*Rambam, Sefer Avodah, Hilkhot Bi'at Mikdash* 1:12; *Hilkhot Klei HaMikdash* 6:11.)

TRANSLATION AND COMMENTARY

ruling and **says:** On **the day before** the date recorded in the scroll **it is forbidden** to fast, lest one come to fast on the minor festival itself, [1]**but** on **the day after** the date recorded in the scroll **it is permitted** to fast, for there is then no longer any concern that a person will fast on the day of the minor festival itself.

אֵין גּוֹזְרִין תַּעֲנִית [2]The Mishnah continues: The court **may not decree a fast on the community beginning on a Thursday, so as not to cause an increase in** food **prices.** On a fast-day there is a great demand for provisions, for everybody goes to the market to buy food to break the fast. If the first of a series of fasts were declared on a Thursday, when there is already a great demand for provisions, for on Thursday people buy supplies for Shabbat, there is concern that the food merchants might raise their prices before the market has time to adjust itself to the rise in demand with a corresponding increase in supply. [3]**Rather, the first three fasts are** arranged so that the first fast is **on Monday,** the second fast is on **Thursday, and** the third fast is on the following **Monday.** [4]**But the second three fasts are** arranged so that the first fast is **on Thursday** (three days after the last fast of the first series of fasts), the second fast is on the following **Monday, and** the third fast is on the following **Thursday.** In this situation there is no concern about starting the second series of fasts on a Thursday, because the second series is a continuation of the first, and the market will have already adjusted itself to the increased demand for food on Thursdays. [5]**Rabbi Yose** disagrees and **says: Just as the first** series of three fasts **may not begin on a Thursday,** [6]**so too** may **the second** series of three fasts **and the last** series of seven fasts **not** begin on a Thursday, but only on a Monday.

אֵין גּוֹזְרִין תַּעֲנִית [7]The Mishnah concludes with a discussion about the days on which a fast may not be decreed. The court **may not decree a fast on the community on the New Moon, on Hanukkah, or on Purim** (and certainly not on Shabbat, on a Festival, or on an intermediate day of a Festival), for these days are regarded as minor festivals on which fasting is forbidden. [8]**But if** the community **have already started** a series of fasts, and one fast in the series falls on the New Moon, or on Hanukkah, or on Purim, **they do not**

אוֹמֵר: לְפָנָיו אָסוּר, [1]לְאַחֲרָיו מוּתָּר.

[2]אֵין גּוֹזְרִין תַּעֲנִית עַל הַצִּבּוּר בַּתְּחִילָּה בַּחֲמִישִׁי, שֶׁלֹּא לְהַפְקִיעַ הַשְּׁעָרִים. [3]אֶלָּא שָׁלֹשׁ תַּעֲנִיּוֹת הָרִאשׁוֹנוֹת שֵׁנִי וַחֲמִישִׁי וְשֵׁנִי, [4]וְשָׁלֹשׁ שְׁנִיּוֹת חֲמִישִׁי שֵׁנִי וַחֲמִישִׁי. [5]רַבִּי יוֹסֵי אוֹמֵר: כְּשֵׁם שֶׁאֵין הָרִאשׁוֹנוֹת בַּחֲמִישִׁי, [6]כָּךְ לֹא שְׁנִיּוֹת וְלֹא אַחֲרוֹנוֹת.

[7]אֵין גּוֹזְרִין תַּעֲנִית עַל הַצִּבּוּר בְּרָאשֵׁי חֳדָשִׁים, בַּחֲנוּכָּה, וּבְפוּרִים. [8]וְאִם הִתְחִילוּ, אֵין

LITERAL TRANSLATION

says: It is forbidden [the day] before, [1][but] it is permitted [the day] after.

[2]We do not decree a fast on the community beginning on Thursday, in order not to raise prices. [3]Rather, the first three fasts are [on] Monday and Thursday and Monday, [4]and the second three [fasts] are on Thursday [and] Monday and Thursday. [5]Rabbi Yose says: Just as the first [ones] do not [begin] on Thursday, [6]so too the second [ones] do not and the last [ones] do not.

[7]We do not decree a fast on the community on New Moons, on Hanukkah, or on Purim. [8]But if they have [already] started, they do not

RASHI

שלא להפקיע את השערים — כשרואין בעלי חניות שקונין למוצאי יום חמישי שתי סעודות גדולות, אחת לליל חמישי ואחת לשבת, סבורים שבא רעב לעולם ומייקרים ומפקיעים השער, אבל משהתחילו להתענות — יודעין שאינו אלא מפני התענית. **בראשי חדשים** — דאיקרי מועד. **ואם התחילו** — שקיבלו תענית מקודם לכן, ונכנס בהן ראש חדש — **אין מפסיקין**, דאף על גב דאקרי מועד — לא כתיב ביה יום משתה ושמחה.

HALAKHAH

אֵין גּוֹזְרִין תַּעֲנִית עַל הַצִּבּוּר בַּתְּחִילָּה בַּחֲמִישִׁי We do not decree a fast on the community beginning on Thursday. "The first of a series of fasts decreed upon the community may not take place on a Thursday, so as not to cause food prices to rise. This ruling applies even in a place where there is no concern that the prices will rise." (*Shulḥan Arukh, Oraḥ Ḥayyim* 572:1.)

אֵין גּוֹזְרִין תַּעֲנִית עַל הַצִּבּוּר בְּרָאשֵׁי חֳדָשִׁים, בַּחֲנוּכָּה, וּבְפוּרִים We do not decree a fast on the community on New Moons, on Hanukkah, or on Purim. "A fast may not be decreed upon the community to take place on Rosh Ḥodesh, on Hanukkah, on Purim, or on the intermediate days of a Festival. If the community has already started to observe a series of fasts because a certain calamity is threatening it, and one of the fasts coincides with one of these days, the fast is observed despite the semi-festive nature of the day and is continued until nightfall. Today, however, when even public fasts are treated as private fasts, the series is interrupted on days of a semi-festive nature, and the fast is observed on another day (*Magen Avraham*, following *Bet Yosef*)." (*Shulḥan Arukh, Oraḥ Ḥayyim* 572:2.)

TRANSLATION AND COMMENTARY

interrupt the series, but observe the fast even though the day is a minor festival. [1]**This is the viewpoint of Rabban Gamliel.** [2]**Rabbi Meir said: Even though Rabban Gamliel said** that **they do not interrupt** the series even if one of the fasts coincides with the New Moon, or with Hanukkah, or with Purim, [3]**he would agree that** in such a case **they do not complete the fast** until nightfall, but break the fast some time before sunset. [4]**And likewise,** if **the Ninth of Av** (a communal fast-day commemorating the destruction of the First and Second Temples) **falls on a Friday** (an impossible situation according to the fixed calendar in use today, but possible when the New Moon was proclaimed after witnesses testified to their sighting of the crescent of the moon), the fast is not prolonged until nightfall, but is broken shortly before the onset of Shabbat, so that people not begin Shabbat while fasting.

GEMARA סֵדֶר תַּעֲנִיּוֹת [5]We learned in the Mishnah: **"What is the order of the service on the fast days** decreed in times of drought? **The ark** is taken from its designated place in the room adjoining the synagogue and **is carried out** to the town square, where the special prayer service is conducted." The Gemara asks: Since the Mishnah does not specify which fasts are being discussed here, [6]can we infer that **even on the first** and second series of three fasts the prayer service is conducted in the manner described in the Mishnah? But if so, [7]**a contradiction may be raised** between our Mishnah and the following Baraita, which stated: **"On the first and second** series of **three fasts** the congregation **enters the synagogue, and** the people **pray in the manner that they pray the entire year.** [8]**But on the last seven fasts** imposed on the community on account of the lack of rain, the service is conducted differently. **The ark is carried out to the town square and ashes are placed on the ark.** [9]Ashes are **also** placed **on the heads of** the most important members of the community, **the Nasi and the president of the court.** [10]In addition, **each and every other person** present at the assembly **takes ashes and places** some **on his** own **head.** Although it is preferable to use ashes to cover the ark and the heads of those assembled for the service, ordinary earth can serve as a substitute. [11]**Rabbi Natan** disagrees and **says: They** must **bring burnt ashes** for this purpose, ordinary earth being an unacceptable alternative." Thus we see that the Baraita states explicitly that on the first and second series of fasts the prayer service is conducted as usual, and this contradicts the interpretation of our Mishnah suggested above.

אָמַר רַב פַּפָּא [12]**Rav Pappa said** in reply: **When we learned** in **our Mishnah** that a special order of service

מַפְסִיקִין. [1]דִּבְרֵי רַבָּן גַּמְלִיאֵל. [2]אָמַר רַבִּי מֵאִיר: אַף עַל פִּי שֶׁאָמַר רַבָּן גַּמְלִיאֵל אֵין מַפְסִיקִין, [3]מוֹדֶה הָיָה שֶׁאֵין מַשְׁלִימִין. [4]וְכֵן תִּשְׁעָה בְּאָב שֶׁחָל לִהְיוֹת בְּעֶרֶב שַׁבָּת.

גמרא [5]״סֵדֶר תַּעֲנִיּוֹת כֵּיצַד? מוֹצִיאִין אֶת הַתֵּיבָה, כו׳״. [6]וַאֲפִילּוּ בְּקַמָּיְיתָא? [7]וּרְמִינְהוּ: ״שָׁלֹשׁ תַּעֲנִיּוֹת רִאשׁוֹנוֹת וּשְׁנִיּוֹת, נִכְנָסִים לְבֵית הַכְּנֶסֶת, וּמִתְפַּלְּלִין כְּדֶרֶךְ שֶׁמִּתְפַּלְּלִין כָּל הַשָּׁנָה כּוּלָּהּ. [8]וּבְשֶׁבַע אַחֲרוֹנוֹת, מוֹצִיאִין אֶת הַתֵּיבָה לִרְחוֹבָהּ שֶׁל עִיר, וְנוֹתְנִין אֵפֶר עַל גַּבֵּי הַתֵּיבָה, [9]וּבְרֹאשׁ הַנָּשִׂיא, וּבְרֹאשׁ אַב בֵּית דִּין, [10]וְכָל אֶחָד וְאֶחָד נוֹטֵל וְנוֹתֵן בְּרֹאשׁוֹ. [11]רַבִּי נָתָן אוֹמֵר: אֵפֶר מִקְלֶה הֵן מְבִיאִין״. [12]אָמַר רַב פַּפָּא: כִּי תְּנַן נַמִי

LITERAL TRANSLATION

interrupt. [1][These are] the words of Rabban Gamliel. [2]Rabbi Meir said: Even though Rabban Gamliel said [that] they do not interrupt, [3]he would agree that they do not complete [the fast]. [4]And likewise the Ninth of Av which falls on the eve of Shabbat.

GEMARA [5]"What is the order [of service] on fasts? They carry the ark out, etc." [6]And even on the first ones? [7]A contradiction was raised (lit., "cast them together"): "[On] the first and second three fasts, they go into the synagogue, and they pray in the way that they pray the entire year. [8]And on the last seven [fasts], they carry the ark out to the open area of the town, and they place ashes on the ark, [9]and on the head of the Nasi, and on the head of the president of the court, [10]and each and every one [else] takes and places [ashes] on his head. [11]Rabbi Natan says: They bring burnt ashes."

[12]Rav Pappa said: When we learned our Mishnah also,

RASHI

שאין משלימין – להתענות כל היום, אלא אוכלין סמוך לערב. מגילת תענית נכתבה בימי חכמים, אף על פי שלא היו כותבין הלכות, והיינו דקתני ״כל הכתוב במגילת תענית״ כאילו היה מקרא.

גמרא אפילו בקמייתא – מוציאין את התיבה? בתמיה. **כי קתני נמי מתניתין** – ״סדר תעניות כילד״ – בסדר תעניות אחרונות קא מיירי. הכי גרסינן בגמרא: **ונותנין אפר על גבי התיבה** – ולא גרסינן אפר מקלה. אפר שריפה עדיף, משום אפרו של יצחק, כדלקמן.

SAGES

רַבִּי נָתָן **Rabbi Natan.** This is Rabbi Natan the Babylonian, who immigrated to Eretz Israel and was one of the greatest Tannaim during the generation before the completion of the Mishnah. Rabbi Natan was the son of the Exilarch in Babylonia, a member of a family descended from King David, the family with the noblest lineage among the Jews. Because of his greatness as a Torah scholar and his noble lineage, he was named deputy to the president of the Sanhedrin. He was famous for his profound knowledge of civil law. Similarly, he was known for his piety, and it is said that Elijah the Prophet used to appear to him.

Rabbi Natan, together with Rabbi Meir, tried to alter the procedure for choosing the president of the Sanhedrin. This effort failed, and as a kind of punishment it was decreed that Rabbi Natan should not be mentioned by name in the Mishnah, but that his teachings be introduced anonymously with the phrase, "Some say." But this decision was not always observed.

Rabbi Natan edited a number of collections of Mishnaic teachings, and the tractate *Avot DeRabbi Natan* is named after him. Many Sages of the following generation were his students, the most prominent of whom was Rabbi Yehudah HaNasi.

מַתְנִיתִין, אַשֶּׁבַע אַחֲרוֹנוֹת תְּנַן.
[1]״וּבְרֹאשׁ הַנָּשִׂיא״. [2]וַהֲדַר תָּנֵי:
״כָּל אֶחָד וְאֶחָד נוֹתֵן בְּרֹאשׁוֹ״.
[3]אִינִי? [4]וְהָתַנְיָא: ״רַבִּי אוֹמֵר:
[5]בִּגְדוּלָּה, מַתְחִילִין מִן הַגָּדוֹל.
[6]וּבִקְלָלָה, מַתְחִילִין מִן הַקָּטָן.
[7]בִּגְדוּלָּה, מַתְחִילִין מִן הַגָּדוֹל,
[8]שֶׁנֶּאֱמַר: ׳וַיֹּאמֶר מֹשֶׁה אֶל
אַהֲרֹן, וּלְאֶלְעָזָר וּלְאִיתָמָר׳.
[9]וּבִקְלָלָה, מַתְחִילִין מִן הַקָּטָן,
[10]שֶׁבַּתְּחִלָּה נִתְקַלֵּל נָחָשׁ,
[11]וְאַחַר כָּךְ נִתְקַלְּלָה חַוָּה,
וְאַחַר כָּךְ נִתְקַלֵּל אָדָם״!
[12]הָא חֲשִׁיבוּתָא לְדִידְהוּ,
[13]דְּאָמְרִי לְהוּ: [14]אַתּוּן חֲשִׁיבִיתוּ
לְמִיבְּעֵי עֲלַן רַחֲמֵי אַכּוּלֵּי
עָלְמָא.
[15]״כָּל אֶחָד וְאֶחָד נוֹתֵן

LITERAL TRANSLATION

we learned [it] with respect to the last seven. [1]"And on the head of the Nasi." [2]And then it teaches: "Each and every one [else] places [ashes] on his head." [3]Is this so? [4]But surely it was taught: "Rabbi says: [5]Regarding greatness, we begin from the greatest. [6]And regarding a curse we begin from the least. [7]Regarding greatness, we begin from the greatest, [8]as it is said: 'And Moses said to Aaron, and to Eleazar and to Ithamar.' [9]And regarding a curse, we begin from the least, [10]for first the serpent was cursed, [11]and afterwards Eve was cursed, and afterwards Adam was cursed"! [12]This is a distinction for them, [13]for they say to them: [14]You are distinguished [enough] to petition for mercy for us on behalf of the entire world. [15]"Each and every one places

RASHI

בגדולה – מלוה בעלמא שלא לפורענות ״וידבר משה אל אהרן ואל אלעזר״ וגו׳

TRANSLATION AND COMMENTARY

is followed on fast days, that ruling **was taught** only **with respect to the last seven** fasts. But on the first and second series of three fasts, the service is conducted in the same manner as during the rest of the year, as stated explicitly in the Baraita.

וּבְרֹאשׁ הַנָּשִׂיא [1]The Mishnah states: "Ashes are **also** placed **on the heads of the Nasi** and of the president of the court." [2]The Mishnah **then** continues and **teaches: "Each and every other person** present at the assembly then **places ashes on his** own **head."** [3]The Gemara asks: **Is this** the appropriate order of events? [4]**But surely** the following **was taught** in a Baraita: **"Rabbi** Yehudah HaNasi **says:** [5]Whenever we deal **with** a matter of **distinction** that applies to more than one person, or with bestowing an honor on more than one person, **we begin with the most important** member of the group meriting that distinction or honor. [6]**And** whenever we deal **with** a matter of **dishonor** relating to more than one person, **we begin with the least important** member of the group upon which the dishonor falls. [7]Whenever we deal **with** a matter of **distinction** that applies to more than one person, **we begin with the most important** member of the group meriting that distinction, [8]**as it is said** [Leviticus 10:6]: **'And Moses said to Aaron, and to Eleazar and to Ithamar,** his sons.' Aaron is mentioned before his sons Eleazar and Ithamar, because he is the most important member of the group meriting the distinction of being anointed with the oil of the Lord [see verse 7]. [9]And whenever we deal **with** a matter of **dishonor, we start with the least important** member of the group on which the dishonor falls, [10]**for** when punishments were meted out in the Garden of Eden, **first the serpent was cursed** [Genesis 3:14-15], [11]**and afterwards Eve was cursed** [verse 16], **and afterwards Adam was cursed** [verses 17-19]. The serpent is mentioned first because he is the inferior member of the group being cursed by God." Why, then, on a fast day are the most important members of the community, the Nasi and the president of the court, the first to suffer the humiliation of having ashes placed on their heads, and only afterwards do the rest of the people place ashes on their own heads?

הָא חֲשִׁיבוּתָא לְדִידְהוּ [12]The Gemara answers: It is right that we should start with the Nasi and with the president of the court, for **this** too **is a** matter of **distinction for them.** [13]**For** when the ashes are placed first on the head of the Nasi and on the head of the president of the court, it is as if **they are being told:** [14]**You are distinguished enough to petition for mercy on behalf of the entire world.**

כָּל אֶחָד [15]We learned in the Mishnah: **"Each and every other person** present at the assembly then **places ashes**

NOTES

שֶׁבַּתְּחִלָּה נִתְקַלֵּל נָחָשׁ **For first the serpent was cursed.** It might have been suggested that the serpent's punishment was given priority for an entirely different reason. The serpent caused the transgression by persuading Eve to partake of the forbidden fruit, and so the serpent's punishment was announced first. However, God initially spoke to Adam and then to Eve, and so the punishments meted out thereafter should also have been announced in that order. The change in order teaches us that, regarding matters of dishonor, we start with the inferior member of the group upon which the dishonor falls (*Nezer HaKodesh*).

SAGES

רַבִּי אַבָּא דְּמִן קֵסָרִי Rabbi Abba of Caesarea. A Palestinian Amora of the third generation, this Sage is mentioned in very few places in the Talmud, and sometimes his name is written as Rabbi Adda of Caesarea. He seems to have been a disciple of Rabbi Yoḥanan and a contemporary of the important Sage, Rabbi Abbahu.

TRANSLATION AND COMMENTARY

on his own **head."** But regarding the Nasi and the president of the court, the Mishnah states that the ashes are placed on their heads by someone else. [1]On this point the Gemara objects: **Let the Nasi and the president of the court also take the ashes by themselves and place** some **on their** own **heads!** [2]**What is the difference** between the common people and the leaders of the community **that** each and every one of the common people places the ashes on his own head, whereas for the leaders **someone else takes ashes and places them on** their heads?

אָמַר רַבִּי אַבָּא דְּמִן קֵסָרִי [3]**Rabbi Abba of Caesarea said** in reply: Ashes are placed on the heads of those assembled for the fast-day service in order to invoke feelings of grief and humility, and they are placed on the people's heads in a way that maximizes those feelings. The more elevated a person is in status, the greater is his humiliation. Thus, with respect to the Nasi and the president of the court, the ashes are placed on their heads by someone else, [4]because the humiliation felt by **someone who humiliates himself cannot be compared to** [16A] the humiliation felt by **someone who is humiliated by others.** But common people are supposedly less sensitive to humiliation, and it makes little difference to them whether they are humiliated by themselves or by others.

וְהֵיכָא מַנַּח לְהוּ [5]The Gemara asks: **Where** precisely on the head **are** the ashes **placed?**

אָמַר רַבִּי יִצְחָק [6]**Rabbi Yitzḥak said** in reply: The ashes are put **on the place** where the **tefillin** are usually laid, in the center of the head slightly above the person's original hairline. [7]This is in keeping with the **verse that says** (Isaiah 61:3): **"To appoint to those who mourn in Zion, to give them an ornament instead of ashes."** The ornament mentioned by the Prophet is understood as a reference to tefillin. This verse, which describes the time when the ashes of the mourners of Zion will be replaced by tefillin, implies that when ashes are put on the head, they are put where tefillin are usually worn.

רְחוֹב [8]The Gemara now examines the various customs associated with the special prayer service conducted on a fast-day, some but not all of which were mentioned in our Mishnah. The words **"town square, ark,**

בְּרֹאשׁוֹ״. [1]נָשִׂיא וְאַב בֵּית דִּין נַמִי נִשְׁקְלוּ אִינְהוּ וְנִינְחוּ בְּרֵאשַׁיְיהוּ! [2]מַאי שְׁנָא דְּשָׁקֵיל אִינִישׁ אַחֲרִינָא וּמַנַּח לְהוּ? [3]אָמַר רַבִּי אַבָּא דְּמִן קֵסָרִי: [4]אֵינוֹ דּוֹמֶה מִתְבַּיֵּישׁ מֵעַצְמוֹ [16A] לְמִתְבַּיֵּישׁ מֵאֲחֵרִים. [5]וְהֵיכָא מַנַּח לְהוּ? [6]אָמַר רַבִּי יִצְחָק: בִּמְקוֹם תְּפִילִּין, [7]שֶׁנֶּאֱמַר: ״לָשׂוּם לַאֲבֵלֵי צִיּוֹן, לָתֵת לָהֶם פְּאֵר תַּחַת אֵפֶר״. [8]רְחוֹב, תֵּיבָה, וְשַׂקִּים, אֵפֶר,

LITERAL TRANSLATION

[ashes] on his head." [1]Let the Nasi and the president of the court also take [ashes] by themselves and place [them] on their heads! [2]What is the difference that another person takes [ashes] and places [them] on them?

[3]Rabbi Abba of Caesarea said: [4]Someone who humiliates himself is not like [16A] someone who is humiliated by others.

[5]And where does one place them?

[6]Rabbi Yitzḥak said: On the place of the tefillin, [7]as it is said: "To appoint to those who mourn in Zion, to give them an ornament instead of ashes."

[8]Mnemonic: Open area, ark, and sackcloth, ashes,

RASHI

הא נמי — דיהבינן בראשייהו דנשיא ואב בית דין ברישא חשיבותא הוא, דאמרי להו אתון חשיבתו טפי כו'. **דשקיל איניש אחרינא כו'** — דקתני: ונותנין על גבי התיבה כו' ועל ראש הנשיא כו' — דמשמע על ידי אחר. וגבי שאר כל אדם לא תני "נותנין", אלא "כל אחד ואחד (נוטל) [נותן]" כו'. **למתבייש מאחרים** — דאיכא עגמת נפש טפי, ומשום חשיבותם הם מתביישים מאחרים, אבל שאר בני אדם דלא חשיבי — לא מתביישי בנתינת אחרים, וסגי להו בנתינת עצמן. **פאר תחת אפר** — שמע מינה במקום תפילין, דכתיב בהו (יחזקאל כד) "פארך חבוש עליך" ואמרינן (ברכות יא,א): אלו תפילין. ומתרגמינן נמי: טוטפתך הוין עלך. והיכא מניחין תפילין — במקום שמוחו של תינוק רופס.

NOTES

כָּל אֶחָד וְאֶחָד נוֹתֵן בְּרֹאשׁוֹ Each and every one places ashes on his head. According to the Jerusalem Talmud it appears that the synagogue attendant placed ashes not only on the heads of the dignitaries but also on the heads of the common people. But there was a difference between the two. If the synagogue attendant did not reach all the common people, those whom he did not reach would place ashes on their own heads. But regarding the Nasi and the president of the court, particular care was taken that the ashes be placed on their heads by someone else, so as to maximize their humiliation, as is explained in our Gemara.

HALAKHAH

בִּמְקוֹם תְּפִילִּין On the place of the tefillin. "When ashes are placed on the head on public fast-days, they are placed on the spot where the tefillin are worn." (*Shulḥan Arukh, Oraḥ Ḥayyim* 579:1.)

אֵפֶר, קְבוּרָה, וּמוֹרִיָּה סִימָן.
[1]לָמָּה יוֹצְאִין לָרְחוֹב?
[2]רַבִּי חִיָּיא בַּר אַבָּא אָמַר: לוֹמַר: [3]״זָעַקְנוּ בִּצְנְעָא וְלֹא נַעֲנֵינוּ. [4]נְבַזֶּה עַצְמֵנוּ בְּפַרְהֶסְיָא״. [5]רֵישׁ לָקִישׁ אָמַר: ״גָּלִינוּ. [6]גָּלוּתֵינוּ מְכַפֶּרֶת עָלֵינוּ״.
[7]מַאי בֵּינַיְיהוּ?
[8]אִיכָּא בֵּינַיְיהוּ דְּגָלֵי מִבֵּי כְנִישְׁתָּא לְבֵי כְנִישְׁתָּא.
[9]וְלָמָּה מוֹצִיאִין אֶת הַתֵּיבָה לִרְחוֹבָהּ שֶׁל עִיר?
[10]אָמַר רַבִּי יְהוֹשֻׁעַ בֶּן לֵוִי: לוֹמַר: [11]״כְּלִי צָנוּעַ הָיָה לָנוּ, וְנִתְבַּזָּה בַּעֲווֹנֵינוּ״.
[12]וְלָמָּה מִתְכַּסִּין בְּשַׂקִּים?

LITERAL TRANSLATION

ashes, burial, and Moriah.

[1]Why do we go out to the open area?

[2]Rabbi Ḥiyya bar Abba said: To say: [3]"We cried out in private but we were not answered. [4]Let us put ourselves to shame in public." [5]Resh Lakish said: "We have been exiled. [6]Let our exile atone for us."

[7]What is [the difference] between them?

[8]There is [a difference] between them where one goes out from [one] synagogue to [another] synagogue.

[9]And why do we carry the ark out to the open area of the town?

[10]Rabbi Yehoshua ben Levi said: To say: [11]"We had a hidden utensil, and it was put to shame on account of our sins."

[12]And why do we cover ourselves with sackcloth?

TRANSLATION AND COMMENTARY

sackcloth, ashes, ashes, burial, and Moriah" are **a mnemonic aid** for the student to remember the issues now to be discussed by the Gemara.

לָמָּה [1]The Gemara asks: **Why do** the people **go out to the town square** on the last seven fasts and conduct the prayer service there?

רַבִּי חִיָּיא בַּר אַבָּא [2]**Rabbi Ḥiyya bar Abba said** in reply: Going out to the town square is a symbolic way of **saying:** [3]**"We** have already **cried out** for mercy **in** the **privacy** of the synagogue **but we were not answered.** [4]**Let us** now **put ourselves to shame in public,** and pour out our hearts to God in the sight of all. Perhaps in that way our prayers will be answered, and the calamity threatening us will be averted." [5]**Resh Lakish said:** Going out to the town square is a way of saying: **"We have been punished with exile** from our usual place of prayer. [6]**Let our exile atone for** the sins that have brought this drought upon us."

מַאי בֵּינַיְיהוּ [7]The Gemara asks: **What is the** practical **difference between** the two explanations just offered?

אִיכָּא בֵּינַיְיהוּ [8]The Gemara answers: **There is a** practical **difference between** the two explanations — whether or not the community **may go out from one synagogue** and conduct the prayer service **in another synagogue.** According to Resh Lakish, who understands that going out to the town square serves as a symbolic act of exile, going from one synagogue to another should be sufficient, for that too should be regarded as an act of exile. But according to Rabbi Ḥiyya bar Abba, who understands that those fasting go out to the town square in order to conduct the prayer service in public, moving the service to another synagogue would not be an acceptable alternative, for the service conducted in the second synagogue would continue to be viewed as a private act.

וְלָמָּה [9]The Gemara asks: We have explained the practice of leaving the synagogue on the last seven fast days and conducting the prayer service outside. But **why is the ark** containing the Torah scroll also **carried out to the town square?** Let the ark remain inside the synagogue and let the service be conducted without the ark!

אָמַר רַבִּי יְהוֹשֻׁעַ בֶּן לֵוִי [10]**Rabbi Yehoshua ben Levi said** in reply: Taking the ark out to the town square is a symbolic way of **saying:** [11]**"We had a hidden utensil,** the ark, which was always kept inside the synagogue building, **and** now **on account of our sins it has been put to shame** by being exposed to the public gaze."

וְלָמָּה [12]The Gemara asks: **Why do** those who fast **cover themselves with sackcloth?**

RASHI

בצינעא — בבית הכנסת. **גלינו** — שיצאנו מכניסתנו. **גלותינו** — תהא מכפרת עלינו. **דגלו מבי כנישתא לבי כנישתא אחריתא** — גלות — איכא, פרהסיא — ליכא. **נתבזה בעוונינו** — וידוי. **[ולמה מתכסין]** — חוגרות שקין. תנינן בירושלמי: שהיו חוגרות שקין ויוצאין לבית הקברות ותוקעין בקרנות, ובעי ליה מיבעיא: שקין למה, ובית הקברות למה, ותקיעת שופר למה?

SAGES

רַבִּי חִיָּיא בַּר אַבָּא Rabbi Ḥiyya bar Abba. An Amora of the third generation, Rabbi Ḥiyya bar Abba was born in Babylonia and immigrated to Eretz Israel in his youth. He studied under members of the first generation of Amoraim in Eretz Israel — Rabbi Ḥanina and Rabbi Yehoshua ben Levi. However, he was mainly a student of Rabbi Yoḥanan, and Rabbi Zera says of him that he was precise in reporting his master's teachings. After the death of Rabbi Yoḥanan, he studied with Rabbi Elazar. Among his colleagues were Rabbi Abbahu, Rabbi Ammi, and Rabbi Assi. His sons also became Sages, the most prominent being Rabbi Abba.

NOTES

וְלָמָּה מִתְכַּסִּין בְּשַׂקִּים? And why do we cover ourselves with sackcloth? The Rishonim note that some of the practices about which the Gemara is asking — wearing sackcloth and visiting the cemetery — are not explicitly mentioned anywhere in the Mishnah or the Baraita. (*Rashi* notes that wearing sackcloth and visiting the cemetery are mentioned in the Jerusalem Talmud.) Some (*Meiri, Mikhtam*) find an allusion to the practice of wearing sackcloth in the message of admonition delivered by the elder (see our Mishnah and the Baraita below) that neither sackcloth nor fasting are effective in winning divine forgiveness, which implies that it was indeed customary for people to wear

¹אָמַר רַבִּי חִיָּיא בַּר אַבָּא: לוֹמַר: ״הֲרֵי אָנוּ חֲשׁוּבִין כִּבְהֵמָה״.
²וְלָמָּה נוֹתְנִין אֵפֶר מִקְלֶה עַל גַּבֵּי תֵיבָה?
³אָמַר רַבִּי יְהוּדָה בֶּן פָּזִי: כְּלוֹמַר: ״עִמּוֹ אָנֹכִי בְצָרָה״.
⁴רֵישׁ לָקִישׁ אָמַר: ״בְּכָל צָרָתָם לוֹ צָר״. ⁵אָמַר רַבִּי זֵירָא: מֵרֵישׁ, כִּי הֲוָה חָזֵינָא לְהוּ לְרַבָּנַן דְּיָהֲבֵי אֵפֶר מִקְלֶה עַל גַּבֵּי תֵיבָה, ⁶מִזְדַּעְזַע לִי כּוּלֵּיהּ גּוּפַאי.
⁷וְלָמָּה נוֹתְנִין אֵפֶר בְּרֹאשׁ כָּל אֶחָד וְאֶחָד?
⁸פְּלִיגִי בָּהּ רַבִּי לֵוִי בַּר חָמָא וְרַבִּי חֲנִינָא. ⁹חַד אָמַר: ״הֲרֵי אָנוּ חֲשׁוּבִין לְפָנֶיךָ כְּאֵפֶר״. ¹⁰וְחַד אָמַר: כְּדֵי שֶׁיִּזְכּוֹר לָנוּ אֶפְרוֹ שֶׁל יִצְחָק.

LITERAL TRANSLATION

[1] Rabbi Ḥiyya bar Abba said: To say: "Behold, we are regarded as animals."

[2] And why do we place burnt ashes on the ark?

[3] Rabbi Yehudah ben Pazi said: As if to say: "I will be with him in trouble." [4] Resh Lakish said: "In all their affliction He was afflicted." [5] Rabbi Zera said: At first, when I would see the Rabbis placing burnt ashes on the ark, [6] my entire body would tremble.

[7] And why do we place ashes on the head of each and every one?

[8] Rabbi Levi bar Ḥama and Rabbi Ḥanina disagreed about this. [9] One said: "Behold, we are regarded before You as ashes." [10] And one said: So that He may remember the ashes of Isaac on our behalf.

RASHI

כבהמה — דמשער בהמה נינהו, מנוצה של עזים.

TRANSLATION AND COMMENTARY

אָמַר רַבִּי חִיָּיא בַּר אַבָּא [1] **Rabbi Ḥiyya bar Abba said** in reply: One covers oneself with sackcloth as an act of self-degradation; it is a way of **saying: We are to be regarded as animals,** whose hair is used in the making of sackcloth."

וְלָמָּה [2] The Gemara asks: **Why are burnt ashes placed on the ark?**

אָמַר רַבִּי יְהוּדָה בֶּן פָּזִי [3] **Rabbi Yehudah ben Pazi said** in reply: The holy ark containing the Torah scroll symbolizes God's presence in the world. Placing ashes on the ark expresses the idea that God Himself participates in the sorrow and distress suffered by His people. It is a way of **saying** in the name of God (Psalms 91:15): **"I will be with him in trouble."** Whenever the Jewish people suffers affliction, God is with it. When circumstances force the Jews to cover themselves with ashes, God does the same — by means of the ashes placed on the holy ark containing His Torah. [4] **Resh Lakish said:** The same idea is found in another verse (Isaiah 63:9): **"In all their affliction He was afflicted."** Recounting his personal reaction to the sight of ashes being placed on the ark, [5] **Rabbi Zera said: At first, when I saw the Rabbis placing burnt ashes on the ark,** [6] I was so overwhelmed with emotion that **my entire body trembled.**

וְלָמָּה [7] The Gemara proceeds to ask about the next practice mentioned in the Mishnah. **Why are ashes placed on the heads of each and every person** assembled at the special prayer service held on the last seven fast days decreed in times of drought?

פְּלִיגִי [8] **Rabbi Levi bar Ḥama and Rabbi Ḥanina disagreed about** the reason for placing ashes on the head. [9] **One** Amora **said:** The people put ashes on their heads in order to humiliate themselves, as if they are saying to God: "On account of our sins, **we are to be regarded before You as** mere **ashes."** [10] **And the other** Amora **said:** The ashes serve as a means of reminding God **to remember the ashes of Isaac on our behalf.** The reference here is to the ashes of the ram substituted for Isaac after he had already been bound and

SAGES

רַבִּי יְהוּדָה בֶּן פָּזִי **Rabbi Yehudah ben Pazi.** A Palestinian Amora of the fourth generation, this Sage is usually called by his full name, Rabbi Yehudah the son of Rabbi Shimon ben Pazi, in the Babylonian Talmud. Rabbi Yehudah's father, Rabbi Shimon ben Pazi, was a disciple of Rabbi Yoḥanan, and Rabbi Yehudah himself was his father's leading disciple. Rabbi Yehudah ben Pazi transmits the Torah teachings of Rabbi Yoḥanan, mainly in his father's name. Rabbi Yehudah ben Pazi was a priest. The members of his family were important members of the household of the Nasi, and they ultimately married into the family of the Nasi. Rabbi Yehudah lived in the city of Lydda and seems to have been one of the judges of the city. His teachings are frequently found in the Jerusalem Talmud and also appear in the Babylonian Talmud.

BACKGROUND

אֶפְרוֹ שֶׁל יִצְחָק **The ashes of Isaac.** Although Isaac was not in fact sacrificed in the Biblical story and God provided a ram to be offered in his place, the ram is regarded as though it were actually the Patriarch Isaac, for both Abraham and Isaac were entirely willing to offer the supreme sacrifice of their own lives. The binding of Isaac became a model for those Jewish martyrs who did in fact offer their lives to sanctify God's Name. This is why reference is sometimes made to the "ashes of Isaac," for with respect to willingness and intention it was as though Isaac had truly offered himself as a sacrifice in obedience to a divine command, and by virtue of that sacrifice Isaac's descendants became the chosen people.

NOTES

sackcloth on these fast-days. *Ritva*, *Ran*, and others argue that the Gemara is inquiring about practices that do not have a literary source in the Mishnah or the Baraita, but which were nonetheless the prevailing custom.

בְּכָל צָרָתָם לוֹ צָר **In all their affliction He was afflicted.** Our commentary follows *Maharsha*, who explains that the holy ark containing the Torah scroll stands in place of the holy ark in the Temple, upon which God's Divine Presence in this world once rested. Placing ashes on the ark is a way of saying that God is with His people in their time of affliction; for just as the people cover themselves with ashes, so too does God.

The Jerusalem Talmud also connects the holy ark that is removed from the synagogue with the holy ark that was in the Holy of Holies in the Temple. Ashes are placed on the ark in order to impress upon the people how different they are from their righteous forefathers: "Our forefathers covered the ark with gold, and here we cover it with ashes."

According to *Maharsha,* the verse should be understood as follows: Whenever the Jewish people finds itself in affliction, God too is afflicted, for He participates in its affliction.

Meiri explains the verse in a slightly different manner: Whenever the Jewish people is afflicted, God too is afflicted, for His existence and unity are revealed in this world primarily through the Jewish People, so that when the Jews suffer, He too suffers.

כְּדֵי שֶׁיִּזְכּוֹר לָנוּ אֶפְרוֹ שֶׁל יִצְחָק **So that He may remember the ashes of Isaac on our behalf.** The Jerusalem Talmud cites an opinion according to which ashes are placed on

TRANSLATION AND COMMENTARY

prepared for sacrifice in compliance with God's command (Genesis 22:9-13). God is called upon to remember how Abraham was ready to offer Him his only son, and how Isaac was willing to submit. The merit of the Patriarchs should cause God to answer the prayers of their descendants.

מַאי בֵּינַיְיהוּ [1]The Gemara asks: **What is the** practical **difference between** these two reasons?

אִיכָּא בֵּינַיְיהוּ [2]The Gemara answers: **There is a difference between them regarding ordinary earth.** The term אפר can refer either to ashes or to earth. According to the Amora who explains that the people put ashes on their heads in order to humiliate themselves, placing earth on their heads (when ashes are not available) is a suitable alternative, for this too is an act of humiliation. But according to the Amora who understands that the ashes serve as a reminder to God of the story of the binding of Isaac, specifically ashes and not earth must be placed on the people's heads.

לָמָּה [3]The Gemara continues: **Why do** the people **go out to the cemetery** on fast days at the conclusion of the prayer service?

פְּלִיגֵי בָּהּ [4]**Rabbi Levi bar Ḥama and Rabbi Ḥanina disagreed about** the reason for visiting the cemetery on public fast days. [5]**One** Amora **said:** Visiting the cemetery is one more way for the people to humiliate themselves, for it is as if they are saying to God: **"We are** to be **regarded before You as dead."** [6]**And the other** Amora **said:** The people visit the cemetery on fast days **so that the dead** will be aware of their plight and **will petition** the Almighty **for mercy** on their **behalf.**

מַאי בֵּינַיְיהוּ [7]Once again the Gemara asks: **What is the** practical **difference between** the two explanations offered for the custom of visiting the cemetery on fast days?

[1]מַאי בֵּינַיְיהוּ?
[2]אִיכָּא בֵּינַיְיהוּ עָפָר סְתָם.
[3]לָמָּה יוֹצְאִין לְבֵית הַקְּבָרוֹת?
[4]פְּלִיגֵי בָּהּ רַבִּי לֵוִי בַּר חָמָא וְרַבִּי חֲנִינָא. [5]חַד אָמַר: "הֲרֵי אָנוּ חֲשׁוּבִין לְפָנֶיךָ כְּמֵתִים". [6]וְחַד אָמַר: כְּדֵי שֶׁיְּבַקְּשׁוּ עָלֵינוּ מֵתִים רַחֲמִים.
[7]מַאי בֵּינַיְיהוּ?

LITERAL TRANSLATION

[1]What is [the difference] between them?
[2][The difference] between them is ordinary earth.
[3]Why do we go out to the cemetery?
[4]Rabbi Levi bar Ḥama and Rabbi Ḥanina disagreed about this. [5]One said: "Behold, we are regarded before You as dead." [6]And one said: So that the dead may petition for mercy on our behalf.
[7]What is [the difference] between them?

RASHI

עפר סתם – שאינו אפר מקלה. זכירת אפרו של יצחק – ליכא. "סתם" לא גרסינן, אלא: איכא בינייהו עפר.

SAGES

רַבִּי לֵוִי בַּר חָמָא **Rabbi Levi bar Ḥama.** A Palestinian Amora of the third generation, Rabbi Levi bar Ḥama (variant readings: Rabbi Levi bar Laḥma) was the disciple and colleague of Rabbi Ḥama bar Ḥanina. Aggadic teachings of his on various topics appear in the Talmud.

NOTES

the head in order to bring to mind the merit of Abraham who said (Genesis 18:27): "I am but dust and ashes." A second opinion is cited by the Jerusalem Talmud — that the people put ashes on their heads in order to bring to mind the merit of Isaac, who is regarded as if he had been burnt to ashes upon the altar. According to the first opinion, ordinary earth can substitute if ashes are not available; but according to the second view, only ashes can be used for this purpose.

Tosafot explains that, since the ashes serve as a reminder to God of the ashes of Isaac, the source of the ashes must be human bones. *Rabbi Ya'akov Emden* rejects this view, arguing that it is inconceivable that human remains should be burned for this purpose. On the contrary, the Gemara's association of this custom with the ashes of Isaac proves that human ashes are *not* required, for Isaac himself was not sacrificed. Rather, the ashes placed on the heads of those fasting serve as a reminder of the ashes of the wood that was burned on the altar when Isaac was made ready for sacrifice. Others explain that the ashes serve as a reminder of the ram that Abraham sacrificed in place of Isaac, the ashes of which are regarded as the ashes of Isaac.

כְּדֵי שֶׁיְּבַקְּשׁוּ עָלֵינוּ מֵתִים רַחֲמִים **So that the dead may petition for mercy on our behalf.** Although *Rif* refers to both of the explanations given here for visiting the cemetery on public fast-days, *Rambam* (*Hilkhot Ta'aniyyot* 4:18) mentions only the first. He explains that the cemetery visit is intended to remind those fasting that if they fail to repent they will soon join the dead who are buried there. It is possible that *Rambam* follows the Jerusalem Talmud, which mentions only the first reason. It has also been suggested that *Rambam* rejects the idea of the living appealing to the dead to petition for mercy on their behalf (*Sefer HaMeorot*).

HALAKHAH

יוֹצְאִין לְבֵית הַקְּבָרוֹת **We go out to the cemetery.** "On public fast-days, after the prayer service is over, the people go out and visit the cemetery, as a reminder that they will be like the dead unless they repent of their evil ways (following *Rambam*, who rules in accordance with the first viewpoint in the Gemara). Thus, if there are no Jewish cemeteries in the area, the people can visit a non-Jewish cemetery (*Rema*). But the common practice follows the second viewpoint in the Gemara, according to which only a Jewish cemetery should be visited (*Magen Avraham*). This is the source of the custom followed in many communities to visit the cemetery on the Ninth of Av (see *Tosafot*)." (*Shulḥan Arukh, Oraḥ Ḥayyim* 579:3.)

BACKGROUND

הַר הַמּוֹרִיָּה Mount Moriah. The meaning of this expression, and similar expressions used in reference to Mount Sinai, is a matter of controversy. Some argue that it means that the Jews were unified and separated from all other nations at Mount Moriah, both because of the binding of Isaac and because the Temple, the heart of the Jewish people, was there. Others say that fear (מוֹרָא) went out of it because of the miracles of God that were manifest in the Temple and in Jerusalem. As Psalm 48:5-7 says: "For behold, the kings were assembled, they passed by together. They saw it and so they marveled, they were troubled, they hastened away. Fear took hold of them there, and pain, as of a woman in labor."

[1]אִיכָּא בֵּינַיְיהוּ קִבְרֵי נָכְרִים. [2]מַאי "הַר הַמּוֹרִיָּה"? [3]פְּלִיגִי בָּהּ רַבִּי לֵוִי בַּר חָמָא וְרַבִּי חֲנִינָא. [4]חַד אָמַר: הַר שֶׁיָּצָא מִמֶּנּוּ הוֹרָאָה לְיִשְׂרָאֵל. [5]וְחַד אָמַר: הַר שֶׁיָּצָא מִמֶּנּוּ מוֹרָא לְאוּמּוֹת הָעוֹלָם. [6]"הַזָּקֵן שֶׁבָּהֶן אוֹמֵר לִפְנֵיהֶן דִּבְרֵי כִבּוּשִׁין". [7]תָּנוּ רַבָּנַן: "אִם יֵשׁ זָקֵן, אוֹמֵר זָקֵן. [8]וְאִם לָאו, אוֹמֵר חָכָם. [9]וְאִם לָאו,

TRANSLATION AND COMMENTARY

אִיכָּא בֵּינַיְיהוּ [1]The Gemara answers: **There is a difference between them regarding the graves of non-Jews.** If the people go out to the cemetery in order to show themselves as being like the dead, then if they cannot reach a Jewish cemetery, they can go to a non-Jewish cemetery instead. But if they visit the cemetery so that the dead will intercede on their behalf, they must visit a Jewish cemetery and go to the graves of the righteous whose petitions for mercy may be answered.

מַאי [2]The Gemara concludes with a question regarding the meaning of the place-name, Mount Moriah, mentioned in our Mishnah. **What is** the significance of the place-name, **Mount Moriah,** the site where Abraham bound his son Isaac to the altar, which later became the site of the Temple in Jerusalem?

פְּלִיגִי בָּהּ [3]**Rabbi Levi bar Ḥama and Rabbi Ḥanina disagreed about** the meaning of the term. [4]**One** Amora **said:** The place is called Mount Moriah (מוֹרִיָּה) because it is **the mountain from which instruction** (הוֹרָאָה) **went out to Israel.** Mount Moriah is so named because the meetings of the Sanhedrin, which served as the final arbiter regarding all matters of Jewish law, took place upon it. [5]**And the other** Amora **said:** The place is called Mount Moriah (מוֹרִיָּה) because it is **the mountain from which fear** (מוֹרָא) **went out to the nations of the world;** for when the nations of the world heard about the wonders that occurred to the Jewish people in Jerusalem, they were overcome with fear and respect.

הַזָּקֵן שֶׁבָּהֶן [6]The Gemara now proceeds to analyze the next clause of the Mishnah, which stated: **"The elder among** those assembled at the special prayer service stands up before the congregation and **rebukes them with words of admonition."** [7]**Our Rabbis taught** a related Baraita, which expands upon the Mishnah's ruling: **"If there is an elder** among those assembled in the town square for the special prayer service, **the elder admonishes** the congregation. [8]**If** there is **no** elder present, then **a** Torah **Sage admonishes** them. [9]**And if**

LITERAL TRANSLATION

[1][The difference] between them is the graves of non-Jews.

[2]What is [meant by] "Mount Moriah"?

[3]Rabbi Levi bar Ḥama and Rabbi Ḥanina disagreed about this. [4]One said: The mountain from which instruction went out to Israel. [5]And one said: The mountain from which fear went out to the nations of the world.

[6]"The elder among them says before them words of admonition." [7]Our Rabbis taught: "If there is an elder, the elder speaks. [8]And if not, a Sage speaks. [9]And if not,

RASHI

קברי נכרים — במקום שאין קברי ישראל. לבקש רחמים, אפילו על עצמן ליכא, כל שכן עלינו. **מאי הר המוריה וכו׳** — איידי דאיירי בפלוגתא דרבי לוי ורבי חנינא תנא נמי הא פלוגתא מאי הר מוריה, דאברהם קרא למקום העקידה "הר יראה", וכתיב (בראשית כב) "אל ארץ המוריה". **חד אמר הר שיצא הוראה** — תורה לישראל "כי מציון תצא תורה" (ישעיה ב), "יורו משפטיך ליעקב" (דברים לג), ולשכת הגזית שבה עמדו הנביאים המוכיחים לישראל. **מורא לאומות העולם** — ששומעין גדולות ישראל וירושלים ומתפחדים עליהם, שמעתי. לישנא אחרינא: הר המוריה — הר סיני, מורא לאומות העולם — במתן תורה, דכתיב (תהלים עו) "ארץ יראה ושקטה".

NOTES

שֶׁיָּצָא מִמֶּנּוּ מוֹרָא לְאוּמּוֹת הָעוֹלָם From which fear went out to the nations of the world. *Rashi* and *Tosafot* quote an opinion that, according to this second explanation, Mount Moriah is to be identified with Mount Sinai. When the Torah was revealed to the Jewish people on Mount Sinai, the rest of the nations of the world were overcome with fear, as the verse says (Psalms 76:9): "You caused judgment to be heard from heaven; the earth feared and was still." A number of Aḥaronim (*Maharsha, Rabbi Zvi Ḥayyot*) point out the difficulty with this opinion: Surely Mount Moriah is the site upon which the Temple was built in Jerusalem, whereas Mount Sinai is outside Eretz Israel.

דִּבְרֵי כִבּוּשִׁין Words of admonition. *Rashi* understands the word כִּבּוּשִׁין in the sense of "pressing" — words that press the heart and force repentance upon it. Others take the word in the sense of "suppressed" — words that uncover what is suppressed in one's heart (*Ein Ya'akov*).

HALAKHAH

הַזָּקֵן שֶׁבָּהֶן אוֹמֵר לִפְנֵיהֶן דִּבְרֵי כִבּוּשִׁין The elder among them says before them words of admonition. "If an elder who is also a Torah Sage is present, he rebukes the congregation. If there is no elderly Sage present, a young Torah Sage is chosen to rebuke the people. If there is no Sage present, a man of imposing physical appearance is appointed to deliver the admonition." (*Shulḥan Arukh, Oraḥ Ḥayyim* 579:1.)

TRANSLATION AND COMMENTARY

there is also **no** Torah Sage present, then **a man of imposing appearance,** who is likely to leave an impression upon his audience, **admonishes** them."

אִטּוּ [1]The Gemara interrupts its presentation of the Baraita with the following question: The Baraita teaches us that if there is no elder present, then the words of admonition are delivered by a Sage. **But is the elder mentioned** here as the preferred speaker **chosen even if he is not a Sage?**

אֲמַר אַבַּיֵי [2]**Abaye said** in reply: This is how we should understand what the Tanna **said: If there is an elder** among those assembled for the special prayer service **who is also a** Torah **Sage,** then **the elder who is** also **a** Torah **Sage admonishes** the congregation. [3]**And if** there is **nobody** present who is both an elder and a Torah Sage, then **a** young Torah **Sage admonishes** the congregation. [4]**And if** there is **not** even a young Torah Sage present, then **a man of imposing appearance** who can persuade the audience to repent **admonishes** the congregation.

אַחֵינוּ [5]The Gemara now resumes its citation of the Baraita: "Whoever is chosen to deliver the admonition says as follows: **'Brothers, neither sackcloth nor fasting are effective** in winning divine forgiveness. [6]**Rather,** sincere **repentance and** the performance of **good deeds are effective** in doing so. [7]**For we find regarding the people of Nineveh that** the verse **does not say about them: "And God saw their sackcloth and their fast,"** [8]**but rather** it says [Jonah 3:10]: **"And God saw their deeds, that they had returned from their evil way."'"**

וְיִתְכַּסּוּ [9]Having mentioned the repentance of the people of Nineveh, which succeeded in averting the calamity that threatened the city, the Gemara now turns its attention to some of the details concerning their repentance. After the Prophet Jonah had warned the people of Nineveh of the impending disaster, the King of Nineveh caused it to be proclaimed (Jonah 3:8): **"But let man and beast be covered with sackcloth."** [10]The Gemara explains: **What did** the people of Nineveh **do** in response to the royal order? [11]**They tied the** mother **animals separately from their young,** [12]**and they said before** God: **"Master of the Universe! If You do not show**

אוֹמֵר אָדָם שֶׁל צוּרָה״. [1]אִטּוּ זָקֵן דְּקָאָמְרִי אַף עַל גַּב דְּלָאו חָכָם הוּא? [2]אָמַר אַבַּיֵי: הָכִי קָאָמַר: אִם יֵשׁ זָקֵן וְהוּא חָכָם, אוֹמֵר זָקֵן וְהוּא חָכָם. [3]וְאִם לָאו, אוֹמֵר חָכָם. [4]וְאִם לָאו, אוֹמֵר אָדָם שֶׁל צוּרָה״. [5]״אַחֵינוּ, לֹא שַׂק וְתַעֲנִית גּוֹרְמִים. [6]אֶלָּא תְּשׁוּבָה וּמַעֲשִׂים טוֹבִים גּוֹרְמִים. [7]שֶׁכֵּן מָצִינוּ בְּאַנְשֵׁי נִינְוֵה שֶׁלֹּא נֶאֱמַר בָּהֶם: ׳וַיַּרְא הָאֱלֹהִים אֶת שַׂקָּם וְאֶת תַּעֲנִיתָם׳, [8]אֶלָּא: ׳וַיַּרְא הָאֱלֹהִים אֶת מַעֲשֵׂיהֶם, כִּי שָׁבוּ מִדַּרְכָּם הָרָעָה׳״. [9]״וְיִתְכַּסּוּ שַׂקִּים הָאָדָם וְהַבְּהֵמָה״. [10]מַאי הֲווּ עָבְדִי? [11]אָסְרָא הַבְּהֵמוֹת לְחוּד וְאֶת הַוּוֹלָדוֹת לְחוּד. [12]אָמְרוּ לְפָנָיו: ״רִבּוֹנוֹ שֶׁל עוֹלָם! אִם אֵין

LITERAL TRANSLATION

a man of [imposing] appearance speaks."

[1]But is the elder whom we mentioned [chosen] even if he is not a Sage?

[2]Abaye said: He says thus: If there is an elder who is [also] a Sage, the elder who is a Sage speaks. [3]And if not, a Sage speaks. [4]And if not, a man of [imposing] appearance speaks.

[5]"Our brothers, neither sackcloth nor fasting are effective. [6]Rather, repentance and good deeds are effective. [7]For so we found regarding the people of Nineveh that it is not said about them: 'And God saw their sackcloth and their fast,' [8]but rather: 'And God saw their deeds, that they had returned from their evil way.'"

[9]"But let man and beast be covered with sackcloth." [10]What did they do? [11]They tied the animals separately and the young separately. [12]They said before Him: "Master of the Universe! If You do not have

RASHI

אף על גב דלאו חכם — אלא עם הארץ, בתמיהה: הא ודאי חכם עדיף! **אם יש זקן והוא חכם** — אומר זקן והוא חכם. **אדם של צורה** — בעל קומה, שישמעו ויקבלו דבריו להמריך את הלב. **מאי אמור** — אנשי נינוה, דכתיב "בחזקה", דמשמע בכח ונילוח דין.

NOTES

אָדָם שֶׁל צוּרָה A man of imposing appearance. A number of different explanations have been offered for this term. Our commentary follows *Rashi,* who explains that this refers to a tall, imposing person, whose words of admonition will surely be heeded. According to the commentary to *Rif* attributed to *Rashi,* the term refers to a person of attractive appearance. *Rosh* suggests that the Baraita is referring to a minor Torah scholar who does not have the status of a Torah Sage. Alternatively, it is referring to a person who is fit to be appointed a communal leader. *Meiri* explains that we are dealing here with a person who is known for his fine moral character and piety. *Maharsha* suggests that the Baraita is referring to a person who is wise in worldly matters.

TRANSLATION AND COMMENTARY

mercy to us, we will not show mercy to them! If we are not deserving, then show us mercy, even if only for the animals' sake!"

וַיִּקְרְאוּ [1]The Gemara continues: The King of Nineveh proclaimed (Jonah 3:8): **"And let them cry mightily to God."** [2]**What did** the people of Nineveh **say** that could be described as a "mighty" and convincing argument? [3]The people of Nineveh **said before** God as follows: **"Master of the Universe! A submissive man and a man who is not submissive, a righteous man and a wicked man, who yields** to whom?" In the natural order of things, submissive and righteous people yield to the demands of those who are arrogant and wicked. Here, too, God who possesses all the qualities of righteousness should submit to the prayers of those who lack these qualities.

וְיָשֻׁבוּ [4]The verse in Jonah continues: **"And let them turn every one from his evil way, and from the violence that is in their hands."** [5]The Gemara asks: **What is the meaning of** the expression **"and from the violence that is in their hands"?**

אֲמַר שְׁמוּאֵל [6]**Shmuel said:** The king ordered as follows: **Even if** a person **has stolen a beam and has** already **built it into a building,** [7]**he must pull down the entire building and restore the** stolen **beam to its** rightful **owner.** Even though it would have been acceptable to leave the building intact and to offer the owner financial compensation for his beam, the King of Nineveh wanted his people to repent fully and to rid themselves of any trace of stolen property.

אָמַר [8]The Gemara continues with a related theme. **Rav Adda bar Ahavah said:** If **a person has** the ill-gotten gains of **a transgression in his possession, and he confesses** to the crime **but does not** fully **repent** of his evil ways and return the stolen property to its rightful owner, [9]**to what may** such a person **be**

אַתָּה מְרַחֵם עָלֵינוּ, אֵין אָנוּ מְרַחֲמִים עַל אֵלּוּ״.

[1]״וְיִקְרְאוּ אֶל אֱלֹהִים בְּחָזְקָה״. [2]מַאי אֲמוּר? [3]אָמְרוּ לְפָנָיו: ״רִבּוֹנוֹ שֶׁל עוֹלָם! עָלוּב וְשֶׁאֵינוֹ עָלוּב, צַדִּיק וְרָשָׁע, מִי נִדְחֶה מִפְּנֵי מִי?״

[4]״וְיָשֻׁבוּ אִישׁ מִדַּרְכּוֹ הָרָעָה, וּמִן הֶחָמָס אֲשֶׁר בְּכַפֵּיהֶם״. [5]מַאי ״וּמִן הֶחָמָס אֲשֶׁר בְּכַפֵּיהֶם״?

[6]אֲמַר שְׁמוּאֵל: אֲפִילּוּ גָּזַל מָרִישׁ וּבְנָאוֹ בְּבִירָה, [7]מְקַעֲקֵעַ כָּל הַבִּירָה כּוּלָּהּ וּמַחֲזִיר מָרִישׁ לִבְעָלָיו.

[8]אָמַר רַב אַדָּא בַּר אַהֲבָה: אָדָם שֶׁיֵּשׁ בְּיָדוֹ עֲבֵירָה, וּמִתְוַדֶּה וְאֵינוֹ חוֹזֵר בָּהּ, [9]לְמָה

LITERAL TRANSLATION

mercy on us, we will not have mercy on these!"

[1]"And let them cry mightily to God." [2]What did they say? [3]They said before Him: "Master of the Universe! A submissive man and a man who is not submissive, a righteous man and a wicked man, who yields to whom?"

[4]"And let them turn every one from his evil way, and from the violence that is in their hands."

[5]What is [meant by] "and from the violence that is in their hands"?

[6]Shmuel said: Even if he stole a beam and built it into a building, [7]he must pull down the entire building and restore the beam to its owner.

[8]Rav Adda bar Ahavah said: A person who has a transgression in his hand, and he confesses but does not retract from it, [9]to what

RASHI

מי נדחה מפני מי – הוי אומר צדיק מפני רשע. **אם אין אתה מרחם כו'** – כלומר: כשם שאתה אומר לרחם על אלו, דכתיב (תהלים קמה) "ורחמיו על כל מעשיו" – כן תרחם עלינו. **מריש** = קורה. **בירה** = מגדל. **שיש בידו עבירה** – גזל. **ואינו חוזר בו** – לשלם את הגזל, למה הוא דומה וכו'.

NOTES

אֲפִילּוּ גָּזַל מָרִישׁ **Even if he stole a beam.** Our Gemara explains that the verse, "And from the violence that is in their hands," teaches that the people of Nineveh went beyond the letter of the law and pulled down a building in order to return a stolen beam that had been incorporated into the structure. By Torah law, such action is indeed necessary, but in order to ease the path to repentance, the Rabbis enacted that the thief could keep the beam and offer financial compensation in its place (see *Gittin* 55a). In their desire to achieve full repentance, the people of Nineveh acted stringently and insisted that the beam itself be returned to its rightful owner. Some commentators explain that this is learned from the term "violence" (חָמָס), which refers to someone who forcibly takes what does not belong to him but pays for it. When the people of Nineveh decided to repent, they wanted not only to cleanse themselves of the crime of theft, but also to rid themselves of the guilt of violence (*Shittah*, *Meiri*). Others derive this from the expression "that is in their hands" (אֲשֶׁר בְּכַפֵּיהֶם). The people of Nineveh wished to turn away from the violence that they had incorporated into their construction with their own hands (*Maharsha*).

HALAKHAH

אָדָם שֶׁיֵּשׁ בְּיָדוֹ עֲבֵירָה **A person who has a transgression in his hand.** "Anyone who confesses to a transgression without wholeheartedly committing himself to refrain from sinning again in the future may be likened to a person who immerses himself while holding a *sheretz* in his hand, and who remains ritually impure until he casts the *sheretz* from his hand." (*Rambam*, *Sefer Mada*, *Hilkhot Teshuvah* 2:3.)

הוּא דּוֹמֶה? [1]לְאָדָם שֶׁתּוֹפֵס שֶׁרֶץ בְּיָדוֹ, [2]שֶׁאֲפִילּוּ טוֹבֵל בְּכָל מֵימוֹת שֶׁבָּעוֹלָם, לֹא עָלְתָה לוֹ טְבִילָה. [3]זְרָקוֹ מִיָּדוֹ, כֵּיוָן שֶׁטָּבַל בְּאַרְבָּעִים סְאָה מִיָּד עָלְתָה לוֹ טְבִילָה, [4]שֶׁנֶּאֱמַר: "וּמוֹדֶה וְעֹזֵב יְרֻחָם". [5]וְאוֹמֵר: "נִשָּׂא לְבָבֵנוּ אֶל כַּפָּיִם אֶל אֵל בַּשָּׁמָיִם". [6]"עָמְדוּ בִּתְפִלָּה. מוֹרִידִין לִפְנֵי הַתֵּיבָה זָקֵן, כו׳". [7]תָּנוּ רַבָּנַן: "עָמְדוּ בִּתְפִלָּה. [8]אַף עַל פִּי שֶׁיֵּשׁ שָׁם זָקֵן וְחָכָם, אֵין מוֹרִידִין לִפְנֵי הַתֵּיבָה אֶלָּא אָדָם הָרָגִיל. [9]רַבִּי יְהוּדָה אוֹמֵר: מְטוּפָּל וְאֵין לוֹ, וְיֵשׁ לוֹ יְגִיעָה בַּשָּׂדֶה, וּבֵיתוֹ רֵיקָם,

LITERAL TRANSLATION

may he be compared? [1]To a person who holds a *sheretz* in his hand, [2]for even if he immerses himself in all the waters in the world, the immersion does not count for him. [3][But] if he casts it from his hand, once he has immersed himself in forty *se'ahs* the immersion immediately counts for him, [4]as it is said: "But whoever confesses and forsakes them shall have mercy." [5]And it says: "Let us lift up our heart with our hands to God in the heavens." [6]"They stand up in prayer. They send down before the ark an elder, etc." [7]Our Rabbis taught: "They stand up in prayer. [8]Even though there is there an elder who is a Sage, they only send down before the ark a person who is well versed [in the prayers]. [9]Rabbi Yehudah says: One who has dependents but no [money], and has labor in the field but his house is empty,

RASHI

נשא לבבנו אל כפים — עם הכפים צריך לישא הלב לשמים, כלומר: שיחזור מקלקולו. **מטופל ואין לו** — יש לו טפלים, ואין לו במה להתפרנס, שלבו דואג עליו, [והוא צריך לקרות מקירות לבו עליהן]. **ויש לו יגיעה** — שמתכוין יותר בתפלת הגשמים.

TRANSLATION AND COMMENTARY

compared? [1]He may be likened **to a person holding a dead *sheretz*** (one of eight species of small rodents and reptiles mentioned in the Torah whose carcasses convey ritual impurity) **in his hand,** who wishes to cleanse himself of the ritual impurity he has contracted by touching the *sheretz*. [2]As long as the *sheretz* is in his hand, then **even if he immerses himself in all the waters in the world, the immersion will not count for him** and will not restore him to a state of ritual purity. [3]**But if he casts the *sheretz* from his hand,** then **once he has immersed himself in** a mikveh containing **forty *se'ah*s** [approximately 100 gallons] of water, **the immersion immediately counts for him** and he becomes ritually pure. [4]**For the verse says** (Proverbs 28:13): "He that covers up his sins shall not prosper; **but whoever confesses and forsakes them shall have mercy."** If someone confesses his sins without forsaking them, he will not win divine forgiveness. But once he has truly forsaken his sins and has rid himself of all that is illegally in his possession, he will immediately be shown mercy. [5]**And another verse says** (Lamentations 3:41): **"Let us lift up our heart with our hands to God in the heavens."** A person must first inspect what is in his hands. Only if his hands are clean of all stolen property may he lift up his heart in prayer and repentance to God in the heavens.

עָמְדוּ בִּתְפִלָּה [6]The Gemara now proceeds to the next clause of the Mishnah, which stated: "When the elder has finished admonishing the assembled congregation, **they stand up** in their places in the town square and prepare themselves **for prayer.** When **they appoint** a person **to come down before the ark** and lead the service, they choose **an elder,** who is well versed in the prayers." [7]**Our Rabbis taught** a related Baraita: "Those who are assembled for the service then **stand up** and prepare themselves **for prayer.** [8]**Even though there may be** among the congregation **an elder who is** also **a** Torah **Sage,** he is not necessarily chosen to lead the prayer. For **they only appoint a person to come down before the ark** and lead the service on fast days if he **is well versed in the prayers,** so that he will be able to recite the special liturgy fluently and without mistakes. [9]**Rabbi Yehudah says:** The prayer leader on a public fast must be **someone who has** young children who are financially **dependent** on him **but** has **no money** with which to support them, for such a person will certainly pray wholeheartedly. He must be **someone who works in the field but whose house is empty,** for

BACKGROUND

שֶׁאֲפִילּוּ טוֹבֵל בְּכָל מֵימוֹת שֶׁבָּעוֹלָם For even if he immerses himself in all the waters in the world. In this parable, immersion serves as a symbol of the things one does to purify oneself before the Lord, and the *sheretz* stands for the actual transgression committed. Hence it is emphasized that, as long as a person continues to grasp the polluting *sheretz* (meaning that he has not entirely eschewed sin), even if he makes a great effort to immerse himself, doing so often, wherever there is much water (meaning, that he prays and fasts frequently), his attempt to purify himself is of no use at all. On the other hand, if he casts away the *sheretz* (the sin), any ritual immersion, even in the minimum amount of water, is sufficient to purify him completely.

HALAKHAH

מְטוּפָּל וְאֵין לוֹ One who has dependents but no money. "On a public fast it is preferable to appoint as prayer leader someone who is well versed in the prayers, and in reading the Torah, the Prophets, and the Writings. He should have children who are financially dependent upon him, but no money with which to support them. He should have work to do in the field. There should be no sinners among the members of his household. He should not have had a bad reputation even as a young man. He should be humble and well liked by the congregation. He should know the proper melodies for the liturgy, and have a voice that is pleasant. It is best if an elder can be found with all these qualities, but if not, a young man with these qualities is chosen." (*Shulḥan Arukh, Oraḥ Ḥayyim* 579:1.)

[1]וּפִרְקוֹ נָאֶה, [2]וּשְׁפַל בֶּרֶךְ, וּמְרוּצֶּה לָעָם, [3]וְיֵשׁ לוֹ נְעִימָה, וְקוֹלוֹ עָרֵב, [4]וּבָקִי לִקְרוֹת בַּתּוֹרָה, וּבַנְּבִיאִים, וּבַכְּתוּבִים, וְלִשְׁנוֹת בַּמִּדְרָשׁ, בַּהֲלָכוֹת, וּבָאַגָּדוֹת, [5]וּבָקִי בְּכָל הַבְּרָכוֹת כּוּלָּן״. [6]וְיָהֲבוּ בֵּיהּ רַבָּנַן עֵינַיְיהוּ בְּרַב יִצְחָק בַּר אַמִּי.

[16B] [7]הַיְינוּ מְטוּפָּל וְאֵין לוֹ, הַיְינוּ בֵּיתוֹ רֵיקָם!

[8]אָמַר רַב חִסְדָּא: זֶהוּ שֶׁבֵּיתוֹ רֵיקָם מִן הָעֲבֵירָה.

[9]״וּפִרְקוֹ נָאֶה״. [10]אָמַר אַבַּיֵי: זֶה שֶׁלֹּא יָצָא עָלָיו שֵׁם רַע בְּיַלְדוּתוֹ.

[11]״הָיְתָה לִּי נַחֲלָתִי כְּאַרְיֵה בַיָּעַר. [12]נָתְנָה עָלַי בְּקוֹלָהּ; עַל

LITERAL TRANSLATION

[1]and whose youth was becoming, [2]and is humble (lit., 'lowly of the knee'), and is acceptable to the people, [3]and has a [melodious] tune, and whose voice is pleasant, [4]and who is expert in reading the Torah, and the Prophets, and the Writings, and in studying Midrash, Halakhot, and Aggadot, [5]and who is expert in all the blessings." [6]And the Rabbis set their eyes on Rav Yitzḥak bar Ammi.

[16B] [7]One who has dependents but no [money] is the same as one whose house is empty!

[8]Rav Ḥisda said: This [refers to] one whose house is empty of transgression.

[9]"And whose youth was becoming." [10]Abaye said: This [refers to] one who did not have a bad reputation in his youth.

[11]"My heritage has become to Me like a lion in the forest. [12]It has cried out against Me with its voice; therefore

TRANSLATION AND COMMENTARY

such a person will pray sincerely for rain. [1]**His youth must have been becoming** (as will be explained below). [2]The prayer leader must be **humble and acceptable to the people,** so that his being chosen to serve as the representative of the people will not create discord among the congregation. [3]He must **know the** traditional **melodies** to be used in the service **and must have a pleasant voice.** [4]The prayer leader on a public fast must **be expert in reading the Torah, the Prophets, and the Writings, and** must be **well versed in Midrash, Halakhah, and Aggadah,** for there are certain passages of the liturgy that are taken from Biblical and Rabbinic sources. [5]**And** the prayer leader must **be familiar with all the blessings** recited in the course of the service, so that he will be able to go through the special liturgy without making mistakes." [6]The Gemara relates that when **the Rabbis** discussed the qualities they wished to find in a prayer leader, they **set their eyes upon Rav Yitzḥak bar Ammi,** who possessed all the qualities mentioned above.

הַיְינוּ מְטוּפָּל [16B] [7]The Gemara seeks to clarify the meaning of some of the qualities mentioned by Rabbi Yehudah: The requirement that the prayer leader be **someone who has** young children who are financially **dependent** on him **but** has **no money** with which to support them **seems to be the same as** the requirement that he be **someone whose house is empty** of possessions and money. Why, then, does Rabbi Yehudah mention the same qualification twice?

אָמַר רַב חִסְדָּא [8]**Rav Ḥisda said** in reply: "Someone whose house is empty" does not **refer to** a person whose house is empty of money, but rather to **someone whose house is empty of transgression.** The prayer leader must be a righteous man, whose house is free of sin.

וּפִרְקוֹ נָאֶה [9]Rabbi Yehudah taught in the Baraita quoted above that the prayer leader on a public fast-day must be someone "**whose youth was becoming.**" [10]**Abaye said: This refers to someone who did not have a bad reputation** even **in his youth.**

הָיְתָה לִּי [11]Having discussed the conditions that determine the choice of the prayer leader on a public fast, the Gemara now explains a Biblical verse that alludes to God's reaction to a prayer leader who lacks the virtues mentioned above. In the verse (Jeremiah 12:8) God says: **"My heritage has become to Me like a lion in the forest.** [12]**It has cried out against Me with its voice; therefore I have hated it."**

RASHI

ופרקו נאה — מפרש לקמן. **ושפל ברך** = עניו. **ומרוצה לעם** = נוח לבריות, ומסכימין לתפלתו. **נעימה** — בסומי קלא, שמושך הלב. **ורגיל לקרות כו׳** — שיהו הפסוקים של תפלה סדורין בפיו. **היינו מטופל ואין לו היינו ביתו ריקן** — היינו כמו (איזהו). **ביתו ריקם מן העבירה** — שאין חמס וגזל בביתו. **ופרקו נאה** — אפילו כשעמד על בחרותו היה נאה, בלי שם רע.

NOTES

שֶׁבֵּיתוֹ רֵיקָם מִן הָעֲבֵירָה **One whose house is empty of transgression.** *Rashi* explains that the term "one whose house is empty of transgression" means that the house of the person appointed to lead the prayers on a fast-day must be free of stolen property and other ill-gotten gains. Thus, by fulfilling the qualification that his house be empty of transgression, and the qualification that his youth must have been becoming, the prayer leader serving on a fast-day is free of all transgressions, because the first qualification bars a person who has committed crimes against another person, and the second bars a person who has committed crimes against God (*Gevurat Ari*). *Rambam* (*Hilkhot Ta'aniyyot* 4:4) maintains that the term "one whose house is empty of transgression" means that the *household* of the prayer leader must be entirely free of transgression. Not only must the prayer leader himself be a righteous man, but his children and grandchildren and all other relatives dependent on him must also be free of sin.

SAGES

רַב יִצְחָק בַּר אַמִּי **Rav Yitzḥak bar Ammi.** A Babylonian Amora of the third generation, Rav Yitzḥak bar Ammi was a student of Rav Ḥisda and transmitted teachings in his name.

A number of Rav Yitzḥak bar Ammi's Halakhic statements and interpretations of Biblical verses are recorded in the Babylonian Talmud.

BACKGROUND

וּפִרְקוֹ נָאֶה **"And whose youth is becoming."** The term פֶּרֶק refers to the time in a person's life when he changes physically and psychologically, the time of adolescence. Often people of that age commit transgressions because of intense drives, or the wildness of youth, or psychological immaturity. Therefore it is emphasized that the prayer leader on a public fast-day must be someone who has never had a bad name, not even in his youth.

נָתְנָה עָלַי בְּקוֹלָהּ **"It has cried out against Me."** This refers to an unfit prayer leader. Not only are his prayers not acceptable, but also, when he raises his voice in prayer ("נָתְנָה עָלַי בְּקוֹלָהּ"), it is damaging, for such prayer is hated by God. Hence the tradition developed that, on special occasions, such as the High Holy Days, special care must be taken to ensure that the prayer leader shall be a God-fearing person.

כֵּן שְׂנֵאתִיהָ״. [1]מַאי ״נָתְנָה עָלַי בְּקוֹלָהּ״?

[2]אָמַר מָר זוּטְרָא בַּר טוֹבִיָּה אָמַר רַב, וְאָמְרִי לָהּ אָמַר רַבִּי חָמָא אָמַר רַבִּי אֶלְעָזָר: [3]זֶה שְׁלִיחַ צִבּוּר שֶׁאֵינוֹ הָגוּן הַיּוֹרֵד לִפְנֵי הַתֵּיבָה.

[4]״וְאוֹמֵר לִפְנֵיהֶם עֶשְׂרִים וְאַרְבַּע בְּרָכוֹת, שְׁמוֹנֶה עֶשְׂרֵה שֶׁבְּכָל יוֹם, וּמוֹסִיף עֲלֵיהֶן עוֹד שֵׁשׁ״. [5]הָנֵי שֵׁשׁ? [6]שֶׁבַע הָוְיָין, כִּדְתְנַן: ״עַל הַשְּׁבִיעִית הוּא אוֹמֵר: [7]׳בָּרוּךְ מְרַחֵם עַל הָאָרֶץ׳״.

[8]אָמַר רַב נַחְמָן בַּר יִצְחָק: מַאי שְׁבִיעִית? [9]שְׁבִיעִית לָאֲרוּכָּה, [10]כִּדְתַנְיָא: ״בְּ׳גוֹאֵל יִשְׂרָאֵל׳ מַאֲרִיךְ, [11]וּבְחוֹתָמָהּ הוּא אוֹמֵר: ׳מִי שֶׁעָנָה אֶת אַבְרָהָם בְּהַר הַמּוֹרִיָּה, הוּא יַעֲנֶה אֶתְכֶם וְיִשְׁמַע בְּקוֹל צַעֲקַתְכֶם הַיּוֹם הַזֶּה. בָּרוּךְ גּוֹאֵל יִשְׂרָאֵל׳. [12]וְהֵן עוֹנִין אַחֲרָיו ׳אָמֵן׳. [13]וְחַזַּן הַכְּנֶסֶת אוֹמֵר לָהֶם: ׳תִּקְעוּ, בְּנֵי

LITERAL TRANSLATION

I have hated it." [1]What is [meant by] "it has cried out against Me with its voice"?

[2]Mar Zutra bar Toviyyah said in the name of Rav, and some say Rabbi Ḥama said in the name of Rabbi Elazar: [3]This [refers to] a prayer leader who is unfit who goes down before the ark.

[4]"And he says before them twenty-four blessings, the eighteen of every day, and he adds to them another six." [5]Are they six? [6]They are seven, as we have learned: "For the seventh he says: [7]'Blessed [are You, O Lord], who has mercy on the land.'"

[8]Rav Naḥman bar Yitzḥak said: What is [meant by] "the seventh"? [9]Seventh from the expanded one, [10]as it was taught: "In [the blessing] 'Redeemer of Israel' he expands, [11]and in its ending he says: 'He who answered Abraham on Mount Moriah, He will answer you and will hearken unto the sound of your crying [on] this day. Blessed [are You, O Lord], the redeemer of Israel.' [12]And they answer after him 'Amen.' [13]And the synagogue attendant says to them: 'Sound a *tekiah,* sons of

TRANSLATION AND COMMENTARY

The Gemara asks: [1]**What is meant by "it has cried out against Me with its voice"?**

אָמַר [2]**Mar Zutra bar Toviyyah said in the name of Rav, and some say** that it was **Rabbi Ḥama** who **said** this **in the name of Rabbi Elazar:** [3]**This refers to a prayer leader who goes down before the** holy **ark** to lead the congregation in prayer, even though **he is unfit** for the task.

וְאוֹמֵר לִפְנֵיהֶם [4]We learned in the Mishnah: "When the prayer leader repeats the Amidah prayer on the last seven fast days, **he recites twenty-four blessings — the eighteen** blessings that are recited **every day and another six** blessings **which he adds."** [5]The Gemara asks: **Are there** really only **six** blessings that are added to the Amidah on these public fasts? [6]Surely **there are seven** extra blessings **as we learn** later in the same Mishnah: **"At the end of the seventh blessing,** the prayer leader **says:** 'He who answered David and Solomon his son in Jerusalem, He will answer you and will hearken unto the sound of your crying on this day. [7]**Blessed are You, O Lord, who has mercy on the land.'"**

אָמַר [8]**Rav Naḥman bar Yitzḥak said** in reply: Only six blessings are added to the Amidah on the final series of fasts decreed upon the community in times of drought. **What,** then, **does** the Mishnah **mean** when it speaks of **"the seventh** blessing"? The meaning is as follows: When the prayer leader repeats the Amidah prayer on these days, he recites an expanded version of the seventh blessing of the regular Amidah, which ends with the words "the redeemer of Israel," and he then continues with six additional blessings which are inserted into the service on account of the fast. Thus the blessing that ends with the words, "who has mercy on the land," [9]is the **seventh** blessing relating to the special nature of the day, if we start the count **from the** blessing, "the redeemer of Israel," which is one of the eighteen regular blessings, but which is recited on the fast in an **expanded** form. [10]**For** the following **was taught** in a Baraita: "On the last seven fast days, the prayer leader **expands the blessing 'Redeemer of Israel'** by inserting special prayers and supplications, [11]**and he recites its concluding formula** as follows: **'He who answered Abraham on Mount Moriah, He will answer you and will hearken unto the sound of your crying on this day. Blessed are You, O Lord, the redeemer of Israel.'** [12]Those assembled for the prayer service then **answer after him, 'Amen,'** the congregation's usual response to a blessing. [13]**The synagogue attendant** then **proclaims: 'Sound a** ***tekiah*** [a long, uninterrupted blast], **sons of**

SAGES

מָר זוּטְרָא בַּר טוֹבִיָּה **Mar Zutra bar Toviyyah.** A second-generation Babylonian Amora, Mar (or Rav) Zutra bar Toviyyah was an outstanding disciple of Rav, and in many Talmudic passages he transmits Rav's Halakhic and Aggadic teachings. After Rav's death, Mar Zutra studied in the yeshivah of Rav Yehudah, where he became a student-colleague of that scholar. His own teachings are also cited in a number of places.

RASHI

זה המעמיד חזן שאינו הגון לפני התיבה – רשע, שהקדוש ברוך הוא שונא אותו יותר מכולן, והוא נותן בקולו לפניו. **שביעית לארוכה** – שביעית לאותה ברכה שהתחיל להאריך בה. ואותה אינה מן התוספת, אלא משמונה עשרה הברכות היא, כדתניא: בגואל ישראל הוא מאריך. **הוא אומר לפניהן** – אותו הזקן הרגיל ומאריך בגאולה, כדקתני מתניתין.

TRANSLATION AND COMMENTARY

Aaron, sound a *tekiah*,' and the trumpets are sounded. [1]**Then** the prayer leader **resumes, and** continues with the first additional blessing inserted into the Amidah, at the conclusion of which **he says: 'He who answered our forefathers at the Red Sea, He will answer you and will hearken unto the sound of your crying on this day. Blessed are You, O Lord, who remembers the forgotten.'** [2]The congregation then **answers after him, 'Amen,'** [3]after which **the synagogue attendant proclaims: 'Sound a *teruah*** [a series of very short blasts], **sons of Aaron, sound a *teruah*,'** and the trumpets are sounded. [4]**And similarly with each of the** special **blessings** recited on account of the fast — the prayer leader completes the blessing, the congregation answers 'Amen' after him, and the synagogue attendant instructs the priests to sound the trumpets. The synagogue attendant alternates his instructions: [5]**After one** blessing **he says, 'Sound a *tekiah*,' and after the next** blessing **he says, 'Sound a *teruah*.'"** [6]The Baraita continues: **"When does this apply?** When does the congregation answer 'Amen' after each of the blessings recited by the prayer leader? [7]Everywhere **in the country** outside the Temple. [8]**But in the Temple it is not so, for we do not answer 'Amen'** to a blessing recited **in the Temple.** In the Temple, the congregation uses a different response to answer the blessings recited by the prayer leader [as will be explained below]. [9]**And from where** in the Bible **do we derive** the principle **that we do not answer 'Amen'** to a blessing recited **in the Temple?** [10]**From the verse** describing a prayer service in the Temple, **which says** [Nehemiah 9:5]: **'Stand up and bless the Lord your God from everlasting to everlasting, and let them bless Your glorious Name,**

אַהֲרֹן, תִּקְעוּ׳. [1]וְחוֹזֵר וְאוֹמֵר: ׳מִי שֶׁעָנָה אֶת אֲבוֹתֵינוּ עַל יַם סוּף, הוּא יַעֲנֶה אֶתְכֶם וְיִשְׁמַע בְּקוֹל צַעֲקַתְכֶם הַיּוֹם הַזֶּה. בָּרוּךְ זוֹכֵר הַנִּשְׁכָּחוֹת׳. [2]וְהֵן עוֹנִין אַחֲרָיו ׳אָמֵן׳. [3]וְחַזַּן הַכְּנֶסֶת אוֹמֵר לָהֶם: ׳הָרִיעוּ, בְּנֵי אַהֲרֹן, הָרִיעוּ׳. [4]וְכֵן בְּכָל בְּרָכָה וּבְרָכָה, [5]בְּאַחַת אוֹמֵר, ׳תִּקְעוּ׳, וּבְאַחַת אוֹמֵר, ׳הָרִיעוּ׳. [6]בַּמֶּה דְּבָרִים אֲמוּרִים? [7]בַּגְּבוּלִין. [8]אֲבָל בַּמִּקְדָּשׁ אֵינוֹ כֵן, לְפִי שֶׁאֵין עוֹנִין ׳אָמֵן׳ בַּמִּקְדָּשׁ. [9]וּמִנַּיִן שֶׁאֵין עוֹנִין ׳אָמֵן׳ בַּמִּקְדָּשׁ? [10]שֶׁנֶּאֱמַר: ׳קוּמוּ בָּרְכוּ אֶת ה׳ אֱלֹהֵיכֶם מִן הָעוֹלָם עַד הָעוֹלָם, וִיבָרְכוּ שֵׁם כְּבֹדֶךָ, וּמְרוֹמַם עַל כָּל בְּרָכָה

LITERAL TRANSLATION

Aaron, sound a *tekiah*.' [1]And he resumes and says: 'He who answered our forefathers at the Red Sea, He will answer you and will hearken unto the sound of your crying [on] this day. Blessed [are you, O Lord], who remembers the forgotten.' [2]And they answer after him 'Amen.' [3]And the synagogue attendant says to them: 'Sound a *teruah*, sons of Aaron, sound a *teruah*.' [4]And similarly with each and every blessing, [5]for one he says, 'Sound a *tekiah*,' and for one he says, 'Sound a *teruah*.' [6]In what [case] are these things said? [7]In the [rest of the] country [lit., 'the boundaries']. [8]But in the Temple it is not so, for we do not answer 'Amen' in the Temple. [9]And from where [do we derive] that we do not answer 'Amen' in the Temple? [10]For it is said: 'Stand up and bless the Lord your God from everlasting to everlasting, and let them bless Your glorious Name, which is exalted above all blessing

RASHI

במה דברים אמורים — דהן עונין אחריו "אמן", בגבולין. **אבל במקדש** — אומר אותו הזקן לאחר הפרשיות: מי שענה את אברהם הוא יענה אתכם וישמע קול צעקתכם ביום הזה ברוך אתה ה׳ אלהי ישראל מן העולם ועד העולם ברוך גואל ישראל. והן עונים אחריו: ברוך שם כבוד מלכותו לעולם ועד. וכן בכל ברכות שבמקדש. **לפי שאין עונין אמן במקדש** — כדיליף לקמן מקרא. **מניין שאין עונין אמן במקדש** — דכתיב בתפלת עזרא בבית שני "קומו וברכו את ה׳ אלהיכם" — והיינו "ברוך ה׳ אלהי ישראל כו׳". **ויברכו שם כבודך** — היינו שעונין אחריו "ברוך שם כבוד מלכותו לעולם ועד", כך הוא הפסוק: "ויברכו שם כבודך ומרומם על כל ברכה ותהלה".

NOTES

אֲבָל בַּמִּקְדָּשׁ אֵינוֹ כֵּן But in the Temple it is not so. Some commentators explain the difference between the congregation's response in the Temple and its response elsewhere as follows: In the Temple, where the personal Name of God is pronounced as it is written, the proper response to a blessing is: "Blessed is the Name of His glorious majesty for ever and ever." But in the areas outside of the Temple, where the Name is pronounced as if it were written "Adonai", those who hear a blessing answer with "Amen" (*Ritva*).

HALAKHAH

אֲבָל בַּמִּקְדָּשׁ אֵינוֹ כֵּן But in the Temple it is not so. "When the fast-day service was said in Jerusalem, the people would congregate on the Temple Mount opposite the Eastern Gate. When the prayer leader reached the passage, 'He who answered Abraham,' he would say: 'Blessed are You, O Lord, our God, the God of Israel, from everlasting to everlasting. Blessed are You, O Lord, redeemer of Israel.' And the congregation would answer after him: 'Blessed is the Name of His majesty for ever and ever.'" (*Rambam, Sefer Zemannim, Hilkhot Ta'aniyyot* 4:15.)

TRANSLATION AND COMMENTARY

which is exalted above all blessing and praise.' We learn from this that each blessing recited in the Temple concludes with the formula: 'Blessed is the Lord, the God of Israel, from everlasting to everlasting,' and the congregation responds, not with 'Amen,' but with: 'Blessed is the Name of His glorious majesty for ever and ever.' [1]**I might have thought that for all the blessings there should only be one praise,** and that the prayer leader should first recite all the blessings and only then should the congregation offer a single response. [2]**Therefore Scripture states: 'Which is exalted above all blessing and praise,'** [3]and this teaches us that **for every blessing** God **should be offered a** different **praise.** In other words, a separate response should be made at the conclusion of each blessing." [4]The Baraita now describes the order of the prayer service in the Temple: **"What does** the prayer leader conducting the fast-day service **in the Temple say** as he concludes each of the special blessings? The prayer leader expands the blessing 'Redeemer of Israel,' and concludes it with the following formula: [5]**'Blessed is the Lord, the God of Israel, from everlasting to everlasting. Blessed is the redeemer of Israel.'** [6]Instead of responding 'Amen,' those assembled for the prayer service in the Temple **answer after him: 'Blessed is the Name of His glorious majesty for ever and ever.'** [7]**The synagogue attendant** then **proclaims: 'Sound a *tekiah*, priests, sons of Aaron, sound a *tekiah*.'** [8]The prayer leader then **resumes** his prayer **and says: 'He who answered Abraham on Mount Moriah, He will answer you and will hearken unto the sound of your crying on this day,'** after which the trumpets are sounded. [9]**The prayer leader** then continues with the first additional blessing inserted into the Amidah, which he **concludes** as follows: **'Blessed is the Lord, the God of Israel,** from everlasting to everlasting. Blessed is He **who remembers the forgotten.'** [10]Once again the congregation **answer after him: 'Blessed is the Name of His glorious majesty for ever and ever.'** [11]**The synagogue attendant** then **proclaims: 'Sound a *teruah*, priests, sons of Aaron, sound a *teruah*.'** The prayer leader then resumes his prayer and says: 'He who answered our forefathers at the Red Sea, He will answer you and will hearken unto the sound of your crying on this day,' after which the trumpets are once again sounded. [12]**And similarly with each of the** special **blessings** inserted into the Amidah: The prayer leader completes the blessing and recites the appropriate concluding formula, the congregation answers with the words, 'Blessed is the name of His glorious majesty for ever and ever,' the synagogue attendant instructs the priests to sound the trumpets, the prayer leader entreats God to answer His people's cries as He did in Biblical times, and the trumpets are sounded.

וּתְהִלָּה׳. [1]יָכוֹל עַל כָּל בְּרָכוֹת כּוּלָּן לֹא תְּהֵא אֶלָּא תְּהִלָּה אַחַת. [2]תַּלְמוּד לוֹמַר: ׳וּמְרוֹמַם עַל כָּל בְּרָכָה וּתְהִלָּה׳ — [3]עַל כָּל בְּרָכָה תֵּן לוֹ תְּהִלָּה. [4]וְאֶלָּא בַּמִּקְדָּשׁ מַהוּ אוֹמֵר? [5]׳בָּרוּךְ ה׳, אֱלֹהֵי יִשְׂרָאֵל, מִן הָעוֹלָם וְעַד הָעוֹלָם. בָּרוּךְ גּוֹאֵל יִשְׂרָאֵל׳. [6]וְהֵן עוֹנִין אַחֲרָיו: ׳בָּרוּךְ שֵׁם כְּבוֹד מַלְכוּתוֹ לְעוֹלָם וָעֶד׳. [7]וְחַזַּן הַכְּנֶסֶת אוֹמֵר לָהֶם: ׳תִּקְעוּ, הַכֹּהֲנִים, בְּנֵי אַהֲרֹן, תִּקְעוּ׳. [8]וְחוֹזֵר וְאוֹמֵר: ׳מִי שֶׁעָנָה אֶת אַבְרָהָם בְּהַר הַמּוֹרִיָּה, הוּא יַעֲנֶה אֶתְכֶם וְיִשְׁמַע בְּקוֹל צַעֲקַתְכֶם הַיּוֹם הַזֶּה׳. [9]׳בָּרוּךְ ה׳, אֱלֹהֵי יִשְׂרָאֵל, זוֹכֵר הַנִּשְׁכָּחוֹת׳. [10]וְהֵם עוֹנִים אַחֲרָיו: ׳בָּרוּךְ שֵׁם כְּבוֹד מַלְכוּתוֹ לְעוֹלָם וָעֶד׳. [11]וְחַזַּן הַכְּנֶסֶת אוֹמֵר לָהֶם: ׳הָרִיעוּ, הַכֹּהֲנִים, בְּנֵי אַהֲרֹן, הָרִיעוּ, וכו׳׳. [12]וְכֵן בְּכָל בְּרָכָה וּבְרָכָה,

LITERAL TRANSLATION

and praise.' [1]I might have thought that for all the blessings there should only be one praise. [2]Therefore Scripture states: 'Which is exalted above all blessing and praise' — [3]for every blessing give Him praise. [4]But in the Temple what does he say? [5]'Blessed is the Lord, the God of Israel, from everlasting to everlasting. Blessed is the redeemer of Israel.' [6]And they answer after him: 'Blessed is the Name of His glorious majesty for ever and ever.' [7]And the synagogue attendant says to them: 'Sound a *tekiah*, priests, sons of Aaron, sound a *tekiah*.' [8]And he resumes and says: 'He who answered Abraham on Mount Moriah, He will answer you and will hearken unto the sound of your crying [on] this day.' [The prayer leader concludes the next blessing:] [9]'Blessed is the Lord, the God of Israel, who remembers the forgotten.' [10]And they answer after him: 'Blessed is the Name of His glorious majesty for ever and ever.' [11]And the synagogue attendant says to them: 'Sound a *teruah*, priests, sons of Aaron, sound a *teruah*, etc.' [12]And similarly with each and every blessing,

BACKGROUND

עַל כָּל בְּרָכָה תֵּן לוֹ תְּהִלָּה For every blessing give Him praise. The ordinary response, "Amen," is an expression of agreement with the words of the blessing and of hope that it will be fulfilled. However, in the Temple such a standard response was not sufficient. Words of praise for God had to be added in response to every blessing, and therefore the following phrase was recited: "Blessed be the Name of His glorious majesty for ever and ever." This was additional praise for God's Name, beyond reciting the blessing itself.

RASHI

הכי גרסינן: יכול על כל הברכות כולן תהלה אחת — תלמוד לומר "על כל ברכה", על כל ברכה תן לו תהלה. **חזן הכנסת** — לא אותו זקן ניהו. וחוזר חזן הכנסת ואומר להן: מי שענה כו׳, אף על פי שאמרו אותו זקן. **כשמריעין** — תחלה הוא אומר להן: הריעו בני אהרן, וכשתוקעין תחלה הוא אומר להן: תקעו בני אהרן כו׳.

TRANSLATION AND COMMENTARY

[1]The synagogue attendant alternates his instructions: **after one** blessing **he says, 'Sound a *tekiah*, and after the next** blessing **he says, 'Sound a *teruah*,' until all the** blessings **are finished.** [2]It is related that **Rabbi Ḥalafta** adopted the practices observed in the Temple and **instituted them in** his home town, **Tzippori, and Rabbi Ḥananyah ben Teradyon** acted likewise **in** his home town, **Sikhnin.** [3]**And when the matter came before the Sages** for consideration, **they said: They only acted this way** in the days of the Temple, when the people congregated **near the Eastern Gate** to pray **on the Temple Mount."**

[1]בְּאַחַת אוֹמֵר, 'תִּקְעוּ', וּבְאַחַת אוֹמֵר, 'הָרִיעוּ', עַד שֶׁגּוֹמֵר אֶת כּוּלָּן. [2]וְכָךְ הִנְהִיג רַבִּי חֲלַפְתָּא בְּצִפּוֹרִי וְרַבִּי חֲנַנְיָה בֶּן תְּרַדְיוֹן בְּסִיכְנִי. [3]וּכְשֶׁבָּא דָּבָר לִפְנֵי חֲכָמִים, אָמְרוּ: לֹא הָיוּ נוֹהֲגִין כֵּן אֶלָּא בְּשַׁעֲרֵי מִזְרָח וּבְהַר הַבַּיִת".

LITERAL TRANSLATION

[1]for one he says, 'Sound a *tekiah*, and for one he says, 'Sound a *teruah*,' until he finishes all of them. [2]And thus did Rabbi Ḥalafta institute in Tzippori, and Rabbi Ḥananyah ben Teradyon in Sikhnin. [3]And when the matter came before the Sages, they said: They would not act this way except at the eastern gates and on the Temple Mount."

RASHI

וכך הנהיג – כל מנהג זה רבי חלפתא בצפורי. לא היו נוהגין כך – שיהו עונין אחריו "ברוך שם כבוד מלכותו לעולם ועד", אלא עונין "אמן" בגבולין.

NOTES

לֹא הָיוּ נוֹהֲגִין כֵּן They would not act this way. There is a wide range of opinions concerning the mistake committed by Rabbi Ḥalafta and Rabbi Ḥananya ben Teradyon. As was explained earlier (15b), *Rashi* maintains that these Rabbis instituted that even those who were assembled for a fast-day service outside the Temple should not answer "Amen" after the prayer leader, but rather "Blessed is the Name of His glorious majesty for ever and ever," as was the custom in the Temple. But, as was explained above, most Rishonim reject this explanation, both because according to the reading found in most texts of the Mishnah the people observing the practice instituted by these Rabbis did in fact answer "Amen" after the prayer leader, and because it would be strange if these Sages had erred in such a serious way.

Some Rishonim (see *Ritva*, *Rid*; see also *Rosh HaShanah* 27a) explain that Rabbi Ḥalafta and Rabbi Ḥananya ben Teradyon adopted the practice of sounding a shofar together with the trumpets that are blown on fast days, even outside the Temple. The Sages disapproved of this practice, for it was only in the Temple itself that the two instruments were sounded together, while anywhere outside the Temple, it was only the trumpets that should have been sounded.

According to others (*Tosafot*, cited by *Ritva*; *Rambam*, *Hilkhot Ta'aniyyot* 4:17), it was only on the Temple Mount that the trumpets were sounded after each of the seven blessings relating to the special nature of the fast-day. In all other places the trumpets were sounded only at the end of the service after all twenty-four blessings had already been recited. Support for this view is brought from our Mishnah, which does not mention that the trumpets are sounded after each of the special blessings. Rabbi Ḥalafta and Rabbi Ḥananya ben Teradyon erred in that they instituted that the trumpets must be sounded after each of the seven special blessings outside the Temple as well. The difficulty with this explanation is that the Baraita states explicitly here that the trumpets were sounded after each of the special blessings, even outside the Temple.

Many Rishonim (*Rabbenu Gershom*, *Ra'avad*, *Ritva*, *Ran*, and others) explain that, outside the Temple, the fast-day service was conducted as outlined in our Mishnah. The prayer leader recited the entreaty "He who answered" as part of the concluding formula of each of the special blessings. The congregation answered each blessing with "Amen," the synagogue attendant then instructed the priests to sound the trumpets, and the trumpets were sounded. But on the Temple Mount the prayer leader did not recite the entreaty "He who answered" as part of the blessing. Instead, he completed the blessing, the congregation answered with "Blessed is the name of His glorious majesty for ever and ever," the synagogue attendant instructed the priests to sound the trumpets, the prayer leader then recited the entreaty that God should answer His people's cry as He had done in Biblical times, and finally the trumpets were sounded. (Alternatively, the prayer leader included the entreaty in the blessing, but repeated it after the congregation's response.) The difference between the Temple and elsewhere can be understood as follows: The trumpet blasts are intended to remind God of the merits of our forefathers, and therefore the trumpets should be sounded immediately after the prayer leader recites each of the entreaties that refer to those merits. The congregational response to the blessings recited in the Temple, "Blessed is the Name of His glorious majesty for ever and ever," would separate the entreaty from the sounding of the trumpets. Thus the prayer leader's entreaty must be deferred until after the congregation has responded to the blessing (or the entreaty must be repeated after the congregation's response), and the trumpets are then sounded immediately. But this is not necessary outside the Temple, where the congregation answers with a simple "Amen." Rabbi Ḥalafta and Rabbi Ḥananya ben Teradyon erred in that they adopted the Temple practice in places outside the Temple.

HALAKHAH

בְּאַחַת אוֹמֵר, "תִּקְעוּ", וּבְאַחַת אוֹמֵר, "הָרִיעוּ". For one he says, "Sound a *tekiah*," and for one he says, "Sound a *teruah*." "After the first special blessing recited by the prayer leader, the synagogue attendant proclaims: 'Sound a *tekiah*,' and after the next blessing he proclaims: 'Sound a *teruah*.' The synagogue attendant alternates these instructions until all seven of the special blessings are completed." (*Rambam*, *Sefer Zemannim*, *Hilkhot Ta'aniyyot* 4:17.)

[1] וְאִית דְּאָמְרִי כִּדְתַנְיָא: [2] ״אוֹמֵר לִפְנֵיהֶן עֶשְׂרִים וְאַרְבַּע בְּרָכוֹת, [3] שְׁמוֹנֶה עֶשְׂרֵה שֶׁבְּכָל יוֹם, וּמוֹסִיף עֲלֵיהֶן עוֹד שֵׁשׁ. [4] וְאוֹתָן שֵׁשׁ הֵיכָן אוֹמְרָן? [5] בֵּין ׳גּוֹאֵל׳ לְ׳רוֹפֵא חוֹלֵי׳. [6] וּמַאֲרִיךְ בִּגְאוּלָּה, [7] וְהֵן עוֹנִין אַחֲרָיו ׳אָמֵן׳ עַל כָּל בְּרָכָה וּבְרָכָה. [8] וְכָךְ הָיוּ נוֹהֲגִין בַּגְּבוּלִין. [9] אֲבָל בַּמִּקְדָּשׁ הָיוּ אוֹמְרִים: ׳בָּרוּךְ ה׳, אֱלֹהֵי יִשְׂרָאֵל, מִן הָעוֹלָם וְעַד הָעוֹלָם. בָּרוּךְ גּוֹאֵל יִשְׂרָאֵל׳. [10] וְלֹא הָיוּ עוֹנִין אַחֲרָיו ׳אָמֵן׳. [11] וְכָל כָּךְ לָמָּה? [12] לְפִי שֶׁאֵין עוֹנִין ׳אָמֵן׳ בַּמִּקְדָּשׁ. [13] וּמִנַּיִן שֶׁאֵין עוֹנִין ׳אָמֵן׳ בַּמִּקְדָּשׁ? שֶׁנֶּאֱמַר: ׳קוּמוּ בָּרְכוּ אֶת ה׳ אֱלֹהֵיכֶם מִן הָעוֹלָם עַד הָעוֹלָם, וִיבָרְכוּ שֵׁם כְּבוֹדֶךָ, וּמְרוֹמַם עַל כָּל בְּרָכָה וּתְהִלָּה׳ — [14] עַל כָּל בְּרָכָה וּבְרָכָה תֵּן לוֹ תְּהִלָּה״.

[15] תָּנוּ רַבָּנַן: [16] ׳עַל הָרִאשׁוֹנוֹת הוּא אוֹמֵר: בָּרוּךְ ה׳, אֱלֹהֵי יִשְׂרָאֵל, מִן הָעוֹלָם. וְעַד הָעוֹלָם בָּרוּךְ גּוֹאֵל יִשְׂרָאֵל׳. [17] וְהֵן עוֹנִין אַחֲרָיו: ׳בָּרוּךְ

LITERAL TRANSLATION

[1] And there are [some] who say [that it is] as was taught: [2] "He says before them twenty-four blessings, [3] the eighteen of every day, and he adds to them another six. [4] And where does he say those six? [5] Between [the blessing] 'Redeemer,' and [the blessing] 'Who heals the sick of [His people Israel].' [6] And he expands [the blessing of] Redemption, [7] and they answer 'Amen' after him after each and every blessing. [8] And this is how they acted in the [rest of the] country. [9] But in the Temple they would say: 'Blessed is the Lord, the God of Israel, from everlasting to everlasting. Blessed is the Redeemer of Israel.' [10] And they would not answer after him 'Amen.' [11] And why all this? [12] Because we do not answer 'Amen' in the Temple. [13] And from where [do we derive] that we do not answer 'Amen' in the Temple? For it is said: 'Stand up and bless the Lord your God from everlasting to everlasting, and let them bless Your glorious Name, which is exalted above all blessing and praise' — [14] for each and every blessing give Him praise."

[15] Our Rabbis taught: [16] "For the first ones he says: 'Blessed is the Lord, the God of Israel, from everlasting to everlasting. Blessed is the Redeemer of Israel.' [17] And they answer after him: 'Blessed is

TRANSLATION AND COMMENTARY

וְאִית דְּאָמְרִי כִּדְתַנְיָא [1] The Gemara now continues with another version of the Baraita just cited. **There are some who say that** the practice **is in accordance with what was taught** in the following Baraita: "When the prayer leader repeats the Amidah prayer on the last seven fast-days decreed in times of drought, [2] **he recites twenty-four blessings** — [3] **the eighteen** blessings that are recited **every day and another six blessings which he adds.** [4] **Where** in the Amidah **does** the prayer leader **say those six** extra blessings? [5] **Between the** seventh **blessing, 'Redeemer** of Israel,' **and the** eighth **blessing, 'Who heals the sick of** His people Israel.' [6] Before he inserts the six additional blessings, the prayer leader **expands the blessing of Redemption** by inserting special entreaties and supplications. [7] Those assembled for the prayer service **answer 'Amen' after him after every blessing.** [8] **This is how** the people **acted** at a fast-day service everywhere **in the country** outside the Temple. [9] **But** when the service was conducted **in the Temple,** the prayer leader expanded the blessing of Redemption and concluded it as follows: **'Blessed is the Lord, the God of Israel, from everlasting to everlasting. Blessed is the Redeemer of Israel.'** [10] And the congregation **would not answer 'Amen' after him.** Instead they said: 'Blessed is the Name of His glorious majesty for ever and ever.' [11] **What is the reason for this** difference? **Because we do not answer 'Amen'** to a blessing recited **in the Temple.** [12] **And from where in the Bible do we derive** the principle **that we do not answer 'Amen'** to a blessing recited **in the Temple?** [13] **From the verse** describing a prayer service in the Temple, which **says** (Nehemiah 9:5): **'Stand up and bless the Lord your God from everlasting to everlasting, and let them bless Your glorious name, which is exalted above all blessing and praise.'** [14] This teaches us that **for every blessing God should be offered a** different **praise.** In other words, a separate response should be made at the conclusion of each blessing, rather than a single response after all the blessings have been recited."

תָּנוּ רַבָּנַן [15] The Gemara now cites another Baraita on the subject of fast-day services in the Temple, in which **our Rabbis taught:** [16] "When the fast-day service is conducted in the Temple, the prayer leader recites **the first** blessing relating to the special nature of the day — the expanded version of the Redemption blessing — at the conclusion of which **he says: 'Blessed is the Lord, the God of Israel, from everlasting to everlasting. Blessed is the Redeemer of Israel.'** [17] Those assembled for the prayer service **answer after him: 'Blessed is**

RASHI

ואית דאמרי כדתנינן כו׳ — כלומר, ואיכא דמתני הכי.

BACKGROUND

וְחַזַּן הַכְּנֶסֶת אוֹמֵר **And the synagogue attendant says.** During the period of the Second Temple, there was a synagogue on the Temple Mount. In that synagogue prayers were held according to the ordinary formula and the Torah was read, whereas in the Temple itself only a few blessings were recited, but not the entire order of prayers. The head of the Temple synagogue was an important man who used to provide for the expenses of that synagogue. (The term חַזָּן — which means "cantor" in modern Hebrew — refers to the warden of the synagogue.) Every time prayers were held or the Torah was read on the Temple Mount, these men would exercise their functions.

TRANSLATION AND COMMENTARY

the Name of His glorious majesty for ever and ever.' [1]**The synagogue attendant** then **proclaims: 'Sound a** ***tekiah*****, priests, sound a** ***tekiah*****.'** [2]The prayer leader then **resumes** his prayer **and says: 'He Who answered Abraham on Mount Moriah, He will answer you and will hearken unto the sound of your crying on this day.'** [3]The priests then **sound a** ***tekiah*****, followed by a** ***teruah*****, and** then another ***tekiah***. The prayer leader then continues with the second blessing relating to the special nature of the day — the first additional blessing inserted into the service. [4]**At the** end of that **second** benediction, the prayer leader **says: 'Blessed is the Lord, the God of Israel, from everlasting to everlasting. Blessed is He who remembers the forgotten.'** [5]Once again, the congregation **answers after him: 'Blessed is the Name of His glorious majesty for ever and ever.'** [6]**The synagogue attendant** then **proclaims: 'Sound a** ***teruah*****, sons of Aaron, sound a** ***teruah*****.'** [7]The prayer leader then **says: 'He who answered our forefathers at the Red Sea, He will answer you and will hearken unto the sound of your crying on this day.'** [8]The priests then **sound a** ***teruah*****, followed by a** ***tekiah*****, and** then another ***teruah***. [9]**And similarly, after each of the** special **blessings** recited on the fast day, the synagogue attendant instructs the priests to sound the trumpets. He alternates his instructions; [10]**after one** blessing **he says, 'Sound a** ***tekiah*****,' and after the next** blessing **he says, 'Sound a** ***teruah*****,' until all the blessings are finished.** It is related that [11]**Rabbi Ḥalafta** adopted the practices observed in the Temple and **instituted them in** his home town, **Tzippori, and Rabbi Ḥananyah ben Teradyon** acted likewise **in** his home town, **Sikhnin.** [12]**And when the matter came before the Sages** for

שֵׁם כְּבוֹד מַלְכוּתוֹ לְעוֹלָם וָעֶד׳. [1]וְחַזַּן הַכְּנֶסֶת אוֹמֵר: ׳תִּקְעוּ, כֹּהֲנִים, תִּקְעוּ׳. [2]וְחוֹזֵר וְאוֹמֵר: ׳מִי שֶׁעָנָה אֶת אַבְרָהָם בְּהַר הַמּוֹרִיָּה, הוּא יַעֲנֶה אֶתְכֶם וְיִשְׁמַע בְּקוֹל צַעֲקַתְכֶם הַיּוֹם הַזֶּה׳. [3]וְהֵן תּוֹקְעִין, וּמְרִיעִין, וְתוֹקְעִין. [4]וְעַל הַשְּׁנִיָּה הוּא אוֹמֵר: ׳בָּרוּךְ ה׳, אֱלֹהֵי יִשְׂרָאֵל, מִן הָעוֹלָם וְעַד הָעוֹלָם. בָּרוּךְ זוֹכֵר הַנִּשְׁכָּחוֹת׳. [5]וְהֵן עוֹנִין אַחֲרָיו: ׳בָּרוּךְ שֵׁם כְּבוֹד מַלְכוּתוֹ לְעוֹלָם וָעֶד׳. [6]וְחַזַּן הַכְּנֶסֶת אוֹמֵר: ׳הָרִיעוּ, בְּנֵי אַהֲרֹן, הָרִיעוּ׳. [7]וְאוֹמֵר: ׳מִי שֶׁעָנָה אֶת אֲבוֹתֵינוּ עַל יַם סוּף, הוּא יַעֲנֶה אֶתְכֶם וְיִשְׁמַע בְּקוֹל צַעֲקַתְכֶם הַיּוֹם הַזֶּה׳. [8]וְהֵם מְרִיעִין, וְתוֹקְעִין, וּמְרִיעִין. [9]וְכֵן בְּכָל בְּרָכָה וּבְרָכָה, [10]בְּאַחַת אוֹמֵר, ׳תִּקְעוּ׳, וּבְאַחַת אוֹמֵר, ׳הָרִיעוּ׳, עַד שֶׁיִּגְמוֹר אֶת הַבְּרָכוֹת כּוּלָּן. [11]וְכָךְ הִנְהִיג רַבִּי חֲלַפְתָּא בְּצִיפּוֹרִי וְרַבִּי חֲנַנְיָה בֶּן תְּרַדְיוֹן בְּסִיכְנִי. [12]וּכְשֶׁבָּא דָּבָר אֵצֶל חֲכָמִים, אָמְרוּ:

LITERAL TRANSLATION

the Name of His glorious majesty for ever and ever.' [1]And the synagogue attendant says: 'Sound a *tekiah*, priests, sound a *tekiah*.' [2]And he resumes and says: 'He who answered Abraham on Mount Moriah, He will answer you and will hearken unto the sound of your crying [on] this day.' [3]And they sound a *tekiah*, and they sound a *teruah*, and they sound a *tekiah*. [4]And for the second one he says: 'Blessed is the Lord, the God of Israel, from everlasting to everlasting. Blessed is He who remembers the forgotten.' [5]And they answer after him: 'Blessed is the Name of His glorious majesty for ever and ever.' [6]And the synagogue attendant says: 'Sound a *teruah*, sons of Aaron, sound a *teruah*.' [7]And he says: 'He who answered our forefathers at the Red Sea, He will answer you and will hearken unto the sound of your crying [on] this day.' [8]And they sound a *teruah*, and they sound a *tekiah*, and they sound a *teruah*. [9]And similarly with each and every blessing, [10]for one he says, 'Sound a *tekiah*,' and for one he says, 'Sound a *teruah*,' until he finishes all the blessings. [11]And thus did Rabbi Ḥalafta institute in Tzippori, and Rabbi Ḥananyah ben Teradyon in Sikhnin. [12]And when the matter came before the Sages, they said:

RASHI

וכן הנהיג — מנהג זה למקדש קאי.

NOTES

וְהֵן תּוֹקְעִין, וּמְרִיעִין, וְתוֹקְעִין **And they sound a** ***tekiah*****,** and they sound a *teruah*, and they sound a *tekiah*. *Rambam* (*Hilkhot Ta'aniyyot* 4:17), who apparently had the reading found in the standard text of the Gemara, maintains that after the first blessing the priests sounded a *tekiah*, then a *teru'ah*, and then a *tekiah*; and after the second blessing they sounded a *teruah*, then a *tekiah*, and then a *teruah*, alternating the order of the blasts after each blessing. According to other readings found in the Rishonim (see *Ritva*), the blasts were sounded in the same order after each blessing — *tekiah*, *teruah*, *tekiah*, or alternatively one blessing was followed by a *tekiah*, the next by a *teruah*, and the next by a *tekiah*.

TRANSLATION AND COMMENTARY

consideration, **they said:** [1]**They only acted this way** in the days of the Temple, when the people congregated **near the Eastern Gate** to pray **on the Temple Mount."**

רַבִּי יְהוּדָה [2]We learned in our Mishnah: **"Rabbi Yehudah says:** The prayer leader **does not recite** the blessings of ***Zikhronot*** and *Shofarot* on fast-days decreed on account of drought. Instead, he says blessings that relate directly to the calamity currently threatening the community." [3]**Rabbi Adda of Yaffo said: What is Rabbi Yehudah's reasoning?** [4]**Because we do not say** the blessings of ***Zikhronot* and *Shofarot*** [17A] **except on Rosh HaShanah, on** Yom Kippur of **the Jubilee Year, and in time of war.** These two blessings are said on Rosh HaShanah because they express the two main characteristics of Rosh Hashanah — its being the day of remembrance and the day of sounding the shofar. They are said on Yom Kippur of the Jubilee Year because of the general analogy drawn between that day and Rosh HaShanah. And they are said in time of war because of the verse (Numbers 10:9) that says: "And if you go to war in your land against the enemy that oppresses you, then you shall blow an alarm with the trumpets, and you shall be remembered before the Lord your God, and you shall be saved from your enemies." But on fast-days decreed on account of drought, blessings based on Biblical passages dealing with famine and drought are more appropriate.

LITERAL TRANSLATION

[1]They would not act this way except at the eastern gates and on the Temple Mount."

[2]"Rabbi Yehudah says: It is not necessary to say *Zikhronot*, etc." [3]Rabbi Adda of Yaffo said: What is the reason of Rabbi Yehudah? [4]Because we do not say *Zikhronot* and *Shofarot* [17A] except on Rosh HaShanah, and in the Jubilee Years, and in time of war.

[5]"For the first he says: "He who answered Abraham, etc."

[6][A Tanna] taught: "There are those who exchange 'crying' to Elijah and 'prayer' to Samuel."

[7]Granted that regarding Samuel "prayer" is written and "crying" is written. [8]But regarding Elijah,

[1]לֹא הָיוּ נוֹהֲגִין כֵּן אֶלָּא בְּשַׁעֲרֵי מִזְרָח וּבְהַר הַבַּיִת״.
[2]״רַבִּי יְהוּדָה אוֹמֵר: לֹא הָיָה צָרִיךְ לוֹמַר זִכְרוֹנוֹת, כו׳״.
[3]אָמַר רַבִּי אַדָּא דְּמִן יָפוֹ: מַאי טַעֲמָא דְּרַבִּי יְהוּדָה? [4]לְפִי שֶׁאֵין אוֹמְרִים זִכְרוֹנוֹת וְשׁוֹפָרוֹת [17A] אֶלָּא בְּרֹאשׁ הַשָּׁנָה, וּבַיּוֹבְלוֹת, וּבִשְׁעַת מִלְחָמָה.
[5]״עַל הָרִאשׁוֹנָה הוּא אוֹמֵר: ׳מִי שֶׁעָנָה אֶת אַבְרָהָם, כו׳׳״.
[6]תָּנָא: ״יֵשׁ מַחֲלִיפִין ׳צְעָקָה׳ לְאֵלִיָּהוּ וּ׳תְפִלָּה׳ לִשְׁמוּאֵל.״
[7]בִּשְׁלָמָא גַּבֵּי שְׁמוּאֵל כְּתִיב בֵּיהּ ״תְּפִלָּה״ וּכְתִיב בֵּיהּ ״צְעָקָה״, [8]אֶלָּא גַּבֵּי אֵלִיָּהוּ,

RASHI

אלא בראש השנה — כדאמרינן בראש השנה (טז, א): אמרו לפני מלכיות וזכרונות וכו׳. **וביובל** — ביום הכפורים של יובל, כדתנן התם (כו,ב): שוה היובל לראש השנה לתקיעה ולברכות כו׳. **ובשעת מלחמה** — דכתיב (במדבר י) ״וכי תבאו מלחמה בארצכם על הצר הצורר אתכם״ וגו׳. ולא ידעינן מנא איתפריש דאומר ברכות ופסוקי מלכיות זכרונות ושופרות בשעת מלחמה. **צעקה לאליהו** — על ״מי שענה את אליהו״ חותם ״שומע צעקה״, ובשמואל ״שומע תפלה״ דכתיב ביה תפלה (שמואל א׳ ז): ״קבצו את כל ישראל המצפתה ואתפלל בעדכם״. **צעקה** — דכתיב (שם) ״ויחר לשמואל ויזעק אל ה׳ כל הלילה״. ואיכא למימר במצפה הוה ההיא צעקה, דבתר פרשת ״קבצו כל ישראל המצפתה״ כתיב בפרשת ״נחמתי כי המלכתי את שאול״ וגו׳. כך שמעתי. **גבי אליהו** — במעשה דהר הכרמל כתיב תפלה, דכתיב ״עניני ה׳ עניני״ דמשמע לשון בקשה ותפלה, ולא לשון צעקה ומשני: ״עניני ה׳ עניני״ — לשון צעקה הוא. כך שמעתי.

עַל הָרִאשׁוֹנָה [5]The Gemara now proceeds to discuss the portion of our Mishnah that deals with the concluding formula of each of the blessings recited on account of the fast. The Mishnah stated: **"At the** end of **the first** blessing, the prayer leader says: **'He who answered Abraham, etc.'** At the end of the fourth blessing, the prayer leader says: 'He who answered Samuel at Mitzpah, He will answer you and will hearken unto the sound of your crying on this day. Blessed are You, O Lord, who hearkens unto crying.' At the end of the fifth blessing, the prayer leader says: 'He who answered Elijah on Mount Carmel, He will answer you and will hearken unto the sound of your crying on this day. Blessed are You, O Lord, who hearkens unto *prayer*.'" [6]**A Tanna taught** a Baraita, which stated: **"There are those who exchage** the concluding formulas of the fourth and fifth blessings, reciting the formula 'Who hearkens unto **crying'** at the end of the blessing referring **to Elijah and** the formula 'Who hearkens unto **prayer'** at the end of the blessing referring **to Samuel."**

בִּשְׁלָמָא [7]The Gemara raises a question regarding this variation in the endings of the blessing. **There is no problem regarding Samuel in using the alternative formula, because we find "prayer" and we find "crying"** written in the Bible in connection with Samuel. For one verse reads (I Samuel 7:5): "And Samuel said, Gather all Israel to Mitzpah, and I will *pray* for you to the Lord," and another verse reads (I Samuel 7:9): "And Samuel *cried* to the Lord for Israel, and the Lord heard him." Thus it is appropriate for either term to be included in the concluding formula of the blessing relating to Samuel. [8]**But regarding Elijah, we find**

SAGES

רַבִּי אַדָּא דְּמִן יָפוֹ Rabbi Adda of Yaffo. A Palestinian Amora, this Sage is seldom mentioned in the Talmud, and it is not known to which generation he belonged, though it seems likely that it was the third generation. Although Yaffo (Jaffa) is not known to have been an important Torah center, Rabbi Adda's name indicates that nevertheless there were significant scholars there. The sources state that this Rabbi Adda had a son, Rabbi Ḥiyya.

BACKGROUND

צְעָקָה וּתְפִלָּה "Crying" and "prayer." The term תְּפִלָּה ("prayer") comprises all forms of prayer, whereas the term צְעָקָה (literally, "a shout") refers to more intense prayer, a demand for an immediate response. In the Bible we find that, on several occasions great men shouted out before God. Indeed, the Gemara's response is that the expression, "Answer me, O Lord, answer me," although it does not use the term צְעָקָה, nevertheless belongs to the category of a shout because of its content, for it demands an immediate response.

TRANSLATION AND COMMENTARY

"prayer" written in the Bible in connection with Elijah. For the verse that reads (I Kings 18:37): "Answer me, O Lord, answer me, so that this people may know that You are the Lord," is a prayer. [1] **But we do not find "crying"** written in the Bible in connection with Elijah. Thus the term "prayer" should be used in the concluding formula of the blessing relating to Elijah, as is described in the Mishnah, and not the term "crying," as is suggested as an alternative in the Baraita.

עֲנֵנִי, ה׳, עֲנֵנִי [2] The Gemara answers: The expression used by Elijah, **"Answer me, O Lord, answer me," is** also **an expression of "crying."** Thus it is fitting to conclude the blessing relating to Elijah with the formula, "Who hearkens unto crying."

עַל הַשִּׁשִּׁית [3] The next clause of the Mishnah states: **"At the end of the sixth** blessing, the prayer leader **says: 'He who answered Jonah** in the belly of the fish, He will answer you and will hearken unto the sound of your crying on this day. Blessed are You, O Lord, who answers in time of trouble.' [4] **At** the end of **the seventh** blessing, the prayer leader **says: 'He who answered David** and Solomon his son in Jerusalem, He will answer you and will hearken unto the sound of your crying on this day. Blessed are You, O Lord, who has mercy on the land.'" The Gemara questions the order of these blessings: [5] **Now since** the Prophet **Jonah lived after** King **David and** King **Solomon** [see II Kings 14:25], [6] **what is the reason that** Jonah **is mentioned** in the blessings **before** David and Solomon?

מִשּׁוּם [7] The Gemara answers: Rather than following the chronological order, the Sages arranged the blessings as they did **because they wished to end** the series **with** the formula, [8] **"Who has mercy on the land,"** which is most directly related to the drought. Thus they had to place the blessing relating to David and Solomon at the end, because David and Solomon ruled the land and prayed on its behalf.

תָּנָא [9] In connection with the concluding formula for the seventh blessing, **a Tanna taught** the following Baraita: **"In the name of Summakhos it was said:** The seventh blessing does not end with the words, 'Who has mercy on the land,' but rather with the following formula: [10] **'Blessed are You, O Lord, who humbles the exalted.'"**

[1] "תְּפִלָּה" כְּתִיב, "צְעָקָה" לָא כְּתִיב!
[2] "עֲנֵנִי, ה׳, עֲנֵנִי" לְשׁוֹן "צְעָקָה" הִיא.
[3] "עַל הַשִּׁשִּׁית הוּא אוֹמֵר: 'מִי שֶׁעָנָה אֶת יוֹנָה, כו׳". [4] עַל הַשְּׁבִיעִית הוּא אוֹמֵר: 'מִי שֶׁעָנָה אֶת דָּוִד, כו׳'". [5] מִכְּדִי יוֹנָה בָּתַר דָּוִד וּשְׁלֹמֹה הֲוָה, [6] מַאי טַעֲמָא מַקְדִּים לֵיהּ בְּרֵישָׁא?
[7] מִשּׁוּם דְּבָעֵי לְמִיחֲתָם: [8] "מְרַחֵם עַל הָאָרֶץ".
[9] תָּנָא: "מִשּׁוּם סוּמָכוֹס אָמְרוּ: [10] 'בָּרוּךְ מַשְׁפִּיל הָרָמִים'".

LITERAL TRANSLATION

"prayer" is written, [1] [but] "crying" is not written!

[2] "Answer me, O Lord, answer me" is an expression of "crying."

[3] "For the sixth he says: 'He who answered Jonah, etc.' [4] For the seventh he says: 'He who answered David, etc.'" [5] Now since Jonah lived after David and Solomon, [6] what is the reason that he places him first?

[7] Because he wishes to end: [8] "Who has mercy on the land."

[9] [A Tanna] taught: "In the name of Summakhos they said: [10] 'Blessed [are You, O Lord,] who humbles the exalted.'"

RASHI

יונה בתר דוד ושלמה — דהוה בימי אמציהו, כסדר עולם. **דבעי למחתם** — בסוף כל ברכות "ברוך מרחם על הארץ" ולהכי בעי באותה חתימה דוד ושלמה. שהן התפללו על ארץ ישראל. כך שמעתי. אי נמי: משום דאינהו תקון בית המקדש, דהוא עיקר הארץ. כך שמעתי. **ברוך משפיל הרמים** — היו אומרים במקום "ברוך מרחם", שהכניעם במטר ששבו בתשובה.

SAGES

סוּמָכוֹס Summakhos. His full name is Summakhos ben Yosef, and he was one of the fifth and last generation of Tannaim. Summakhos was Rabbi Meir's most distinguished disciple and was responsible for transmitting much of his master's legacy of teachings. Even after Rabbi Meir's death, Summakhos devoted much effort to resolving possible contradictions in those teachings.

Like Rabbi Meir, Summakhos was famous for his חֲרִיפוּת — acute powers of reasoning. The Talmud (*Eruvin* 13b) praises him as being capable of providing forty-eight explanations to substantiate every ruling he made in matters of ritual purity.

He was apparently considered one of the leading Sages of his generation, for we even find mention of him contesting the Halakhic opinions of the greatest of the contemporaries of Rabbi Meir, including Rabbi Yose and Rabbi Eliezer ben Ya'akov. Even a Sage as distinguished as Rabbi Natan sought out Summakhos's opinion.

Summakhos appears to have lived to a great age, for even the Amora, Rav, met him and was taught by him.

LANGUAGE

סוּמָכוֹס Summakhos. The source for this name is the Greek word σύμμαχος, *summakhos*, which means "ally."

NOTES

בָּרוּךְ מַשְׁפִּיל הָרָמִים Blessed are You, O Lord, who humbles the exalted. The Rishonim disagree about how this concluding formula relates to David and Solomon. *Ritva* (following the Jerusalem Talmud) explains that both David and Solomon became overly proud — David, when he conducted a census of the nation, and Solomon, when he glorified his achievement in building the Temple (I Kings 8:13). Both of them were then humbled by God, after which they repented before Him and their prayers were once again answered. Thus the blessing expresses the hope that, just as the repentance of David and Solomon was accepted by God, so too will the repentance of those who fast be accepted by Him, and the calamity threatening the community will thereby be averted.

Shittah explains this concluding formula in a very different manner: During the reigns of David and Solomon, the elevated were humbled. In other words, the nations of the world became subjugated to Israel. Thus the series of special blessings recited on account of drought concludes with a general expression of praise to God. A variant reading is cited by a number of Rishonim: "Blessed are You, O Lord, who humbles and elevates [מַשְׁפִּיל וּמֵרִים]."

TRANSLATION AND COMMENTARY

שָׁלֹשׁ תַּעֲנִיּוֹת הָרִאשׁוֹנוֹת [1] **A later clause of the** Mishnah states: **"On the first three fasts** imposed on the community when the rain is late, **the members of the** *mishmar* whose week it is to serve in the Temple **fast, but** they **do not prolong their fast** until nightfall." The Mishnah continues with further rulings regarding the members of the *mishmar* and the *bet av* whose turn it is to serve in the Temple. [2] **Our Rabbis taught** the following Baraita: **"Why did** the Sages **say that the members of the** *mishmar* whose week it is to serve in the Temple **are permitted to drink wine during the night, but not during the day?** [3] They may not drink wine during the day, **lest the Temple service** on a particular day become too **burdensome for the members of the** *bet av* serving in the Temple at the time, [4] **and** as a result the other members of the *mishmar* whose week it is to serve **will be required to come in and help them** complete their tasks. Thus the Sages forbade all the members of that week's *mishmar* to drink wine **during the day,** lest they enter the Temple and perform the Temple service while intoxicated. But the members of the *mishmar* may drink wine during the night, when only a small amount of work has to be done in the Temple, and it is unlikely that the members of that day's *bet av* will require assistance. [5] **And why did** the Sages **say that the members of the** *bet av* whose day it is to serve in the Temple **may not drink wine** at all, neither **during the day nor during the night?** [6] They may not drink wine at all, **because** on the day that it is their turn to serve in the Temple **they are constantly engaged in the Temple service,** day and night. [7] **From here** the Sages **derived** the following law: Even today, when the Temple is no longer in existence, a priest is forbidden to drink wine at a time when it would theoretically be his turn to serve in the Temple, for the Temple may speedily be rebuilt and the priest may be summoned to serve there. [8] Thus, **if a priest knows** to which *mishmar* he belongs, because he can trace back his ancestry to a particular *mishmar*, and he knows the week during which that *mishmar* used to serve in the Temple, **and** if **he** also **knows** to which *bet av* he belongs and the day on which that *bet av* used to

LITERAL TRANSLATION

[1] "[On] the first three fasts, the members of the *mishmar* fast but do not complete [their fast], etc." [2] Our Rabbis taught: "Why did they say [that] the members of the *mishmar* are permitted to drink wine in the nights, but not in the days? [3] Lest the [Temple] service weigh heavily on the members of the *bet av*, [4] and they will come and they will help them. [5] Why did they say [that] the members of the *bet av* [may not drink wine,] neither in the day nor in the night? [6] Because they are always engaged in the [Temple] service. [7] From here they said: [8] Any priest who can identify his *mishmar* and his *bet av*,

[1]"שָׁלֹשׁ תַּעֲנִיּוֹת הָרִאשׁוֹנוֹת, אַנְשֵׁי מִשְׁמָר מִתְעַנִּין וְלֹא מַשְׁלִימִין כו׳". [2]תָּנוּ רַבָּנַן: "מִפְּנֵי מָה אָמְרוּ אַנְשֵׁי מִשְׁמָר מוּתָּרִין לִשְׁתּוֹת יַיִן בַּלֵּילוֹת, אֲבָל לֹא בַּיָּמִים? [3]שֶׁמָּא תִּכְבַּד הָעֲבוֹדָה עַל אַנְשֵׁי בֵּית אָב, [4]וְיָבוֹאוּ וִיסַיְּיעוּ לָהֶם. [5]מִפְּנֵי מָה אָמְרוּ אַנְשֵׁי בֵּית אָב לֹא בַּיּוֹם וְלֹא בַּלַּיְלָה? [6]מִפְּנֵי שֶׁהֵן עֲסוּקִין תָּמִיד בַּעֲבוֹדָה. [7]מִכָּאן אָמְרוּ: [8]כָּל כֹּהֵן שֶׁמַּכִּיר מִשְׁמַרְתּוֹ וּמִשְׁמֶרֶת בֵּ׳׳וּ אָב

RASHI

מִכָּאן וְגוֹמְרוּ מְדַקְתָּנֵי הָכָא, דַּאֲפִילוּ אַנְשֵׁי מִשְׁמָר שֶׁלֹּא הָיוּ עוֹבְדִין בְּאוֹתוֹ הַיּוֹם כְּלָל — אֲפִילוּ הָכִי אֲסוּרִין לִשְׁתּוֹת יַיִן. כֹּהֵן — בַּזְּמַן הַזֶּה. הַמַּכִּיר מִשְׁמַרְתּוֹ — הַיּוֹדֵעַ מֵאֵיזוֹ מִשְׁמֶרֶת הוּא, מִיְּשֹעֲרִיב אוֹ מִידַעְיָה, אוֹ אַחַת מֵעֶשְׂרִים וְאַרְבָּעָה מִשְׁמָרוֹת, שֶׁיּוֹדֵעַ שְׁמוֹת אֲבוֹתָיו וַאֲבוֹת אֲבוֹתָיו עַד יְהוֹיָרִיב, וְיוֹדֵעַ אֵיזֶה יוֹם וְאֵיזֶה שַׁבָּת הָיוּ עוֹבְדִים.

CONCEPTS

מִשְׁמָר וּבֵית אָב *Mishmar* and *bet av*. The priests who served in the Temple were divided into twenty-four groups, called *mishmarot* ("watches"). Each *mishmar* served for one week at a time. Thus each *mishmar* performed the Temple service for approximately two weeks every year. During the Pilgrim Festivals, all the *mishmarot* went to the Temple and performed the Temple service together. Each *mishmar* received the priestly gifts (מַתְּנוֹת כְּהוּנָּה) that were contributed to the Temple during their week of Temple service. The *mishmarot* were divided into *batei av* (בָּתֵּי אָב — "families"), which served in the Temple for one day of the week. Corresponding to each *mishmar* there was a *ma'amad* ("post" or "division"), a group of non-priests, who accompanied the members of the *mishmar* to Jerusalem. The priests were originally divided into *mishmarot* in the time of King David. During the Second Temple period, when many of the Jews who had been exiled to Babylonia after the destruction of the First Temple returned to Eretz Israel, some of the *mishmarot* remained in Babylonia. Those priests who did return to Eretz Israel had to be divided once again into twenty-four *mishmarot*.

BACKGROUND

כָּל כֹּהֵן שֶׁמַּכִּיר מִשְׁמַרְתּוֹ **Any priest who can identify his** *mishmar*. For many generations after the destruction of the Temple, the memory of the *mishmarot* was preserved, along with the lists of priestly families belonging to each *mishmar*. Such lists are found in a significant number of hymns and also in inscriptions found in ancient synagogues in Galilee, centuries after the destruction of the Temple.

NOTES

אַנְשֵׁי בֵּית אָב לֹא בַּיּוֹם וְלֹא בַּלַּיְלָה **The members of the** *bet av* **may drink wine neither in the day nor in the night.** Most Rishonim explain that the members of the *bet av* whose turn it is to serve in the Temple are forbidden to drink wine not only during the day but also at night, because certain tasks — for example, the burning of fats — are carried out at night as well as by day.

Rambam (*Hilkhot Bi'at HaMikdash* 1:6) explains that the members of the *bet av* may not drink wine at night, lest they rise early in the morning and begin to serve in the Temple before they are entirely sober, and they thus violate

the prohibition against performing the Temple service while intoxicated.

Ḥasdei David notes that there is a practical difference between these two explanations: According to *Rambam*, the members of the *bet av* are forbidden to drink wine on the night prior to the day on which they are to serve in the Temple, whereas according to the other Rishonim, they are forbidden to drink wine on the night following the day on which they performed their service.

כָּל כֹּהֵן שֶׁמַּכִּיר מִשְׁמַרְתּוֹ **Any priest who can identify his** *mishmar*. Our commentary follows *Rashi* and many other

HALAKHAH

אַנְשֵׁי מִשְׁמָר מוּתָּרִין לִשְׁתּוֹת יַיִן בַּלֵּילוֹת, אֲבָל לֹא בַּיָּמִים **The members of the** *mishmar* **are permitted to drink wine in the nights, but not in the days.** "The members of the *mishmar* whose week it is to serve in the Temple are permitted to drink wine during the night, but not during

the day. The members of the *bet av* whose day it is to serve in the Temple are forbidden to drink wine both during the day and during the night." (*Rambam, Sefer Avodah, Hilkhot Bi'at HaMikdash* 1:6.)

TRANSLATION AND COMMENTARY

serve, [1]**and** if **he** also **knows that the members of his** ***bet av*** **were established** as fit to serve in the Temple, never having been disqualified from taking part in the Temple service, he **is forbidden to drink wine all that day** that his *bet av* used to serve, for the Temple may speedily be rebuilt and he must be prepared to serve there. [2]**If** the priest **knows** to which ***mishmar*** he belongs and the week during which that *mishmar* used to serve in the Temple, **but he does not know** to which ***bet av*** he belongs and so cannot know the particular day of the week that his *bet av* used to serve, [3]**but he does know that the members of his** ***bet av*** **were established** as fit to serve in the Temple, **he is forbidden to drink wine throughout the week** that his *mishmar* used to serve in the Temple. Every day of that week may be the day on which the priest's *bet av* used to serve. [4]And **if the** priest **does not know** to which ***mishmar*** he belongs **or** to which ***bet av*** he belongs, **but he knows that the members of his** ***bet av*** were indeed **established** as fit to serve in the Temple, [5]**he is forbidden to drink wine throughout the year,** for any day may be the turn of his *bet av* to serve in the Temple. [6]**Rabbi** Yehudah HaNasi disagrees with the anonymous first Tanna of the Baraita and **says: I say** that if we are concerned that the rebuilding of the Temple may take place very soon, then every priest **should forever be forbidden to drink wine,** for when the Temple is rebuilt, the entire priesthood may be summoned to serve at the rededication ceremonies, or the *mishmarot* may be entirely rearranged, and therefore no priest should ever be allowed to become intoxicated. [7]**But what can I do?** The extended period of time that **the Temple** has remained

שֶׁלּוֹ, [1]וְיוֹדֵעַ שֶׁבָּתֵּי אֲבוֹתָיו קְבוּעִין שָׁם, אָסוּר לִשְׁתּוֹת יַיִן כָּל אוֹתוֹ הַיּוֹם. [2]בְּמַכִּיר מִשְׁמַרְתּוֹ וְאֵין מַכִּיר מִשְׁמֶרֶת בֵּית אָב שֶׁלּוֹ, [3]וְיוֹדֵעַ שֶׁבָּתֵּי אֲבוֹתָיו קְבוּעִין שָׁם, אָסוּר לִשְׁתּוֹת יַיִן כָּל אוֹתָהּ שַׁבָּת. [4]אֵינוֹ מַכִּיר מִשְׁמַרְתּוֹ וּמִשְׁמֶרֶת בֵּית אָב שֶׁלּוֹ, וְיוֹדֵעַ שֶׁבָּתֵּי אֲבוֹתָיו קְבוּעִין שָׁם, [5]אָסוּר לִשְׁתּוֹת יַיִן כָּל הַשָּׁנָה. [6]רַבִּי אוֹמֵר: אוֹמֵר אֲנִי: אָסוּר לִשְׁתּוֹת יַיִן לְעוֹלָם. [7]אֲבָל מָה

LITERAL TRANSLATION

[1]and who knows that [the members of] his *bet av* were established there, is forbidden to drink wine all that day. [2]If he can identify his *mishmar* but cannot identify his *bet av*, [3]but he knows that [the members of] his *bet av* were established there, he is forbidden to drink wine all that week. [4][If] he cannot identify his *mishmar* or his *bet av*, but knows that [the members of] his *bet av* were established there, [5]he is forbidden to drink wine all the year. [6]Rabbi says: I say: He is forever forbidden to drink wine. [7]But what

RASHI

קבועין — שיודע ודאי שבית אב שלו עובד במקדש, לפי שהרבה היו מבתי אבות הכהנים שלא הוקבעו. שוב אמר לי רבי: קבועין — שלא נתחלל בית אב שלו להיות מגואל מן הכהונה, ויודע שראוי בית אב שלו לעבוד. **אסור לשתות יין כל אותו היום** — ותו לא, שמא יבנה בית המקדש ותכבד העבודה, ויהיה זה צריך לעבוד. **מכיר משמרתו** — שיודע איזה שבת בשנה עובדין. **ואינו יודע מאיזה בית אב** — דעכשיו אינו מכיר באיזה יום בשבת עובדין, ויודע שבתי אבותיו קבועין — אסור כל אותה שבת מספיקא. בכולהו גרסינן: ויודע שבתי אבותיו קבועין הן, דאם אינו יודע שבתי אבותיו קבועין לעבוד — מותר הוא לשתות יין כל השנה, ולא חיישינן שמא יבנה, ושמא בית אב שלו יעבדו היום. **רבי אומר אומר אני כהן אסור כו'** — כלומר, אי חיישינן לשמא יבנה — יהא אסור לעולם, אפילו המכיר משמרתו ומשמרת בית אבותיו, דחיישינן שמא ישתנה סדר משמרות, ושמא יעבדו כולם לחנוכת הבית בבת אחת, ונמצא זה צריך לעבוד. אבל מה אעשה שתקנתו קלקלתו. דהוי כמה שנים שלא חזרה בירה, וקלקלה זו תקנתו לשתות יין בהדיא, ולשמא יבנה לא חיישינן.

NOTES

Rishonim who maintain that the Baraita is referring to the period after the Temple was destroyed. Even though the Temple is no longer standing, the priests who know that they belong to a certain *mishmar* or to a certain *bet av* are required to abstain from wine at certain times, so that they will be ready to serve in the Temple should it suddenly be rebuilt. *Rambam* (*Hilkhot Bi'at HaMikdash* 1:7), however, seems to understand that the Baraita is dealing with the period when the Temple still stood. During that time, even if a priest was abroad or for some other reason could not serve in the Temple, he was required to abstain from wine during the day or week that his *bet av* or *mishmar* was due to serve. (see also *Gevurat Ari* and *Sfat Emet*).

שֶׁבָּתֵּי אֲבוֹתָיו קְבוּעִין שָׁם That the members of his ***bet av*** **were established there.** Our commentary follows *Rashi* and others who explain that the expression, "He knows that the members of his *bet av* were established there," means that the priest knows that his family was fit to serve in the Temple, never having been disqualified from participating in the Temple service on account of the personal status of one of the family's ancestors.

Some Rishonim (see *Ramban, Hassagot* to *Rambam's Sefer HaMitzvot*, positive commandment 36; *Ritva*) explain that some of the priests were not assigned to a particular *mishmar*, and so did not have a set time to serve in the Temple. Rather, they would come to the Temple as they wished, and would assist those who had been assigned to a particular *mishmar* and whose turn to serve had arrived. Thus the expression, "He knows that the members of his *bet av* were established there," refers to a priest who knows that his family had been attached to a particular *mishmar* which had a set time to work in the Temple.

TRANSLATION AND COMMENTARY

in ruins works to **the** priests' **advantage.** So many years have passed without the Temple being rebuilt that we need not take into consideration the possibility that this may speedily occur and that the priests will suddenly be called upon to serve in the Temple. Hence the restrictions once imposed on priests against drinking wine are no longer in force."

אָמַר אַבַּיֵי [1]Concluding the discussion about the limitations on drinking wine imposed on the priesthood, **Abaye said: In accordance with whose** viewpoint **do the priests nowadays drink wine** without any restrictions? [2]They act **in accordance with** the viewpoint of **Rabbi** Yehudah HaNasi, who said that we do not anticipate that the Temple will speedily be rebuilt, and therefore the restrictions on drinking wine that were once imposed on the priesthood no longer apply.

אַנְשֵׁי מִשְׁמָר [3]The Gemara now proceeds to analyze the next clause of the Mishnah, which states: **"The members of the *mishmar*** whose week it is to serve in the Temple **and the members of the** *ma'amad* whose week it is to stand in the Temple when the communal sacrifices are offered **are forbidden to cut their hair or wash their clothes** throughout the week of their service. [4]**But on the Thursday** of the week of their service, **they are permitted** to cut their hair and launder their clothing **in honor of Shabbat."** [5]The Gemara asks: **What is the reason** for the restrictions regarding the cutting of hair and the laundering of clothes that were placed on the members of the *mishmar* and the *ma'amad* during their week of service?

אָמַר [6]**Rabbah bar Bar Hanah said** in reply **in the name of Rabbi Yohanan:** The members of the *mishmar* and the *ma'amad* are forbidden to cut their hair or do their laundry throughout the week, except on Thursday, [7]**so that they should not enter their watch when they are unkempt.** If they were permitted to cut

אֶעֱשֶׂה? שֶׁתַּקָּנָתוֹ קַלְקָלָתוֹ"?
[1]אָמַר אַבַּיֵי: כְּמַאן שָׁתוּ הָאִידָּנָא כַּהֲנֵי חַמְרָא? [2]כְּרַבִּי.
[3]"אַנְשֵׁי מִשְׁמָר וְאַנְשֵׁי מַעֲמָד אֲסוּרִים לְסַפֵּר וּלְכַבֵּס.
[4]וּבַחֲמִישִׁי מוּתָּרִין מִפְּנֵי כְבוֹד הַשַּׁבָּת". [5]מַאי טַעְמָא?
[6]אָמַר רַבָּה בַּר בַּר חָנָה אָמַר רַבִּי יוֹחָנָן: [7]כְּדֵי שֶׁלֹּא יִכָּנְסוּ לְמִשְׁמַרְתָּם כְּשֶׁהֵן מְנוּוָּלִין.

LITERAL TRANSLATION

can I do? For his remedy is its [the Temple's] ruin." [1]Abaye said: In accordance with whom do the priests drink wine today? [2]In accordance with Rabbi.

[3]"The members of the *mishmar* and the members of the *ma'amad* are forbidden to cut their hair or wash their clothes. [4]But on Thursday they are permitted because of the honor of Shabbat." [5]What is the reason? [6]Rabbah bar Bar Hanah said in the name of Rabbi Yohanan: [7]So that they should not enter their watch when they are unkempt.

RASHI

כשהן מנוולין – שלא יהו סומכין על יום אחד מימי שבת, ואין מסתפרין בשבת שעברה.

NOTES

שֶׁתַּקָּנָתוֹ קַלְקָלָתוֹ For his remedy is the Temple's ruin. A number of different interpretations have been suggested for this expression. Some authorities explain that the fact that the Temple has been destroyed works to the advantage of the priests, for there is no reason to require them to abstain from wine when there is no Temple and no Temple service (*Geonim*). Our commentary follows *Rashi* and others who suggest a slight variation of the previous interpretation: The fact that the Temple has lain in its ruined state for such a long time benefits the priests, for it seems unlikely that the Temple will be rebuilt in the immediate future, and the restrictions against drinking wine that were once imposed on the priests are suspended.

Rambam (*Hilkhot Bi'at HaMikdash* 1:7) explains that Rabbi Yehudah HaNasi's comment applies only in the case of a priest who does not know to which *mishmar* and to which *bet av* he belongs. Such a priest is permitted to drink wine whenever he wants, for he cannot serve in the Temple until his *mishmar* and *bet av* are determined. Thus the priest's ruin — his ignorance — is also his remedy.

Others (*Mikhtam, Kaftor VaFerah*) offer an entirely different explanation: Every priest should forever be forbidden to drink wine, but that enactment would lead to the priests' ruin, for they would not be able to observe the prohibition.

HALAKHAH

כְּמַאן שָׁתוּ הָאִידָּנָא כַּהֲנֵי חַמְרָא In accordance with whom do the priests drink wine today? "If a priest knows to which *mishmar* and to which *bet av* he belongs, and also knows that his family was established as fit to serve in the Temple, he is forbidden to drink wine throughout the day that his *bet av* used to serve. If he knows to which *mishmar* he belongs, but does not know to which *bet av* he belongs, he is forbidden to drink wine throughout the week that his *mishmar* used to serve in the Temple. If the priest knows neither to which *mishmar* nor to which *bet av* he belongs, by right he should be forever forbidden to drink wine. But his difficulty works to his advantage, and he is permitted to drink wine, because he will not be able to serve in the Temple (even if it is speedily rebuilt) until his *mishmar* and *bet av* are reestablished." (*Rambam, Sefer Avodah, Hilkhot Bi'at HaMikdash* 1:7.)

אַנְשֵׁי מִשְׁמָר וְאַנְשֵׁי מַעֲמָד אֲסוּרִים לְסַפֵּר וּלְכַבֵּס The members of the *mishmar* and the members of the *ma'amad* are forbidden to cut their hair or wash their clothes. "The members of the *mishmar* and the *ma'amad* whose week it is to be in the Temple are forbidden to cut their hair or do their laundry during the period of their service, so that they do not enter their watch with untrimmed hair and dirty clothing." (*Rambam, Sefer Avodah, Hilkhot Bi'at HaMikdash* 1:12.)

TRANSLATION AND COMMENTARY

their hair and wash their clothing during their week of service, they might begin their service with untrimmed hair and dirty clothing, thinking that they will cut their hair and do their laundry sometime during the week. But now that the Rabbis have forbidden them to cut their hair or do their laundry all week, they will take care to attend to these things before they begin their service, and will therefore be neat and clean when they arrive.

תָּנוּ רַבָּנַן [1]The Gemara continues with a related Baraita. **Our Rabbis taught: "A king must cut his hair every day;** [2]**a High Priest** must cut his hair at least once a week, **on Fridays;** and **an ordinary priest** must cut his hair at least **once in thirty days."**

מֶלֶךְ מִסְתַּפֵּר [3]The Gemara now analyzes each of the rulings found in the Baraita just cited. The Baraita taught: **"A king must cut his hair every day."** [4]The Gemara asks: **What is the reason** for this?

אָמַר [5]**Rabbi Abba bar Zavda said in reply:** [6]This obligation is derived from **the** Biblical **verse** that **says** (Isaiah 33:17): **"Your eyes shall see the king in his beauty."** This verse teaches us that the king must ensure that he is always immaculate in appearance. Thus he is required to trim his hair daily and keep himself properly groomed.

כֹּהֵן גָּדוֹל [7]The next clause of the Baraita states: **"A High Priest** must cut his hair at least once a week, **on Fridays."** [8]The Gemara asks: **What is the reason** for this?

אָמַר רַב שְׁמוּאֵל [9]**Rav Shmuel bar Yitzḥak said** in reply: As was explained earlier, the priests who served in the Temple were divided into twenty-four *mishmarot*, each *mishmar* officiating in the Temple for one week at a time. The *mishmarot* changed every Shabbat, the outgoing *mishmar* offering the morning and additional sacrifices, and the incoming *mishmar* offering the evening sacrifice and laying the fresh shewbread on the table. [10]**Since the *mishmarot* change every Shabbat,** it is fitting that the High Priest have his hair cut on Fridays, so that the incoming *mishmar* first see him when he is perfectly groomed.

כֹּהֵן הֶדְיוֹט [11]The Baraita concluded: **"An ordinary priest** must cut his hair at least **once in thirty days."** [12]The Gemara asks: **From where do we know** this law?

[1]תָּנוּ רַבָּנַן: ״מֶלֶךְ מִסְתַּפֵּר בְּכָל יוֹם, [2]כֹּהֵן גָּדוֹל מֵעֶרֶב שַׁבָּת לְעֶרֶב שַׁבָּת, כֹּהֵן הֶדְיוֹט אַחַת לִשְׁלֹשִׁים יוֹם״.
[3]״מֶלֶךְ מִסְתַּפֵּר בְּכָל יוֹם״. [4]מַאי טַעְמָא?
[5]אָמַר רַבִּי אַבָּא בַּר זַבְדָּא:
[6]אָמַר קְרָא: ״מֶלֶךְ בְּיָפְיוֹ תֶּחֱזֶינָה עֵינֶיךָ״.
[7]״כֹּהֵן גָּדוֹל מֵעֶרֶב שַׁבָּת לְעֶרֶב שַׁבָּת״. [8]מַאי טַעְמָא?
[9]אָמַר רַב שְׁמוּאֵל בַּר יִצְחָק:
[10]הוֹאִיל וּמִשְׁמָרוֹת מִתְחַדְּשׁוֹת.
[11]״כֹּהֵן הֶדְיוֹט אַחַת לִשְׁלֹשִׁים יוֹם״. [12]מְנָלַן?

LITERAL TRANSLATION

[1]Our Rabbis taught: "A king cuts his hair every day, [2]a High Priest from Friday to Friday, an ordinary priest once in thirty days."

[3]"A king cuts his hair every day." [4]What is the reason?

[5]Rabbi Abba bar Zavda said: [6]The verse says: "Your eyes shall see the king in his beauty."

[7]"A High Priest from Friday to Friday." [8]What is the reason?

[9]Rav Shmuel bar Yitzḥak said: [10]Because the *mishmarot* change.

[11]"An ordinary priest once in thirty days." [12]From where [do we know this]?

RASHI

מסתפר בכל יום – מלוה. **מערב שבת לערב שבת** – ולא יהיה מגודל יותר. **ומשמרות מתחדשות** – בכל שבת ושבת, ומשמרה שלא ראתהו עד עכשיו ובאה לראותו – הדבר נאה שתראהו ביופיו.

SAGES

רַבִּי אַבָּא בַּר זַבְדָּא **Rabbi Abba bar Zavda.** A Palestinian Amora of the second and third generations. He went to Babylonia, became a disciple of Rav, and transmitted teachings in his name. He also studied with Rav Huna. He later returned to Eretz Israel and studied with Rabbi Elazar. After Rabbi Elazar's death he was considered the most important Sage in Eretz Israel.

רַב שְׁמוּאֵל בַּר יִצְחָק **Rav Shmuel bar Yitzḥak.** A Babylonian Amora of the third generation, Rav Shmuel bar Yitzḥak was apparently one of Rav's younger students. He later became a disciple of Rav Huna. Like many of Rav Huna's students, he immigrated to Eretz Israel (he seems to have been middle-aged at the time). Though we do not find teachings of his in the name of Rabbi Yoḥanan, we do find him in discussion with Rabbi Yoḥanan's students, some of whom quote him. Rav Shmuel bar Yitzḥak's Aggadic and Halakhic teachings are found in both the Babylonian and Jerusalem Talmuds. We do not know what he did for a living, but we know he had a daughter who was married to Rabbi Hoshaya.

Rav Shmuel bar Yitzḥak behaved with humility, and deferred to those younger than himself. He used to dance before brides, as we learn from tractate *Ketubot* in the Babylonian Talmud, and from tractate *Pe'ah* in the Jerusalem Talmud.

NOTES

Thus it is preferable to have an enactment permitting priests to drink wine, rather than that they should be guilty of willfully violating the prohibition.

שֶׁלֹּא יִכָּנְסוּ לְמִשְׁמַרְתָּם כְּשֶׁהֵן מְנוּוָּלִין **So that they should not enter their watch when they are unkempt.** *Ra'avad* asks: Why is there concern that the members of the *mishmar* whose week it is to serve in the Temple will enter their watch with untrimmed hair? Surely priests are required to cut their hair at least once in thirty days (see Gemara below), and therefore in any case the hair of the priests entering their watch will not be very long!

Rosh answers: If a priest enters his watch without first trimming his hair, he will be unkempt to a certain extent, even if he has cut his hair within the last thirty days so as not to violate the prohibition against letting his hair grow long.

HALAKHAH

מֶלֶךְ מִסְתַּפֵּר בְּכָל יוֹם **A king cuts his hair every day.** "A king must cut his hair every day and groom himself, and he must dress himself in becoming and splendid clothing, as the verse says, 'Your eyes shall see the king in his beauty.'" (*Rambam, Sefer Shofetim, Hilkhot Melakhim* 2:5.)

כֹּהֵן גָּדוֹל מֵעֶרֶב שַׁבָּת לְעֶרֶב שַׁבָּת **A High Priest from Friday to Friday.** "The High Priest must never let his hair grow long, even if he does not enter the Temple, but must cut his hair at least once a week, on Fridays." (*Rambam, Sefer Avodah, Hilkhot Klei HaMikdash* 5:6.)

כֹּהֵן הֶדְיוֹט אַחַת לִשְׁלֹשִׁים יוֹם **An ordinary priest once in thirty days.** "An ordinary priest who serves in the Temple must cut his hair at least once in thirty days." (*Rambam, Sefer Avodah, Hilkhot Bi'at HaMikdash* 1:11.)

TRANSLATION AND COMMENTARY

אָתְיָא [1]The Gemara answers: This regulation is inferred on the basis of the hermeneutical principle of *gezerah shavah*, an analogy based on similar expressions. If the same word or expression appears in two Biblical passages, the law applying in the one may be applied to the other as well. The meaning of the expression *"pera"* (פֶּרַע — "locks of hair") mentioned with respect to a priest **is derived from** another mention of the same expression ***"pera"* regarding a Nazirite** (a person who has taken Nazirite vows and who must refrain, among other things, from cutting his hair). [2]**Here** (Ezekiel 44:20) **the verse says** with respect to priests: **"And they shall not shave their heads, and their locks** [*pera*] **they shall not let grow,"** from which we learn that a priest must not let his hair grow long. [3]**And there** (Numbers 6:5) **the verse says** with reference to a Nazirite: **"He shall be holy, and he shall let the long locks** [*pera*] **of the hair of his head grow,"** from which we learn that a Nazirite must let his hair grow long. [4]**Just as there,** in the case of the Nazirite, the obligation to let his hair grow long **means** that the Nazirite may not cut his hair for at least **thirty days,** [5]**so too here,** in the case of a priest, the prohibition against allowing the hair to grow long **means** that the priest must not let his hair go uncut for **thirty days.**

וְנָזִיר [6]The Gemara asks: As for **the Nazirite himself, from where do we know** that the expression *"pera"* indicates a period of thirty days?

אָמַר רַב מַתְנָה [7]**Rav Matenah said** in reply: A person can vow to be a Nazirite for any period he wishes, but the minimum is thirty days. [8]And **someone who does not specify how long he wishes to be a Nazirite** also assumes the obligations of a Nazirite **for** a period of **thirty days.** Now, since a Nazirite must not cut his hair during the entire period of his vow, it follows that the minimum time during which a Nazirite must refrain from cutting his hair is thirty days, by which time the Torah regards his hair as having grown long enough to be called *"pera."* [9]And **from where** do we know that the minimum period of being a Nazirite is thirty days? [10]This is derived from **the** very same **verse** (Numbers 6:5), which **says: "He shall be** [יִהְיֶה] holy." [11]**The numerical value of** the word יִהְיֶה **is thirty** (י = 10, ה = 5, י = 10, ה = 5), from which we learn that the minimum period of being a Nazirite is thirty days.

אָמַר לֵיהּ [12]**Rav Pappa said to Abaye:** [13]**But perhaps Scripture** meant to **say as follows:** The priests **shall not let** their locks **grow long at all,** but must cut their hair every day! And if you argue that we learn from the case of the Nazirite that the expression *"pera"* means growing one's hair for thirty days, perhaps the verse can be understood in the following manner: The priests must not let their locks grow for thirty days; instead they must cut their hair daily!

אָמַר לֵיהּ [14]Abaye **said to** Rav Pappa in reply: **If the** Biblical **verse had been formulated** thus:

LITERAL TRANSLATION

[1]*"Pera"* [here] is derived (lit., "comes") from *"pera"* regarding a Nazirite. [2]It is written here: "And they shall not shave their heads, and their long locks [*pera*] they shall not let grow," [3]and it is written there: "He shall be holy, and he shall let the long locks [*pera*] of the hair of his head grow." [4]Just as there [it means] thirty [days], [5]so too here [it means] thirty [days].

[6]And from where [do we know about] the Nazirite himself?

[7]Rav Matenah said: [8]An unspecified Nazariteship is thirty days. [9]From where [do we know this]? [10]The verse says: "He shall be [יִהְיֶה]," [11]the numerical value [of which] is thirty.

[12]Rav Pappa said to Abaye: [13]But perhaps Scripture (lit., "the Merciful One") meant (lit., "said") this: They shall not let them grow long at all!

[14]He said to him: If it had been written:

[1]אָתְיָא ״פֶּרַע״ ״פֶּרַע״ מִנָּזִיר. [2]כְּתִיב הָכָא: ״וְרֹאשָׁם לֹא יְגַלֵּחוּ, וּפֶרַע לֹא יְשַׁלֵּחוּ״, [3]וּכְתִיב הָתָם: ״קָדֹשׁ יִהְיֶה, גַּדֵּל פֶּרַע שְׂעַר רֹאשׁוֹ״. [4]מַה לְהַלָּן שְׁלֹשִׁים, [5]אַף כָּאן שְׁלֹשִׁים.

[6]וְנָזִיר גּוּפֵיהּ מְנָלַן?

[7]אָמַר רַב מַתְנָה: [8]סְתַם נְזִירוּת שְׁלֹשִׁים יוֹם. [9]מְנָלַן? [10]אָמַר קְרָא: ״יִהְיֶה״, [11]בְּגִימַטְרִיָּא תְּלָתִין הָוֵי.

[12]אֲמַר לֵיהּ רַב פַּפָּא לְאַבַּיֵי: [13]וְדִלְמָא הָכִי קָאָמַר רַחֲמָנָא: לָא לִירַבּוּ כְּלָל!

[14]אֲמַר לֵיהּ: אִי הֲוָה כָּתַב:

RASHI

לא לירבו כלל אלא יסתפרו בכל יום. דהכי משמע "ופרע" דהיינו שלשים לא ישלחו, אלא יגלחו. **שלוחי לא משלחי** — הכי משמע פרע שגדלו — אינן רשאין לגדל עוד.

SAGES

רַב מַתְנָה Rav Matenah. A second-generation Babylonian Amora, he studied with the Amoraim of the first generation in Babylonia. His name may be a shortened form of the Biblical name Matanyah. He was a disciple of Shmuel, though he also transmits teachings in the name of Rav. Rav Matenah's colleague, Rav Yehudah, was also a disciple of Rav and Shmuel. Many of the Amoraim of the third generation were Rav Matenah's pupils and transmit teachings in his name. He lived in Papunya, near Pumbedita. He was the Rabbi of that town and may also have been the head of a small yeshivah there. According to a Geonic tradition, he was the son of the great Palestinian Amora Rabbi Yohanan, ten of whose sons died during his lifetime, and he was sent by Rabbi Yohanan to Babylonia to study with Shmuel.

LANGUAGE

גִּימַטְרִיָּא Numerical value. Many efforts have been made to find the precise source of this word in the Greek language. It is probably derived from γεωμετρία, *geometria,* which was understood in general terms as referring to calculations (and it is used in that sense in Rabbinic literature). From this it was applied more specifically to calculating the numerical value of letters of the alphabet.

HALAKHAH

סְתַם נְזִירוּת An unspecified Naziriteship. "If a person vows to be a Nazirite but does not specify for how long, he assumes Nazirite obligations for a period of thirty days." (*Rambam, Sefer Hafla'ah, Hilkhot Nezirut* 3:1.)

TRANSLATION AND COMMENTARY

[1] **"They** [the priests] **shall not let their locks grow long** [לֹא יְשַׁלְּחוּ פֶּרַע]," then **I might have interpreted** the verse **as you have suggested** — that the priests must not let their hair grow long at all. [2] But **now that the verse has been formulated: "And their long locks they shall not let grow** [וּפֶרַע לֹא יְשַׁלֵּחוּ]," the verse must be understood as saying that the priests' locks **may indeed be** grown **long** and need not be cut for thirty days; but once they have been allowed to grow long, [3] **they** must **not be** allowed to **grow without restriction,** but must periodically be cut. Hence a priest must cut his hair at least once in thirty days.

אִי הָכִי [4] The Gemara asks: **If it is true** that the priest's obligation to cut his hair at least once in thirty days is derived from the Bible, then **even nowadays,** when there is no Temple, priests **should be** obligated to have their hair cut at least once a month! Why are priests not concerned nowadays about the prohibition against letting their hair grow long?

דּוּמְיָא [5] The Gemara answers: The law forbidding priests to grow their hair long **is similar to** the law forbidding priests to become **intoxicated with wine.** The verse in Ezekiel (44:20) forbidding priests to grow their hair long is followed by a verse forbidding them to drink wine, and this implies that an analogy may be drawn between the two prohibitions. [6] **Just as with respect to** the prohibition forbidding priests to become **intoxicated with wine,** [7] **it is** only **at a time when entry** into the Temple is possible — when the Temple is standing — that drinking wine **is forbidden, but** if it is **not a time when entry** into the Temple is possible, drinking wine **is permitted,** [8] **so too here** with respect to the prohibition forbidding priests to grow their hair long. Regarding the prohibition against drinking wine, the verse says (Ezekiel 44:21): "Nor shall any priest drink wine, when they enter the inner court." This teaches us that the prohibition forbidding priests to drink wine applies only when the Temple is standing and the priests can enter it to perform the Temple service. By analogy it follows that the prohibition forbidding priests to grow their hair long also applies only when the Temple is standing and the priests can enter it and serve there. But nowadays, when the Temple is no longer standing, the priests need not be concerned about the prohibition against letting their hair grow long.

וְהָתַנְיָא [9] The Gemara raises an objection: **But surely it was taught** in the Baraita cited above: [10] **"Rabbi** Yehudah HaNasi **says: I say** that if we are concerned that the rebuilding of the Temple may take place very soon, then all **priests should forever be forbidden to drink wine. But what can I do?** [11] The extended period of time that **the Temple** has remained **in ruins** works to **the** priests' **advantage.** Since so many years have passed without the Temple being rebuilt, we need not take into consideration the possibility that this may speedily occur. Hence there are no restrictions on priests nowadays regarding the drinking of wine." [12] **And**

[1] ״לֹא יְשַׁלְּחוּ פֶּרַע״, כִּדְקָאָמְרַתְּ. [2] הַשְׁתָּא דִּכְתִיב: ״וּפֶרַע לֹא יְשַׁלֵּחוּ״, פֶּרַע לֶיהֱוֵי, [3] שִׁלּוּחֵי הוּא דְּלָא לִישַׁלְּחוּ.
[4] אִי הָכִי, אֲפִילּוּ הָאִידָּנָא נַמִי!
[5] דּוּמְיָא דִּשְׁתוּיֵי יַיִן. [6] מָה שְׁתוּיֵי יַיִן, [7] בִּזְמַן בִּיאָה הוּא דְּאָסוּר, שֶׁלֹּא בִּזְמַן בִּיאָה שָׁרֵי, [8] אַף הָכָא נַמִי.
[9] וְהָתַנְיָא: [10] רַבִּי אוֹמֵר: אוֹמֵר אֲנִי: כֹּהֲנִים אֲסוּרִים לִשְׁתּוֹת יַיִן לְעוֹלָם. [11] אֲבָל מָה אֶעֱשֶׂה? שֶׁתַּקָּנָתוֹ קַלְקָלָתוֹ״. [12] וַאֲמַר

LITERAL TRANSLATION

[1] "They shall not let their locks grow long [לֹא יְשַׁלְּחוּ פֶּרַע]," [2] [it might have been] as you said. Now that it is written: "And their long locks they shall not let grow [וּפֶרַע לֹא יְשַׁלֵּחוּ]," they may be long, [3] [but] they may not be grown [without restriction].

[4] If so, even nowadays too [this should apply]!

[5] It is similar to those who have drunk wine. [6] Just as [regarding] those who have drunk wine, [7] it is at the time of entry that it is forbidden, [but] not at the time of entry it is permitted, [8] so too here.

[9] But surely it was taught: [10] "Rabbi says: I say: Priests are forever forbidden to drink wine. [11] But what can I do? For his remedy is its [the Temple's] ruin." [12] And

RASHI

אי הכי – כיון דמקרא מפקת לה, האידנא נמי לא לישלחו! **ומשני: כיין,** דומיא דיין, דכתיב בסמוך להאי ״ופרע לא ישלחו ויין לא ישתו כל כהן״. **מה יין בזמן ביאה הוא דאסור** – דכתיב (יחזקאל מד) ״בבואם אל החצר״ וגו׳ בזמן שבית המקדש קיים, שבאין שם לעבוד. **שלא בזמן ביאה** – כגון האידנא, שהבית חרב, ולאו זמן ביאה היא.

HALAKHAH

בִּזְמַן בִּיאָה הוּא דְּאָסוּר It is at the time of entry that it is forbidden. "Just as a priest is forbidden to drink wine only at a time when he enters the Temple, he is likewise forbidden to let his grow long only at a time when he enters the Temple. According to *Ra'avad*, a priest may not let his hair grow long, even when he does not actually enter the Temple. It is only when there is no Temple that he is permitted to let his hair grow long." (*Rambam, Sefer Avodah, Hilkhot Bi'at HaMikdash* 1:10.)

TRANSLATION AND COMMENTARY

Abaye said on this matter: **In accordance with whose** viewpoint **do the priests nowadays drink wine** without any restrictions?

כְּרַבִּי [17B] [1]They act **in accordance with** the viewpoint of **Rabbi** Yehudah HaNasi. [2]Now, argues the Gemara, surely **this proves by implication that the Rabbis** who disagree with Rabbi Yehudah HaNasi **forbid** priests to drink wine even today. It therefore follows that they should maintain that the prohibition forbidding priests to grow their hair long is also still in force today.

מַאי טַעֲמָא [3]The Gemara answers: **What is the reason** why the Rabbis who disagree with Rabbi Yehudah HaNasi forbid priests to drink wine even today? [4]It is because they believe that **the Temple will speedily be rebuilt, and** that **a priest** belonging to the *mishmar* and *bet av* whose turn it is to serve in the Temple and **who is fit for service will** suddenly **be needed,** [5]**but no** priest **will be available,** as they will all be disqualified because they have drunk wine. The resumption of the Temple service will then have to be delayed until the priests are once again fit to serve. [6]But **here,** regarding the prohibition forbidding the priests to let their hair grow long, even the Rabbis agree that it is no longer in force, for even if the Temple were to be rebuilt, and all the priests had let their hair grow long, **it would be possible for** the priests **to cut their hair** in a very short time **and** prepare themselves to **enter** the Temple and perform the service.

אִי הָכִי [7]The Gemara raises another objection: But **if** this is **so,** then the prohibition forbidding priests to **drink wine** should **also** no longer be in force, for even if the Temple were speedily rebuilt, and all the priests had drunk wine, **it would be possible for them to sleep a little** and thus prepare themselves in a very short time to **reenter** the Temple and perform the service. [8]This solution is **in accordance with** the viewpoint of **Rami bar Abba.** [9]**For Rami bar Abba said: A walk of a mile or** even **the slightest amount of sleep** following the drinking of wine **dissipates the** intoxicating **effects of the wine.** Thus even the Rabbis should agree that nowadays priests are permitted to drink wine without any restrictions.

אַבַּיֵי: כְּמַאן שָׁתוּ הָאִידָּנָא כַּהֲנֵי חַמְרָא?

[17B] [1]כְּרַבִּי. [2]מִכְּלָל דְּרַבָּנַן אָסְרִי.

[3]מַאי טַעֲמָא? [4]מְהֵרָה יִבָּנֶה בֵּית הַמִּקְדָּשׁ, וּבָעֵינַן כֹּהֵן הָרָאוּי לַעֲבוֹדָה, [5]וְלֵיכָּא. [6]הָכָא, אֶפְשָׁר דִּמְסַפֵּר וְעָיֵיל.

[7]אִי הָכִי, שָׁתוּי יַיִן נַמִי, אֶפְשָׁר דְּגָנֵי פּוּרְתָּא וְעָיֵיל, [8]כִּדְרָמִי בַּר אַבָּא. [9]דְּאָמַר רָמִי בַּר אַבָּא: דֶּרֶךְ מִיל וְשֵׁינָה כָּל שֶׁהוּא מְפִיגִין אֶת הַיַּיִן.

LITERAL TRANSLATION

Abaye said: In accordance with whom do the priests drink wine today?

[17B] [1]In accordance with Rabbi. [2][This proves] by implication that the Rabbis forbid [this].

[3]What is the reason? [4]The Temple will speedily be rebuilt, and we [will] need a priest who is fit for service, [5]and there will be none. [6]Here, it is possible for him to cut his hair and enter.

[7]If so, [regarding] one who has drunk wine also, it is possible [for him] to sleep a little and enter, [8]in accordance with [9]Rami bar Abba. For Rami bar Abba said: A walk of a mile and the slightest amount of sleep dissipate the [effects of] wine.

RASHI

והתניא רבי אומר אני כו׳ ואמר אביי כו׳ — מכלל דרבנן אסרי, דחיישינן לשמא יבנה. ומאי נמי מייתי רישא דברייתא, מפני מה אמרו אנשי משמר כו׳ ואייתי סיפא בלשון קצרה ודייק מינה: מכלל דרבנן אסרי. **כרבי הא רבנן מיסר אסרי** — אפילו שלא בזמן הזה. ומשני: **מאי טעמא כו׳ והכא כו׳** — "מאי טעמא" תירוצא הוא, כלומר, דטעמא מאי גזור רבנן ביין — שמא יבנה כו׳. אבל גבי פרועי ראש — לא גזרו. דאפשר דמסתפר מיד, והדר עייל לבית המקדש לעבודה. **דרך מיל ושינה כל שהוא כו׳.**

NOTES

מִכְּלָל דְּרַבָּנַן אָסְרִי **This proves by implication that the Rabbis forbid this.** According to *Rabbenu Ḥananel,* Abaye himself, who was a priest descended from the family of Eli, did not act in accordance with the opinion of Rabbi Yehudah HaNasi. For it is related elsewhere (*Ketubot* 65a) that Rava told Abaye's widow that he knew that Abaye never used to drink wine. Thus, when Abaye asked how the priests of his day could drink wine without any restrictions, he was asking about the custom prevailing among the rest of the priests, a custom which he himself did not follow.

מְהֵרָה יִבָּנֶה בֵּית הַמִּקְדָּשׁ **The Temple will speedily be rebuilt.** Some of the Rishonim note that one of the reasons why the priests act in accordance with the viewpoint of Rabbi Yehudah HaNasi nowadays, against the viewpoint of the Sages, is that the decree imposed by the Sages is based on a very distant concern. Even if the Temple were speedily to be rebuilt, the *mishmarot* might be totally rearranged, or the entire priesthood might possibly serve together at the rededication ceremonies. Thus there is no reason to say

HALAKHAH

דֶּרֶךְ מִיל וְשֵׁינָה כָּל שֶׁהוּא **A walk of a mile or the slightest amount of sleep.** "A mile walk or the slightest amount of sleep dissipates the intoxicating effects of wine, provided that only a *revi'it* or less has been consumed. But if a person has drunk more than a *revi'it,* sleep makes him more intoxicated, and walking makes him more unsteady." (*Shulḥan Arukh, Oraḥ Ḥayyim* 99:2.)

[1]לָאו מִי אִיתְּמַר עֲלָהּ: [2]אָמַר רַב נַחְמָן אָמַר רַבָּה בַּר אֲבוּהּ: לֹא שָׁנוּ אֶלָּא בְּשֶׁשָּׁתָה שִׁיעוּר רְבִיעִית? [3]אֲבָל שָׁתָה יוֹתֵר מֵרְבִיעִית כָּל שֶׁכֵּן שֶׁדֶּרֶךְ מַטְרִידָתוֹ וְשֵׁינָה מְשַׁכַּרְתּוֹ. [4]רַב אַשִׁי אֲמַר: שְׁתוּיֵי יַיִן דִּמְחַלֵּי עֲבוֹדָה, [5]גָּזְרוּ בְּהוּ רַבָּנַן. [6]פְּרוּעֵי רֹאשׁ דְּלָא מְחַלֵּי עֲבוֹדָה, [7]לָא גָּזְרוּ בְּהוּ רַבָּנַן. [8]מֵיתִיבִי: ״וְאֵלּוּ שֶׁהֵן בְּמִיתָה: שְׁתוּיֵי יַיִן, וּפְרוּעֵי רֹאשׁ״.

LITERAL TRANSLATION

[1]Has it not been said regarding this: [2]Rav Naḥman said in the name of Rabbah bar Avuha: They did not teach [this] except when he drank the measure of a *revi'it*? [3]But [if] he drank more than a *revi'it*, how much more so does walking make him unsteady and sleep make him drunk.

[4]Rav Ashi said: [Regarding] those who have drunk wine who disqualify [their] service, [5]the Rabbis decreed concerning them. [6][Regarding] those with long hair who do not disqualify [their] service, [7]the Rabbis did not decree concerning them.

[8]They raised an objection: "And these are those who are [liable] to death: Those who have drunk wine, and those with long hair."

TRANSLATION AND COMMENTARY

לָאו [1]The Gemara rebuts this objection: **Has not** a restriction **been made regarding this** statement of Rami bar Abba? [2]**For Rav Naḥman said in the name of Rabbah bar Avuha:** The statement that a mile walk or even the slightest amount of sleep dissipates the intoxicating effects of wine **applies only where** a person **drank** wine **to the amount of a** ***revi'it*** (a quarter of a *log*). [3]**But if** a person **has drunk more than a** ***revi'it*** of wine, then **walking** about **makes him all the more unsteady** on his feet, **and sleep,** too, only **adds to his intoxication.** Thus the Rabbis maintain that the prohibition forbidding priests to drink wine is still in effect today, but they agree that the prohibition forbidding priests to let their hair grow long no longer applies, for even if the Temple were suddenly to be rebuilt, the priests could quickly cut their hair and begin their service.

רַב אַשִׁי אֲמַר [4]**Rav Ashi suggested** another way to distinguish between the prohibition forbidding priests to drink wine and the prohibition forbidding them to let their hair grow long. If a priest entered the Temple while **intoxicated with wine** and took part in the Temple service, **his service was disqualified.** This is derived from the verses (Leviticus 10:9-10): "Do not drink wine or strong drink...so that you may differentiate between holy and unholy...," which teach us that if a priest serves in the Temple while intoxicated, his service is unholy and therefore disqualified. [5]Thus **the Rabbis decreed** that, even today, priests are forbidden to drink wine on the days on which it would be their turn to serve in the Temple. [6]But if a priest served in the Temple while his **hair was overgrown, his service was not disqualified,** for there is no Biblical verse indicating that the service of a priest with overgrown hair is indeed disqualified. [7]Thus **the Rabbis did not decree** that priests today are forbidden to let their hair grow long, for even if the Temple were speedily to be rebuilt and the priests were to serve with overgrown hair, their service would not be disqualified.

מֵיתִיבִי [8]**An objection was raised** against Rav Ashi's distinction from the following Baraita: **"And these are** the transgressors **who are liable to death** at the hand of Heaven: Priests **who** serve in the Temple while **intoxicated with wine, and** priests who serve while **their hair is overgrown."** The Gemara asks: From where

RASHI

ושינה משכרתו — והאי שינוי איכא בהך מיהא. **שתוי יין דמחלי עבודה** — דכתיב "יין ושכר אל תשת" וסמיך ליה "ולהבדיל בין הקדש ובין החול" בין עבודה קדושה למחוללת, דאי עביד עבודה שתוי יין — חילל. **פרועי ראש** — דלא כתיב ביה חלל, דלא נראה חילול. **ואילו שבמיתה** — בידי שמים, במסכת סנהדרין, ב"אלו הן הנשרפין" (פג,א). **שתויי יין** — במיתה, דכתיב "יין ושכר אל תשת בבואכם אל אהל מועד ולא תמותו" — דהיינו מיתה בידי שמים, מדלא כתיב "יומת", ואמר בשלמא כו'.

SAGES

רַבָּה בַּר אֲבוּהּ **Rabbah bar Avuha.** A Babylonian Amora of the second generation, Rabbah bar Avuha was a pupil of Rav, and transmitted many teachings in his name. Rabbah bar Avuha was a member of the Exilarch's family, and Rav Naḥman was his pupil and son-in-law.

NOTES

that a particular priest should be forbidden to drink wine on a particular day on account of the *mishmar* to which his ancestors belonged during the Second Temple period (see *Meiri*).

HALAKHAH

שְׁתוּיֵי יַיִן **Those who have drunk wine.** "If a priest who is fit for service in the Temple has drunk wine, he is forbidden to go beyond the altar in the Temple Courtyard. If he enters and serves, his service is disqualified and he is liable to death at the hand of Heaven." (*Rambam, Sefer Avodah, Hilkhot Bi'at HaMikdash* 1:1.)

פְּרוּעֵי רֹאשׁ **Those with long hair.** "If a priest has let his hair grow long, he is forbidden to go beyond the altar in the Temple Courtyard. If he enters and serves, he is liable to death at the hand of Heaven, but his service is not disqualified. (*Rambam,* Ibid., 1:8-9.)

[1]בִּשְׁלָמָא שְׁתוּיֵי יַיִן בְּהֶדְיָא כְּתִיב בְּהוּ: ״יַיִן וְשֵׁכָר אַל תֵּשְׁתְּ״. [2]אֶלָּא פְּרוּעֵי רֹאשׁ מְנָלַן? [3]דִּכְתִיב: ״וְרֹאשָׁם לֹא יְגַלֵּחוּ, וּפֶרַע לֹא יְשַׁלֵּחוּ״. [4]וּכְתִיב בַּתְרֵיהּ: ״וְיַיִן לֹא יִשְׁתּוּ כָּל כֹּהֵן, בְּבוֹאָם אֶל הֶחָצֵר הַפְּנִימִית״. [5]וְאִיתְקוּשׁ פְּרוּעֵי רֹאשׁ לִשְׁתוּיֵי יַיִן: [6]מַה שְׁתוּיֵי יַיִן בְּמִיתָה, [7]אַף פְּרוּעֵי רֹאשׁ בְּמִיתָה. [8]וּמִינָּהּ, אִי מַה שְׁתוּיֵי יַיִן דִּמְחַלֵּי עֲבוֹדָה, [9]אַף פְּרוּעֵי רֹאשׁ דִּמְחַלֵּי עֲבוֹדָה!

[10]לָא. כִּי אִיתְקוּשׁ, לְמִיתָה הוּא דְּאִתְקוּשׁ. [11]אֲבָל לְאַחוּלֵי עֲבוֹדָה, לָא אִתְקוּשׁ.

LITERAL TRANSLATION

[1]Granted [regarding] those who have drunk wine, it is written explicitly regarding them: "Do not drink wine or strong drink." [2]But from where [do we know about] those with long hair? [3]For it is written: "And they shall not shave their heads, and their locks they shall not let grow." [4]And it is written after that: "Nor shall any priest drink wine, when they enter the inner court." [5]And those with long hair are compared to those who have drunk wine: [6]Just as those who have drunk wine are [liable] to death, [7]so too are those with long hair [liable] to death. [8]And from this, just as those who have drunk wine disqualify [their] service, [9]so too do those with long hair disqualify [their] service!

[10]No. When they are compared, it is regarding the death penalty that they are compared. [11]But regarding the disqualification of [their] service they are not compared.

TRANSLATION AND COMMENTARY

do we know that these two transgressions are capital offenses? [1]**Granted that with respect to those** priests **who** serve in the Temple **while intoxicated with wine, the verse states explicitly** (Leviticus 10:9): **"Do not drink wine or strong drink,** neither you nor your sons with you, when you enter the Tent of Meeting, lest you die," which implies that if a priest serves while intoxicated, he will be liable to the death penalty. [2]**But from where do we know that those** priests who serve in the Temple **while their hair is overgrown** are also liable to death at the hand of Heaven? [3]This is derived from **the verse** which **states** (Ezekiel 44:20): **"And they shall not shave their heads, and their locks they shall not let grow,"** [4]**and** from **the following verse** (21) **which states: "Nor shall any priest drink wine, when they enter the inner court."** [5]The juxtapostition of these two verses teaches us that the prohibition that applies to **those who** serve in the Temple **with overgrown hair may be compared to** the prohibition regarding **those who** serve while **intoxicated with wine:** [6]**Just as those who** serve in the Temple while **intoxicated with wine are liable to death** at the hand of Heaven (as is learned from the verse in Leviticus), [7]**so too are those who** serve **with overgrown hair liable to death** at the hand of Heaven. [8]Now that we have drawn an analogy between the two prohibitions, it should be legitimate **to extend** that analogy **as follows: Just as those who** serve in the Temple while **intoxicated with wine disqualify their service,** [9]**so too do those** who serve **with overgrown hair disqualify their service!** Thus the Rabbis should have decreed that, even today, priests are forbidden to let their hair grow long, for the Temple may speedily be rebuilt and the priests whose turn it is to serve may find themselves doing so with overgrown hair and thereby disqualify their service. This conclusion surely contradicts the statement of Rav Ashi!

לָא [10]The Gemara responds to this objection: **No,** the analogy drawn between the two prohibitions cannot be extended. **When** the two prohibitions **were compared,** it was only **regarding the death penalty,** which was mentioned with respect to the one but not with respect to the other, that **they were compared.** [11]**But regarding the disqualification of their service,** the two prohibitions **were not compared.** Thus a priest who serves in the Temple while drunk disqualifies his service, but a priest who serves with overgrown hair does not disqualify his service. And the distinction drawn by Rav Ashi between the two prohibitions, regarding whether or not they are still in force today, is still valid.

RASHI

הכי גרסינן: ומינה מה שתויי יין מחלי עבודה אף פרועי ראש מחלי עבודה – קשיא לא גרס. **כי גמירי הלכה למיתה** – לאחולי עבודה לא גמירי. **מחלי עבודה** – חולין היא כל עבודתו שעבד. **אף פרועי ראש** – עבודתם מחוללת, דלכל מילי איתקוש, ותיובתא דרב אשי דאמר: פרועי ראש לא מחלי עבודה. **דרב חסדא** – בפרק שני דזבחים, וקא בעי התם: כהן ערל שמתו אחיו מחמת מילה מהו, ואמר רב חסדא כו׳: ערל לב וערל בשר.

NOTES

לָא. כִּי אִיתְקוּשׁ No. When they are compared. Our commentary follows the reading found in the standard text of the Talmud, according to which a rebuttal is offered here to the objection just raised against Rav Ashi's contention that the service of a priest who is intoxicated with wine is disqualified, whereas the service of a priest with unkempt hair is not. The Gemara had argued that since an analogy is drawn between the prohibition against serving in the Temple while intoxicated and the prohibition against serving there with unkempt hair regarding the punishment

BACKGROUND

וַאֲתָא יְחֶזְקֵאל וְאַסְמְכָהּ אַקְּרָא And Ezekiel came and supported it with a verse. Some commentators have understood this expression to mean that the Prophet Ezekiel found some proof in the Torah to serve as the basis for an oral tradition. Others have explained that Ezekiel did not issue this Halakhic ruling as an act of prophecy, since a Prophet is neither able nor permitted to issue a Halakhic innovation on this basis. Rather, these teachings were supported by an oral tradition, and Ezekiel included them within a prophecy. Thus the Bible merely provides support for an oral tradition.

[1] אֲמַר לֵיהּ רָבִינָא לְרַב אַשִׁי: הָא מִקַּמֵּי דַּאֲתָא יְחֶזְקֵאל, מַאן אֲמָרָהּ? [2] אֲמַר לֵיהּ: וּלְטַעֲמִיךְ, הָא דְּאָמַר רַב חִסְדָּא: [3] דָּבָר זֶה מִתּוֹרַת מֹשֶׁה לֹא לָמַדְנוּ, וּמִדִּבְרֵי קַבָּלָה לָמַדְנוּ: [4] ״כָּל בֶּן נֵכָר, עֶרֶל לֵב, וְעֶרֶל בָּשָׂר, לֹא יָבוֹא אֶל מִקְדָּשִׁי״. [5] הָא מִקַּמֵּי דַּאֲתָא יְחֶזְקֵאל, מַאן אֲמָרָהּ? [6] אֶלָּא, גְּמָרָא גְּמִיר לַהּ, וַאֲתָא יְחֶזְקֵאל וְאַסְמְכָהּ אַקְּרָא. [7] הָכָא נַמִי גְּמָרָא גְּמִיר לַהּ,

LITERAL TRANSLATION

[1] Ravina said to Rav Ashi: Before Ezekiel came, who said this?

[2] He said to him: And according to your opinion, [there is a difficulty with] what Rav Ḥisda said: [3] This matter we did not learn from the Torah of Moses, but we learned it from the words of the Prophets: [4] "Any stranger, uncircumcised in heart, or uncircumcised in flesh, shall not enter My sanctuary." [5] Before Ezekiel came, who said this? [6] Rather, it was learned as a tradition, and Ezekiel came and supported it with a verse. [7] Here too it was learned as a tradition,

TRANSLATION AND COMMENTARY

אֲמַר לֵיהּ [1] Continuing on the same theme, **Ravina said to Rav Ashi: Before Ezekiel came** and made his pronouncement, **who said** that a priest is forbidden to let his hair grow long? As we learned above, no such prohibition is recorded in the Torah itself, the source of the prohibition being the verse in Ezekiel (44:20): "And they shall not shave their heads, and their locks they shall not let grow." But surely a Prophet is not authorized to issue new laws that were not mentioned in the Torah!

אֲמַר לֵיהּ [2] Rav Ashi **said to** Ravina: **But according to your reasoning, there is a** similar **difficulty with what Rav Ḥisda said** concerning the source of the law that an uncircumcised priest may not serve in the Temple. [3] For Rav Ḥisda said: **We did not learn this matter from the Torah of Moses, but** rather **we learned it from the words of the Prophets,** from the verse that says (Ezekiel 44:9): [4] **"Any stranger, uncircumcised in heart, or uncircumcised in flesh, shall not enter in My sanctuary."** And another verse in that same chapter (verse 7) says: "In that you have brought into My sanctuary strangers, uncircumcised in heart and uncircumcised in flesh, to be in My sanctuary, to pollute it, even My house," which teaches us that the service performed by an uncircumcised priest is considered polluted. Now, the same objection that was raised against the derivation of the prohibition forbidding a priest to let his hair grow long can be raised against the derivation of these laws regarding the service of an uncircumcised priest: [5] **Before Ezekiel came** and made his pronouncement, **who said** that an uncircumcised priest is forbidden to serve in the Temple, and that, if he serves, his service is disqualified? Surely these regulations cannot be based solely on the verses in Ezekiel, because a Prophet does not have the authority to promulgate new laws on his own initiative! [6] **Rather,** continued Rav Ashi, you are forced to the conclusion that until the days of Ezekiel this matter **was accepted as an** oral **tradition** going back to the giving of the Torah on Mount Sinai, just like the rest of the Oral Law, **and** then **Ezekiel came and supported** the oral tradition **with a** written **verse.** Thus Ezekiel did not issue a new law. Instead, he provided Scriptural support for a law whose real source was an oral tradition from Sinai. [7] **Here too,** regarding the prohibition forbidding a priest to let his hair grow long, we can say the same thing: The matter **was** originally **accepted as an** oral **tradition** going back to

NOTES

to which the violator is liable, an analogy should also be drawn between the two prohibitions regarding the disqualification of the service performed by the violator, for there is a general rule that there is no such thing as half an analogy (אֵין הֶיקֵּשׁ לְמֶחֱצָה). Indeed, in the parallel passage found in *Sanhedrin* 22b, the Gemara concludes its objection with the word קַשְׁיָא, "it is difficult" (a reading also found in some manuscripts of our Gemara here), and no resolution of the difficulty is offered. But in the standard texts of our Gemara the objection is answered with the argument that the analogy drawn between the two prohibitions regarding the death penalty to which the transgressor is liable is not to be extended to the disqualification of his service.

Ritva explains that the continuation of the Gemara is actually an answer to the objection raised against Rav Ashi. Ravina asks: "Before Ezekiel came, who said that a priest is forbidden to let his hair grow long?" Since the prohibition is derived from a verse in Ezekiel and does not appear in the text of the Torah itself, the rule that there is no such thing as half an analogy does not apply. Thus the source of the prohibition cannot be the verse in Ezekiel; the prohibition must be based on an oral tradition going back to Sinai. But since an oral tradition from Sinai has the authority of a Torah law, the rule that there is no such thing as half an analogy should apply here as well! Rav Ashi now explains himself: Before Ezekiel came, who said that a priest is forbidden to let his hair grow long? There must indeed have been an oral tradition on the matter going back to Sinai, and Ezekiel must merely have provided Scriptural support for a law that was already known. And according to that tradition, a priest who serves with unkempt hair is liable to the death penalty, but his service is not disqualified.

TRANSLATION AND COMMENTARY

Sinai, **and** then **Ezekiel came and supported** the oral tradition **with a** written **verse.** [1]And **when they learned the law** forbidding a priest to let his hair grow long, **it was** only **with regard to the death penalty** to which the transgressor of the prohibition is liable. According to the oral tradition received at Sinai, a priest who serves in the Temple with unkempt hair is liable to death at the hand of Heaven. [2]But **with regard to the disqualification of the service** of a priest with unkempt hair, **they did not learn anything.**

כָּל הַכָּתוּב [3]The Gemara now proceeds to discuss the next clause of the Mishnah, which stated: "With regard to **all the days that are recorded in** ***Megillat Ta'anit***, upon which it is **not permitted to eulogize** the dead, [4]**it is** also **forbidden** to deliver a eulogy on **the day before** the date recorded in the scroll, [5]but on **the day after** the date recorded in the scroll, **it is permitted** to deliver a eulogy." The Gemara now cites the opening section of *Megillat Ta'anit*. [6]**Our Rabbis taught: "These are the days on which it is forbidden to fast, and some of them are days on which it is even forbidden to eulogize** the dead: [7]**From the New Moon of Nisan until the eighth** day **of the month,** [8]when the Rabbinic tradition regarding **the daily sacrifice was** firmly **established** as law, [9]**it is not** even **permitted to eulogize** the dead." During the Second Temple period, there were a number of Jewish sects, particularly the Sadducees and Boethusians, who did not accept the Oral Law. Instead, they interpreted the written Torah in their own way. Regarding the daily sacrifice offered in the Temple, the verse says (Numbers 28:4): "The one lamb you shall offer in the morning, and the other lamb you shall offer in the afternoon." From the fact that the Torah uses the singular verb, "you shall offer [תַּעֲשֶׂה]," the Sadducees concluded that a private individual could donate the animal to be used for the daily sacrifice. The Rabbis countered that there is another verse which says (Numbers 28:2): "My offering, the provision of My sacrifices made by fire, for a sweet savor to Me, shall you observe to offer to Me in their due season." Here the Torah uses the plural verb, "you shall observe [תִּשְׁמְרוּ]," which teaches that the daily sacrifice is a communal offering that must be purchased with the money collected by the Temple treasury from the half-shekels donated by the entire people each year. One year, during the period between the first of Nisan and the eighth day of that month, the Rabbinic tradition regarding the daily sacrifice was firmly established as law, in commemoration

וַאֲתָא יְחֶזְקֵאל וְאַסְמְכָהּ אַקְּרָא. [1]כִּי גְּמִירֵי הֲלָכָה, לְמִיתָה. [2]לְאַחוּלֵי עֲבוֹדָה, לָא גְּמִירֵי. [3]״כָּל הַכָּתוּב בִּמְגִילַּת תַּעֲנִית ׳דְּלָא לְמִיסְפַּד׳, [4]לְפָנָיו אָסוּר, [5]לְאַחֲרָיו מוּתָּר״. [6]תָּנוּ רַבָּנַן: ״אִלֵּין יוֹמַיָּא דְּלָא לְהִתְעַנָּאָה בְּהוֹן, וּמִקְצָתְהוֹן דְּלָא לְמִיסְפַּד בְּהוֹן. [7]מֵרֵישׁ יַרְחָא דְּנִיסָן וְעַד תְּמַנְיָא בֵּיהּ, [8]אִיתּוֹקַם תְּמִידָא. [9]דְּלָא לְמִיסְפַּד בְּהוֹן.

LITERAL TRANSLATION

and Ezekiel came and supported it with a verse. [1]When they learned the law, [it was] with regard to the death penalty. [2]Regarding the disqualification of service, they did not learn [it].

[3]"[On] all [the days] that are written in the *Megillat Ta'anit* 'not to eulogize,' [4]it is forbidden [the day] before, [5][but] it is permitted [the day] after." [6]Our Rabbis taught: "These are the days on which one may not fast, and some of them [are days] on which one may not eulogize. [7]From the New Moon of Nisan until the eighth of [the month], [8]the daily sacrifice was established. [9][Therefore] it is not [permitted] to eulogize on them.

RASHI

הלכתא גמירי לה — מסיני. **מריש ירחא דניסן עד תמניא ביה** — דכל שמונה ימים נשאו ונתנו בדבר, עד שנצחו את הצדוקין, ועשו אותם יום טוב. ודבר זה מפורש במנחות בפרק ״רבי ישמעאל״ ובמגילת תענית המצויה אצלנו. **דלא להתענאה בהון** — שכולן אסורין בתענית, ומקצתהון שיש בהן קצת חמורין כל כך שבהספד נמי אסורין.

NOTES

אִלֵּין יוֹמַיָּא דְּלָא לְהִתְעַנָּאָה בְּהוֹן These are the days on which one may not fast. Most Rishonim explain that the prohibition against eulogizing is a greater stringency than the prohibition against fasting. Thus the prohibition against fasting applies on all the days recorded in *Megillat Ta'anit*, whereas the prohibition against eulogizing applies on only some of them, on the more festive days. *Ritva* argues that fasting is a graver violation of the festive nature of a day than is the delivery of a eulogy, for the person fasting suffers affliction throughout the day. *Rabbenu Yehonatan* adds that a eulogy is delivered to honor the deceased or those who survive him, and this is why a prohibition against eulogizing was instituted only on the more festive days recorded in *Megillat Ta'anit*.

Rabbenu Efrayim (cited by *Ritva* and *Shittah,* and cited more fully by *Ba'al HaMa'or)* explains the relationship between the two prohibitions in just the opposite manner: The prohibition against fasting is a greater stringency than the one against eulogizing. According to this interpretation, the delivery of a eulogy is regarded as a greater violation of the festive nature of a holiday, because a eulogy is delivered in public. Hence the prohibition against eulogizing applies on all the days recorded in *Megillat Ta'anit,* whereas fasting is only prohibited on some of the days. The standard text of the Talmud supports the viewpoint accepted by the majority of the Rishonim, whereas the viewpoint of *Rabbenu Efrayim* requires a considerable number of textual emendations.

TRANSLATION AND COMMENTARY

of which a minor festival was declared, on which fasting and eulogizing the dead were forbidden. [1]The quotation from *Megillat Ta'anit* continues: "**From the eighth** day of the month of Nisan **until the end of the Festival** of Pesaḥ, [2]when **the Festival of Shavuot was restored** so that it was henceforth celebrated on the proper date according to Rabbinic tradition, it is **not** even permitted **to eulogize** the dead." The Torah prescribes that the Omer-offering must be brought to the Temple "on the day after the Sabbath [Leviticus 23:11]." According to Rabbinic tradition, the word "Sabbath" mentioned here does not refer to the weekly Shabbat, but rather to the first day of Pesaḥ. Thus the Omer-offering was to be brought to the Temple on the sixteenth of Nisan, the day after of the first day of Pesaḥ, whatever day of the week that might be. The Boethusians disagreed with the Rabbis about the meaning of the expression, "the day after the Sabbath," and maintained that the Omer ceremony was to be performed on the day after the Shabbat immediately following the first day of Pesaḥ. Thus there was no fixed date for the Omer-offering, but it was always brought on a Sunday. Now, the date of the Festival of Shavuot is directly related to the date of the Omer-offering, for the verse says (Leviticus 23:15): "And you shall count for yourselves from the day after the Sabbath, from the day that you brought the Omer of the wave-offering; there shall be seven complete Sabbaths." When seven complete weeks have been counted, the Festival of Shavuot is celebrated. Since the Boethusians disagreed with the Rabbis about the date of the Omer-offering, they disagreed with them about the date of Shavuot as well. Whereas the Rabbis maintained that Shavuot must always fall seven weeks after the sixteenth of Nisan, whatever day of the week that date happens to be, the Boethusians maintained that Shavuot must always fall on a Sunday. One year, during the period between the eighth of Nisan and the end of the Festival of Pesaḥ, the Rabbinic tradition regarding the date on which the Festival of Shavuot was to be celebrated was reestablished, in commemoration of which a minor festival was instituted, on which fasting and eulogizing the dead were forbidden.

אֲמַר מָר [3]The Gemara now wishes to analyze this section of *Megillat Ta'anit* in the light of the rulings found in our Mishnah. **It was said above: "From the New Moon of Nisan until the eighth** day **of the month,** [4]when the Rabbinic tradition regarding **the daily sacrifice was** firmly **established** as law, **it is not** even **permitted to eulogize** the dead." [5]The Gemara asks: **Why** does *Megillat Ta'anit* say that in commemoration of the Rabbis' victory over the Sadducees regarding the daily sacrifice, eulogizing the dead is forbidden "**from the New Moon** of Nisan until the eighth day of the month"? [6]**Let it say** "**from the second** day **of** the month of **Nisan,"** [7]**for** surely **the New Moon is itself a festive day** on which delivering a eulogy is **forbidden!** Even without the Rabbis' victory over the Sadducees, eulogizing the dead should be forbidden on the first day of Nisan, for the New Moon is regarded as a minor festival in its own right!

[1]מִתְּמַנְיָא בֵּיהּ עַד סוֹף מוֹעֲדָא, [2]אִיתּוֹתַב חַגָּא דִּשְׁבוּעַיָּא, דְּלָא לְמִיסְפַּד בְּהוֹן".
[3]אֲמַר מָר: "מֵרֵישׁ יַרְחָא דְּנִיסָן עַד תְּמַנְיָא בֵּיהּ, [4]אִיתּוֹקַם תְּמִידָא. דְּלָא לְמִיסְפַּד". [5]לָמָּה לִי "מֵרֵישׁ יַרְחָא"? [6]לֵימָא "מִתְּרֵי בְּנִיסָן", [7]וְרֹאשׁ חוֹדֶשׁ גּוּפֵיהּ יוֹם טוֹב הוּא וְאָסוּר!

LITERAL TRANSLATION

[1]From the eighth [of the month] until the end of the Festival, [2]the Festival of Shavuot was restored. [Therefore] it is not [permitted] to eulogize on them."

[3]The Master said: "From the New Moon of Nisan until the eighth of [the month], [4]the daily sacrifice was established. [Therefore] it is not [permitted] to eulogize [on them]." [5]Why do I need "from the New Moon"? [6]Let him say "from the second of Nisan," [7]for the New Moon itself is a festive day and forbidden!

RASHI

איתוקם תמידא ואיתותב חגא דשבועיא – בעניינים רבים חלקו ביתוסין עם חכמים, ומפורשין במנחות ובמגילת תענית [פרק א], והכי גרסינן התם בפרק "ר' ישמעאל" [סה,א], תנו רבנן: אלין יומיא דלא להתענאה בהון. ומקצתהון דלא למיספד בהון, מריש ירחא דניסן עד תמניא ביה איתוקם תמידא, דלא למיספד. ומתמניא ביה עד סוף מועדא איתותב חגא דשבועיא, דלא למיספד. **מריש ירחא דניסן ועד תמניא ביה איתוקם תמידא דלא למיספד** – שהיו הצדוקים אומרים יחיד מתנדב ומביא תמיד, מאי דרוש – "את הכבש אחד תעשה בבקר ואת הכבש השני תעשה בין הערביים". מאי אהדרו להו – "את קרבני לחמי לאשי תשמרו להקריב" לשון רבים הוא, שיהו כולן באין מתרומת הלשכה.

NOTES

וְרֹאשׁ חוֹדֶשׁ גּוּפֵיהּ יוֹם טוֹב הוּא For the New Moon itself is a festive day. *Rashi* and others explain that the assumption that the New Moon is regarded as a festive day is based on the Rabbinic interpretation of the verse (Lamentations 1:15): "He has called against me a 'time' [מוֹעֵד]" as referring to the New Moon (see below, 29a), the term מוֹעֵד being one of the Biblical synonyms for a festive day. Others suggest that the New Moon's being regarded as a festive day is derived from the verse (Numbers 10:10): "And on the day of your gladness, and on your times, and on your New Moons." The verse implies that an analogy is to be drawn between "your times" and "your New Moons," which teaches us that both are festive days on which fasting and eulogizing are forbidden (*Rabbenu Elyakim*).

[1] אָמַר רַב: לֹא נִצְרְכָה אֶלָּא לֶאֱסוֹר יוֹם שֶׁלְּפָנָיו.
[2] וְשֶׁלְּפָנָיו נַמִי — תֵּיפּוֹק לֵיהּ דַּהֲוָה לֵיהּ יוֹם שֶׁלִּפְנֵי רֹאשׁ חֹדֶשׁ!
[3] רֹאשׁ חֹדֶשׁ דְּאוֹרַיְיתָא הוּא, וּדְאוֹרַיְיתָא לָא בָּעֵי חִיזּוּק.
[4] דְּתַנְיָא: ״הַיָּמִים הָאֵלֶּה הַכְּתוּבִין בִּמְגִילַּת תַּעֲנִית — לִפְנֵיהֶם וּלְאַחֲרֵיהֶם אֲסוּרִין.
[5] שַׁבָּתוֹת וְיָמִים טוֹבִים — הֵן אֲסוּרִין, לִפְנֵיהֶן וּלְאַחֲרֵיהֶן מוּתָּרִין.
[6] וּמַה הֶפְרֵשׁ בֵּין זֶה לָזֶה?
[7] הַלָּלוּ דִּבְרֵי תוֹרָה, וְדִבְרֵי תוֹרָה אֵין צְרִיכִין חִיזּוּק.
[8] הַלָּלוּ דִּבְרֵי סוֹפְרִים, וְדִבְרֵי סוֹפְרִים צְרִיכִין חִיזּוּק״.
[9] אָמַר מָר: מִתְּמַנְיָא בֵּיהּ עַד סוֹף מוֹעֲדָא, אִיתּוֹתַב חַגָּא דִּשְׁבוּעַיָּא.
[10] דְּלָא לְמִיסְפַּד״.

LITERAL TRANSLATION

[1] Rav said: It was not needed except to forbid the day before it.

[2] But the day before also — let him derive it from [the fact] that it is the day before the New Moon!

[3] The New Moon is by Torah law, and a Torah law does not require reinforcement, [4] as it was taught: "Those days that are written in *Megillat Ta'anit* — [the day] before them and [the day] after them are forbidden. [5] Shabbat and Festivals — they themselves are forbidden, [the day] before them and [the day] after them are permitted. [6] And what is the difference between this and that? [7] These are matters of Torah [law], and matters of Torah [law] do not require reinforcement. [8] These are matters [instituted] by the Scribes, and matters [instituted] by the Scribes require reinforcement."

[9] The Master said: "From the eighth [of the month] until the end of the Festival, the Festival of Shavuot was restored. [10] [Therefore] it is not [permitted] to eulogize [on them]."

RASHI

מתמניא ביה כו׳ עד דלא למיספד — שהיו ביתוסים אומרים

TRANSLATION AND COMMENTARY

אָמַר רַב [1] **Rav said: It was only necessary** to include the first day of Nisan in *Megillat Ta'anit* in order **to forbid** eulogizing on **the day before it** (the twenty-ninth day of the month of Adar) as well. For we learned in our Mishnah that, with respect to the days recorded in *Megillat Ta'anit* on which it is not permitted to eulogize the dead, it is also not permitted to deliver a eulogy on the day before the date mentioned.

וְשֶׁלְּפָנָיו נַמִי [2] The Gemara asks: How can it be argued that the first of Nisan was mentioned in *Megillat Ta'anit* in order to forbid eulogizing on the day before as well? Even if the first of Nisan had not been mentioned there, we would in any case have known that delivering a eulogy on **the day before** the first day of Nisan is **also** forbidden, for this **can be derived from the fact that it is the day before the New Moon.** If delivering a eulogy is forbidden not only on the minor festivals recorded in *Megillat Ta'anit*, but also on the day before those festivals, then eulogizing should surely be forbidden not only on the day of the New Moon, which is a Biblical festival, but also on the preceding day!

רֹאשׁ חֹדֶשׁ [3] The Gemara answers: Indeed, the reason why the New Moon of Nisan was included in *Megillat Ta'anit* among the days on which delivering a eulogy is forbidden was in order to forbid eulogizing on the last day of the month of Adar as well, as was argued above. The prohibition against eulogizing on the twenty-ninth of Adar could not have been derived from the fact that it is the day before the New Moon, for in general there is no prohibition against fasting or eulogizing on the day before the New Moon. The days recorded in *Megillat Ta'anit* are minor festivals instituted by the Rabbis, on which they forbade fasting, and in some cases eulogizing as well. The Rabbis reinforced their enactment by extending these prohibitions to the day before these minor festivals. But **the** institution of the **New Moon is based on Torah law, and a Torah law does not require** any **reinforcement,** [4] **as was taught** in the following Baraita: "On **those days that are recorded in *Megillat Ta'anit*,** fasting, and in some cases eulogizing, is forbidden. On **the day before and** on **the day after** the dates actually recorded in *Megillat Ta'anit* these activities **are** also **forbidden.** [5] But as for **Shabbat and the Festivals**, on those days **themselves** fasting and eulogizing **are forbidden,** but on **the day before and** on **the day after them,** these activities **are permitted.** [6] **What is the** basis for the **difference between** the laws that apply to the days recorded in *Megillat Ta'anit* and those that apply to Shabbat and to the Festivals? [7] The restrictions on Shabbat and the Festivals **are Torah laws, and Torah laws do not require** any **reinforcement.** [8] But the prohibitions against fasting and eulogizing are **Rabbinic enactments, and Rabbinic enactments do require reinforcement."**

אָמַר מָר [9] The Gemara now proceeds to the next minor festival recorded in *Megillat Ta'anit.* **It was said above: "From the eighth** day of the month of Nisan **until the end of the Festival** of Pesaḥ, when **the Festival of Shavuot was restored** so that it was henceforth celebrated on the proper date according to Rabbinic tradition, [10] **it is not**

BACKGROUND

וְדִבְרֵי סוֹפְרִים צְרִיכִין חִיזּוּק And matters instituted by the Scribes require reinforcement. In certain matters that were originally Rabbinic decrees, the Sages ruled particularly stringently by issuing supplementary rulings or by extreme insistence upon observing a certain Halakhah. This was because some people are contemptuous of Rabbinic rulings and might come to abandon them completely. People are not, however, contemptuous of Torah rulings. Hence the Sages were not required to add supplementary decrees to emphasize their importance.

אִיתּוֹקַם תְּמִידָא...אִיתּוֹתַב חַגָּא דִּשְׁבוּעַיָּא The daily sacrifice was established...the Festival of Shavuot was restored. These minor festivals, like a number of others recorded in *Megillat Ta'anit,* are connected with the struggles of the Rabbinic Sages against the Sadducees and the Boethusians. These sects apparently enjoyed significant support from the Hasmonean kings, and even after the end of the Hasmonean dynasty they seem to have had high-ranking supporters even among the important priestly families.

The "establishment of the daily sacrifice" (הַקְרָבַת הַתָּמִיד) was a victory in an important controversy with the Sadducees, who permitted using individual donations for the daily sacrifice. This involved a matter of principle, for it removed the Temple service from the realm of individuals and made it a sacrifice in which everyone had a share through the half-shekel contributions made by all Jews.

The "restoration of the Festival of Shavuot" is related to another prolonged controversy with the Boethusians, who believed that the expression "the day after the Sabbath" in relation to bringing the Omer-offering referred to the day after Shabbat, with the result that Shavuot would always be celebrated on a Sunday. As is described in tractate *Rosh HaShanah,* the Boethusians used a variety of methods to reinforce their opinion. They even bribed witnesses in their attempts to mislead the court. The victory in this controversy with them meant the removal of an important obstacle to the proper observance of the Jewish Festivals.

TRANSLATION AND COMMENTARY

even permitted **to eulogize** the dead." [1]The Gemara asks: **Why** does *Megillat Ta'anit* say that eulogizing the dead is forbidden from the eighth day of the month of Nisan **"until the end of the Festival** of Pesaḥ"? [2]**Let it say "until the Festival"** of Pesaḥ, [3]**for** surely **the Festival** of Pesaḥ **is itself a holiday** on which delivering a eulogy is forbidden!

אֲמַר רַב פַּפָּא [4]**Rav Pappa said:** This question can be answered in the same way that Rav answered the similar question raised above about the first date recorded in *Megillat Ta'anit*. **For Rav said: It was only necessary** to include the first day of Nisan in *Megillat Ta'anit* [18A] in order **to forbid** eulogizing on **the day before it** (the twenty-ninth of Adar) as well. [5]**Here too** a similar argument can be put forward: **It was only necessary** to include the days of Pesaḥ in *Megillat Ta'anit* in order **to forbid** eulogizing on **the day after** Pesaḥ as well. If *Megillat Ta'anit* had said that eulogizing is forbidden from the eighth of Nisan until the Festival of Pesaḥ, then eulogizing would indeed be forbidden during the Festival of Pesaḥ itself, but it would be permitted on the twenty-second day of Nisan, the day after Pesaḥ, for the Torah prohibition against delivering a eulogy on Pesaḥ does not need to be reinforced by extending the prohibition to the next day. But now that *Megillat Ta'anit* says that eulogizing is forbidden until the end of the Festival of Pesaḥ, delivering a eulogy is forbidden on the day after Pesaḥ as well, because the Rabbis reinforced their enactment by extending the prohibition for another day.

כְּמַאן [6]The Gemara raises an objection: **In accordance with whose** viewpoint was this solution proposed? [7]It could only have been proposed **in accordance with** the viewpoint of **Rabbi Yose, who said** in our Mishnah: "Regarding the days on which according to *Megillat Ta'anit* eulogizing is forbidden, **both** on **the day before** the date recorded in the scroll **as well as** on **the day after** the date recorded in the scroll, **it is forbidden** to deliver a eulogy." For according to the anonymous first Tanna of the Mishnah, it is only on the day before the date recorded in *Megillat Ta'anit* that eulogizing is forbidden, but on the day after the date recorded there delivering a eulogy is permitted. [8]But **if it is true** that the solution proposed above assumes that the ruling in *Megillat Ta'anit* was formulated in accordance with the viewpoint of Rabbi Yose, then another difficulty arises: It was argued above that the first day of Nisan was included in *Megillat Ta'anit* in order to forbid eulogizing on the day before it, on the twenty-ninth of Adar. But if the ruling in *Megillat Ta'anit* was formulated in accordance with the viewpoint of Rabbi Yose, then **why say** that eulogizing is forbidden on **the twenty-ninth** of Adar because **it is the day before** the first of Nisan, **the day on which**

[1]לָמָּה לִי "עַד סוֹף מוֹעֵד"? [2]לֵימָא "עַד הַמּוֹעֵד", [3]וּמוֹעֵד גּוּפֵיהּ יוֹם טוֹב הוּא וְאָסוּר!
[4]אֲמַר רַב פַּפָּא: כְּדַאֲמַר רַב: לָא נִצְרְכָא [18A] אֶלָּא לֶאֱסוֹר יוֹם שֶׁלְּפָנָיו, [5]הָכָא נַמִי לָא נִצְרְכָה אֶלָּא לֶאֱסוֹר יוֹם שֶׁלְּאַחֲרָיו.
[6]כְּמַאן? [7]כְּרַבִּי יוֹסֵי, דְּאָמַר: בֵּין לְפָנָיו וּבֵין לְאַחֲרָיו אָסוּר? [8]אִי הָכִי, בְּעֶשְׂרִים וְתִשְׁעָה נַמִי, מַאי אִירְיָא דְּהָוֵי יוֹמָא דְּמִקַּמֵּי יוֹמָא

LITERAL TRANSLATION

[1]Why do I need "until the end of the Festival"? [2]Let him say "until the Festival," [3]for the Festival itself is a festive day and forbidden!

[4]Rav Pappa said: As Rav said: It was not needed [18A] except to forbid the day before it. [5]Here too it was not needed except to forbid the day after it. [6]In accordance with whom? [7][Is it] in accordance with Rabbi Yose, who said: "It is forbidden both [the day] before and [the day] after"? [8]If so, regarding the twenty-ninth [of Adar] also, why specifically [mention] that it was the day before the day

RASHI

עצרת אחר השבת הוא, שהעומר מתחיל אחד בשבת שנאמר "וספרתם לכם ממחרת השבת". ניטפל להן רבן יוחנן בן זכאי ואמר להם: שוטים מניין לכם. ולא היה אדם שהחזירו דבר, חוץ מזקן אחד שהיה מפטפט כנגדו, ואמר: משה רבינו אוהב ישראל היה, ויודע שעצרת יום אחד הוא, עמד ותיקנה אחר שבת, כדי שיהיו מתענגים שני ימים וכו'. ודחו אותן, והלכו להן בייתוסים מכח הפסוקין על כרחן, וחזרו בהן. (עד כאן הגהה). איתוקס תמידא דלא למיספד גרסינן, ולא גרסינן להתענאה, כדמוכח בסמוך דקתני: לא נצרכה אלא לאסור את שלפניו, ואי גרסינן להתענאה — אם כן היינו רבי יוסי, דאמר: לפניו אסור. והא ליכא למימר דרבי יוסי היא, דקא פריך: כמאן — כרבי יוסי בתמיהה. מכלל דכרבנן פסיקא ליה. **עד סוף מועדא** — פסח. **חגא דשבועיא דלא למיספד** — במגילת תענית [פרק א] מפרש מאי "איתוקס". **וראש חדש יום טוב הוא** — דכתיב "קרא עלי מועד" והוי ראש חודש אב, בהאי מסכתא לקמן (כט,א). **לאסור את שלפניו** — להכי נקט מריש ירחא דניסן, לאסור את יום שלפני ראש חדש בתענית, כדתניא בסמוך: לפניהן אסורין. דאי משום ראש חדש לא היה נאסר, כדמפרש: דדברי תורה אין צריכין חיזוק. **כמאן כרבי יוסי** — דמתניתין, דאמר אף לאחריו? בתמיהה, ושבקת רבנן. אי הכי, דאליבא דרבי יוסי מוקמת לה למגילת תענית — עשרים ותשעה באדר נמי, דקתרצת לעיל דלהכי נקט "ריש ירחא דניסן", דהיינו יום שלשים, דאדר הסמוך לניסן לעולם חסר, מעשרים ותשעה יום הוא, משום דקא בעי למיסר יום עשרים ותשעה — תיפוק ליה דבלאו הכי הוי אסור יום עשרים ותשעה, דהוה ליה יום דבתר עשרים ושמונה, שהוא תשעה עשר כו' ואסור יום שלאחריו כרבי יוסי, ואמאי נקט "ריש ירחא", לאסור את שלפניו?

TRANSLATION AND COMMENTARY

the Rabbinic tradition regarding **the daily** … **rifice was** firmly **established** as law? [1]**Let this** … oition **be derived from the fact that it is the d**… **er the twenty-eighth of Adar,** another of the m… stivals recorded in *Megillat Ta'anit.* [2]**For it was taught** in *Megillat Ta'anit*: **"On the twenty-eighth of Adar,** the day on which the **good tidings came to the Jews that they would not be forced to refrain from Torah** study, one is not permitted to eulogize the dead. The circumstances which led to the establishment of … minor festival on the tw… ty-eighth of Adar were a… lows: [3]It **once** happen… **the evil kingdom** of … sued a series of … **apostasy against** t… ple, declaring t… engage in t… , [4]**and that** … cum- cise th… at they **must** … Shabbat. [5]**W**… **ehudah ben** S… **his colleagues do** … se decrees were is- … **They went and sought** … e **from a certain** Roman …**atron in whose company all** the **distinguished men of Rome were** to be **found.** [7]Sympathetic to their cause, the matron **said to** Yehudah ben Shamu'a and his colleagues: **'Rise up and cry out in the night.'** [8]Accepting her advice, **they went and cried out in the night.** [9]First **they** cried out to God in prayer and **said: 'O God in Heaven,** do not give the nations of the world reason to doubt Your existence and Your power to save us!' Then they cried out to the Romans, saying: [10]**'Are we not** all **brothers, are we not** all **the children of one father, are we not** all **the children of one mother?** [11]**How are we different from every** other **nation and tongue that you** single us out and **impose on us** such **evil decrees?'** [12]These cries of protest were effective **and** the decrees **were canceled.** [13]**And that very day** on which the evil decrees were canceled, which was the twenty-eighth day of the month of Adar, the Sages **made** into **a** minor **festival** on which fasting and eulogizing are forbidden." Now, according to Rabbi Yose, eulogizing is forbidden not only on the twenty-eighth of Adar, but also on the next day, the twenty-ninth. Thus the question raised earlier remains: If *Megillat Ta'anit* represents Rabbi Yose's opinion, why must it state that delivering a eulogy is forbidden on the New Moon of Nisan? It cannot be argued that *Megillat Ta'anit* mentioned that date in order to forbid eulogizing on the day before it, the twenty-ninth of Adar, for according to Rabbi Yose eulogizing on that day is in any case forbidden on account of its being the day after the twenty-eighth!

אָמַר אַבַּיֵי [14]**Abaye said: It was only necessary** to include the first day of Nisan in *Megillat Ta'anit,* in order

דְּמִיתּוֹקַם תְּמִידָא? [1]תֵּי… ה
דַּהֲוָה לֵיהּ יוֹמָא דְּבָתַר… ן
וּתְמַנְיָא בֵּיהּ, [2]דְּתַנְיָא: בְּ…
וּתְמַנְיָא בֵּיהּ אָתַת בְּ…
טַבְתָּא לִיהוּדָאֵי דְּלָא יְעִי…
אוֹרַיְיתָא. [3]שֶׁפַּעַם אַחַת
מַלְכוּת הָרְשָׁעָה שְׁמָד
יִשְׂרָאֵל שֶׁלֹּא יַעַסְקוּ בַּתּ…
[4]וְשֶׁלֹּא יָמוּלוּ אֶת בְּנֵיהֶ…
וְשֶׁיְּחַלְּלוּ שַׁבָּתוֹת. [5]מֶה עָשָׂ…
יְהוּדָה בֶּן שַׁמּוּעַ וַחֲבֵרָיו
[6]הָלְכוּ וְנָטְלוּ עֵצָה מִמַּטְרוֹנִיתָא
אַחַת שֶׁכָּל גְּדוֹלֵי רוֹמִי מְצוּיִין
אֶצְלָהּ. [7]אָמְרָה לָהֶם: עִמְדוּ
וְהַפְגִּינוּ בַּלַּיְלָה. [8]הָלְכוּ וְהִפְגִּינוּ
בַּלַּיְלָה, [9]אָמְרוּ: אִי שָׁמַיִם!
[10]לֹא אַחִים אֲנַחְנוּ, לֹא בְּנֵי אָב
אֶחָד אֲנַחְנוּ, לֹא בְּנֵי אֵם אַחַת
אֲנַחְנוּ? [11]מַה נִּשְׁתַּנֵּינוּ מִכָּל
אוּמָּה וְלָשׁוֹן שֶׁאַתֶּם גּוֹזְרִין
עָלֵינוּ גְּזֵירוֹת רָעוֹת! [12]וּבִטְּלוּם.
[13]וְאוֹתוֹ יוֹם עֲשָׂאוּהוּ יוֹם טוֹב".
[14]אָמַר אַבַּיֵי: לֹא נִצְרְכָה אֶלָּא

LITERAL TRANSLATION

on which the daily sacrifice was established. [1]Let him derive it [from the fact] that it is the day after the twenty-eighth of [Adar], [2]as it was taught: "On the twenty-eighth of [Adar] good tidings came to the Jews that they would not be removed from the Torah. [3]For once the evil kingdom decreed apostasy on Israel, that they must not engage in [the study of] Torah, [4]and that they must not circumcise their sons, and that they must desecrate Sabbaths. [5]What did Yehudah ben Shamu'a and his colleagues do? [6]They went and took advice from a certain matron at whose [home] were found all the great men of Rome. [7]She said to them: Rise and cry out in the night. [8]They went and cried out in the night. [9]They said: 'O, Heavens! [10]Are we not brothers, are we not the children of one father, are we not the children of one mother? [11]How are we different from every nation and tongue that you decree against us evil decrees?' [12]And they canceled them. [13]And that day they made a festival."

[14]Abaye said: It was not needed

RASHI

דלא יעידון — שלא יהו צריכין ליבטל מתלמוד תורה, שגזור עליהן שלא יעסקו בתורה. **הפגינו** = לעקו. כך מתרגמינן בתהלים כל לשון שַׁוְעָה ולעקה — לשון פגיה. **אי שמים** גרסינן. אהה ה', להקדוש ברוך הוא היו לועקים, על אותם שגזרו עליהם גזרות קשות, והיו אומרים להם לפני הקדוש ברוך הוא: וכי לא אחיכם וכו'. **לא נצרכה אלא לחדש מעובר** — בשנה מעוברת, שיש

LANGUAGE

מַטְרוֹנִיתָא Matron. This Aramaic word is derived from the Latin word *matrona,* meaning matron.

הַפְגִּינוּ And cry out. The root פגן (occasionally בגן) is found in Aramaic and means "to cry," or "to wail." The root is close to and probably derived from the Persian *afgan,* meaning "a shout," or "a cry." And it may possibly have the more precise meaning of a cry of protest to a ruler, begging him to act justly.

SAGES

יְהוּדָה בֶּן שַׁמּוּעַ Yehudah ben Shamu'a. Of this Tanna of the last generation of Tannaim very little is known, the main thing being that he was a disciple of Rabbi Meir. Apparently Yehudah ben Shamu'a was one of the oldest of Rabbi Meir's disciples, because other Sages of the last generation of Tannaim transmit his teachings.

BACKGROUND

מַלְכוּת הָרְשָׁעָה The evil kingdom. This was the term used by the Sages for the Roman Empire, because during most of the time that it ruled over Eretz Israel, both under the pagan emperors and under the Christian ones, it persecuted the Jews in various ways, by discriminatory and restrictive laws and by special decrees against the Jewish religion.

הָלְכוּ וְנָטְלוּ עֵצָה מִמַּטְרוֹנִיתָא אַחַת They went and took advice from a certain matron. During this period and even many years earlier, in Temple times, Judaism had great influence on prominent Romans. In particular, there were many women, some belonging to the highest classes in society, who had a positive attitude toward Judaism and were ready to help Jews and Judaism in various ways.

אָתַת בְּשׂוֹרְתָא טַבְתָּא לִיהוּדָאֵי Good tidings came to the Jews. The date and character of this decree are not known with certainty, just as we have no information about Yehudah ben Shamu'a. However, from the context and the chronology it seems that the events took place after the decrees of Hadrian, which followed the Bar Kokhba rebellion, had been somewhat reduced in severity. The story recorded here may have occurred during the reign of Marcus Aurelius (161- 180 C.E.). Although this emperor had a low regard for the Jews, he did not actively persecute them. Perhaps intervention by means of a demonstration had the effect of moderating the decrees.

TRANSLATION AND COMMENTARY

to forbid eulogizing on the preceding day, when Adar is **a full month** of thirty days. According to the Jewish calendar, a month may be "defective," having only twenty-nine days, or "full," having thirty days. When the month of Adar is full, eulogizing the dead is forbidden on the twenty-ninth day of the month on account of the minor festival celebrated the day before, on the twenty-eighth. But the prohibition against delivering a eulogy on the twenty-eighth is not extended to the thirtieth. Thus *Megillat Ta'anit* mentioned the first of Nisan in order to forbid eulogizing on the last day of Adar in those years when Adar is a full month of thirty days.

רַב אַשִׁי [1]**Rav Ashi said: You can even say that it was necessary** to include the first of Nisan in *Megillat Ta'anit* in order to forbid eulogizing on the preceding day, even when Adar is **a defective month** of only twenty-nine days; for if restrictions had been imposed on the twenty-ninth of Adar only because it is the day after the minor festival celebrated on the twenty-eighth, then fasting would have been forbidden on the twenty-ninth of Adar, but eulogizing on that day would have been permitted. [2]**For** the general rule **regarding any day** on which restrictions were imposed on account of its being the day before or the day **after** one of the minor festivals recorded in *Megillat Ta'anit* is that **fasting is forbidden but eulogies are permitted.** [3]**But since this day,** the twenty-ninth of Adar, **is placed between two** of the minor **festivals** recorded in the scroll, the twenty-eighth of Adar and the first of Nisan, [4]the Rabbis **made it like a** minor **festival itself, and even eulogies are forbidden** on it.

אֲמַר מָר [5]The Gemara now returns to the section of *Megillat Ta'anit* that **was cited above: "From the eighth**

לְחֹדֶשׁ מְעוּבָּר.

[1]רַב אַשִׁי אֲמַר: אֲפִילּוּ תֵּימָא לְחוֹדֶשׁ חָסֵר. [2]כָּל שֶׁלְּאַחֲרָיו, בְּתַעֲנִית אָסוּר בְּהֶסְפֵּד מוּתָּר. [3]וְזֶה, הוֹאִיל וּמוּטָּל בֵּין שְׁנֵי יָמִים טוֹבִים, [4]עֲשָׂאוּהוּ כְּיוֹם טוֹב עַצְמוֹ, וַאֲפִילּוּ בְּהֶסְפֵּד נַמִי אָסוּר.

[5]אֲמַר מָר: "מִתְּמַנְיָא בֵּיהּ וְעַד

LITERAL TRANSLATION

except for a full month.

[1]Rav Ashi said: You can even say [that it was necessary] for a defective month. [2][For on] any [day] that is after it, fasting is forbidden [but] eulogies are permitted. [3]But this [day], since it is placed between two festivals, [4]they made it like a festival itself, and even eulogies are forbidden.

[5]The Master said: "From the eighth [of the month] until

RASHI

בה שני אדר והאחד חסר. דהשתא, כי הוה אדר שני מלא — הוה יום שלשים לפני ראש חדש ניסן. אי נמי, דעברוה לאדר, כגון שלא נראה החדש יום שלשים. דמשום יום טוב דעשרים ושמונה לא מיתסר אלא עשרים ותשעה. רבא אמר אפילו תימא חדש חסר — ואהכי נקט "מריש ירחא", דאי הוה אסר ליה ליום עשרים ותשעה משום בתר עשרים ושמונה — לא הוה אסר ליה אלא בתענית לחודיה. דכל שלאחריו כו׳ — כלומר, כל שאסור משום אחר יום טוב — בתענית הוא דאסור, הא בהספד — מותר. ואהכי נקט "מריש ירחא", דלהוי האי "עשרים ותשעה" דנקט מוטל בין שני ימים, משום דאי מיתסר משום דלפני יום טוב — אימור לא איתסר בהספד, דהאי דנקט "כל שלאחריו" כו׳ — לאו משום דלפניו נמי אסור בהספד, אלא איידי דפריך דליתסר יום עשרים ותשעה משום בתר עשרים ושמונה הוא דמיהדר ליה "כל שלאחריו" כו׳.

NOTES

הוֹאִיל וּמוּטָּל בֵּין שְׁנֵי יָמִים טוֹבִים **Since it is placed between two festivals.** Support is brought from this passage for the view adopted by most of the Rishonim that the prohibition against fasting applies on all the days recorded in *Megillat Ta'anit,* whereas the prohibition against eulogizing applies on only some of them. *Megillat Ta'anit* says that on the twenty-eighth of Adar and on the first of Nisan eulogizing is forbidden. Now, if this means that eulogizing is forbidden in addition to fasting, we can understand why both are forbidden on the twenty-ninth of Adar, it being the day between the two minor festivals recorded in the scroll. But according to *Rabbenu Efrayim,* who maintains that the prohibition against eulogizing applies on all of the days recorded in *Megillat Ta'anit,* whereas the prohibition against fasting applies only when fasting is specifically forbidden, there is a difficulty. If on the twenty-eighth of Adar and on the first of Nisan only eulogizing is forbidden, but fasting is permitted, why should both be forbidden on the twenty-ninth of Adar, on account of its being between two days recorded in the scroll? (See *Ritva, Shittah.*)

הוֹאִיל וּמוּטָּל בֵּין שְׁנֵי יָמִים טוֹבִים **Since it is placed between two festivals.** As will be explained below (19a), the rulings found in *Megillat Ta'anit* were later rescinded, so that henceforth fasting and eulogizing were permitted even on the days recorded in the scroll. Thus Rav Ashi's position, that a day between two festivals assumes the character of a festival, has no practical significance with respect to the prohibitions against fasting and eulogizing on the minor festivals listed in the scroll. But it does have ramifications even today with respect to an entirely different issue. The *taḥanun* prayer — a supplication recited after the prayer leader's repetition of the Amidah in the daily morning and afternoon services, but omitted on Shabbat, Festivals, and minor festivals — is not said on the second of Sivan, because that day occurs between the first of Sivan (the New Moon) and the third of Sivan (the first of the three days immediately preceding the Shavuot Fesival (שְׁלוֹשֶׁת יְמֵי הַגְבָּלָה), which are treated in some respects as a minor festival).

TRANSLATION AND COMMENTARY

day **of the month** of Nisan **until the end of the Festival** of Pesah, when **the Festival of Shavuot was restored** so that it was henceforth celebrated on the proper date according to Rabbinic tradition, [1]it is **not** permitted to fast or even **to eulogize** the dead." [2]The Gemara asks: **Why was it necessary** for *Megillat Ta'anit* **to say** that fasting and eulogizing the dead are forbidden **"from the eighth of the month** of Nisan until the end of the Festival of Pesah"? [3]**It could have said** that fasting and eulogizing the dead are forbidden **"from the ninth of** Nisan until the end of Pesah," for surely on **the eighth** of Nisan **itself** it **is forbidden** to fast or to deliver a eulogy, [4]**because it is** one of **the days on which** the Rabbinic tradition regarding **the daily sacrifice was** firmly **established** as law, in commemoration of which another minor festival was declared, on which fasting and eulogizing the dead are forbidden!

כֵּיוָן [5]The Gemara answers: It was necessary for the *Megillat Ta'anit* to say that fasting and eulogizing the dead are forbidden on the eighth of Nisan on account of the Rabbis' victory regarding the dating of Shavuot, because a situation could arise in which fasting and delivering a eulogy on that day would cease to be forbidden on account of the minor festival celebrated from the first of Nisan to the eighth in commemoration of the Rabbis' victory regarding the daily sacrifice. **If some** calamitous **event occurred,** the Rabbis could decide that a communal fast would have to be observed during the first week of Nisan. In that case the minor festival commemorating the Rabbis' victory regarding the daily sacrifice would have to be **canceled**. The prohibitions against fasting and eulogizing would be canceled only on **the first seven days of Nisan,** [6]but on **the eighth day itself** fasting and eulogizing **would** still **be forbidden,** [7]**for** that day **is the first day** of the minor festival commemorating the Rabbis' victory over the Boethusians, **at which** time **the Festival of Shavuot was restored** to its proper date according to Rabbinic tradition.

הָשְׁתָּא דְּאָתֵית לְהָכִי [8]The Gemara notes: **Now that you have come to this** conclusion, that the eighth of Nisan was mentioned twice in *Megillat Ta'anit* so that fasting and eulogizing would be forbidden on that day even if one of the festivals of which it is a part were to be canceled, **a similar solution can be offered**

סוֹף מוֹעֲדָא אִיתּוֹתַב חַגָּא דִשְׁבוּעַיָּא [1]דְּלָא לְמִיסְפַּד". [2]לָמָּה לִי לְמֵימַר מִתְּמַנְיָא בֵּיהּ? [3]לֵימָא מִתִּשְׁעָה בֵּיהּ, [4]וּתְמַנְיָא גּוּפֵיהּ אָסוּר, דַּהֲוָה לֵיהּ יוֹמָא דְּאִיתּוּקַם בֵּיהּ תְּמִידָא!

[5]כֵּיוָן דְּאִילּוּ מִקְלַע לֵיהּ מִילְּתָא וּבָטְלִינֵיהּ לְשִׁבְעָה, [6]תְּמַנְיָא גּוּפֵיהּ אָסוּר, [7]דַּהֲוָה לֵיהּ יוֹמָא קַמָּא דְּאִיתּוֹתַב בֵּיהּ חַגָּא דִשְׁבוּעַיָּא.

[8]הָשְׁתָּא דְּאָתֵית לְהָכִי,

LITERAL TRANSLATION

the end of the Festival the Festival of Shavuot was restored. [1][Therefore] it is not permitted to eulogize [on them]." [2]Why do I need to say "from the eighth of the [month]"? [3]Let him say "from the ninth of [the month]," [4]and the eighth itself is forbidden, for it is the day on which the daily sacrifice was established!

[5]Because if something happened and we canceled [any of] the [first] seven [days], [6]the eighth [day] itself would be forbidden, [7]for it is the first day on which the Festival of Shavuot was restored.

[8]Now that you have come to this,

RASHI

לימא מתשעה ותמניא גופיה — יום טוב הוא, דהא הוה ליה מהנך ימים טובים דאיתוקם בהו תמידא, כדכתיב ביה: מריש ירחא עד תמניא. הכי **גרסינן: דאי איקלע מילתא ובטליניה לשבעה תמניא גופיה אסור דהוה ליה יומא דאיתותב חגי דשבועיא** — דאי איקלע מילתא, שאם נגזר גזירה וצריכין להתענות תוך אלו ימים טובים דתמיד, ובטלו אותן להתענות בכולן, שאין לבטלה לחצאין. **אבתי יומא תמניא אסור משום חגא דשבועיא** — ואי קשיא: אכתי לימא תשעה, ואפילו אם אירע מילתא דבטלי — אכתי הוא אסור, תמניא גופיה, משום קמא יומא דחג שבועיא, דהוה יום שלפניו! לאו פירכא הוא, דהא יום טוב גופיה בטיל, ואנא ליקום וליגזור קמיה יומא דאיתותב חגא דשבועיא? וכהאי גוונא מתרץ לקמן ביום טוריינוס.

NOTES

כֵּיוָן דְּאִילּוּ מִקְלַע לֵיהּ מִילְּתָא וּבָטְלִינֵיהּ **Because if something happened and we canceled it.** The Jerusalem Talmud also deals with the difficulty that arises from the fact that *Megillat Ta'anit* records certain dates as being days on which fasting and eulogizing are forbidden on acco[illegible] joyous events that occurred on [illegible] Second Temple period, even tho[illegible] are already forbidden on thos[illegible] — either because they are [illegible] law, or because they commemorate other events recorded in *Megillat Ta'anit* itself. The Jerusalem Talmud argues that *Megillat Ta'anit* is simply a list of dates on which miracles were performed for the Jewish people, on account of which [illegible] reason.

¹כֵּיוָן עֶשְׂרִים וְתִשְׁעָה נַמִּי, דְּאִילּוּ מִיקְלַע מִילְּתָא וּבַטְלִינֵיהּ לְעֶשְׂרִים וּתְמָנְיָא, ²עֶשְׂרִין וְתִשְׁעָה גּוּפֵיהּ אָסוּר, ³דַּהֲוָה לֵיהּ יוֹמָא דְּמִקַּמֵּי יוֹמָא דְּאִיתּוֹקַם תְּמִידָא.

⁴אִיתְּמַר: ⁵רַב חִיָּיא בַּר אַסִּי אָמַר רַב: הֲלָכָה כְּרַבִּי יוֹסֵי. ⁶וּשְׁמוּאֵל אָמַר: הֲלָכָה כְּרַבִּי מֵאִיר.

⁷וּמִי אָמַר שְׁמוּאֵל הָכִי? ⁸וְהָתַנְיָא: "רַבָּן שִׁמְעוֹן בֶּן גַּמְלִיאֵל אוֹמֵר: ⁹וּמָה תַּלְמוּד לוֹמַר 'בְּהוֹן', ¹⁰'בְּהוֹן' שְׁתֵּי פְּעָמִים? ¹¹לוֹמַר לְךָ שֶׁהֵן אֲסוּרִין, לִפְנֵיהֶן וּלְאַחֲרֵיהֶן מוּתָּרִין". ¹²וְאָמַר שְׁמוּאֵל:

LITERAL TRANSLATION

[the same applies to] the twenty-ninth [of Adar] also, [1]because if something happened and we canceled the twenty-eighth [day], [2]the twenty-ninth [day] itself would be forbidden, [3]for it is the day before the day on which the daily sacrifice was established.

[4]It was stated: [5]Rav Ḥiyya bar Assi said in the name of Rav: The Halakhah is in accordance with Rabbi Yose. [6]And Shmuel said: The Halakhah is in accordance with Rabbi Meir.

[7]But did Shmuel say this? [8]But surely it was taught: "Rabban Shimon ben Gamliel says: [9]And what does it teach by saying 'on them,' [10]'on them' twice? [11]To say to you that *they* are forbidden, [but the days] before them and after them are permitted." [12]And Shmuel said:

RASHI

עשרים ותשעה נמי — דתרצת לה לעיל: לא נצרכה כו', להכי נקט "בריש ירחא", דאי מיקלע כו'. **כרבי יוסי** — דאמר: בין לפניו בין לאחריו אסור. **כרבי מאיר** — סתם מתניתין, דקתני: לאחריו מותר. **מה תלמוד לומר בהון בהון** — דלא להתענאה בהון, ומקצתהון דלא למספד בהון. וקא דריש לה כדדייק לקמן "בהון" משמע מיעוט. **ואמר שמואל** — גרס.

TRANSLATION AND COMMENTARY

for the difficulty raised earlier **regarding the twenty-ninth** of Adar. The question was raised above as to why *Megillat Ta'anit* states that fasting and delivering a eulogy is forbidden on the first of Nisan. Surely, it was argued, fasting and eulogizing are forbidden on that day because it is the New Moon! In reply to this question, it was suggested that *Megillat Ta'anit* mentions the first of Nisan in order to forbid fasting and eulogizing on the previous day, the twenty-ninth of Adar. The Gemara then raised the objection that we already know that fasting and eulogizing on the twenty-ninth of Adar are forbidden, because it is the day after the twenty-eighth of that month, which is one of the minor festivals recorded in the scroll. In the light of what has just been said regarding the ninth of Nisan, this previous objection can be answered as follows: *Megillat Ta'anit* mentions the first of Nisan in order to forbid fasting and eulogizing on the twenty-ninth of Adar, because a situation could arise in which fasting and eulogizing on that day would not be forbidden on account of its being the day after one of the dates recorded in *Megillat Ta'anit*. [1]**For if a** calamitous **event occurred,** as a result of which the Rabbis **canceled** the minor festival previously celebrated on **the twenty-eighth** of Adar in order to allow a communal fast to be proclaimed on that day, [2]then fasting and eulogizing on **the twenty-ninth** of Adar **itself would** still **be forbidden,** [3]because that is the day before the day on which the Rabbinic tradition regarding the daily sacrifice was firmly established as law.

אִיתְּמַר [4]It was stated that there was a disagreement between Amoraim about the following matter: [5]**Rav Ḥiyya bar Assi said in the name of Rav: The Halakhah is in accordance with the viewpoint of Rabbi Yose,** who said that regarding those days on which *Megillat Ta'anit* states that eulogizing is forbidden, eulogizing is also forbidden on the day before and on the day after the date recorded in the scroll; and regarding those days on which fasting is forbidden, fasting is also forbidden on the day before, but is permitted on the day after. [6]**But Shmuel said: The Halakhah is in accordance with** the viewpoint of **Rabbi Meir,** the author of the ruling recorded anonymously in the Mishnah, who said that regarding those days on which *Megillat Ta'anit* states that eulogizing is forbidden, eulogizing is also forbidden on the day before, but is permitted on the day after; and regarding those days on which fasting is forbidden, fasting is permitted both on the day before and on the day after.

וּמִי אָמַר [7]The Gemara asks: **But did Shmuel** really **say** that the law is in accordance with the viewpoint of Rabbi Meir? **Surely** Shmuel is known to have ruled on this matter in accordance with a third viewpoint not mentioned in the Mishnah, [8]for the following **was taught** in a Baraita: **"Rabban Shimon ben Gamliel says:** [9]**Why does** *Megillat Ta'anit* **state:** 'These are the days ***on which*** one may not fast, and some of them are days ***on which*** it is even forbidden to eulogize the dead,' [10]emphasizing **twice** that the restrictions referred to here apply on those specific days mentioned in the scroll? [11]*Megillat Ta'anit* is formulated in this way in order **to teach you** that fasting and eulogizing **are forbidden** only on the days actually recorded in the scroll, whereas on **the days before and after** those dates fasting and eulogizing **are permitted."** [12]**And Shmuel said:**

SAGES

רַב חִיָּיא בַּר אַסִּי Rav Ḥiyya bar Assi (correct reading: Rav Ḥiyya bar Ashi). A Babylonian Amora of the second generation, Rav Ḥiyya bar Ashi was a very close disciple of Rav, and he presents teachings in his master's name in dozens of places in the Talmud. He was also the teacher of Rav's son. He also studied with Shmuel and with Ze'iri. He apparently lived in the city of Korkonya, close to Sura, and seems to have been an artisan (a netmaker). His relationship with Rav Huna was that of a colleague. Several Sages of his generation and of the following generation present Halakhic teachings in his name. The Talmud also speaks of his righteousness and great piety.

הֲלָכָה כְּרַבָּן שִׁמְעוֹן בֶּן גַּמְלִיאֵל!
[1]מֵעִיקָּרָא סָבַר כֵּיוָן דְּלֵיכָּא תַּנָּא דְּמֵיקֵל כְּרַבִּי מֵאִיר, [2]אֲמַר הֲלָכָה כְּרַבִּי מֵאִיר. [3]כֵּיוָן דִּשְׁמָעֵיהּ לְרַבָּן שִׁמְעוֹן דְּמֵיקֵל טְפֵי, [4]אָמַר הֲלָכָה כְּרַבָּן שִׁמְעוֹן בֶּן גַּמְלִיאֵל.
[5]וְכֵן אָמַר בָּאלִי אָמַר רַבִּי חִיָּיא בַּר אַבָּא אָמַר רַבִּי יוֹחָנָן: [6]הֲלָכָה כְּרַבִּי יוֹסֵי. [7]אָמַר לֵיהּ רַבִּי חִיָּיא לְבָאלִי: אַסְבְּרָא לָךְ. [8]כִּי אֲמַר רַבִּי יוֹחָנָן הֲלָכָה כְּרַבִּי יוֹסֵי, [9]אַדִּלָּא לְהִתְעַנָּאָה.
[10]וּמִי אֲמַר רַבִּי יוֹחָנָן הָכִי? [11]וְהָאֲמַר רַבִּי יוֹחָנָן: הֲלָכָה כִּסְתַם מִשְׁנָה. [12]וּתְנַן: ״אַף עַל

LITERAL TRANSLATION

The Halakhah is in accordance with Rabban Shimon ben Gamliel!

[1]At the outset he thought [that] since there is no Tanna who is as lenient as Rabbi Meir, [2]he said [that] the Halakhah is in accordance with Rabbi Meir. [3]Once he heard that Rabban Shimon [ben Gamliel] is [even] more lenient, [4]he said [that] the Halakhah is in accordance with Rabban Shimon ben Gamliel.

[5]And similarly Bali said in the name of Rabbi Hiyya bar Abba who said in the name of Rabbi Yoḥanan: [6]The Halakhah is in accordance with Rabbi Yose. [7]Rabbi Ḥiyya said to Bali: I will explain [this] to you. [8]When Rabbi Yoḥanan said [that] the Halakhah is in accordance with Rabbi Yose, [9][it was] regarding not fasting.

[10]But did Rabbi Yoḥanan say this? [11]But surely Rabbi Yoḥanan said: The Halakhah is in accordance with the anonymous Mishnah. [12]And we have learned: "Although

RASHI

הלכה כרבן שמעון — דמדרבנן נינהו, ולא מחמרינן כולי האי.
באלי — שם אדם. הכי גרסינן: כי אמר רבי יוחנן הלכה אדלא להתענאה — דימים הכתובים במגילת תענית דלא להתענאה — לפניהן אסורים ולאחריו מותרין, כרבי יוסי ולא כרבי מאיר, דאמר: אף לפניהם מותר, אבל אדלא למספד — דאין הלכה כרבי יוסי [דאמר] לפניו ולאחריו אסור, אלא כרבי מאיר, דאמר: לפניו — אסור, ולאחריו — מותר. ומי אמר רבי יוחנן הכי — דלפניו מיהא אסור, כרבי יוסי.

TRANSLATION AND COMMENTARY

The Halakhah on this matter **is in accordance with** the viewpoint of **Rabban Shimon ben Gamliel,** that the prohibitions imposed by *Megillat Ta'anit* are restricted to the days it specifically mentions! How, then, can Shmuel rule in accordance with the viewpoint of Rabbi Meir, if elsewhere he rules in accordance with the viewpoint of Rabban Shimon ben Gamliel?

מֵעִיקָּרָא סָבַר [1]The Gemara answers: It is true that the two rulings issued by Shmuel cannot be reconciled, but they reflect the same principle — that since we are dealing here with Rabbinic prohibitions, the most lenient position should be accepted as law. **Initially** Shmuel was familiar only with the two positions found in the Mishnah, that of Rabbi Yose and that of Rabbi Meir. **Since he thought that there was no** other **Tanna who was as lenient** on this matter **as Rabbi Meir,** [2]**he ruled that the Halakhah is in accordance with** the viewpoint of **Rabbi Meir** [3]But **once he** became aware of the third position, stated in the Baraita, and **heard that Rabban Shimon ben Gamliel was even more lenient** on this matter than Rabbi Meir, [4]**he** changed his ruling and **said that the Halakhah is in accordance with** the most lenient viewpoint of all, that of **Rabban Shimon ben Gamliel.**

וְכֵן אָמַר בָּאלִי [5]The Gemara continues: **And on the same topic** the Sage **Bali said in the name of Rabbi Ḥiyya bar Abba, who said in the name of Rabbi Yoḥanan:** [6]**The Halakhah is in accordance with** the viewpoint of **Rabbi Yose.** [7]**Rabbi Ḥiyya bar Abba said to Bali: I will explain** Rabbi Yoḥanan's ruling **to you.** [8]**When Rabbi Yoḥanan said that the Halakhah is in accordance with** the viewpoint of **Rabbi Yose,** [9]**it was** only **regarding** those days about which *Megillat Ta'anit* states that one is **not** permitted **to fast.** Rabbi Yoḥanan ruled in accordance with the viewpoint of Rabbi Yose that fasting is also forbidden on the day before the date recorded in the scroll, and against the viewpoint of Rabbi Meir that fasting on the day before is permitted. But as for the days about which *Megillat Ta'anit* states that one is not permitted to eulogize the dead, Rabbi Yoḥanan did not rule in accordance with the viewpoint of Rabbi Yose that eulogizing is also forbidden both on the day before and on the day after the date recorded in the scroll, but rather he ruled in accordance with the viewpoint of Rabbi Meir that eulogizing is forbidden only on the day before, but is permitted on the day after.

וּמִי אֲמַר [10]The Gemara now questions this tradition regarding Rabbi Yoḥanan's ruling: **But did Rabbi Yoḥanan** really **say** that the Halakhah is in accordance with Rabbi Yose that, regarding those days when *Megillat Ta'anit* forbids fasting, one is also not permitted to fast on the day before the date recorded in the scroll? [11]**Surely Rabbi Yoḥanan formulated** the following general rule: **The Halakhah is** always **in accordance with** the viewpoint of **the anonymous Mishnah,** a Mishnah whose contents are not attributed to a named authority and which records no controversy on the issue discussed there. [12]**And we have learned** an

SAGES

בָּאלִי Bali. A Palestinian Amora of the third generation, Bali was a student of Rabbi Ḥiyya bar Abba, though he also transmits teachings by other Sages. His name is apparently derived from a foreign language; some scholars believe that it comes from Arabic.

BACKGROUND

הֲלָכָה כִּסְתַם מִשְׁנָה The Halakhah is in accordance with the anonymous Mishnah. Some Amoraim, such as Rabbi Yoḥanan, took this principle as a consistent basis for their decisions. It derives from the assumption that the anonymous presentation of a certain opinion in the Mishnah proves that Rabbi Yehudah HaNasi and his court decided that this was the Halakhah, and there was no court greater and more important than that of Rabbi Yehudah HaNasi in the following generations. This principle has a number of refinements. In some cases we find both an anonymous Mishnah and a difference of opinion between Tannaim. If the difference of opinion precedes the anonymous Mishnah, then the Halakhah agrees with the anonymous Mishnah. But if the anonymous Mishnah is followed by the difference of opinion, the Halakhah does not necessarily agree with the anonymous Mishnah. These principles regarding anonymous statements in the Mishnah are complicated by the fact that such statements cited in various places occasionally disagree with each other, or a difference of opinion in connection with an anonymous statement may appear elsewhere in the Mishnah. The details of these matters are a matter of controversy among Rabbinical authorities.

TRANSLATION AND COMMENTARY

5a) in which it is stated: **"Even though** the Sages **said that** there are times when **we bring forward** the reading of *Megillat Esther* ['The Scroll of Esther'] **but we may never delay** its reading, [18B] **eulogies and fasting are** nevertheless **permitted** on those days to which the reading of *Megillat Esther* is brought forward." The Rabbis enacted various dates for the reading of *Megillat Esther*. Those living in cities that were walled in the days of Joshua read the *Megillah* on the fifteenth of Adar. Those living in other towns or villages read the *Megillah* on the fourteenth of Adar. Those living in smaller villages sometimes read the *Megillah* before the fourteenth of Adar, because the Rabbis permitted them to read the *Megillah* on the Monday or the Thursday preceding the fourteenth of Adar — the days on which they would gather in the larger towns. Similarly, if the fourteenth or fifteenth of Adar falls on Shabbat, those who should read the *Megillah* on Shabbat bring the reading forward to Thursday or Friday. Thus, the *Megillah* may be read on the eleventh, the twelfth, the thirteenth, the fourteenth, or the fifteenth of Adar. How so? If the fourteenth of Adar falls on a Monday, those living in the unwalled towns and villages read it on the fourteenth, and those living in the walled cities read it on the fifteenth. If the fourteenth of Adar falls on a Tuesday or a Wednesday, those living in the villages bring their reading of the *Megillah* forward to the previous Monday, the twelfth or the thirteenth of Adar; those living in the unwalled towns read it on the fourteenth, and those living in the walled cities read it on the fifteenth. If the fourteenth of Adar falls on a Thursday, those living in the unwalled towns and villages read it on the fourteenth, and those living in the walled cities read it on the fifteenth. If the fourteenth of Adar falls on a Friday, those living in the villages read it on Thursday the thirteenth, and those living in the walled cities and the unwalled towns read it on the fourteenth. If the fourteenth of Adar falls on Shabbat, those living in the unwalled towns and villages bring their reading of the *Megillah* forward to Thursday the twelfth, and those living in the walled cities read it on the fifteenth. And if the fourteenth of Adar falls on a Sunday, those living in the villages read it on the previous Thursday, the eleventh of Adar; those living in the unwalled towns read it on the fourteenth; and those living in the walled cities read it on the fifteenth. Now, the Mishnah in tractate *Megillah* said that eulogies and fasting are permitted on those days to which the reading of the *Megillah* is brought forward. [1]**When** does this ruling apply? [2]**If we say that** the Mishnah **is referring** to **those** people living in walled cities, **who generally read** the *Megillah* **on the fifteenth of Adar, but** the fifteenth of Adar fell on Shabbat and so **they** had to **read** the *Megillah* that year **on the fourteenth,** and it is in such a case that the Mishnah allows those who bring their reading of the *Megillah* forward to fast and to eulogize on the day of their *Megillah* reading, there is a difficulty. [3]**Are** those people living in the walled cities really **permitted** to fast and eulogize on the fourteenth, the day they read the *Megillah*? [4]**Surely it is written in *Megillat Ta'anit*: "The fourteenth and fifteenth days of Adar are the days of Purim,** and **on them it is not permitted** to fast or **to eulogize** the dead." [5]**And** regarding this passage from *Megillat Ta'anit*, **Rava said: It was necessary** to include the days of Purim in *Megillat Ta'anit* **only in order to forbid those** living

פִּי שֶׁאָמְרוּ מַקְדִּימִין וְלֹא מְאַחֲרִין, [18B] מוּתָּרִין בְּהֶסְפֵּד וְתַעֲנִית". [1]אֵימַת? [2]אִילֵימָא בְּנֵי חֲמֵיסַר וְקָא קָרוּ לֵיהּ בְּאַרְבֵּיסַר, [3]וּמִי שָׁרֵי? [4]וְהָכְתִיב בִּמְגִילַּת תַּעֲנִית: "יוֹם אַרְבָּעָה עָשָׂר בּוֹ וְיוֹם חֲמִשָּׁה עָשָׂר בּוֹ יוֹמֵי פוּרַיָּא אִינּוּן, דְּלָא לְמִיסְפַּד בְּהוֹן". [5]וַאֲמַר רָבָא: לָא נִצְרְכָא

LITERAL TRANSLATION

they said [that] we bring forward but we do not delay, [18B] eulogies and fasting are permitted." [1]When? [2]If we say [that this refers to] those who [should read on] the fifteenth [of Adar] but read on the fourteenth, [3]is it permitted? [4]But surely it is written in *Megillat Ta'anit*: "The fourteenth day and the fifteenth day [of Adar] are the days of Purim, on which [it is] not [permitted] to eulogize." [5]And Rava said: It was not needed

RASHI

מקדימין — שקראו קודם זמנה. **מותרין בהספד ובתענית** — בני חמשה עשר [דכרכין ובני ארבעה עשר דכפרים ועיירות שקראו מגילה] דכרכין קודם זמנה, כדמפרש התם: באחד עשר, בשנים עשר, בשלשה עשר, בארבעה עשר, בחמשה עשר, שהכפרים מקדימין ליום הכניסה — מותרין, אותן ימים שקראוה קודם זמנה, בהספד ותענית. **בני חמיסר** — דהיינו כרכים המוקפין חומה מימות יהושע בן נון, וקא קרי בארביסר — כגון שהלך לכפר וקרא עמהן, דפרוז בן יומו נקרא פרוז, כדאמרינן במגילה (יט,א). **מי שרי** — ארבעה עשר אפילו לבני חמשה עשר בהספד ותענית. **ואמר רבא לא נצרכה** — לכתוב במגילת תענית לגזור ההספד ותענית לבני ארבעה עשר בארבעה עשר ולבני חמישה עשר בחמשה עשר — דהא קרא כתיב בהדיא "להיות עושים את ימי הפורים האלה" וגו׳.

HALAKHAH

יוֹמֵי פוּרַיָּא אִינּוּן, דְּלָא לְמִיסְפַּד בְּהוֹן Are the days of Purim, on which it is not permitted to eulogize. "Eulogizing and fasting are forbidden on the fourteenth and fifteenth of Adar for all people and in all places, both for those living in walled cities, who celebrate Purim only on the fifteenth, and for those living in unwalled towns, who celebrate Purim only on the fourteenth." (*Shulḥan Arukh, Oraḥ Ḥayyim* 696:3.)

אֶלָּא לֶאֱסוֹר אֶת שֶׁל זֶה בְּזֶה וְאֶת שֶׁל זֶה בְּזֶה.
[1]וְאֶלָּא, בְּנֵי אַרְבֵּיסַר וְקָא קָרֵי לֵיהּ בִּתְלֵיסַר. [2]יוֹם נִיקָנוֹר הוּא!
[3]וְאֶלָּא, בְּנֵי אַרְבֵּיסַר וְקָא קָרֵי לֵיהּ בִּתְרֵיסַר. [4]יוֹם טוּרְיָינוּס הוּא!
[5]אֶלָּא לָאו דְּקָא קָרוּ לֵיהּ בַּחֲדֵיסַר, [6]וְקָתָנֵי: "מוּתָּר בְּהֶסְפֵּד וּבְתַעֲנִית"!
[7]לָא. בְּנֵי אַרְבָּעָה עָשָׂר [8]וְקָא

LITERAL TRANSLATION

except to forbid those of this [day to read] on that and those of that [day to read] on this.

[1]Rather, [it refers to] those who [should read] on the fourteenth [of Adar] but read on the thirteenth. [2][But] it is the day of Nicanor!

[3]Rather, [it refers to] those who [should read] on the fourteenth [of Adar] but read on the twelfth. [4][But] it is the day of Trajan!

[5]Rather, is it not that they read it on the eleventh, [6]and it teaches: "Eulogies and fasting are permitted"!

[7]No. [It refers to] those who [should read] on the fourteenth [of Adar] [8]but

TRANSLATION AND COMMENTARY

in walled cities to fast and eulogize **on** the fourteenth of Adar, **and** to forbid **those** living in unwalled towns to fast and eulogize **on** the fifteenth. *Megillat Ta'anit* did not have to mention that fasting and eulogies are forbidden on the fifteenth of Adar to those living in walled cities and on the fourteenth of Adar to those living in unwalled towns, for the verse in Esther (9:22) says explicitly: "That they should make them days of feasting and joy." If *Megillat Ta'anit* includes the days of Purim, it can only be in order to teach us that someone who is celebrating Purim on the fifteenth of Adar is forbidden to fast and to eulogize even on the fourteenth, and that someone who is celebrating Purim on the fourteenth of Adar is forbidden to fast and to eulogize even on the fifteenth. This being the case, those living in walled cities who bring their reading of the *Megillah* forward to the fourteenth are certainly forbidden to fast and eulogize on that day!

וְאֶלָּא [1]**Rather,** continues the Gemara, the Mishnah must be referring to **those** people living in villages, **who generally read** the *Megillah* **on the fourteenth of Adar. But** the fourteenth of Adar fell on a Tuesday or a Friday, and so **they** had to **read** the *Megillah* that year **on** the previous Monday or Thursday, **the thirteenth** of Adar, and it is in such cases that the Mishnah allows those who bring their reading of the *Megillah* forward to fast and eulogize on the day they read the *Megillah*. [2]But this too poses a difficulty, for the thirteenth of Adar **is the day of Nicanor,** a minor festival recorded in *Megillat Ta'anit* in its own right, and on which fasting is forbidden!

וְאֶלָּא [3]**Rather,** continues the Gemara, the Mishnah must be understood as referring to **those** people living in villages, **who generally read** the *Megillah* **on the fourteenth of Adar, but** the fourteenth of Adar fell on a Wednesday, and so **they** had to **read** the *Megillah* that year **on** the previous Monday, **the twelfth** of Adar. And the Mishnah teaches us that though the villagers brought their reading of the *Megillah* forward to the twelfth of Adar, they were permitted to fast and eulogize on that day. But this understanding of the Mishnah, too, must be rejected, [4]for the twelfth of Adar **is the day of Trajan,** another of the minor festivals recorded in *Megillat Ta'anit*, and on which fasting is forbidden!

אֶלָּא לָאו [5]**Rather,** concludes the Gemara, the Mishnah must be referring to those people living in villages, who generally read the *Megillah* on the fourteenth of Adar; but the fourteenth of Adar fell on a Sunday, and so **they** had to **read** the *Megillah* that year **on** the previous Thursday, **the eleventh** of Adar. **And** regarding such a case the Mishnah **teaches:** "Those who bring their reading of the *Megillah* forward **are permitted to eulogize and fast** on the day of their *Megillah* reading." Thus we see that the anonymous Mishnah in tractate *Megillah* permits fasting on the eleventh of Adar, even though the eleventh of Adar is the day before the day of Trajan, a day when fasting is forbidden. Hence there is a contradiction between the two rulings of Rabbi Yohanan, for it was said above (18a) that Rabbi Yohanan ruled in accordance with Rabbi Yose that fasting is forbidden on the days before the dates recorded in *Megillat Ta'anit,* and Rabbi Yohanan also ruled that the law is always in accordance with the viewpoint of an anonymous Mishnah, which in the case of the Mishnah in tractate *Megillah* disagrees with the viewpoint of Rabbi Yose!

לָא [7]The Gemara resolves the difficulty: **No,** the Mishnah in tractate *Megillah* can indeed be understood as **referring to those** people living in villages, **who generally read** the Megillah **on the fourteenth of Adar;** [8]**but** the fourteenth of Adar fell on a Wednesday, and so **they** had to **read** the *Megillah* that year **on** the

RASHI

אלא לאסור את של זה בזה – כגון בני חמשה עשר (דקרו) בארבעה עשר ובני ארבעה עשר בחמשה עשר. **בני ארביסר** – ניהו, כפרים ועיירות. **וקא קרי בשלשה עשר** – כגון שחל ארבעה עשר בשלישי בשבת, ומקדימין ליום הכניסה. **יום ניקנור הוא** – לקמן מפרש, ואסור בהספד ותענית. **אלא בני ארבעה עשר וקרו בשנים עשר** – שחל ארבעה עשר ברביעי בשבת, והקדימו ליום הכניסה, דהיינו שנים עשר. **טוריינוס** – בסמוך מפרשה. **בחדיסר** – שחל להיות ארבעה עשר באחד בשבת, וכפרים מקדימין ליום הכניסה דהוו אחד עשר. ושמע מינה, דאף על גב שהוא יום שלפני טוריינוס – שרי בהספד ותענית.

BACKGROUND

טוּרְיָינוּס Trajan. The available material from non-Jewish sources is not sufficient to explain the matter completely. However, it seems that the event is connected with the major revolts of the Jews against Rome at the end of the reign of the Emperor Trajan (98-117 C.E.). The man who ordered the killing of Pappus and Lulianus seems to have been one of Trajan's officers, who was later defeated and killed. Pappus and Lulianus were apparently not killed on the day of this officer's death, and the day of his death was therefore declared a festive day.

BACKGROUND

שְׁמַעְיָה וַאֲחִיָּה Shemayah and Aḥiyyah. We do not know who Shemayah and his brother were, and some authorities maintain that they were "the martyrs of Lydda." According to one tradition, they assumed the responsibility for the assassination of the daughter of the emperor in their native city of Lydda, in order to save all the inhabitants of the city from death.

נִיקָנוֹר Nicanor (in Greek, Νικάνωρ). He was a general in the army of Antiochus Epiphanes, who served as the commander of the elephant corps and was apparently appointed by the king to govern Eretz Israel. On 13 Adar 161 B.C.E., his army was defeated near Adasa, northwest of Jerusalem, and he was killed in that battle.

קָרוּ לֵיהּ בִּתְרֵיסַר. [1]וּדְקָאָמְרַתְּ יוֹם טְרָיָינוּס הוּא, [2]יוֹם טְרָיָינוּס גּוּפֵיהּ בַּטּוּלֵי בַטְלוּהוּ, [3]הוֹאִיל וְנֶהֶרְגוּ בּוֹ שְׁמַעְיָה וַאֲחִיָּה אָחִיו. [4]כִּי הָא דְּרַב נַחְמָן גְּזָר תַּעֲנִיתָא בִּתְרֵיסַר. [5]אֲמַרוּ לֵיהּ רַבָּנַן: "יוֹם טוּרְיָינוּס הוּא!" [6]אֲמַר לְהוּ: "יוֹם טוּרְיָינוּס גּוּפֵיהּ בַּטּוּלֵי בַטְלוּהוּ, [7]הוֹאִיל וְנֶהֶרְגוּ בּוֹ שְׁמַעְיָה וַאֲחִיָּה אָחִיו".

[8]וְתֵיפּוֹק לֵיהּ דַּהֲוָה לֵיהּ יוֹם שֶׁלִּפְנֵי נִיקָנוֹר!

[9]אֲמַר רַב אַשִׁי: הָשְׁתָּא אִיהוּ גּוּפֵיהּ בַּטְלוּהוּ, [10]מִשּׁוּם יוֹם נִיקָנוֹר נֵיקוּם וְנִגְזַר?

LITERAL TRANSLATION

read on the twelfth. [1]And as for what you said [that] it is the day of Trajan, [2]they canceled the day of Trajan itself, [3]since Shemayah and Aḥiyyah his brother were killed on it. [4]As when Rav Naḥman decreed a fast on the twelfth [of Adar, [5]and] the Rabbis said to him: "It is the day of Trajan!" [6]He said to them: "They canceled the day of Trajan itself, [7]since Shemayah and Aḥiyyah his brother were killed on it."

[8]But let him derive it from [the fact] that it is the day before [the day of] Nicanor!

[9]Rav Ashi said: Now [that] they have canceled that [day] itself, [10]shall we get up and decree on account of the day of Nicanor?

RASHI

שמעיה ואחיה – חסידים היו, ולא פירש מי הם. דאותו שאכלו הארי – עידו היה ולא שמעיה.

TRANSLATION AND COMMENTARY

previous Monday, **the twelfth.** It is in such a case that the Mishnah permits those who bring their *Megillah* reading forward to fast and eulogize on the day they read the *Megillah*. [1]**And as for the objection that was raised** earlier, that the Mishnah could not have permitted fasting on the twelfth of Adar because **that** day **is the day of Trajan,** there is really no difficulty. [2]Although *Megillat Ta'anit* records **the day of Trajan** as a minor festival, the Rabbis themselves later **canceled** the festival, [3]because **Shemayah and his brother Aḥiyyah were killed on** that day. The abolition of the day of Trajan as a minor festival is attested to by the following incident: [4]Once **Rav Naḥman decreed a** public **fast on the twelfth of Adar,** [5]and **the Rabbis said to him:** "How can you decree a public fast on the twelfh of Adar? Surely **it is the day of Trajan!**" [6]Rav Naḥman **said to** his colleagues: "**The day of Trajan** is indeed recorded in *Megillat Ta'anit* as a minor festival on which fasting is forbidden, but the Rabbis later **canceled** the festival, [7]because **Shemayah and his brother Aḥiyyah were killed on** that day." Now, since the day of Trajan was canceled, the Mishnah could indeed have permitted those who read the *Megillah* on the twelfth of Adar to fast on that day.

וְתֵיפּוֹק לֵיהּ [8]The Gemara now argues that even after the cancelation of the day of Trajan, fasting on the twelfth of Adar should still be forbidden. **Let** the prohibition against fasting on the twelfth of Adar **be derived from the fact that it is the day before the day of Nicanor,** which is celebrated on the thirteenth of Adar, for according to Rabbi Yose fasting is forbidden not only on the date actually recorded in *Megillat Ta'anit*, but also on the day before!

אֲמַר רַב אַשִׁי [9]Rav Ashi said: Now that the Rabbis **have canceled** the prohibition against fasting on the day of Trajan itself on account of the deaths of Shemayah and Aḥiyyah, which took place on that day, [10]**is it possible that we would decree** a prohibition against fasting on that day **on account of** its being the day before **the day of Nicanor?** If the mourning for the deaths of Shemayah and Aḥiyyah is sufficient reason to

NOTES

אֲמַרוּ לֵיהּ רַבָּנַן: "יוֹם טוּרְיָינוּס הוּא!" The Rabbis said to him: "It is the day of Trajan!" Elsewhere (*Rosh HaShanah* 19b), the Gemara concludes that *Megillat Ta'anit* was rescinded, so that henceforth fasting and eulogizing were permitted even on the days recorded in the scroll, with the exceptions of Hanukkah and Purim, on which the prohibitions against fasting and delivering eulogies remained in force. Most Rishonim maintain that the prohibitions against fasting and eulogizing on all the days other than Hanukkah and Purim were totally rescinded, so that both individual fasts and public fasts are now permitted on the days recorded in the scroll. But according to *Ra'avad* (*Hassagot* to *Rif, Megillah* 4a, which is cited by a number of Rishonim to our passage), only the prohibition against individual fasts on the days recorded in the scroll was rescinded, but the prohibition against public fasts on those days was never canceled. *Ra'avad* adduces support for his viewpoint from our passage. Rav Naḥman justified his decree of a public fast on the twelfth of Adar with the argument that the day of Trajan had been canceled because of a particular calamity that had occurred on that day. Now, if *Megillat Ta'anit* had been rescinded even with respect to public fasts, such an argument would have been unnecessary. *Rabbenu Meshullam* and others explain that Rav Naḥman put forward this argument in order to justify his decree even according to the opinion that *Megillat Ta'anit* had not been rescinded.

יוֹם נִיקָנוֹר The day of Nicanor. Many Rishonim address the issue of the Fast of Esther, which is observed on the day before Purim, on the thirteenth of Adar. As was mentioned in the previous note, the prohibitions against fasting and eulogizing on Hanukkah and Purim were never canceled, even after *Megillat Ta'anit* was rescinded. And since Rav and Rabbi Yoḥanan ruled in accordance with the viewpoint

TRANSLATION AND COMMENTARY

cancel the prohibition against fasting on a day that is itself mentioned in *Megillat Ta'anit*, then it is certainly sufficient reason to cancel the prohibition against fasting on a day preceding a day recorded in the scroll!

Now that we have explained the Mishnah in tractate *Megillah* as permitting fasting on the twelfth of Adar, the apparent contradiction between Rabbi Yoḥanan's two rulings falls away. Rabbi Yoḥanan rules in accordance with the viewpoint of Rabbi Yose that fasting is forbidden on the days before the dates recorded in *Megillat Ta'anit*. And he also rules in accordance with the viewpoint of the anonymous Mishnah in tractate *Megillah* that fasting is permitted on the twelfth of Adar, even though it is a day preceding a date recorded in *Megillat Ta'anit*, because the minor festival that was to be celebrated on that day was itself canceled by the later Rabbis. In such a case, even Rabbi Yose agrees that we cannot prohibit fasting on the grounds that the day is the day before a date recorded in *Megillat Ta'anit*.

[1]מַאי נִיקָנוֹר, וּמַאי טוּרְיָינוּס? [2]דְּתַנְיָא: ״נִיקָנוֹר אֶחָד מֵאִפַּרְכֵי יְוָונִים הָיָה. [3]וּבְכָל יוֹם וָיוֹם הָיָה מֵנִיף יָדוֹ עַל יְהוּדָה וִירוּשָׁלַיִם, [4]וְאוֹמֵר: ׳אֵימָתַי תִּפּוֹל בְּיָדִי וְאֶרְמְסֶנָּה׳? [5]וּכְשֶׁגָּבְרָה מַלְכוּת בֵּית חַשְׁמוֹנַאי וְנִצְּחוּם, [6]קִצְּצוּ בְּהוֹנוֹת יָדָיו וְרַגְלָיו וּתְלָאוּם בְּשַׁעֲרֵי יְרוּשָׁלַיִם, [7]וְאָמְרוּ: ׳פֶּה שֶׁהָיָה מְדַבֵּר בְּגַאֲוָה וְיָדַיִים

LITERAL TRANSLATION

[1]What is [the day of] Nicanor, and what is [the day of] Trajan?

[2]For it was taught: "Nicanor was one of the Greek generals. [3]And on every single day he would wave his hand against Judea and Jerusalem, [4]and say: 'When will it fall into my hand and I will trample upon it?' [5]And when the kingdom of the Hasmonean House prevailed and defeated them, [6]they cut off his thumbs and big toes and hung them on the gates of Jerusalem, [7]and they said: 'The mouth that used to speak with haughtiness and the hands

RASHI

איפרכי = דוכוס.

LANGUAGE

אִפַּרְכֵי Generals. This word is derived from the Greek ἔπαρχος, *aparkhos*, or "ὕπαρχος, *hyparkhos*, meaning "the commander of an important military unit."

מַאי נִיקָנוֹר [1]The Gemara now seeks to clarify the circumstances that brought the Rabbis to declare minor festivals on the twelfth and the thirteenth of Adar. The Gemara asks: **What is the origin of the day of Nicanor, and what is the origin of the day of Trajan?**

דְּתַנְיָא [2]The Gemara answers: As for the day of Nicanor, **it was taught** in a Baraita: **"Nicanor was one of the Greek generals.** [3]**Every day he would wave his hand in the direction of** the province of **Judea and** the city of **Jerusalem,** [4]**and** would **say: 'When will** that city **fall into my hands, so that I can trample upon it?'** [5]**When the Hasmonean kingdom prevailed and defeated** the Greek army, Nicanor was killed in the battle. [6]**His thumbs and big toes were cut off and hung on the gates of Jerusalem.** [7]When people saw this, **they said: 'The mouth that used to speak with** such **haughtiness and the hands that used to wave** so scornfully **in**

NOTES

of Rabbi Yose, that fasting is forbidden not only on the days recorded in the scroll, but also on the day before each of the minor festivals listed there (see above, 18a), it stands to reason that the prohibition against fasting on the day before Purim should also still be in force. How, then, is a public fast observed on the thirteenth of Adar, the day before Purim?

Ra'avad suggests that, although the prohibition against fasting on Hanukkah and on Purim was never canceled, the prohibition against fasting on the day before each of those festivals was indeed rescinded together with the rest of *Megillat Ta'anit*. According to *Ra'avad* himself, this answer does not suffice, for he maintains that only the prohibition against individual fasts was canceled, whereas the prohibition against public fasts is still in force (see previous note). Thus he argues that the Fast of Esther is different, because it was not instituted as an act of mourning, but rather as part of the commemoration of the miracle performed for the Jewish people at the time of Esther. Moreover, the fast was already accepted in the days of Esther and Mordecai, and it was observed even when *Megillat Ta'anit* was in force and the day of Nicanor was celebrated as a minor festival.

Ramban and *Rabbenu Meshullam* suggest that the prohibition against fasting on the thirteenth of Adar on account of its being the day of Nicanor was canceled when *Megillat Ta'anit* was rescinded. Therefore the prohibition against fasting on that day because it is the day before Purim is also no longer in force. This is similar to the argument put forward by the Gemara itself, that once the prohibition against fasting on the twelfth of Adar on account of its being the day of Trajan was canceled, the prohibition against fasting on that day because it is the day before the day of Nicanor was also no longer in effect.

Some Rishonim (*Ritva, Shittah, Meiri*) argue that the law is in accordance with the view of Shmuel, who ruled in accordance with Rabban Shimon ben Gamliel that there is no prohibition against fasting or eulogizing on the days before the dates recorded in *Megillat Ta'anit*. Thus, with the cancelation of the day of Nicanor, there is no longer any prohibition against fasting on the thirteenth of Adar.

Ba'al HaMa'or argues that there was never a prohibition against fasting on the thirteenth of Adar on account of its being the day before Purim, because Purim is a Scriptural holiday, and Scriptural laws do not require reinforcement.

LANGUAGE

לוּלְיָנוּס Lulianus. This was how the Latin name *Julianus* was pronounced in Hebrew.

דְּיוֹפְלֵי Two officials. This word has been explained in various ways, and several readings of our text have been proposed. The reading in our possession seems to be derived from a Greek expression, διπλοῖ, *diploi*, meaning "two people."

BACKGROUND

הַרְבֵּה דּוּבִּין וַאֲרָיוֹת יֵשׁ לוֹ לַמָּקוֹם And God has many bears and lions. In other words, if because of our sins we are condemned to die, our fate is sealed in any case and we cannot be saved from it, for God will cause us to die in a similar way, by means of a wild beast, if not by human hands. But the fact that we have been condemned to die for our sins does not give you the right to kill us — you are doing so because of your wickedness, and you will be punished for ordering us to be killed.

שֶׁהָיוּ מְנִיפוֹת עַל יְרוּשָׁלַיִם — [1]תֵּעָשֶׂה בָּהֶם נְקָמָה׳״.
[2]מַאי טוּרְיָינוּס?
[3]״אָמְרוּ: כְּשֶׁבִּקֵּשׁ טוּרְיָינוּס לַהֲרוֹג אֶת לוּלְיָנוּס וּפַפּוֹס אָחִיו בְּלוּדְקִיָא, [4]אָמַר לָהֶם: ׳אִם מֵעַמּוֹ שֶׁל חֲנַנְיָה, מִישָׁאֵל, וַעֲזַרְיָה אַתֶּם, יָבֹא אֱלֹהֵיכֶם וְיַצִּיל אֶתְכֶם מִיָּדִי כְּדֶרֶךְ שֶׁהִצִּיל אֶת חֲנַנְיָה, מִישָׁאֵל, וַעֲזַרְיָה מִיַּד נְבוּכַדְנֶצַּר׳. [5]אָמְרוּ לוֹ: ׳חֲנַנְיָה, מִישָׁאֵל, וַעֲזַרְיָה צַדִּיקִים גְּמוּרִין הָיוּ, וּרְאוּיִין הָיוּ לֵיעָשׂוֹת לָהֶם נֵס, [6]וּנְבוּכַדְנֶצַּר מֶלֶךְ הָגוּן הָיָה, וְרָאוּי לַעֲשׂוֹת נֵס עַל יָדוֹ. [7]וְאוֹתוֹ רָשָׁע הֶדְיוֹט הוּא, וְאֵינוֹ רָאוּי לַעֲשׂוֹת נֵס עַל יָדוֹ. [8]וְאָנוּ נִתְחַיַּיבְנוּ כְּלָיָה לַמָּקוֹם. [9]וְאִם אֵין אַתָּה הוֹרְגֵנוּ, הַרְבֵּה הוֹרְגִים יֵשׁ לוֹ לַמָּקוֹם, [10]וְהַרְבֵּה דּוּבִּין וַאֲרָיוֹת יֵשׁ לוֹ לַמָּקוֹם בְּעוֹלָמוֹ שֶׁפּוֹגְעִין בָּנוּ וְהוֹרְגִין אוֹתָנוּ. [11]אֶלָּא לֹא מְסָרָנוּ הַקָּדוֹשׁ בָּרוּךְ הוּא בְּיָדְךָ אֶלָּא שֶׁעָתִיד לִיפָּרַע דָּמֵינוּ מִיָּדְךָ׳. [12]אַף עַל פִּי כֵן, הֲרָגָן מִיָּד. [13]אָמְרוּ: לֹא זָזוּ מִשָּׁם עַד שֶׁבָּאוּ דְּיוֹפְלֵי מֵרוֹמִי וּפָצְעוּ אֶת

LITERAL TRANSLATION

that used to wave against Jerusalem — [1]may vengeance be taken against them.'"

[2]What is [the day of] Trajan?

[3]"They said: When Trajan sought to kill Lulianus and Pappus his brother in Laodicea, [4]he said to them: 'If you are from the people of Hananiah, Mishael, and Azariah, let your God come and save you from my hand in the way that He saved Hananiah, Mishael, and Azariah from the hand of Nebuchadnezzar.' [5]They said to him: 'Hananiah, Mishael, and Azariah were perfectly righteous, and they were worthy that a miracle should be performed for them, [6]and Nebuchadnezzar was a fit king, and he was worthy that a miracle should be performed through him. [7]But this wicked man is a commoner, and he is not worthy that a miracle should be performed through him. [8]And we have been condemned to destruction by God. [9]And if you do not kill us, God has many executioners, [10]and God has many bears and lions in His world who can attack us and kill us. [11]But the Holy One, blessed be He, did not hand us over to you except in order ultimately to avenge our blood from your hand.' [12]Even so, he killed them immediately. [13]They said: They did not move from there before two officials arrived from Rome and split

TRANSLATION AND COMMENTARY

the direction of Jerusalem — [1]may vengeance now **be taken against them.'"** A minor festival was later proclaimed on the thirteenth of Adar to commemorate this victory and was named the day of Nicanor.

מַאי טוּרְיָינוּס [2]The Gemara continues: **What is** the origin of **the day of Trajan?**

אָמְרוּ [3]The Gemara answers: It was taught in a Baraita: **"It was said** that **when Trajan intended to execute Lulianus and Pappus his brother,** two important leaders of the Jewish people, **in Laodicea, [4]he** first **said to them** in scorn: **'If** indeed **you are from the people of Hananiah, Mishael, and Azariah, let your God come** now, perform a miracle, **and save you from my hand in the** same **way that He** once **saved Hananiah, Mishael, and Azariah from the hand of Nebuchadnezzar,** King of Babylonia!' [5]Lulianus and Pappus then **said to him:** 'There is no comparison between the two situations. **Hananiah, Mishael, and Azariah were perfectly righteous men and were worthy that a miracle should be performed for them. [6]And,** furthermore, **Nebuchadnezzar was a legitimate king** who rightfully ascended the throne of Babylonia, **and he was worthy** that a miracle should be performed for Hananiah, Mishael, and Azariah **through him. [7]But this wicked man,** Trajan, **is** nothing but **a commoner** who seized the throne by force, **and he is not worthy that a miracle should be performed** for us **through him.** What is more, we are not righteous men like Hananiah, Mishael, and Azariah. [8]**We have been condemned to destruction by God** on account of the sins that we have committed against Him. [9]So, even **if you do not execute us** now, **God has many** other **executioners** who can perform the task. [10]**And** even if we are not put to death by man, **God has many bears and lions in His world who can attack us and kill us.** [11]**The Holy One, blessed be He, handed us over to you only so that in the future** you will receive a fitting punishment and **our blood will be avenged from your hand.'** [12]**Even so,** Trajan disregarded what Lulianus and Pappus had said and **executed them immediately.** [13]**It was said** that **nobody** had time to **move from** the scene of the execution **before two officials arrived from Rome** with instructions to depose Trajan

RASHI

לוליינוס ופפוס אחיו — צדיקים גמורים היו. **בלודקיא** — היא לוד. והיינו דאמרינן בכל דוכתא (בבא בתרא י,ב): הרוגי לוד אין כל בריה יכולה לעמוד במחיצתן בגן עדן. ויש אומרין: שנהרגו על בתו של מלך שנמצאת הרוגה, ואמרו: היהודים הרגוה, וגזרו גזרה על שונאיהן של ישראל, ועמדו אלו ופדו את ישראל, ואמרו: אנו הרגנוה, והרג המלך לאלו בלבד. **אם מעמו — כו׳. נתחייבנו הריגה** — על חטא חייבי מיתות בית דין. **דיופלין** — שני שרים, וכן מטרופולין של מלכים — לשון שרים.

מוֹחוֹ בְּגִיזְרִין״.

[1]״אֵין גּוֹזְרִין תַּעֲנִית עַל הַצִּבּוּר בַּתְּחִלָּה בַּחֲמִישִׁי, כו׳. [2]אֵין גּוֹזְרִין תַּעֲנִית בְּרָאשֵׁי חֳדָשִׁים, כו׳ ״.

[3]וְכַמָּה הָוְיָא הַתְחָלָה?

[4]רַב אַחָא אָמַר: שָׁלשׁ. [5]רַבִּי אַסִי אָמַר: אַחַת.

[6]אָמַר רַב יְהוּדָה אָמַר רַב: זוֹ דִּבְרֵי רַבִּי מֵאִיר שֶׁאָמַר מִשּׁוּם רַבָּן גַּמְלִיאֵל. [7]אֲבָל חֲכָמִים אוֹמְרִים: מִתְעַנֶּה וּמַשְׁלִים.

[8]דָּרַשׁ מָר זוּטְרָא מִשְּׁמֵיהּ דְּרַב הוּנָא: [9]הֲלָכָה: מִתְעַנֶּה וּמַשְׁלִים.

הדרן עלך סדר תעניות כיצד

LITERAL TRANSLATION

his skull open with clubs."

[1]"We do not decree a fast on the community beginning on a Thursday, etc. [2]We do not decree a fast [on the community] on New Moons, etc."

[3]And how much is a start?

[4]Rav Aḥa said: Three [fasts]. [5]Rabbi Assi said: One.

[6]Rav Yehudah said in the name of Rav: These are the words of Rabbi Meir who said [them] in the name of Rabban Gamliel. [7]But the Sages say: He fasts and completes [the fasts].

[8]Mar Zutra expounded in the name of Rav Huna: [9]The Halakhah is: He fasts and completes [the fast].

RASHI

בגזירין — מקלות, כמו גזירי עלים. **שלש** — תעניות שני וחמישי ושני. **וכמה הויא התחלה** — שאינו מפסיק לאחר מכאן. **רבי אחא ורבי יוסי** — אמוראי נינהו, דלאו אורחא דתנאי לאשתעויי בגמרא כי האי גוונא. **זו דברי רבי מאיר** — ואדברי רבי מאיר דמתניתין קאי, דקתני אין משלימין. **מתענה ומשלים** — עד חשיכה.

הדרן עלך סדר תעניות קמא

TRANSLATION AND COMMENTARY

and they split his skull open with clubs and killed him." Interpreting Trajan's end as an act of divine punishment, the Rabbis commemorated the event with a minor festival on the twelfth of Adar.

אֵין [1]We learned in our Mishnah (above, 15b): "The court **may not decree a fast on the community beginning on a Thursday,** so as not to raise food prices. [2]The court **may not decree a fast on the community on the New Moon,** on Hanukkah, or on Purim. But if the community has already started a series of fasts, and one fast in the series falls on the New Moon, or on Hanukkah, or on Purim, it does not interrupt the series, but observes the fast even though the day is a minor festival. This is the viewpoint of Rabban Gamliel."

וְכַמָּה [3]The Gemara asks: **How much is** considered **a start** in this matter?

רַב אַחָא אָמַר [4]**Rav Aḥa said:** If the community has already observed **three** fasts, and the next fast in the series falls on the New Moon, on Hanukkah, or on Purim, it does not interrupt the series. [5]**Rabbi Assi said:** Even if the community has already observed only **one** fast, it does not interrupt the series, even if the next fast falls on one of these minor festivals.

אָמַר רַב יְהוּדָה [6]We learned in the next clause of our Mishnah: "Rabbi Meir said: Even though Rabban Gamliel said that they do not interrupt the series even if one of the fasts coincides with the New Moon, or with Hanukkah, or with Purim, he would agree that in such a case they do not fast until nightfall, but break the fast some time before sunset." **Rav Yehudah said in the name of Rav: This is the viewpoint of Rabbi Meir who gave his ruling in the name of Rabban Gamliel.** [7]**But the Sages** disagree and say: In those situations in which a fast is observed on one of the minor festivals, **we fast and prolong** the fast until nightfall.

דָּרַשׁ [8]The Gemara concludes the chapter with a practical ruling on this last matter. **Mar Zutra expounded in the name of Rav Huna:** [9]**The Halakhah is** in accordance with the viewpoint of the Sages, that in those situations where a fast is observed on a minor festival, **we fast and prolong** the fast until nightfall.

NOTES

וְכַמָּה הָוְיָא הַתְחָלָה And how much is a start? *Rambam,* in his *Commentary to the Mishnah,* apparently understands that when the Mishnah speaks of a start, it is not referring to the start of a series of fasts before one of the minor festivals, but rather to the start of a fast on one of the minor festivals itself. Thus the Mishnah teaches as follows: The court may not decree a fast on the New Moon, on Hanukkah, or on Purim. But if the court mistakenly decreed a fast on one of these days, and the community began to observe the fast — for three hours according to Rav Aḥa, or for one hour according to Rabbi Assi — and then it was realized that the fast had been decreed in error, they do not interrupt the fast. *Ritva* attributes *Rambam*'s view to a scribal error, for it is inconceivable that the community should continue a fast that should never have been decreed in the first place, just because the people have already fasted for a few hours. In his *Mishneh Torah* (*Hilkhot Ta'aniyyot* 1:7), *Rambam* follows the view of the rest of the Rishonim that the Mishnah is referring to the start of a series of fasts before one of the minor festivals.

HALAKHAH

אֵין גּוֹזְרִין תַּעֲנִית בְּרָאשֵׁי חֳדָשִׁים We do not decree a fast on the community on New Moons. "We do not decree a fast on the community on the New Moon, or on Hanukkah, or on Purim, or on the intermediate days of a Festival. But if the community has already started a series of fasts, even if it has observed only a single fast, and the next fast of the series falls on one of these minor festivals, the fast is observed and prolonged until nightfall." (*Shulḥan Arukh, Oraḥ Ḥayyim* 572:2.)

Conclusion to Chapter Two

The great public fasts proclaimed by the court because of drought or other calamities are marked by a number of rituals and practices intended to stress the gravity of the situation and to move the hearts of the people to repentance. For example, the special prayer service is conducted in the open, rather than in the synagogue; ashes are placed on the heads of the communal leaders and the rest of the assembly; and the holy ark is taken outside and covered with ashes. Six blessings are added to the Amidah prayer, and one of the regular blessings is expanded. These blessings, the texts of which are recorded in the Mishnah and the Gemara, are recited by the prayer leader on the public fasts when he repeats the Amidah. In the Temple, and according to many authorities even outside the Temple, each of these special blessings is followed by the blowing of the shofar or trumpets. Scriptural passages and special supplications referring to the fast and the themes of remorse and repentance are inserted into the service.

As to the question of who is exempt from observing the public fasts, it is concluded that the members of the *mishmar* whose week it is to serve in the Temple, and even more so the members of the *bet av* whose day it is to perform the Temple service, are to a large extent exempt from the communal fasts proclaimed in times of danger. At times, however, they are required to participate in the distress of the community and to observe the fast in a symbolic way, refraining from food and drink for part of the day. As the fasts become increasingly more severe, so too does the obligation falling upon the priests to participate in the communal fasts increase, though the members of the *bet av* whose day it is to serve in the Temple are never required to observe a public fast for the entire day. A number of other regulations pertaining to the members of the *mishmar* and the *bet av*, but unrelated to fasting, are discussed in this chapter. Restrictions on drinking wine and on letting one's hair grow long are placed on the members of the *mishmar* and *bet av* whose week or day it is to serve in the Temple, in order that they should be prepared to perform the Temple service and not violate the Biblical prohibitions against serving in the Temple with unkempt hair or when intoxicated with wine.

As for the days on which fasting is forbidden, it is concluded that the days recorded in *Megillat Ta'anit* which were once declared semi-festive days on which fasting and eulogizing are forbidden are no longer regarded as semi-festivals, with the exception of Hanukkah and Purim. Thus a fast may not be proclaimed on Hanukkah, on Purim or on the New Moon, but if the community has already started to observe a series of fasts proclaimed on account of a particular calamity threatening the community, and one of the fasts falls on one of these minor festivals, the series is not interrupted, and the fast is observed despite the semi-festive nature of the day.

Introduction to Chapter Three

סֵדֶר תַּעֲנִיּוֹת אֵלּוּ

"If there be famine in the land, if there be pestilence, blight, mildew, locust, or if there be caterpillar; if their enemy besiege them in the land of their cities; whatever plague, whatever sickness there be. Whatever prayer and whatever supplication is made by any man, or by all Your people Israel, who shall know every man the plague of his own heart, and spread forth his hands towards this house. Then hear You in heaven Your dwelling place, and forgive, and do, and give to every man according to his ways, those whose heart You know; for You, You only, know the heart of all the children of men." (I Kings 8:37-39.)

Until now tractate *Ta'anit* has dealt primarily with the fasts proclaimed in response to drought, the most common calamity to threaten a community. But clearly there are other calamities that threaten a community and may be cause for communal repentance and prayer, and justify the decree of a public fast. A number of questions arise with respect to this issue. It is necessary to clarify the circumstances under which it is appropriate for fasts to be proclaimed. A public fast cannot be proclaimed for every approaching trouble or difficulty, and therefore the events regarded as serious calamities must be clearly defined. It is also necessary to determine the modes of conduct that are appropriate when fasts are not proclaimed but it is nevertheless fitting that the community be aroused to repentance through special prayers and supplications. Just as we must determine the circumstances under which fasts should be proclaimed, it is also necessary to clarify when those fasts ought to be observed. The times for fasts in periods of drought are more or less fixed, for they are connected to the change of seasons. But there are situations where the community is faced with an immediate danger, so that it is not possible to put off the declaration of a fast.

Another question arises regarding the applicability of the fast: Who is required to observe it? It stands to reason that a distinction must be made between national calamities that threaten the entire Jewish people and local disasters threatening specific communities or limited groups. When is it necessary to be concerned that a local calamity may attain national proportions, and when is it necessary for a community not directly affected by a calamity to participate in the distress of those communities that are struck by disaster?

Another issue dealt with in this chapter is the proper conduct to be observed if the community's prayers are answered during the course of the fast, so that the fast is no longer necessary. Should the fast be observed until completion, or may it be interrupted, since the calamity in response to which the fast was proclaimed no longer threatens? Also, how should the people express their feelings of joy and gratitude when their prayers are answered? An analysis of these and related issues constitutes the main subject matter of this chapter.

LITERAL TRANSLATION

MISHNAH [1] The order of these fasts that was said [above applies] with respect to [the period of] the first rainfall. [2] But [if] plants have changed, they sound the alarm for them immediately.

סֵדֶר

[1] תַּעֲנִיּוֹת אֵלּוּ הָאָמוּר בִּרְבִיעָה רִאשׁוֹנָה. [2] אֲבָל צְמָחִים שֶׁשָּׁנוּ, מַתְרִיעִין עֲלֵיהֶן מִיָּד.

RASHI

סדר תעניות אלו — האמור בפרק ראשון (י,א), שבתחילה יחידים מתענין סדר תעניות, ואחר כך צבור הולכין ומתענין עד שלשה עשר, אם לא נענו. **ברביעה ראשונה** — אם עבר זמן רביעה ראשונה של יורה, ולא ירדו גשמים — מתענין והולכין כסדר הזה. **אבל צמחים ששנו** — שנשתנו ממנהגן, תחת חטה יצא חוח, תחת שעורה באשה, שלא היו חטים בשבולים או שינוי אחר — מתריעין עליהן מיד, אפילו בראשונות, שכל חומר האחרונות נוהג בהן.

TRANSLATION AND COMMENTARY

MISHNAH **סֵדֶר תַּעֲנִיּוֹת** In the first chapter of our tractate, the Mishnah described the fasts that were observed when the rain was late in falling. If no rain had fallen by the seventeenth day of Marḥeshvan, pious individuals would begin to observe a series of three fasts. If rain had still not fallen by the beginning of the month of Kislev, the court would decree a series of three fasts to be observed by the entire community (above, 10a). If those fasts passed and it had still not rained, the court would decree another series of three communal fasts. And if this second series of fasts passed and the rain had not fallen, the court would decree seven additional fasts upon the community (above, 12b). As was explained in the first chapter, each series of fasts was increasingly severe. [1] Our Mishnah establishes that **this order of fasts that was recorded** in the first chapter of our tractate **applies** only if **the first rainfall** fails to arrive. [2] **But if** the rain has fallen as expected and the crops have begun to grow, but **the plants look different,** and are considered to have an unusual appearance, **the alarm is immediately sounded for the** stricken crops. In such a case, we do not follow the order laid down for the fasts observed if the rain is late, with each series of fasts becoming increasingly more severe than the previous one. When the court decrees fasts on account of the rain being late, it is not until the final series of seven fasts that the alarm is sounded with the blowing of a shofar and the insertion of special supplications into the prayers. But if the rain fell on time but the crops start to grow strangely, the court immediately proclaims a series of fasts with all the stringencies of the last series of fasts observed when the rain is late, so that the alarm is sounded on the first fast.

NOTES

צְמָחִים שֶׁשָּׁנוּ If plants have changed. Most of the Rishonim explain the Mishnah as referring to crops that have started to wither or have been struck by disease (*Rabbenu Ḥananel, Rabbenu Gershom, Meiri,* and others). *Rashi* explains the passage by citing the verse (Job 31:40): "Let thistles grow instead of wheat, and weeds instead of barley," and argues that the Mishnah is referring to a case where the crops grew in an entirely unusual manner, where, for example, the wheat plants grew without wheat kernels.

מַתְרִיעִין עֲלֵיהֶן מִיָּד They sound the alarm for them immediately. The expression "they sound the alarm [מַתְרִיעִין]" is repeated many times in the course of this chapter. *Ra'avad* explains that, whenever this expression is used, it means that the shofar is sounded without a fast being proclaimed. If the rain is late, the court proclaims a series of fasts, on the last seven of which the shofar is sounded. But in the cases discussed in our chapter, only the shofar is sounded, but fasts are not proclaimed. This interpretation is based on the argument that the circumstances described in this chapter are less threatening than a delay in the first rainfall of the season. The case in which the rain fell as usual but the crops took on an unusual appearance, or the case in which there was a forty-day interval between the first and the second rains of the season, require a less drastic response than a case in which the rain fails totally to fall. If when there is no rain at all the court first decrees a series of less stringent fasts, and only when the drought persists does it decree the more stringent fasts on which the shofar is sounded, then it stands to reason that when there is rain but the crops appear unusual, or when there is an interval between rainstorms, the court should not immediately decree a series of severe fasts on which the shofar is sounded.

But most Rishonim (*Rashi, Tosafot, Ramban, Ritva, Ran,* and others) maintain that whenever the expression "they sound the alarm" is used, it means that the court immediately decrees a series of the most severe fasts on which the shofar is sounded. This definition of the term "they sound the alarm" is consistently applied unless it is obvious from the context that the term means that the

HALAKHAH

סֵדֶר תַּעֲנִיּוֹת אֵלּוּ The order of these fasts. "The order of three series of fasts of increasing severity applies only when it did not rain at all. But if the rain fell on time and the plants began to grow but then started to wither, or if the rain did not fall in the manner or in the quantities that are useful for small plants, trees and storage cisterns, the community must proclaim fasts and sound the alarm immediately." (*Shulḥan Arukh, Oraḥ Ḥayyim* 575:8.)

[1] וְכֵן שֶׁפָּסְקוּ גְּשָׁמִים בֵּין גֶּשֶׁם לְגֶשֶׁם אַרְבָּעִים יוֹם, [2] מַתְרִיעִין עֲלֵיהֶן, מִפְּנֵי שֶׁהִיא מַכַּת בַּצּוֹרֶת.

[3] יָרְדוּ לַצְּמָחִין אֲבָל לֹא יָרְדוּ לָאִילָן, [4] לָאִילָן וְלֹא לַצְּמָחִין, [5] לָזֶה וְלָזֶה אֲבָל לֹא לַבּוֹרוֹת, לַשִּׁיחִין, וְלַמְּעָרוֹת, [6] מַתְרִיעִין עֲלֵיהֶן מִיָּד.

[7] וְכֵן עִיר שֶׁלֹּא יָרְדוּ עָלֶיהָ גְּשָׁמִים, דִּכְתִיב: [8] "וְהִמְטַרְתִּי עַל עִיר אֶחָת, וְעַל עִיר אַחַת לֹא אַמְטִיר, חֶלְקָה אַחַת תִּמָּטֵר, וגו׳", [19A] אוֹתָהּ הָעִיר מִתְעַנָּה וּמַתְרַעַת,

LITERAL TRANSLATION

[1] And similarly, [if] the rains stopped between [one] rain and [the next] rain [for] forty days, [2] they sound the alarm for them, because it is a plague of drought.

[3] If [rains] fell for the plants, but did not fall for the trees, [4] [or] for the trees but not for the plants, [5] [or] for this and that but not for the pits, for the ditches, and for the caves, [6] they sound the alarm for them immediately.

[7] And similarly, [regarding] a city on which rain did not fall, as it is written: [8] "And I will cause it to rain on one city, but on one city I will not cause it to rain, one portion will be rained upon, etc.," [19A] that city fasts and sounds the alarm,

TRANSLATION AND COMMENTARY

וְכֵן שֶׁפָּסְקוּ [1] This ruling also applies to other cases: **Similarly, if** the first rainfall arrived on time, but then **the rain stopped** and there was an interval of **forty days between the first and the second rains,** the court immediately proclaims a series of severe fasts, [2] and **the alarm is sounded** on the first fast; for a forty-day interval between the first two rainfalls of the season **is** surely the sign of **a calamity** which will lead to **drought.**

יָרְדוּ לַצְּמָחִין [3] The Mishnah continues: And similarly, **if rain fell** in a gentle manner that is beneficial **for** small **plants but did not fall** heavily in a way that is useful **for trees,** [4] **or** if rain fell heavily in a way that is useful **for trees, but** did **not** fall in a gentle manner that is beneficial **for** small **plants,** [5] **or** if rain fell in ways that are beneficial **both for** trees and for small plants **but** did not fall in large enough quantities to fill the storage **pits, ditches, and caves,** and provide enough drinking water for the dry summer months, [6] severe fasts are proclaimed and **the alarm is sounded immediately.**

וְכֵן עִיר [7] **And similarly, if rain did not fall on a particular city,** but it did rain as usual in all the surrounding areas, proving that it was by divine decree that the rain did not fall upon the city, **as the verse says** (Amos 4:7): [8] **"And I will cause it to rain on one city, but on one city I will not cause it to rain; one portion will be rained upon,** and one portion on which it will not rain will dry up," [19A] the people living in **that city** where the rain has not fallen must begin to fast immediately and must sound the alarm by blowing the shofar.

RASHI

בין גשם לגשם — בין רביעה ראשונה לשניה — סימן בצורת היא. **ירדו לצמחים אבל לא לאילן** — מפרש בגמרא. **לבורות שיחין ומערות** — בבבא בתרא מפרש מאי בור ומאי שיח ומאי מערה, וכולן בית כניסיות מי גשמים לשתיה. **שלא ירדו עליה גשמים דכתיב והמטרתי על עיר אחת ועל עיר אחת לא אמטיר וגו׳** — כגון שהמטיר בעיר זו, ובחבירתה לא המטיר, דקללה היא. **הכי גרסינן: אותה העיר מתענה ומתרעת**

BACKGROUND

מַכַּת בַּצּוֹרֶת A plague of drought. When the rains begin late, this is cause for alarm, which is why the fasts and the prayers for rain were instituted. However, if rain eventually falls in sufficient quantities, at the proper intervals, the damage is not severe. In contrast, a long dry spell between one rainfall and another during the growing season can entirely destroy plants that have already sprouted. This is a true drought, causing the crop to be insufficient. Therefore it is proper to declare stringent fasts immediately and to pray for the nullification of the evil decree.

בּוֹרוֹת, שִׁיחִין, וּמְעָרוֹת Pits, ditches, and caves. All these terms refer to essentially the same thing — an excavation in the earth for use as a container (generally to hold water). But there are technical differences between these terms (and other terms in the same context): A pit (בּוֹר) is an excavation in the earth with a round opening; a ditch (שִׁיחַ) is long, narrow, and rectangular; while a cave (מְעָרָה) is covered by a roof of sorts.

עִיר שֶׁלֹּא יָרְדוּ עָלֶיהָ גְּשָׁמִים A city on which rain did not fall. Residents of a city where rain has not fallen, while it has rained normally in the surrounding areas, cannot expect that rain will subsequently fall in a natural way only on that very place so as to make up the shortfall. The residents of that city must therefore fear that there will be a severe shortage of grain, and they must also view the lack of rainfall in their city as a decree from Heaven, in response to which they must pray.

NOTES

shofar is sounded without a fast being proclaimed (for example, "Rabbi Akiva says: They sound the alarm, but do not fast"), or that an alarm is sounded by the recitation of special prayers (for example, "For these they sound the alarm on Shabbat"). Although the total failure of rain is a greater calamity than the disasters discussed in our chapter, it is in response to the disasters discussed in our chapter that the court immediately decrees a series of fasts of the most severe kind, whereas when the rain is late, the court first proclaims a series of less stringent fasts, and gradually increases their severity. If the beginning of the month of Kislev has arrived, and rain has still not fallen, the failure of the rain is not yet of calamitous proportions and the situation may still correct itself, and therefore the fasts that are declared are not so stringent. It is only after the drought has lasted for some time and the difficulties caused by the failure of rain have become more serious that the most severe fasts are proclaimed and the shofar is sounded. But if the crops begin to grow strangely or if there is a forty-day interval between rainstorms, the serious threat with which the community is faced already exists, and so the court immediately proclaims fasts of the most severe kind. Moreover, a minor delay in the first rainfall of the season is not regarded as a clear sign that a heavenly decree of drought has been issued, for it is not unusual for the rain to be late, and this is why the court initially proclaims fasts of lesser stringency. It is only after the drought has lasted for some time that the lack of rain must be regarded as a divine punishment, so that fasts of the greatest severity must be proclaimed. But when the crops begin to grow strangely or when there is a forty-day interval between rainfalls, it is immediately apparent that a heavenly decree has been issued, and it is therefore fitting that fasts of the most severe kind be proclaimed immediately.

אוֹתָהּ הָעִיר מִתְעַנָּה וּמַתְרַעַת That city fasts and sounds the alarm. *Rashi* explains that the people living in the outlying areas must also fast, because they are indirectly affected by the lack of rain in the neighboring city. For if there is no rainfall in the city, its residents will purchase food in the outlying areas, causing food shortages and higher prices.

Rabbenu Yehonatan and others suggest that the people

LITERAL TRANSLATION

[1] and all its surrounding areas fast but do not sound the alarm. [2] Rabbi Akiva says: They sound the alarm but do not fast.

[3] And similarly, [regarding] a city in which there is plague or a collapse [of buildings], [4] that city fasts and sounds the alarm, [5] and all its surrounding areas fast but do not sound the alarm. [6] Rabbi Akiva says: They sound the alarm but do not fast.

[7] What is plague? [8] A city that sends out five hundred foot soldiers, [9] and three dead went out on three days one after the other — [10] this is plague. [11] Less than that, this is not plague.

[1] וְכָל סְבִיבוֹתֶיהָ מִתְעַנּוֹת וְלֹא מַתְרִיעוֹת. [2] רַבִּי עֲקִיבָא אוֹמֵר: מַתְרִיעוֹת וְלֹא מִתְעַנּוֹת.

[3] וְכֵן עִיר שֶׁיֵּשׁ בָּהּ דֶּבֶר אוֹ מַפּוֹלֶת, [4] אוֹתָהּ הָעִיר מִתְעַנָּה וּמַתְרַעַת, [5] וְכָל סְבִיבוֹתֶיהָ מִתְעַנּוֹת וְלֹא מַתְרִיעוֹת. [6] רַבִּי עֲקִיבָא אוֹמֵר: מַתְרִיעוֹת וְלֹא מִתְעַנּוֹת.

[7] אֵיזֶהוּ דֶּבֶר? [8] עִיר הַמּוֹצִיאָה חֲמֵשׁ מֵאוֹת רַגְלִי, [9] וְיָצְאוּ מִמֶּנָּה שְׁלֹשָׁה מֵתִים בִּשְׁלֹשָׁה יָמִים זֶה אַחַר זֶה — [10] הֲרֵי זֶה דֶּבֶר. [11] פָּחוֹת מִכָּאן, אֵין זֶה דֶּבֶר.

TRANSLATION AND COMMENTARY

[1] **All** the people living in **the surrounding areas** where rain has fallen as usual must **fast** together with their neighbors in the city, **but they are not required to sound the alarm** by sounding the shofar. [2] **Rabbi Akiva** disagrees and **says:** The people living in the surrounding areas **must sound the alarm** by blowing the shofar, **but they are not required to observe** any **fasts.**

וְכֵן עִיר [3] The Mishnah applies the same distinction to another type of calamity: **And similarly,** if **a** certain **city was struck by plague or by the collapse of buildings** caused by stormy weather or by an earthquake, [4] the people living in **that city** must begin to **fast** immediately **and** must **sound the alarm** by blowing the shofar. [5] **All** the people living in **the surrounding areas** not directly struck by the disaster must **fast** together with their neighbors in the city, **but they are not required to sound the alarm.** [6] **Rabbi Akiva** disagrees and **says:** The people who live outside the stricken city **must sound the alarm** by blowing the shofar, **but they are not required to observe** any **fasts.**

אֵיזֶהוּ דֶּבֶר [7] The Mishnah asks: **What is** the definition of a **plague** that requires the residents of a city to fast? [8] The Mishnah answers: If **the city sends out five hundred foot soldiers** — in other words, if the city has an able-bodied male population of five hundred — [9] **and three corpses** of men who have died of the disease **have been taken out** of the city for burial **over** a period of **three days one after the other,** one man having died each day for three days, [10] **that is a plague.** [11] But if the death rate is **less than this, this is not a plague** that requires fasting or the sounding of the alarm.

RASHI

וכל סביבותיה מתענות ולא מתריעות — ולפיכך מתענות שאותה העיר שלא ירדו עליה גשמים תלך לקנות התבואה באותה העיר ויהיה בה רעב. **או מפולת** — שחומותיה והבתים נופלין ברוח.

NOTES

living in the outlying areas must fast to participate in the distress affecting their neighbors in the city and must offer prayers on their behalf.

The Jerusalem Talmud explains the dispute between the anonymous first Tanna of the Mishnah and Rabbi Akiva as follows: The first Tanna of the Mishnah derives the regulations that apply to those living outside the stricken city from the laws pertaining to Yom Kippur, on which fasting is required and the shofar is not sounded. Rabbi Akiva derives these regulations from laws pertaining to Rosh HaShanah, on which the shofar is sounded but a fast is not observed.

HALAKHAH

אוֹתָהּ הָעִיר...וְכָל סְבִיבוֹתֶיהָ That city...and all its surrounding areas. "If a specific city is visited by a calamity, the people living there must fast and sound the alarm by blowing the shofar. The people living in the surrounding areas must also fast, but they do not sound the alarm," following the first Tanna of the Mishnah. (*Shulḥan Arukh, Oraḥ Ḥayyim* 576:1,12.)

עִיר שֶׁיֵּשׁ בָּהּ דֶּבֶר A city in which there is plague. "If a city is struck by a plague, its residents must fast and sound the alarm. What is considered a plague? If a city has an able-bodied male population of 500 (women, children and old people are not included; *Rambam*), and three men die from the disease over a period of three days, one each day, the city is regarded as having been struck by a plague. A city with a larger population is regarded as having been struck by a plague if it has a proportionately higher mortality rate. *Magen Avraham* notes that fasts are not observed today during periods of plague, for there is concern that those who refrain from eating and drinking will weaken themselves and make themselves more susceptible to the disease." (*Shulḥan Arukh,* Ibid., 576:1-2.)

מַפּוֹלֶת Collapse of buildings. "If in a certain city there is an increase in the incidence of buildings collapsing for no apparent reason, or if the city is struck by an earthquake or a storm which causes buildings to collapse, the residents of that city must fast and sound the alarm." (*Shulḥan Arukh,* Ibid., 576:4.)

BACKGROUND

דֶּבֶר Plague. Generally this term, which is mentioned in the Torah and other ancient sources, is associated with bubonic plague, a very contagious disease transmitted from rats by fleas. Bubonic plague caused widespread epidemics, such as the Black Death, during the Middle Ages in Europe. Nevertheless it is not clear that the Mishnah is referring specifically to this disease, because its symptoms were well known, and there was no reason to decide whether it had broken out on the basis of the number of victims. Hence the Mishnah could be referring to various other contagious diseases, regarding which it was necessary to determine whether they had reached epidemic proportions.

עִיר הַמּוֹצִיאָה חֲמֵשׁ מֵאוֹת רַגְלִי A city that sends out five hundred foot soldiers. Most likely this refers to men between the ages of twenty and sixty, like the definition of men of military age in the Torah. Hence it probably refers to a town with a total of nearly four thousand residents.

שְׁלֹשָׁה מֵתִים בִּשְׁלֹשָׁה יָמִים Three dead went out on three days. The reason for framing the definition in this way was to be certain that there was a plague, that death occurred every day and with regularity. For a number of deaths in a single day could also indicate that an illness had struck a particular family or area, or could be due to simple coincidence.

TRANSLATION AND COMMENTARY

עַל אֵלּוּ מַתְרִיעִין [1]With respect to drought, plague and the collapse of buildings, a distinction was made between the city that was struck by the calamity and the surrounding areas that were not affected by it. The Mishnah now presents a list of calamities requiring those living outside the disaster area to fast and to sound the alarm. **For the following** calamities, fasts must be proclaimed and **the alarm must be sounded in all places,** even those far away from the place struck by the calamity: [2]If the crops in a certain area have been struck by **blight or mildew,** or if an area has been devastated by swarms of ordinary **locusts or** of ***hasil*** (a particularly destructive type of locust), or if a place has been invaded by **wild beasts,** which usually refrain from entering populated areas, or by **sword-carrying** soldiers, even if the army is only passing through — [3]in all these cases, wherever word of the calamity arrives, fasts must be proclaimed and **the alarm must be sounded,** [4]**because these are** all **calamities that spread.**

מַעֲשֶׂה [5]The Mishnah now cites a number of incidents to illustrate this ruling. **It once happened that the elders** of the Sanhedrin **went down from Jerusalem to their cities** in other parts of Eretz Israel [6]**and decreed a fast** everywhere, **because blight in an amount to fill the opening of an oven was sighted on** grain **in Ashkelon,** a city on the Mediterranean coast close to the southern border of the country. [7]**And** it also happened that the Sages **decreed a fast** throughout Eretz Israel **because wolves** were seen **eating two children on the** eastern **side of the Jordan** River. [8]**Rabbi Yose says:** These fasts were **not** decreed **because** the wolves had actually **eaten** the children, **but because** the wolves **were seen** in a populated area.

עַל אֵלּוּ [9]The Mishnah continues: **For the following** impending calamities **the alarm is sounded** even on

[1]עַל אֵלּוּ מַתְרִיעִין בְּכָל מָקוֹם: [2]עַל הַשִּׁדָּפוֹן, וְעַל הַיֵּרָקוֹן, וְעַל הָאַרְבֶּה, וְעַל הֶחָסִיל, וְעַל הַחַיָּה רָעָה, וְעַל הַחֶרֶב. [3]מַתְרִיעִין עָלֶיהָ, [4]מִפְּנֵי שֶׁהִיא מַכָּה מְהַלֶּכֶת.
[5]מַעֲשֶׂה שֶׁיָּרְדוּ זְקֵנִים מִירוּשָׁלַיִם לְעָרֵיהֶם, [6]וְגָזְרוּ תַּעֲנִית עַל שֶׁנִּרְאָה כִּמְלֹא פִּי תַנּוּר שִׁדָּפוֹן בְּאַשְׁקְלוֹן. [7]וְעוֹד גָּזְרוּ תַּעֲנִית עַל שֶׁאָכְלוּ זְאֵבִים שְׁנֵי תִינוֹקוֹת בְּעֵבֶר הַיַּרְדֵּן. [8]רַבִּי יוֹסֵי אוֹמֵר: לֹא עַל שֶׁאָכְלוּ, אֶלָּא עַל שֶׁנִּרְאוּ.
[9]עַל אֵלּוּ מַתְרִיעִין בַּשַּׁבָּת:

LITERAL TRANSLATION

[1]For these they sound the alarm in all places: [2]For blight, and for mildew, and for locusts, and for *hasil*, and for wild beasts, and for the sword. [3]They sound the alarm for it, [4]because it is a calamity that spreads (lit., "a walking calamity").

[5]It once happened that elders went down from Jerusalem to their cities, [6]and they decreed a fast because blight [in an amount] to fill the opening of an oven was seen in Ashkelon. [7]And they also decreed a fast because wolves ate two children on the other side of the Jordan. [8]Rabbi Yose says: Not because they ate [the children], but because they were seen.

[9]For these they sound the alarm on Shabbat:

RASHI

מתריעים בבכל מקום — אם יראו באספמיא — מתריעין בבבל, בבבל — מתריעין באספמיא. כדקתני טעמא בסיפא: מפני שהיא מכה מהלכת, אם במקום אחד היא — מתריעין עליה כל השומעין, כדי שלא תבא עליהן. **שדפון** — בתבואות. **ירקון** — חולי. **חיה רעה** — משכלת בני אדם. **חרב** — חיילות ההולכין להרוג ולהשחית בכל מקום. **מלא תנור** — מפרש בגמרא. **לעריהם** — בארץ ישראל. **באשקלון** — בארץ פלשתים. **ועל שאכלו זאבים** — שהיא חיה רעה, ומכה מהלכת היא. **שנראו** — ובאו בעיר. **מתריעין** — ב"עננו".

NOTES

עַל אֵלּוּ מַתְרִיעִין **For these they sound the alarm.** Citing a number of Talmudic sources referring to other calamities in response to which the alarm is sounded even on Shabbat, *Gevurat Ari* notes that the list found in our Mishnah is incomplete, perhaps because it mentions only the more common situations.

עַל אֵלּוּ מַתְרִיעִין בַּשַּׁבָּת **For these they sound the alarm on Shabbat.** In the first chapter of the tractate (above, 14a), the Gemara argued that our Mishnah cannot mean that the shofar is sounded on Shabbat in response to these calamities, for surely the sounding of a shofar is forbidden on Shabbat. Rather, the first Tanna of the Mishnah allows

HALAKHAH

עַל אֵלּוּ מַתְרִיעִין בְּכָל מָקוֹם **For these they sound the alarm in all places.** "If the crops in a certain area are struck by blight or mildew (even if only a small amount of grain is affected), or if the area is struck by locusts or by any other type of calamity that can easily spread from one place to another, fasts must be proclaimed and the alarm must be sounded everywhere (even in places which are far away from the stricken area, provided that they are in the same country; *Rema* in the name of *Ran*)." (*Shulḥan Arukh, Oraḥ Ḥayyim* 576:8-9.)

עַל אֵלּוּ מַתְרִיעִין בַּשַּׁבָּת **For these they sound the alarm on Shabbat.** "On Shabbat and on Festivals, fasts are not observed, nor is the alarm sounded, nor are special prayers recited for any type of calamity, with the following

TRANSLATION AND COMMENTARY

Shabbat: For a city that is being surrounded by a non-Jewish army, **and** for a city that is in danger of being inundated by **a river** that has overflowed its banks, **and for a ship that is being tossed about at sea** in a severe storm. [1]**Rabbi Yose says:** In all these cases an alarm may be sounded even on Shabbat in order **to summon help, but** an alarm may **not** be sounded **as** a means of **crying out** to God in prayer for divine intervention. [2]**Shimon HaTimni says: For plague, too,** the alarm is sounded even on Shabbat. **But the Sages did not agree with him.**

עַל כָּל צָרָה [3]The Mishnah ends its discussion of the calamities for which an alarm is sounded by laying down the following general rule: **For any trouble that may strike the community the alarm is sounded, except** when the community is affected by **too much rain.** Even if it rains excessively and the people suffer as a result, the alarm should not be sounded because rain in general is a blessing, and blessings should not be rejected.

מַעֲשֶׂה [4]The Mishnah relates: **It once happened** during a period of drought **that** the people **said to Ḥoni HaMe'aggel:** [5]**"Pray** on our behalf **that rain should fall,** so that this drought will come to an end." Confident that his prayers would immediately be answered, [6]Ḥoni **said to them:** "Before I offer my prayers, **go out and bring in the** earthenware **ovens** that you use **for your Paschal sacrifices** and that are left out in the courtyards, **so that they do not dissolve** when the rain falls on them." [7]Ḥoni began to **pray, but rain did not fall.** [8]**What did** Ḥoni **do? He drew a circle** on the ground **and stood within it.** [9]**He** then **said to** God: **"Master of the Universe! Your children have**

עַל עִיר שֶׁהִקִּיפוּהָ נָכְרִים אוֹ נָהָר, וְעַל הַסְּפִינָה הַמִּיטָּרֶפֶת בַּיָּם. [1]רַבִּי יוֹסֵי אוֹמֵר: לְעֶזְרָה, וְלֹא לִצְעָקָה. [2]שִׁמְעוֹן הַתִּימְנִי אוֹמֵר: אַף עַל הַדֶּבֶר. וְלֹא הוֹדוּ לוֹ חֲכָמִים.

[3]עַל כָּל צָרָה שֶׁלֹּא תָּבוֹא עַל הַצִּבּוּר מַתְרִיעִין עֲלֵיהֶן, חוּץ מֵרוֹב גְּשָׁמִים.

[4]מַעֲשֶׂה שֶׁאָמְרוּ לוֹ לְחוֹנִי הַמְעַגֵּל: [5]"הִתְפַּלֵּל שֶׁיֵּרְדוּ גְשָׁמִים". [6]אָמַר לָהֶם: "צְאוּ וְהַכְנִיסוּ תַּנּוּרֵי פְסָחִים בִּשְׁבִיל שֶׁלֹּא יִמּוֹקוּ". [7]הִתְפַּלֵּל, וְלֹא יָרְדוּ גְשָׁמִים. [8]מֶה עָשָׂה? עָג עוּגָה וְעָמַד בְּתוֹכָהּ, [9]וְאָמַר לְפָנָיו: "רִבּוֹנוֹ שֶׁל עוֹלָם! בָּנֶיךָ

LITERAL TRANSLATION

For a city that non-Jews or a river have surrounded, and for a ship that is being tossed about at sea. [1]Rabbi Yose says: For help, but not for crying out. [2]Shimon of HaTimni says: Also for plague. But the Sages did not agree with him.

[3]For any trouble that may come (lit., "may not come") upon the community, they sound the alarm for them, except for excessive rain.

[4]It once happened that they said to Ḥoni HaMe'aggel: [5]"Pray that rains may fall." [6]He said to them: "Go out and bring in the ovens for the Paschal sacrifices so that they will not dissolve." [7]He prayed, but rains did not fall. [8]What did he do? He drew a circle and stood within it, [9]and he said before Him: "Master of the Universe! Your children

RASHI

המטורפת — מלשון טרף אבנא (ברכות כח,א), ומלשון בילה טרופה (עדיות פרק ב׳ משנה ד׳) כו׳. כדמפרש בפרק שלמעלה (יד,א). **שמעון התימני** — מתמנה היה. **שלא תבוא** — לישנא מעליא נקט. **מרוב גשמים** — לאו כגון שירדה על עיר אחת ועל עיר אחת לא ירדה, שהם ודאי שתיהן לקללה, כדאמר רב יהודה (לעיל ו,ב) "תמטר" — מקום מטר, שמקלקל תבואה, אלא כבר ירדו, וטורח הם לבני אדם, אבל אינן מקלקלין תבואות. וטעמא מפרש בגמרא למה אין מתריעין. **תנורי פסחים** — שהם בחצרות, ושל חרס הן, ומטלטלין אותן שלא ימוקו בגשמים.

SAGES

חוֹנִי הַמְעַגֵּל **Ḥoni HaMe'aggel.** Our information about Ḥoni HaMe'aggel comes mainly from this passage. Josephus mentions his death in *The Antiquities of the Jews,* saying that he was killed in the civil war between Hyrcanus and Aristobulus, the sons of King Alexander Jannaeus.

From the Jerusalem Talmud it appears that there was an earlier Sage of this name, of whom the story is told that he slept for seventy years, and that the Ḥoni who was active in the time of Shimon ben Shetaḥ was one of his descendants. As we see from the story below, (23a-b), these special powers to perform miracles remained in the family.

The epithet "HaMe'aggel" is usually understood as meaning someone who drew circles and stood in the center of them. However, *Rav Tzemaḥ Gaon* explains that it comes from the name of his home town, Megalo. Others maintain that the epithet comes from his profession — that he used to plaster roofs with a roller (מַעְגִּילָה).

NOTES

the reciting of the *anenu* prayer even on Shabbat. Rabbi Yose disagrees, arguing that the people may cry out for help in times of danger, but he does not allow them to cry out to God in prayer, for (as *Rashi* explains) there is no assurance that their prayers will be effective. Many Rishonim maintain that in general the term מַתְרִיעִין — "they sound the alarm" — means that an alarm is sounded as part of the observance of a fast. But even they agree that here the term does not imply that a fast is proclaimed, for a fast may not be proclaimed on Shabbat. But according to one reading of *Rambam* (*Hilkhot Ta'aniyyot* 1:6), a fast must be proclaimed even on Shabbat if the community is threatened with one of the calamities listed here in the Mishnah.

HALAKHAH

exceptions: If the community faces serious difficulties regarding earning a livelihood, the community may include special prayers even on Shabbat. Similarly, if a city is threatened by an enemy army or by floodwaters, or if an individual is in a life-threatening situation, special prayers may be recited even on Shabbat. But the shofar may not be sounded, except to summon help." (*Shulḥan Arukh, Oraḥ Ḥayyim* 576:12-13, 288:9.)

חוּץ מֵרוֹב גְּשָׁמִים **Except for too much rain.** "Fasts are not proclaimed in Eretz Israel in times of excessive rainfall, except in places where there is concern that the water will cause buildings to collapse." (*Shulḥan Arukh,* Ibid., 576:11.)

TRANSLATION AND COMMENTARY

turned to me to pray for rain on their behalf, [1]**because I am** considered by them **a member of Your household**, who can elicit Your mercy and bring an end to the drought. [2]Therefore, **I swear by Your great Name that I will not move from here** and will not leave this circle **until You have mercy on Your children** and send rain." [3]As soon as he finished speaking, **rain began to come down** in tiny **drops.** [4]Ḥoni then **said** to God: "**I did not ask for** rain like **this, but rather for rain** that falls in sufficient quantity to fill up the storage **cisterns, ditches, and caves** with water, so that there will be enough water for the entire year." [5]Immediately the rain **began to come down** very **heavily,** causing a great deal of damage. [6]Again Ḥoni **said** to God: "**I did not ask for rain** like this either, **but for rains of benevolence, blessing, and generosity,** that fall to the ground gently, but in sufficient amounts." [7]**The rain** then began to **fall in the normal way,** not in tiny drops and not with excessive force, but in a gentle but steady stream. [8]The rain continued for a long time, **until** it became necessary for the people of **Israel to leave** the lower parts of **Jerusalem** and to go up **to** the higher region of **the Temple Mount because the rain** was flooding the lower areas of the city. [9]The people then **came** back to Ḥoni **and said to him: "Just as you prayed for** the rain to fall, so you must pray for the rain **to cease** before any further damage is done." [10]But Ḥoni **said to** them: "Go out and see if the *Even HaTo'in* is covered by the water." A large stone, called the *Even HaTo'in,* stood at one of the high points of the city of Jerusalem. Anyone who found a lost object would go there and announce his find, in an attempt to locate the object's rightful owner. "As long as that stone is not covered by water," said Ḥoni, "I will not pray for the rain to stop, for one should not reject a blessing." [11]**Shimon ben Shetaḥ**, the head of the Sanhedrin in that generation, **sent** a message **to** Ḥoni: **"If you were not Ḥoni, I would** surely **place you under a ban,** for you addressed God disrespectfully, as if God did not

שָׂמוּ פְּנֵיהֶם עָלַי, [1]שֶׁאֲנִי כְּבֶן בַּיִת לְפָנֶיךָ. [2]נִשְׁבָּע אֲנִי בְּשִׁמְךָ הַגָּדוֹל שֶׁאֵינִי זָז מִכָּאן עַד שֶׁתְּרַחֵם עַל בָּנֶיךָ". [3]הִתְחִילוּ גְּשָׁמִים מְנַטְּפִין. [4]אָמַר: "לֹא כָּךְ שָׁאַלְתִּי, אֶלָּא גִּשְׁמֵי בוֹרוֹת, שִׁיחִין, וּמְעָרוֹת". [5]הִתְחִילוּ לֵירֵד בְּזַעַף. [6]אָמַר: "לֹא כָּךְ שָׁאַלְתִּי, אֶלָּא גִּשְׁמֵי רָצוֹן, בְּרָכָה, וּנְדָבָה". [7]יָרְדוּ כְּתִקְנָן, [8]עַד שֶׁיָּצְאוּ יִשְׂרָאֵל מִירוּשָׁלַיִם לְהַר הַבַּיִת מִפְּנֵי הַגְּשָׁמִים. [9]בָּאוּ וְאָמְרוּ לוֹ: "כְּשֵׁם שֶׁהִתְפַּלַּלְתָּ עֲלֵיהֶם שֶׁיֵּרְדוּ, כָּךְ הִתְפַּלֵּל שֶׁיֵּלְכוּ לָהֶן". [10]אָמַר לָהֶם: "צְאוּ וּרְאוּ אִם נִמְחֵית אֶבֶן הַטּוֹעִין". [11]שָׁלַח לוֹ שִׁמְעוֹן בֶּן שֶׁטַח: "אִלְמָלֵא חוֹנִי אַתָּה, גּוֹזְרֵנִי עָלֶיךָ נִידּוּי.

LITERAL TRANSLATION

have turned their faces to me, [1]for I am like a member of Your household. [2]I swear by Your great Name that I will not move from here until You have mercy on Your children." [3]Rains began to come down in drops. [4]He said: "I did not ask [for] this, but [for] rains [to fill] pits, ditches, and caves." [5]They began to come down heavily (lit., "in anger"). [6]He said: "I did not ask [for] this, but [for] rains of benevolence, blessing, and generosity." [7]They fell in their normal way, [8]until Israel went out of Jerusalem to the Temple Mount because of the rains. [9]They came and said to him: "Just as you prayed for them that they should fall, so pray that they should go away." [10]He said to them: "Go out and see if the *Even HaTo'in* is covered." [11]Shimon ben Shetaḥ sent to him: "If you were not Ḥoni, I would decree a ban

RASHI

גשמי בורות – שיפוע גשמים למלאות בורות. **ונדבות** – רצון ועין יפה. **אבן הטוען** – אבן טוען היתה בירושלים, וכל מי שאבדה לו אבידה כו'. בבבא מציעא (כח,ב). **לנדות** – על כבוד הרב.

NOTES

אִם נִמְחֵית אֶבֶן הַטּוֹעִין If the *Even HaTo'in* is covered. The reference here is to a large stone located in Jerusalem which served as the center for announcements regarding lost property (see *Bava Metzia* 28b). Here, the stone is called אֶבֶן הַטּוֹעִין, literally "the error stone," whereas in *Bava Metzia* it is called אֶבֶן הַטּוֹעֵן, literally "the claiming stone," because it marked the place in Jerusalem where claims were put forward regarding lost objects.

Our translation of the word נִמְחֵית as "is covered" follows *Rashi* (in *Bava Metzia*), *Rambam, Meiri* and others who explain that when this stone was covered with water, it was time to cease praying for rain, as this level of water indicated that abundant rain had already fallen. The Jerusalem Talmud (cited by *Tosafot* in *Bava Metzia*) understands the word according to its usual sense of "to obliterate." According to this interpretation, Ḥoni HaMe'aggel was using hyperbole to inform his listeners: "Just as water cannot dissolve the *Even HaTo'in*, I cannot annul the blessed arrival of the rain."

BACKGROUND

אֶבֶן הַטּוֹעִין *Even HaTo'in*. This was apparently a large boulder or a very high stone column. The expression used by Honi HaMe'aggel was certainly an exaggeration, since he spoke of a flood so severe that it not only penetrated low-lying houses, but also covered the whole area with deep water.

SAGES

שִׁמְעוֹן בֶּן שֶׁטַח Shimon Ben Shetaḥ. President of the Sanhedrin during the reign of King Alexander Yannai, Shimon Ben Shetaḥ was one of the most important Jewish leaders and exponents of the Oral Law. He was an authoritative leader, insisting on observing the minutiae of the Torah and acting vigorously against any effort to challenge the authority of the accepted Halakhah, whether because of pressure from the outside or from sectarians of all kinds within the camp.

In his time witchcraft was expunged from the land with special decrees, and he established the laws of giving testimony. He also improved marriage contracts and gave them more force. Because he insisted on the obligatory power of the Sanhedrin, he also summoned the king to judgment and demanded that he behave like an ordinary citizen in giving respect to the court. For this and many other reasons, he came into conflict with King Yannai and was forced to hide several times to avoid his vengeance. However, as can be seen in tractate *Berakhot* (48a), he did not succumb either to threats or to honors and flattery. When people took revenge against him and testified falsely against his son, he and his son accepted punishment so as not to invalidate the established laws.

Although his sister (Queen Shlomzion) was the king's wife, Shimon Ben Shetaḥ continued to practice his profession, which was apparently connected with tanning leather. After Yannai's death, his widow Shlomzion continued to rule, and her reign, when internal affairs were in Shimon Ben Shetaḥ's hands, is regarded as a time of contentment in every respect.

TRANSLATION AND COMMENTARY

understand what it was that you wanted. [1]**But what can I do to you, for you act like a spoiled child before God and** nevertheless **He accedes to your request,** you are **like a son who acts like a spoiled child before his father, and** his father nevertheless **accedes to his request?** [2]It is **to you** that **the verse** is referring when it **says** (Proverbs 23:24-25): 'The father of the righteous shall greatly rejoice, and he who begets a wise child shall have joy of him. **Your father and your mother shall be glad, and she who bore you shall rejoice.**' It is obvious that you have found grace in God's eyes, so how can I place you under a ban?"

הָיוּ מִתְעַנִּין [3]The Mishnah continues: **If people** have taken it upon themselves to **observe a fast** on account of drought, **and rain falls for them before sunrise** on the day of the fast in sufficient quantities to make the fast unnecessary, **they do not** have to **complete their fast.** [4]But if the rain falls only **after sunrise, they** must **complete their fast.** [5]**Rabbi Eliezer** disagrees with the first Tanna of the Mishnah and **says:** If a fast has been proclaimed on account of drought, and rain falls **before noon** on the day of the fast, **the people do not** have to **complete their fast.** [6]But if the rain falls **after noon, they** must **complete their fast.** Most people take their main meal at noon, and so it is only at noon that a day begins to be regarded as a fast-day in the practical sense. If a fast was proclaimed but became unnecessary before noon, before it was actually regarded as a fast, it does not have to be observed until completion. But if the fast became unnecessary only after noon, after the day was already regarded as a fast-day, for most people will have already refrained from eating their midday meal, the fast must be observed until completion.

מַעֲשֶׂה [7]The Mishnah now cites an incident to illustrate this ruling. **It once happened that a fast was decreed in Lod** [Lydda] on account of the rain being late, **and rain** began to **fall before noon** on the very day of the fast. Following the viewpoint of Rabbi Eliezer, that if it rains before noon on the day of a fast, the fast need not be observed until completion, [8]**Rabbi Tarfon said to** the people of Lod: **"Go out, and eat and drink, and celebrate a festive day,** for your prayers have been answered and the drought has come to an end." [9]**And** the people of Lod **went out, and ate and drank, and celebrated** the day as a festive day. [10]**And** they came back to the synagogue **in the afternoon and recited the great Hallel** (Psalm 136, which includes the verse: "Who gives bread to all flesh, for His loving-kindness endures forever") to thank God for answering their prayers.

GEMARA סֵדֶר תַּעֲנִיּוֹת [11]We learned in our Mishnah: "**This order of fasts that was recorded** in the first chapter

[1]אֲבָל מָה אֶעֱשֶׂה לְךָ, שֶׁאַתָּה
מִתְחַטֵּא לִפְנֵי הַמָּקוֹם, וְעוֹשֶׂה
לְךָ רְצוֹנְךָ, כְּבֵן שֶׁהוּא מִתְחַטֵּא
עַל אָבִיו, וְעוֹשֶׂה לוֹ רְצוֹנוֹ?
[2]וְעָלֶיךָ הַכָּתוּב אוֹמֵר: ׳יִשְׂמַח
אָבִיךָ וְאִמֶּךָ, וְתָגֵל יוֹלַדְתֶּךָ׳״.
[3]הָיוּ מִתְעַנִּין, וְיָרְדוּ לָהֶם
גְּשָׁמִים קוֹדֶם הָנֵץ הַחַמָּה, לֹא
יַשְׁלִימוּ. [4]לְאַחַר הָנֵץ הַחַמָּה,
יַשְׁלִימוּ. [5]רַבִּי אֱלִיעֶזֶר אוֹמֵר:
קוֹדֶם חֲצוֹת, לֹא יַשְׁלִימוּ.
[6]לְאַחַר חֲצוֹת, יַשְׁלִימוּ.
[7]מַעֲשֶׂה שֶׁגָּזְרוּ תַּעֲנִית בְּלוֹד,
וְיָרְדוּ לָהֶם גְּשָׁמִים קוֹדֶם
חֲצוֹת. [8]אָמַר לָהֶם רַבִּי טַרְפוֹן:
״צְאוּ, וְאִכְלוּ וּשְׁתוּ, וַעֲשׂוּ יוֹם
טוֹב״. [9]וְיָצְאוּ, וְאָכְלוּ וְשָׁתוּ,
וְעָשׂוּ יוֹם טוֹב. [10]וּבָאוּ בֵּין
הָעַרְבַּיִם וְקָרְאוּ הַלֵּל הַגָּדוֹל.

גמרא [11]״סֵדֶר תַּעֲנִיּוֹת
הָאֵלּוּ הָאָמוּר בִּרְבִיעָה

LITERAL TRANSLATION

upon you. [1]But what shall I do to you, for you act like a spoiled child before God and He does your will for you, like a son who acts like a spoiled child with his father, and he does his will for him? [2]And about you the verse says: 'Your father and your mother shall be glad, and she who bore you shall rejoice.'"

[3][If] they were fasting, and rains fell for them before sunrise, they do not complete [their fast]. [4]After sunrise, they complete [their fast]. [5]Rabbi Eliezer says: Before noon, they do not complete [their fast]. [6]After noon, they complete [their fast].

[7]It once happened that they decreed a fast in Lod, and rains fell for them before noon. [8]Rabbi Tarfon said to them: "Go out, and eat and drink, and celebrate a festive day." [9]And they went out, and they ate and drank, and they celebrated a festive day. [10]And in the afternoon they came and recited the great Hallel.

GEMARA [11]"The order of these fasts that was said [above applies] with respect to

RASHI

מתחטא — *פורפיי״ש בלעז ״ישמח אביך ואמך ותגל יולדתך״.

LANGUAGE

מִתְחַטֵּא Who acts like a spoiled child. Although many commentators have argued that this word is derived from the root חטא (to sin), this is difficult to understand. Others maintain that it is derived from a different root, חטי, found in Arabic, meaning to obtain things by imploring for them. Hence מִתְחַטֵּא means to beg, implore, indulge oneself.

LANGUAGE (RASHI)

פורפיי״ש* From the Old French *forfais,* which means "evildoer," or "sinner."

SAGES

רַבִּי טַרְפוֹן Rabbi Tarfon. He was a priest who served in the Temple at the end of the Second Temple period. However, his main period of activity came later, to a large extent in association with Rabbi Eliezer and Rabbi Yehoshua. Rabbi Tarfon was wealthy and extremely generous. He seems to have been one of the Sages to acknowledge the greatness of Rabbi Akiva. Although he was initially superior to the latter in wisdom and was probably older, he came to consider himself Rabbi Akiva's disciple. Rabbi Tarfon also trained a number of disciples, and we know that Rabbi Yehudah bar Il'ai was one of his students. His grandson was a Sage during the time of Rabbi Yehudah HaNasi.

NOTES

בִּרְבִיעָה רִאשׁוֹנָה With respect to the first rainfall. *Ritva* explains that the expression "the first rainfall" can be used in two different senses. It can refer to the *yoreh* in general, the first rain of the season, which itself may be divided into

רִאשׁוֹנָה״. [1] וּרְמִינְהִי: ״רְבִיעָה רִאשׁוֹנָה וּשְׁנִיָּה, לִשְׁאוֹל; [2] שְׁלִישִׁית, לְהִתְעַנּוֹת״.
[3] אָמַר רַב יְהוּדָה: הָכִי קָאָמַר: סֵדֶר תַּעֲנִיּוֹת הָאָמוּר אֵימָתַי? [4] בִּזְמַן שֶׁיָּצְאָה רְבִיעָה רִאשׁוֹנָה, וּשְׁנִיָּה, וּשְׁלִישִׁית, וְלֹא יָרְדוּ גְּשָׁמִים. [5] אֲבָל יָרְדוּ גְּשָׁמִים בִּרְבִיעָה רִאשׁוֹנָה, וְזָרְעוּ וְלֹא צָמְחוּ, [6] אִי נַמִי צָמְחוּ וְחָזְרוּ וְנִשְׁתַּנּוּ, מַתְרִיעִין עֲלֵיהֶן מִיָּד.
[7] אָמַר רַב נַחְמָן: דַּוְקָא נִשְׁתַּנּוּ, [8] אֲבָל יָבְשׁוּ, לֹא.
[9] פְּשִׁיטָא, ״נִשְׁתַּנּוּ״ תְּנַן!

LITERAL TRANSLATION

the first rainfall." [1] A contradiction was raised (lit., "and cast them together"): "[If] the first and second rainfalls [fail, we are obliged] to pray; [2] [if] the third [fails, we are obliged] to fast."

[3] Rav Yehudah said: He says thus: The order of fasts that was said [above applies] when? [4] When [the times for] the first, second, and third rainfalls have passed, and rains have not fallen. [5] But if rains fell at [the time of] the first rainfall, and they planted but they did not grow, [6] or else they grew but then they changed, they sound the alarm for them immediately.

[7] Rav Naḥman said: Only [if] they changed, [8] but [if] they dried up, no.

[9] This is obvious, [for] we have learned: "[If] they changed"!

TRANSLATION AND COMMENTARY

of our tractate **applies** only if the time when **the first rainfall** is supposed to have fallen passed but there was still no rain." According to this Mishnah, once the time when the first rainfall was expected has passed without rain having fallen, the court immediately begins to proclaim the series of fasts described in the first chapter. [1] But this is difficult to understand, for **a contradiction can be raised** between the Mishnah and a Baraita in which it was taught: "Even if **the first and second rainfalls** have failed to arrive on time, it is not yet time to begin fasting, but only **to entreat** God for rain by inserting the supplication, 'And give dew and rain for a blessing upon the face of the earth,' in the ninth blessing of the Amidah prayer. [2] But if **the third** rainfall fails to arrive, it is time **to** begin **observing the** series of **fasts** decreed in times of drought." When, then, should the fasts observed in times of drought begin — at the time when the first rainfall was expected or only at the time when the third rainfall was supposed to fall?

אָמַר רַב יְהוּדָה [3] **Rav Yehudah said** in reply: **This is what** the Tanna of our Mishnah **meant to say: The order of fasts that was recorded** in the first chapter of our tractate — **when does** that order **apply?** [4] **When the time for the first, second and third rainfalls** — all of which come under the category of *yoreh,* the first rain of the season — has passed, and the rain has still not fallen. [5] But if rain fell at the time when the first rainfall was expected, and crops were planted but they did not grow at all, [6] or else they began to grow but then they started to change and took on an unusual appearance, the alarm is immediately sounded for the stricken crops.

אָמַר רַב נַחְמָן [7] **Rav Naḥman said:** Our Mishnah's ruling applies **only** if the crops started to **grow strangely.** In such a case, the alarm is sounded immediately, for there is still hope that the crops will recover. [8] **But if** the crops have **dried up** completely, so that there is no longer any chance of saving them, there is **no** purpose in sounding the alarm, for any prayers offered in this case would be considered prayers said in vain.

פְּשִׁיטָא [9] The Gemara objects: Surely **this is obvious, for we have learned** in the Mishnah: "But **if** the plants start to **change,** the alarm is sounded immediately," implying that the alarm is not sounded when the crops have dried up completely! Why, then, was it necessary for Rav Naḥman to state explicitly something that is implicit in the Mishnah?

RASHI

גמרא רביעה ראשונה ושניה לשאול — שאף על פי שלא ירדו גשמים לא בראשונה ולא בשניה — לא היו מתענין אלא שואלין. וקשיין מתניתין, דקתני: סדר תעניות אלו האמור ברביעה ראשונה, וברייתא, — אהדדי. **הכי קאמר כו׳** — וכגון רביעה ראשונה שניה ושלישית דכולי יורה קרי ליה רביעה, כך שמעתי. **דוקא נשתנו** — דכי נשתנו ודאי הוא דמתריעין מיד, דצריך להתפלל עליה שיחזיר ביופי כתקנן. **אבל יבשו** — לא צריך, דמכאן ואילך לא יועיל, והוא תפלת שוא. אפילו יבשו כשהן חטין עדיין דקין — אפילו הכי לא מתריעין. הכי גרסינן — פשיטא שנו תנן לא צריכא דאקון מהו דתימא כו׳.

NOTES

a number of separate rainfalls. And it can also refer to the very first rainfall of the *yoreh*. The Gemara first understood the Mishnah as referring to "the first rainfall" according to the second sense, and therefore it raised the objection that another Tannaitic source states that the fasts do not begin until the time of the third rainfall. Rav Yehudah answered that the Mishnah is using the term according to the first sense. Thus the Mishnah is teaching us that the fasts do not begin until the entire first rainfall — which includes all the rains of the *yoreh* — has failed to arrive on time.

TRANSLATION AND COMMENTARY

לָא [1]The Gemara explains: **No, it was necessary** for Rav Naḥman to inform us that even **when** the crops have dried up, but have then **produced stalks** again, the alarm is not sounded. [2]For **you might have thought that producing stalks is something** significant, an indication that the crops may yet recover. [3]**Therefore** Rav Naḥman **teaches us that this is not so.** If the crops have already dried up, there is no longer any chance of saving them, and so there is no reason to proclaim a fast or to pray on their behalf.

וְכֵן שֶׁפָּסְקוּ גְּשָׁמִים [4]The next clause of our Mishnah states: **"And similarly, if** the first rainfall fell on time, but then **the rain stopped** and there was an interval of forty days **between the first and second rains,** the alarm is sounded immediately, for a forty-day interval between the first two rainfalls of the season is surely the sign of a plague of drought." [5]The Gemara asks: **What is** the meaning of the expression, **"a plague of drought"?**

אָמַר רַב יְהוּדָה [6]**Rav Yehudah said in the name of Rav:** The expression means that a forty-day interval between the first two rainfalls of the season is the sign of **a plague that will lead to drought.** If the first rainfall of the season falls on time, but it does not rain again for another forty days, the soil will ultimately be affected by drought, the year will end with a small yield, and as a result there will be a scarcity of food.

אָמַר רַב נַחְמָן [7]The Gemara now establishes criteria for distinguishing between drought that causes a temporary shortage of food and drought that causes famine. **Rav Naḥman said:** If the crops fail in a particular region through lack of rain, and thereby cause a food shortage, but it is possible to **transport food** by boat **from** another area **by way of a river** connecting the area where the produce is available with the region

[1]לָא, צְרִיכָא דְּאַקּוּן. [2]מַהוּ דְּתֵימָא אַקְנָתָא מִילְּתָא הִיא. [3]קָמַשְׁמַע לָן.
[4]"וְכֵן שֶׁפָּסְקוּ גְשָׁמִים בֵּין גֶּשֶׁם לְגֶשֶׁם כו'". [5]מַאי "מַכַּת בַּצּוֹרֶת"?
[6]אָמַר רַב יְהוּדָה אָמַר רַב: מַכָּה הַמְּבִיאָה לִידֵי בַּצּוֹרֶת.
[7]אָמַר רַב נַחְמָן: נַהֲרָא אַנַּהֲרָא,

LITERAL TRANSLATION

[1]No, it was necessary where they produced stalks. [2]You might have said [that] producing stalks is something. [3][Therefore] he tells us [that this is not so].

[4]"And similarly, [if] the rains stopped between [one] rain and [the next] rain, etc." [5]What is "a plague of drought"?

[6]Rav Yehudah said in the name of Rav: A plague that leads to drought.

[7]Rav Naḥman said: [When food is transported from] river to river,

RASHI

דאקון – שעלו בקנה, שנתקנו מעט לאחר שנתייבשו. **מהו דתימא: אקנתא מילתא היא** – דהואיל ונתקנו מעט, אם יתפלל – מועיל להם. קא משמע לן רב נחמן דאקנתא לאו מילתא. לשון אחר: אבל יבשו לא – דממילא חוזרין. **לא צריכא דאקון** – שעלו בקנה, מהו דתימא אקנתא מילתא היא, דכיון שעלו בקנה ועדיין לא בשלו כל צרכן – ודאי, אי לא מתריעין – תו לא גדלי, קמשמע לן דלאו מילתא היא, דאף על גב דאקון אכתי גדלי טפי. **נהרא אנהרא בצורתא** – כשאין תבואה בעיר אחת, ויש בעיירות אחרות, ואפשר להביא מזה לזה דרך נהר בספינה.

BACKGROUND

דְּאַקּוּן Where they produced stalks. The phenomena described here are connected with various stages in the desiccation of plants. Sometimes a temporary water deficit of some 5 to 10 percent occurs in a plant. This deficit can take place during the summer and does not impair the growth of the plant. However, a water deficit of 30 percent causes permanent blight, in which the plant is weakened, and its leaves shrivel. If that condition lasts no more than a short time, the plant will revive if water is supplied. But if this blight continues for some time, the absorptive capacity of the roots is impaired, and the plant will die, despite any temporary recovery.

SAGES

רַבִּי שִׁמְעוֹן בֶּן מְנַסְיָא Rabbi Shimon ben Menasya. A fifth-generation Tanna. His father's name, Menasya, is apparently an Aramaic or Hellenized form of the Hebrew מְנַשֶּׁה, Menasheh. Rabbi Shimon ben Menasya was an outstanding disciple of Rabbi Meir, but he also studied with other Tannaim, such as Rabbi Shimon ben Yoḥai. A colleague of Rabbi Yehudah HaNasi, Rabbi Shimon ben Menasya nevertheless took issue with him on a number of occasions, although he greatly respected him. Some authorities maintain that Rabbi Shimon ben Menasya was a member of the "holy congregation of Jerusalem" (קְהָלָא קַדִּישָׁא דִּבִירוּשָׁלַיִם), a select group of men who engaged in Torah study and prayer, attempting to remain in Jerusalem after the Jews were expelled from the city. Rabbi Shimon ben Menasya's Halakhic and Aggadic teachings are cited once in the Mishnah (*Ḥagigah* 1:7) and in a number of places in the Tosefta and the Talmud.

NOTES

לָא צְרִיכָא דְּאַקּוּן No, it was necessary where they produced stalks. The Rishonim agree that the term אַקּוּן refers to some positive development in the growth of the plants, but they disagree about the precise meaning of the word. *Rashi* and *Ra'avad* maintain that the word is derived from the root קנה, meaning "stalk," and that the plants produced stalks after they had dried up (*Rashi*), or before they dried up (*Ra'avad*). *Rabbenu Gershom* derives the word from the root תקן, meaning "improve," and explains that the plants showed some sign of improvement after they had already dried up. *Rabbenu Ḥananel* suggests that after the plants had already dried up, they once again "turned green." Citing the *Geonim,* he writes that after the plants had already dried up, they once again "became strong."

Most Rishonim understand the Gemara as follows: The Mishnah's ruling applies only if the crops have started to grow strangely, in which case they might recover. But if the crops dry up completely, even if they then produce stalks, or improve, or turn green, or become strengthened, there is no point in sounding the alarm, for there is no longer any hope of saving them, and any prayers offered on their behalf would be in vain.

Rashi suggests another intepretation: The Mishnah's ruling applies when the crops start to grow strangely, in which case the alarm must be sounded so that the plants may recover. But if the crops have dried up, even if they already produced stalks beforehand, there is no need to sound the alarm, for they will recover on their own.

נַהֲרָא אַנַּהֲרָא River to river. Our commentary follows *Rashi,* who explains that Rav Naḥman distinguishes between drought, when it is possible to transport food from another region by river, and famine, when it is necessary to transport food overland. *Rashi* suggests a second interpretation, according to which, in a drought, water can be diverted from one river to another, whereas in a famine, all the rivers in the region have dried up.

TRANSLATION AND COMMENTARY

where the crops have failed, [19B] the cause of that scarcity of food **is** regarded as a **drought.** [1]But if it is necessary to transport produce overland **from one province to the next,** this is **famine,** a much more serious calamity.

וַאֲמַר רַבִּי חֲנִינָא [2]**Rabbi Ḥanina said:** If a shortage of grain has caused prices to rise, so that **a** ***se'ah*** of wheat sells **for a sela, but** the produce **is** nonetheless readily **available** at that price to those who have money, this is **drought.** But if produce prices are low because no one has money, [3]so that **four** ***se'ah*s** of wheat sell for a sela, **but** produce **is** simply **not available,** this is **famine.**

אָמַר רַבִּי יוֹחָנָן [4]**Rabbi Yoḥanan said:** The Rabbis needed **only** to **teach** us about the case **where money is cheap and produce is** nevertheless **expensive,** because of the shortage of food. In such a case the alarm must be sounded immediately, for this is a situation where those with money will be able to purchase food, but those without will be unable to do so. [5]**But if money is expensive** because there is little currency in circulation, then even if **produce is cheap** and the shortage of currency keeps prices depressed, [6]it is obvious that **the alarm is sounded immediately,** because nobody has enough money to buy food. [7]The following story describes such a situation: Rabbi Yoḥanan said: I remember a time when four *se'ahs* of wheat were being sold for the relatively modest price of one sela, [8]and nevertheless there **were many** people **in Tiberias** whose stomachs were **distended by famine** because they did not have **an isar** of money with which to buy food.

יָרְדוּ לִצְמָחִין [9]The Gemara now proceeds to analyze the next clause of the Mishnah, which stated: **"If rain fell** in a way that is beneficial **for** small **plants but not for trees,** or if it fell in a way that is beneficial for trees but not for small plants, or if it fell in a way that is beneficial both for trees and for plants but not for storage pits, ditches, and caves, the alarm is sounded immediately." [10]The Gemara argues: **Granted** that **you can find rain which fell** in a way that is beneficial **for** small **plants but not for trees** — [11]in a case **where gentle rain fell, but heavy rain did not fall.** You can

[19B] בַּצּוֹרְתָּא; [1]מְדִינְתָּא אַמְּדִינְתָּא, כַּפְנָא.
[2]וַאֲמַר רַבִּי חֲנִינָא: סְאָה בְּסֶלַע, וּשְׁכִיחָא, בַּצּוֹרְתָּא; [3]אַרְבָּעָה, וְלָא שְׁכִיחָא, כַּפְנָא.
[4]אָמַר רַבִּי יוֹחָנָן: לֹא שָׁנוּ אֶלָּא בִּזְמַן שֶׁהַמָּעוֹת בְּזוֹל וּפֵירוֹת בְּיוֹקֶר. [5]אֲבָל מָעוֹת בְּיוֹקֶר וּפֵירוֹת בְּזוֹל, [6]מַתְרִיעִין עָלֶיהָ מִיָּד. [7]דְּאָמַר רַבִּי יוֹחָנָן: נְהִירְנָא כַּד הֲווּ קַיְימֵי אַרְבָּעָה סָאִין בְּסֶלַע, [8]וַהֲווּ נְפִישֵׁי נְפִיחֵי כָפָן בִּטְבֶרְיָא, מִדְּלֵית אִיסָּר.
[9]"יָרְדוּ לִצְמָחִין אֲבָל לֹא לָאִילָן". [10]בִּשְׁלָמָא לִצְמָחִים וְלֹא לָאִילָן — [11]מַשְׁכַּחַתְּ לַהּ דַּאֲתָא נִיחָא, וְלָא אֲתְיָא רַזְיָא.

LITERAL TRANSLATION

[19B] [it is] drought; [1][from] province to province, [it is] famine.

[2]And Rabbi Ḥanina said: [If] a *se'ah* [is sold] for a sela, but it is found, [this is] drought; [3][if] four, but it is not found, [this is] famine.

[4]Rabbi Yoḥanan said: They did not teach [this] except at a time when money is cheap and produce is expensive. [5]But [if] money is expensive and produce is cheap, [6]they sound the alarm for it immediately. [7]For Rabbi Yoḥanan said: I remember when four *se'ah*s stood at a sela, [8]and there were many swollen from famine in Tiberias, because there was not an isar [coin].

[9]"If [rains] fell for the plants, but not for the trees." [10]Granted [that rain can fall] for plants but not for trees — [11]you find it where gentle [rain] fell, but heavy [rain] did not fall.

RASHI

בצורתא — בצורת היא זו ולא רעב, הואיל ויכולין לישא בספינות. **מדינתא אמדינתא** — וצריכין להוליך ממדינה למדינה על ידי חמרים, כפנא — רעב. ורעב קשה מבצורת, לפי שאי אפשר להביא בשופי, מפי רבי. לשון אחר: נהרא אנהרא, אם יבש מעיין זה וצריך להסב מעיין אחר בכאן, אי נמי להמתין עד שיגדל נהר אחרת ויבא כאן — בצורת הוא זה. **מדינתא אמדינתא** — אם יבשו כל הנהרות שבתוך העיר, וצריכין להביא מים מעיר אחרת, כפנא — רעב הוא זה, תקיפא מבצורתא. **סאה בסלע ושכיחא** — כי זבני סאה של חיטין בסלע דהיינו יוקר ומצויה לקנות בכל עת — בצורתא. **מעות ביוקר** — אין מעות מצויות להן. **נהירנא** — אני זוכר. **מדלית איסר** — מאין מעות. **דאתיא ניחא** — ואמרינן בפירקא דלעיל (ג,ב): מיטרא ניחא לפירי ולתבואה, ומיטרא רזיא לאילני, דאתיא ניחא לפירי ואתיא רזא לאילנות.

NOTES

בִּזְמַן שֶׁהַמָּעוֹת בְּזוֹל וּפֵירוֹת בְּיוֹקֶר **At a time when money is cheap and produce is expensive.** Our commentary follows *Ritva,* who explains that Rabbi Ḥanina's distinction between drought and famine parallels Rabbi Yoḥanan's distinction between a case where money is cheap and produce is expensive and a case where money is expensive and produce is cheap. In all cases, argues *Ritva,* the alarm is sounded immediately, because the Mishnah implies that if the alarm is sounded for drought, it must also be sounded for famine, which is a more desperate situation. Thus Rabbi Yoḥanan's statement that the Rabbis made their regulation only in a case where money was cheap and produce was expensive, but not in the reverse case, cannot be understood as implying that the alarm was not sounded in the latter case, but rather that the Rabbis did not need to make their regulation in the latter case, for the law in that case was obvious.

[1]לָאִילָן וְלֹא לַצְּמָחִין — [2]דְּאָתְיָא רַזְיָא, וְלָא אָתְיָא נִיחָא. [3]לָזֶה וְלָזֶה, אֲבָל לֹא לַבּוֹרוֹת, וְלֹא לַשִּׁיחִין וּמְעָרוֹת — [4]מַשְׁכַּחַת לָהּ, דְּאָתְיָא רַזְיָא וְנִיחָא, [5]מִידּוּ טוּבָא לָא אָתְיָא. [6]אֶלָּא הָא דְּתַנְיָא: ״יָרְדוּ לַבּוֹרוֹת, לַשִּׁיחִין, וְלַמְּעָרוֹת, אֲבָל לֹא לָזֶה וְלָזֶה״, [7]הֵיכִי מַשְׁכַּחַת לָהּ?

[8]דְּאָתְיָא בְּשַׁפִּיכוּתָא.

[9]תָּנוּ רַבָּנַן: ״מַתְרִיעִין עַל הָאִילָנוֹת בִּפְרוֹס הַפֶּסַח. [10]עַל הַבּוֹרוֹת, וְשִׁיחִין, וּמְעָרוֹת, בִּפְרוֹס הֶחָג. [11]וְאִם אֵין לָהֶן

LITERAL TRANSLATION

[1]For trees but not for plants — [2]where heavy [rain] fell, but gentle [rain] did not fall. [3]For this and for that, but not for pits, and not for ditches and caves — [4]you will find it where heavy [rain] and gentle [rain] fell, [5]but abundant [rain] did not fall. [6]But [regarding] what was taught: "[If rains] fell for pits, for ditches, and for caves, but not for this and that," [7]how do you find it?

[8]Where it fell in torrents.

[9]Our Rabbis taught: "They sound the alarm for trees close to Pesaḥ. [10]For pits, and ditches, and caves, close to the Festival [of Sukkot]. [11]And if they do not have

TRANSLATION AND COMMENTARY

also find rain that fell in a manner useful [1]**for trees but not for** small **plants** — [2]in a case **where heavy rain fell, but gentle rain did not fall.** [3]And **you can** also **find** rainfall that is beneficial **both for** trees and for small plants but **not for** storage **pits, ditches, and caves** — [4]in a case **where heavy rain** fell (benefiting the trees) **and gentle rain fell** (helping the smaller plants), [5]**but** the rain **did not fall** in such **abundance** that it filled up the storage areas. [6]**But** a question remains **regarding what was taught** in a related Baraita: **"If rain fell** in a way that was beneficial **for** storage **pits, ditches, and caves, but not for** trees **or** small plants, the alarm is sounded immediately." [7]**How can we find** such a case? For if rain fell in a quantity sufficient to fill the storage pits, ditches, and caves, then surely there was enough rain for the small plants and trees. If it fell gently, it would have been beneficial for small plants; and if it fell heavily, it would have been beneficial for trees. How, then, can we construct a case where the rain fell in a way that was beneficial for pits, ditches, and caves, but not for small plants or trees?

דְּאָתְיָא בְּשַׁפִּיכוּתָא [8]The Gemara answers: We can find such a case **where** the rain **fell in torrents.** Such rain is beneficial for storage pits because it fills them quickly with water. But it does not benefit any of the vegetation, for it falls so heavily that it causes damage to everything in its path.

תָּנוּ רַבָּנַן [9]**Our Rabbis taught** in a Baraita: **"The alarm is sounded for trees close to Pesaḥ,** the time when the trees are supposed to blossom in Eretz Israel, for if the trees do not have enough water when they are supposed to blossom, they will suffer irreparable damage. Fasts are observed and prayers for rain are offered until either the trees receive sufficient rain or the rainy season is over. [10]The alarm is sounded **for** storage **pits, ditches, and caves close to the Festival of Sukkot.** If the storage pits, ditches, and caves are dry, the alarm is sounded with the approach of Sukkot. Prayers for rain could not be recited during the summer dry season, because prayers are not offered in expectation of a miracle. But with the approach of Sukkot and the rainy season, the alarm is sounded until it rains and the storage facilities are filled with water. [11]**And** there is such a deterioration in the water supply that **there is no water** left for the people **to drink,**

RASHI

בשפיכתא — בכח גדול יותר מדאי, דאינה טובה לא לזה ולא לזה. שוב אמר רבי: שפיכותא — מטר דק ועבה יותר מדאי, לאילני לא מהניא — דלאו רזיא היא, לצמחים נמי לא — שהגשמים מרובין באין ושוטפין אותן. **בפרוס הפסח** — בימי הפסח, על בורות שיחין ומערות אם לא ירדו להן גשמים. **אפילו בפרוס החג** — להשקות זרעים ואת בהמתם.

NOTES

בִּפְרוֹס הַפֶּסַח Close to Pesaḥ. The precise meaning of the term as it is used here is unclear. Elsewhere (*Bekhorot* 58a), the Gemara explains that the expression בִּפְרוֹס הַפֶּסַח refers to the first of Nisan, the midpoint of the thirty-day period before Pesaḥ during which the laws pertaining to the holiday must be studied (see *Mikhtam*, *Meiri*, and others). *Rashi* writes here that the alarm is sounded for trees *during* Pesaḥ. *Rambam* (*Hilkhot Ta'aniyyot* 2:17) maintains that if the time of Pesaḥ has arrived or is close to arriving, and rain has not yet fallen in quantities sufficient for the trees, the alarm is sounded immediately.

בִּפְרוֹס הֶחָג Close to the Festival of Sukkot. *Rambam* (*Hilkhot Ta'aniyyot* 2:17) and others understand the term חַג, literally "festival," in its usual sense as referring to the Festival of Sukkot. *Ritva* asks: How is it possible that the alarm was not sounded all summer long when the rainfall

HALAKHAH

עַל הָאִילָנוֹת בִּפְרוֹס הַפֶּסַח For trees close to Pesaḥ. If Pesaḥ is approaching and rain has not fallen in sufficient quantities for the trees, fasts are proclaimed and special prayers are recited until there is adequate rain or the rainy

BACKGROUND

שְׁפִיכוּתָא Torrents. Heavy rains can fall within a short time. It has happened in Eretz Israel that more than 100 mm. of rain fell within an hour-and-a-half. This causes flooding which can seriously damage crops, and can even sweep away a layer of topsoil. This type of rain is useful only to fill cisterns, but it damages every kind of vegetation.

מַיִם לִשְׁתּוֹת, מַתְרִיעִין עֲלֵיהֶן מִיָּד. [1]וְאֵיזֶהוּ ׳מִיָּד׳ שֶׁלָּהֶן? [2]שֵׁנִי, וַחֲמִישִׁי, וְשֵׁנִי. וְעַל כּוּלָּן אֵין מַתְרִיעִין עֲלֵיהֶן אֶלָּא בְּאִפַּרְכְיָא שֶׁלָּהֶן. [3]וְאַסְכָּרָא, בִּזְמַן שֶׁיֵּשׁ בָּהּ מִיתָה, מַתְרִיעִין עָלֶיהָ, [4]בִּזְמַן שֶׁאֵין בָּהּ מִיתָה, אֵין מַתְרִיעִין עָלֶיהָ. [5]וּמַתְרִיעִין עַל הַגּוֹבַאי בְּכָל שֶׁהוּא. [6]רַבִּי שִׁמְעוֹן בֶּן אֶלְעָזָר אוֹמֵר: אַף עַל הֶחָגָב״.

[7]תָּנוּ רַבָּנַן: ״מַתְרִיעִין עַל הָאִילָנוֹת בִּשְׁאָר שְׁנֵי שָׁבוּעַ.

LITERAL TRANSLATION

water to drink, they sound the alarm for them immediately. [1]And what is 'immediately' for them? Monday, and Thursday, and Monday. [2]And for all of them they do not sound the alarm for them except in their own province. [3]As for diphtheria, when there is death from it, they sound the alarm for it, [4][but] when there is no death from it, they do not sound the alarm for it. [5]And they sound the alarm for the *govai* for the smallest quantity. [6]Rabbi Shimon ben Elazar says: Also for the *ḥagav*." [7]Our Rabbis taught: "They sound the alarm for trees during the other years of the Sabbatical cycle.

TRANSLATION AND COMMENTARY

the alarm is sounded immediately even during the summer months, for in the face of such danger the people have no choice but to pray for a miracle. [1]**And what is** the meaning of the expression **'immediately'** used here with respect to sounding the alarm? It does not necessarily mean that public fasts are proclaimed on that very day, but that they are proclaimed on the first **Monday** following the declaration of the emergency, the next **Thursday, and** the following **Monday.** [2]**And in all** these **cases, the alarm is sounded** only **in the province** where the calamity has occurred. [3]**As for diphtheria** and other infectious diseases, if **people have died from** the illness, fasts are proclaimed and **the alarm is sounded,** because this is regarded as a communal disaster. [4]**But if nobody has died** from the illness, fasts are not proclaimed and **the alarm is not sounded.** [5]**The alarm is sounded upon the** sighting of *govai*, a type of locust that causes immense damage to crops, if even **the smallest number** of such insects is seen. [6]**Rabbi Shimon ben Elazar says:** The alarm is **also** sounded **upon the** sighting of *ḥagav*, another type of locust that can cause considerable damage to crops."

תָּנוּ רַבָּנַן [7]The Gemara continues with another Baraita, in which **our Rabbis taught: "During the** first six **years of the Sabbatical cycle, the alarm is sounded** if rain has not fallen in a manner that is beneficial for trees. But during the seventh year of the cycle, when working the land is forbidden and all the produce that grows is ownerless, the alarm is not sounded if rain has not fallen in a manner that is beneficial

RASHI

אם אין להם לשתות מתריעין וכו׳ — אפילו בפרוס החג, דימות החמה נינהו, אפילו הכי — מתריעין, משום דכולן צריכות לשתות. **וכולן** — כל אלו. **בהיפרכיא שלהן** — באותו מלכות שכלו שם מי בורות שיחין ומערות. **ואסכרא** — *בוצמל״ע בלעז. פעמים שנקבע בתוך פיו של אדם ומת. לשון ״כי יסכר פי דוברי שקר״ (תהלים סג) והיא סרונכה, מיתה משונה. **בזמן שיש בה מיתה** — שהיא משולחת — מהלכת, ומתים בה. **על הגובאי** — שמכלה את התבואה, כל שהוא — אפילו לא נראה אלא קצת, בידוע שעתידין לבוא לרוב. אבל חגב כל שהוא מצוי הוא, ואינו מכלה כל כך כארבה. **בשאר שני שבוע** — דשמיטה, אבל בשמיטה — לא, דהפקר נינהו.

LANGUAGE

אִפַּרְכְיָא This word is derived from the Greek επαρχια, *eparkhia,* meaning "a district."

BACKGROUND

אַסְכָּרָא Diphtheria. From the description, this disease appears to be diphtheria, which first affects the mouth and throat. In some cases, when the disease spreads deep into the throat, it can cause death by suffocation. The infection can also spread to other parts of the body and is liable to weaken the heart and even to cause death. This disease mainly affects children under the age of ten (see below, 27b).

LANGUAGE (RASHI)

בוצמל״ע* (correct reading: בונמלנ״ט). From the Old French *bonmalant,* which means "diphtheria," or "croup."

NOTES

was most desperately needed, and only when Sukkot approaches is the alarm sounded? *Ritva* explains that while the need for rain is greatest during the summer months, prayers for rain cannot be offered then, because one should not pray for a miracle. But with the approach of Sukkot, prayers may be offered, for the water shortage has already been felt for a long time and the rainy season is now at hand. *Ran* argues that the water shortage is only really felt when it comes close to Sukkot, for all summer long there is still some water left in the storage cisterns from the previous winter. *Ritva* suggests alternatively that the term חַג should be understood as referring to the Festival of Shavuot. Indeed, according to the Jerusalem Talmud's version of the Baraita, the alarm is sounded concerning pits, ditches, and caves close to the Festival of Shavuot.

HALAKHAH

season passes. Similarly, if Sukkot is approaching and the storage cisterns contain little water, fasts must be observed until there is adequate rainfall. If there is a shortage of drinking water, fasts are proclaimed at any time, even during the summer months." (*Shulḥan Arukh, Oraḥ Ḥayyim* 575:8.)

אַסְכָּרָא Diphtheria. "If a community is struck by a particular illness, such as diphtheria, and people are dying from the disease, the alarm is sounded and fasts are proclaimed." (Ibid., 576:5.)

עַל הַגּוֹבַאי בְּכָל שֶׁהוּא For the *govai* for the smallest quantity. "If even one specimen of the destructive locusts *ḥasil* or *govai* is sighted, the alarm is sounded and fasts are proclaimed. If the *ḥagav* is sighted, special prayers are recited, but the alarm is not sounded and fasts are not proclaimed. Now that we are unable to distinguish between the various types of locust, the alarm is sounded in all cases." (Ibid., 576:9.)

[1]עַל הַבּוֹרוֹת, וְעַל הַשִּׁיחִין, וְעַל הַמְּעָרוֹת, אֲפִילּוּ בַּשְּׁבִיעִית. [2]רַבָּן שִׁמְעוֹן בֶּן גַּמְלִיאֵל אוֹמֵר: אַף עַל הָאִילָנוֹת בַּשְּׁבִיעִית, [3]מִפְּנֵי שֶׁיֵּשׁ בָּהֶן פַּרְנָסָה לָעֲנִיִּים". [4]תַּנְיָא אִידָךְ: "מַתְרִיעִין עַל הָאִילָנוֹת בִּשְׁאָר שְׁנֵי שָׁבוּעַ. [5]עַל הַבּוֹרוֹת, עַל הַשִּׁיחִין, וְעַל הַמְּעָרוֹת, אֲפִילּוּ בַּשְּׁבִיעִית. [6]רַבָּן שִׁמְעוֹן בֶּן גַּמְלִיאֵל אוֹמֵר: אַף עַל הָאִילָנוֹת. [7]מַתְרִיעִין עַל הַסְּפִיחִין בַּשְּׁבִיעִית, [8]מִפְּנֵי שֶׁיֵּשׁ בָּהֶן פַּרְנָסָה לָעֲנִיִּים". [9]תַּנְיָא: "אָמַר רַבִּי אֶלְעָזָר בֶּן פְּרָטָא: מִיּוֹם שֶׁחָרַב בֵּית הַמִּקְדָּשׁ, נַעֲשׂוּ גְּשָׁמִים צִימוּקִין

LITERAL TRANSLATION

[1]For pits, and for ditches, and for caves, even during the Sabbatical Year. [2]Rabban Shimon ben Gamliel says: Also for trees during the Sabbatical Year, [3]because they furnish sustenance for the poor."

[4]It was taught in another [Baraita]: "They sound the alarm for trees during the other years of the Sabbatical cycle. [5]For pits, for ditches, and for caves, even during the Sabbatical Year. [6]Rabban Shimon ben Gamliel says: Also for trees. [7]They sound the alarm for the aftergrowths of the Sabbatical Year, [8]because they furnish sustenance for the poor."

[9]It was taught: "Rabbi Elazar ben Perata said: Since the day that the Temple was destroyed, rains have become meager

RASHI

אפילו בשביעית – כל שעה צריכין לשתיה, ואף על פי שהגשמים מועילין לקרקע בשביעית. רבן שמעון בן גמליאל אומר – מתריעין על האילנות, ואף על הספיחין של שביעית שאינן חשובין כל כך. צמוקין – שיורדין בקושי, מלשון "ושדיים צומקים" (הושע ט).

TRANSLATION AND COMMENTARY

to trees. [1]But if not enough rain has fallen to fill the storage **pits, ditches, and caves,** the alarm is sounded **even during the Sabbatical Year,** for drinking water is always needed. [2]**Rabban Shimon ben Gamliel says:** The alarm is sounded **even for trees during the Sabbatical Year,** [3]**because** the produce growing on the trees **serves as** an important source of **sustenance for the poor** during that year." All the produce of the Sabbatical Year is ownerless and must be left unguarded so that everybody can have free access to it. If rain does not fall in a manner that is beneficial to trees, it is the poor who will suffer the most, for they are the most dependent on the fruit that grows during the Sabbatical Year. Thus the alarm must be sounded on their behalf, if the trees have not had enough rain.

תַּנְיָא אִידָךְ [4]A slightly different version of this dispute was **taught in another Baraita: "During the** first six **years of the Sabbatical cycle, the alarm is sounded** if rain has not fallen in a manner that is beneficial **for trees.** But during the seventh year of that cycle the alarm is not sounded. [5]However, if rain has not fallen in sufficient quantities to fill the storage **pits, ditches, and caves,** the alarm is sounded **even during the Sabbatical Year.** [6]**Rabban Shimon ben Gamliel says:** The alarm is sounded **even for trees** during the Sabbatical Year. [7]**The alarm is** also **sounded for produce that has grown of itself in the Sabbatical Year as a result** of what was sown in the previous year, [8]**because this** produce, which is permitted to be eaten during the Sabbatical Year, **is** an important source of **sustenance for the poor** during that year."

תַּנְיָא [9]**It was taught** in a Baraita: **"Rabbi Elazar ben Perata said: Since the day that the Temple was**

BACKGROUND

צִימּוּקִין **Meager.** According to the version in our possession, this must be understood according to the normal meaning of the root צמק, which is to dry up. Since the destruction of the Temple, rainfall has not been plentiful, but sparse and irregular, like something shriveled and reduced in size and shape. In the *Arukh* a different reading is found: סְקִימִיּוֹן. He explains that this means that the world is placed on trial to determine the quantity of rainful. The word is apparently Greek, but its origin and meaning have not yet been clarified.

NOTES

מִפְּנֵי שֶׁיֵּשׁ בָּהֶן פַּרְנָסָה לָעֲנִיִּים **Because they contain sustenance for the poor.** The Tannaim disagree about whether the alarm is sounded during the Sabbatical Year only for the trees, or even for the aftergrowth of vegetables and grain planted during the previous year. Some explain that the disagreement reflects a more fundamental dispute regarding the Rabbinic prohibition imposed upon the aftergrowth of what was planted during the sixth year — whether the Rabbis forbade the produce for consumption, or whether they only forbade the purchase of such produce from a person who is suspected of having planted during the Sabbatical Year (see *Rash* [*Shevi'it* 9:1, end], *Rid*, and *Gevurat Ari*).

According to the versions of the Baraita found in the Babylonian Talmud, the alarm is sounded even during the Sabbatical Year if there is no rain, because the produce growing on the trees and the aftergrowths of what was planted the previous year, which was be eaten during the Sabbatical Year, are an important source of sustenance for the poor. But according to the version of the Baraita found in the Tosefta and in the Jerusalem Talmud, the alarm is sounded on account of drought even during the Sabbatical Year, for the benefit of "others." The Jerusalem Talmud cites two explanations for this cryptic term: Some say that the alarm is sounded for the benefit of the non-Jews who are not bound by the restrictions imposed during the Sabbatical Year. Others explain that it is sounded for the benefit of those Jews who are suspected of violating the restrictions and planting during the Sabbatical Year.

מִיּוֹם שֶׁחָרַב בֵּית הַמִּקְדָּשׁ **Since the day that the Temple was destroyed.** *Maharsha* explains that, during the time that the Temple was standing, the High Priest offered a special prayer on Yom Kippur that rain should fall at the

TRANSLATION AND COMMENTARY

destroyed, rains have become meager and irregular **in the world.** [1]**There are years when the rain falls in abundance and there are years when it falls in small amounts.** [2]**There are years when the rain falls at the right time, and there are years when it does not fall at the right time.** [3]**To what may a year in which the rain falls at the right time be compared?** [4]It may be compared **to a slave whose master provides him with** everything he needs for **his sustenance** for the week **on Sunday,** so that he has the entire week during which to prepare food for his household. [5]**In such a case, his dough is baked as it should be** baked, **and it can be eaten as it should** be eaten. [6]**To what may a year in which the rain does not fall at the right time be compared?** [7]It may be compared **to a slave whose master provides him with** everything he needs for **his sustenance** for the week **on Friday,** so that he has little time to prepare the food before Shabbat. [8]**In such a case, he cannot bake his dough as it should be baked and it cannot be eaten as it should be** eaten. Similarly, during a year in which the rain falls at the appropriate time, agricultural work can be done in an orderly way and a successful yield can be expected. But during a year when rain does not fall at the appropriate time, then even if it falls in adequate amounts, the agricultural calendar is disturbed and the yield is poor as a result. [9]**To what may a year in which the rain falls in abundant quantities be compared?** [10]It may be compared **to a slave whose master provides him with his sustenance all at once.** [11]**Millstones cause** the same amount of **waste when they grind a** ***kor*** of wheat **as when they grind a** ***kav*** [1/180 of a *kor*], **and dough is diminished** by the same amount **when a** ***kor*** of flour is kneaded **as when a** ***kav*** is kneaded.

לָעוֹלָם. [1]יֵשׁ שָׁנָה שֶׁגְּשָׁמֶיהָ מְרוּבִּין, וְיֵשׁ שָׁנָה שֶׁגְּשָׁמֶיהָ מוּעָטִין. [2]יֵשׁ שָׁנָה שֶׁגְּשָׁמֶיהָ יוֹרְדִין בִּזְמַנָּן, וְיֵשׁ שָׁנָה שֶׁאֵין גְּשָׁמֶיהָ יוֹרְדִין בִּזְמַנָּן. [3]שָׁנָה שֶׁגְּשָׁמֶיהָ יוֹרְדִין בִּזְמַנָּן — לְמָה הוּא דּוֹמֶה? [4]לְעֶבֶד שֶׁנָּתַן לוֹ רַבּוֹ פַּרְנָסָתוֹ בְּאֶחָד בְּשַׁבָּת. [5]נִמְצֵאת עִיסָּה נֶאֱפֵית כְּתִיקְנָהּ וְנֶאֱכֶלֶת כְּתִיקְנָהּ. [6]שָׁנָה שֶׁאֵין גְּשָׁמֶיהָ יוֹרְדִין בִּזְמַנָּן — לְמָה הוּא דּוֹמֶה? [7]לְעֶבֶד שֶׁנָּתַן לוֹ רַבּוֹ פַּרְנָסָתוֹ בְּעֶרֶב שַׁבָּת. [8]נִמְצֵאת עִיסָּה נֶאֱפֵית שֶׁלֹּא כְּתִיקְנָהּ וְנֶאֱכֶלֶת שֶׁלֹּא כְּתִיקְנָהּ. [9]שָׁנָה שֶׁגְּשָׁמֶיהָ מְרוּבִּין — לְמָה הוּא דּוֹמֶה? [10]לְעֶבֶד שֶׁנָּתַן לוֹ רַבּוֹ פַּרְנָסָתוֹ בְּבַת אַחַת. [11]נִמְצְאוּ רֵיחַיִם טוֹחֲנוֹת מִן הַכּוֹר מַה שֶּׁטּוֹחֲנוֹת מִן הַקַּב, וְנִמְצֵאת עִיסָּה אוֹכֶלֶת מִן הַכּוֹר כְּמוֹ אוֹכֶלֶת מִן הַקַּב.

LITERAL TRANSLATION

for the world. [1]There is a year whose rains are abundant, and there is a year whose rains are few. [2]There is a year whose rains fall at their [right] time, and there is a year whose rains do not fall at their [right] time. [3]A year whose rains fall at their [right] time — to what is it compared? [4]To a slave whose master gave him his sustenance on Sunday. [5]It turns out that [his] dough is baked as it should be and is eaten as it should be. [6]A year whose rains do not fall at their [right] time — to what is it compared? [7]To a slave whose master gave him his sustenance on Friday. [8]It turns out that [his] dough is not baked as it should be and is not eaten as it should be. [9]A year whose rains are abundant — to what is it compared? [10]To a slave whose master gave him his sustenance all at once. [11]The millstones turn out to grind from a *kor* what they grind from a *kav*, [and] and the dough turns out to consume from a *kor* as it consumes from a *kav*.

RASHI

למה הוא דומה — פרנסתו של כל השבת כולה. **נאפת כתקנה** — שיש לו פנאי לאפותה. **פרנסתו בבת אחת** — פרנסת כל השנה, וטוחן אותה ביחד. **נמצאת רחיים במה שאוכלת מן הכור כו'** — שכן דרך שמשתייר מן הקמח ברחיים. וכן כשהגשמים יורדין מרובים ומרביעין את הארץ, ומה שהיו טרשים — בולעים מן הרוב בולעין מן המיעוט, ומה שהרוח מנשבת ובולעת מן הרוב — בולעת מן המיעוט. **נמצאת עיסה** — עריבה שלשין בה את הבצק, שמשתייר בשוליה מן העיסה. אף גשמים, כשיורדין מעט מעט — נבלעין בטרשין ואין מרביעין את הארץ.

BACKGROUND

נֶאֱפֵית כְּתִיקְנָהּ וכו׳ Baked as it should be. When there is enough time to prepare dough and bake it, the process takes place in proper order, the dough rises well, and the baking is done at the proper temperature. But when these things must be done in a hurry, the dough is not kneaded properly, and lumps of flour remain in it. It is also baked at too high a temperature (to finish it faster), so that the bread is liable to be only partially baked or burned. Similarly, rainfall after the proper time and with gaps that are too long between rains can prevent all the plants from sprouting. And even those which do sprout often do not flourish because of the shortage of water when they need a lot of it. Thus, even if the overall quantity of rain is the same, only the proper distribution of rainfall throughout the season can guarantee proper growth.

רֵיחַיִם טוֹחֲנוֹת מִן הַכּוֹר The millstones turn out to grind from a *kor*. Every time grain is milled, a certain amount is lost. Some of this loss occurs when the millstones themselves, which are rough in order to grind the grain, are filled with pieces of the ground grain. This wastage can be reduced by the proper adjustment of the space between the millstones, but some very fine flour always blows away. Some of this loss is a constant amount, so that when a small quantity of grain is ground, the percentage of the loss is higher.

עִיסָּה אוֹכֶלֶת מִן הַכּוֹר Dough turns out to consume from a *kor*. When dough is made, some flour is always spilled or scattered, and some dough sticks to the sides of the vessel. In this case, too, the percentage of loss is greater when a small amount of flour is mixed.

NOTES

appointed time and in abundant amounts. But after the Temple was destroyed, that prayer was no longer offered, and since then rain has fallen at irregular intervals and in disappointing quantities.

Arukh has a different reading in our passage: "Since the day that the Temple was destroyed, the rain has become a means of judging the world." While the Temple stood, the generation could see whether it was judged innocent or guilty by means of the scarlet thread that hung in the Temple. On Yom Kippur it turned white, to show that the people's sins had been forgiven, or it remained scarlet, to show that they had not. But since the Temple was destroyed, rain has become the primary test by which a generation can see that it has been vindicated or found guilty in the eyes of God.

TRANSLATION AND COMMENTARY

[1] **To what may a year in which the rain falls in meager quantities be compared?** [2] It may be compared **to a slave whose master provides him with** the raw foodstuffs that he needs for **his sustenance little by little.** [3] When food is processed in small quantities, the total waste increases, for **the same amount** of waste that **the millstones** cause **when they grind a** *kor* of wheat **they** cause **when they grind a** *kav*, [4] **and dough is diminished** by **the same amount when a** *kav* of flour is kneaded **as when a** *kor* is kneaded. Similarly, much more benefit can be derived when rain falls in abundant quantities than when it falls in meager amounts, even if the total rainfall is the same. [5] **Another analogy** may be offered: **To what may a year in which the rain falls in abundant quantities be compared?** [6] It may be compared **to a person who kneads clay.** [7] **If he has much water** at his disposal, **the water will not be used up, and** as a result **the clay will be kneaded well.** To what may a year in which the rain falls in meager quantities be compared? [8] It may be compared to a person **who has** only a **little water** with which to knead his clay, so that when **the water is used up,** he must go and fetch more. By the time he comes back with the additional water, [9] the clay will once again have become as dry as it was at the outset, **and** as a result **the clay will not be kneaded well.** Similarly, when the rain falls in abundant quantities, the crops will grow well, but when it falls in meager quantities, there is never enough water in the ground to ensure a successful yield.

תָּנוּ רַבָּנַן [10] **Our Rabbis taught** the following Baraita: **"On one occasion all Israel went up to Jerusalem for** one of the **Pilgrim Festivals, and there was not** enough **water** in the city for everyone **to drink.** [11] **Nakdimon ben Guryon,** one of the wealthy men living in Jerusalem before the destruction of the Second Temple, **approached a certain** Roman **official,** [12] **and said to him: 'Lend me twelve wells of water for the pilgrims, and I will give you** back **twelve wells of water** after the cisterns have been replenished by the rain. [13] **And if I do not return** the water to you, **I will give you twelve talents of silver** in their stead.' The Roman official agreed,

LITERAL TRANSLATION

[1] A year whose rains are few — to what is it compared? [2] To a slave whose master gave him his sustenance little by little. [3] The millstones turn out to grind from a *kav* what they grind from a *kor*, [4] [and] the dough turns out to consume from a *kav* what is consumed from a *kor*. [5] Another explanation (lit., 'thing'): When its rains are abundant, to what is it compared? [6] To a person who kneads clay. [7] If he has much water, the water is not used up and the clay is kneaded well. [8] If he has little water, [9] the water is used up and the clay is not kneaded well."

[10] Our Rabbis taught: "Once all Israel went up on pilgrimage to Jerusalem, and they did not have water to drink. [11] Nakdimon ben Guryon approached a certain governor, [12] [and] said to him: 'Lend me twelve wells of water for the pilgrims, and I will give you twelve wells of water. [13] And if I do not give [them] to you, I will give you twelve talents of silver.'

[1] שָׁנָה שֶׁגְּשָׁמֶיהָ מוּעָטִין — לְמָה הוּא דּוֹמֶה? [2] לְעֶבֶד שֶׁנָּתַן לוֹ רַבּוֹ פַּרְנָסָתוֹ מְעַט מְעַט. [3] נִמְצְאוּ רֵיחַיִּים מַה שֶּׁטּוֹחֲנוֹת מִן הַכּוֹר טוֹחֲנוֹת מִן הַקַּב, [4] נִמְצֵאת עִיסָּה כַּמָּה שֶׁנֶּאֱכֶלֶת מִן הַכּוֹר אוֹכֶלֶת מִן הַקַּב. [5] דָּבָר אַחֵר: בִּזְמַן שֶׁגְּשָׁמֶיהָ מְרוּבִּין, לְמָה הוּא דּוֹמֶה? [6] לְאָדָם שֶׁמְּגַבֵּל אֶת הַטִּיט. [7] אִם יֵשׁ לוֹ מַיִם רַבִּים, מַיִם אֵינָן כָּלִין וְהַטִּיט מְגוּבָּל יָפֶה. [8] אִם יֵשׁ לוֹ מַיִם מוּעָטִין, [9] מַיִם כָּלִים וְהַטִּיט אֵינוֹ מִתְגַּבֵּל יָפֶה".

[10] תָּנוּ רַבָּנַן: "פַּעַם אַחַת עָלוּ כָּל יִשְׂרָאֵל לָרֶגֶל לִירוּשָׁלַיִם, וְלֹא הָיָה לָהֶם מַיִם לִשְׁתּוֹת. [11] הָלַךְ נַקְדִּימוֹן בֶּן גּוּרְיוֹן אֵצֶל הֶגְמוֹן אֶחָד, [12] אָמַר לוֹ: 'הַלְוֵינִי שְׁתֵּים עֶשְׂרֵה מַעְיְינוֹת מַיִם לְעוֹלֵי רְגָלִים, וַאֲנִי אֶתֵּן לְךָ שְׁתֵּים עֶשְׂרֵה עֵינוֹת מַיִם. [13] וְאִם אֵינִי נוֹתֵן לְךָ, הֲרֵינִי נוֹתֵן לְךָ שְׁתֵּים עֶשְׂרֵה כִּכַּר כֶּסֶף'.

RASHI

הכי גרסינן: מימיו מרובין — [אינן] כלין, וטיט מתגבל יפה. **מימיו מועטין** — הטיט אינו מתגבל יפה. מים אינן כלין, ויוכלו לגבל טיט הרבה כמה שירצה. **נקדימון בן גוריון** — עשיר גדול היה. **ואני אתן לך שנים עשר מעיינות מים** — כלומר, שירדו גשמים ויתמלאו כל המעיינות מים. אותן מעיינות לא היו נובעים מים כל כך, ואינן מתמלאין מאליהן כשאר מעיינות.

BACKGROUND

וְהַטִּיט מְגוּבָּל יָפֶה The clay is kneaded well. Mixing flour and water to make dough, like mixing earth with water to create mortar, does not simply produce a mixture, but changes the structure of the flour. This change is connected with certain chemical processes, the creation of molecules of a different structure. When there is enough water (provided in the right amount and at the right time), this process absorbs all the flour (or earth). But when there is a shortage of water, only some of the material is properly mixed in, and the rest sticks to the kneaded portions without being changed. Insufficient rain can make the plants sprout, but their growth will be impeded, and they will not ripen well because of the shortage of water.

SAGES

נַקְדִּימוֹן בֶּן גּוּרְיוֹן Nakdimon ben Guryon. He is mentioned several times in our sources as one of the richest men in Jerusalem at the time of the destruction of the Second Temple. He is also mentioned in the writings of Josephus. His Hebrew name was "Buni," as mentioned here in the text. He also had a Greek name, as was customary at that time, and this name was interpreted by the Sages in memory of the event associated with him.

LANGUAGE

נַקְדִּימוֹן Nakdimon ben Guryon. The source of this name seems to be the Greek Νικόδημος, *Nikodemos,* which means "the victor over the people."

הֶגְמוֹן Ruler. From the Greek ἡγεμών, *hegemon*, which has the meaning of "leader," especially a military leader, and which in a later period was used with specific reference to the Roman prefects. In the Talmud, the word is used in the sense of "ruler" or "high official."

NOTES

שְׁתֵּים עֶשְׂרֵה מַעְיָינוֹת Twelve wells. *Maharsha* writes that Nakdimon asked for twelve wells of water, hoping that the merits of the twelve tribes of Israel would help him to repay the loan, and that if their merits proved to be insufficient, the twelve talents of silver would atone for their transgressions.

TRANSLATION AND COMMENTARY

and set Nakdimon a **deadline.** [1]**When the day arrived** for the water to be returned, **and the rain had** still **not fallen,** [2]the Roman official **sent** Nakdimon a message early **in the morning:** 'The time has come for you to repay the loan. [3]**Send me** immediately **either the water or the money that you owe me.'** [4]Nakdimon **sent** the Roman official the following reply: **'I still have time** before I am required to repay the loan, **for the entire day is mine.** When we agreed that the loan would be extended until today, we meant that the loan would only become due at the end of the day.' [5]**At noon** the Roman official **sent him** another message: **'Send me** immediately **either the water or the money that you owe me.'** [6]Nakdimon **sent** the official the following reply: **'I still have time left in the day** to repay your loan.' [7]**In the afternoon** the Roman official **sent** back a message to Nakdimon: **'Send me** immediately **either the water or the money that you owe me!'** [8]Nakdimon **sent** back a reply, saying: **'I still have time left in the day.** The day is not over until sunset.' [9]**The Roman official scoffed at** Nakdimon, **saying:** [10]**'All year long, rain has** not fallen, [20A] and yet you still think that rain will fall now before the day is over?' [11]He entered the bathhouse joyfully, contemplating the money that he was shortly to receive. [12]**As the Roman official joyfully entered the bathhouse, Nakdimon sadly entered the Temple.** [13]**He wrapped himself** in his prayer shawl **and stood up in prayer,** [14]and **said to God: 'Master of the Universe!** [15]**You know full well that** when I made the agreement with the Roman official, **I did not act for my own** personal **honor, nor did I act for the honor of my father's house.** [16]**Rather, I acted for Your honor,** O God, **so that water would be available for** all **the pilgrims** who arrived in Jerusalem for the Festival. Cause it to rain now, so that Your holy Name is not desecrated.' [17]**Immediately the sky became filled with clouds, and rain fell** heavily **until the twelve wells** that Nakdimon had promised to replenish **were filled** with water **and overflowed.**

[1]וְקָבַע לוֹ זְמַן. כֵּיוָן שֶׁהִגִּיעַ
הַזְּמַן וְלֹא יָרְדוּ גְּשָׁמִים,
[2]בְּשַׁחֲרִית שָׁלַח לוֹ: [3]'שַׁגֵּר לִי
אוֹ מַיִם אוֹ מָעוֹת שֶׁיֵּשׁ לִי
בְּיָדְךָ'. [4]שָׁלַח לוֹ: 'עֲדַיִין יֵשׁ לִי
זְמַן, כָּל הַיּוֹם כּוּלּוֹ שֶׁלִּי הוּא'.
[5]בַּצָּהֳרַיִים שָׁלַח לוֹ: 'שַׁגֵּר לִי
אוֹ מַיִם אוֹ מָעוֹת שֶׁיֵּשׁ לִי
בְּיָדְךָ'. [6]שָׁלַח לוֹ: 'עֲדַיִין יֵשׁ לִי
שָׁהוּת בַּיּוֹם'. [7]בַּמִּנְחָה שָׁלַח
לוֹ: 'שַׁגֵּר לִי מַיִם אוֹ מָעוֹת
שֶׁיֵּשׁ לִי בְּיָדְךָ'. [8]שָׁלַח לוֹ:
'עֲדַיִין יֵשׁ לִי שָׁהוּת בַּיּוֹם'.
[9]לִגְלֵג עָלָיו אוֹתוֹ הֶגְמוֹן, אָמַר:
[10]'כָּל הַשָּׁנָה כּוּלָּהּ לֹא יָרְדוּ
גְּשָׁמִים, [20A] וְעַכְשָׁיו יֵרְדוּ
גְּשָׁמִים'? [11]נִכְנַס לְבֵית הַמֶּרְחָץ
בְּשִׂמְחָה. [12]עַד שֶׁהָאָדוֹן נִכְנַס
בְּשִׂמְחָתוֹ לְבֵית הַמֶּרְחָץ,
נַקְדִּימוֹן נִכְנַס לְבֵית הַמִּקְדָּשׁ
כְּשֶׁהוּא עָצוּב. [13]נִתְעַטֵּף וְעָמַד
בִּתְפִלָּה. [14]אָמַר לְפָנָיו: 'רִבּוֹנוֹ
שֶׁל עוֹלָם! [15]גָּלוּי וְיָדוּעַ לְפָנֶיךָ
שֶׁלֹּא לִכְבוֹדִי עָשִׂיתִי, וְלֹא
לִכְבוֹד בֵּית אַבָּא עָשִׂיתִי.
[16]אֶלָּא לִכְבוֹדְךָ עָשִׂיתִי, שֶׁיְּהוּ
מַיִם מְצוּיִין לְעוֹלֵי רְגָלִים'.
[17]מִיָּד נִתְקַשְּׁרוּ שָׁמַיִם בְּעָבִים,
וְיָרְדוּ גְּשָׁמִים עַד שֶׁנִּתְמַלְּאוּ
שְׁתֵּים עֶשְׂרֵה מַעְיָנוֹת מַיִם

LITERAL TRANSLATION

[1]And he set a time for him. When the time arrived and the rain had not fallen, [2]he sent to him in the morning: [3]'Send me either the water or the money that you owe me (lit., "that I have in your hand").' [4]He sent to him: 'I still have time, [for] the entire day is mine.' [5]At midday he sent to him: 'Send me either the water or the money that you owe me.' [6]He sent to him: 'I still have time left in the day.' [7]In the afternoon he sent to him: 'Send me the water or the money that you owe me.' [8]He sent to him: 'I still have time left in the day.' [9]That governor sneered at him [and] said: [10]'All year long rains have not fallen, [20A] and rains will fall now?' [11]He entered the bathhouse joyfully. [12]As the lord entered the bathhouse joyfully, Nakdimon entered the Temple in sadness. [13]He wrapped himself and stood in prayer. [14]He said before Him: 'Master of the Universe! [15]It is revealed and known before You that I did not do [this] for my [own] honor, nor did I do [it] for the honor of my father's house. [16]Rather, I did [it] for Your honor, so that water would be available for the pilgrims.' [17]Immediately the sky became covered with clouds, and rain fell until the twelve wells were filled

RASHI

ועכשיו ירדו גשמים — בתמיה.

NOTES

נִכְנַס לְבֵית הַמֶּרְחָץ He entered the bathhouse. *Maharsha* reads between the lines of this story and offers a number of insights into the actions and statements of the Roman official and of Nakdimon. The Roman official added insult to injury by entering the bathhouse when the Jews who had arrived in Jerusalem for the Festival did not even have water to drink. And similarly, Nakdimon meant to insult the official when he demanded payment for the extra water that had been added to his wells when it rained.

וְהוֹתִירוּ. [1]עַד שֶׁיָּצָא אָדוֹן מִבֵּית הַמֶּרְחָץ נַקְדִּימוֹן בֶּן גּוּרְיוֹן יָצָא מִבֵּית הַמִּקְדָּשׁ. [2]כְּשֶׁפָּגְעוּ זֶה בָּזֶה, אָמַר לוֹ: ׳תֵּן לִי דְּמֵי מַיִם יוֹתֵר שֶׁיֵּשׁ לִי בְּיָדְךָ׳. [3]אָמַר לוֹ: ׳יוֹדֵעַ אֲנִי שֶׁלֹּא הִרְעִישׁ הַקָּדוֹשׁ בָּרוּךְ הוּא אֶת עוֹלָמוֹ אֶלָּא בִּשְׁבִילְךָ. [4]אֶלָּא עֲדַיִין יֵשׁ לִי פִּתְחוֹן פֶּה עָלֶיךָ שֶׁאוֹצִיא מִמְּךָ אֶת מְעוֹתַיי, שֶׁכְּבָר שָׁקְעָה חַמָּה, וּגְשָׁמִים בִּרְשׁוּתִי יָרְדוּ׳. [5]חָזַר וְנִכְנַס לְבֵית הַמִּקְדָּשׁ, נִתְעַטֵּף וְעָמַד בִּתְפִלָּה, וְאָמַר לְפָנָיו: [6]׳רִבּוֹנוֹ שֶׁל עוֹלָם! הוֹדַע שֶׁיֵּשׁ לְךָ אֲהוּבִים בְּעוֹלָמְךָ׳. [7]מִיָּד נִתְפַּזְּרוּ הֶעָבִים וְזָרְחָה הַחַמָּה. [8]בְּאוֹתָהּ שָׁעָה אָמַר לוֹ הָאָדוֹן: ׳אִילּוּ לֹא נִקְדְּרָה הַחַמָּה, [9]הָיָה לִי פִּתְחוֹן פֶּה עָלֶיךָ שֶׁאוֹצִיא מִמְּךָ מְעוֹתַיי׳״. [10]תָּנָא: ״לֹא נַקְדִּימוֹן שְׁמוֹ, אֶלָּא בּוּנִי שְׁמוֹ. [11]וְלָמָּה נִקְרָא שְׁמוֹ נַקְדִּימוֹן? [12]שֶׁנִּקְדְּרָה חַמָּה בַּעֲבוּרוֹ״.

LITERAL TRANSLATION

and overflowed. [1]As the lord left the bathhouse, Nakdimon ben Guryon left the Temple. [2]When they met each other, he said to him: 'Give me the money of the extra water that you owe me.' [3]He said to him: 'I know that the Holy One, blessed be He, did not shake His world except on account of you. [4]But I still have a claim (lit., "an opening of the mouth") against you that I may collect my money from you, for the sun has already set, and the rains fell in my possession.' [5]He went back and entered the Temple, wrapped himself and stood in prayer, and said before Him: [6]'Master of the Universe! Make it known that You have loved ones in Your world.' [7]Immediately the clouds dispersed and the sun shone. [8]At that time the lord said to him: 'If the sun had not broken through, [9]I would have had a claim against you that I could have collected my money from you.'"

[10][A Sage] taught: "Nakdimon was not his name, but Buni was his name. [11]And why was his name called Nakdimon? [12]Because the sun broke through for his sake."

TRANSLATION AND COMMENTARY

[1]**As the** Roman **official was leaving the bathhouse, Nakdimon ben Guryon left the Temple.** [2]**When they met each other,** Nakdimon **said to** the Roman: 'Your wells have been replenished, and I owe you nothing more. But you must **give me the money you owe** *me* **for the extra water** that is now in your wells.' [3]The Roman official **said to** Nakdimon: **'I know that the Holy One, blessed be He, shook His world** and caused the rain to fall **only on account of you.** [4]**But I still have a claim against you on the basis of which** I can **collect from you the money** you owe me, **for** the day is already over, **the sun has already set, and** therefore **the rain** that just came down **fell in my possession.** We had agreed on a date by which my wells would have to be replenished, or else you would be obligated to hand over to me twelve talents of silver. Even though those wells have now been replenished, nevertheless since they were refilled after the date agreed upon had already passed, you still owe me the twelve talents of silver.' [5]Nakdimon **went back into the Temple, wrapped himself** again in his prayer shawl, **and stood up** a second time **in prayer, and said to God:** [6]**'Master of the Universe! Make it known** to all **that You have loved ones in Your world.** Just as you performed a miracle for us and caused it to rain, perform another miracle for us and allow the sun to shine, and thereby demonstrate the special relationship You maintain with the Jewish people.' [7]**Immediately, the clouds dispersed and the sun shone,** proving that it was still day and that the water that Nakdimon had borrowed had been returned in time. [8]**At that time the** Roman **official said to** Nakdimon: **'If the sun had not broken through** the clouds, [9]**I would** indeed **have had a claim against you on the basis of which I could have collected my money from you,** for I could have argued that my water had not been returned in time.'"

תָּנָא [10]**A Sage taught** the following Baraita: **"Nakdimon was not his** real **name; his** real **name was Buni.** [11]**Why, then, was he called Nakdimon?** [12]**Because the sun broke through** the clouds and shone **on his account."** The name Nakdimon (נַקְדִּימוֹן) is connected here with the word "broke through" (נִקְדְּרָה) and alludes to the story related in the Baraita cited above.

RASHI

בוני — שמו. **נקדרה** — זרחה, לשון מקדיר, שהיתה חמה קודרת ברקיע וזורחת, *פירטוז״ר בלעז.

LANGUAGE (RASHI)

פירטוצ״ר* From the Old French *forfais,* which means "to penetrate," or "to break through."

NOTES

שֶׁנִּקְדְּרָה חַמָּה בַּעֲבוּרוֹ The sun broke through for his sake. According to the reading found in the standard text of our Gemara (נִקְדְּרָה), as well as according to the reading (נָקְדָה) found in a parallel passage in *Gittin* (56a), the sun "broke through" the clouds and shone for Nakdimon's sake. But according to the readings found in certain manuscripts and editions, as well as in certain Rishonim — נִקְדְּמָה לוֹ חַמָּה (see *Rabbenu Ḥananel*), or עָמְדָה לוֹ חַמָּה (see *Baḥ*) — it

[1]תָּנוּ רַבָּנַן: ״שְׁלֹשָׁה נִקְדְּמָה
לָהֶם חַמָּה בַּעֲבוּרָן: [2]מֹשֶׁה,
וִיהוֹשֻׁעַ, וְנַקְדִּימוֹן בֶּן גּוּרְיוֹן״.
[3]בִּשְׁלָמָא נַקְדִּימוֹן בֶּן גּוּרְיוֹן,
גְּמָרָא. [4]יְהוֹשֻׁעַ נַמִּי קְרָא,
דִּכְתִיב: ״וַיִּדֹּם הַשֶּׁמֶשׁ וְיָרֵחַ
עָמָד, וגו׳״. [5]אֶלָּא מֹשֶׁה מְנָלַן?
[6]אֲמַר רַבִּי אֶלְעָזָר: אָתְיָא
״אָחֵל״, ״אָחֵל״. [7]כְּתִיב הָכָא:
״אָחֵל תֵּת פַּחְדְּךָ״. [8]וּכְתִיב
הָתָם: ״אָחֵל גַּדֶּלְךָ״.
[9]רַבִּי שְׁמוּאֵל בַּר נַחְמָנִי אֲמַר:
אָתְיָא ״תֵּת״, ״תֵּת״. [10]כְּתִיב
הָכָא: ״אָחֵל תֵּת פַּחְדְּךָ״.
[11]וּכְתִיב הָתָם: ״בְּיוֹם תֵּת ה׳
אֶת הָאֱמֹרִי״.

TRANSLATION AND COMMENTARY

תָּנוּ רַבָּנַן [1]The Gemara adds: **Our Rabbis taught** the following Baraita: **"For three** people **the sun delayed its setting** and continued to shine: [2]**Moses, Joshua, and Nakdimon ben Guryon."**

בִּשְׁלָמָא [3]The Gemara explains: **Granted** that regarding **Nakdimon ben Guryon, we have** the **tradition** mentioned above that the sun continued to shine beyond its normal time for setting. [4]Regarding **Joshua also, there is a verse** that teaches that the sun continued to shine for him and sunset was delayed, **for the verse says** (Joshua 10:13): **"And the sun stood still, and the moon stayed,** until the people had avenged themselves upon their enemies." [5]**But** as for **Moses, from where do we know** that the sun continued to shine beyond its usual time for setting?

אֲמַר רַבִּי אֶלְעָזָר [6]**Rabbi Elazar said** in reply: This can be derived from an inference based on the hermeneutical principle of *gezerah shavah*, the comparison of similar expressions used in two Biblical texts. If the same word appears in two Biblical passages, what is stated explicitly with respect to one passage may also be applied to the other. In our case, the expression, **"I will begin,"** mentioned with respect to Moses, **can be understood in the light of** the same expression, **"I will begin,"** mentioned with respect to Joshua. [7]**Here** (Deuteronomy 2:25), regarding Moses, **the verse says:** "This day **I will begin** [אָחֵל] **to give your dread** and your fear upon the nations that are under the whole heaven, who shall hear the report of you, and shall tremble and quake because of you." [8]**And elsewhere** (Joshua 3:7), regarding Joshua, **the verse says:** "This day **I will begin** [אָחֵל] **to magnify you** in the sight of all Israel, that they may know that as I was with Moses, so I will be with you." Since the Bible uses the same expression, "I will begin," with respect to both Moses and Joshua, we can infer that just as the sun delayed setting on behalf of Joshua, it likewise delayed setting on behalf of Moses.

רַבִּי שְׁמוּאֵל בַּר נַחְמָנִי [9]**Rabbi Shmuel bar Nahmani said:** The matter is indeed derived by means of a *gezerah shavah*, but not the one suggested by Rabbi Elazar. The word **"give"** mentioned with respect to Moses **can be interpreted in the light of** the same word **"give"** mentioned with respect to Joshua. [10]**Here** (Deuteronomy 2:25), regarding Moses, **the verse says:** "This day **I will begin to give** [תֵּת] **your dread** and your fear upon the nations, etc." [11]**And elsewhere** (Joshua 10:12), regarding Joshua, **the verse says:** "Then Joshua spoke to the Lord **on the day when the Lord gave** [תֵּת] **the Amorite** before the children of Israel, and he said in the sight of Israel: Sun, stand still upon Gibeon; and moon, in the valley of Ajalon." The appearance of the word "give" in both passages allows us to infer that just as the sun delayed setting on behalf of Joshua, it also did so for Moses.

LITERAL TRANSLATION

[1]Our Rabbis taught: "For three the sun was delayed: [2]Moses, Joshua, and Nakdimon ben Guryon."

[3]Granted [regarding] Nakdimon ben Guryon [we have] a tradition. [4][Regarding] Joshua too [we have] a verse, for it is written: "And the sun stood still, and the moon stayed, etc." [5]But [regarding] Moses from where do we [know this]?

[6]Rabbi Elazar said: It is learned (lit., "it comes") [from] "I will begin," "I will begin." [7]It is written here: "I will begin to give your dread." [8]And it is written there: "I will begin to magnify you."

[9]Rabbi Shmuel bar Nahmani said: It is learned from "give," "give." [10]It is written here: "I will begin to give your dread." [11]And it written there: "On the day when the Lord gave the Amorite."

RASHI

הכי גרסינן — נקדימון בן גוריון הא דאמרן. אתיא אחל אחל — כתיב במלחמת יהושע (יהושע ג) ״אחל גדלך״ ובמלחמת משה כתיב (דברים ב) ״אחל תת פחדך״, מה יהושע נקדמה לו חמה במלחמתו, כדכתיב בהדיא — אף משה כן. שכן דרך הכתובין, למד סתום מן המפורש ברמז בדיבור דומה לחבירו. וגזירה שוה אחת מן שלש עשרה מדות שניתנו לו למשה מסיני, ובתחילת סיפרא מפורש.

NOTES

would seem that the sun shone for Nakdimon's sake at a time when it should already have set. This is also consistent with the next Baraita, which lists Nakdimon together with Joshua — suggesting that the sun shone for Nakdimon at a time when it should already have set, just as it had for Joshua. *Maharsha* explains that the miracle performed for Nakdimon was that the sun did not set at the appointed time, but remained in the sky until the clouds dispersed, proving to the Roman official that it was still day and that his claim for payment was invalid.

[1]רַבִּי יוֹחָנָן אֲמַר: אָתְיָא מִגּוּפֵיהּ דִּקְרָא: [2]״אֲשֶׁר יִשְׁמְעוּן שִׁמְעֲךָ, וְרָגְזוּ וְחָלוּ מִפָּנֶיךָ״. [3]אֵימָתַי רָגְזוּ וְחָלוּ מִפָּנֶיךָ? [4]בְּשָׁעָה שֶׁנִּקְדְּמָה לוֹ חַמָּה לְמשֶׁה.

[5]״וְכֵן עִיר שֶׁלֹּא יָרְדוּ עָלֶיהָ גְּשָׁמִים, כו׳״. [6]אָמַר רַב יְהוּדָה אָמַר רַב: וּשְׁתֵּיהֶן לִקְלָלָה.

[7]״הָיְתָה יְרוּשָׁלַיִם לְנִדָּה בֵּינֵיהֶם״. [8]אָמַר רַב יְהוּדָה אָמַר רַב: לִבְרָכָה. [9]כְּנִדָּה — מַה נִּדָּה יֵשׁ לָהּ הֶיתֵּר, [10]אַף יְרוּשָׁלַיִם יֵשׁ לָהּ תַּקָּנָה.

[11]״הָיְתָה כְּאַלְמָנָה״. [12]אָמַר רַב יְהוּדָה: לִבְרָכָה. כְּאַלְמָנָה, [13]וְלֹא אַלְמָנָה מַמָּשׁ. [14]אֶלָּא כְּאִשָּׁה שֶׁהָלַךְ בַּעְלָהּ לִמְדִינַת הַיָּם, [15]וְדַעְתּוֹ לַחֲזוֹר עָלֶיהָ.

LITERAL TRANSLATION

[1]Rabbi Yoḥanan said: It is learned from the verse itself: [2]"Who shall hear the report of you, and shall tremble and quake because of you." [3]When did they tremble and quake because of you? [4]At the time when the sun was delayed for Moses.

[5]"And similarly, [regarding] a city on which rains did not fall, etc." [6]Rav Yehudah said in the name of Rav: And both of them are for a curse.

[7]"Jerusalem is like a menstruating woman among them." [8]Rav Yehudah said in the name of Rav: For a blessing. [9]Like a menstruating woman — just as a menstruating woman will become permitted, [10]so too will Jerusalem be restored.

[11]"She has become like a widow." [12]Rav Yehudah said: For a blessing. Like a widow, [13]but not actually a widow. [14]Rather, [she is] like a woman whose husband has gone abroad (lit., "to a country overseas"), [15]but his intention is to return to her.

TRANSLATION AND COMMENTARY

רַבִּי יוֹחָנָן אֲמַר [1]**Rabbi Yoḥanan said:** That the sun continued to shine especially for Moses need not be derived by means of a *gezerah shavah*, for **it can be learned from the verse itself** that refers to Moses (Deuteronomy 2:25): "This day I will begin to give your dread and your fear upon the nations that are under the whole heaven, [2]**who shall hear the report of you, and shall tremble and quake because of you."** [3]And it may be asked: **When did** all the nations that are under Heaven **tremble and quake because of** Moses? [4]Surely, it was **when the sun delayed setting for Moses** and shone especially for him.

וְכֵן עִיר [5]The Gemara now proceeds to analyze the next clause of the Mishnah, which stated: **"And similarly, if rain did not fall on a** particular **city,** but it did rain as usual in all of the surrounding areas, as the verse says (Amos 4:7): 'And I will cause it to rain on one city, but on one city I will not cause it to rain,' the people living in that city where the rain has not fallen must fast and sound the alarm, whereas the people living in the surrounding areas must fast, but they are not required to sound the alarm." [6]**Rav Yehudah said in the name of Rav: The two** cities mentioned in the verse — both the city where there was no rainfall, as well as the city on which it rained — **were cursed.** God punished both cities, one with excessive rain and the other with drought.

הָיְתָה יְרוּשָׁלַיִם [7]Having cited Rav Yehudah's interpretation of what appears to be a blessing as in fact being a curse, the Gemara continues with four cases in which Rav Yehudah interprets Biblical verses in the opposite direction, taking a seeming curse and explaining it as in fact being a blessing. (1) The verse says (Lamentations 1:17): **"Jerusalem is like a menstruating woman among them."** According to the plain meaning of the verse, Jerusalem is viewed as a place from which people wish to keep their distance, just as is the case with a menstruating woman. [8]But **Rav Yehudah said in the name of Rav:** This verse should be understood **as a blessing.** [9]Jerusalem is **like a menstruating woman. Just as a menstruating woman will become permitted** to her husband after her days of ritual impurity come to an end, [10]**so too will Jerusalem be restored** one day to its former greatness.

הָיְתָה כְּאַלְמָנָה [11](2) According to its plain meaning, the verse (Lamentations 1:1), **"She has become like a widow,"** should also be understood as a curse. The city of Jerusalem, which had once been teeming with people, is described as sitting solitary, just like a widow who has lost her husband. [12]But **Rav Yehudah said:** This verse should be understood **as a blessing.** [13]Jerusalem is ***like*** **a widow, but** she is **not actually a widow.** [14]**Rather,** Jerusalem **is to be compared to a woman whose husband has gone abroad** for an extended period of time, [15]but **his intention is to return to her.** Jerusalem may be compared to such a woman, for her heavenly husband has temporarily taken leave of her, but He too is sure to return.

RASHI

שתיהן לקללה — אקרא קאי, האי דכתיב "על עיר אחת אמטיר ועל עיר אחת לא אמטיר" — שניהם לקללה: אותה שימטיר עליה — רוב גשמים שמקלקלין את התבואה, ואת שלא ימטיר — אין גשמים ואין תבואה גדילה. "אשר לא תמטיר עליה" מוסב הדבר על העב, שהעב בלשון נקיבה, דכתיב (מלכים א׳ יח) "הנה עב קטנה ככף איש עולה מים". **ולא אלמנה גמורה** — דהא לא כתיב "אלמנה" אלא "היתה כאלמנה" — כאשה העומדת באלמנות חיות על בעלה שהלך ועתיד לחזור.

LANGUAGE

גְּזִירִיפַּטֵי Police officers. This seems to be the Persian word *gazir-pat*, which means "the chief of police," "the head of the local force."

LANGUAGE (RASHI)

פורק״א* From the Old French *forche,* which means "fork."

אינקרי״ש** From the Old French *encres,* which means "superfluous," or "unnecessary."

BACKGROUND

קָנֶה Reed.

The reed mentioned in the sources could be the common reed, *Phragmites communis,* or else the *Arundo dopax.* These are species of perennial grasses with straight stems two to four meters in height. Normally these reeds grow in dense clumps along the banks of rivers or next to other bodies of water. Reeds were used to make fences and to weave coarse mats. They were also used to make pens, mainly for writing large letters with ink.

TRANSLATION AND COMMENTARY

וְגַם אֲנִי [1](3) At first glance, the verse (Malachi 2:9), **"And I too have made you contemptible and base** before all the people," is also a curse. [2]But **Rav Yehudah said:** This verse should be understood **as a blessing** in disguise. Their non-Jewish captors will find the Jews so contemptible [3]**that they will refrain from appointing them** to serve **as river officials** in charge of collecting customs duties, **or** as **police officers** in charge of maintaining public order, two difficult and unpleasant positions.

וְהִכָּה ה׳ [4](4) It was stated in the curse pronounced upon the people of Israel by Ahijah the Shilonite (I Kings 14:15): **"And the Lord shall smite Israel as a reed is shaken in the water."** Although the simple meaning of the verse is that Ahijah the Shilonite meant these words as a curse foretelling the destruction of the Kingdom of Israel, [5]**Rav Yehudah said in the name of Rav:** This verse should be understood **as a blessing,** [6]**as Rabbi Shmuel bar Naḥmani explained in the name of Rabbi Yonatan:** [7]**What is meant by** the verse (Proverbs 27:6): **"Faithful are the wounds of a friend; but the kisses of an enemy are deceitful"?** This can be illustrated by a comparison of the curse pronounced upon Israel by Ahijah the Shilonite and the blessing given to them by Balaam. [8]Far **better is the curse that Ahijah the Shilonite laid upon Israel, than the blessing that Balaam the wicked bestowed upon them.** [9]The Gemara explains: **Ahijah the Shilonite cursed** the Jewish people by comparing it **to a reed,** [10]for **he said** with respect **to Israel: "And the Lord shall smite Israel as a reed is shaken in the water."** Ostensibly, this appears to be a malediction, but when one analyzes the comparison more carefully, Ahijah's words reveal themselves as containing a blessing. [11]The Jewish people will be **like a reed** that **stands in a place where there is** much **water, and** when it is cut down **its stem grows new shoots, and its roots are many** in proportion to its size, [12]**so that even if all the winds of the world come and blow on it, they cannot uproot it from its place,** [13]**but** the reed **moves back and forth** together **with** the **wind, and when the winds have subsided, the reed** still **stands in its** original

[1]״וְגַם אֲנִי נָתַתִּי אֶתְכֶם נִבְזִים וּשְׁפָלִים״. [2]אָמַר רַב יְהוּדָה: לִבְרָכָה, [3]דְּלָא מוֹקְמִי מִינַּן לָא רֵישֵׁי נַהֲרֵי וְלָא גְּזִירִיפַּטֵי. [4]״וְהִכָּה ה׳ אֶת יִשְׂרָאֵל כַּאֲשֶׁר יָנוּד הַקָּנֶה בַּמַּיִם״. [5]אָמַר רַב יְהוּדָה אָמַר רַב: לִבְרָכָה. [6]דְּאָמַר רַבִּי שְׁמוּאֵל בַּר נַחְמָנִי אָמַר רַבִּי יוֹנָתָן: [7]מַאי דִּכְתִיב: ״נֶאֱמָנִים פִּצְעֵי אוֹהֵב וְנַעְתָּרוֹת נְשִׁיקוֹת שׂוֹנֵא״? [8]טוֹבָה קְלָלָה שֶׁקִּילֵּל אֲחִיָּה הַשִּׁילוֹנִי אֶת יִשְׂרָאֵל יוֹתֵר מִבְּרָכָה שֶׁבֵּרְכָן בִּלְעָם הָרָשָׁע. [9]אֲחִיָּה הַשִּׁילוֹנִי קִלְּלָן בְּקָנֶה. [10]אָמַר לָהֶם לְיִשְׂרָאֵל: ״וְהִכָּה ה׳ אֶת יִשְׂרָאֵל כַּאֲשֶׁר יָנוּד הַקָּנֶה״. [11]מַה קָּנֶה זֶה עוֹמֵד בִּמְקוֹם מַיִם, וְגִזְעוֹ מַחֲלִיף, וְשָׁרָשָׁיו מְרוּבִּין, [12]וַאֲפִילּוּ כָּל הָרוּחוֹת שֶׁבָּעוֹלָם בָּאוֹת וְנוֹשְׁבוֹת בּוֹ, אֵין מְזִיזוֹת אוֹתוֹ מִמְּקוֹמוֹ, [13]אֶלָּא הוֹלֵךְ וּבָא עִמָּהֶן, דָּמְמוּ הָרוּחוֹת, עָמַד הַקָּנֶה בִּמְקוֹמוֹ.

LITERAL TRANSLATION

[1]"And I too have made you contemptible and base." [2]Rav Yehudah said: For a blessing, [3]that they do not appoint from us river officials (lit., "heads") or police officers.

[4]"And the Lord shall smite Israel as a reed is shaken in the water." [5]Rav Yehudah said in the name of Rav: For a blessing. [6]For Rabbi Shmuel bar Naḥmani said in the name of Rabbi Yonatan: [7]What is [it] that is written: "Faithful are the wounds of a friend; but the kisses of an enemy are deceitful"? [8]The curse that Ahijah the Shilonite cursed Israel is better than the blessing that Balaam the wicked blessed them. [9]Ahijah the Shilonite cursed them with a reed. [10]He said to Israel: "And the Lord shall smite Israel as a reed is shaken [in the water]." [11]Just as this reed stands in a place of water, and its stem grows again, and its roots are many, [12]and even [if] all the winds of the world come and blow on it, they do not move it from its place, [13]but it goes and comes with them, [and when] the winds have subsided, the reed stands

RASHI

דלא מוקמי מינן רישי נהרי — מוכסין. גזיריפטי — סרדיוטין, מרוב בזיון. ונעתרות נשיקות שונא — ״נעתרות״ לשון הפך, כדאמרינן במסכת סוכה (יד,א): ״ויעתר לו״, מה עתר זה מהפך את התבואה — *פורקא בלעז. אי נמי: ״נעתרות״ — לשון רבוי וייתור, **אינקרי״ש בלעז, כמו ״העתרתם עלי דבריכם״ (יחזקאל לה).

NOTES

דְּלָא מוֹקְמִי מִינַּן רֵישֵׁי נַהֲרֵי That they do not appoint from us river officials. *Rabbenu Gershom* explains that it was beneficial for the Jews not to be appointed as customs officials or as police officers, for were they appointed to such positions, they would surely stir up the anger and jealousy of their non-Jewish neighbors. *Rabbenu Elyakim* adds that if they were not assigned such tasks, they would have more time to devote to Torah study.

[1]אֲבָל בִּלְעָם הָרָשָׁע בֵּירְכָן בְּאֶרֶז, שֶׁנֶּאֱמַר: [2]״כַּאֲרָזִים עֲלֵי מָיִם״ [3]מָה אֶרֶז זֶה אֵינוֹ עוֹמֵד בִּמְקוֹם מַיִם, וְאֵין גִּזְעוֹ מַחֲלִיף, וְאֵין שָׁרָשָׁיו מְרוּבִּין, [4]אֲפִילּוּ כָּל הָרוּחוֹת שֶׁבָּעוֹלָם נוֹשְׁבוֹת בּוֹ, אֵין מְזִיזוֹת אוֹתוֹ מִמְּקוֹמוֹ, [5]כֵּיוָן שֶׁנָּשְׁבָה בּוֹ רוּחַ דְּרוֹמִית, עוֹקַרְתּוֹ וְהוֹפַכְתּוֹ עַל פָּנָיו. [6]וְלֹא עוֹד אֶלָּא שֶׁזָּכָה קָנֶה לִיטּוֹל הֵימֶנּוּ קוּלְמוֹס לִכְתּוֹב בּוֹ סֵפֶר תּוֹרָה, נְבִיאִים, וּכְתוּבִים.

[7]תָּנוּ רַבָּנַן: ״לְעוֹלָם יְהֵא אָדָם רַךְ כְּקָנֶה וְאַל יְהֵא קָשֶׁה כְּאֶרֶז. [8]מַעֲשֶׂה שֶׁבָּא רַבִּי אֶלְעָזָר בְּרַבִּי שִׁמְעוֹן מִמִּגְדַּל גְּדוֹר מִבֵּית רַבּוֹ, [9]וְהָיָה רָכוּב עַל חֲמוֹר וּמְטַיֵּיל עַל שְׂפַת נָהָר. [10]וְשָׂמֵחַ שִׂמְחָה גְּדוֹלָה, וְהָיְתָה דַּעְתּוֹ גַּסָּה עָלָיו מִפְּנֵי שֶׁלָּמַד תּוֹרָה הַרְבֵּה.

LITERAL TRANSLATION

in its place. [1]But Balaam the wicked blessed them with a cedar, as it is said: [2]"Like cedar trees beside the waters." [3]Just as this cedar does not stand in a place of water, and its stump does not grow again, and its roots are not many, [4][and] even [if] all the winds of the world blow on it, they do not move it from its place, [5][but] if a southerly wind blows on it, it uproots it and turns it over on its face. [6]And moreover, the reed merited that a pen be taken from it with which to write the scroll of the Torah, the Prophets, and the Writings.

[7]Our Rabbis taught: "A person should always be soft as a reed, and should not be hard as a cedar. [8]It once happened that Rabbi Elazar the son of Rabbi Shimon was coming from Migdal Gedor from the house of his teacher, [9]and he was riding on an ass and traveling along a riverbank. [10]And he was very happy, and he was proud of himself because he had learned much Torah.

TRANSLATION AND COMMENTARY

place. [1]**But Balaam the wicked blessed** the Jewish people by comparing it **to a cedar tree, as it is said** (Numbers 24:5-6): "How goodly are your tents, O Jacob, and your tabernacles, O Israel. Like the winding brooks, like gardens by the river's side, like aloes which the Lord has planted, [2]and **like cedar trees beside the waters."** Ostensibly, Balaam seems to be blessing the Jewish people, but upon closer examination his words reveal a hidden curse. [3]The Jewish people will be **like a cedar** tree that **does not stand in a place where there is** much **water, and** when it is cut down **its stump does not grow new shoots, and its roots are not many** in proportion to its great size, [4]**so that even though all the** weaker **winds may blow on it and are unable to move it from its place,** [5]yet **if a** strong **southerly wind blows on it,** it **can uproot** the tree **and turn it over.** [6]**Moreover,** there is another reason why we should understand the comparison of the Jewish people to a reed as a blessing. For **the reed was privileged to supply the pen used to write the scrolls of the Torah, the Prophets, and the Writings.** In Talmudic times, the handwritten scrolls of the Torah, the Prophets, and the Writings were written with pens made of reed. But the cedar tree has no such sacred purpose. The woodcutters merely fashion the cedar into beams for building, or chop it into firewood. Thus we see that the curse that Ahijah the Shilonite laid upon Israel by comparing them to a reed is preferable to the blessing bestowed upon them by Balaam by comparing them to a cedar.

תָּנוּ רַבָּנַן [7]The Gemara now cites a Baraita in which the qualities of a reed are found to be preferable to those of a cedar. **Our Rabbis taught: "A person should always** endeavor to **be soft** in his relations with other people, like **a reed** that yields even to a gentle breeze, **and should not be hard** on others, **like a cedar** that stands firm even against a strong wind. [8]This lesson may be illustrated by the following story: **It once happened that Rabbi Elazar the son of Rabbi Shimon was returning** home **from the house of his teacher in Migdal Gedor.** [9]**He** made his way home **riding on an ass, and traveled** happily **along a riverbank.** [10]While he had been away, **he had become** very **proud of himself**

RASHI

בירכן בארז – ״כארזים עלי מים״ (במדבר כד). **ארז זה אינו עומד במקום מים כו׳** – ואף על גב דכתיב בקרא ״כארזים עלי מים״ – ההוא לאו בלעם קאמר ליה, דבלעם אמר ״כארזים״ והמלאך השיבו ״עלי מים״. וכן כולהו, דבלעם אמר ״כנחלים״ דזימנין מתייבשין – וקאמר ליה המלאך ״נטיו״, דאין יבישין לעולם. והיינו דכתיב ״ויהפוך ה׳ אלהיך לך את הקללה לברכה״ על ידי מלאך, שהשיבו על ידי מלאך. **ואפילו כל הרוחות** – שאינן קשות. **רוח דרומית** – שהיא קשה, כדאמרינן (בבא בתרא כה,ב): אילמלא בן נץ שמעמידה – אין כל בריה יכולה לעמוד מפניה, שנאמר ״המבינתך יאבר נץ יפרש כנפיו לתימן״. **ומטייל** – לשמות.

LANGUAGE

קוּלְמוֹס Pen. The source of this word is the Greek κάλαμος, *kalamos*, which means "reed," for pens were made from reeds.

BACKGROUND

אֶרֶז Cedar. The cedar tree can attain enormous size. However, since it grows in the mountains, where the soil is not deep, its roots tend to be shallow. Since the prevailing winds in the Middle East blow from the west or the north, the tree develops roots to resist those winds. But if a storm comes from the south, which is not common but does occasionally happen, it may uproot the tree.

מִגְדַּל גְּדוֹר Migdal Gador. The precise location of Migdal Gador is not known. Some authorities maintain that it was a small settlement between Hamat Gader and Gader. According to that view, Rabbi Elazar walked along the Yarmuk River.

HALAKHAH

זָכָה קָנֶה The reed merited. "According to some authorities, a Torah scroll must be written with a pen made from a reed, and not with a quill (*Rema*, in the name of *Mordekhai*). But *Shakh* (following *Levush*) states that the common custom does not follow this ruling. Today, Ashkenazi scribes use a quill, while their Sephardi counterparts use a reed." (*Shulḥan Arukh*, *Yoreh De'ah* 271:7.)

LANGUAGE

רֵיקָה **Worthless person.** This expression was apparently very commonly used by people of that time, for it also appears in non-Jewish sources. It is the Aramaic form of the Hebrew word רֵיק, meaning "empty," as used, for example, in Judges 11:3: "Men of low character [אֲנָשִׁים רֵיקִים] gathered around Jephthah." As translated here, it means people without manners or morals.

TRANSLATION AND COMMENTARY

and felt himself superior to others **because he had learned much Torah** in his teacher's house. [20B] [1]On his way, Rabbi Elazar the son of Rabbi Shimon **happened to meet a certain man who was extremely ugly.** [2]Recognizing the Torah scholar, the man **said to** Rabbi Elazar: **'Peace be unto you, my teacher.'** [3]But Rabbi Elazar **did not return his greeting.** [4]Instead, **he said to him: 'Worthless person, how ugly you are! [5]Are all the people of your city as ugly as you?'** [6]The man **said to** Rabbi Elazar: **'I do not know, [7]but you should go and tell the craftsman who fashioned me: "How ugly is this vessel that you made!"** It is not my fault that I am ugly. If you have any complaints, you can go and make them to God Himself, for it is He who made me the way I am.' [8]**As soon as** Rabbi Elazar **understood that he had sinned** and had gratuitously humiliated another person, **he got down from his ass, prostrated himself before** the man whom he had insulted, [9]**and said to him: 'I have sinned toward you. Forgive me!'** [10]The man refused to accept his apology and **said to him: 'I will not forgive you until you go to the craftsman who** made me and say to him: [11]**"How ugly is this vessel that you made!"'** [12]The man walked away, and Rabbi Elazar the son of Rabbi Shimon **followed after him,** continuing in his efforts to appease him, **until he reached his** own **city.** [13]When **the people of** Rabbi Elazar's **city** sighted the returning Talmudic scholar, they **went out to greet him, and said to him:** [14]**'Peace be unto you, teacher, teacher, master, master.'** [15]The man whom Rabbi Elazar had insulted **said to** the townsmen: **'Whom do you address** with such deference, calling him your **teacher?'** [16]They said to him: 'We are greeting the man **who is following you,** Rabbi Elazar the son of Rabbi Shimon.' [17]The man **said to them: 'If this man is a** Torah **scholar, let there not be many like him in Israel!'** [18]Astonished by his remark, the townsmen **said to him: 'Why** do you say such things?' [19]The man **said to them: 'He did such-and-such to me,'** and he recounted the entire episode to them. [20]Shocked as they were by the story, Rabbi Elazar's townsmen **said to** the man whom their master had insulted: **'Even so,** you must **forgive him, for he is a man who is great in Torah** knowledge.' The man

LITERAL TRANSLATION

[20B] [1]A certain man happened to meet him who was extremely ugly. [2]He said to him: 'Peace be unto you, my teacher.' [3]But he did not return his [greeting]. [4]He said to him: 'Worthless person, how ugly is that man! [5]Are all the people of your city as ugly as you?' [6]He said to him: 'I do not know, [7]but go and say to the craftsman who made me: "How ugly is this vessel that you made!"' [8]When he understood that he had sinned, he got down from the ass and prostrated himself before him, [9]and said to him: 'I have sinned toward you, forgive me!' [10]He said to him: 'I will not forgive you until you go to the craftsman who made me and say to him: [11]"How ugly is this vessel that you made!"' [12]He traveled behind him until he came to his city. [13]The people of his city went out toward him, and they said to him: [14]'Peace be unto you, teacher, teacher, master, master.' [15]He said to them: 'Whom do you call "teacher, teacher"?' [16]They said to him: 'The man who is traveling after you.' [17]He said to them: 'If this [man] is a teacher let there not be many like him in Israel!' [18]They said to him: 'Why?' [19]He said to them: 'He did such-and-such to me.' [20]They said to him: 'Even so, forgive him, for he is a man [who is] great in Torah.'

[20B] [1]נִזְדַּמֵּן לוֹ אָדָם אֶחָד שֶׁהָיָה מְכוֹעָר בְּיוֹתֵר. [2]אָמַר לוֹ: 'שָׁלוֹם עָלֶיךָ, רַבִּי'. [3]וְלֹא הֶחֱזִיר לוֹ. [4]אָמַר לוֹ: 'רֵיקָה, כַּמָּה מְכוֹעָר אוֹתוֹ הָאִישׁ! [5]שֶׁמָּא כָּל בְּנֵי עִירְךָ מְכוֹעָרִין כְּמוֹתְךָ?' [6]אָמַר לוֹ: 'אֵינִי יוֹדֵעַ, [7]אֶלָּא לֵךְ וֶאֱמוֹר לָאוּמָּן שֶׁעֲשָׂאַנִי: "כַּמָּה מְכוֹעָר כְּלִי זֶה שֶׁעָשִׂיתָ!"' [8]כֵּיוָן שֶׁיָּדַע בְּעַצְמוֹ שֶׁחָטָא, יָרַד מִן הַחֲמוֹר וְנִשְׁתַּטַּח לְפָנָיו, [9]וְאָמַר לוֹ: 'נֶעֱנֵיתִי לְךָ, מְחוֹל לִי!' [10]אָמַר לוֹ: 'אֵינִי מוֹחֵל לְךָ עַד שֶׁתֵּלֵךְ לָאוּמָּן שֶׁעֲשָׂאַנִי וֶאֱמוֹר לוֹ: [11]"כַּמָּה מְכוֹעָר כְּלִי זֶה שֶׁעָשִׂיתָ!"' [12]הָיָה מְטַיֵּיל אַחֲרָיו עַד שֶׁהִגִּיעַ לְעִירוֹ. [13]יָצְאוּ בְּנֵי עִירוֹ לִקְרָאתוֹ, וְהָיוּ אוֹמְרִים לוֹ: [14]'שָׁלוֹם עָלֶיךָ, רַבִּי, רַבִּי, מוֹרִי, מוֹרִי'. [15]אָמַר לָהֶם: 'לְמִי אַתֶּם קוֹרִין "רַבִּי, רַבִּי"?' [16]אָמְרוּ לוֹ: 'לָזֶה שֶׁמְטַיֵּיל אַחֲרֶיךָ'. [17]אָמַר לָהֶם: 'אִם זֶה רַבִּי, אַל יִרְבּוּ כְּמוֹתוֹ בְּיִשְׂרָאֵל!' [18]אָמְרוּ לוֹ: 'מִפְּנֵי מָה?' [19]אָמַר לָהֶם: 'כָּךְ וְכָךְ עָשָׂה לִי'. [20]אָמְרוּ לוֹ: 'אַף עַל פִּי כֵן, מְחוֹל לוֹ, שֶׁאָדָם גָּדוֹל בַּתּוֹרָה

RASHI

נזדמן לו אדם — יש ספרים שכתוב נהן: אליהו זכור לטוב.

NOTES

כַּמָּה מְכוֹעָר אוֹתוֹ הָאִישׁ **How ugly is that man.** *Iyyun Ya'akov* explains that Rabbi Elazar the son of Rabbi Shimon was not commenting on the physical ugliness of the man's face, but was castigating him for the ignorance and

הוא׳. [1]אָמַר לָהֶם: ׳בִּשְׁבִילְכֶם הֲרֵינִי מוֹחֵל לוֹ, וּבִלְבַד שֶׁלֹּא יְהֵא רָגִיל לַעֲשׂוֹת כֵּן׳. [2]מִיָּד נִכְנַס רַבִּי אֶלְעָזָר בְּרַבִּי שִׁמְעוֹן וְדָרַשׁ: [3]לְעוֹלָם יְהֵא אָדָם רַךְ כְּקָנֶה וְאַל יְהֵא קָשֶׁה כְּאֶרֶז. [4]וּלְפִיכָךְ זָכָה קָנֶה לִיטּוֹל הֵימֶנָּה קוּלְמוֹס לִכְתּוֹב בּוֹ סֵפֶר תּוֹרָה, תְּפִילִּין, וּמְזוּזוֹת״.

[5]״וְכֵן עִיר שֶׁיֵּשׁ בָּהּ דֶּבֶר אוֹ מַפּוֹלֶת, כו׳״. [6]תָּנוּ רַבָּנַן: ״מַפּוֹלֶת שֶׁאָמְרוּ בְּרִיאוֹת וְלֹא רְעוּעוֹת; [7]שֶׁאֵינָן רְאוּיוֹת לִיפּוֹל, וְלֹא הָרְאוּיוֹת לִיפּוֹל״.

[8]הֵי נִיהוּ בְּרִיאוֹת הֵי נִיהוּ שֶׁאֵינָן רְאוּיוֹת לִיפּוֹל; [9]הֵי נִיהוּ רְעוּעוֹת הֵי נִיהוּ רְאוּיוֹת לִיפּוֹל!

[10]לָא, צְרִיכָא דְּנָפְלוּ מֵחֲמַת

LITERAL TRANSLATION

[1]He said to them: 'For your sakes I will forgive him, provided that he does not become accustomed to act in this way.' [2]Immediately Rabbi Elazar the son of Rabbi Shimon entered and expounded: [3]A person should always be soft as a reed, and should not be hard as a cedar. [4]And therefore, the reed merited that a pen be taken from it with which to write the Torah scroll, tefillin, and mezuzot."

[5]"And similarly, [regarding] a city in which there is plague or a collapse [of buildings], etc." [6]Our Rabbis taught: "The collapse of which they spoke [refers to walls that were] sound and not dilapidated; [7]those that were not liable to collapse, and not those that were liable to collapse."

[8]Those that are sound are surely the same as those that are not liable to collapse; [9]those that are dilapidated are surely the same as those that are liable to collapse!

[10]No, it is necessary where they collapsed on account

TRANSLATION AND COMMENTARY

[1]**said to them: 'For your sakes I will forgive him, provided that** he agrees to guard himself against arrogance and pride and **does not become accustomed to behave in the** way he did.' [2]**Immediately Rabbi Elazar the son of Rabbi Shimon entered** the Academy **and expounded:** [3]**A person should always** endeavor to **be soft** in his relations with other people, **like a reed** that yields even to a gentle breeze, **and should not be hard, like a cedar** that stands firm against a strong wind, for it is a person's hardness and arrogance toward other people that lead him to sin. [4]**And it is on account of** its pliant nature that **the reed was privileged to supply the pen used to write the Torah scroll, tefillin, and mezuzot."**

וְכֵן עִיר [5]The Gemara now proceeds to analyze the next clause of our Mishnah, which stated: **"And similarly,** if a certain **city was struck by plague or by the collapse of buildings,** the people living in that city must begin to fast immediately and sound the alarm." [6]**Our Rabbis taught** a Baraita which clarifies the case discussed in our Mishnah: "When the Rabbis **spoke of** fasting in response to **the collapse** of the walls of buildings, **they were speaking of walls** that had been **sound, and not of dilapidated** walls. [7]Similarly, when the Rabbis spoke of fasting as a result of the collapse of walls, they were speaking of a case where the walls that fell down **had not been liable to collapse, and not** of a case where **they were liable to collapse."**

הֵי נִיהוּ בְּרִיאוֹת [8]The Gemara seeks to understand the difference between the two criteria mentioned in the Baraita and asks: **Surely walls that are sound are the same as** walls **that are not liable to collapse,** [9]and **surely** walls **that are dilapidated are the same as** walls **that are liable to collapse!** Why did the Baraita need to say the same thing twice?

לָא [10]The Gemara answers: **No, it was necessary** to mention both criteria in order to teach us that a fast is proclaimed only if the walls that collapsed had been both sound and not liable to collapse, for it is

RASHI

הכי גרסינן: מפולת שאמרו בריאות ולא רעועות שאינן ראויות ליפול ולא שראויות ליפול הי ניהו בריאות והי ניהו שאינן ראויות ליפול הי ניהו רעועות והי ניהו ראויות ליפול לא צריכא דקיימן אגודא דנהרא — מפולת שיש שם רוח חזק שמפיל החומות. מפולת שאמרו מתריעין עליהן — בבריאות קאמרינן, שיהו החומות בריאות ואף על פי כן נופלות מכח נשיבת הרוח. אבל אם היו החומות הנופלות רעועות — אין מתריעין עליהן. וכשאינן ראויות ליפול — מתריעין עליהן, ולא בראויות ליפול. **לא צריכא** — הא דקתני: שאינן רעועות וראויות ליפול אלא כגון דקאי אגודא דנהרא, על שפת הנהר, שאף על פי שהיא בריאה — ראויה היא ליפול, שהמים מפילין אותה, שמקלקלין את הקרקע ושוחקין את היסוד.

NOTES

boorishness he thought were expressed in the man's face. When the man responded with his wise retort, Rabbi Elazar understood that he had been mistaken and that the man's ugliness was merely physical, and he immediately expressed his regret for having humiliated him.

HALAKHAH

מַפּוֹלֶת **A collapse of buildings.** "If the walls of the buildings in a certain city begin to collapse, and these walls are sound and do not stand on a riverbank, the people of that city must begin to fast and sound the alarm." (*Shulḥan Arukh, Oraḥ Ḥayyim* 576:4.)

גּוּבְהַיְיהוּ. [1]אִי נַמִי, דְּקַיְימָן אַגּוּדָא דְּנַהֲרָא. [2]כִּי הַהִיא אֲשִׁיתָא רְעוּעָה דַּהֲוַאי בִּנְהַרְדְּעָא, דְּלָא הֲוָה חָלֵיף רַב וּשְׁמוּאֵל תּוּתָהּ, [3]אַף עַל גַּב דְּקַיְימָא בְּאַתְרָהּ תְּלֵיסַר שְׁנִין. [4]יוֹמָא חַד אִיקְלַע רַב אַדָּא בַּר אַהֲבָה לְהָתָם. [5]אֲמַר לֵיהּ שְׁמוּאֵל לְרַב: ״נֵיתֵי מָר, נַקִּיף״. [6]אֲמַר לֵיהּ: ״לָא צְרִיכְנָא הָאִידָּנָא, [7]דְּאִיכָּא רַב אַדָּא בַּר אַהֲבָה בַּהֲדַן דִּנְפִישׁ זְכוּתֵיהּ, וְלָא מִסְתְּפֵינָא״.

[8]רַב הוּנָא הֲוָה לֵיהּ הַהוּא חַמְרָא בְּהַהוּא בֵּיתָא רְעִיעָא, וּבָעֵי לְפַנּוּיֵיהּ. [9]עַיְילֵיהּ לְרַב אַדָּא בַּר אַהֲבָה לְהָתָם, [10]מְשָׁכֵיהּ בִּשְׁמַעְתָּא עַד דְּפַנְּיֵיהּ. [11]בָּתַר דִּנְפַק, נְפַל בֵּיתָא. [12]אַרְגִּישׁ רַב אַדָּא בַּר אַהֲבָה אִיקְפַּד. [13]סָבַר לָהּ כִּי הָא דְּאָמַר רַבִּי יַנַּאי: לְעוֹלָם אַל יַעֲמוֹד אָדָם בִּמְקוֹם סַכָּנָה וְיֹאמַר: [14]״עוֹשִׂין לִי נֵס״, שֶׁמָּא אֵין עוֹשִׂין לוֹ נֵס. [15]וְאִם תִּימְצֵי לוֹמַר עוֹשִׂין לוֹ נֵס, [16]מְנַכִּין לוֹ מִזְּכֻיּוֹתָיו.

[17]אֲמַר רַב חָנָן: מַאי קְרָא?

LITERAL TRANSLATION

of their height. [1]Or alternatively, where they were standing on the bank of a river. [2]Like a certain dilapidated wall that was in Neharde'a, under which Rav and Shmuel would not pass, [3]although it stood in its place for thirteen years. [4]One day Rav Adda bar Ahavah happened to come there. [5]Shmuel said to Rav: "Let us come, Sir, [and] go around [it]." [6]He said to him: "We do not need [to do so] now, [7]for Rav Adda bar Ahavah is with us whose merit is great, and I am not afraid."

[8]Rav Huna had some wine in a certain dilapidated building, and he wished to remove it. [9]He brought Rav Adda bar Ahavah into it. [10]He delayed him with a legal discussion until he had removed [the wine]. [11]After he went out, the building collapsed. [12]Rav Adda bar Ahavah noticed [and] became angry. [13]He agreed with what Rabbi Yannai said: A person should never stand in a place of danger and say: [14]"A miracle will be performed for me," in case a miracle will not be performed for him. [15]And [even] if you say [that] a miracle will be performed for him, [16]it will be deducted from his merits.

[17]Rav Hanan said: What is the verse?

TRANSLATION AND COMMENTARY

possible to construct a case in which the walls were sound but nevertheless liable to collapse. How so? For example, **where** the walls **collapsed on account of their** great **height.** [1]**Or** alternatively, **if** the walls that collapsed **had been standing on the bank of a river,** and the ground on which they stood was being slowly eroded. The Gemara now demonstrates that a wall may be sound but liable to collapse, or dilapidated but not liable to collapse, by means of the following anecdote: [2]**There was a certain dilapidated wall in Neharde'a, under which Rav and Shmuel would not pass,** [3]**even though it had stood in its place** without falling **for thirteen years.** Since the wall was nevertheless dilapidated, Rav and Shmuel considered it a dangerous place, and therefore avoided passing near it, lest it fall on them. [4]**One day Rav Adda bar Ahavah happened to come** to Neharde'a, and was walking with Rav and Shmuel. As they approached the place where the dilapidated wall stood, [5]**Shmuel said to Rav: "Come** with me, **Sir, and go around** the dilapidated wall as we always do." [6]Rav **said to** Shmuel: **"We** do not need to do so today, [7]for Rav Adda bar Ahavah, whose merit is great, is with us, so that I am not afraid that the wall will collapse on us."

רַב הוּנָא [8]A similar story was related about **Rav Huna,** who **had wine** stored **in a certain dilapidated building from which he wished to remove it**. But he was afraid to enter the building, lest it collapse. [9]**He brought Rav Adda bar Ahavah into** the building, ostensibly to discuss a matter of law with him. [10]Rav Huna **prolonged his discussion** with Rav Adda **until he** had succeeded in having all the wine **removed** from the building. [11]**After** Rav Huna and Rav Adda bar Ahavah **went out, the building collapsed.** [12]**Rav Adda bar Ahavah** then **understood** what had happened **and became angry.** [13]For **he agreed with what Rabbi Yannai used to say: A person should never stand in a dangerous place and say:** [14]"There is no need for me to worry, because **a miracle will be performed for me," in case a miracle is not performed for him.** [15]**And even if we say that** a certain person is justified in thinking that **a miracle will be performed for him,** he should still not put himself in danger and then rely on miraculous, divine protection, for if a miracle is in fact performed for him, [16]**it will be deducted from his merits.** Thus it is better for a person to keep out of danger and to preserve his merits for a time when they are really needed.

אֲמַר רַב חָנָן [17]**Rav Hanan said: Which verse** in the Torah teaches us that a person's merits are reduced if

RASHI

כי ההיא אשיתא רעועה כו׳. באתרה – במקומה, אף על גב דאינה ראויה ליפול, דהא קמה באתרה כולי האי – אפילו הכי, כיון דרעועה היא – לא הוו חלפי תותה, אלא היה מקיף סביבותיה. **מנכין** – ממעטין.

SAGES

רַב אַדָּא בַּר אַהֲבָה Rav Adda bar Ahavah. A famous Babylonian Amora of the first and second generations. He was born (or was circumcised) on the day Rabbi Yehudah HaNasi died. Rav Adda was a disciple of Rav, and transmitted several teachings in his name. Among his colleagues were Rav Huna, Rav Hisda, and Rav Nahman. Many teachings are transmitted in Rav Adda's name in the Talmud. He was renowned for his piety, righteousness, and modesty, and lived to an advanced age.

TRANSLATION AND COMMENTARY

miracles are performed on his behalf? [1]He answered: This principle is derived from **the** following **verse,** which **says** (Genesis 32:10): **"I am not worthy of all the mercies and all the truth** that You have showed Your servant." When Jacob was returning to Eretz Israel after having spent the previous twenty years in Laban's home in Haran, he was overcome by fear when he was told that his brother Esau was approaching him with a force of four hundred men. Before entreating God to save him from his brother, Jacob confessed that he was unworthy (קָטֹנְתִּי) of all the mercy that had been bestowed upon him in the past. Rav Ḥanan argues that Jacob's confession can also be understood as follows: "I have become small because of all the mercies and all the truth that You have showed Your servant." Jacob was afraid that his merits had been diminished as a result of the kindness that God had shown him in the past, and felt that he might not have sufficient merits to allow for miracles to be performed on his behalf in the future.

[1]דִּכְתִיב: "קָטֹנְתִּי מִכֹּל הַחֲסָדִים וּמִכָּל הָאֱמֶת". [2]מַאי הֲוָה עוֹבָדֵיהּ דְּרַב אַדָּא בַּר אַהֲבָה? [3]כִּי הָא דְּאִתְּמַר: [4]שָׁאֲלוּ תַּלְמִידָיו לְרַב אַדָּא בַּר אַהֲבָה: בַּמֶּה הֶאֱרַכְתָּ יָמִים? [5]אָמַר לָהֶם: מִיָּמַי לֹא הִקְפַּדְתִּי בְּתוֹךְ בֵּיתִי, [6]וְלֹא צָעַדְתִּי בִּפְנֵי מִי שֶׁגָּדוֹל מִמֶּנִּי, וְלֹא הִרְהַרְתִּי בַּמְּבוֹאוֹת הַמְטוּנָּפוֹת, [7]וְלֹא הָלַכְתִּי אַרְבַּע אַמּוֹת בְּלֹא תּוֹרָה וּבְלֹא תְּפִילִּין, [8]וְלֹא יָשַׁנְתִּי בְּבֵית הַמִּדְרָשׁ, לֹא שֵׁינַת קֶבַע וְלֹא שֵׁינַת עֲרַאי, [9]וְלֹא שַׂשְׂתִּי בְּתַקָּלַת חֲבֵרִי, [10]וְלֹא קָרָאתִי לַחֲבֵירִי בַּהֲכִינָתוֹ.

LITERAL TRANSLATION

[1]As it is written: "I am not worthy of all the mercies and of all the truth."

[2]What were the deeds of Rav Adda bar Ahavah?

[3][It was] like [the following] that was stated: [4]His disciples asked Rav Adda bar Ahavah: On account of what have you lived so long? [5]He said to them: In [all] my days I have never become angry in my house, [6]and I have not walked in front of someone who was greater than me, and I have not meditated in filthy alleyways, [7]and I have not walked four cubits without Torah or without tefillin, [8]and I have not slept in the study hall, neither regular sleep nor momentary sleep, [9]and I have not rejoiced in the mishap of my fellow, [10]and I have not called my fellow by his nickname.

RASHI

הכי גרסינן: לא הקפדתי בתוך ביתי ולא הלכתי בלא תורה — דכל שעתא הוה גריס. **בהכינתו** — שמכנים לו בני אדם, כגון סס לווי.

מַאי הֲוָה עוֹבָדֵיהּ [2]It was stated earlier that Rav Adda bar Ahavah was known for his meritorious deeds, which led Rav and Rav Huna to believe that they would be protected from danger as long as they remained in his company. The Gemara now asks: **What were the** exceptional **deeds of Rav Adda bar Ahavah?**

כִּי הָא דְּאִתְּמַר [3]The Gemara answers: **The following statement was made** on this subject: [4]**Rav Adda bar Ahava was asked by his disciples: On account of what** good deeds **have you** merited to **live so long?** [5]Rav Adda bar Ahavah **said to** his disciples: Throughout my life I have **never** become **angry** with the members of my family who live **in my house. And I have never walked in front of someone who was greater than me.** [6]**I have not meditated** on Torah matters **in filthy alleyways,** so as not to defile such thoughts by bringing them to mind in dirty places. [7]Moreover, **I have never walked four cubits without** thinking about the **Torah or** wearing **tefillin.** [8]**I have never slept in the study hall, neither regular sleep nor** even a **nap,** for this is an offense that causes a person to forget the Torah he has learned (*Sanhedrin* 71a). [9]**And I have never rejoiced when someone else has suffered a mishap,** nor have I tried to take advantage of his misfortune. [10]**I have never called another person by** a derogatory **nickname,** a transgression which is included among those that cannot be expiated (*Bava Metzia* 58b).

NOTES

בַּמֶּה הֶאֱרַכְתָּ יָמִים? **On account of what have you lived so long?** *Keren Orah* explains at length that a person can live a long life only if his soul finds contentment and pleasure in his body, and he demonstrates how each of the righteous acts mentioned here assisted Rav Adda bar Ahavah to achieve long life.

HALAKHAH

וְלֹא הִרְהַרְתִּי בַּמְּבוֹאוֹת הַמְטוּנָּפוֹת **And I have not meditated in filthy alleyways.** "One may not discuss or even meditate upon sacred matters when in a toilet, a bathhouse, or any other dirty place." (*Rambam, Sefer Ahavah, Hilkhot Keriyat Shema* 3:4.)

וְלֹא קָרָאתִי לַחֲבֵירִי בַּהֲכִינָתוֹ **And I have not called my fellow by his nickname.** "It is forbidden to call people by derogatory names in order to humiliate them, even if they are used to such names." (*Shulhan Arukh, Hoshen Mishpat* 228:5.)

LANGUAGE

גוּהַרְקָא Carriage. This is apparently the Middle Persian word *"gahvarak"* meaning "a chair," "a litter," or "a bed."

TRANSLATION AND COMMENTARY

[1]**And some say** that Rav Adda bar Ahavah said: I have never called another person **by** a derogatory **name that has been applied to his family.** Even though some of the sins listed here are serious, most people treat them lightly. Thus Rav Adda bar Ahavah could attribute his long life to the special care he had taken to avoid these transgressions.

אֲמַר לֵיהּ רָבָא [2]The Gemara continues with another story about the righteous deeds of one of the Amoraim. **Rava said to Rafram bar Pappa: Tell us, Sir, about some of the fine deeds that Rav Huna used to perform.** [3]Rafram **said to** Rava: **I do not remember** the righteous deeds that Rav Huna performed **in his youth,** [4]**but I remember** well those that he performed **in his old age.** [5]On **every cloudy day** when there was a threat of strong winds and heavy rains, Rav Huna's attendants **would take him out in a golden carriage,** [6]**and he would survey** the buildings **all over the city.** [7]**Every wall that** he found to be **dilapidated he would** arrange to have **pulled down,** so that it would not collapse during the storm and cause injury or damage. [8]**If the owner** of such a wall **was in a** financial **position** to rebuild it on his own, Rav Huna **would** have him **rebuild it.** [9]**And if** the owner of the wall **was not in a** financial **position** to rebuild it on his own, Rav Huna **would rebuild it himself with his own money.** Another expression of Rav Huna's righteousness can be found in the following practice: [10]**Every Friday afternoon** as Shabbat was approaching and the vegetable merchants were closing their stalls, Rav Huna **would send a servant to the market,** [11]and **he would buy all the vegetables that were left with the dealers and** would **throw** them **into the river.** Vegetables not sold before Shabbat would go to waste. Therefore Rav Huna would buy them, so that the merchants would not be deterred from bringing large quantities of produce to market on a Friday for fear of wasting their unsold stock.

וְלֵיתְבֵיהּ לַעֲנִיִּים [12]The Gemara asks: Why did Rav Huna throw the vegetables into the river? **He should have distributed them** free of charge **to the poor!** In that way everybody would have benefited: the public would have found an abundant supply of produce in the marketplace, the vegetable dealers would have been protected from loss, and the poor would have had food!

[1]וְאָמְרִי לָהּ: בַּחֲנִיכָתוֹ.
[2]אֲמַר לֵיהּ רָבָא לְרַפְרָם בַּר פַּפָּא: לֵימָא לָן מָר מֵהָנֵי מִילֵּי מְעַלְּיָיתָא דַּהֲוָה עָבֵיד רַב הוּנָא. [3]אֲמַר לֵיהּ: בְּיַנְקוּתֵיהּ לָא דְּכִירְנָא. [4]בְּסִיבוּתֵיהּ דְּכִירְנָא: [5]דְּכָל יוֹמָא דְּעֵיבָא הָווּ מַפְּקִין לֵיהּ בְּגוּהַרְקָא דְּדַהֲבָא, [6]וְסָיֵיר לָהּ לְכוּלָּהּ מָתָא. [7]וְכָל אֲשִׁיתָא דַּהֲוַות רְעִיעָתָא הֲוָה סָתַר לָהּ. [8]אִי אֶפְשָׁר לְמָרָהּ, בָּנֵי לָהּ. [9]וְאִי לָא אֶפְשָׁר, בָּנֵי לָהּ אִיהוּ מִדִּידֵיהּ. [10]וְכָל פַּנְיָא דְּמַעֲלֵי שַׁבְּתָא הֲוָה מְשַׁדֵּר שְׁלוּחָא לְשׁוּקָא, [11]וְכָל יַרְקָא דַּהֲוָה פָּיֵישׁ לְהוּ לְגִינָּאֵי זָבֵין לֵיהּ וּשְׁדֵי לֵיהּ לְנַהֲרָא.
[12]וְלֵיתְבֵיהּ לַעֲנִיִּים!

LITERAL TRANSLATION

[1]And some say: By his surname.

[2]Rava said to Rafram bar Pappa: Tell us, Sir, some of those fine things that Rav Huna did. [3]He said to him: [What he did] in his youth I do not remember, [4][but what he did] in his old age I do remember. [5]Every cloudy day they would take him out in a golden carriage, [6]and he would survey the entire city. [7]And every wall that was dilapidated he would pull down. [8]If its owner was able, he would rebuild it. [9]And if he was unable, [Rav Huna] himself would rebuild it with his own [money]. [10]And every Friday afternoon he would send a deputy to the market, [11]and all the vegetables that were left with the vegetable dealers he would buy and throw into the river.

[12]But let him give them to the poor!

RASHI

חניכתו – כמו: חניכת אבות בגיטין עד עשרה דורות (גיטין פח,א). **ביומא דעיבא** – יום המעונן, דהוי רוח מנשבת, ומסתפי דלא תפיל חומות. **בגוהרקא** – תיבה תלויה בעגלה, ושרות יושבות בהן. **וסייר** – בודק, תרגום "פוקד" (שמות לד), מסער, כמו: האי טבחא דלא סר סכינא קמיה חכם.

NOTES

הַכִּינָתוֹ...חֲנִיכָתוֹ His nickname...his surname. Our commentary follows *Rashi* and *Tosafot,* who explain the distinction between the two terms as follows: The former refers to a derogatory nickname applied to a particular person, whereas the latter refers to a derogatory name applied to an entire family.

Rabbenu Ḥananel and *Arukh* (who had the readings חֲנִיכָתִי and חֲנִיכָתוֹ) explain that, according to the first version of the story, Rav Adda bar Ahavah himself did not make up a derogatory nickname, while according to the second version Rav Adda bar Ahavah did not call another person by the nickname used by other people. *Shittah* writes that Rav Adda bar Ahavah was careful not to call another person even by a nickname that was not intended to be disparaging.

[1] זְמְנִין דְּסָמְכָא דַּעְתַּיְיהוּ, [2] וְלָא אָתוּ לְמִיזְבַּן.
[3] וּלְשַׁדְיֵיהּ לִבְהֵמָה!
[4] קָסָבַר מַאֲכַל אָדָם אֵין מַאֲכִילִין לִבְהֵמָה.
[5] וְלָא לִיזְבְּנֵיהּ כְּלָל!
[6] נִמְצֵאתָ מַכְשִׁילָן לֶעָתִיד לָבֹא.
[7] כִּי הֲוָה לֵיהּ מִילְּתָא דְּאָסוּתָא, [8] הָוֵי מָלֵי כּוּזָא מִינֵּיהּ וְתָלֵי לֵיהּ בְּסֵיפָּא דְּבֵיתָא וְאָמַר: [9] "כָּל דְּבָעֵי, לֵיתֵי וְלִישְׁקוֹל".

LITERAL TRANSLATION

[1] Sometimes they would rely [on this], [2] and would not come to buy.

[3] But let him throw them to animals!

[4] He maintained [that] food fit for humans should not be fed to animals.

[5] But let him not buy them at all!

[6] You would cause them to sin in the future.

[7] When he had some medicine, [8] he would fill a water jug with it and hang it on the doorpost of his house and say: [9] "Whoever needs [it], let him come and take."

TRANSLATION AND COMMENTARY

זְמְנִין [1] The Gemara answers: If Rav Huna had distributed the leftover vegetables to the poor for nothing, people **would rely** on receiving free produce, [2] **and would refrain from buying** from the vegetable dealers. In that case, some people might have no vegetables for Shabbat, if none were still unsold on Friday afternoon. Moreover, some people who could afford vegetables might pretend to be paupers and take the produce he was distributing free of charge.

וּלְשַׁדְיֵיהּ לִבְהֵמָה [3] The Gemara now raises another question: Why did Rav Huna throw the vegetables into the river? **He should have given** the produce **to** animals, so that at least some benefit would be derived from the vegetables!

קָסָבַר [4] The Gemara answers: Rav Huna **maintained that food fit for humans should not be fed to animals.** To do so shows contempt for food and a rejection of the bounty that God has bestowed upon man.

וְלָא [5] The Gemara asks one further question about Rav Huna's behavior: If the vegetables cannot be distributed to the poor, and they must not be given to animals, then **should** Rav Huna **have bought** the unsold produce **at all?**

נִמְצֵאתָ [6] The Gemara answers: If Rav Huna had not bought the unsold vegetables from the merchants, **he would have caused them to act wrongly in the future.** If the vegetable dealers had not found a buyer for their produce, they would have brought smaller quantities of vegetables to market the next week. In order to encourage the merchants to stock abundant quantities of vegetables, Rav Huna guaranteed them that he would buy all the produce that they failed to sell, even though he would be forced to throw it into the river.

כִּי הֲוָה לֵיהּ [7] Rav Huna also had this custom: **When a** new **medicine** that was not readily available **came** into his hands, [8] **he would fill a water jug** with the medicine **and hang it on the doorpost of his house and say:** [9] **"Whoever needs** this medicine **may come and take** some."

RASHI

כי הוה ליה מילתא דאסותא רמי ליה אכוזא דמיא כו' לא גרסינן.
זבין ליה ושדי ליה בנהרא – להכי זבין להו, דאי הוה משתייר מידי לגננין – אזלא לאיבוד, דמכמשא בשבת, ונמצא מכשילן לעתיד לבא, דלא מייתי ירקי לסעודת שבת. **דסמכא דעתייהו** – שנסמכין עניים לאותו ירק, ואומרים: אין אנו צריכין לקנות, ושמא ישתייר שם כלום ואין להם מה לאכול בשבת. **אין מאכילין אותן לבהמה** – משום ביזוי אוכלין, ומחזי כבועט בטובה שהשפיע הקדוש ברוך הוא בעולם. אי נמי: משום דחסה תורה על ממונן של ישראל. וזרק לנהר, והולכין למקום אחר, ומוצאין אותם בני אדם ואוכלין אותן, כך שמעתי.

LANGUAGE

כּוּזָא Water jug. This word is derived from the Persian word *koz,* meaning "a pitcher."

NOTES

מַאֲכַל אָדָם אֵין מַאֲכִילִין לִבְהֵמָה Food fit for humans should not be fed to animals. *Ra'avad* points out that, according to numerous sources, there is no prohibition against feeding animals food fit for human consumption. Some commentators explain that while one may indeed feed animals with food fit for humans, one may not go out and buy such food with the intention of using it as animal fodder. Alternatively, one may feed animals with a small amount of food fit for human consumption, but not with large quantities of such food. Alternatively, a distinction can be drawn between food that is clearly intended for humans and food that is fit for humans but is also commonly given to animals, like carobs or gourds. Lastly, a distinction can be drawn between places where animal fodder is available and places where only food fit for human consumption is available (see *Meiri* and *Maḥatzit HaShekel*).

The commentators ask: If it is not permitted to use food that is fit for human consumption as animal fodder because this would be considered a demonstration of disrespect for the food, how could Rav Huna have thrown the vegetables

HALAKHAH

מַאֲכַל אָדָם אֵין מַאֲכִילִין לִבְהֵמָה Food fit for humans should not be fed to animals. "One may not feed food that is fit for human consumption to animals, for this would be a disrespectful use of the food." (*Magen Avraham, Shulḥan Arukh, Oraḥ Ḥayyim* 171:1.)

BACKGROUND

מִילְּתָא דְּשִׁיבְתָּא A tradition concerning Shivta. In other places in the Talmud (*Yoma* 77b, *Hullin* 107b) it is explained that Shivta is an evil spirit present on the hands of someone who does not wash them when required. In the responsa of the Geonim it is a disease that strikes small children and causes them to waste away and die.

SAGES

אִילְפָא Ilfa. He was a first-generation Palestinian Amora. In the Jerusalem Talmud he is called Hilfi (חִילְפִי). He was a disciple of Rabbi Yehudah HaNasi and studied under him and his senior disciples. As is related here, Ilfa was a friend of Rabbi Yohanan, and Rabbi Yohanan's students reported teachings in his name. He had an extremely sharp mind and was one of the greatest Torah authorities of his generation. He is also known as a teacher of Aggadah, and some Aggadic teachings are reported in his name. His great piety and righteousness are also reported.

TRANSLATION AND COMMENTARY

וְאִיכָּא דְּאָמְרִי [1]**There are some who report** a slightly different version of Rav Huna's practice: [2]Rav Huna **had** received **a tradition concerning** the evil spirit called **Shivta,** that it endangered those who would eat without first washing their hands. [3]**Therefore he would take a water jug and hang it** in his house **and say:** [4]**"Whoever needs** water, **let him come into** the house and wash his hands, **so that he will not be in danger."**

כִּי הֲוָה [5]Rafram bar Pappa concludes with a further example of the meritorious deeds performed by Rav Huna: **When** Rav Huna began **to eat bread, he would open the doors** of his house **and proclaim:** [6]**"Whoever is in need** of food **may come** in **and eat** at my table."

אֲמַר רָבָא [7]Having heard Rafram's review of Rav Huna's righteous practices, **Rava said: All those** good deeds that were performed by Rav Huna **I** too **can do,** [8]**except for this** last one, **which I cannot do.** [21A] I cannot open the doors of my house to all who are needy, [9]**because the** hungry **soldiers** stationed **in** my city of **Mehoza are** so **numerous.** If I were to open my doors to all of them, I would very soon be left with nothing.

אִילְפָא וְרַבִּי יוֹחָנָן [10]The Gemara now continues with another story about a dilapidated wall. **Ilfa and Rabbi Yohanan** once **studied Torah** together, devoting all their time and effort to their scholarly pursuits, so that they were unable to go out and earn a living. [11]As a result **they were very hard pressed for money.** Seeing that their situation was getting desperate, [12]**they said** to each other: **"Let us get up** and break off our studies, **and go and establish** some sort of **a business, and fulfill in ourselves** the verse that says (Deuteronomy 15:4:): [13]**'But there shall be no poor among you.'** Let us understand this verse as imposing a personal obligation on us to remove the poverty in our midst." [14]Rabbi Yohanan and Ilfa **went** off in search of an appropriate business venture, and on their way they happened to **sit down under a dilapidated wall and** began to **eat their bread.** [15]**Two ministering angels came** and began to consider what should be done with these two Rabbinical students who had decided to leave the Academy and go out into the world of business. [16]**Rabbi Yohanan heard one** angel **saying to the other: "Let us throw this wall down upon them**

[1]וְאִיכָּא דְּאָמְרִי: [2]מִילְּתָא דְּשִׁיבְתָּא הֲוָה גְּמִיר, [3]וַהֲוָה מַנַּח כּוּזָא דְּמַיָּא וְדָלֵי לֵיהּ וְאָמַר: [4]"כָּל דִּצְרִיךְ, לֵיתֵי וְלֵיעוּל, דְּלָא לִסְתַּכֵּן".

[5]כִּי הֲוָה כָּרֵךְ רִיפְתָּא, הֲוָה פָּתַח לְבָבֵיהּ וְאָמַר: [6]"כָּל מַאן דִּצְרִיךְ, לֵיתֵי וְלֵיכוּל".

[7]אֲמַר רָבָא: כּוּלְּהוּ מָצֵינָא מְקַיֵּימְנָא, לְבַר [8]מֵהָא דְּלָא מָצֵינָא לְמֶיעֱבַד, [21A] [9]מִשּׁוּם דִּנְפִישִׁי בְּנֵי חֵילָא דִּמְחוֹזָא.

[10]אִילְפָא וְרַבִּי יוֹחָנָן הָווּ גָּרְסִי בְּאוֹרַיְיתָא, [11]דְּחִיקָא לְהוּ מִילְּתָא טוּבָא. [12]אָמְרִי: "נֵיקוּם וְנֵיזִיל וְנֶיעֱבַד עִיסְקָא, וּנְקַיֵּים בְּנַפְשִׁין: [13]'אֶפֶס כִּי לֹא יִהְיֶה בְּךָ אֶבְיוֹן'". [14]אֲזַלוּ, אוֹתְבֵי תּוּתֵי גּוּדָא רְעִיעָא. הָווּ קָא כָּרְכִי רִיפְתָּא. [15]אָתוּ תְּרֵי מַלְאֲכֵי הַשָּׁרֵת. [16]שְׁמָעֵיהּ רַבִּי יוֹחָנָן דַּאֲמַר חַד לְחַבְרֵיהּ: "נִישְׁדֵי עֲלַיְיהוּ הַאי גּוּדָא

LITERAL TRANSLATION

[1]And there are [some] who say: [2]He had a tradition concerning Shivta, [3]and he would set down a water jug and hang it and say: [4]"Whoever needs [it], let him come and enter, so that he will not be in danger."

[5]When he would prepare to eat bread, he would open his door and say: [6]"Whoever is needy, let him come and eat."

[7]Rava said: All of them I can do, [8]except for this which I cannot do, [21A] [9]because the troops of Mehoza are many.

[10]Ilfa and Rabbi Yohanan were studying Torah, [11][and] they were very hard pressed [for money]. [12]They said: "Let us get up and go and establish a business, and let us fulfill in ourselves: [13]'But there shall be no poor among you.'" [14]They went, sat down under a dilapidated wall, [and] ate bread. [15]Two ministering angels came. [16]Rabbi Yohanan heard that one was saying to his fellow: "Let us throw this wall down upon them

RASHI

מילתא דשיבתא – מנהג שֵׁדִים, שמזיקין למי שאוכל ואינו נוטל ידיו. דשיבתא כהך דגרסינן במסכת יומא (עז,ב): אמר אביי משום שיבתא, והוה תלי ליה לההוא כוזא דמיא, כי היכי דלימשו ידייהו מינה. **בר מהא** – חוץ מזו, דכל מאן דבעי הוה עייל ואכל. **משום דנפישי בני מחוזא** – דאיכא עניי טפי, וקא מיכלי קרנא. **דחיקא להו** – עניות. **כי לא יהיה בך אביון** – בך בעצמך.

NOTES

into the river? *Rashi* explains that Rav Huna meant the vegetables to drift downstream and be eaten by whoever found them. Others suggest that there was no recognizable show of disrespect, for those who saw the vegetables in the river would assume that they were already rotten when discarded (*Petah Enayim* in the name of *Rosh*).

נִישְׁדֵי עֲלַיְיהוּ הַאי גּוּדָא Let us throw this wall down upon them. *Rabbi Ya'akov Emden* suggests that this story should

TRANSLATION AND COMMENTARY

and kill them, for they are forsaking their study of Torah, which can bring them eternal **life in the World-to-Come, and are** instead determined to **engage** in business, which can only improve their lot **in** this **temporary life** in the present world." [1]**The second** angel **said to** the first: [2]**"Leave them** alone, **for among them there is one whose hour** of greatness **is** still **waiting for him."** [3]**Rabbi Yoḥanan heard** this conversation between the two angels, **but Ilfa did not hear** it. [4]**Rabbi Yoḥanan asked Ilfa: "Sir, did you hear anything?"** [5]Ilfa **replied: "No,** I did not." [6]Rabbi Yoḥanan then **said** to himself: **"Since I heard** the angels talking to each other **and Ilfa did not hear** their conversation, [7]it seems reasonable to **conclude that** it is **for me** that **the hour** of greatness **is** still **waiting,** and not for Ilfa." [8]**Rabbi Yoḥanan** then reconsidered his decision to abandon his studies and **said to** Ilfa: **"I will go back** to the Academy and resume my studies, **and** I will **fulfill in myself** the verse which says [Deuteronomy 15:11]: [9]**'For the poor will never cease out of the land.'** After having thought the matter over, I have decided that I must devote myself entirely to my studies, even if this means that I will be forced to lead a life of poverty." [10]**Rabbi Yoḥanan went back** to the Academy, **but Ilfa did not go back** with him. Instead, he went away to distant places pursuing business ventures. [11]**By the time Ilfa returned** from his travels, **Rabbi Yoḥanan had** developed into a great Torah Sage and had **become the head of the Academy.** With his appointment as head of the Academy, Rabbi Yoḥanan's financial situation had improved dramatically, for it was customary for the person who filled that position to be maintained in comfort by the community. [12]When Ilfa reentered the Academy, his former colleagues **said to him: "If you, Sir, had remained** in the Academy **and continued to study** Torah, **would you not** now **be head of the Academy** instead of Rabbi Yoḥanan?" [13]Ilfa immediately **went and suspended himself from the mast of a ship, and proclaimed:** "Even though I left the Academy in order to engage in business, I never abandoned my Torah studies. To prove this, I am ready to submit to the following test.

וְנִקְטְלִינְהוּ, שֶׁמַּנִּיחִין חַיֵּי עוֹלָם הַבָּא וְעוֹסְקִין בְּחַיֵּי שָׁעָה". [1]אֲמַר לֵיהּ אִידָךְ: [2]"שָׁבְקִינְהוּ, דְּאִיכָּא בְּהוּ חַד דְּקַיְימָא לֵיהּ שַׁעְתָּא". [3]רַבִּי יוֹחָנָן שְׁמַע, אִילְפָא לָא שְׁמַע. [4]אֲמַר לֵיהּ רַבִּי יוֹחָנָן לְאִילְפָא: "שְׁמַע מָר מִידֵי?" [5]אֲמַר לֵיהּ: "לָא". [6]אֲמַר: "מִדְּשָׁמְעִי אֲנָא וְאִילְפָא לָא שְׁמַע, [7]שְׁמַע מִינָּהּ לְדִידִי קַיְימָא לִי שַׁעְתָּא". [8]אֲמַר לֵיהּ רַבִּי יוֹחָנָן: "אִיהֲדַר וְאוֹקֵי בְּנַפְשַׁאי: [9]'כִּי לֹא יֶחְדַּל אֶבְיוֹן מִקֶּרֶב הָאָרֶץ'". [10]רַבִּי יוֹחָנָן הֲדַר, אִילְפָא לָא הֲדַר. [11]עַד דַּאֲתָא אִילְפָא, מְלִיךְ רַבִּי יוֹחָנָן. [12]אָמְרוּ לוֹ: "אִי אֲתִיב מָר וְגָרִיס, לָא הֲוָה מָלֵיךְ מָר?" [13]אֲזַל תְּלָא נַפְשֵׁיהּ בְּאַסְקַרְיָא דִּסְפִינְתָּא, אֲמַר:

LITERAL TRANSLATION

and kill them, for they are forsaking the life of the World-to-Come and are engaging in life for the moment." [1]The other one said to him: [2]"Leave them, for there is among them one whose hour is waiting (lit., 'standing') for him." [3]Rabbi Yoḥanan heard, [but] Ilfa did not hear. [4]Rabbi Yoḥanan said to Ilfa: "Sir, did you hear anything?" [5]He said: "No." [6]He said: "Since I heard and Ilfa did not hear, [7][I can] infer from this [that] it is for me that the hour is waiting." [8]Rabbi Yoḥanan said to him: "I will go back and fulfill in myself: [9]'For the poor will never cease out of the land.'" [10]Rabbi Yoḥanan went back, [but] Ilfa did not go back. [11]By the time Ilfa came, Rabbi Yoḥanan was head [of the Academy]. [12]They said to him: "If you, Sir, had sat and studied, would you, Sir, not be head [of the Academy]?" [13]He went and suspended himself from the mast of a ship, [and] said:

RASHI

חיי העולם הבא — תורה. **חיי שעה** — עולם הזה, זה סחורה. **קיימא ליה שעתא** — עתיד להתגדל, ואין זמנו למות. **שמע מינה** — מדאנא שמעתיה. **איהדר** — איזיל לתורתי. **עד דאתא אילפא** — ממקום שהלך שם לסחורה. **מלך רבי יוחנן** — מינוהו ראש ישיבה עליהן. מנהג הוא: מי שהוא ראש ישיבה היו מגדלין אותו משלהן, ומעשירין אותו, כדאמרינן לגבי כהן גדול בסיפרא וביומא (יח, א): "והכהן הגדול מאחיו" — גדלוהו משל אחיו. **אמרו לו** — אנשי המקום לאילפא. **אי אתיב מר וגריס** — אם היית יושב ועוסק בתורה היינו ממליכין אותך כמו שעשינו לרבי יוחנן. דאילפא הוי גמיר טפי מרבי יוחנן. **תלא נפשיה באסקריא** — כלונס עץ ארוך תקוע, בלב הספינה, שמניחין עליה מכסה, *וילו"ן בלעז.

LANGUAGE

אַסְקַרְיָא Mast. This word is probably derived from the Greek ἱστοκεραία, *histokeraia,* meaning "a mast."

LANGUAGE (RASHI)

וילו"ן* Possibly from the Old French *veile,* which means "a sail."

NOTES

be understood in the light of the Talmudic dictum that Satan brings charges against a man only in his hour of danger. After Ilfa and Rabbi Yoḥanan left their Torah studies, the angels waited until the two men entered a dangerous situation before considering what should be done with them.

[1]״אִי אִיכָּא דְּשָׁאֵיל לִי בְּמַתְנִיתָא דְּרַבִּי חִיָּיא וְרַבִּי אוֹשַׁעֲיָא [2]וְלָא פָּשְׁטִינָא לֵיהּ מִמַּתְנִיתִין [3]נָפֵילְנָא מֵאַסְקָרְיָא דִּסְפִינְתָּא וְטָבַעְנָא״. [4]אֲתָא הַהוּא סָבָא, תְּנָא לֵיהּ: [5]״הָאוֹמֵר: ׳תְּנוּ שֶׁקֶל לְבָנַיי בְּשַׁבָּת׳, [6]וְהֵן רְאוּיִין לָתֵת לָהֶם סֶלַע, נוֹתְנִין לָהֶם סֶלַע. [7]וְאִם אָמַר: ׳אַל תִּתְּנוּ לָהֶם אֶלָּא שֶׁקֶל׳, אֵין נוֹתְנִין לָהֶם אֶלָּא שֶׁקֶל. [8]אִם אָמַר: ׳אִם מֵתוּ, יִרְשׁוּ אֲחֵרִים תַּחְתֵּיהֶם׳,

LITERAL TRANSLATION

[1]"If there is someone who asks me about a Baraita of Rabbi Ḥiyya and Rabbi Oshaya, [2]and I do not derive it from our Mishnah, [3]I will drop from the mast of the ship and drown." [4]A certain old man came, [and] taught before him: [5]"[If] someone says: 'Give my sons a shekel a week,' [6]and they are fit to be given a sela, we give them a sela. [7]But if he said: 'Give them only a shekel,' we give them only a shekel. [8]If he said: 'If they die, let others inherit in their place,'

TRANSLATION AND COMMENTARY

[1]**If there is anyone who can ask me about** a matter discussed in **a Baraita of Rabbi Ḥiyya and Rabbi Oshaya** [the Tosefta compiled by these two Sages on the basis of the traditions they had received from their teacher, Rabbi Yehudah HaNasi], [2]**and I will not** be able to **derive it from** a ruling found in **the Mishnah** itself, [3]**I will drop from the mast of this ship and drown** myself." Ilfa was ready to stake his life on his total mastery of Tannaitic literature. [4]**A certain elder came, and taught** the following Baraita **before** Ilfa: [5]**"If a person** on his deathbed deposits all his assets in the hands of a trustee and **says** to him: 'I want you to **give my sons a shekel** [half a sela] **a week** to cover their expenses until they reach majority, and only then will the rest of my assets pass into their hands,' [6]but as it turns out **they need to be given a** full **sela** each week, a shekel being insufficient to cover all their expenses, **they must be given a sela.** In such a case, we assume that the father did not wish to limit his children's allowance to a shekel a week if that amount were insufficient to cover their expenses. All that he meant was that his children should be maintained at a moderate level, and that they should not be given more than what they needed. But if they really did need more than a shekel for their basic subsistence, he would surely not have objected to their being given a larger allowance. [7]**But if** the father **says**: 'When I die, I wish you to **give** my sons *only* a shekel a week,' **they are given only a shekel**, even if that amount does not suffice to provide for their needs. Since the father made use of the word 'only' in formulating his instructions, we must assume that he meant his words to be followed strictly. [8]**And if** the father **says: 'When my sons die,** I do not wish my estate to pass to their heirs, my grandsons, but I want **other** people to **inherit in their place,'**

RASHI

דשאיל לי כו׳ — כלומר, אף על גב דעבדי עיסקא — גריסנא אנא טפי מיניה. **דבי רבי חייא ודבי רבי אושעיא** — דהוו מסדרי מתניתא על פי רבינו הקדוש, שהיה רבס. **ולא פשיטנא ליה ממתניתין** — דאשכחנא משנה כוותיה דההיא ברייתא. **תנא ליה** — שנה לפניו, כלומר: בעא מיניה. **האומר תנו שקל לבניי** — מי שמת, והניח ממונו ביד איש נאמן, ואמר: תנו שקל, חצי סלע, לבניי להוצאה בשבוע. **וראויין לתת להן סלע** — שיש לו נכסים הרבה, ואין מספקין לשבת בפחות מסלע. **נותנין להם סלע** — דאי הוה בדעתיה דלא למיתן להו אלא שקל — היה מצוה: אל תתנו להן אלא שקל, והאי דקאמר ״תנו להן שקל״ ולא אמר ״תנו סלע״ — משום דבעי לזרוזינהו, כדאמרן בכתובות (ע, א): כדי לזרזן במשא ובמתן, כדי שיטרחו וילמדו דרך ארץ, וירויחו. **אם מתו ירשו אחרים תחתיהן** — אף על גב דאמר ״תנו שקל״ ולא אמר ״אל תתנו אלא שקל״ — גלי בדעתיה דלא בעי למיתב להו אלא שקל בשבת, כי היכי דאי מתו — ירשו אחרים תחתיהן.

NOTES

וְלָא פָּשְׁטִינָא לֵיהּ מִמַּתְנִיתִין And I do not derive it from our Mishnah. Elsewhere (*Eruvin* 92a), the principle is stated: "If Rabbi Yehudah HaNasi did not teach it, from where did Rabbi Ḥiyya know it?" Thus, all that is included in the Baraitot compiled by Rabbi Ḥiyya and by Rabbi Oshaya must be based on traditions they received from Rabbi Yehudah HaNasi, and to which allusions can be found in the Mishnah.

אִם אָמַר: ״אִם מֵתוּ, יִרְשׁוּ אֲחֵרִים תַּחְתֵּיהֶם״ If he said: "If they die, let others inherit in their place." The Rishonim ask: There is a general rule that an inheritance cannot be terminated (*Bava Batra* 129b). Therefore, if a man bequeaths his property to his legal heir, saying: "To you and afterwards to someone else," the property does not pass to the other person upon the heir's death, but rather to the heir's heirs. Why, then, does the Baraita rule that the

HALAKHAH

הָאוֹמֵר: ״תְּנוּ שֶׁקֶל לְבָנַיי בְּשַׁבָּת״ If someone says: "Give my sons a shekel a week." "If a person who is on his deathbed says: 'Give my sons a shekel a week,' or if he says: 'Give them only a shekel a week,' and it turns out that they need a sela a week, they must be given a sela a week as needed, following the Gemara's conclusion in

TRANSLATION AND COMMENTARY

[1]then **whether he said, 'Give** my sons a shekel a week,' [2]**or** he said, **'Give** them **only** a shekel a week,' [3]the sons **are given only a shekel a week.** Since the father said that he wished his estate to be transferred to people other than his grandchildren on the death of his sons, we assume that he meant to restrict his children's allowance, so that assets would remain after their deaths that could be passed on to the other parties." Where, asked the elder, do we find a ruling in the Mishnah on which this Baraita is based? [4]**Ilfa said to him: Whose opinion does this** Baraita **follow?** [5]**It follows the opinion of Rabbi Meir, who said: It is a duty to fulfill the words of the deceased.** We learned this opinion of Rabbi Meir elsewhere in the Mishnah (*Ketubot* 69b): "If a father entrusts money to another person on behalf of his daughter — for example, to buy real estate for her or to pay for her dowry — and the father dies, and after her betrothal the daughter asks the trustee to hand over the money to her bridegroom, for she trusts him to carry out her father's wishes, the trustee must not do so, but must himself execute the father's instructions as he received them." As the Gemara explains (ibid.), Rabbi Meir maintains that the trustee must carry out the father's instructions because it is a duty to fulfill the words of the deceased. Our Baraita's rulings are based on the same principle.

אָמְרוּ עָלָיו [6]The Gemara now relates another story connected with a dilapidated building. **It was related about** a certain Sage named **Naḥum of Gam Zu that he was blind in both eyes, both his hands were cut off, both his legs were amputated, and his entire body was covered with boils.** [7]**And he was lying** in his bed in that unfortunate condition **in a dilapidated house.** [8]He was so completely helpless that **the legs of his bed had to be placed in bowls of water so that ants would not climb up** the legs of the bed and distress **him.**

[1]בֵּין שֶׁאָמַר, ׳תְּנוּ׳, [2]בֵּין שֶׁאָמַר, ׳אַל תִּתְּנוּ׳, [3]אֵין נוֹתְנִין לָהֶם אֶלָּא שֶׁקֶל״. [4]אֲמַר לֵיהּ: הָא מַנִּי? [5]רַבִּי מֵאִיר הִיא, דְּאָמַר: מִצְוָה לְקַיֵּים דִּבְרֵי הַמֵּת. [6]אָמְרוּ עָלָיו עַל נַחוּם אִישׁ גַּם זוּ שֶׁהָיָה סוּמָא מִשְּׁתֵּי עֵינָיו, גִּדֵּם מִשְּׁתֵּי יָדָיו, קִיטֵּעַ מִשְּׁתֵּי רַגְלָיו, וְכָל גּוּפוֹ מָלֵא שְׁחִין. [7]וְהָיָה מוּטָּל בְּבַיִת רָעוּעַ [8]וְרַגְלֵי מִטָּתוֹ מוּנָּחִין בִּסְפָלִין שֶׁל מַיִם כְּדֵי שֶׁלֹּא יַעֲלוּ עָלָיו נְמָלִים.

LITERAL TRANSLATION

[1]whether he said, 'Give,' [2]or, 'Give only,' [3]we give them only a shekel." [4]He [Ilfa] said to him: Whose [opinion] is this? [5]It is [that of] Rabbi Meir, who said: It is a duty to fulfill the words of the deceased.

[6]They related about Naḥum of Gam Zu that he was blind in both eyes, both his hands were cut off, both his legs were amputated, and his entire body was full of boils. [7]And he was lying in a dilapidated house, [8]and the legs of his bed were placed in bowls of water so that ants would not climb on him.

RASHI

אמר ליה — אילפא. **הא מני** — דקתני: אף על גב דלא ספקי בצליר מסלע לא יהבינן להו אלא שקל — רבי מאיר היא, דאמר במסכת כתובות במתניתין (סט, ב): מצוה לקיים דברי המת. דאי לאו מצוה — מן הדין נותנין להן כל הראוי להן, שהרי כל הממון שלהן הוא, ואין בו לאותן אחרים כלום, אלא לאחר מיתתן, אם יש מותר — יש להן, ואם לאו — לא יטלו. ומתוך שרוצין אנו לקיים דבריו שירשו אחרים תחתיהם — אנו מקמצין את הממון, כדי שיהא שם מותר. **והיה מטתו מונחת כו׳** — רגלי המטה מונחין בספלים מלאים מים, שלא יעלו אליו נמלים דרך רגלי המטה, מפני שהיה גידם, ואם היו עולים — אינו יכול ליטלם בידיו ולזורקן.

SAGES

נַחוּם אִישׁ גַּם זוּ Naḥum of Gam Zu. A Tanna of the end of the Second Temple period, he apparently came from the town of Gimzo in Judea, after which he is named. Apart from what is told here about his righteousness, we know that Rabbi Akiva was his student and learned his method of Halakhic Midrash from him. It appears that the difference between the method of Rabbi Akiba and that of Rabbi Yishmael is ancient (see *Shevuot* 26a), and related to the respective methods of Naḥum of Gam Zu and Rabbi Neḥunya ben HaKanah.

LANGUAGE

סְפָלִין Bowls. From the use of this term here and in many other sources it seems clear that the reference is to big vessels used to hold a large quantity of a beverage or for washing feet. In modern Hebrew the word סֵפֶל refers to a small drinking cup, a usage that has no basis in the sources.

NOTES

father's instructions are effective when he says that, upon his sons' death, others are to inherit in their place?

Rambam (*Hilkhot Zekhiyyah U'Mattanah* 12:6) explains that the Baraita's ruling is restricted to a case where the father states explicitly that his heirs are not to receive his property as an inheritance, but as a gift, for a gift may indeed be terminated. *Ra'avad* maintains that the Baraita's ruling applies only in a case where the father deposited his assets in the hands of a trustee; but if the heirs actually received the property, the inheritance cannot be terminated. Others (see *Meiri*) explain that the Baraita's ruling is restricted to a case where the father limited his heirs to a shekel a week, for in such a case they never received the estate itself and so it can be passed on to others upon their death.

HALAKHAH

Ketubot that there is no practical difference between the two formulations. But if the father says: 'When my sons die, I wish my estate to pass to other people and not to my grandsons,' the sons are given only a shekel a week." (*Shulḥan Arukh, Ḥoshen Mishpat* 253:17.)

מִצְוָה לְקַיֵּים דִּבְרֵי הַמֵּת It is a duty to fulfill the words of the deceased. "It is a duty to fulfill the instructions of the deceased, even if he was well when the instructions were issued. This applies only where the deceased had deposited in the hands of a third party the funds that were to be used to fulfill his directives." (*Shulḥan Arukh, Ḥoshen Mishpat* 252:2; *Even HaEzer* 54.)

TRANSLATION AND COMMENTARY

פַּעַם אַחַת [1] **On one occasion, his disciples** were concerned that their teacher was in danger, and they wished to move him to a safer place. Since their principal concern was their master's well-being, they **planned** first **to remove** Naḥum from the building on his **bed, and** only **afterwards to remove his utensils.** [2] But Naḥum **said to them: "My sons,** I would advise you first to **remove the utensils and** only **afterwards** to **remove** me in **my bed,** [3] **for I assure you that as long as I am in the house, the house will not fall."** [4] The disciples heeded their teacher's advice, and first **removed the utensils and** only **afterwards removed** Naḥum on **his bed.** [5] No sooner had the utensils been removed and Naḥum safely evacuated, than **the house collapsed.** [6] **His disciples** turned to Naḥum and **said to him: "Our teacher, since** it is clear that **you are a perfectly righteous man,** for we ourselves have seen that it was through your merit that this dilapidated house did not collapse as long as you were inside it, [7] **why did this happen to you?** What could you possibly have done to justify the suffering you have been made to endure?" [8] Naḥum **said** to his disciples: "My sons, I myself am the cause of my misfortune. [9] For once I was traveling along the road on the way **to my father-in-law's house.** [10] **I had with me a load** that was distributed among **three asses, one** carrying **food, one** carrying **drink, and one** carrying **all sorts** of special **delicacies.** [11] At one point on my journey I stopped to rest, and **a poor man came and stood in front of me on the road, and said to me: 'My teacher, give me something to eat!'** [12] Not realizing how desperate the man was, **I said to him: 'Wait** a few minutes **until I have unloaded the ass.'** [13] But **I did not have time to unload the ass before** the poor man **died** of hunger. [14] **I went and fell on his face,** and I reproached myself bitterly for not coming more quickly to his aid. [15] **I said: 'Let my eyes, which had no compassion for your eyes, become blind. Let my hands, which had no compassion for your hands, be cut off. Let my legs, which had no compassion for your legs, be amputated.'** [16] **And my mind did not become calm until I said: 'Let my entire body be covered with boils.'** Thus it was I myself who prayed for these afflictions, hoping that through them I might be granted atonement." [17] Having heard their master's story, **his disciples said to him: "Alas for us that we have seen you like this,** enduring so much suffering." [18] Naḥum **said to them: "Alas for me, if you had not seen me like this.** I am glad to be subjected to

[1] פַּעַם אַחַת בִּקְּשׁוּ תַּלְמִידָיו
לְפַנּוֹת מִטָּתוֹ וְאַחַר כָּךְ לְפַנּוֹת
אֶת הַכֵּלִים. [2] אָמַר לָהֶם: ״בָּנַיי,
פַּנּוּ אֶת הַכֵּלִים וְאַחַר כָּךְ פַּנּוּ
אֶת מִטָּתִי, [3] שֶׁמּוּבְטָח לָכֶם
שֶׁכָּל זְמַן שֶׁאֲנִי בַּבַּיִת, אֵין
הַבַּיִת נוֹפֵל״. [4] פִּינּוּ אֶת הַכֵּלִים
וְאַחַר כָּךְ פִּינּוּ אֶת מִטָּתוֹ,
[5] וְנָפַל הַבַּיִת. [6] אָמְרוּ לוֹ
תַּלְמִידָיו: ״רַבִּי, וְכִי מֵאַחַר
שֶׁצַּדִּיק גָּמוּר אַתָּה, [7] לָמָּה
עָלְתָה לְךָ כָּךְ?״ [8] אָמַר לָהֶם:
״בָּנַיי, אֲנִי גָּרַמְתִּי לְעַצְמִי.
[9] שֶׁפַּעַם אַחַת הָיִיתִי מְהַלֵּךְ
בַּדֶּרֶךְ לְבֵית חָמִי, [10] וְהָיָה עִמִּי
מַשּׂוֹי שְׁלֹשָׁה חֲמוֹרִים, אֶחָד
שֶׁל מַאֲכָל, וְאֶחָד שֶׁל מִשְׁתֶּה,
וְאֶחָד שֶׁל מִינֵי מְגָדִים. [11] בָּא
עָנִי אֶחָד וְעָמַד לִי בַּדֶּרֶךְ, וְאָמַר
לִי: ׳רַבִּי, פַּרְנְסֵנִי!׳ [12] אָמַרְתִּי
לוֹ: ׳הַמְתֵּן עַד שֶׁאֶפְרוֹק מִן
הַחֲמוֹר׳. [13] לֹא הִסְפַּקְתִּי לִפְרוֹק
מִן הַחֲמוֹר עַד שֶׁיָּצְתָה נִשְׁמָתוֹ.
[14] הָלַכְתִּי וְנָפַלְתִּי עַל פָּנָיו,
[15] וְאָמַרְתִּי: ׳עֵינַי, שֶׁלֹּא חָסוּ עַל
עֵינֶיךָ, יִסּוֹמוּ. יָדַיי, שֶׁלֹּא חָסוּ
עַל יָדֶיךָ, יִתְגַּדְּמוּ. רַגְלַי, שֶׁלֹּא
חָסוּ עַל רַגְלֶיךָ, יִתְקַטְּעוּ׳. [16] וְלֹא
נִתְקָרְרָה דַּעְתִּי עַד שֶׁאָמַרְתִּי:
׳כָּל גּוּפִי יְהֵא מָלֵא שְׁחִין׳״.
[17] אָמְרוּ לוֹ: ״אוֹי לָנוּ שֶׁרְאִינוּךָ
בְּכָךְ״. [18] אָמַר לָהֶם: ״אוֹי לִי
אִם לֹא רְאִיתוּנִי בְּכָךְ״.

LITERAL TRANSLATION

[1] Once his disciples wished to remove his bed and afterwards to remove the utensils. [2] He said to them: "My sons, remove the utensils and afterwards remove my bed, [3] for it is assured (lit., 'promised to you') that as long as I am in the house, the house will not fall." [4] They removed the utensils and afterwards they removed his bed, [5] and the house fell. [6] His disciples said to him: "Teacher, since you are a perfectly righteous man, [7] why did this happen to you?" [8] He said to them: "My sons, I caused [it] to myself. [9] For once I was traveling on the road to the house of my father-in-law, [10] and I had with me a load [that was being carried] on three asses, one of food, and one of drink, and one with various kinds of delicacies. [11] A poor man came and stood in front of me on the road, and said to me: 'My teacher, sustain me!' [12] I said to him: 'Wait until I unload the ass.' [13] I did not have time to unload the ass before his soul departed. [14] I went and fell on his face, [15] and I said: 'Let my eyes, which had no compassion for your eyes, become blind. Let my hands, which had no compassion for your hands, be cut off. Let my legs, which had no compassion for your legs, be amputated.' [16] And my mind did not become calm (lit., 'become cool') until I said: 'Let my entire body be full of boils.'" [17] They said to him: "Alas for us that we have seen you like this." [18] He said to them: "Alas for me, if you had not seen me like this."

TRANSLATION AND COMMENTARY

all this suffering, for in this way I may expiate for the insensitivity I showed to a poor, hungry man."

וְאַמַּאי קָרוּ לֵיהּ [1]The Gemara now relates another story about Naḥum of Gam Zu. **Why was he called Naḥum of Gam Zu?** The designation "of Gam Zu" probably refers to his home town, Gimzu, in the center of Eretz Israel near Lod. [2]But the Gemara suggests that he was called Naḥum of Gam Zu **because whatever happened to him,** whether good or bad, [3]**he would** always **say: "This too** [*gam zu* — גַּם זוּ] **is for the best."** He remained permanently convinced that, no matter how bleak the situation, there is a favorable aspect to all that God does in this world which will eventually reveal itself. The Gemara illustrates this custom of Naḥum's with the following story: [4]It **once** happened that the Jewish community in Eretz **Israel wished to send a gift to the** Roman **emperor.** [5]**They asked** themselves: **"Who will go** to Rome with the gift?" [6]And they answered: **"Let Naḥum of Gam Zu** go, **for he is experienced in miracles.** If a difficulty arises that threatens the success of the mission, Naḥum's extreme piety will merit that a miracle be performed on his behalf, and this will assure a favorable outcome." [7]So he **was sent** to Rome **with a chest full of precious stones and pearls** as a gift for the emperor. During Naḥum's journey, [8]**he spent a night at a certain inn.** [9]**That night**, while Naḥum was asleep, **the innkeepers got up, took his chest,** removed the precious stones and other jewels, **and refilled** the chest **with earth.** [10]**When Naḥum arrived** at his destination and presented the gift to the emperor, the emperor's servants **opened the chest and saw that it was filled with earth.** [11]Enraged by the insult, **the emperor wished to put** Naḥum and the rest of his delegation **to death.** [12]**He said:** "Surely **the Jews are mocking me!"** [13]Unperturbed, Naḥum **said: "This too must** surely **be for the best!"** [14]Before the emperor could carry out the execution, **Elijah** the Prophet **came, and appeared to** the emperor **as one of** the Roman officers. [15]Elijah **said to** the emperor: "It is inconceivable that the Jews sent you a chestful of earth merely in order to anger you. **Perhaps the earth** they presented to you **was** taken **from the earth of their father Abraham.** [16]Legend has it that **when** Abraham **would throw** a clod of **earth** into the air, **it would be turned into swords,** [17]and similarly when he would throw **straw, it would be** turned into **arrows."** [18]The legend is based on **the verse** that **says** (Isaiah 41:2): "Who raised up a man from the East, whom righteousness met wherever he set his foot, gave the nations before him, and made him rule over kings? [19]**He makes his sword as dust, his bow as driven straw."** The Rabbis understood that "the man from the East" is an allusion to the Patriarch Abraham who left his birthplace in the East and moved to Eretz Israel. Thus the verse can be understood as referring to the dust that Abraham could convert into swords,

[1]וְאַמַּאי קָרוּ לֵיהּ נַחוּם אִישׁ גַּם זוּ? [2]דְּכָל מִילְּתָא דַּהֲוָה סָלְקָא לֵיהּ, [3]אָמַר: "גַּם זוּ לְטוֹבָה". [4]זִימְנָא חֲדָא בָּעוּ לְשַׁדּוּרֵי יִשְׂרָאֵל דּוֹרוֹן לְבֵי קֵיסָר. [5]אָמְרוּ: "מַאן יֵיזִיל? [6]יֵיזִיל נַחוּם אִישׁ גַּם זוּ, דִּמְלוּמָּד בְּנִיסִּין הוּא". [7]שַׁדְּרוּ בִּידֵיהּ מְלֹא סִיפְטָא דַּאֲבָנִים טוֹבוֹת וּמַרְגָּלִיּוֹת. [8]אֲזַל בָּת בְּהַהוּא דִּירָא. [9]בְּלֵילְיָא קָמוּ הָנָךְ דִּיוֹרָאֵי, וְשַׁקְלִינְהוּ לְסִיפְטֵיהּ וּמְלוּנְהוּ עַפְרָא. [10]כִּי מְטָא הָתָם, שְׁרִינְהוּ לְסִיפְטָא, חֲזַנְהוּ דִּמְלוּ עַפְרָא. [11]בְּעָא מַלְכָּא לְמִקְטְלִינְהוּ לְכוּלְּהוּ. [12]אֲמַר: "קָא מְחַיְּיכוּ בִּי יְהוּדָאֵי!" [13]אֲמַר: גַּם זוּ לְטוֹבָה. [14]אֲתָא אֵלִיָּהוּ, אִדַּמִּי לֵיהּ כְּחַד מִינַּיְיהוּ. [15]אֲמַר לֵיהּ: "דִּלְמָא הָא עַפְרָא מֵעַפְרָא דְּאַבְרָהָם אֲבוּהוֹן הוּא. [16]דְּכִי הֲוָה שָׁדֵי עַפְרָא, הָווּ סַיְיפֵיהּ; [17]גִּילֵי, הָווּ גִּירֵי. [18]דִּכְתִיב: [19]'יִתֵּן כֶּעָפָר חַרְבּוֹ, כְּקַשׁ נִדָּף קַשְׁתּוֹ'".

LITERAL TRANSLATION

[1]And why did they call him Naḥum of Gam Zu? [2]Because whatever happened to him, [3]he would say: "This too is for the best." [4]Once Israel wished to send a gift to the house of the emperor. [5]They said: "Who will go? [6]Let Naḥum of Gam Zu go, for he is experienced in miracles." [7]They sent with him a chest full of precious stones and pearls. [8]He went [and] spent the night at a certain inn. [9]In the night the inhabitants got up, and took his chest and filled it with earth. [10]When he reached there, they opened the chest, [and] saw that it was filled with earth. [11]The emperor wished to put them all to death. [12]He said: "The Jews are laughing at me!" [13]He said: "This too is for the best." [14]Elijah came, [and] appeared to him as one of them. [15]He said to him: "Perhaps this earth is from the earth of their father Abraham. [16]For when he would throw earth, it would become swords; [17]straw, it would become arrows. [18]For it is written: [19]'He makes his sword as dust, his bow as driven straw.'"

RASHI

דסלקי ליה — כל המאורע לו, אפילו רעה. **בת בההיא דיורא** — לן לילה אחת באותו המלון. **לסיפטיה** — ארגז שלו. **לכולהו** — שותפיהן של ישראל. **כחד מינייהו** — כאחד משרי קיסר. **מעפרא דאברהם הוא** — כשנלחם עם המלכים. **גילי** — קשין.

LANGUAGE

דּוֹרוֹן A gift. From the Greek δῶρον, *doron,* meaning "a gift," especially a gift given to honor someone.

סִיפְטָא A chest. This word is probably derived from the Persian *sapad,* meaning "a basket," especially an object in which valuable things are hidden. This is its meaning in several Iranian dialects.

TRANSLATION AND COMMENTARY

and the straw that he could turn into arrows. [1]Now, **there was a certain country that** the Romans **were unable to conquer.** The emperor decided to test the earth that the Jews had presented to him, and to see whether or not it had any miraculous qualities. [2]The emperor's men **tested** the earth in actual battle, **and** with its help **they** were able to **conquer** the country that had previously withstood them. When the Romans were convinced that the Jews had sent them an invaluable gift, [3]**they entered the** imperial **treasury, filled** Naḥum's **chest with precious stones and pearls, and sent him** and his delegation **away with great honor.** [4]**On their way home, they spent a night at the same inn** where they had stayed on their way to Rome. Surprised to see that Naḥum had been well received in Rome, [5]the innkeepers **said to him: "What did you take with you that** the Roman officials **treated you with such great honor?"** [6]Naḥum **said to them: "What I brought from here I took there."** The innkeepers concluded that the earth on which their inn was standing must have some sort of miraculous power. [7]They pulled down their inn, and took the earth on which it stood to the house of the emperor. [8]They said to him: "The **earth that was brought here** by Naḥum **was** really **ours,** and now we have brought you an additional supply." [9]The emperor's men **tested** the earth in battle, **but did not find** that it had any miraculous powers, [10]and **so they put the innkeepers to death.**

אֵי זוֹ הִיא דֶּבֶר [11]The Gemara now proceeds to discuss the next clause of our Mishnah, which stated: **"What is** the definition of a **plague** that requires the residents of the city struck by the disease to fast? If **the city sends out five hundred foot-soldiers,** and three corpses of men who have died of the disease have been taken out of the city for burial over a period of three days, one after the other, that is the plague which requires the city's residents to begin fasting and to sound the alarm." [12]**Our Rabbis taught** a related Baraita which says that a city with a larger population is regarded as having been struck by a plague if it has a proportionately higher mortality rate: [13]"If **a city sends out fifteen hundred foot-soldiers** — in other words, if the city has an able-bodied male population of fifteen hundred, **as in Kfar Akko — and nine corpses** of men who died of the disease **have been taken out of** the city for burial **over** a period of **three days, one after the other,** three men having died each day for three days, [14]**that is the plague** which requires the city's residents to begin fasting and to sound the alarm. [15]But if all nine men died **on one day, or** if they died **over** a period of **four days, this is not a plague** that requires fasting or the sounding of the alarm. [16]If **a city sends out five hundred foot-solders** — in other words, if five hundred able-bodied men live in the city,

[1]הֲוָיא חֲדָא מְדִינְתָּא דְּלָא מָצוּ לְמִיכְבְּשָׁהּ. [2]בַּדְקוּ מִינֵּיהּ וּכְבָשׁוּהָ. [3]עָיְילוּ לְבֵי גְּנָזֵיהּ, וּמַלּוּהוּ לְסִיפְטֵיהּ אֲבָנִים טוֹבוֹת וּמַרְגָּלִיּוֹת, וְשַׁדְּרוּהוּ בִּיקָרָא רַבָּה. [4]כִּי אָתוּ בָּיְתוּ בְּהַהוּא דִּיוֹרָא. [5]אָמְרוּ לֵיהּ: "מַאי אַיְיתִית בַּהֲדָךְ דַּעֲבַדִי לָךְ יְקָרָא כּוּלֵּי הַאי?" [6]אֲמַר לְהוּ: "מַאי דְּשָׁקְלִי מֵהָכָא אַמְטֵי לְהָתָם". [7]סָתְרוּ לְדִירַיְיהוּ וְאַמְטְינְהוּ לְבֵי מַלְכָּא. [8]אָמְרוּ לֵיהּ: "הַאי עַפְרָא דְּאַיְיתֵי הָכָא מִדִּידַן הוּא". [9]בַּדְקוּהּ, וְלָא אַשְׁכְּחוּהּ. [10]וְקַטְלִינְהוּ לְהָנָךְ דִּיוֹרָאֵי.

[11]"אֵי זוֹ הִיא דֶּבֶר? עִיר הַמּוֹצִיאָה חֲמֵשׁ מֵאוֹת רַגְלִי, כו'". [12]תָּנוּ רַבָּנַן: [13]"עִיר הַמּוֹצִיאָה חֲמֵשׁ מֵאוֹת וְאֶלֶף רַגְלִי, כְּגוֹן כְּפַר עַכּוֹ, וְיָצְאוּ הֵימֶנָּה תִּשְׁעָה מֵתִים בִּשְׁלֹשָׁה יָמִים זֶה אַחַר זֶה — [14]הֲרֵי זֶה דֶּבֶר. [15]בְּיוֹם אֶחָד אוֹ בְּאַרְבָּעָה יָמִים — אֵין זֶה דֶּבֶר. [16]וְעִיר הַמּוֹצִיאָה חֲמֵשׁ מֵאוֹת רַגְלִי,

LITERAL TRANSLATION

[1]There was one country that they were unable to conquer. [2]They tested some of it and they conquered it. [3]They entered the treasury, and filled his chest with precious stones and pearls, and sent him [away] with great honor. [4]When they came, they spent the night in that same inn. [5]They said to him: "What did you take with you that they treated you with such great honor?" [6]He said to them: "What I brought from here I took there." [7]They pulled down their inn and took it to the house of the emperor. [8]They said to him: "That earth which came here was ours." [9]They tested it, but did not find in it [the same miraculous power]. [10]So they put those innkeepers to death.

[11]"What is plague? A city that sends out five hundred foot soldiers, etc." [12]Our Rabbis taught: "A city that sends out one-thousand-five-hundred foot soldiers, [13]like Kfar Akko, and nine dead went out from it on three days one after the other — [14]this is plague. [15]On one day or on four days — this is not plague. [16]And a city that sends out five hundred foot soldiers,

RASHI

ביתו = לנו במלון.

[1]כְּגוֹן כְּפַר עָמִיקוֹ, וְיָצְאוּ מִמֶּנָּה שְׁלֹשָׁה מֵתִים בִּשְׁלֹשָׁה יָמִים זֶה אַחַר זֶה — [2]הֲרֵי זֶה דֶּבֶר. [21B] [3]בְּיוֹם אֶחָד אוֹ בְּאַרְבָּעָה יָמִים — [4]אֵין זֶה דֶּבֶר.

[5]דְּרוֹקַרְתְּ עִיר הַמּוֹצִיאָה חֲמֵשׁ מֵאוֹת רַגְלִי הֲוָה, וְיָצְאוּ מִמֶּנָּה שְׁלֹשָׁה מֵתִים בְּיוֹם אֶחָד. [6]גְּזַר רַב נַחְמָן בַּר רַב חִסְדָּא תַּעֲנִיתָא. [7]אֲמַר רַב נַחְמָן בַּר יִצְחָק: כְּמַאן? [8]כְּרַבִּי מֵאִיר, [9]דְּאָמַר: ״רִיחֵק נְגִיחוֹתָיו חַיָּיב, [10]קֵירֵב נְגִיחוֹתָיו לֹא כָּל שֶׁכֵּן!״

LITERAL TRANSLATION

[1]like Kfar Amiko, and three dead went out from it on three days one after the other — [2]this is plague. [21B] [3]On one day or on four days — [4]this is not plague."

[5]Drokart was a city that sends out five hundred foot soldiers, and three dead went out from it on one day. [6]Rav Naḥman bar Rav Ḥisda decreed a fast. [7]Rav Naḥman bar Yitzḥak said: In accordance with whom? [8]In accordance with Rabbi Meir, [9]who said: "[If where] it did its gorings at intervals he is liable, [10][then where] it did its gorings close together, how much more so!"

TRANSLATION AND COMMENTARY

[1]**as in Kfar Amiko — and three corpses** of men who have died of the disease **have been taken out of** the city for burial **over** a period of **three days, one after the other**, one man having died each day for three days, [2]**that is the plague** which requires the city's residents to begin fasting and to sound the alarm. [21B] [3]But if all three men died **on one day, or** if they died **over** a period of **four days,** [4]**this is not a plague** which requires fasting or the sounding of the alarm."

דְּרוֹקַרְתְּ [5]The Gemara now relates an incident which appears to contradict our Mishnah and the Baraita just cited: **Drokart was a city in which five hundred** able-bodied **men lived, and three corpses** of men who had died of a certain disease **were taken out of** the city **in one day.** [6]**Rav Naḥman bar Rav Ḥisda** immediately **decreed a fast.** [7]**Rav Naḥman bar Yitzḥak said: In accordance with whose** viewpoint did Rav Naḥman bar Rav Ḥisda proclaim the fast? Surely the Baraita states explicitly that if three people die on one day, and nobody else dies during the next two days, this is not regarded as a plague that requires fasting and the sounding of an alarm. Why, then, did Rav Naḥman bar Rav Ḥisda decree that the residents of Drokart must fast when a certain disease caused three people to die in a single day? [8]He must have proclaimed the fast **in accordance with** the opinion of **Rabbi Meir** regarding a *shor mu'ad* (שׁוֹר מוּעָד — "a goring ox"), whose owner has been forewarned. If an ox causes damage by goring or by some other malicious act, then the first three times that it causes damage it is regarded as a *shor tam* (שׁוֹר תָּם — "an innocent ox"), and the owner is liable for only half of the damage it has caused. But if the ox gores a fourth time, and the owner was officially notified about his ox's behavior after each of the first three gorings, the animal is considered a *shor mu'ad*, a habitually goring ox, and the owner must pay in full for the damage. We have learned elsewhere in the Mishnah (*Bava Kamma* 23b) that, according to Rabbi Yehudah, an ox is only regarded as a *mu'ad* if it gores on three consecutive days, whereas according to Rabbi Meir it is treated as a *mu'ad* even if it gores three times in one day. [9]And it was taught in a Baraita (ibid., 23b-24a) that Rabbi Meir justified his position, **saying: "If where** the ox **did its gorings at intervals,** goring on three separate days, its owner **is liable** to pay full damages if his ox gores a fourth time, [10]**then** it stands to reason that **when** the ox **did its gorings close together,** goring three times in one day, its owner should **all the more** be required to pay in full for the damage caused by his ox if it gores again!" Rav Naḥman bar Yitzḥak is suggesting that Rav Naḥman bar Rav Ḥisda must follow the opinion of Rabbi Meir regarding a *shor mu'ad*, applying Rabbi Meir's rationale to the subject of fasts: If where a disease has caused three people to die over a period of three days, one person dying on each of three consecutive days, the community is required to fast and to sound the alarm, then it stands to reason that where the disease has caused three people to die in a single day, the community should all the more be obligated to fast and to sound the alarm! But this presents a difficulty, for with respect to a *shor mu'ad* the law is not in accordance with the viewpoint of Rabbi Meir.

RASHI

כפר עמיקו שלשה מתים בשלשה ימים — מת אחד בכל יום. **ביום אחד אין זה דבר** — לאקראי בעלמא הוא.
הכי גרסינן: עיר גדולה המוציאה אלף וחמש מאות רגלי יצאו הימנה תשעה מתים וכו׳ — אלף וחמש מאות איש דהיינו פי שלשה בעיר קטנה. **כפר עכו דרוקרת** — נוסח אחר: דיוקרא, עיר ששמה יו״ד, והיא קטנה, על שם שיו״ד קטנה באותיות. **הכי גרסינן: יצאו הימנה שלשה מתים בשלשה ימים.**
ריחק נגיחותיו — בשור מוּעָד קאי, בבבא קמא, בפרק ״כיצד הרגל מועדת״ (כד,א) אי זהו תם ואי זהו מועד, כל שהעידו בו שלשה ימים — דברי רבי יהודה. רבי מאיר אומר: כל שהעידו בו שלש פעמים ביום אחד. רבי יהודה סבר: כתיב ״או נודע כי שור נגח הוא מתמול שלשום״, ״מתמול״ — תרי, ״שלשום״ — תלת, הרי שלשה ימים. ורבי מאיר סבר: ריחק נגיחותיו, כשנגח בשלשה ימים זה אחר זה — חייב, קירב נגיחותיו שנגח שלש פעמים ביום אחד — לא כל שכן?

BACKGROUND

דְּרוֹקַרְתְּ Drokart. The location of this place is not known precisely. Some scholars believe that it is Darucarra, on the ruins of which the city of Wasit was built during the Arab period. It seems that several important Sages lived in or near this city, for Rav Huna, Rav Naḥman bar Yitzḥak, and others are mentioned in the Talmud in connection with it.

TRANSLATION AND COMMENTARY

אָמַר לֵיהּ [1]The Gemara continues: Impressed by this argument, **Rav Naḥman bar Rav Ḥisda said to Rav Naḥman bar Yitzḥak: "Rise, Sir, get up and come to** live with **us!"** Rav Naḥman bar Rav Ḥisda suggested to Rav Naḥman bar Yitzḥak that Drokart would be a community more fitting for a person of his stature. [2]But Rav Naḥman bar Yitzḥak refused the offer and **said to him: "We have learned** in a Baraita: [3]**'Rabbi Yose says: It is not the place that a person occupies which bestows honor upon him, but rather it is the person who bestows honor upon the place he occupies.** [4]Support for this maxim can be brought from two Biblical precedents. **We find regarding Mount Sinai that as long as the Divine Presence rested upon** the mountain during the period that God revealed the Torah to the Jewish people, [5]**the Torah said** [Exodus 34:3]: "And no man shall come up with you, neither let any man be seen throughout all the mountain, **neither let the flocks nor the herds feed before that mountain."** [6]But **when the Divine Presence withdrew from** the mountain, **the Torah said** [Exodus 19:13]: **"When the horn sounds long, they shall come up to the mountain."** When the horns were sounded, heralding the departure of the Divine Presence, the mountain once again became open to all. Thus we see that the mountain itself had no intrinsic sanctity. Its sanctity was wholly dependent on the Divine Presence. [7]**And similarly we find with respect to the Tent of Meeting** [the Tabernacle] **in the wilderness, that as long as** the Tent of Meeting **was pitched** and the Israelites remained encamped around it, [8]**the Torah said** [Numbers 5:2]: **"And they shall put out of the camp every leper,** and everyone suffering from gonorrhea, and whoever has been defiled by the dead." As long as the Tent of Meeting was standing and the Divine Presence rested upon it, the place where it stood was endowed with a certain sanctity that required that

[1]אָמַר לֵיהּ רַב נַחְמָן בַּר רַב חִסְדָּא לְרַב נַחְמָן בַּר יִצְחָק: "לֵיקוּם מָר, לֵיתֵי לְגַבָּן". [2]אָמַר לֵיהּ: "תְּנֵינָא: [3]'רַבִּי יוֹסֵי אוֹמֵר: לֹא מְקוֹמוֹ שֶׁל אָדָם מְכַבְּדוֹ, אֶלָּא אָדָם מְכַבֵּד אֶת מְקוֹמוֹ. [4]שֶׁכֵּן מָצִינוּ בְּהַר סִינַי, שֶׁכָּל זְמַן שֶׁהַשְּׁכִינָה שְׁרוּיָה עָלָיו, [5]אָמְרָה תּוֹרָה: "גַּם הַצֹּאן וְהַבָּקָר אַל יִרְעוּ אֶל מוּל הָהָר הַהוּא". [6]נִסְתַּלְּקָה שְׁכִינָה מִמֶּנּוּ, אָמְרָה תּוֹרָה: "בִּמְשֹׁךְ הַיֹּבֵל, הֵמָּה יַעֲלוּ בָהָר". [7]וְכֵן מָצִינוּ בְּאֹהֶל מוֹעֵד שֶׁבַּמִּדְבָּר, שֶׁכָּל זְמַן שֶׁהוּא נָטוּי, [8]אָמְרָה תּוֹרָה: "וִישַׁלְּחוּ מִן הַמַּחֲנֶה כָּל צָרוּעַ".

LITERAL TRANSLATION

[1]Rav Naḥman bar Rav Ḥisda said to Rav Naḥman bar Yitzḥak: "Rise, Sir, [and] come to us." [2]He said to him: "We have learned: [3]'Rabbi Yose says: It is not a person's place that bestows honor upon him, but rather a person bestows honor upon his place. [4]For thus we find with respect to Mount Sinai, that all the time that the Divine Presence rested upon it, [5]the Torah said: "Let neither the flocks nor the herds feed before that mountain." [6][When] the Divine Presence withdrew from it, the Torah said: "When the horn sounds long, they shall come up to the mountain." [7]And similarly we find with respect to the Tent of Meeting in the wilderness, that all the time that it was pitched, [8]the Torah said: "And they shall put out of the camp every leper."

RASHI

ליקום מר להכא — דרב נחמן בר יצחק הוה יתיב בין גברי דלא חשיבי כולי האי, וקאמר ליה רב נחמן בר רב חסדא: ליקום מר מהתם וליתי ליתיב גבאי. **תנינא** — אני תנא, שונה אני ברייתא זו: רבי יוסי אומר כו'. **לא מקומו של אדם מכבדו** — ואם אלך ואשב שם — אין המקום מכבדני. **גם הצאן והבקר אל ירעו** — דמשום שכינה היה הר סיני מכובד ומקודש. **אל מול ההר ההוא** — מדכתיב "ההוא" משמע: כל זמן שהוא בגדולתו, שהשכינה עליו. נסתלקה השכינה "במשוך היובל" וגו'. ואף על גב דהאי קרא בלוחות הראשונות כתיב — לא נסתלקה שכינה עד לוחות האחרונות שניתנו ביום הכפורים. וגם כל ימות החורף שעסקו במלאכת המשכן שהתה שכינה בהר, ומשם ניתנו כל המצות בקולי קולות ולפידים ביום קבלת עשרת הדברות, עד אחד בניסן שהוקם המשכן. ונסעה וזזה שכינה מן ההר וישבה לה על הכפורת, ושם באהל מועד נשנית התורה כללותיה ופרטותיה. ועל אותה שעה היה מתיר להם בלוחות הראשונות לעלות, כדאמרינן במסכת ביצה (ה,א): כל דבר שבמנין — צריך מנין אחר להתירו. ובראש קונטרס רומי אתה מוצא תשובת רבים בכך. **במשוך היובל** — בסיום השופר, כשמסתלק השכינה. דרך הוא להאריך ולמשוך התקיעה בשעת סיום.

NOTES

אֶל מוּל הָהָר הַהוּא Before that mountain. As *Rashi* points out, the maxim that it is the person who bestows honor on the place he occupies, and not vice versa, is derived from the two verses mentioned here. The word "that" (הַהוּא) in the expression "that mountain" is superfluous, and teaches us that no man was permitted to ascend Mount Sinai while it was "that mountain," the mountain on which the Divine Presence was resting. But once the Divine Presence withdrew from the mountain, it once again became accessible to all, as the second verse states, "When the horn sounds long, they shall come up to the mountain." According to *Rashi*, the prohibition against ascending Mount Sinai continued after the Tablets of the Covenant were given, both after the first set was given and after the second set, for the Divine Presence remained on the mountain for almost another year until the Tabernacle was erected on the first of Nisan and the Divine Presence moved from the mountain and rested upon the ark in the

TRANSLATION AND COMMENTARY

those who were defiled should be sent away. [1]But **when the curtain was rolled up** and the Tent of Meeting was made ready for transporting, **lepers and those suffering from gonorrhea were allowed to come into** the area where the Tent of Meeting had previously stood.' Thus we see that the site of the Tent of Meeting had no intrinsic sanctity. It was endowed with special sanctity only as long as the Tent of Meeting was standing and the Divine Presence was resting upon it. This being the case, there is no reason for me to leave my community and to move to the more distinguished city of Drokart. For Drokart has no intrinsic honor that will be bestowed on me when I arrive there. If I indeed deserve it, I will find honor and distinction anywhere." [2]Determined to benefit from his colleague's learning, Rav Naḥman bar Rav Ḥisda **said to** Rav Naḥman bar Yitzḥak: **"If so, I will rise and come to you, Sir."** [3]Rav Naḥman bar Yitzḥak **said to** Rav Naḥman bar Rav Ḥisda: "If one of us is to move, it is better that I come to you, rather than that you come to me. [4]For **it is preferable that a maneh who is the son of half** a maneh **should come to a maneh who is the son of a maneh, rather than that a maneh who is the son of a maneh should go to a maneh who is the son of half** a maneh. While I may be an accomplished scholar, my father was not a particularly learned man. But you are not only an accomplished scholar in your own right, but your father, Rav Ḥisda, was also a great Sage. It is fitting that the scholar from an undistinguished family should visit the scholar of distinguished lineage, and not the other way round."

בְּסוּרָא הֲוַות דִּבַרְתָּא [5]The Gemara continues with the following anecdote: **In** the city of **Sura there was** once an outbreak of **plague, but in Rav's neighborhood there was no** incidence of the **disease**. Many **people thought that it was on account of Rav's great merit** that his neighborhood was not visited by the disease. [6]But **it was revealed to them in a dream** that the neighborhood's good fortune in being spared the disease was not to be attributed to the good deeds of Rav. [7]**Rav's merit was** so **very great that this matter was** too

[1]הוּגְלְלוּ הַפָּרוֹכֶת, הוּתְּרוּ זָבִין וְהַמְצוֹרָעִים לִיכָּנֵס שָׁם׳״. [2]אֲמַר לֵיהּ: ״אִי הָכִי, נֵיקוּם אֲנָא לְגַבֵּי מָר״. [3]אֲמַר לֵיהּ: [4]״מוּטָב יָבֹא מָנֶה בֶּן פְּרָס אֵצֶל מָנֶה בֶּן מָנֶה, וְאַל יָבֹא מָנֶה בֶּן מָנֶה אֵצֶל מָנֶה בֶּן פְּרָס״.
[5]בְּסוּרָא הֲוַות דִּבַרְתָּא, בְּשִׁיבָבוּתֵיהּ דְּרַב לָא הֲוָות דִּבַרְתָּא. [6]סְבַרוּ מִינֵּיהּ מִשּׁוּם זְכוּתֵיהּ דְּרַב, דְּנָפֵישׁ. [7]אִיתְחֲזִי לְהוּ בְּחִילְמָא: רַב דִּנְפִישָׁא זְכוּתֵיהּ טוּבָא, הָא מִילְּתָא

LITERAL TRANSLATION

[1][When] the curtain was rolled up, those suffering from gonorrhea and the lepers were permitted to enter there.'" [2]He said to him: "If so, I will rise [and come] to you, Sir." [3]He said to him: [4]"It is preferable that a maneh [who is] the son of a half should come to a maneh [who is] the son of a maneh, and that a maneh [who is] the son of a maneh should not come to a maneh [who is] the son of a half."

[5]In Sura there was a plague, [but] in Rav's neighborhood there was no plague. [6]They thought [that it was] on account of the merit of Rav, which was great. [7]It was revealed to them in a dream: Rav whose merit is very great, this matter

RASHI

הוגללו הפרוכת — שהיו נגללין בשעת נסיעתן היו נוסעין כולן, ובאין זבים ומצורעים ונכנסין במחנה. **פרס** — חצי מנה, ולשון פרוסה, כמו ״פרס פריסת מלכותך״ (דניאל ה). שאביו של רב נחמן בר רב חסדא גדול מיצחק אביו של רב נחמן, מדמיתקרי בר רב חסדא ואידך רב נחמן בר יצחק, מכלל שלא נסמך. **דברתא** — דֶבֶר. **בשיבבותיה** — בשכונתו. **איתחזי להו בחילמא** — להנך אינשי דסברי משום זכותיה דרב הוא.

BACKGROUND

מָנֶה בֶּן פְּרָס A maneh who is the son of a half. Since Rav Naḥman bar Yitzḥak's father is not given the title "Rav," it is likely that he was not learned in Torah, though he married into a family of Sages. In any event, Rav Ḥisda (the father of Rav Naḥman bar Rav Ḥisda), was one of the greatest Sages of the second and third generations of Amoraim in Babylonia, and Rav Naḥman bar Yitzḥak was one of his students. Hence it is understandable that he gave great honor to the son of his teacher.

יָבֹא מָנֶה בֶּן פְּרָס That a maneh who is the son of a half. This is apparently what he actually did, for we find in several places in the Talmud that Rav Naḥman bar Yitzḥak issued Halakhic rulings in Drokart, which is where he lived, or where he went to live for some time.

LANGUAGE

פְּרָס A half. The main meaning of this root is to cut or break, and the meaning of לִפְרֹס is generally "to cut," or "to count." However, this word is often used to mean a half, the half of something (hence half a maneh).

NOTES

Tabernacle. *Rabbi Ya'akov Emden* maintains that the verse, "When the horn sounds long," teaches us that the prohibition against ascending the mountain was removed immediately after the Torah was revealed and the first set of tablets of stone were given to Moses. It was therefore necessary for the Torah to state once again, before the second set of tablets was given, that "no man shall come up with you...before that mountain," for in the meantime access to the mountain had been permitted.

אֵצֶל מָנֶה בֶּן פְּרָס To a maneh who is the son of a half. *Rashi* and *Tosafot* note the difference in the way that the Gemara refers to the two scholars featured in this story: The one is called Rav Naḥman bar Rav Ḥisda, while the other is called Rav Naḥman bar Yitzḥak. The first was the son of the great Sage Rav Ḥisda, while the second was the son of a man who had never been ordained with the title Rav.

Rabbi Ya'akov Emden argues that it would have been disrespectful for Rav Naḥman bar Yitzḥak to consider himself his father's superior in knowledge of Torah, referring to himself as a maneh and to his father as half a maneh. Rather, Rav Naḥman bar Yitzḥak was referring not to scholarly accomplishment but to material wealth. Rav Naḥman bar Yitzḥak himself was a wealthy man, but his father Yitzḥak was not. Rav Naḥman bar Rav Ḥisda, on the other hand, was a rich man and also the son of a rich man.

LANGUAGE

מָרָא A hoe. The source of this word is the Latin *marra*, which means "a hoe."

זְבִילָא Shovel. This word is apparently related to זֶבֶל, meaning "garbage," and denotes a tool used for carrying garbage. From the description in the Talmud, it seems that it was some kind of shovel.

LANGUAGE (RASHI)

פושיי״ר* From the Old French *fossoir,* which means "a hoe."

פלי״א** From the Old French *pele,* meaning "a spade."

REALIA

מָרָא A hoe. From descriptions in the Talmud it seems that the hoe referred to looked something like this:

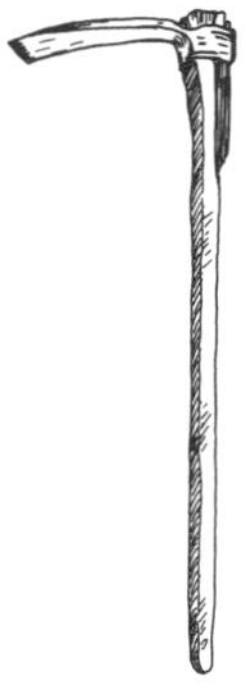

TRANSLATION AND COMMENTARY

small for Rav's merit to have played a role. [1]**Rather,** the neighborhood **was** spared the disease **on account of a certain** righteous **person,** [2]**who** was accustomed to **lend** out **his hoe and his shovel** when a grave had to be dug **for burial.** That man's acts of kindness in lending out his tools were rewarded measure for measure when those tools remained idle while similar tools were being used in other parts of the city to dig graves for the victims of the plague.

בְּדְרוֹקַרְתְּ [3]It was also reported that **in Drokart there was** once **a fire** which spread throughout most of the city, **but in Rav Huna's neighborhood there was no fire.** [4]Many **people thought that it was on account of Rav Huna's great merit** that the fire did not reach his neighborhood. [5]But **it was revealed to them in a dream** that **that matter was** too **small for Rav Huna's** great merit to have played a role. [6]**Rather,** the fire did not reach Rav Huna's neighborhood **on account of a certain** righteous **woman, who** was accustomed to **heat her oven** with her own firewood **and** then to **lend out** the heated oven **to her neighbors,** saving them the cost of fuel. Because she generously made her fire available, her neighborhood was spared from the fire that consumed a large part of the city.

אָמְרוּ לֵיהּ [7]The Gemara continues with a series of stories about fasts that were decreed by certain Amoraim in times of calamity. **It was reported to Rav Yehudah: "Locusts have arrived** in our area." [8]Rav Yehudah immediately **decreed a fast** in order to arouse God's compassion and to avert the calamity. Hearing that Rav Yehudah had proclaimed a fast, [9]certain **people said to him:** "There is no reason to decree a fast, for the locusts **are not** eating the crops or **causing** any other **damage."** [10]Rav Yehudah **said to** those who objected to the fast that he had decreed: **"Have** the locusts **brought provisions with them?"** Even if they have not yet caused damage, they will certainly do so in the future, for they have certainly not brought their own food with them!

אָמְרוּ לֵיהּ [11]The Gemara now relates that **it was reported to Rav Yehudah: "There is pestilence** spreading **among the pigs."** [12]Rav Yehudah immediately **decreed a fast.** The Gemara asks: Rav Yehudah appears to

זוּטְרָא לֵיהּ לְרַב. [1]אֶלָּא מִשּׁוּם הַהוּא גַּבְרָא, [2]דְּשַׁיֵּיל מָרָא וּזְבִילָא לִקְבוּרָה.
[3]בִּדְרוֹקַרְתְּ הֲוַות דְּלֵיקְתָא, וּבְשִׁיבָבוּתֵיהּ דְּרַב הוּנָא לָא הֲוַות דְּלֵיקְתָא. [4]סְבוּר מִינָּהּ בִּזְכוּתָא דְּרַב הוּנָא, דְּנָפֵישׁ. [5]אִיתְחֲזִי לְהוּ בְּחֶילְמָא: הַאי זוּטְרָא לֵיהּ לְרַב הוּנָא. [6]אֶלָּא מִשּׁוּם הַהִיא אִיתְּתָא דִּמְחַמְּמַתְּ תַּנּוּרָא וּמְשַׁיְּילֵי לְשִׁיבָבוּתֵיהּ.
[7]אָמְרוּ לֵיהּ לְרַב יְהוּדָה: "אָתוּ קַמְצֵי". [8]גְּזַר תַּעֲנִיתָא. [9]אֲמַרוּ לֵיהּ: "לָא קָא מַפְסְדָן". [10]אֲמַר לְהוּ: זַוְודָּא אַיְיתוּ בַּהֲדַיְיהוּ"?
[11]אֲמַרוּ לֵיהּ לְרַב יְהוּדָה: "אִיכָּא מוֹתָנָא בַּחֲזִירֵי". [12]גְּזַר

LITERAL TRANSLATION

is small for Rav. [1]Rather, [it was] on account of a certain person, [2]who lent a hoe and a shovel for burial.

[3]In Drokart there was a fire, but in Rav Huna's neighborhood there was no fire. [4]They thought [that it was] on account of the merit of Rav Huna, which was great. [5]It was revealed to them in a dream: This is small for Rav Huna. [6]Rather, [it was] on account of a certain woman who heated her oven and lent it to her neighbors.

[7]They said to Rav Yehudah: "Locusts have come." [8]He decreed a fast. [9]They said to him: "They are not causing damage." [10]He said to them: "Have they brought provisions with them?"

[11]They said to Rav Yehudah: "There is pestilence among the pigs." [12]He decreed

RASHI

הא זוטר ליה לרב — גם זה קטן הוא לפי גדולת רב. **מרא** — *פושיי״ר בלעז. **זבילי** — **פלי״א בלעז. **לקבורה** — ומשום זכותיה דקבורה מדדו בו מדה כנגד מדה. **ומשיילא לשיבבותיה** — ומשאילתו לשכנותיה לאחר שהסיקתו משלה, לפיכך נמדדת השכר בה במדה. **קמצא** — ארבה שמכלה את התבואה. **לא קא מפסדא** — לא בעינן למיגזר תעניתא. **זוודא איתו בהדייהו** — בתמיה: וכי צידה הביאו עמם שלא יפסידו את התבואה?

NOTES

הָא מִילְּתָא זוּטְרָא לֵיהּ לְרַב This matter is small for Rav. *Maharsha* explains that, while it is clear that Rav's great merit contributed to his neighborhood being saved, it was revealed to the people in a dream that they would have been saved even without Rav, by virtue of the merit of that righteous man who lent out his grave-digging tools for the benefit of the community. Alternatively, Rav's community was not saved by virtue of its great leader's merit, so that he would not have to pay for the miracle performed on its behalf with the merits that he had accumulated through his righteous behavior in the past (see above, 20b).

אִיכָּא מוֹתָנָא בַּחֲזִירֵי There is pestilence among the pigs.

HALAKHAH

אִיכָּא מוֹתָנָא בַּחֲזִירֵי There is pestilence among the pigs. "If plague has spread among pigs, a fast must be proclaimed, for a pig's intestines are similar to those of human beings, and there is concern that the disease will

TRANSLATION AND COMMENTARY

have been concerned that the disease among the pigs would eventually spread to people as well. [1]**Shall we conclude** from this **that Rav Yehudah maintains that** in general **an epidemic that has spread among one** particular **species can** be expected to **spread among all other** species?

לָא [2]The Gemara answers: **No.** In general, a disease afflicting one species does not spread to another. [3]But **pigs are different, because their intestines are** anatomically **similar to those of human beings,** and there is concern that a disease affecting pigs may be equally harmful to people.

אָמְרוּ לֵיהּ [4]The Gemara continues: **It was reported to Shmuel: "There is pestilence in** the region of **Bei Ḥoza'i."** [5]**He** immediately **decreed a fast** in his own city of Neharde'a, far away from the area affected by the disease. [6]The Neharde'ans **said to** Shmuel: **"But surely** Bei Ḥoza'i **is far away** from here!" [7]Shmuel **said** to them: "Distant as Bei Ḥoza'i may be, **there is no crossing** between **here** and there **to stop** the disease from spreading. Thus it is necessary to decree a fast, even here in Neharde'a."

אָמְרוּ לֵיהּ [8]A similar incident occurred in which **it was reported to Rav Naḥman: "There is pestilence** spreading **in Eretz Israel."** [9]On the basis of this report Rav Naḥman **decreed a fast** in his own city of Neharde'a. [10]**He explained** his action, saying: **"If the mistress,** Eretz Israel, **is afflicted,** [11]then **the maidservant,** Babylonia, **how much more so** is she afflicted!"

טַעֲמָא [12]The Gemara now asks: Rav Naḥman argued that **the reason** why he decreed a fast in Neharde'a when pestilence broke out in Eretz Israel **was that** he regarded Eretz Israel as **the mistress** with respect to the rest of the Jewish world **and** Babylonia as **the maidservant.** [13]**But** it follows from Rav Naḥman's argument that with respect to two places in Babylonia, both of which are regarded as **maidservants,** there is **no** reason to proclaim a fast in one on account of a plague that has broken out in the other. [14]**But** this poses a

תַּעֲנִיתָא. [1]נֵימָא קָסָבַר רַב יְהוּדָה מַכָּה מְשׁוּלַּחַת מִמִּין אֶחָד מְשׁוּלַּחַת מִכָּל הַמִּינִין? [2]לָא. [3]שָׁאנֵי חֲזִירֵי, דְּדָמְיָין מֵעַיְיהוּ לִבְנֵי אֱינָשֵׁי.

[4]אֲמַרוּ לֵיהּ לִשְׁמוּאֵל: ״אִיכָּא מוֹתָנָא בֵּי חוֹזַאי. [5]גְּזַר תַּעֲנִיתָא. [6]אֲמַרוּ לֵיהּ: ״וְהָא מְרַחֵק״! [7]אֲמַר: ״לֵיכָּא מַעַבְּרָא הָכָא דְּפָסֵיק לֵיהּ״.

[8]אֲמַרוּ לֵיהּ לְרַב נַחְמָן: ״אִיכָּא מוֹתָנָא בְּאַרְעָא דְּיִשְׂרָאֵל״. [9]גְּזַר תַּעֲנִיתָא. [10]אָמַר: ״אִם גְּבִירָה לוֹקָה, [11]שִׁפְחָה לֹא כָּל שֶׁכֵּן!״ [12]טַעֲמָא דִּגְבִירָה וְשִׁפְחָה. [13]הָא שִׁפְחָה וְשִׁפְחָה, לָא. [14]וְהָא אֲמַרוּ לֵיהּ לִשְׁמוּאֵל: ״אִיכָּא

LITERAL TRANSLATION

a fast. [1]Shall we say [that] Rav Yehudah maintains [that] an epidemic that is spread among one species will spread among all the species?

[2]No. [3]Pigs are different, because their intestines are similar to those of human beings.

[4]They said to Shmuel: "There is pestilence in Bei Ḥoza'i." [5]He decreed a fast. [6]They said to him: "But surely it is far away!" [7]He said: "There is no crossing here to stop it."

[8]They said to Rav Naḥman: "There is pestilence in Eretz Israel." [9]He decreed a fast. [10]He said: "If the mistress is afflicted, [11]the maidservant how much more so!"

[12]The reason is that [one is] a mistress and [the other is] a maidservant. [13]But [if one is] a maidservant and [the other is] a maidservant, no. [14]But surely they said to Shmuel: "There is

RASHI

מעייהו — בני מעיין שלהן, שאין להן כרס הפנימי כשאר בהמה, וסימן רע הוא. **בי חוזאי** — מקום במלכות בבל. **גזר תעניתא** — בעירו. **הא מרחק** — ואין לחוש שמא יבא עד כאן. **אמר להו וכי מעברא פסיק להו** — וכי מעברות ושאר מחילות מפסיקין לפני הדבר שלא יבא? **שפחה לא כל שכן** — ויש לחוש שמא ישתלח עד כאן. **הא שפחה ושפחה** — שתי עיירות של חוצה לארץ, כגון בי חוזאי ונהרדעא דאתריה דשמואל.

BACKGROUND

דְּדָמְיָין מֵעַיְיהוּ לִבְנֵי אֱינָשֵׁי Because their intestines are similar to those of human beings. There are a number of parasitic diseases, such as trichinosis, that can be passed from pigs to human beings. Most of these diseases are transmitted by eating the meat of pigs, which would not have happened in this case.

However, the internal anatomical similarity between pigs and human beings is well known, and pigs' intestines can be surgically transplanted into human beings because of the relatively low level of rejection. Rav Yehudah's concern was based on his fear that a disease that had struck pigs might also strike human beings.

בֵּי חוֹזַאי Bei Ḥoza'i. This is the Aramaic name for an area of the Persian kingdom at the confluence of the Tigris and Euphrates rivers (Shatt-al-Arab). Today the region is known as Huzistan, which means "the home of the Ḥoza'i" in Persian. The journey from this region to the main Jewish centers of population in Babylonia was long, taking more than a month. Nevertheless, because of the close commercial ties between Bei Ḥoza'i and northern Babylonia, it was feared that disease could be communicated from one region to the other, although it might take a considerable time.

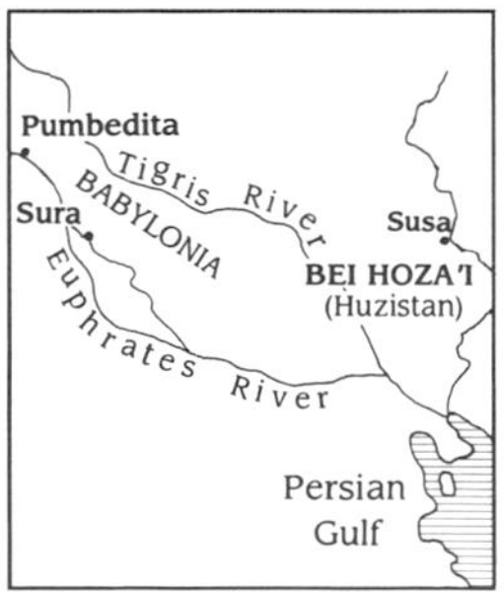

NOTES

Tosafot infers from this incident that if a plague is spreading among the non-Jewish inhabitants of a particular community, their Jewish neighbors must proclaim a fast. For if there is concern that a disease afflicting pigs will spread to human beings, because the intestines of a pig are anatomically similar to those of a human being, there should surely be concern that the disease will spread from the non-Jews to the Jews, for they are anatomically identical. *Ritva* cites a view according to which the Jewish community is not required to proclaim a fast, if its non-Jewish neighbors have been struck by disease, for while Jews and non-Jews constitute one biological species, the divine decrees issued against the one group do not necessarily apply to the other.

HALAKHAH

spread from the pigs to people. All the more so must a fast be proclaimed if the plague has reached the Jewish community's non-Jewish neighbors." (*Shulḥan Arukh, Oraḥ Ḥayyim* 576:3.)

אִיכָּא מוֹתָנָא בֵּי חוֹזַאי There is pestilence in Bei Ḥoza'i. "If plague has spread across a certain area, and caravans travel regularly between that place and other places, a fast must be proclaimed in those other places, even if they are far away from the plague-struck area, following Shmuel. If plague breaks out in Eretz Israel, a fast must be proclaimed throughout the Diaspora, following Rav Naḥman." (Ibid., 576:2.)

מוֹתָנָא בֵּי חוֹזַאי״, [1]גְּזַר תַּעֲנִיתָא!
[2]שָׁאנֵי הָתָם, כֵּיוָן דְּאִיכָּא שַׁיָּירָתָא דִּלְוַוי וְאָתְיָא בַּהֲדֵיהּ.
[3]אַבָּא אוּמָּנָא הֲוָה אָתֵי לֵיהּ שְׁלָמָא מִמְּתִיבְתָּא דִּרְקִיעָא כָּל יוֹמָא, [4]וּלְאַבַּיֵי כָּל מַעֲלֵי יוֹמָא דְּשַׁבְּתָא, לְרָבָא כָּל מַעֲלֵי יוֹמָא דְּכִיפּוּרֵי. [5]הֲוָה קָא חָלְשָׁא דַּעְתֵּיהּ דְּאַבַּיֵי מִשּׁוּם דְּאַבָּא אוּמָּנָא. [6]אֲמַרוּ לֵיהּ: ״לָא מָצֵית לְמֶיעֱבַד כְּעוֹבָדֵיהּ״. [7]וּמַאי הָווּ עוֹבָדֵיהּ דְּאַבָּא אוּמָּנָא? [8]דְּכִי הֲוָה עָבֵיד מִילְּתָא, הֲוָה מָחֵית גַּבְרֵי לְחוּד וְנָשֵׁי לְחוּד. [9]וְאִית לֵיהּ לְבוּשָׁא דְּאִית בֵּיהּ קַרְנָא, דַּהֲוַות בְּזִיעָא כִּי כּוּסִילְתָּא. [10]כִּי הֲוַות אָתְיָא לֵיהּ אִיתְּתָא, הֲוָה מַלְבִּישׁ לָהּ, כִּי הֵיכִי דְּלָא נִיסְתַּכֵּל בָּהּ. [11]וְאִית לֵיהּ דּוּכְתָּא דִּצְנִיעָא דְּשָׁדֵי בֵּיהּ פְּשִׁיטֵי דְּשָׁקֵיל. [12]דְּאִית לֵיהּ שָׁדֵי בֵּיהּ; [13]דְּלֵית לֵיהּ לָא

LITERAL TRANSLATION

pestilence in Bei Ḥoza'i," [1][and] he decreed a fast!

[2]It is different there, since there are caravans which it accompanies and goes with.

[3]Greetings from the Heavenly Academy would come to Abba the bloodletter every day, [4]and to Abaye every Friday, [and] to Rava every [year on] the eve of Yom Kippur. [5]Abaye was dejected on account of Abba the bloodletter. [6]They said to him: "You are unable to do as he does." [7]And what were the deeds of Abba the bloodletter? [8]When he would do something, he would place the men separately and the women separately. [9]And he had a garment which had a [bloodletting] horn, which had a slit for the bloodletting lancet. [10]When a woman would come to him, he would dress her in it, so that he would not look upon her. [11]And he had a hidden place where they would put the money that he would take. [12]Whoever had [money] would put [it] in; [13]whoever did not have would not be embarrassed.

TRANSLATION AND COMMENTARY

difficulty, for **surely** when **it was reported to Shmuel: "There is a pestilence in** the region of **Bei Ḥoza'i,"** [1]Shmuel **decreed a fast** in his own city of Neharde'a!

שָׁאנֵי הָתָם [2]The Gemara answers: Ordinarily, a fast would not be proclaimed in one place in Babylonia because of an outbreak of plague elsewhere, but the situation **is different** regarding Bei Ḥoza'i and Neharde'a. **Since there are caravans** that travel regularly between the two places, it is likely that the disease will **accompany** the travelers **and be carried with them** from one place to the other.

אַבָּא אוּמָּנָא הֲוָה [3]Having earlier cited several stories relating to the righteous deeds of the Sages, the Gemara now continues with another such story. **Greetings from the Heavenly Academy would come every day to Abba the bloodletter.** Every day a heavenly voice would speak to Abba the bloodletter, saying: "Peace be with you." [4]**To Abaye** the heavenly greetings would come **every Friday, and Rava** would be greeted by the heavenly voice **every year on the day before Yom Kippur.** [5]**Abaye was dejected on account of Abba the bloodletter,** for he could not understand why Abba the bloodletter merited being greeted daily by the heavenly voice, whereas he himself received such greetings only once a week before Shabbat. [6]Attempting to console Abaye, people **said to him: "You are unable to perform the** good **deeds that he performs,** on account of which he receives daily greetings from Heaven." [7]The Gemara asks: **And what were the** righteous **deeds** that **Abba the bloodletter** performed in the course of his work? [8]The Gemara answers: **When he engaged in bloodletting, he would set the men apart from women** for reasons of modesty. [9]**And he had a** special **garment containing the bloodletting cup, which had a slit for the bloodletting lancet.** [10]**When a woman came to him** for treatment, **he would have her dress in** that garment, **so that** she would be able to remain fully dressed during the bloodletting procedure and **he would not** come to **see her** exposed in even the slightest way. Moreover, he would not accept payment from his clients directly. [11]Instead, at his place of work **he had a hidden place where** his clients **would put the money he charged** for his services. Neither he nor anybody else would see who paid and who did not pay. [12]So **whoever had money** with which to pay him **would put** a coin **in,** [13]and **whoever did not**

RASHI

שיירתא — דאזלי מבי חוזאי לנהרדעא. **דלווי** — מתלוה ובא עמהן. **שלמא מרקיעא** — בת קול אומרת לו: שלום עליך. **אבא אומנא** — מקיז דם. **כי הוה עביד מילתא** — כשהיה מקיז דם לבני אדם. **ודנשים לחודייהו** — לצניעותא. **דאית ביה קרנא** — *וינטוס״א, שהיה תקוע בו הקרן שהוא מקיז בו, ולנשים הוי מלביש לה. **ולא מכסיף** — דלאחר שהכה לא הוה ידע מאן רמי (בכסילתיה) פשיטי להתם, ומאן דלא רמי.

BACKGROUND

אוּמָּנָא Bloodletter. An *ummana* is someone with a trade and a skill, but the term is used especially in reference to handicrafts and medical skills (similar to the use of the word "surgeon" in Greek culture). An *ummana* would let blood, circumcise, and perform simple operations.

PEOPLE

אַבָּא אוּמָּנָא Abba the bloodletter. For generations, physicians believed that letting blood was beneficial to the body, both to weaken various illnesses, and, more importantly, as a means of preserv ing health. Therefore people would have their blood let frequently in order to strengthen their bodies. Nevertheless it was also known that the letting of blood weakened the body, and that in certain cases it could be dangerous. Therefore the Sages recommended various foods to be eaten after the letting of blood, which were designed to provide energy for the body.

LANGUAGE

כּוּסִילְתָּא The bloodletting lancet. A Syrian-Aramaic word meaning "a scratch made in the skin for the purpose of letting blood."

פְּשִׁיטֵי Coins. Some scholars take this word to mean "simple" (פָּשׁוּט) — that is, simple coins, mainly of copper. Others associate the word with the Middle Persian *pasec*, meaning "a small coin."

LANGUAGE (RASHI)

וינטוש״א* From the Old French *ventose,* which means "a vessel used to let blood."

NOTES

לָא מָצֵית לְמֶיעֱבַד כְּעוֹבָדֵיהּ You are unable to do as he does. *Maharsha* points out that although Abaye surely engaged in charitable activities, he first and foremost served as the head of the Talmudic Academy at Pumbedita, and so he was unable to contribute as much of his time and money to charity as Abba the bloodletter.

TRANSLATION AND COMMENTARY

have any money **would** be able to **leave without embarrassment.** [1] **When a Talmudic scholar would come to** Abba to have his blood let, **he would not take a fee from him.** [2] On the contrary, **after** the scholar **stood up** at the end of the procedure, Abba **would give him money,** [3] **and say to him: "Go and** buy yourself some nourishing food so that you may **regain your strength."** [4] **One day Abaye sent a pair of Sages** to Abba the bloodletter **to check** how far his righteousness extended. [5] When the Sages arrived at his house, Abba **seated them, fed them** a meal, **gave them to drink,** [6] **and spread out rags for them** to sleep on **during the night.** [22A] [7] When they woke **in the morning,** the two visiting Sages **rolled up** their host's rugs, **got up and went out to the market with them** as if to sell them. The two Sages intended to see how Abba the bloodletter would react when he saw them putting the rugs up for sale. [8] Abba **found** the Sages in the market and saw that they were trying to sell his rugs. [9] The two Sages **said to him:** "Please **estimate, Sir, how much they are worth,** and we will sell them to you." [10] Instead of charging them with theft, Abba **said to them:** "They are worth **such-and-such."** [11] The two Sages then **said to him: "But perhaps they are** really **worth more."** [12] Abba **said to them: "I bought these** rugs myself **for that amount."** Seeing that Abba was not about to accuse them of stealing the mats from him, [13] the two Sages **said to him:** "These rugs **are yours, and we took them from you** in order to test your righteousness." [14] The two Sages continued: **"With your permission,** please tell us **what you thought of us** when you saw that we had taken your rugs? Why did you not say a word to us about the matter?" [15] Abba the bloodletter **said to them: "I said** to myself: [16] **These Sages must surely be involved in a case of redeeming captives.** [17] They need money, **but they were** too **embarrassed to tell me** and to ask me directly, so they took the rugs without asking my permission." [18] The Sages **said to him:**

מִיכְסִיף. [1] כִּי הֲוָה אִתְרַמֵי לֵיהּ צוּרְבָא מֵרַבָּנַן, אַגְרָא מִינֵּיהּ לָא שָׁקֵיל, [2] וּבָתַר דְּקָאֵי, יָהֵיב לֵיהּ פְּשִׁיטֵי, [3] וַאֲמַר לֵיהּ: ״זִיל בְּרִיא נַפְשָׁךְ״. [4] יוֹמָא חַד שְׁדַר אַבַּיֵי זוּגָא דְּרַבָּנַן לְמִיבְדְּקֵיהּ. [5] אוֹתְבִינְהוּ, וְאָכְלִינְהוּ, וְאַשְׁקִינְהוּ, [6] וּמָךְ לְהוּ בִּיסְתַּרְקֵי בְּלֵילְיָא. [22A] [7] לְצַפְרָא כָּרְכִינְהוּ וְשָׁקְלִינְהוּ, וְקָמוּ וּנְפַקוּ לְהוּ לְשׁוּקָא, [8] וְאַשְׁכַּחִינְהוּ. [9] אֲמַרוּ לֵיהּ: ״לְשַׁיְּימֵיהּ מָר הֵיכִי שָׁווּ״. [10] אֲמַר לְהוּ: ״הָכִי וְהָכִי״. [11] אֲמַרוּ לֵיהּ: ״וְדִלְמָא שָׁווּ טְפֵי״. [12] אֲמַר לְהוּ: ״בְּהָכִי שָׁקְלִינְהוּ״. [13] אֲמַרוּ לֵיהּ: ״דִּידָךְ נִיהוּ, וְשָׁקְלִינְהוּ מִינָּךְ״. [14] אמרו לֵיהּ: ״בְּמָטוּתָא מִינָּךְ, בְּמַאי חֲשַׁדְתִּינַן?״ [15] אֲמַר לְהוּ: ״אָמִינָא: [16] פִּדְיוֹן שְׁבוּיִים אִיקְלַע לְהוּ לְרַבָּנַן, [17] וְאִכְסִיפוּ לְמֵימַר לִי״. [18] אֲמַרוּ לֵיהּ:

LITERAL TRANSLATION

[1] When a Talmudic scholar would happen to come to him, he would not take a fee from him, [2] and after he got up, he would give him coins, [3] and would say to him: "Go [and] strengthen yourself."

[4] One day Abaye sent a pair of Sages to check him. [5] He seated them, and fed them, and gave them to drink, [6] and spread out rugs for them in the night. [22A] [7] In the morning, they rolled them up and took them, and they got up and went out to the market, [8] and he found them. [9] They said to him: "Estimate, Sir, how much they are worth." [10] He said to them: "Such-and-such." [11] They said to him: "But perhaps they are worth more." [12] He said to them: "I bought them for that [amount]." [13] They said to him: "They are yours, and we took them from you." [14] They said to him: "With your permission, of what did you suspect us?" [15] He said to them: "I said: [16] [A case of] redemption of captives happened to the Rabbis, [17] and they were embarrassed to tell me." [18] They said to him:

RASHI

בריא נפשך — תבריא עצמך. **למיבדקיה** — לבדקו במעשיו. **ומך להו בסתרקי** — קיפל תחתיהן תכשיטי צמר, *טפיד״ו בלעז, ליתן בהן. **לצפרא כרכינהו** — רבנן לביסתרקי דאבא אומנא, ואייתינהו לשוקא לזבינינהו. **אמרו ליה** — לאבא אומנא: לשיימינהו מר, והב לן דמייהו. והיו בודקין אותו אם יחשדם כגזלנין, או אם יהא שָׁם אותם פחות מכדי דמיהם. **במאי חשדתינן** — כשלקחנום. **וכסיפא** — לכו מילתא למימר לי לאלתר ליתן אותם, ואהכי אתו למיגני גבאי, למיעבד כולי האי.

LANGUAGE

בִּיסְתַּרְקֵי Rugs. The source of this word is apparently the Persian *bistar* (in Pahlavi, or Middle Persian, it is *vistarg*), meaning "a rug," "a couch" or "a carpet."

LANGUAGE (RASHI)

טפיד״ו* From the Italian *tapedo,* which means "a carpet" or "a rug."

NOTES

אַסְחְתִּינְהוּ מִדַּעְתַּאי לִצְדָקָה I dismissed them from my mind and gave them to charity. *Meiri* concludes from here that, whereas a mental commitment to give charity is not binding until that commitment is given verbal formulation, it is commendable that a person not withdraw a mental commitment to give charity, even if he took the obligation upon himself in error.

SAGES

רַבִּי בְּרוֹקָא חוֹזָאָה **Rabbi Beroka of Bei Ḥoza'i.** This Sage is mentioned only here, hence we do not know to which generation he belonged. Rabbi Beroka came from Bei Ḥoza'i, which was not an important Torah center.

BACKGROUND

בֵּי לֶפֶט **Bei Lefet.** This city, the Aramaic name of which was apparently *Bel-apat*, the city of the god Bel, was a large commercial center in the northern part of Bei Ḥoza'i. It was rebuilt by King Shavor and called "Gunde-Sabur" after him. However, the name Bei Lefet remained in use for many generations.

מְסָאנֵי אוּכָּמֵי **Black shoes.**

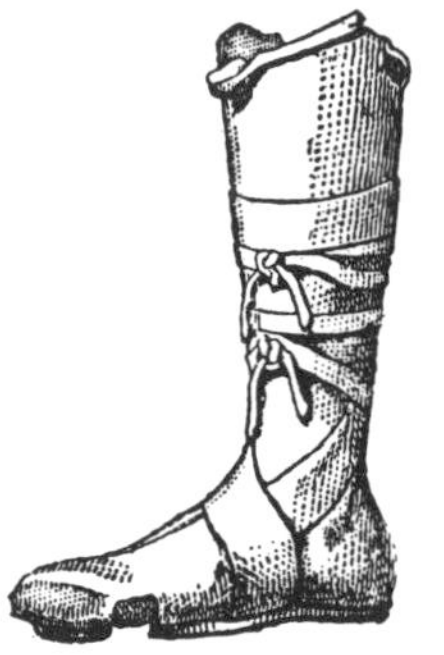

Shoe of a member of the senatorial class in Rome.

Shoes were generally like this, though there were differences in the number of straps and laces on the shoe. Each social class had straps of a distinctive color and shoes of a specific form, and it seems that there was a similar difference between the shoes worn by Jews and those worn by non-Jews.

The Jews apparently wore shoes with white straps, whereas the non-Jews had black straps. This was a sign which enabled people immediately to distinguish between Jews and non-Jews, and the Sages were very strict with those who changed the color of their shoes in order to resemble non-Jews.

TRANSLATION AND COMMENTARY

"Now, please take the rugs back, for they still belong to you!" [1]Abba **said to them: From the time** that I thought that you had taken the rugs in order to raise money for the redemption of captives, I **dismissed them** totally **from my mind** and renounced my ownership of them, so that they could be used **for charity.** I cannot now take them back."

הֲוָה [2]The Gemara concludes this story by noting that **Rava was distressed on account of Abaye,** for Abaye merited being greeted by the heavenly voice every week before Shabbat, whereas Rava received heavenly greetings only once a year on the day before Yom Kippur. [3]People attempted to console him, **saying: "It should be enough for you that your** good deeds serve to **protect the entire** population of the **city** where you live."

רַבִּי בְּרוֹקָא חוֹזָאָה [4]The Gemara now relates another anecdote about the righteous behavior of seemingly simple people. **Rabbi Beroka of Bei Ḥoza'i used to frequent the market of Bei Lefet,** [5]where the Prophet **Elijah would often appear to him.** Once, as he was passing through the market, [6]Rabbi Beroka met Elijah and **said to him:** "Among the great crowd found in this market is there someone who is worthy of entering the World-to-Come?" [7]Elijah said to him: "No." [8]Meanwhile, Elijah saw a certain man who was **wearing black shoes,** which was against the prevailing Jewish custom. [9]This man **had** also **not placed** white and **blue threads on his garment,** and was thus violating the Biblical commandment to wear ritual fringes on the four corners of one's garment. [10]Elijah **said** to Rabbi Beroka: "This man **is worthy of** entering **the World-to-Come."** [11]Rabbi Beroka immediately **ran after** the man **and said to him: "What is your occupation?"** [12]The man **said to him: "Go away now, but come** back **tomorrow** and I will discuss the matter with you."

"הָשְׁתָּא נִשְׁקְלִינְהוּ מָר!" [1]אֲמַר לְהוּ: "מֵהַהוּא שַׁעְתָּא אַסַּחְתִּינְהוּ מִדַּעְתָּאִי לִצְדָקָה". [2]הֲוָה קָא חָלְשָׁא דַּעְתֵּיהּ דְּרָבָא מִשּׁוּם דְּאַבַּיֵי. [3]אֲמַרוּ לֵיהּ: "מִסְתַּיֵּיךְ דְּקָא מַגְנִית אַכּוּלָּא כְּרַכָּא".

[4]רַבִּי בְּרוֹקָא חוֹזָאָה הֲוָה שְׁכִיחַ בְּשׁוּקָא דְּבֵי לֶפֶט. [5]הֲוָה שְׁכִיחַ אֵלִיָּהוּ גַּבֵּיהּ. [6]אֲמַר לֵיהּ: "אִיכָּא בְּהַאי שׁוּקָא בַּר עָלְמָא דְּאָתֵי?" [7]אֲמַר לֵיהּ: "לָא". [8]אַדְּהָכִי וְהָכִי, חֲזָא לְהַהוּא גַּבְרָא דַּהֲוָה סַיֵּים מְסָאנֵי אוּכָּמֵי [9]וְלָא רָמֵי חוּטָא דִּתְכֶלְתָּא בִּגְלִימֵיהּ. [10]אֲמַר לֵיהּ: "הַאי בַּר עָלְמָא דְּאָתֵי הוּא". [11]רְהַט בַּתְרֵיהּ, אֲמַר לֵיהּ: "מַאי עוֹבָדָךְ?" [12]אֲמַר לֵיהּ: "זִיל הָאִידָּנָא, וְתָא לִמְחָר".

LITERAL TRANSLATION

"Now, Sir, take them!" [1]He said to them: "From that time I dismissed them from my mind [and gave them] to charity."

[2]Rava was distressed on account of Abaye. [3]They said to him: "It is enough for you that you protect the entire city."

[4]Rabbi Beroka of Bei Ḥoza'i was often found in the market of Bei Lefet. [5]Elijah would often appear to him. [6]He said to him: "Is there in this market someone worthy of (lit., 'a son of') the World-to-Come?" [7]He said to him: "No." [8]In the meantime, he saw a certain man who was wearing black shoes [9]and did not place a blue thread on his garment. [10]He said to him: "This [man] is worthy of the World-to-Come." [11]He ran after him [and] said to him: "What is your occupation?" [12]He said to him: "Go now, and come tomorrow."

RASHI

לשקלינהו מר – שלא היינו רוצין אלא לנסותך. **חלשא דעתיה דרבא אדאביי** – דלרבא לא אתי שלמא אלא ממעלי יומא דכיפורי למעלי יומא דכיפורי, ולאביי כל מעלי שבתא. **אכולא כרכא** – על כל בני עירך. **רב ברוקא חוזאה** – שהיה מבי חוזאי. **דבי לפט** – מקום. **אמר ליה** – רב ברוקא לאליהו: מי איכא בהאי שוקא כו'. מסאני אוכמי = מנעלים שחורים, שלא כמנהג היהודים. ולא רמי חוטא = לא הטיל ציצית בטליתו. אמר ליה – אליהו לרב ברוקא: האי בר עלמא דאתי הוא. קרא ליה – רב ברוקא לההוא גברא.

NOTES

מַגְנִית אַכּוּלָּא כְּרַכָּא **You protect the entire city.** *Rabbi Ya'akov Emden* points out that these words of consolation assume special significance in the light of what is stated elsewhere (*Rosh HaShanah* 17a), that the residents of Meḥoza, the city in which Rava lived, were evil people who merited destruction. Thus it was only Rava's unusually righteous behavior that saved them from immediate punishment.

בַּר עָלְמָא דְּאָתֵי **Worthy of the World to Come.** Although it is stated elsewhere (*Sanhedrin* 90a) that with few exceptions all Israel have a share in the World to Come, most people must first pass through Gehenna and be punished for the transgressions they committed in this world; and only after they have been purified of sin are they fit to enjoy the pleasures of the World to Come. When Rabbi Beroka met the Prophet Elijah in the marketplace, he asked that Elijah point out to him a man worthy of entering the World to Come directly, without having first to suffer in Gehenna, so that he could learn what righteous behavior merits that reward.

[1]לְמָחָר אֲמַר לֵיהּ: "מַאי עוֹבָדָךְ?" [2]אֲמַר לֵיהּ: "זַנְדּוּקָנָא אֲנָא, וְאָסַרְנָא גַּבְרֵי לְחוּד וְנָשֵׁי לְחוּד. [3]וּרְמִינָא פּוּרְיַיאי בֵּין הָנֵי לְהָנֵי כִּי הֵיכִי דְּלָא לֵיתוּ לִידֵי אִיסּוּרָא. [4]כִּי חָזֵינָא בַּת יִשְׂרָאֵל דִּיהָבִי נָכְרִים עֲלָהּ עֵינַיְיהוּ, [5]מָסַרְנָא נַפְשַׁאי וּמַצֵּילְנָא לָהּ. [6]יוֹמָא חַד הֲוָות נַעֲרָה מְאוֹרָסָה גַּבָּן דִּיהֲבוּ בָּהּ נָכְרִים עֵינַיְיהוּ. [7]שְׁקַלִי דּוּרְדַּיָּיא דְּחַמְרָא וּשְׁדַאי לָהּ בְּשִׁיפּוּלָהּ, [8]וַאֲמַרִי: 'דִּיסְתְּנָא הִיא'." [9]אֲמַר לֵיהּ: "מַאי טַעֲמָא לֵית לָךְ חוּטֵי [10]וְרָמֵית מְסָאנֵי אוּכָּמֵי?" [11]אֲמַר לֵיהּ: "עָיֵילְנָא וְנָפֵיקְנָא בֵּינֵי נָכְרִים כִּי הֵיכִי דְּלָא לֵידְעוּ דִּיהוּדָאָה אֲנָא. [12]כִּי הָווּ גָּזְרֵי גְּזֵירְתָא, מוֹדַעֲנָא לְהוּ לְרַבָּנַן, וּבָעוּ רַחֲמֵי וּמְבַטְּלֵי לִגְזֵירָתַיְיהוּ". [13]"וּמַאי טַעֲמָא כִּי אָמִינָא לָךְ אֲנָא, 'מַאי עוֹבָדָךְ?' [14]וַאֲמַרְתְּ לִי: 'זִיל הָאִידָּנָא וְתָא לִמְחָר'?" [15]אֲמַר לֵיהּ: "בְּהַהִיא שַׁעְתָּא גָּזְרֵי גְּזֵירְתָא, [16]וְאָמִינָא: בְּרֵישָׁא אֵיזִיל וְאַשְׁמַע לְהוּ לְרַבָּנַן דְּלִבָעֵי רַחֲמֵי עֲלָהּ דְּמִילְּתָא". [17]אַדְּהָכִי וְהָכִי, אָתוּ הָנָךְ תְּרֵי אָחֵי. [18]אֲמַר לֵיהּ:

LITERAL TRANSLATION

[1]The next day he said to him: "What is your occupation?" [2]He said to him: "I am a prison guard, and I imprison the men by themselves and the women by themselves. [3]And I put my bed between these and those so that they may not come to [violate] a prohibition. [4]When I see a Jewish woman upon whom the non-Jews are setting their eyes, [5]I risk my life and save her. [6]One day there was a betrothed girl among us upon whom the non-Jews set their eyes. [7]I took wine dregs and put them on the lower part [of her dress], [8]and I said: She is a menstruating woman." [9]He said to him: "What is the reason [that] you do not have threads [10]and you wear black shoes?" [11]He said to him: "I go in and out among the non-Jews [like this] so that they will not know that I am a Jew. [12]When they issue a decree, I inform the Rabbis, and they pray for [God's] mercy and annul their decrees." [13]"And what is the reason [that] when I said to you, 'What is your occupation?' [14]you said to me: 'Go now and come tomorrow'?" [15]He said to him: "At that time they had issued a decree. [16]And I said: First I will go and inform the Rabbis so that they will pray for mercy regarding the matter." [17]In the meantime, two brothers came. [18]He said to him:

TRANSLATION AND COMMENTARY

[1]Rabbi Beroka sought the man out **the next day** and **asked him** a second time: **"What is your occupation?"** [2]The man **said to** Rabbi Beroka: **"I am a prison guard** and I work in the local prison run by the non-Jewish authorities, **and I imprison the men by themselves and the women by themselves** for reasons of modesty. [3]As an extra precaution, **I place my** own **bed between the** men's section **and that** of the women, **so that they do not come to violate** any **prohibition** involving forbidden sexual relations. [4]Moreover, **when I see a female Jewish** prisoner **upon whom the non-Jews are setting their eyes,** [5]I am ready to **risk my life in order to save her.** [6]For example, **one day a betrothed girl was** imprisoned **in our** jail, and **the non-Jews set their eyes upon her.** What did I do? [7]**I took wine dregs** the same color as blood, **and I put them on the lower part of** the girl's **dress,** [8]**and I said** to the men: Leave her alone, for you can see that **she is** menstruating and is at present unfit for sexual relations." [9]Rabbi Beroka then **said to him**: "But **why do you not** place **the threads** of the required fringes on the four corners of your garments? [10]**And** why do **you wear black shoes** when all the other Jews here refrain from wearing shoes of that color?" [11]The man **said to** Rabbi Beroka: **"I go in and out among the non-Jews** dressed **like this so that they will not recognize me as a Jew.** In that way I can mingle freely with the non-Jewish authorities and find out what they are planning. [12]**When** I hear that **they** intend to **issue a decree** detrimental to the Jewish community, I go and **inform the Rabbis, and they pray** to God **for mercy and** the decree is **annulled.**" [13]Rabbi Beroka asked the man one more question: **"And what is the reason** why, **when I asked you** the first time, **'What is your occupation?,'** [14]**you** put me off and **said to me: 'Go** away **now and come** back **tomorrow'**? Why could you not tell me yesterday what I just heard from you now?" [15]The man **said to** Rabbi Beroka: **"At the time** when you first approached me, the non-Jews **had** just **issued a decree** detrimental to the Jewish community. [16]**So I said** to myself: **First** of all **I must go and inform the Rabbis** about what has happened, **so that they will pray for mercy regarding the matter.** This is why I was forced to ask you to come back today." [17]**Meanwhile,** as Rabbi Beroka was talking with this man, **two brothers came** to the marketplace. [18]The Prophet Elijah **said to** Rabbi Beroka:

RASHI

זנדוקנא — שומר בית האסורין.
רמינא פורייאי כו' — מטיל אני מטתי בין אנשים לנשים. **דיהבי נכרים עינייהו עלה** — בעלי בית האסורים. **איתרמי נערה כו'** — דהואי בבית הסוהר. **דורדיא דחמרא** — שמרים של יין, האדומים כדם. **בשיפולה** — בשולי בגדיה. **דיסתנא** — דרך נשים לה, ומאוסה היא, והוא לשון פרסי. **אמר ליה** — אליהו לרב ברוקא: הני נמי בני עלמא דאתי נינהו.

LANGUAGE

זַנְדּוּקָנָא Prison guard. This word derives from the Persian, apparently the combined form *zendanakan,* meaning "the man in charge of a prison."

דּוּרְדַּיָּיא Wine dregs. This word, meaning "dregs," derives from the Persian *durd,* whence it was borrowed by both Arabic and Aramaic.

דִּיסְתְּנָא A menstuating woman. This is the Persian word *datan,* meaning "menstruation" or "menstrual blood."

BACKGROUND

שִׁדָּפוֹן Blight. This term apparently refers to blight (*ustilago*), a disease affecting grain. Blight is caused by a fungus that attacks the seeds of the grain, so that instead of an ear of corn, a pouch of black spores is formed. These spores are scattered by the wind and infect other plants in the vicinity. The disease can spread over large areas and cause significant damage to harvests.

כָּנָף אֶחָד One winged creature. Locusts are not generally found in populated areas, but during a plague of locusts they arrive from their permanent habitat, which is slightly north of the Sahara Desert in Africa. Therefore, even an individual locust indicates the start of a mass invasion (which has various ecological causes), and this requires special prayer.

TRANSLATION AND COMMENTARY

They too are worthy of entering **the World to Come."** [1]So Rabbi Beroka **went up to them and asked them: "What is your occupation?"** [2]The brothers **said** to Rabbi Beroka: **"We are jesters who** go about and **cheer up** people who are **sad.** [3]**In addition, when we see two people quarreling,** [4]**we work untiringly to make peace between them."** These were significant accomplishments, for we have learned in the Mishnah (*Pe'ah* 1:1) that making peace between people is included in the list of things the fruit of which a person enjoys in this world, while the principal remains for him in the World to Come.

עַל אֵלּוּ מַתְרִיעִין [5]The Gemara now proceeds to analyze the next clause of our Mishnah: **"For the following** calamities, fasts must be proclaimed **and the alarm must be sounded in all places,** even those far away from the place struck by the calamity." [6]The Gemara cites a related Baraita in which **our Rabbis taught: "For the following** calamities, fasts must be proclaimed and **the alarm must be sounded in all places,** even those far away from the place struck by the calamity. [7]If the crops in a certain area have been struck by **blight or mildew, or** if an area has been devastated by **locusts or** by ***hasil*** locusts [a particularly destructive type], **or** if a place has been invaded by **wild beasts** — in all these cases, fasts must be proclaimed and the alarm must be sounded, for these are all calamities that can spread quickly from one place to another. [8]**Rabbi Akiva says:** The alarm must be sounded **for blight and for mildew,** even if only **the smallest amount** of grain was damaged by the disaster. [9]As **for locusts and *hasil*** locusts, **even if only one specimen** of the destructive insect **was seen in** all **Eretz Israel,** [10]**the alarm must be sounded** everywhere, for that single specimen is the harbinger of swarms of locusts that are yet to come."

וְעַל חַיָּה [11]We learned in our Mishnah: "If a place has been invaded by wild **beasts,** the alarm must be sounded everywhere." [12]**Our Rabbis taught** a Baraita clarifying the cases in which the alarm is sounded on

"הָנָךְ נַמִּי בְּנֵי עָלְמָא דְאָתֵי נִינְהוּ". [1]אֲזַל לְגַבַּיְיהוּ אֲמַר לְהוּ: "מַאי עוֹבָדַיְיכוּ?" [2]אָמְרוּ לֵיהּ: "אֱינָשֵׁי בָּדוּחֵי אֲנַן, מְבַדְּחִינַן עֲצִיבֵי. [3]אִי נַמִּי, כִּי חָזֵינַן בֵּי תְרֵי דְאִית לְהוּ תִּיגְרָא בַּהֲדַיְיהוּ, [4]טָרְחִינַן וְעָבְדִינַן לְהוּ שְׁלָמָא".

[5]"עַל אֵלּוּ מַתְרִיעִין בְּכָל מָקוֹם כו'". [6]תָּנוּ רַבָּנַן: "עַל אֵלּוּ מַתְרִיעִין בְּכָל מָקוֹם: [7]עַל הַשִּׁדָּפוֹן, וְעַל הַיֵּרָקוֹן, וְעַל אַרְבֶּה וְחָסִיל, וְעַל חַיָּה רָעָה. [8]רַבִּי עֲקִיבָא אוֹמֵר: עַל הַשִּׁדָּפוֹן וְעַל הַיֵּרָקוֹן, בְּכָל שֶׁהוּא. [9]אַרְבֶּה וְחָסִיל, אֲפִילּוּ לֹא נִרְאָה בְּאֶרֶץ יִשְׂרָאֵל אֶלָּא כָּנָף אֶחָד, [10]מַתְרִיעִין עֲלֵיהֶן". [11]"וְעַל חַיָּה וכו'". [12]תָּנוּ רַבָּנַן:

LITERAL TRANSLATION

"These too are worthy of the World to Come." [1]He went up to them [and] said to them: "What is your occupation?" [2]They said to him: "We are jesters, [and] we cheer up the sad. [3]Or alternatively, when we see two people between whom there is a quarrel, [4]we work hard and make peace between them."

[5]"For these they sound the alarm in all places, etc." [6]Our Rabbis taught: "For these they sound the alarm in all places: [7]For blight, and for mildew, and for locusts and *hasil*, and for wild beasts. [8]Rabbi Akiva says: For blight and for mildew, for any amount. [9][For] locusts and *hasil*, even if only one winged creature (lit., 'wing') was seen in Eretz Israel, [10]they sound the alarm for them."

[11]"And for wild beasts, etc." [12]Our Rabbis taught:

RASHI

בדוחי = שמחים, ומשמחים בני אדם. **טרחינן** – במילי דבדיחותא ביניהו. **עד דעבדי שלמא** – שהן דברים שאדם אוכל פירותיהן בעולם הזה והקרן קיימת וכו': הבאת שלום בין אדם לחבירו. **שדפון וירקון** – כיון שנראה כל שהוא מתריעין. ומלא תנור דמתניתין להתענות. אי נמי, מעשה היה כך. **כנף אחד** – עוף אחד של אותו מין, כענין "צפור כל כנף" (בראשית ז).

HALAKHAH

וְעַל אַרְבֶּה וְחָסִיל And for locusts and *hasil*. "As for locusts of one kind or another, even if only one specimen of the insect was seen in all of Eretz Israel, the alarm must be sounded and fasts proclaimed." (*Shulhan Arukh, Orah Hayyim* 576:9.)

וְעַל חַיָּה And for wild beasts. "Fasts must be proclaimed and the alarm must be sounded upon the sighting of wild beasts, provided that they appear to be a visitation. Under what circumstances do we say that the animals are a visitation? If a wild beast is seen in the city during the day, or if it is seen during the day in a field and it sees two people but does not run away from them, or if it is seen during the day in a field that is close to a marsh and it sees two people and chases after them, or if it is seen in the marsh itself and it not only chases after the two people but attacks them and eats one of them — in all these cases the presence of the animal is regarded as a divine visitation. But if the animal attacks two people in the marsh and eats both of them, it is not regarded as a visitation, for it was clearly acting out of hunger. If a building is constructed in an otherwise unpopulated area, and a wild beast climbs onto the roof and removes an infant from its cradle, it is regarded as a visitation." (Ibid., 576:6-7.)

”[1]חַיָּה רָעָה שֶׁאָמְרוּ, [1]בִּזְמַן שֶׁהִיא מְשׁוּלַּחַת, [2]מַתְרִיעִין עָלֶיהָ; [3]אֵינָהּ מְשׁוּלַּחַת, אֵין מַתְרִיעִין עָלֶיהָ. [4]אֵי זוֹ הִיא מְשׁוּלַּחַת וְאֵי זוֹ הִיא שֶׁאֵינָהּ מְשׁוּלַּחַת? [5]נִרְאֵית בָּעִיר, מְשׁוּלַּחַת; [6]בַּשָּׂדֶה, אֵינָהּ מְשׁוּלַּחַת. [7]בַּיּוֹם, מְשׁוּלַּחַת; [8]בַּלַּיְלָה, אֵינָהּ מְשׁוּלַּחַת. [9]רָאֲתָה שְׁנֵי בְּנֵי אָדָם וְרָצְתָה אַחֲרֵיהֶן, מְשׁוּלַּחַת; [10]נֶחְבֵּאת מִפְּנֵיהֶן, אֵינָהּ מְשׁוּלחת. [11]טָרְפָה שְׁנֵי בְּנֵי אָדָם וְאָכְלָה אֶחָד מֵהֶן, מְשׁוּלַּחַת; [12]אָכְלָה שְׁנֵיהֶן, אֵינָהּ מְשׁוּלַּחַת. [13]עָלְתָה לַגַּג וְנָטְלָה תִּינוֹק מֵעֲרִיסָהּ, מְשׁוּלַּחַת“.

[14]הָא גּוּפָהּ קַשְׁיָא. [15]אָמְרַתְּ: ”נִרְאֲתָה בָּעִיר, מְשׁוּלַּחַת“. [16]לָא שְׁנָא בַּיּוֹם וְלָא שְׁנָא בַּלַּיְלָה. [17]וַהֲדַר אָמְרַתְּ: ”בַּיּוֹם, מְשׁוּלַּחַת; [18]בַּלַּיְלָה, אֵינָהּ מְשׁוּלַּחַת“!

LITERAL TRANSLATION

"The dangerous animals of which they spoke, [1]at a time when it is a visitation, [2]they sound the alarm for it; [3][when] it is not a visitation, they do not sound the alarm for it. [4]Which is a visitation, and which is not a visitation? [5]If [a wild beast] was sighted in the city, it is a visitation; [6]in the field, it is not a visitation. [7]During the day, it is a visitation; [8]at night, it is not a visitation. [9][If] it saw two people and chased after them, it is a visitation; [10][if] it hid from them, it is not a visitation. [11][If] it attacked two people and ate one of them, it is a visitation; [12][if] it ate both of them, it is not a visitation. [13][If] it went up on the roof and took an infant from a cradle, it is a visitation."

[14]This itself is difficult. [15]You said: "If [a wild beast] was sighted in the city, it is a visitation." [16]There is no difference if [it happens] during the day and there is no difference [if it happens] at night: [17]And then you said: "During the day, it is a visitation; [18]at night, it is not a visitation"!

TRANSLATION AND COMMENTARY

account of an invasion of wild beasts: "As for **the wild beasts mentioned by** the Rabbis, the following distinction must be made: [1]**At a time when** the animals appear to be **a visitation** by divine decree, as alluded to in the verse [Leviticus 26:22]: 'And I will send wild beasts among you, that will rob you of your children, and destroy your cattle, and make you few in number,' [2]fasts are proclaimed and **the alarm is sounded.** [3]But **at a time when** the animals do **not** appear to be **a visitation,** and seem to be acting in their usual manner, **the alarm is not sounded,** even if the animals have already caused considerable damage." [4]The Baraita explains. "In **which** case do we say that the animals are **a visitation, and in which** case do we say that they **are not a visitation?** [5]**If a wild beast is sighted in the city, it is** regarded as being **a visitation,** because wild animals usually refrain from entering populated areas. [6]But if the animal is sighted **in the fields, it is not** considered **a** divine **visitation,** because it is the customary behavior of wild animals to roam the fields. [7]If the wild beast was sighted **during the day, it is** regarded as **a visitation,** [8]for wild animals usually come out only at night. But if the animal was sighted **at night, it is not** considered **a visitation.** [9]If the wild beast **saw two people and chased after them, it is** regarded as **a visitation,** for wild animals generally refrain from attacking more than one person at a time. [10]But **if** the animal saw the two and **hid from them, it is not** considered **a visitation.** [11]**If** a wild animal **attacked** and killed **two people but** then **ate** only **one of them, it is** regarded as **a visitation**, for the animal clearly had not attacked the people merely out of hunger. [12]But **if** the animal attacked and killed two people and then **ate both of them, it is not** considered **a visitation,** for we can assume that it was hungry. [13]And finally, **if** the wild beast **went up onto the roof** of a home **and took an infant from its cradle, it is** regarded as **a visitation,** for it is highly unusual for an animal to act in such a way."

הָא גּוּפָהּ קַשְׁיָא [14]The Gemara now proceeds to analyze this Baraita clause by clause. It begins by pointing out that the Baraita **itself is difficult** to understand, because there seems to be an internal contradiction between two of its rulings. [15]The Baraita first **states: "If a wild beast is sighted in the city, it is** regarded as **a visitation."** [16]**No distinction is made** in this ruling **between** a case in which the wild animal is sighted **during the day and** a case in which it is sighted **at night.** It follows, therefore, that whenever the beast is sighted in the city, it is regarded as a visitation. [17]**But** the Baraita **then continues:** "If the wild beast was sighted **during the day, it is** regarded as a visitation, [18]but if it was sighted only **at night, it is not** considered **a visitation."** How can these two rulings be reconciled with each other?

RASHI

משולחת — מן השמים. **בשדה אינה משולחת** — דהיינו אורחה. **טרפה שני בני אדם** — ולא אכלה אלא אחד מהם — ודאי משולחת, דכיון דלא היתה רעבה אלא לאחד — מאי טעמא קטלה ליה לאידך? **שניהן אינה משולחת** — שמפני הרעב אכלתם. **עלתה לגג** — רגילין היו להשתמש כל תשמישיהן בגגות, שלא היו משופעים אלא חלקים ושוין, והוא הדין לבית שתחתיו. **עריסה** — *ברצו״ל בלעז.

BACKGROUND

מְשׁוּלַּחַת **A visitation.** This expression is based on Biblical language (Deuteronomy 32:24, 2 Kings 17:25, and elsewhere). It means an incursion of wild animals into human settlements. Such an incursion may be caused by hunger. Although wild animals normally avoid all contact with humans and their settlements, hunger may cause them to break into settlements and attack people. Some sources indicate another cause for this phenomenon — an outbreak of rabies among wild animals, causing them to be more aggressive.

LANGUAGE (RASHI)

ברצו״ל* From the Old French *brecol,* which means "a cradle."

BACKGROUND

אַגְמָא A marsh. Like the Hebrew word אֲגַם, this refers to an area, near a river or a pond, in which reeds (אַגְמוֹן), low trees, and grass grow densely. Because Babylonia is a flat country, and because of the silt deposits from the rivers, there are many swamps. Because marshes are muddy and the earth is soft and frequently flooded by overflow from the river, they are usually uninhabited, and are frequented by animals, including beasts of prey.

LANGUAGE (RASHI)

מרשי״ק* From the Old French *marsc*, which means "a marsh."

HEBREW TEXT

[1] לָא קַשְׁיָא. [2] הָכִי קָאָמַר: נִרְאֲתָה בָּעִיר בַּיּוֹם, מְשׁוּלַּחַת; [3] בָּעִיר בַּלַּיְלָה, אֵינָהּ מְשׁוּלַּחַת. [4] אִי נַמִי, בַּשָּׂדֶה אֲפִילּוּ בַּיּוֹם, אֵינָהּ מְשׁוּלַּחַת.

[5] "רָאֲתָה שְׁנֵי בְּנֵי אָדָם וְרָצְתָה אַחֲרֵיהֶן, מְשׁוּלַּחַת". [6] הָא עוֹמֶדֶת, אֵינָהּ מְשׁוּלַּחַת. [7] וַהֲדַר אָמְרַתְּ: "נֶחְבֵּאת מִפְּנֵיהֶן, אֵינָהּ מְשׁוּלַּחַת". [8] הָא עוֹמֶדֶת, מְשׁוּלַּחַת!

[9] לָא קַשְׁיָא. [10] כָּאן, בְּשָׂדֶה הַסְּמוּכָה לַאֲגַם; [11] כָּאן, בְּשָׂדֶה שֶׁאֵינָהּ סְמוּכָה לַאֲגַם.

[12] "טָרְפָה שְׁנֵי בְּנֵי אָדָם כְּאֶחָד וְאָכְלָה אֶחָד מֵהֶן, מְשׁוּלַּחַת; [13] שְׁנֵיהֶם, אֵינָהּ מְשׁוּלַּחַת". [14] וְהָא אָמְרַתְּ: [15] "אֲפִילּוּ רָצְתָה"!

[16] אֲמַר רַב פַּפָּא: [17] כִּי תָּנֵי הַהִיא, בְּאַגְמָא.

LITERAL TRANSLATION

[1] There is no difficulty. [2] He says thus: If [a wild beast] was sighted in the city during the day, it is a visitation; [3] in the city at night, it is not a visitation. [4] Or also, in the field even during the day, it is not a visitation.

[5] "[If] it saw two people and chased after them, it is a visitation." [6] But [if] it stands [in its place], it is not a visitation. [7] And then you said: "[If] it hid from them, it is not a visitation." [8] But [if] it stands [in its place], it is a visitation!

[9] There is no difficulty. [10] Here, [it is] in a field that is near a marsh; [11] here, [it is] in a field that is not near a marsh.

[12] "[If] it attacked two people together and ate one of them, it is a visitation; [13] both of them, it is not a visitation." [14] But surely you said: [15] "Even if it chased [them]"!

[16] Rav Pappa said: When that was taught, [17] [it referred] to a marsh.

TRANSLATION AND COMMENTARY

לָא קַשְׁיָא [1] The Gemara answers: **There is** really **no difficulty.** The second ruling, according to which a distinction is made between a wild beast sighted during the day and one sighted at night, refers to a case where the animal was seen roaming in the city, for if it is seen wandering in the fields, it is never regarded as a visitation. [2] What the Tanna of the Baraita means to **say** is **as follows: If a wild beast is sighted in the city during the day, it is** regarded as **a visitation.** [3] But if it is seen roaming in **the city at night, it is not** considered **a visitation.** [4] **And similarly,** if the animal is sighted **in the fields even during the day, it is not** regarded as **a visitation.**

רָאֲתָה [5] The Gemara now suggests that there is an internal contradiction in the next clause of the Baraita as well. The Baraita first states: **"If** the wild beast **saw two people and chased them, it is** regarded as a **visitation."** [6] It follows from this ruling that **if** the animal **stood** still and neither chased the two people nor ran and hid, **it is not** considered **a visitation.** [7] **But** then the Baraita **continues: "If** the wild animal ran away and **hid from** the two people it had seen, **it is not** considered **a visitation."** [8] But it follows from this second ruling that if the animal **stood** still without hiding, then even if it did not chase after the two people it had seen, **it is** indeed considered **a visitation!**

לָא קַשְׁיָא [9] The Gemara answers: **There is** really **no difficulty,** because the two rulings refer to different cases. [10] **Here,** in the first ruling, the Baraita is referring to a case where the wild beast saw the two people **in a field near a marsh,** the animal's natural habitat. In such a case, the fact that this animal did not run away **does not prove that** its presence is a divine visitation. [11] **But there,** in the second ruling, the Baraita is referring to a case where the wild animal saw the two people **in a field** that was **not close to a marsh.** In such a case, the presence of the animal is viewed as a divine visitation, even if the animal does not chase the two people but stays still.

טָרְפָה [12] The Gemara now points out another difficulty in the Baraita. The Baraita states: **"If** the animal **attacked** and killed **two people together, but** then **ate** only **one of them, it is** regarded as **a visitation.** [13] But if the animal attacked and killed two people and then ate **both of them, it is not** considered **a visitation.** [14] **But** this is difficult to understand, for **surely** the Baraita stated earlier that the animal's behavior is regarded as a visitation, [15] **even if it** only **chased after** the two people and did not eat either of them!

אֲמַר רַב פַּפָּא [16] **Rav Pappa said** in reply: Here, too, there is really no difficulty, because the Baraita's two rulings refer to different cases. [17] **When** the Baraita **taught** that the presence of the animal is regarded as a visitation only if it ate one of the two people it attacked, but not if it merely chased them, **it was referring**

RASHI

הכי קאמר — האי דקתני "נראתה בעיר כו'" הכי קאמר: נראתה בעיר, כגון שנראתה ביום, דסתם "נראתה" — ביום משמע. אבל בלילה — אינה משולחת. והאי דקתני "נראתה ביום" — א"שדה" קאי, דאם נראתה בשדה ביום — אינה משולחת. **הא עמדה** — בשדה, דלא רצתה ולא נחבאת. **בשדה הסמוכה לאגם** — עמדה — אינה משולחת, דכיון דסמוכה לאגם — היינו רביתה, ולא ברחה, סברה: אי אתי בתראי — עריקנא לאגם מיד. **בשדה שאינה סמוכה לאגם** — עמדה — משולחת, דכיון דלאו מקום רביתה הוא וקיימא — ודאי משולחת גזירה היא. **אגם** — *מרשי"ק בלעז. והוא מלא קנים. **כי תניא ההיא** — דאכלה אין, רצתה — לא באגם, דכיון דהיינו דוכתה — סמכה אדעתה ורהטא אבתרייהו.

LITERAL TRANSLATION

[1]It was taught above (lit., "the thing itself"): "[If] it went up on the roof and took an infant from a cradle, it is a visitation." [2]It is obvious!

[3]Rav Pappa said: [In buildings] such as hunters' hideouts.

[4]"For the sword, etc." [5]Our Rabbis taught: "[Regarding] the sword of which they spoke, it is not necessary to mention a sword that is not of peace, [6]but even a sword of peace. [7]For you do not have a sword more peaceful than [that of] Pharaoh Necho, [8]and even so King Josiah came to grief on account of it, [9]as it is said: [22B] [10]'And he sent messengers to him, saying: What have I to do with you, King of Judah? [11]Not against you do I come this day, but against the house with which I am at war;

[1]גּוּפָא: ״עָלְתָה לַגַּג וְנָטְלָה תִּינוֹק מֵעֲרִיסָה, מְשׁוּלַּחַת״.
[2]פְּשִׁיטָא!
[3]אֲמַר רַב פַּפָּא: כְּכוּכֵי דְּצַיָּיְדֵי.
[4]״עַל הַחֶרֶב וְכוּ׳״. [5]תָּנוּ רַבָּנַן: ״חֶרֶב שֶׁאָמְרוּ, אֵינוֹ צָרִיךְ לוֹמַר חֶרֶב שֶׁאֵינוֹ שֶׁל שָׁלוֹם, [6]אֶלָּא אֲפִילּוּ חֶרֶב שֶׁל שָׁלוֹם. [7]שֶׁאֵין לְךָ חֶרֶב שֶׁל שָׁלוֹם יוֹתֵר מִפַּרְעֹה נְכֹה, [8]וְאַף עַל פִּי כֵן נִכְשַׁל בָּהּ הַמֶּלֶךְ יֹאשִׁיָּהוּ, [9]שֶׁנֶּאֱמַר: [22B] [10]׳וַיִּשְׁלַח אֵלָיו מַלְאָכִים, לֵאמֹר: מַה לִּי וָלָךְ, מֶלֶךְ יְהוּדָה? [11]לֹא עָלֶיךָ אַתָּה הַיּוֹם, כִּי אֶל בֵּית מִלְחַמְתִּי;

RASHI

כוכא דציידי — כוך קטן של ציידין, שיחפרו למארב העופות, ואף על גב דלאו בנין קבוע הוא, ולא הוה כיישוב — הויא משולחת. **אין צריך לומר חרב שאינו של שלום** — שמתריעין עליה. **אלא אפילו חרב של שלום** — העוברת דרך אותו מלכות לילך להלחם במקום אחרת. **וישלח אליו מלאכים לאמר מה לי ולך מלך יהודה לא עליך אתה היום כי אל בית מלחמתי**

TRANSLATION AND COMMENTARY

to a case where it chased them **in a marsh.** An animal acts more boldly in its own habitat. But when the Baraita taught that the presence of the animal is considered a visitation if it saw two people and chased them, it was referring to a case where it saw the two and chased them in a field.

גּוּפָא [1]The Gemara now considers the last clause of the Baraita. **It was taught above: "If** the wild beast **went up onto the roof of a home and took an infant from its cradle, it is** regarded as **a visitation."** The Gemara objects: Why did the Baraita have to issue this ruling? [2]Surely **it is obvious** that in such a case the action of the animal is considered a divinely-inspired visitation, for the animal exhibited extraordinary behavior by entering the town, climbing up onto the roof of a building, and snatching the baby from its cradle!

אֲמַר רַב פַּפָּא [3]**Rav Pappa said** in reply: The Baraita is referring here to a case where the animal snatched the infant **from the roof of a hunter's hideout,** which was constructed outside town in an unpopulated area. The Baraita teaches us that if the animal climbed onto the roof of the hideout, and snatched a baby from its cradle, that indeed is highly unusual behavior and serves as proof that the presence of the animal was a visitation.

עַל הַחֶרֶב [4]We learned in our Mishnah: "The alarm is sounded **on account of the** threat imposed by **sword-carrying** soldiers." [5]**Our Rabbis taught** a Baraita that expands on this ruling: "As for **the sword-carrying** soldiers **mentioned** by the Sages, **it was not necessary to state** that the alarm must be sounded when the soldiers carry **swords that are not of peace** — when an enemy army threatens to attack the community. [6]The sword-carrying soldiers were mentioned in order to teach us that the alarm must be sounded **even** if those soldiers are carrying **swords of peace** — when the invading army is only passing through the country. [7]**For there was no sword more peaceful than that of Pharaoh Necho,** King of Egypt, who wished to pass through Eretz Israel with his forces in order to join the Assyrians in their war against the Babylonians. [8]**And even so King Josiah came to grief on account of** Pharaoh Necho's campaign and met his death as a result. [9]**For the verse says** [II Chronicles 35:20-22]: [22B] 'After all this, when Josiah had prepared the Temple, Necho King of Egypt came up to fight against Carchemish on the Euphrates, and Josiah went out against him. [10]**And he sent messengers to him, saying: What have I to do with you, King of Judah?** [11]**Not against you do I**

BACKGROUND

כְּכוּכֵי דְּצַיָּיְדֵי Such as hunter's hideouts. Professional hunters, especially those who hunt large and cautious animals, normally build small huts in which they sit for a long time waiting for the animals to appear. Sometimes these hideouts are built on stilts, at a significant height above the ground.

NOTES

חֶרֶב שֶׁל שָׁלוֹם A sword of peace. The alarm must be sounded even if the invading army does not wish to attack the Jewish people, but only to cross its territory in order to wage war with its true enemy, because it is likely that the soldiers passing through the country will cause serious damage (*Meiri*). Moreover, there is concern that the people's transgressions will cause the invading army to turn their weapons against the Jewish people, even though the foreign soldiers had originally planned to pass through the country in peace (*Ritva*).

HALAKHAH

עַל הַחֶרֶב For the sword. "If an enemy army comes to wage war against Israel, or even if it only wishes to pass through the land in order to wage war against another country, fasts must be proclaimed and the alarm must be sounded." (*Shulḥan Arukh, Oraḥ Ḥayyim* 576:1.)

[1]וֵאלֹהִים אָמַר לְבַהֲלֵנִי: חֲדַל לְךָ מֵאֱלֹהִים, אֲשֶׁר עִמִּי, וְאַל יַשְׁחִיתֶךָ׳״.
[2]מַאי ״אֱלֹהִים, אֲשֶׁר עִמִּי״?
[3]אָמַר רַב יְהוּדָה אָמַר רַב: זוֹ עֲבוֹדָה זָרָה. [4]אָמַר: ״הוֹאִיל וְקָא בָּטַח בַּעֲבוֹדָה זָרָה, יָכֵילְנָא לֵיהּ״.
[5]״וַיֹּרוּ הַיֹּרִים לַמֶּלֶךְ יֹאשִׁיָּהוּ, וַיֹּאמֶר הַמֶּלֶךְ לַעֲבָדָיו: [6]הַעֲבִירוּנִי, כִּי הָחֳלֵיתִי מְאֹד״.
[7]מַאי ״כִּי הָחֳלֵיתִי מְאֹד״?
[8]אָמַר רַב יְהוּדָה אָמַר רַב: מְלַמֵּד שֶׁעָשׂוּ כָּל גּוּפוֹ כִּכְבָרָה.
[9]אָמַר רַבִּי שְׁמוּאֵל בַּר נַחְמָנִי אָמַר רַבִּי יוֹנָתָן: מִפְּנֵי מַה נֶּעֱנַשׁ יֹאשִׁיָּהוּ? [10]מִפְּנֵי שֶׁהָיָה לוֹ לִימָּלֵךְ בְּיִרְמְיָהוּ, וְלֹא נִמְלַךְ.

LITERAL TRANSLATION

[1]and God has commanded me to make haste: Forbear from interfering with God, who is with me, so that he will not destroy you.'"
[2]What is [meant by] "God, who is with me"?
[3]Rav Yehudah said in the name of Rav: This [means] idols. [4]He said: "Since he trusts in idolatry, I can [defeat] him."
[5]"And the archers shot at King Josiah, and the king said to his servants: [6]Move me away, for I am very seriously wounded."
[7]What is [meant by] "for I am very seriously wounded"?
[8]Rav Yehudah said in the name of Rav: This teaches that they made his entire body like a sieve.
[9]Rabbi Shmuel bar Naḥmani said in the name of Rabbi Yonatan: Why was Josiah punished? [10]Because he should have consulted with Jeremiah, but he did not consult [with him].

TRANSLATION AND COMMENTARY

come this day, but against the house with which I am at war; [1]**and God has commanded me to make haste: Forbear from interfering with God, who is with me, so that he will not destroy you.** Nevertheless Josiah would not turn his face from him, but he sought an opportunity to fight with him, and he did not hearken to the words of Necho from the mouth of God, and came to fight in the valley of Megiddo.' Although Pharaoh Necho stated explicitly that he had no wish to fight against Josiah, but wished merely to pass through Eretz Israel, Josiah tried to stop him at Megiddo, but was killed in battle (verses 23-24). Thus even 'the sword of peace' can pose great danger, and therefore the alarm must be sounded on account of an invading army, even if its intentions are peaceful."

״מַאי ״אֱלֹהִים [2]The Gemara now discusses the story of the death of Josiah in greater detail and asks: **What did** Necho **mean** when he spoke of **"God, who is with me"**?

אָמַר רַב יְהוּדָה [3]**Rav Yehudah said in the name of Rav: This** does not **refer** to the Holy One, blessed be He, but rather **to** Necho's **idols.** When Necho announced that he had brought his idols with him in the hope that they would assist him in battle, Josiah decided to attack him, [4]**saying** to himself: "Since Necho **trusts in idols, I** will surely **be able to defeat him** in battle."

וַיֹּרוּ הַיֹּרִים [5]The verse describing Josiah's fall in battle says (II Chronicles 35:23): **"And the archers shot at King Josiah, and the king said to his servants:** [6]**Move me away, for I am very seriously wounded."** [7]The Gemara asks: **What did** Josiah **mean** when he said: **"For I am very seriously wounded"?**

אָמַר רַב יְהוּדָה [8]**Rav Yehudah said in the name of Rav: This teaches that** the Egyptian archers shot so many arrows at Josiah that **his entire body became like a sieve.**

אָמַר רַבִּי שְׁמוּאֵל בַּר נַחְמָנִי [9]**Rabbi Shmuel bar Naḥmani said in the name of Rabbi Yonatan: Why was Josiah,** the righteous King of Judah who made such great efforts to purge Eretz Israel of idolatry, **punished** so severely for going to war against Pharaoh Necho? [10]**Because he should have consulted with** the Prophet **Jeremiah,** and asked his advice as to whether or not he should go out to battle, **but he did not consult with**

RASHI

ואלהים אמר לבהלני חדל לך מאלהים אשר עמי וגו׳ לא עליך אני הולך היום — יאשיה יצא לקראתו למלחמה, ולא נתנו לעבור בארצו, ושלח לו פרעה נכה מלאכים לאמר כו׳. **מאן אלהים** — דקאמר ליה פרעה נכה ״חדל לך מאלהים אשר עמי״. **מלמד** — מדכתיב ״ויורו המורים״ דמשמע: יריות רבות יורו המורים. **אמר רב יהודה אמר רב** — מלמד שעשו כל גופו ככברה.

NOTES

שֶׁעָשׂוּ כָּל גּוּפוֹ כִּכְבָרָה **That they made his entire body like a sieve.** *Rashi* explains that this interpretation is derived from the words: "And the archers shot [וַיֹּרוּ הַיֹּרִים]." The use of two words deriving from the same root, ירה, "to shoot," suggests that each of the archers shot many arrows. *Rashash*, however, suggests that Rav's comment is based on the word הָחֳלֵיתִי, which has been translated here as "wounded" (from the root חלה, "to be sick"). Rav understands the word as being derived from the root חלל, "to make a hole." Thus, Josiah asked to be taken away because his body had been pierced with holes like a sieve.

מִפְּנֵי מָה נֶעֱנַשׁ יֹאשִׁיָּהוּ **Why was Josiah punished?** The Midrash (Lamentations Rabbah 1:53) interprets the verse (II Chronicles 35:22): "And he did not hearken to the words of

TRANSLATION AND COMMENTARY

him. [1]Rabbi Shmuel bar Naḥmani continues: On **what exposition** of Scripture did Josiah rely in deciding to fight Pharaoh Necho? He relied on the following verse which says (Leviticus 26:6): "And I will give peace in the land, and you shall lie down and none shall make you afraid; and I will remove evil beasts from the land, [2]**and a sword shall not go through your land."** [3]**What is meant** here **by "a sword"? If we say** that this refers to **a sword that is not of peace** but a sword raised in war against the Jewish people, this is difficult to understand, [4]for **surely** the first part of **the verse** has already **said: "And I will give peace in the land"!** If God has already promised to establish peace in the land, why should He add that a sword will not pass through it? [5]**Rather,** the verse must mean that **even a sword of peace** will not pass through the land. Not only will peace reign in the land, but no foreign army will even pass through the country in order to fight its enemy elsewhere. Josiah thought that these blessings would be realized in his day, and that he would be successful in his attempt to deny Pharaoh Necho free passage through the land. [6]**But he did not realize that his generation was not deserving** of these blessings.

[1]מַאי דָּרַשׁ? [2]"וְחֶרֶב לֹא תַעֲבֹר בְּאַרְצְכֶם". [3]מַאי "חֶרֶב"? אִילֵימָא: חֶרֶב שֶׁאֵינָהּ שֶׁל שָׁלוֹם, [4]וְהָכְתִיב: "וְנָתַתִּי שָׁלוֹם בָּאָרֶץ"! [5]אֶלָּא, אֲפִילּוּ שֶׁל שָׁלוֹם. [6]וְהוּא אֵינוֹ יוֹדֵעַ שֶׁאֵין דּוֹרוֹ דּוֹמֶה יָפֶה.

[7]כִּי הֲוָה נִיחָא נַפְשֵׁיהּ, חֲזָא יִרְמְיָהוּ שִׂפְוָותֵיהּ דְּקָא מְרַחֲשָׁן, [8]אָמַר: "שֶׁמָּא, חַס וְחָלִילָה, מִילְּתָא דְּלָא מְהַגְּנָא אָמַר אַגַּב צַעֲרֵיהּ". [9]גְּחִין וּשְׁמְעֵיהּ דְּקָא מַצְדִּיק עֲלֵיהּ דִּינָא אַנַּפְשֵׁיהּ, [10]אָמַר: "צַדִּיק הוּא ה׳, כִּי פִיהוּ מָרִיתִי". [11]פָּתַח עֲלֵיהּ הַהִיא שַׁעְתָּא: "רוּחַ אַפֵּינוּ, מְשִׁיחַ ה׳".

[12]"מַעֲשֶׂה וְיָרְדוּ זְקֵנִים מִירוּשָׁלַיִם לְעָרֵיהֶם, כו׳". [13]אִיבַּעְיָא לְהוּ: כִּמְלֹא תַנּוּר

LITERAL TRANSLATION

[1]What did he expound? "And a sword shall not go through your land." [2]What is [meant by] "a sword"? [3]If we say: A sword that is not of peace, [4]but surely it is written: "And I will give peace in the land"! [5]Rather, even [a sword] of peace. [6]But he did not know that his generation did not appear worthy.

[7]When he was dying, Jeremiah saw that his lips were moving, [8][and] said: "Perhaps, God forbid, he is saying something improper on account of his pain." [9]He bent over and heard him justifying the judgment on himself, [10]saying: "The Lord is righteous, for I have rebelled against His word." [11]He began [his tribute] over him at that hour: "The breath of our nostrils, the anointed of the Lord."

[12]"It once happened that elders went down from Jerusalem to their cities, etc." [13]It was asked of them: In an amount to fill an oven

RASHI

הא כתיב ונתתי שלום בארץ — ולמאי הלכתא כתביה רחמנא לאידך קרא "וחרב לא תעבור בארצכם" — אלא אפילו חרב של שלום. **שאין דורו דומה יפה** — בעיני המקום. **איבעיא להו כמלא תנור תבואה** — דהיינו שיעור גדול יותר ממלא תנור פת. דשיעור קטן הוא, שאין דרך למלאות כל חלל התנור פת, אלא בדפנות מדביקין אותו.

כִּי הֲוָה נִיחָא נַפְשֵׁיהּ [7]The Gemara continues: **When** Josiah **was lying on his deathbed,** the Prophet **Jeremiah** stood near him and **saw that his lips were moving.** [8]Jeremiah **said** to himself: **"Perhaps, God forbid,** Josiah **is saying something improper on account of his** great **distress,** and is complaining that he has been punished unfairly." [9]But when **he bent over** in order to hear what the king was saying, **he heard him justifying the divine judgment on himself,** [10]**citing** the verse (Lamentations 1:18): **"The Lord is righteous, for I have rebelled against His word."** [11]Jeremiah **immediately began his tribute** for the dying king, with words of praise, citing the following verse (Lamentations 4:20): **"The breath of our nostrils, the anointed of the Lord,** was trapped in their pits."

מַעֲשֶׂה [12]The Gemara now proceeds to examine the next clause of the Mishnah, which stated: **"It once happened that the elders of the Sanhedrin went down from Jerusalem to their cities** in other parts of Eretz Israel, and decreed a fast everywhere, because blight in an amount to fill the opening of an oven was sighted on grain in Ashkelon." [13]When this Mishnah was studied in the Academy, **the following question arose:** Does this mean that enough of the crop was stricken by blight to **fill an oven with the** blighted **grain?**

BACKGROUND

כִּמְלֹא תַנּוּר תְּבוּאָה In an amount to fill an oven with grain. In those days ovens were made in the form of very large urns. Firewood was burned inside them, and pieces of dough would be placed on the inner walls. Thus there was a big difference between estimating the quantity according to the amount of grain that an oven could contain and according to the amount of bread that could be baked in it.

NOTES

Necho from the mouth of God," as an allusion to a warning issued by Jeremiah to Josiah in the name of Isaiah that he should not involve himself in the war being waged by Pharaoh Necho, because it is about such conflicts that the Prophet said (Isaiah 19:2): "And I will set Egypt against Egypt: and they shall fight every one against his brother, and every one against his neighbor; city against city, and kingdom against kingdom."

TRANSLATION AND COMMENTARY

[1]**Or** does it **perhaps** mean that there was blighted grain **in an amount** that would suffice **to fill an oven with bread** prepared from the grain? The latter amount is much smaller than the former, for when a person fills an oven with bread, he does not fill the entire internal space of the oven but places loaves of bread against the walls of the oven, and leaves the middle empty.

תָּא שְׁמַע [2]The Gemara answers: **Come and hear** what we have learned in our Mishnah: "They decreed a fast because blight in an amount **to fill the opening of an oven** was sighted on grain in Ashkelon." The Mishnah's mention of the "opening" of the oven proves that it is talking about filling the oven with bread and not with grain, for when a person fills an oven with grain he fills the entire internal space and not just its opening, but when he fills an oven with bread he fills the opening, attaching loaves of bread to the walls of the oven near its opening.

וַעֲדַיִין תִּיבָּעֵי לְהוּ [3]**But,** continues the Gemara, **the** following **question still remains,** even if we concede that the Mishnah is talking about filling an oven with bread: [4]Does the Mishnah mean that there was enough blighted grain to prepare a single loaf of bread to fill **the cover** placed on the opening **of the oven?** [5]**Or** does it **perhaps** mean that there was blighted grain in an amount that would suffice to prepare **the row of bread that surrounds the opening of the oven?**

תֵּיקוּ [6]The Gemara offers no solution to the problem posed here, and concludes: The problem **remains** unresolved.

וְעוֹד גָּזְרוּ [7]The next clause of the Mishnah states: "And it **also** happened that the Sages **decreed a fast** throughout Eretz Israel **because wolves** were seen **eating** two children on the eastern side of the Jordan River." The Gemara now considers a separate Halakhic issue that could arise in connection with a tragedy of this type. [8]**Ulla said in the name of Rabbi Shimon ben Yehotzadak: It once happened that** a pair of **wolves swallowed two children** whole **and** later **their** remains **were passed out by way of the** wolves' **excretory channels.** [9]**The incident came before the Sages** for a ruling regarding the status of those remains. Ordinarily, a corpse or parts of a dead body impart ritual impurity. The question arose whether ritual impurity can be

תְּבוּאָה, [1]אוֹ דִּלְמָא כִּמְלֹא תַּנּוּר פַּת?

[2]תָּא שְׁמַע: ״כִּמְלֹא פִּי תַּנּוּר״.

[3]וַעֲדַיִין תִּיבָּעֵי לְהוּ: [4]כְּכִיסּוּיָא דְּתַנּוּרָא, [5]אוֹ דִּלְמָא כִּי דָּרָא דְּרִיפְתָּא דְּהָדַר לֵיהּ לְפוּמָא דְּתַנּוּרָא?

[6]תֵּיקוּ.

[7]״וְעוֹד גָּזְרוּ תַּעֲנִית עַל שֶׁאָכְלוּ זְאֵבִים, כו׳״. [8]אָמַר עוּלָּא מִשּׁוּם רַבִּי שִׁמְעוֹן בֶּן יְהוֹצָדָק: מַעֲשֶׂה וּבָלְעוּ זְאֵבִים שְׁנֵי תִינוֹקוֹת וֶהֱקִיאוּם דֶּרֶךְ בֵּית הָרְעִי. [9]וּבָא מַעֲשֶׂה לִפְנֵי

LITERAL TRANSLATION

with grain, [1]or perhaps in an amount to fill an oven with bread?

[2]Come [and] hear: "In an amount to fill the opening of an oven."

[3]But it may still be asked of them: [4]Like the cover of the oven, [5]or perhaps like the row of bread that surrounds the opening of the oven?

[6]Let it stand [undecided].

[7]"And they also decreed a fast because wolves ate, etc." [8]Ulla said in the name of Rabbi Shimon ben Yehotzadak: It once happened that wolves swallowed two children and passed them out by way of the excretory channel. [9]And the incident came before

RASHI

תא שמע – דקתני הדא כי האי לישנא כמלא פי התנור, דהיינו פת, דאילו תבואה לא מלי קיימא על פי התנור. **או דלמא כי דרא דריפתא** – שורה של לחם הדבוקין זה אצל זה בפי התנור, אי נמי: שמדביקין זה למעלה מזה עד פי התנור. **ובלען** – כשהן שלימין.

BACKGROUND

כְּכִיסּוּיָא דְּתַנּוּרָא Like the cover of the oven. The mouth of the oven was the opening, facing upward, on either side of which, in the interior of the oven, pieces of dough would be placed. Such an oven also had an earthenware cover with which it was closed in order to retain the heat.

זְאֵבִים Wolves. Wolves, even in packs, seldom attack human beings. But the wolves in Eretz Israel were reputedly larger and stronger than those in Europe, and there were cases of wolves entering settlements and attacking children.

SAGES

רַבִּי שִׁמְעוֹן בֶּן יְהוֹצָדָק Rabbi Shimon ben Yehotzadak. A Palestinian Sage who lived in the transition period between the Tannaim and the Amoraim, he taught the famous Amora Rabbi Yoḥanan, who transmits many teachings in Rabbi Shimon's name.

Little is known of his life, other than that he was a priest and probably lived in the southern part of the country. The Jerusalem Talmud recounts that he died in the city of Lydda, and that the Sages of the generation, his companions in study, attended his funeral.

NOTES

כִּמְלֹא פִּי תַּנּוּר In an amount to fill the opening of an oven. Our commentary follows *Rashi, Rabbenu Gershom, Tosafot,* and others, who explain that the amount of grain required to fill an oven is greater than the amount of grain required if bread prepared from that grain is to fill that oven. *Rabbenu Elyakim* assumes just the opposite — that more grain is needed if the opening of the oven is to be filled with bread prepared from that grain than if it is to be filled with the grain itself.

HALAKHAH

כִּמְלֹא פִּי תַּנּוּר In an amount to fill the opening of an oven. "If the crops in a certain area are struck by blight or mildew, even if only a small amount of grain — enough to fill the opening of an oven — is so affected (the precise definition of this measure not having been determined: *Leḥem Mishneh*), fasts must be proclaimed and the alarm must be sounded." (*Shulḥan Arukh, Oraḥ Ḥayyim* 576:8.)

TRANSLATION AND COMMENTARY

imparted by a corpse or by parts of a dead body that have already passed through an animal's digestive tract. [1]The Sages who were asked to rule on the matter **declared the flesh** of the devoured children **ritually pure,** because it could be considered as the animals' own excretions. [2]**But they declared the bones ritually impure,** because they were intact.

עַל אֵלּוּ מַתְרִיעִין בְּשַׁבָּת [3]The Gemara proceeds to analyze the next clause of our Mishnah, which stated: **"For the following** impending calamities **the alarm is sounded** even **on Shabbat."** [4]**Our Rabbis taught** a related Baraita: "If **a city is being surrounded by an enemy army, or** is in danger of being inundated by **a river** that has overflowed its banks, **or** if a **ship is being tossed about in a storm at sea** and there is concern that it may capsize, **or** if **an individual is being pursued by non-Jews or by bandits, or** if an individual is possessed by **an evil spirit** and there is concern that he may cause himself injury — in all these cases the alarm may be sounded even on Shabbat. [5]And **in all these cases, an individual is permitted to afflict himself by** observing many individual **fasts** in order to petition God for compassion. [6]But **Rabbi Yose** disagrees and **says: An individual is not permitted to afflict himself by** observing a great number of individual **fasts,** [7]**lest** by spending his days in fasting he grows too weak to maintain himself through his own labors and **becomes** totally **dependent on** the mercies of other **people, and nobody is prepared to show him compassion."**

אָמַר רַב יְהוּדָה [8]**Rav Yehudah said in the name of Rav: What is the reasoning of Rabbi Yose?** Is there Biblical support for his opinion that a person may not afflict himself by undertaking a great number of fasts? [9]Rav explains: Rabbi Yose bases his opinion on **the** following **verse** which **states** (Genesis 2:7): "And the Lord God formed man out of the dust of the ground, and breathed into his nostrils the breath of life; **and man became**

חֲכָמִים, [1]וְטִיהֲרוּ אֶת הַבָּשָׂר, [2]וְטִמְּאוּ אֶת הָעֲצָמוֹת.

[3]״עַל אֵלּוּ מַתְרִיעִין בְּשַׁבָּת, כו׳״. [4]תָּנוּ רַבָּנַן: ״עִיר שֶׁהִקִּיפוּהָ נָכְרִים אוֹ נָהָר, וְאֶחָד סְפִינָה הַמִּיטָּרֶפֶת בַּיָּם, וְאֶחָד יָחִיד שֶׁנִּרְדָּף מִפְּנֵי נָכְרִים אוֹ מִפְּנֵי לִסְטִין, וּמִפְּנֵי רוּחַ רָעָה מַתְרִיעִין בְּשַׁבָּת, [5]וְעַל כּוּלָּן יָחִיד רַשַּׁאי לְסַגֵּף אֶת עַצְמוֹ בְּתַעֲנִית. [6]רַבִּי יוֹסֵי אוֹמֵר: אֵין הַיָּחִיד רַשַּׁאי לְסַגֵּף אֶת עַצְמוֹ בְּתַעֲנִית, [7]שֶׁמָּא יִצְטָרֵךְ לַבְּרִיּוֹת, וְאֵין הַבְּרִיּוֹת מְרַחֲמוֹת עָלָיו״.

[8]אָמַר רַב יְהוּדָה אָמַר רַב: מַאי טַעֲמָא דְּרַבִּי יוֹסֵי? [9]דִּכְתִיב: ״וַיְהִי הָאָדָם לְנֶפֶשׁ חַיָּה״.

LITERAL TRANSLATION

the Sages, [1]and they declared the flesh ritually pure, [2]and they declared the bones ritually impure.

[3]"For these they sound the alarm on Shabbat, etc." [4]Our Rabbis taught: "[For] a city surrounded by non-Jews or a river, and for a ship that is being tossed about at sea, and for an individual who is being pursued by non-Jews or by bandits, or by an evil spirit, they sound the alarm on Shabbat, [5]and for all of them an individual is permitted to afflict himself by a fast. [6]Rabbi Yose says: An individual is not permitted to afflict himself by a fast, [7]lest he come to need people, and people will not have mercy on him."

[8]Rav Yehudah said in the name of Rav: What is the reason of Rabbi Yose? [9]For it is written: "And man became a living soul."

RASHI

וטהרו את הבשר — שאינו מטמא טומאת מת, דנתעכל ונתבטל תוך מעיו, וכגון ששהו ימי עיכול, ופירשא בעלמא הוא. **וטימאו את העצמות** — דלא מתעכלו. **מפני רוח רעה** — שנכנס בו רוח שידה, ורץ והולך, ושמא יטבע בנהר או יפול וימות. **לסגף** — ״לענות נפש״ מתרגמינן: לסגפא נפש (במדבר ל). **יצטרך לבריות** — כי אין בו כח להרויח ולהתפרנס מיגיעו. **דכתיב לנפש חיה** — החייה.

BACKGROUND

וְטִיהֲרוּ אֶת הַבָּשָׂר And they declared the flesh ritually pure. Most predators are incapable of chewing their food. They either swallow it whole or tear it into pieces. Although their intestines are relatively short, their digestive juices are very potent. Therefore they can quickly digest anything they swallow. For this reason, any meat swallowed by an animal is regarded as having been fully digested (even if it was in the predator's intestines only a short time), and the laws of meat no longer apply to it.

NOTES

וְאֵין הַבְּרִיּוֹת מְרַחֲמוֹת עָלָיו And people will not have mercy on him. *Maharsha* adds that there is reason to fear that people will refrain from showing compassion to someone who engages in excessive fasting, for if a person fasts for many days and weakens his body so that he can no longer work in order to support himself, it is likely that he will be viewed as having brought this desperate situation upon himself.

HALAKHAH

וְטִיהֲרוּ אֶת הַבָּשָׂר And they declared the flesh ritually pure. "If a wolf swallows a child whole, and later its remains are passed out through the wolf's excretory channel, the flesh is ritually pure, but the bones are ritually impure." (*Rambam, Sefer Tahorah, Hilkhot Tum'at Met* 20:4.)

יָחִיד רַשַּׁאי לְסַגֵּף אֶת עַצְמוֹ בְּתַעֲנִית An individual is permitted to afflict himself by a fast. "Just as the community must observe fasts and offer special prayers when threatened by calamity, so too must each and every individual observe a fast when faced by some personal affliction (following *Maggid Mishneh* that the individual is obligated to fast in such situations; see also *Bah, Pri Megadim*)," following the anonymous first Tanna of the Baraita, and against Rabbi Yose. (*Shulhan Arukh, Orah Hayyim* 578:1.)

SAGES

רַבִּי חָנָן בֶּן פִּיטוֹם Rabbi Ḥanan ben Pitom. This Sage is mentioned only here. He seems to have been one of the students of Rabbi Akiva who perished during the Bar Kokhba rebellion.

TRANSLATION AND COMMENTARY

a living soul [נֶפֶשׁ חַיָּה]." Rabbi Yose understands this verse as implying a divine command. [1]God said: "**The soul that I placed within you, give it life.**" The verse implies that it is forbidden to endanger one's life by excessive fasting.

שִׁמְעוֹן הַתִּימְנִי אוֹמֵר [2]Our Mishnah continues: **"Shimon HaTimni says: For plague,** too, the alarm is sounded even on Shabbat. But the Sages did not agree with him." [3]**A question was raised** in the Academy as to the extent of the dispute between Shimon HaTimni and the Sages: When the Mishnah says that **the Sages did not agree with** Shimon HaTimni, does it mean that they disagreed with him **regarding Shabbat, but agreed with him regarding weekdays?** If so, Shimon HaTimni maintains that the alarm is sounded for plague even on Shabbat, whereas according to the Sages the alarm is sounded for plague only on the other days of the week, but not on Shabbat. [4]**Or perhaps the Sages did not agree with** Shimon HaTimni **at all,** and maintained that the alarm is never sounded for plague.

תָּא שְׁמַע [5]The Gemara answers: **Come, and hear, for** the following **was taught** in a Baraita: **"The alarm is sounded for plague** even **on Shabbat, and it is not necessary to say that** the alarm is sounded for plague **on weekdays.** [6]**Rabbi Ḥanan ben Pitom, the disciple of Rabbi Akiva, says in the name of Rabbi Akiva:** [7]**The alarm is not sounded for plague at all,** not even on weekdays, lest the alarm for plague be sounded on Shabbat." It is reasonable to assume that the Sages who disagreed with Shimon HaTimni accepted the opinion of Rabbi Akiva, leaving only two Tannaitic opinions on the matter and not three. Thus it follows that the Sages maintain that the alarm is never sounded for plague.

עַל כָּל צָרָה [8]We learned in our Mishnah: "For any trouble that may strike the community the alarm is sounded, except when the community is afflicted by too much rain." [9]**Our Rabbis taught** the same thing in the following Baraita, which stated: **"For any trouble that may strike the community the alarm is sounded,**

[1] "נְשָׁמָה שֶׁנָּתַתִּי בְּךָ, הַחֲיֵיהָ".
[2] "שִׁמְעוֹן הַתִּימְנִי אוֹמֵר: אַף עַל הַדֶּבֶר כו'". [3] אִיבַּעְיָא לְהוּ: לֹא הוֹדוּ לוֹ חֲכָמִים בְּשַׁבָּת, אֲבָל בְּחוֹל הוֹדוּ לוֹ? [4] אוֹ דִּלְמָא לֹא הוֹדוּ לוֹ כְּלָל?
[5] תָּא שְׁמַע, דְּתַנְיָא: "מַתְרִיעִין עַל הַדֶּבֶר בְּשַׁבָּת, וְאֵין צָרִיךְ לוֹמַר בְּחוֹל. [6] רַבִּי חָנָן בֶּן פִּיטוֹם, תַּלְמִידוֹ שֶׁל רַבִּי עֲקִיבָא, [7] מִשּׁוּם רַבִּי עֲקִיבָא אוֹמֵר: אֵין מַתְרִיעִין עַל הַדֶּבֶר כָּל עִיקָּר".
[8] "עַל כָּל צָרָה שֶׁלֹּא תָּבוֹא עַל הַצִּבּוּר כו'". [9] תָּנוּ רַבָּנַן: עַל כָּל צָרָה שֶׁלֹּא תָּבוֹא עַל הַצִּבּוּר

LITERAL TRANSLATION

[1][God said]: "The soul I placed within you, give it life."

[2]"Shimon HaTimni says: Also for plague, etc." [3]It was asked of them: Did the Sages not agree with him regarding Shabbat, but agreed with him regarding weekdays? [4]Or did they perhaps not agree with him at all?

[5]Come [and] hear, for it was taught: "They sound the alarm for plague on Shabbat, and it is not necessary to say [that they do so] on weekdays. [6]Rabbi Ḥanan ben Pitom, the disciple of Rabbi Akiva, says in the name of Rabbi Akiva: [7]They do not sound the alarm for plague at all."

[8]"For any trouble that may come upon the community, etc." [9]Our Rabbis taught: "For any trouble that may come upon the community,

RASHI

חנן בן פטום אומר אין מתריעין על הדבר – אפילו בחול, דגזירה היא.

NOTES

אוֹ דִּלְמָא לֹא הוֹדוּ לוֹ כְּלָל Or did they perhaps not agree with him at all? Many Rishonim ask: Here it is reported by Rabbi Ḥanan ben Pitom that, according to his teacher, Rabbi Akiva, the alarm is not sounded for plague at all, even on weekdays. But it was stated explicitly in our Mishnah that, according to Rabbi Akiva, people living outside a city affected by plague must sound the alarm but not fast. Surely, then, the residents of the city itself must sound the alarm if their city is affected by plague!

Ra'avad resolves this difficulty by amending the Baraita to read: "Rabbi Ḥanan ben Pitom said in the name of Rabbi Akiva: They do not sound the alarm for plague on Shabbat." But most Rishonim explain that when Rabbi Akiva said that they do not sound the alarm for plague at all, he was referring to the communities outside the city affected by the disease and beyond its surrounding areas. Surely Rabbi Akiva agrees that the alarm is sounded for plague by the residents of the city afflicted by the plague, as well as by the people living in the surrounding areas. But he disagrees with Shimon HaTimni, who maintains that the alarm is sounded even in other cities, for Rabbi Akiva maintains that outside the city afflicted by the plague and beyond the immediately surrounding areas the alarm is not sounded for plague even on weekdays (*Ramban, Ritva, Rid,* and others).

HALAKHAH

עַל הַדֶּבֶר For plague. "The alarm is not sounded for plague on Shabbat, but during the rest of the week the alarm is sounded and fasts are proclaimed." (*Shulḥun Arukh, Oraḥ Ḥayyim* 576:2; 288:9.)

LITERAL TRANSLATION

they sound the alarm, except for too much rain." [1]What is the reason?

[2]Rabbi Yoḥanan said: Because we do not pray on account of too much good. [3]And Rabbi Yoḥanan said: From where [do we derive] that we do not pray on account of too much good? [4]For it is said: "Bring all the tithes into the storehouse, etc." [5]What is [the meaning of] "until it is more than enough"? [6]Rami bar Ḥama said: Until your lips wear out from saying: "Enough."

[7]Rami bar Rav Yud said: [8]But in the Diaspora they sound the alarm for it.

[9]It was also taught thus: "[In] a year whose rains are abundant, the men of the *mishmar*

מַתְרִיעִין עָלֶיהָ, חוּץ מֵרוֹב גְּשָׁמִים.
[1]מַאי טַעֲמָא?
[2]אָמַר רַבִּי יוֹחָנָן: לְפִי שֶׁאֵין מִתְפַּלְּלִין עַל רוֹב הַטּוֹבָה.
[3]וְאָמַר רַבִּי יוֹחָנָן: מִנַּיִין שֶׁאֵין מִתְפַּלְּלִין עַל רוֹב הַטּוֹבָה?
[4]שֶׁנֶּאֱמַר "הָבִיאוּ אֶת כָּל הַמַּעֲשֵׂר אֶל בֵּית הָאוֹצָר", וגו׳
[5]מַאי "עַד בְּלִי דָי"?
[6]אָמַר רָמִי בַּר חָמָא: עַד שֶׁיִּבְלוּ שִׂפְתוֹתֵיכֶם מִלּוֹמַר: "דַּי".
[7]אָמַר רָמִי בַּר רַב יוּד:
[8]וּבַגּוֹלָה מַתְרִיעִין עָלֶיהָ.
[9]תַּנְיָא נַמִּי הָכִי: שָׁנָה שֶׁגְּשָׁמֶיהָ מְרוּבִּין, אַנְשֵׁי מִשְׁמָר

RASHI

רמי בר רב יוד — חכם ששמו יוד. **ובגולה** — בבל, שהיא במצולה. **מתריעין על רוב גשמים** — שלא ירדו.

TRANSLATION AND COMMENTARY

except when there is **too much rain."**

מַאי טַעֲמָא [1]The Gemara asks: **What is the reason** that the alarm is not sounded for excessive rain?

אָמַר רַבִּי יוֹחָנָן [2]**Rabbi Yoḥanan said** in reply: **Because prayers should not be offered on account of too much good.** In general, rain is considered to be a blessing for the world, and is one of the main objects of our prayers. Thus it is improper to offer prayers that the rain should cease. [3]**And Rabbi Yoḥanan said: From where** in the Bible **do we derive** the ruling **that prayers should not be offered on account of too much good?** [4]This principle is learned from **the following verse,** which **says** (Malachi 3:10): **"Bring all the tithes into the storehouse** that there may be food in My house, and test Me now by this, said the Lord of Hosts, if I will not open for you the windows of heaven, and pour out for you a blessing until it is more than enough."

אָמַר רַבִּי יוֹחָנָן [5]**What is the meaning of** the words **"until it is more than enough"?** The Prophet uses an unusual construction (עַד בְּלִי דָי), which literally means "until without enough." Perhaps Malachi means that there will not be enough space for all the bounty bestowed by Heaven.

אָמַר רָמִי בַּר חָמָא [6]**Rami bar Ḥama said** that the meaning of the verse can be brought out even more forcefully if the phrase is taken as a play on words. The word בְּלִי, which means "without," can also be interpreted as a verb meaning "to wear out." Thus the Prophet is saying that the blessing will be poured out **until your lips wear out from saying: "Enough."**

אָמַר רָמִי בַּר רַב יוּד [7]The Gemara continues: **Rami bar Rav Yud said:** When the Mishnah stated that the alarm is not sounded for too much rain, it was referring to Eretz Israel, which is a mostly hilly region, so that excess rainwater flows into the sea. Moreover, the buildings in Eretz Israel are constructed largely from stone, and stand up well to abundant rain. [8]**But in the Diaspora** — Babylonia, the main Jewish community outside Eretz Israel — **the alarm is sounded for** too much rain, for excessive rain poses a real danger to the population there. Babylonia is mainly a low-lying region and suffers severely from flooding. Moreover, the mud-brick buildings in Babylonia may well collapse if there is excessive rainfall. Thus it is proper to sound the alarm in Babylonia when there is too much rain.

תַּנְיָא נַמִּי הָכִי [9]**The same** ruling **was also taught** in a Baraita referring to the priests who served in the Temple. The priests were divided into twenty-four groups, called *mishmarot* ("watches"). Each *mishmar* served for one week at a time, so that each *mishmar* performed the Temple service for approximately two weeks a year. Corresponding to each of the *mishmarot* was a group of non-priests, called a ma'amad ("post" or

SAGES

רָמִי בַּר רַב יוּד Rami bar Rav Yud. He was a Babylonian Amora of the second generation. The name "Yud" is probably an abbreviation of "Yehudah," and he is mentioned elsewhere as Rami bar Rav Yehudah.

BACKGROUND

וּבַגּוֹלָה מַתְרִיעִין But in the Diaspora they sound the alarm. In the Talmud the word גּוֹלָה ("diaspora"), when unqualified, means Babylonia. The reason why they sounded the alarm for too much rain there was that, being flat and low-lying country, it suffered serious damage from floods, which could casue fatalities. Moreover, in Eretz Israel most buildings were constructed of stone, whereas in Babylonia they were made of mud bricks and thus likely to collapse as a result of excessive rain.

HALAKHAH

חוּץ מֵרוֹב גְּשָׁמִים Except for too much rain. "If there is an excessive amount of rainfall, prayers must be offered that the rain should stop, for there is concern that the water will cause buildings to collapse. In Eretz Israel such prayers are usually not recited, because in Eretz Israel abundant rain is regarded as a blessing and there is no concern that the excessive rainfall will cause the collapse of buildings. Even in Eretz Israel, however, prayers that the rain should stop must be offered in places such as Safed, where there is reason to believe that excessive rain will cause damage to the buildings." (*Shulḥan Arukh, Oraḥ Ḥayyim* 576:11.)

שׁוֹלְחִין לְאַנְשֵׁי מַעֲמָד: [1]תְּנוּ עֵינֵיכֶם בַּאֲחֵיכֶם שֶׁבַּגּוֹלָה שֶׁלֹּא יְהֵא בָּתֵּיהֶם קִבְרֵיהֶם. [2]שָׁאֲלוּ אֶת רַבִּי אֱלִיעֶזֶר: עַד הֵיכָן גְּשָׁמִים יוֹרְדִין וְיִתְפַּלְּלוּ שֶׁלֹּא יֵרְדוּ? [3]אָמַר לָהֶם: כְּדֵי שֶׁיַּעֲמוֹד אָדָם בְּקֶרֶן אֹפֶל, וִישַׁכְשֵׁךְ רַגְלָיו בַּמַּיִם.

[4]וְהָתַנְיָא ״יָדָיו״!

[5]רַגְלָיו כְּיָדָיו קָאָמִינָא.

[6]אֲמַר רַבָּה בַּר בַּר חָנָה: [7]לְדִידִי חֲזְיָא לִי קֶרֶן אֹפֶל, דְּקָם הַהוּא טַיָּיעָא כִּי רָכֵיב גַּמְלָא וְנָקֵיט רוֹמְחָא בִּידֵיהּ מִיתְחֲזֵי אִינִבָא.

[8]תָּנוּ רַבָּנַן: ״׳וְנָתַתִּי גִשְׁמֵיכֶם

LITERAL TRANSLATION

send to the men of the *ma'amad*: [1]'Set your eyes on your brethren in the Diaspora so that their houses may not become their graves.' [2]They asked Rabbi Eliezer: Up to where should the rain fall, that they should pray that they not fall? [3]He said to them: So that a man may stand on Keren Ofel, and paddle his feet in the water."

[4]But surely it was taught: "His hands"!

[5]I meant his feet [must be] like his hands.

[6]Rabbah bar Bar Ḥanah said: [7]I personally saw Keren Ofel, where a certain Arab was standing [below] while riding a camel and was holding a spear in his hand, [and] he looked like a worm.

[8]Our Rabbis taught: "'And I will give your rains

TRANSLATION AND COMMENTARY

"division"). Each time a *mishmar* went to Jerusalem to serve in the Temple, part of the corresponding *ma'amad* would go there as well, and would represent the entire people when the communal sacrifices were offered. The rest of the *ma'amad* would remain at home, and during that week would fast each day from Monday to Thursday, read special portions from the Torah, and say special prayers. The Baraita states: **"In a year when rains were abundant, the members of the *mishmar*** whose week it was to serve in the Temple **would send** the following message **to the members of the** corresponding ***ma'amad*** to offer special prayers on behalf of the Jewish people everywhere: [1]**'Set your eyes on your brethren in the Diaspora,** and offer prayers on behalf of the Jewish community there, **so that their houses may not** collapse on account of excessive rain and floodwaters and **become their graves.'"** Thus we see that it is proper to offer prayers that there not be too much rainfall in Babylonia. [2]The Baraita continues: **"Rabbi Eliezer was asked** about the following matter: **How much rain must fall** before **people may** begin to **pray** even in Eretz Israel **that no more rain should fall?** [3]Rabbi Eliezer **answered:** Such prayers may not be offered **until** there is so much rain that a person standing on Keren Ofel, one of the high points of the city of Jerusalem, can **paddle his feet in the water** flowing through the Kidron Valley. But as long as such a quantity of rain has not fallen, and indeed so much rain has never fallen and it is most improbable that such an amount will ever fall in the future, one may not pray that the rain should stop."

וְהָתַנְיָא ״יָדָיו״ [4]The Gemara raises an objection against one of the details mentioned in the Baraita: **But surely it was taught** in another Baraita: "One may not pray that the rain should stop falling until a person standing on Keren Ofel can paddle **his *hands*** in the water flowing through the Kidron Valley"!

רַגְלָיו כְּיָדָיו קָאָמִינָא [5]The Gemara answers: There is no contradiction between the two sources. **His feet must be like his hands.** If there was so much rainfall that a person can paddle his feet in the water, he can bend down and immerse his hands in the water as well.

אֲמַר רַבָּה בַּר בַּר חָנָה [6]Having mentioned Keren Ofel and emphasized its impressive height, the Gemara now offers this vivid description of the place: **Rabbah bar Bar Ḥanah said:** [7]**I personally was** once **looking from Keren Ofel** and I saw **a certain Arab standing below while riding a camel, and he was holding a spear in his hand, and** the distance from Keren Ofel to the valley below was so great that **he looked** as small **as a worm.**

תָּנוּ רַבָּנַן [8]**Our Rabbis taught** a Baraita, which stated: "If the people of Israel walk in God's statutes and keep His commandments, they will be rewarded with the fulfillment of God's promise [Leviticus 26:4]: **And I will give your rains in their season,** and the land will yield its produce, and the trees of the field will yield their fruit.' Rain will fall at the proper time and in the proper amounts, not too much and not too little.

RASHI

שלא יהו בתיהם קבריהן – שעמוקה היא, ונטבעים בתיהם במים. **אנשי משמר ואנשי מעמד** – מפרש בשלשה פרקים לקמן (כו,א). **תנו עיניכם** – התבוננו בתפלתכם בתעניות עליהם, שלא ירדו רוב גשמים. **קרן אפל** – שן סלע גבוה, וכך שמו. **וישכשך רגליו במים** – כלומר: לעולם אין מתפללין. **והתניא ידו** – עד שישכשך ידו. **רגלו כידו** – וכיון דיכול לשכשך ברגלו, אי שוחה – יכול לשכשך בידו נמי. **טייעא** = סוחר ישמעאל. **ומיתחזי** – האי טייעא וגמליה ורומחא לרבה בר בר חנה דהוה על קרן אפל. **איניבא** – תולעת, לשון אחר: כי אנבא – *לינדינ״א בלעז.

BACKGROUND

קֶרֶן אֹפֶל Keren Ofel. It is thought that Keren Ofel is another word for the Ofel (עוֹפֶל), the fortress of ancient Jerusalem. The difference in height between the Keren Ofel and the Kidron stream below it is more than a hundred meters.

LANGUAGE

אִינִיבָא Worm. This word probably derives from a Semitic root also found in Aramaic, which appears in Assyrian as *nabu*. It means "lice" or "fleas."

LANGUAGE (RASHI)

לינדינ״א* From the Italian *lendena*, which means "eggs of lice."

TRANSLATION AND COMMENTARY

[1]Thus **the earth will neither become over-saturated** by rain **nor** will it remain **thirsty** for water, **but** rather it **will receive a moderate amount** of rainfall. [2]**For whenever the rains are abundant, the earth is made muddy, and** as a result **it does not yield** high-quality **fruit.** [3]**Another explanation** of God's promise may be offered: [23A] [4]When the verse uses the expression: 'And I will give your rains **in their season,**' it means that rain will fall at its proper time, [5]**on Tuesday nights and on Friday nights,** when people find it most convenient for rain to fall. On Tuesday nights people do not wander in the streets, for that is the time when it is believed demonic forces walk abroad. And on Friday nights people stay at home in order to enjoy their Shabbat rest. Thus God promises that the rain will fall when most people are least inconvenienced by inclement weather. And should you argue that rainfall on Tuesday and Friday nights is not enough for a successful harvest, that is not the case. [6]**For we find that in the days of** the Sage **Shimon ben Shetah the rain** always **fell** only 'in its season' — **on Tuesday nights and on Friday nights.** [7]Nevertheless there was **enough** rain **so that** the grains of **wheat grew** to be as big **as kidneys, and the barley** grains were as big **as the pits of olives, and** the **lentils** grew to be as big **as dinarim of gold.** [8]**And they tied up some of the** unusually large grains of wheat and barley and lentils, and saved them **as an example for** all **future generations, to let them know how much damage sin causes** by diminishing the size and quality of each year's harvest. [9]This is in **accordance with the verse, which says** [Jeremiah 5:24-25]: 'Neither do they say in their heart, Let us now fear the Lord our God, Who gives rain, the former rain and the latter rain, in its season, Who keeps for us the appointed weeks of the harvest. [10]**Your iniquities have turned away these things, and your sins have withheld the good from you.'** The bountiful produce served as proof that God is willing to cause the rain to fall in its season and in quantities sufficient for a most abundant crop, and it is only because the people are undeserving that this does not occur every year. [11]And similarly we find in the days of King Herod that, when the people were engaged in the reconstruction of the Temple in Jerusalem, [12]the rain would fall only at night. [13]Early the next day the wind would blow,

בְּעִתָּם׳. [1]לֹא שִׁכּוֹרָה וְלֹא צְמֵאָה, אֶלָּא בֵּינוֹנִית. [2]שֶׁכָּל זְמַן שֶׁהַגְּשָׁמִים מְרוּבִּין — מְטַשְׁטְשִׁין אֶת הָאָרֶץ, וְאֵינָהּ מוֹצִיאָה פֵּירוֹת. [3]דָּבָר אַחֵר: [23A] [4]׳בְּעִתָּם׳ — [5]בְּלֵילֵי רְבִיעִיּוֹת וּבְלֵילֵי שַׁבָּתוֹת. [6]שֶׁכֵּן מָצִינוּ בִּימֵי שִׁמְעוֹן בֶּן שֶׁטַח, שֶׁיָּרְדוּ לָהֶם גְּשָׁמִים בְּלֵילֵי רְבִיעִיּוֹת וּבְלֵילֵי שַׁבָּתוֹת, [7]עַד שֶׁנַּעֲשׂוּ חִטִּים כִּכְלָיוֹת וּשְׂעוֹרִים כְּגַרְעִינֵי זֵיתִים וַעֲדָשִׁים כְּדִינְרֵי זָהָב. [8]וְצָרְרוּ מֵהֶם דּוּגְמָא לְדוֹרוֹת, לְהוֹדִיעַ כַּמָּה הַחֵטְא גּוֹרֵם, [9]שֶׁנֶּאֱמַר: ׳עֲוֹנוֹתֵיכֶם הִטּוּ אֵלֶּה, [10]וְחַטֹּאתֵיכֶם מָנְעוּ הַטּוֹב מִכֶּם׳. [11]וְכֵן מָצִינוּ בִּימֵי הוֹרְדוֹס שֶׁהָיוּ עוֹסְקִין בְּבִנְיַן בֵּית הַמִּקְדָּשׁ, [12]וְהָיוּ יוֹרְדִין גְּשָׁמִים בַּלַּיְלָה. [13]לְמָחָר נָשְׁבָה הָרוּחַ,

LITERAL TRANSLATION

in their season, [1][so that the earth will be] neither over-watered (lit., 'drunk') nor thirsty, but [will receive] a moderate amount, [2]for whenever the rains are abundant, they make the earth muddy, and it does not yield fruit. [3]Another explanation: [23A] [4]'In their season' — [5]on Tuesday nights and on Friday nights (lit., 'on the nights of fourth days and on the nights of Sabbaths'). [6]For so we find in the days of Shimon ben Shetah that rains fell for them on Tuesday nights and on Friday nights, [7]until wheat became like kidneys, and barley like the pits of olives, and lentils like dinarim of gold. [8]And they tied up [some] of them [as] an example for [future] generations, to let [them] know how much [damage] sin causes, [9]as it is said: 'Your iniquities have turned away these things, [10]and your sins have withheld the good from you.' [11]And similarly we find in the days of Herod that they were engaged in the construction of the Temple, [12]and rains would fall at night. [13]The next day the wind would blow,

RASHI

לא שכורה — לא שתויה יותר מדאי, שמטשטשין את הארץ. **דכתיב בעתם** — זהו בלילי רביעיות ובלילי שבתות, דאין טורח לבני אדם. דאינם הולכים לדרכים בלילי רביעיות מפני אגרת בת מחלת, בפסחים (קיב,ב). **שכן מצינו** — כלומר: ושמא תאמר אין סיפק בגשמים של שני לילות בשבת — מצינו בימי שמעון בן שטח כו׳. **וצררו** — קשרו ואצרו. **הורדוס** — סתר בנין דעזרא, ובנה בנין יפה ממנו, בבבא בתרא (ד,א).

NOTES

בְּלֵילֵי רְבִיעִיּוֹת On Tuesday nights. Most commentators explain the term as referring to the eves of the fourth (רְבִיעִי) day of the week, Tuesday nights. But some understand the expression as referring to the nights on which the downpours of rain (רְבִיעָה) are expected. The latter explanation is supported by the reading found in some manuscripts and early sources: בִּימֵי רְבִיעִיּוֹת — "on the days of the downpours."

BACKGROUND

כִּכְלָיוֹת, כְּדִינְרֵי זָהָב Like kidneys, like dinarim of gold. Today the length of a grain of wheat or barley is about 6 mm., and lentils are 3-4 mm. The plants here are thus two or three times larger than normal.

LANGUAGE

דּוּגְמָא Example. This word is derived from the Greek δεῖγμα, *deigma*, meaning "an example" or "a model."

PEOPLE

בִּימֵי הוֹרְדוֹס In the days of Herod. King Herod, who reigned from 37-4 B.C.E., usurped the monarchy from the Hasmonean kings. He was regarded by the Jewish Sages as an evil king, because he seized power by force, because he was cruel and assimilated, and because he submitted to the domination of the Romans.

On the other hand, the Sages made favorable mention of his great deed, the renewal of the building of the Temple. The Temple built by Herod was considered the most splendid building of its day. Most of the construction was finished in nine years, though it was still not entirely completed at the time of its destruction.

TRANSLATION AND COMMENTARY

the clouds would disperse, the sun would shine, and the people would go out for another day's **work.** When the people saw that the rain fell only when it would not interfere with the building of the Temple, [1]**they knew that they were involved in work** that was pleasing to **Heaven."**

מַעֲשֶׂה [2]The Gemara now proceeds to the next portion of the Mishnah, which opened as follows: **"It once happened** during a period of drought **that** the people **sent for Ḥoni HaMe'aggel,** asking him to pray that rain should fall." [3]The same story is also reported in the following Baraita in which **our Rabbis taught:** "It **once** happened that **most** of the month **of Adar had** already **passed but rain had** still **not fallen.** [4]Worried, the people **sent for Ḥoni HaMe'aggel,** who was noted for his successful intercessions with God on behalf of the Jewish community, and said to him: [5]**'Pray** on our behalf **that rain will fall** and the drought will come to an end.' Ḥoni began to **pray, but rain did not fall.** [6]**He drew a circle** on the ground, **and stood within it, just as the Prophet Habakkuk had done, as the verse says** [Habakkuk 2:1]: **'I will stand upon my watch,** [7]**and** set myself upon the tower, and I will watch to see what He will say to me, and what I shall answer when I am reproved.' Habakkuk stood within a circle and swore to God that he would not move until he had received an answer to his question regarding the future redemption of the people of Israel. [8]In similar fashion, Ḥoni addressed God and **said to Him: 'Master of the Universe! Your children have turned to me** to pray for rain, **because I am** considered by them **a member of Your household,** who can elicit Your mercy. [9]Therefore, **I swear by Your great Name that I will not move from here** and will not leave this circle **until You have mercy on Your children** and cause the rain to fall.' [10]As soon as he finished speaking, **rain began to come down in** tiny **drops.** [11]Ḥoni's **disciples said to him: 'Master, we have seen that you** can call upon God to perform miracles, but this does not help us. You must pray again on our behalf so that

וְנִתְפַּזְּרוּ הֶעָבִים, וְזָרְחָה הַחַמָּה, וְיָצְאוּ הָעָם לִמְלַאכְתָּן, [1]וְיָדְעוּ שֶׁמְּלֶאכֶת שָׁמַיִם בִּידֵיהֶם״.

[2]״מַעֲשֶׂה שֶׁשָּׁלְחוּ לְחוֹנִי הַמְעַגֵּל, וכו׳״. [3]תָּנוּ רַבָּנַן: ״פַּעַם אַחַת, יָצָא רוֹב אֲדָר וְלֹא יָרְדוּ גְּשָׁמִים. [4]שָׁלְחוּ לְחוֹנִי הַמְעַגֵּל: ׳הִתְפַּלֵּל וְיֵרְדוּ גְּשָׁמִים׳. [5]הִתְפַּלֵּל וְלֹא יָרְדוּ גְּשָׁמִים. [6]עָג עוּגָה, וְעָמַד בְּתוֹכָהּ, כְּדֶרֶךְ שֶׁעָשָׂה חֲבַקּוּק הַנָּבִיא, [7]שֶׁנֶּאֱמַר: ׳עַל מִשְׁמַרְתִּי אֶעֱמֹדָה, וְאֶתְיַצְּבָה עַל מָצוֹר, וגו׳״. [8]אָמַר לְפָנָיו: ׳רִבּוֹנוֹ שֶׁל עוֹלָם! בָּנֶיךָ שָׂמוּ פְּנֵיהֶם עָלַי, שֶׁאֲנִי כְּבֶן בַּיִת לְפָנֶיךָ. [9]נִשְׁבָּע אֲנִי בְּשִׁמְךָ הַגָּדוֹל שֶׁאֵינִי זָז מִכָּאן עַד שֶׁתְּרַחֵם עַל בָּנֶיךָ׳. [10]הִתְחִילוּ גְּשָׁמִים מְנַטְּפִין. [11]אָמְרוּ לוֹ תַּלְמִידָיו: ׳רַבִּי, רְאִינוּךָ, וְלֹא נָמוּת.

LITERAL TRANSLATION

and the clouds would disperse, and the sun would shine, and the people would go out to their work, [1]and they would know that the work of Heaven [was] in their hands."

[2]"It once happened that they sent for Ḥoni HaMe'aggel, etc." [3]Our Rabbis taught: "Once, most of Adar had passed and rains had not fallen. [4]They sent for Ḥoni HaMe'aggel: 'Pray that rains may fall.' [5]He prayed, but rains did not fall. [6]He drew a circle, and stood within it, in the way that the Prophet Habakkuk had done, [7]as it is said: 'I will stand upon my watch, and set myself upon the tower, etc.' [8]He said before Him: 'Master of the Universe! Your children have turned (lit., "put their faces") to me, for I am like a member of Your household. [9]I swear by Your great Name that I will not move from here until You have mercy on Your children.' [10]Rains began to come down in drops. [11]His disciples said to him: 'Master, we have seen you, but let us not die.

RASHI

עוגה – שורה עגולה, כמו עוגה שהיא עגולה. **כדרך שעשה חבקוק** – כדמפרש בתרגום של תפלת חבקוק "על משמרתי אעמדה" – כמין בית האסורים עשה וישב. **ראינוך ולא נמות** – נראה אותך ולא נמות, בניחותא: השתדל שלא נמות ברעב מפני עצירת גשמים.

NOTES

כְּבֶן בַּיִת לְפָנֶיךָ Like a member of Your household. *Maharsha* explains this term as an expression of modesty: Ḥoni HaMe'aggel compared himself to an unimportant member of God's household, who on account of his insignificance is able to enter his Master's house and put forward his requests whenever he wishes. This is reminiscent of Rabbi Yoḥanan ben Zakkai's explanation (*Berakhot* 34b) as to why he himself did not pray for his son's recovery but asked Rabbi Ḥanina ben Dosa to pray for him instead. Rabbi Yoḥanan ben Zakkai viewed himself as the king's officer, whereas Rabbi Ḥanina he regarded as the king's slave. The king's slave, who appears regularly before his master, is more suited to place a request before the king than is the king's officer, who is not accustomed to speak to him.

רְאִינוּךָ, וְלֹא נָמוּת We have seen you, but let us not die. Many commentators explain this expression as follows: We

[1]כִּמְדוּמִּין אָנוּ שֶׁאֵין גְּשָׁמִים יוֹרְדִין אֶלָּא לְהַתִּיר שְׁבוּעָתְךָ׳. [2]אָמַר: ׳לֹא כָּךְ שָׁאַלְתִּי, אֶלָּא גִּשְׁמֵי בוֹרוֹת, שִׁיחִין, וּמְעָרוֹת׳. [3]יָרְדוּ בְּזַעַף, עַד שֶׁכָּל טִפָּה וְטִפָּה כִּמְלֹא פִּי חָבִית. [4]וְשִׁיעֲרוּ חֲכָמִים שֶׁאֵין טִפָּה פְּחוּתָה מִלּוֹג. [5]אָמְרוּ לוֹ תַּלְמִידָיו: ׳רַבִּי, רְאִינוּךָ, וְלֹא נָמוּת. [6]כִּמְדוּמִּין אָנוּ שֶׁאֵין גְּשָׁמִים יוֹרְדִין אֶלָּא לְאַבֵּד הָעוֹלָם׳. [7]אָמַר לְפָנָיו: ׳לֹא כָּךְ שָׁאַלְתִּי, אֶלָּא גִּשְׁמֵי רָצוֹן, בְּרָכָה, וּנְדָבָה׳. [8]יָרְדוּ כְּתִיקְנָן, עַד שֶׁעָלוּ כָּל הָעָם לְהַר הַבַּיִת מִפְּנֵי הַגְּשָׁמִים. [9]אָמְרוּ לוֹ: ׳רַבִּי, כְּשֵׁם שֶׁהִתְפַּלַּלְתָּ שֶׁיֵּרְדוּ, כָּךְ הִתְפַּלֵּל וְיֵלְכוּ לָהֶם׳. [10]אָמַר לָהֶם: ׳כָּךְ מְקוּבְּלָנִי שֶׁאֵין מִתְפַּלְּלִין עַל רוֹב הַטּוֹבָה. [11]אַף עַל פִּי כֵן, הָבִיאוּ לִי פַּר הוֹדָאָה׳. [12]הֵבִיאוּ לוֹ פַּר הוֹדָאָה. [13]סָמַךְ שְׁתֵּי יָדָיו עָלָיו, וְאָמַר לְפָנָיו: ׳רִבּוֹנוֹ שֶׁל עוֹלָם!

LITERAL TRANSLATION

[1]It seems to us that the rains are falling only in order to free [you from] your oath.' [2]He said: 'I did not ask [for] this, but [for] rains [to fill] pits, ditches, and caves.' [3]They came down strongly (lit., 'in anger'), until each and every drop was enough to fill the mouth of a barrel. [4]And the Sages estimated that no drop was less than a *log*. [5]His disciples said to him: 'Master, we have seen you, but let us not die. [6]It seems to us that the rains are falling only in order to destroy the world.' [7]He said before Him: 'I did not ask [for] this, but [for] rains of goodwill, blessing, and generosity.' [8]They fell in their normal way, until all the people went up to the Temple Mount because of the rains. [9]They said to him: 'Master, just as you prayed that they should fall, so pray that they should go away.' [10]He said to them: 'So have I received [the tradition] that we do not pray on account of too much good. [11]Even so, bring me a bullock for confession.' [12]They brought him a bullock for confession. [13]He laid his two hands on it, and said before Him: 'Master of the Universe!

TRANSLATION AND COMMENTARY

we do not die from the drought. [1]For **it seems to us that the rain is falling only in order to free you from your oath** and allow you to leave the circle. [2]Honi then **addressed** God again: **'I did not ask for** rain like **this, but rather** enough **rain** to fill up the storage **cisterns, ditches, and caves** with water for the entire year.' [3]Immediately the rain began to **come down** very **strongly, so that each and every drop was** large **enough to fill the mouth of a barrel.** [4]**And the Sages estimated that there was no drop** of rain that measured **less than a *log*** [a liquid measure equal to the volume of six eggs]. [5]Honi's **disciples said to him: 'Master,** again **we have seen that you** can call upon God to perform miracles, but again this does not help us. Please pray again so that **we do not die** from this violent rainstorm. [6]For **it seems to us that the rain is falling** not **in order** to bring an end to the drought but **rather to destroy the world.'** [7]Honi then **addressed** God again: **'I did not ask for rain like this** either, **but rather for rain of goodwill, blessing, and generosity,** that falls gently, but in sufficient quantities to meet the people's needs.' [8]**The rain** then began to **fall in the normal way until** it became necessary for **all the people** to leave the lower parts of Jerusalem and **to go up to** the higher region of **the Temple Mount because of the rain.** [9]Honi's disciples then came back to him and **said: 'Master, just as you prayed for** the rain **to fall, so you must** now **pray for** the rain **to stop** before the city is completely flooded.' [10]But Honi **said to them: 'I have received a tradition** from my teachers **that prayers should not be offered on account of too much good.** Since rain in general is considered to be a blessing, it would be improper for me to pray for it to cease, for I would seem to be rejecting the blessing that God has bestowed. [11]**Even so, bring me a bullock,** and I will offer it as a peace-offering and recite over it a **confessional** prayer. Perhaps God will hearken to my prayer and will cause the rain to cease.' [12]Immediately, **they brought him a bullock** so that he could recite over it the **confessional** prayer. [13]**He** laid his two hands on the animal's head, **and said before** God: **'Master of the Universe!**

RASHI

פר הודאה — להתודות עליו, ועשה לו סמיכה, והביאו שלמים. חוני בזמן הבית היה.

NOTES

have seen you — we have seen that God performs miracles on your behalf. But let us not die — pray for us now so that we do not die, for we are still in a desperate situation. *Rabbenu Gershom* understands this expression as a question: Just because we have seen you, shall we not die? Surely the rain you have caused to fall has not been beneficial to us in any way!

BACKGROUND

כְּמֵהִין **Truffles.**

Truffles (*Tuberaceae*) belong to a special genus of fungi which grow entirely underground, including the fruit. The body of the fruit looks like a slightly rounded clump in various colors (black, brown, and whitish). Truffles generally grow from 3-5 cm. up to 10 cm. in diameter, and a large truffle can weigh as much as a kilogram. Truffles are harvested by removing the earth from above them, sometimes by animals trained to do this. Most truffles, while still young, are edible and are regarded as a delicacy.

LANGUAGE (RASHI)

בולי״ץ* From the Old French *boleiz,* which means "a mushroom."

TRANSLATION AND COMMENTARY

[1] **Your people Israel whom You brought out of Egypt cannot bear too much good or too much punishment.** [2] When **You displayed Your anger toward them** and withheld the rain from them or caused it to come down in tiny drops, **they were unable to bear it.** [3] And when **You bestowed upon them** too much **good** and caused the rain to come down with great force, **they were** also **unable to bear it.** [4] **May it be Your will that the rain will stop, so that there will be relief in the world.'** [5] **Immediately, the wind** began to **blow, the clouds dispersed, the sun shone** through, **and the people went out to the fields and collected truffles and mushrooms** that had sprung up after the rain, and were understood to be a sign that the rain that had fallen would be a blessing for them. [6] **Shimon ben Shetaḥ,** the head of the Sanhedrin in that generation, **sent** a message **to** Ḥoni, saying: **'If you were not Ḥoni, I would** surely **place you under a ban,** for you addressed God disrespectfully. [7] And moreover, **if the years were like the years of** the Prophet **Elijah, when the keys of rain were** entrusted **in his hands** and he swore that it would not rain, saying [I Kings 17:1]: "As the Lord God of Israel lives, before whom I stand, there shall not be dew or rain these years, but according to my word," [8] **would the Name of Heaven not have been desecrated by you** who swore that you would not move from your place until the rain fell, for surely one oath or the other would have been seen to be false? [9] **But what can I do to you, for you act like a spoiled child before God and** nevertheless **He accedes to your request, like a son who acts like a spoiled child before his father and** his father nevertheless **accedes to his request.** [10] For example, the boy **says to his** father: **"Father, take me to be washed in hot water,"** and then he says: "Father, **rinse me in cold water,"** or he says to him:

[1] עַמְּךָ יִשְׂרָאֵל שֶׁהוֹצֵאתָ מִמִּצְרַיִם אֵינָן יְכוֹלִין לֹא בְּרוֹב טוֹבָה וְלֹא בְּרוֹב פּוּרְעָנוּת. [2] כָּעַסְתָּ עֲלֵיהֶם — אֵינָן יְכוֹלִין לַעֲמוֹד. [3] הִשְׁפַּעְתָּ עֲלֵיהֶם טוֹבָה — אֵינָן יְכוֹלִין לַעֲמוֹד. [4] יְהִי רָצוֹן מִלְּפָנֶיךָ שֶׁיִּפָּסְקוּ הַגְּשָׁמִים וִיהֵא רֶיוַח בָּעוֹלָם'. [5] מִיָּד נָשְׁבָה הָרוּחַ, וְנִתְפַּזְּרוּ הֶעָבִים, וְזָרְחָה הַחַמָּה, וְיָצְאוּ הָעָם לַשָּׂדֶה וְהֵבִיאוּ לָהֶם כְּמֵהִין וּפִטְרִיּוֹת. [6] שָׁלַח לוֹ שִׁמְעוֹן בֶּן שֶׁטַח: 'אִלְמָלֵא חוֹנִי אַתָּה, גּוֹזֵרְנִי עָלֶיךָ נִידּוּי. [7] שֶׁאִילּוּ שָׁנִים כִּשְׁנֵי אֵלִיָּהוּ שֶׁמַּפְתְּחוֹת גְּשָׁמִים בְּיָדוֹ שֶׁל אֵלִיָּהוּ, [8] לֹא נִמְצָא שֵׁם שָׁמַיִם מִתְחַלֵּל עַל יָדְךָ? [9] אֲבָל מָה אֶעֱשֶׂה לְךָ, שֶׁאַתָּה מִתְחַטֵּא לִפְנֵי הַמָּקוֹם וְעוֹשֶׂה לְךָ רְצוֹנְךָ, כְּבֵן שֶׁמִּתְחַטֵּא עַל אָבִיו וְעוֹשֶׂה לוֹ רְצוֹנוֹ. [10] וְאוֹמֵר לוֹ: "אַבָּא, הוֹלִיכֵנִי לְרַחֲצֵנִי בְּחַמִּין, שָׁטְפֵנִי בְּצוֹנֵן, תֵּן לִי

LITERAL TRANSLATION

[1] Your people Israel whom You brought out of Egypt cannot [bear] too much good nor too much punishment. [2] You became angry with them — they cannot stand. [3] You bestowed good upon them — they cannot stand. [4] May it be Your will that the rains will stop and there will be relief in the world.' [5] Immediately the wind blew, and the clouds dispersed, and the sun shone, and the people went out to the field and brought for themselves truffles and mushrooms. [6] Shimon ben Shetaḥ sent to him: 'If you were not Ḥoni, I would decree a ban upon you. [7] For if the years were like the years of Elijah when the keys of rains were in Elijah's hand, [8] would the Name of Heaven not have been desecrated by you? [9] But what shall I do to you, for you act like a spoiled child before God and He does your will for you, like a son who acts like a spoiled child with his father, and he does his will for him. [10] And he says to him: "Father, take me to wash me in hot water, rinse me in cold water, give me

RASHI

כמהין ופטריות — *בולי״ן בלעז, שיצאו מחמת הגשמים וידעו כי של ברכה היו. **אלמלא חוני אתה** — ואדם גדול. **לנדות** — שמנדין על כבוד הרב, שהטיח דברים ואמר: לא כך שאלתי. **שאלמלא היו שנים כשני אליהו** — גזירת עצירת גשמים, ומפתח של גשמים בידו של אליהו גרסינן. **לא נמצא שם שמים מתחלל** — בתמיה, שאליהו נשבע "חי ה' אם יהיה השנים האלה טל ומטר כי אם לפי דברי" (מלכים א' יז) ואתה נשבע שאין אתה זז עד שירדו גשמים. **נמצא שם שמים מתחלל על ידך** — דזה או זה בא לידי שבועת שוא. **מתחטא** — לשון חטא, כלומר: הוי הולך וחוטא.

NOTES

שֶׁאִילּוּ שָׁנִים כִּשְׁנֵי אֵלִיָּהוּ For if the years were like the years of Elijah. Shimon ben Shetaḥ argued that Ḥoni deserved to be placed under a ban for two reasons: First, because he addressed God in a disrespectful manner. And second, because he might have created a situation where the name of Heaven was desecrated. Thus the word שֶׁאִילּוּ ("for if") should be understood as וְאִילּוּ ("and if"), and it introduces the second argument put forward by Shimon ben Shetaḥ (*Gevurat Ari*). According to the reading of *Gra*, the text reads explicitly: "And moreover [וְלֹא עוֹד אֶלָּא]."

According to the Jerusalem Talmud, the name of Heaven would have been desecrated if a decree had been issued *that the rain should be withheld* as in the days of Elijah, for in such a case all would see that Ḥoni's prayers were not

אֱגוֹזִים, שְׁקֵדִים, אֲפַרְסְקִים,
וְרִמּוֹנִים״, [1]וְנוֹתֵן לוֹ. [2]וְעָלֶיךָ
הַכָּתוּב אוֹמֵר: ״יִשְׂמַח אָבִיךָ
וְאִמֶּךָ וְתָגֵל יוֹלַדְתֶּיךָ״״.
[3]תָּנוּ רַבָּנַן: ״מָה שָׁלְחוּ בְּנֵי
לִשְׁכַּת הַגָּזִית לְחוֹנִי הַמְעַגֵּל?
[4]״וְתִגְזַר אֹמֶר, וְיָקָם לָךְ, וְעַל
דְּרָכֶיךָ נָגַהּ אוֹר׳. [5]׳וְתִגְזַר אֹמֶר׳
— אַתָּה גָּזַרְתָּ מִלְּמַטָּה,
וְהַקָּדוֹשׁ בָּרוּךְ הוּא מְקַיֵּים
מַאֲמָרְךָ מִלְמַעְלָה. [6]׳וְעַל דְּרָכֶיךָ
נָגַהּ אוֹר׳ — דּוֹר שֶׁהָיָה אָפֵל
הֵאַרְתָּ בִּתְפִלָּתְךָ. [7]׳כִּי הִשְׁפִּילוּ,
וַתֹּאמֶר: גֵּוָה׳ — דּוֹר שֶׁהָיָה
שָׁפֵל, הִגְבַּהְתּוֹ בִּתְפִלָּתְךָ. [8]׳וְשַׁח
עֵינַיִם יוֹשִׁעַ׳ — דּוֹר שֶׁשָּׁח
בַּעֲוֹנוֹ, הוֹשַׁעְתּוֹ בִּתְפִלָּתְךָ.
[9]׳יְמַלֵּט אִי נָקִי׳ — דּוֹר שֶׁלֹּא
הָיָה נָקִי, מִלַּטְתּוֹ בִּתְפִלָּתְךָ.
[10]׳וְנִמְלַט בְּבֹר כַּפֶּיךָ׳ — מִלַּטְתּוֹ
בְּמַעֲשֵׂה יָדֶיךָ הַבְּרוּרִין״.

LITERAL TRANSLATION

nuts, almonds, peaches, and pomegranates," [1]and he gives him. [2]And about you the verse says: "Your father and mother shall be glad, and she who bore you shall rejoice."'"

[3]Our Rabbis taught: "What did the men in the Chamber of Hewn Stone send to Honi HaMe'aggel? [4]'You shall also decree a thing, and it shall be established for you, and the light shall shine on your ways.' [5]'You shall also decree a thing' — you have decreed from below, and the Holy One, blessed be He, fulfills your word from above. [6]'And the light shall shine upon your ways' — a generation that was in darkness you have enlightened with your prayer. [7]'When men have been humbled, you say: There is lifting up' — a generation that was humbled, you have lifted it up with your prayer. [8]'And he will save him with lowered eyes' — a generation that was lowered by its sin, you have saved it with your prayer. [9]'He will deliver one who is not innocent' — a generation that was not innocent, you have delivered it with your prayer. [10]'And he will be delivered by the pureness of your hands' — you have delivered him with your pure deeds."

TRANSLATION AND COMMENTARY

"Give me nuts, almonds, peaches, and pomegranates," [1]**and** his father **grants him** each of these requests. Similarly, you placed various requests before God, first asking for more rain, and then for less, and finally that the rain should stop altogether, and God has granted you each of your requests. [2]It is **to you** that **the verse** is referring when it **says** [Proverbs 23:25]: **"Your father and your mother shall be glad, and she who bore you shall rejoice."'"**

תָּנוּ רַבָּנַן [3]**Our Rabbis taught** another Baraita, in which the story related above is continued: **"What** words of praise **did the** Sages sitting **in the Chamber of Hewn Stone,** the chamber of the Temple that served as the seat of the Great Sanhedrin [ancient Israel's supreme legislative and religious body], **send to Ḥoni HaMe'aggel** after he succeeded in ending the drought? [4]The members of the Great Sanhedrin applied to Ḥoni the following verses [Job 22:28-30]: **'You shall also decree a thing, and it shall be established for you; and the light shall shine on your ways.** When men have been humbled, you say: There is lifting up, and he will save him with lowered eyes. He will deliver the one who is not innocent, and he will be delivered by the pureness of your hands.' [5]**'You shall also decree a thing' — you,** Ḥoni, **have decreed from below** that God must cause rain to fall, **and the Holy One, blessed be He, has fulfilled your words from above.** [6]**'And the light shall shine upon your ways' — a generation that was in darkness** because of the distress caused by the long drought, **you have enlightened with your prayer** which was answered with rain. [7]**'When men have been humbled, you say: There is lifting up' — a generation that was humbled** by a rainless winter **you have lifted up with your prayer.** [8]**'And he will save him with lowered eyes' — a generation that was lowered by its sin** and threatened with famine, **you have saved** from death **with your prayer.** [9]**'He will deliver one who is not innocent' — a generation that was not innocent** of wrongdoing, and was punished with drought, **you have delivered with your prayer.** [10]**'And he will be delivered by the pureness of your hands'** — it is you who **have delivered** that unrighteous generation with your pure deeds."

RASHI

לשכת הגזית — סנהדרין. **דור שהיה אפל** — מרוב צער שלא ירדו גשמים. **הושעת בתפלתך** — מן המיתה, שהבאת עליהם שובע.

BACKGROUND

לִשְׁכַּת הַגָּזִית The Chamber of Hewn Stone. There were chambers (לְשָׁכוֹת) used for various purposes within the Temple. The name of the Chamber of Hewn Stone derived from the large, hewn stones used in its walls. It was the official meeting-place of the Great Sanhedrin, the highest tribunal of the Jewish people. About forty years before the destruction of the Second Temple, the Sanhedrin was prevented from continuing to hold sessions in this chamber. From that time onward, no Rabbinical Courts were empowered to administer capital punishment.

NOTES

answered. *Maharsha* explains that in such a case the Name of Heaven would have been desecrated because Ḥoni's oath would prove to have been false. Our commentary follows *Rashi*, who writes that in such a case one oath or the other — either Ḥoni's oath not to move from the circle until there was rain or the divine decree withholding rain — would have been false, causing the Name of Heaven to be desecrated.

כִּי הִשְׁפִּילוּ **When men have been humbled.** The Jerusalem Talmud explains this verse in an even bolder manner:

¹אָמַר רַבִּי יוֹחָנָן: כָּל יָמָיו שֶׁל אוֹתוֹ צַדִּיק, הָיָה מִצְטַעֵר עַל מִקְרָא זֶה: ²״שִׁיר הַמַּעֲלוֹת: בְּשׁוּב ה׳ אֶת שִׁיבַת צִיּוֹן, הָיִינוּ כְּחֹלְמִים״. ³אֲמַר: ״מִי אִיכָּא דְּנָיֵים שִׁבְעִין שְׁנִין בְּחֶלְמָא״? ⁴יוֹמָא חַד הֲוָה אֲזַל בְּאוֹרְחָא, חַזְיֵיהּ לְהַהוּא גַּבְרָא דַּהֲוָה נָטַע חָרוּבָא. ⁵אֲמַר לֵיהּ: ״הַאי עַד כַּמָּה שְׁנִין טָעֵין״? ⁶אֲמַר לֵיהּ: ״עַד שִׁבְעִין שְׁנִין״. ⁷אֲמַר לֵיהּ: ״פְּשִׁיטָא לָךְ דְּחָיֵית שִׁבְעִין שְׁנִין״? ⁸אֲמַר לֵיהּ: ״הַאי גַּבְרָא עָלְמָא בְּחָרוּבָא אַשְׁכַּחְתֵּיהּ. ⁹כִּי הֵיכִי דְּשָׁתְלִי לִי אֲבָהֲתַי, שָׁתְלִי נַמִי לִבְרַאי״. ¹⁰יְתֵיב קָא כָּרֵיךְ רִיפְתָּא. ¹¹אֲתָא לֵיהּ שֵׁינְתָא נִים. ¹²אֲהַדְרָא לֵיהּ מְשׁוּנִיתָא אִיכַּסֵּי מֵעֵינָא, וְנִים שִׁבְעִין שְׁנִין. ¹³כִּי קָם, חַזְיֵיהּ לְהַהוּא גַּבְרָא דְּהוּא קָא מְלַקֵּט מִינַּיְיהוּ.

TRANSLATION AND COMMENTARY

אָמַר רַבִּי יוֹחָנָן ¹The Gemara continues with another story relating to Ḥoni HaMe'aggel. **Rabbi Yoḥanan said: All his life, that righteous man** Ḥoni HaMe'aggel **was distressed by** his inability to understand the following **verse** (Psalm 126:1): ²**"A song of degrees: When the Lord brought back the captivity of Zion, we were like men in a dream."** Ḥoni understood the Psalmist as saying that when the people of Israel would return from their exile, they would view their seventy-year captivity in Babylonia as a dream. ³But Ḥoni **asked** himself: **Is there anyone who sleeps for seventy years** and dreams a single **dream?** ⁴**One day he was going along the road, when he saw a man planting a carob tree.** ⁵Ḥoni called to the man and **said to him: "In how many years will this tree** that you are planting bear fruit?" ⁶The man **answered him:** "It should be possible to harvest carobs from this tree **in** about **seventy years."** ⁷Ḥoni **said to him: "Are you certain that you will live** another **seventy years** so that you will be able to derive benefit from this tree?" ⁸The man **explained to** Ḥoni: **"I found a world** filled **with carob trees.** Those trees were planted for the benefit of future generations. ⁹Just as my forefathers once planted carob trees for my benefit, so too must I now plant carob trees for the benefit of my children and grandchildren." ¹⁰Ḥoni sat down **and ate** his **bread.** ¹¹When he had finished eating, **slumber overcame him, and he fell into a** deep **sleep.** ¹²**A cliff was formed around** the place where he lay, **so that he remained hidden from view, and he slept** there **for seventy years.** ¹³**When he** finally **awoke, he saw someone picking** carobs from the tree whose planting he had witnessed shortly before he had gone to sleep.

LITERAL TRANSLATION

¹Rabbi Yoḥanan said: All the days of that righteous man, he was distressed about this verse: ²"A song of degrees: When the Lord brought back the captivity of Zion, we were like men in a dream." ³He said: "Is there anyone who sleeps seventy years in a dream?" ⁴One day he was going along the road, [and] he saw a man who was planting a carob tree. ⁵He said to him: "In how many years will this [tree] bear [fruit]?" ⁶He said to him: "In seventy years." ⁷He said to him: "Is it obvious to you that you will live seventy years?" ⁸He said to him: "I (lit., 'this man') found a world with carob trees. ⁹Just as my forefathers planted for me, I too plant for my children." ¹⁰He sat down [and] ate bread. ¹¹Slumber overcame him [and] he fell asleep. ¹²A cliff was formed around him [and] he was hidden from the eye, and he slept [for] seventy years. ¹³When he awoke, he saw a man who was picking [some] of them.

RASHI

של אותו צדיק – חוני המעגל היה מצטער על המקרא הזה. **שיר המעלות** – לשון עילוי. **היינו כחולמים** – כחלום נדמה גלות בבל שהיה שבעים שנה. **שבעין שני בחלמא** – בתמיה: מי איתא דניים שבעין שנין בחלמיה = ויש אדם ישן שבעים שנה בשינה אחת? **עד שבעין שנין** – לא טעין פירא בטעינא קמייתא. **יתיב** – חוני המעגל וקא כריך ריפתא. **הכי גרסינן** – עלמא בחרובא אשכחתיה, כי היכי דשתלי לי אבהתיי אנא נמי אישתיל לברי. **אהדרא ליה משוניתא** = עלתה סביבותיו שן סלע. **ואיכסי מעינא דאינשי** – ולא אשכחוהו התם.

BACKGROUND

חָרוּבָא A carob tree. Carob trees live for a long time, but in general they produce crops of commercial quantities within six to eight years of their planting. One explanation of the seventy-year period mentioned here is related to the fact that carob trees are dioecious — either male, which do not bear fruit, or female. But after sixty or seventy years male trees become androgynous and can bear fruit. When it is planted it is not clear what the sex of the tree will be, and thus it can happen that a carob tree will not produce fruit for seventy years.

NOTES

"When men have been humbled, you say: There is lifting up." When God said that His people would be humbled, you, Ḥoni, said that they would be lifted up. And as it turned out it was God's decree that was canceled, and Ḥoni's oath that was fulfilled.

כָּל יָמָיו שֶׁל אוֹתוֹ צַדִּיק All the days of that righteous man. According to the Jerusalem Talmud, there were two different Ḥonis, the Ḥoni who slept for seventy years being an ancestor of the Ḥoni who petitioned God for rain. The first Ḥoni lived at the end of the First Temple period, and slept for the seventy years during which the people of Israel were in captivity in Babylonia. The second Ḥoni lived during the Second Temple period.

Many commentators see this story, either in whole or in part, as a parable explaining the essence of the exilic experience as a period of sleep, and emphasizing the present need to make adequate preparations for the generations to come (see *Maharsha, Keren Orah,* and *Derash Moshe*).

TRANSLATION AND COMMENTARY

[1]Ḥoni **said to** the man: **"Are you the one who planted** this tree?" [2]The man **answered:** "I did not plant this tree myself. **I am the grandson** of the man who planted the tree many years ago." [3]Ḥoni realized what must have happened and **said:** "I can **infer from this that I have been asleep for** the past **seventy years.** Thus we see that it is possible to dream a single dream for seventy years, and so the Psalmist was justified in comparing Israel's seventy-year captivity in Babylonia to a dream." [4]Ḥoni **saw his ass to which had been born several generations of mules** during the seventy years that he had slept. [5]Ḥoni then **went to his** old **house and asked: "Is the son of Ḥoni HaMe'aggel** still **alive?"** [6]The people **said to him: "His son is no** longer alive, but **his grandson is** still living." [7]**He** then **proclaimed: "I am Ḥoni HaMe'aggel."** [8]But his family **did not believe him.** [9]**He went to the Academy.** There **he heard the Rabbis saying:** [10]**"The decisions** we have arrived at today **are** as perfectly **clear to us as** if they had been studied **in the days of Ḥoni HaMe'aggel,** [11]**who whenever he entered the Academy would resolve for the Rabbis any difficulty that they might have."** [12]Ḥoni immediately **proclaimed: "I am he,** Ḥoni HaMe'aggel." [13]**But,** just like Ḥoni's family, the Rabbis **did not believe him, and they did not give him the respect to which he was entitled.** [14]Ḥoni **was** greatly **distressed** about his inability to persuade anyone of his identity. [15]**He petitioned** God **for mercy,** asking that an end be put to his life, **and** soon thereafter **he died.** [16]Commenting on Ḥoni's death, **Rava said:** This is what **people** mean when they say the popular proverb: [17]**"Either companionship or death."** Man is in great need of companionship. A person who is unable to satisfy that need prefers death to a life of solitude.

אַבָּא חִלְקִיָּה [18]The Gemara continues with a story about a descendant of Ḥoni HaMe'aggel, who was also known for his great piety. **Abba Ḥilkiyyah was a grandson of Ḥoni HaMe'aggel.** [19]**Whenever the world was in** desperate **need of rain, the Rabbis would send word to him, he would petition** God **for mercy, and rain would come.** [20]**Once the world was in** great **need of rain, and the Rabbis sent two of their number to Abba Ḥilkiyyah**

[1]אֲמַר לֵיהּ: "אַתְּ הוּא דִּשְׁתַלְתֵּיהּ"? [2]אֲמַר לֵיהּ: "בַּר בְּרֵיהּ אֲנָא". [3]אֲמַר לֵיהּ: "שְׁמַע מִינָּהּ דְּנַיְימִי שִׁבְעִין שְׁנִין". [4]חֲזָא לַחֲמָרֵיהּ דְּאִתְיְילִידָא לֵיהּ רַמָּכֵי רַמָּכֵי. [5]אֲזַל לְבֵיתֵיהּ אֲמַר לְהוּ: "בְּרֵיהּ דְּחוֹנִי הַמְעַגֵּל מִי קַיָּים"? [6]אָמְרוּ לֵיהּ: "בְּרֵיהּ לֵיתָא, בַּר בְּרֵיהּ אִיתָא". [7]אֲמַר לְהוּ: "אֲנָא חוֹנִי הַמְעַגֵּל". [8]לָא הֵימְנוּהוּ. [9]אֲזַל לְבֵית הַמִּדְרָשׁ שְׁמַעִינְהוּ לְרַבָּנַן דְּקָאָמְרִי: [10]"נְהִירָן שְׁמַעְתְּתִין כְּבִשְׁנֵי חוֹנִי הַמְעַגֵּל, [11]דְּכִי הָוֵי עָיֵיל לְבֵית מִדְרְשָׁא כָּל קוּשְׁיָא דַּהֲווּ לְהוּ לְרַבָּנַן הֲוָה מְפָרֵק לְהוּ". [12]אֲמַר לְהוּ: "אֲנָא נִיהוּ", [13]וְלָא הֵימְנוּהוּ, וְלָא עָבְדִי לֵיהּ יְקָרָא כִּדְמִבָּעֵי לֵיהּ. [14]חֲלַשׁ דַּעְתֵּיהּ, [15]בָּעֵי רַחֲמֵי, וּמִית. [16]אֲמַר רָבָא, הַיְינוּ דְּאָמְרִי אֱינָשֵׁי: [17]"אוֹ חַבְרוּתָא אוֹ מִיתוּתָא".

[18]אַבָּא חִלְקִיָּה בַּר בְּרֵיהּ דְּחוֹנִי הַמְעַגֵּל הֲוָה, [19]וְכִי מִצְטְרִיךְ עָלְמָא לְמִיטְרָא הֲווּ מְשַׁדְּרִי רַבָּנַן לְגַבֵּיהּ, וּבָעֵי רַחֲמֵי וְאָתֵי מִיטְרָא. [20]זִימְנָא חֲדָא אִיצְטְרִיךְ עָלְמָא לְמִיטְרָא, שַׁדּוּר רַבָּנַן זוּגָא דְּרַבָּנַן לְגַבֵּיהּ לְמִבָּעֵי

LITERAL TRANSLATION

[1]He said to him: "Are you he who planted it?" [2]He said to him: "I am the son of his son." [3]He said to him: "Conclude from this that I have slept [for] seventy years." [4]He saw his ass to which had been born many descendants. [5]He went to his house [and] said to them: "Is the son of Ḥoni HaMe'aggel alive?" [6]They said to him: "His son is not [alive, but] the son of his son is." [7]He said to them: "I am Ḥoni HaMe'aggel." [8]They did not believe him. [9]He went to the Academy [and] heard the Rabbis saying: [10]"Our decisions are as clear as in the years of Ḥoni HaMe'aggel, [11]who when he entered the Academy would resolve for them any difficulty that the Rabbis had." [12]He said to them: "I am he," [13]but they did not believe him, and they did not give him the respect that was due to him. [14]He was distressed, [15]he petitioned for mercy, and he died. [16]Rava said: This is what people say: [17]"Either companionship or death."

[18]Abba Ḥilkiyyah was a grandson of Ḥoni HaMe'aggel, [19]and when the world was in need of rain the Rabbis would send to him, and he would petition for mercy and rain would come. [20]Once the world was in need of rain, [and] the Rabbis sent a pair of Rabbis to him [to ask him] to petition for

SAGES

אַבָּא חִלְקִיָּה Abba Ḥilkiyyah. This Sage is mentioned only here and in *Makkot* 24a; his conduct, which was held up as an example, is described further on in our passage. In this case the name "Abba" is an honorific title given to an older man or to various Sages before they began to use the title "Rabbi."

RASHI

רמכי רמכי — וולדי וולדות באלו השנים דנייס. מעוברת זכר היתה, וחזר ובא עליה, והולידו. **אמר להו** — שאל להון: בנו של חוני המעגל קיים הוא. **נהירנא לן הנך שמעתתא** — מוגהת לנו שמועה זו כאילו למדנוה בחייו של חוני המעגל, שהיה מפרקה לנו ומגיה לנו יפה יפה. **או חברותא או מיתותא** — ולא גרסינן הכא כחברי דאיוב, אלא בבבא בתרא (טז, ב), גבי מעשה דאיוב, אם אין חביריו של אדם נוהגין בו כבוד כבתחילה — נוח לו שימות. אי נמי משום הנך בריוני לא כתוב בספרינו.

BACKGROUND

הִיזְמֵי **Prickly shrubs.**

Young Rest-harrow Bush
This is most probably the thorny rest-harrow, *Ononis antiquorum L.,* of the Papilinaceae family, a thorny bush growing to a height of 20-75 cm. and common in fields and near streams. Its leaves are mainly trifoliate, and its lateral branches tend to be thorny and brachiate.

הִיגֵי **Thorns.**

Henna Plant
Common henna, *Alhagi maurorum Medik* belongs to the Papilinaceae family. It is a thorny bush with simple, nondentate leaves. It grows to a height of 30 cm., but can grow as high as a meter. It is mainly found in fields and salt marshes.

TRANSLATION AND COMMENTARY

to ask him **to petition** God **for mercy, so that rain would come.** [1]The messengers **went to** Abba Ḥilkiyyah's **house, but they did not find him** there. [2]**They went** out **to** look for him in **the field, and they found him** there **hoeing** the soil. [3]**They offered him greetings,** [23B] **but he did not return their greetings.** The Rabbis thought that Abba Ḥilkiyyah's conduct was strange, but they did not say anything at the time. While they were waiting for him, they observed him doing a number of other things they found puzzling. [4]**Toward evening, when he** stopped working and started **gathering firewood** to take home with him, **he carried the wood and his hoe on one shoulder,** [5]**and** he took off **the cloak** he had been wearing and draped it **over the other shoulder.** [6]**The whole way** home Abba Ḥilkiyyah **did not wear** his **shoes,** [7]**but when he reached water, he put on his shoes,** removing them as soon as he was again on dry land. [8]**When he reached** an area of **prickly shrubs and thorns, he lifted up his clothes,** to keep them from getting caught on the thorns, though this meant that his legs were exposed. [9]When he reached the city, his wife came out to greet him and she was **dressed** in her best clothes and wearing her jewelry. [10]**When he reached his house, his wife entered first, he entered** after her, **and then the Rabbis entered** after him. [11]**He sat down** for his meal **and ate** his **bread, but he did not say to the Rabbis** who had entered after him, **"Come** and join me **and eat** some bread," as would have been customary. [12]**He** then **distributed bread to his** two **children; to the older** child **he** gave **one piece** of bread, **and to the younger one** he gave **two** pieces. [13]He then took his wife aside and **said to her: "I know that** these two **Rabbis have come** here to ask me to pray **for rain.** [14]**Let us go up to the roof** before they say anything, **and** let us privately **ask** God **for mercy.** [15]**Perhaps the Holy One, blessed be He, will be appeased** by our prayers **and will bring rain.** [16]**Then we can avoid taking credit** for the rain, for nobody will know that it was we who petitioned God to show compassion." [17]**They went up to the roof,** [18]and Abba Ḥilkiyyah **stood in one corner and** his wife stood **in the opposite corner,** and they both offered prayers for rain. [19]**Clouds began to form on the side** where **his wife**

רַחֲמֵי דְּנֵיתֵי מִיטְרָא. [1]אֲזוּל לְבֵיתֵיהּ וְלָא אַשְׁכְּחוּהוּ. [2]אֲזוּל בְּדַבְרָא וְאַשְׁכְּחוּהוּ דַּהֲוָה קָא רָפֵיק. [3]יְהַבוּ לֵיהּ שְׁלָמָא [23B] וְלָא אַסְבַּר לְהוּ אַפֵּיהּ. [4]בְּפַנְיָא, כִּי הֲוָה מְנַקֵּט צִיבֵי, דָּרָא צִיבֵי וּמָרָא בְּחַד כַּתְפָּא, [5]וּגְלִימָא בְּחַד כַּתְפָּא. [6]כּוּלָּהּ אוֹרְחָא לָא סַיֵּים מְסָאנֵי. [7]כִּי מָטֵי לְמַיָּא, סַיֵּים מְסָאנֵיהּ. [8]כִּי מְטָא לְהִיזְמֵי וְהִיגֵי, דָּלֵינְהוּ לְמָנֵיהּ. [9]כִּי מְטָא לְמָתָא, נְפָקָה דְּבֵיתְהוּ לְאַפֵּיהּ כִּי מִיקַּשְׁטָא. [10]כִּי מְטָא לְבֵיתֵיהּ, עֲלַת דְּבֵיתְהוּ בְּרֵישָׁא, וַהֲדַר עָיֵיל אִיהוּ, וַהֲדַר עָיְילֵי רַבָּנַן. [11]יָתֵיב וְכָרֵיךְ רִיפְתָּא, וְלָא אֲמַר לְהוּ לְרַבָּנַן, "תּוּ כְּרוֹכוּ". [12]פְּלַג רִיפְתָּא לִינוּקֵי; לְקַשִּׁישָׁא חֲדָא, וּלְזוּטְרָא תְּרֵי. [13]אֲמַר לָהּ לִדְבֵיתְהוּ: "יָדַעְנָא דְּרַבָּנַן מִשּׁוּם מִיטְרָא קָא אָתוּ. [14]נֵיסַּק לְאִיגְּרָא, וְנִיבָּעֵי רַחֲמֵי. [15]אֶפְשָׁר דְּמִרַצֵּי הַקָּדוֹשׁ בָּרוּךְ הוּא וְיֵיתֵי מִיטְרָא, [16]וְלָא נַחֲזִיק טִיבוּתָא לְנַפְשִׁין. [17]סַקוּ לְאִיגְּרָא; [18]קָם אִיהוּ בַּחֲדָא זָוִיתָא, וְאִיהִי בַּחֲדָא זָוִיתָא. [19]קַדִּים סְלוּק עֲנָנֵי מֵהָךְ זָוִיתָא

LITERAL TRANSLATION

mercy so that rain would come. [1]They went to his house but they did not find him. [2]They went into a field and they found him hoeing. [3]They greeted him, [23B] but he did not show them a [kind] face.

[4]In the evening, when he was gathering wood, he carried the wood and the hoe on one shoulder, [5]and a cloak on one shoulder. [6]The whole way he did not wear shoes. [7]When he reached water, he put on his shoes. [8]When he reached prickly shrubs and thorns, he lifted up his clothes. [9]When he reached the city, his wife went out toward him dressed up. [10]When he reached his house, his wife entered first, and then he entered, and then the Rabbis entered. [11]He sat down and ate bread, but he did not say to the Rabbis, "Come [and] eat." [12]He divided bread among the children; to the older [he gave] one [piece], and to the younger two. [13]He said to his wife: "I know that the Rabbis have come on account of rain. [14]Let us go up to the roof, and ask for mercy. [15]Perhaps the Holy One, blessed be He, will be appeased and will bring rain, [16]and we will not give credit to ourselves." [17]They went up to the roof; [18]he stood in one corner, and she in one corner. [19]Clouds first came up from his wife's corner.

RASHI

רפיק בדברא = עודר בשדה. **לא אסבר להו אפיה** — לא החזיר להם פניו. **בפניא** — לפנות ערב, כשהלך לביתו. **דלינהו למניה** — הגביה בגדיו אחר כתיפיו, כדי שלא יקרעו. **כי מיקשטא** — בתכשיטין. **לאיגרא** — עלייה. **זויתא** — זוית. **מזויתא דדביתהו** — מאותו הרוח שאשתו שם עלו העבים תחלה, שהיא נענית תחילה.

דִּדְבֵיתְהוּ. [1]כִּי נָחֵית, אֲמַר לְהוּ: ״אַמַּאי אָתוּ רַבָּנַן״? [2]אֲמַרוּ לֵיהּ: ״שַׁדְּרִי לָן רַבָּנַן לְגַבֵּי דְּמָר לְמִיבָּעֵי רַחֲמֵי אַמִּיטְרָא״. [3]אֲמַר לְהוּ: ״בָּרוּךְ הַמָּקוֹם שֶׁלֹּא הִצְרִיךְ אֶתְכֶם לְאַבָּא חִלְקִיָּה״. [4]אֲמַרוּ לֵיהּ: ״יָדְעִינַן דְּמִיטְרָא מֵחֲמַת מָר הוּא דַּאֲתָא, [5]אֶלָּא לֵימָא לָן מָר הָנֵי מִילֵּי דִּתְמִיהָא לָן: [6]מַאי טַעֲמָא כִּי יָהֵיבְנָא לְמָר שְׁלָמָא לָא אַסְבַּר לָן מָר אַפֵּיהּ״? [7]אֲמַר לְהוּ: ״שְׂכִיר יוֹם הֲוַאי, [8]וְאָמִינָא לָא אִיפַּגַּר״. [9]״וּמַאי טַעֲמָא דָּרָא מָר צִיבֵי אַחַד כַּתְפֵיהּ וּגְלִימָא אַחַד כַּתְפֵיהּ״? [10]אֲמַר לְהוּ: ״טַלִּית שְׁאוּלָה הָיְתָה. לְהָכִי שְׁאַלִי, וּלְהָכִי לֹא שְׁאַלִי״. [11]״מַאי טַעֲמָא כּוּלָּהּ אוֹרְחָא לָא סַיֵּים מָר מְסָאנֵיהּ, וְכִי מָטֵי לְמַיָּא סַיֵּים מְסָאנֵיהּ״? [12]אֲמַר לְהוּ: ״כּוּלָּהּ אוֹרְחָא חָזֵינָא; [13]בְּמַיָּא לָא קָא חָזֵינָא״. [14]״מַאי טַעֲמָא כִּי מְטָא מָר לְהִיזְמֵי וְהִיגֵי, דַּלֵּינְהוּ לְמָנֵיהּ״? [15]אֲמַר לְהוּ: ״זֶה מַעֲלֶה אֲרוּכָה, וְזֶה אֵינָהּ מַעֲלָה אֲרוּכָה״. [16]״מַאי טַעֲמָא כִּי מְטָא מָר לְמָתָא, נָפְקָא

LITERAL TRANSLATION

[1]When he went down, he said to them: "Why have the Rabbis come?" [2]They said to him: "The Rabbis have sent us to you, Sir, [to ask you] to petition for mercy regarding rain." [3]He said to them: "Blessed is God who did not cause you to need Abba Ḥilkiyyah." [4]They said to him: "We know that the rain has come on account of you, Sir. [5]But tell us, Sir, those things that seem strange to us: [6]What is the reason why when we gave you greetings, Sir, you did not show us a [kind] face?" [7]He said to them: "I was a day-worker, [8]and I said I would not take time off." [9]"And what is the reason why you carried wood [on] one of your shoulders and a cloak [on] one of your shoulders?" [10]He said to them: "It was a borrowed garment. For this I borrowed [it], but for this I did not borrow [it]." [11]"What is the reason why the whole way you did not wear shoes, but when you reached water you put on your shoes?" [12]He said to them: "The whole way I could see; [13]in the water I could not see." [14]"What is the reason why when you reached prickly shrubs and thorns, you lifted up your clothing?" [15]He said to them: "This heals, but this does not heal." [16]"What is the reason why when you reached the city, your wife went

TRANSLATION AND COMMENTARY

stood, showing that her prayers were effective. [1]**When** Abba Ḥilkiyyah **came down** from the roof, he addressed his guests and **said to them: "Why have the Rabbis come** to my house?" [2]**They said to him: "The Rabbis have sent us to you, Sir, to ask you to petition** God **for mercy regarding** the grave shortage of **rain."** [3]Abba Ḥilkiyyah **said to them: "Blessed is God who did not cause you to need Abba Ḥilkiyyah.** There is no longer any reason for me to pray for rain. Clouds already fill the skies, and rain is sure to follow." Shortly afterwards it began to rain. [4]The Rabbis **said to him: "We know that the rain has come on account of you, Sir.** [5]**But** please **explain to us, Sir, those things** that you did during the course of the day that **seemed** so **strange to us:** [6]**What is the reason why, when we offered you greetings, you did not return our greetings?"** [7]Abba Ḥilkiyyah **said to them: "I was a day-worker,** and I was therefore required to work throughout the day. [8]When you greeted me, **I said** to myself **that I must not take time off** to answer you, and thereby deprive my employer of work to which he is entitled." [9]The guests then asked him: **"And what is the reason why you carried** the **fire-wood** and the hoe **on one of your shoulders, and** you took off **your cloak** and draped it **over your other shoulder?** Why did you not wear your cloak in the usual manner and support the wood and the hoe on it?" [10]Abba Ḥilkiyyah **explained to them: "The cloak was** not mine. It was **borrowed. I borrowed it for** the purpose of wearing it, **but I did not borrow it for** the purpose of putting wood on top of it." [11]The Rabbis now asked Abba Ḥilkiyyah about another unusual aspect of his behavior: **"What is the reason why, all the way** home, **you did not wear** your **shoes, but when you reached water you put on your shoes?"** [12]**He** answered **them** as follows: **"The whole way,** while I was walking on dry land, **I could see** what was before me and avoid stepping on anything that might hurt me. [13]But as I was walking **in the water, I could not see** where I was placing my feet, and so I put on my shoes for protection." [14]Abba Ḥilkiyyah was then asked about something else that he had done: **"What is the reason why, when you reached** an area of **prickly shrubs and thorns, you lifted up your clothing,** thus exposing your legs to possible injury?" [15]**He explained** this matter **to them** as well: "If I am scratched by thorns, my flesh will **heal, but** if my clothing gets torn, it **will not heal."** [16]Abba Ḥilkiyyah's guests then continued: **"What is the reason why, when you reached the city, your wife came out** to greet you

RASHI

לא אפגר — לא אתבטל ממלאכתי, כמו: יומא דמיפגרי רבנן (שבת קכט,ב). **מאי טעמא דרת** — מדוע נשאת הטלית על כתף אחת, ולא נתת בכתף תחת המשאוי. **להכי שאלה לי** — להתעטף בה. **ולהכי לא שאלה לי** — להטיל עליה קוצין, לקרעה. **במיא לא חזינן** — מה דאית בה, ושמא ישכנו דג או נחש.

דְּבֵיתְהוּ דְּמָר כִּי מִיקַּשְׁטָא״? [1]אֲמַר לְהוּ: ״כְּדֵי שֶׁלֹּא אֶתֵּן עֵינַי בְּאִשָּׁה אַחֶרֶת״. [2]״מַאי טַעֲמָא עָיְילָא הִיא בְּרֵישָׁא, וַהֲדַר עָיֵיל מָר אַבַּתְרָהּ, וַהֲדַר עָיְילִינַן אֲנַן״? [3]אֲמַר לְהוּ: ״מִשּׁוּם דְּלָא בְּדַקִיתוּ לִי״. [4]״מַאי טַעֲמָא כִּי כָּרֵיךְ מָר רִיפְתָּא, לָא אֲמַר לָן ׳אַיְתוּ כְּרוֹכוּ׳״? [5]״מִשּׁוּם דְּלָא נְפִישָׁא רִיפְתָּא, וְאָמִינָא לָא אַחֲזִיק בְּהוּ בְּרַבָּנַן טִיבוּתָא בְּחִנָּם״. [6]״מַאי טַעֲמָא יָהֵיב מָר לִינוּקָא קַשִּׁישָׁא חֲדָא רִיפְתָּא וּלְזוּטְרָא תְּרֵי״? [7]אֲמַר לְהוּ: ״הַאי קָאֵי בְּבֵיתָא, [8]וְהַאי יָתֵיב בְּבֵי כְּנִישְׁתָּא״. [9]״וּמַאי טַעֲמָא קַדֵּים סְלוּק עֲנָנֵי מֵהַךְ זָוִיתָא דַּהֲוַות קָיְימָא דְּבֵיתְהוּ דְּמָר לַעֲנָנָא דִּידֵיהּ״? [10]״מִשּׁוּם דְּאִיתְּתָא שְׁכִיחָא בְּבֵיתָא, וִיהֲבָא רִיפְתָּא לַעֲנִיֵּי, וּמְקַרְבָא הֲנָיָיתָהּ, [11]וַאֲנָא יָהֵיבְנָא זוּזָא, וְלָא מְקַרְבָא הֲנָיָיתֵיהּ. [12]אִי נַמִי, הָנְהוּ בִּירְיוֹנֵי דַּהֲווּ בְּשִׁיבָבוּתָן,

LITERAL TRANSLATION

out dressed up?" [1]He said to them: "So that I should not set my eyes on another woman." [2]"What is the reason why she entered first, and then you entered after her, and then we entered?" [3]He said to them: "Because you are not known to me." [4]"What is the reason why when you ate bread, you did not say to us, 'Come [and] eat'?" [5]"Because there was not enough bread, and I said [that] I should not gain credit from the Rabbis for nothing." [6]"What is the reason why you gave the older child one [piece of] bread and the younger one two?" [7]He said to them: "This one stays at home, [8]and this one sits in the synagogue." [9]"And what is the reason why the clouds came up from that corner in which your wife was standing before your cloud?" [10]"Because a woman is found at home, and gives bread to the poor, and its benefit is immediate, [11]but I give money, and its benefit is not immediate. [12]Or else, [regarding] those brutish men who were in our neighborhood,

TRANSLATION AND COMMENTARY

dressed in her best clothes and wearing her jewelry?" [1]**He said to them:** "She tried to make herself attractive, **so that I would not set my eyes on another woman** as I walked through the town." [2]The Rabbis continued with another question: **"What is the reason why,** when you reached your house, your wife **entered first, you then entered after her, and then we entered** after you?" [3]Abba Ḥilkiyyah **replied:** "I had us enter the house in that order **because I did not know** whether **you** were men of virtue or not. I had my wife enter first, and you behind me, because I did not want you to be alone with her." [4]The Rabbis then asked: **"What is the reason why, when you** sat down to **eat** your **bread, you did not say to us, 'Come** and **eat** with me'?" [5]Abba Ḥilkiyyah replied: "I did not ask you to join me in my meal **because there was not enough bread** for all of us, **and I said** to myself that it would be better if I did not invite you to join me, so **that I should not gain credit from you for nothing.** Had I asked you to join us, you would not have eaten anything, for you would have realized that I did not have enough food in the house. But you would still have felt indebted to me for extending the invitation. Now that I did not ask you to join me, you owe me nothing." [6]The Rabbis then asked: **"What is the reason why,** when **you** distributed bread to your two children, you **gave the older child one** piece of **bread and** gave **the younger child two** pieces?" [7]Abba Ḥilkiyyah **answered them: "The older child stays at home,** so if he is hungry he can always find something to eat. [8]**But the younger child sits in the synagogue** the whole day and studies Torah with his teacher. That is why I gave him an extra piece of bread." [9]The Rabbis asked Abba Ḥilkiyyah one further question: **"What is the reason why,** when the weather started to change, the **clouds began to form on the side where your wife was standing, before they** began to form on the side where you were standing? Why were the prayers offered by your wife better received than yours?" [10]Abba Ḥilkiyyah explained: "My wife's prayers were answered first **because** most of the time **she is found at home, and she gives bread to the poor** who come begging at our door, **and the benefit** of the charity she gives **is immediate. Her righteous behavior was rewarded measure for measure, and her prayers were answered immediately.** [11]**But** I am not usually at home, and when I am approached for charity, **I give money, and** in that way **the benefit** of my gift **is not immediate,** because the recipient must buy something with it. [12]**Alternatively,** my wife's prayers may have been answered first for another reason. **Certain brutish men were** once living **in our neighborhood,**

BACKGROUND

לָא אַחֲזִיק בְּהוּ בְּרַבָּנַן טִיבוּתָא בְּחִנָּם That I should not gain credit from the Rabbis for nothing. It is common practice to invite a guest who has arrived at mealtime to join you at the table, even when it is clear that the guest does not intend to eat. However, Abba Ḥilkiyyah was very scrupulous in his actions, and he viewed this custom as a form of deceit. Since he did not have enough food for the guests, he did not really intend to offer them anything to eat, and he did not wish to extend an empty invitation for courtesy's sake.

LANGUAGE

בִּרְיוֹנֵי Brutish men. The derivation of this word is not clear. Some authorities claim that it is derived from the Aramaic root בר, *bar,* meaning "exterior" or "wild," and means wild people, who do not belong to the community. But the form of the word indicates that the root is non-Semitic, and some authorities derive it from the Latin *Praetoriani,* members of the Imperial Guard. These soldiers achieved great power over the years and were known to behave coarsely and savagely.

RASHI

דלא בדקיתו לי — אם כשרים אם פריצים. דאמר מר (במסכת דרך ארץ רבה פרק ה): כל אדם יהי בעיניך כלסטים. **טובת הנאה חנם** — דאינהו לא הוו קא אכלי, דליכא ריפתא, וקא מחזקינן בהו טובה חנם. **ינוקא קאי בבי כנישתא** — קמי רביה, ולא אתי כולי יומא. **דאיתתא שכיחא בביתא** — כל יומא, וכי מיצטריך ענייא מידי — אזלא ויהבה. **ועוד דמקרבא הנייתה** — שדבר אכילה היא נותנת לעני, והוא בלא טורח, ממה שהיתה נותנת מעות ויטריח העני עד שיקנה. **אי נמי** — אהכי קדים ענני דידה. **משום בריוני** — בורים עמי הארץ.

TRANSLATION AND COMMENTARY

[1]and **I prayed that they should die, whereas she prayed that they should repent** from their evil ways. **And** indeed my wife's prayers, which show her superior qualities, were accepted, for the brutish men **repented."**

חָנָן הַנֶּחְבָּא [2]The Gemara now relates a story about another descendant of Ḥoni HaMe'aggel: **Ḥanan HaNeḥba was a grandson of Ḥoni HaMe'aggel.** [3]**When the world was** in dire **need of rain, the Rabbis sent schoolchildren to** Ḥanan HaNeḥba to influence him to pray for rain. [4]The children **grabbed him by the hem of his cloak,** and begged him to do all in his power to bring an end to the drought. Addressing him as if they were orphans who had been entrusted to his care, [5]**they said to him: "Father, Father, give us rain!"** [6]Ḥanan HaNeḥba then **said before the Holy One, blessed be He: "Master of the Universe!** If for no other reason, **act** on behalf **of these** young children **who are unable to distinguish between their Father** in Heaven, **Who is the** actual **giver of rain, and their father** on earth **who does not** have the power to **give** them **rain."** [7]The Gemara asks: **Why was he called Ḥanan HaNeḥba,** i.e., "Ḥanan the Hidden One"? The Gemara answers: He was given that name on account of his great modesty, [8]**for he used to hide himself in the lavatory** to avoid the honors that people sought to bestow on him.

[1]אֲנָא בְּעַי רַחֲמֵי דְּלֵימוּתוּ, וְהִיא בָּעֲיָא רַחֲמֵי דְּלִיהַדְרוּ בִּתְיוּבְתָּא, וְאַהֲדָרוּ. [2]חָנָן הַנֶּחְבָּא בַּר בְּרַתֵּיהּ דְחוֹנִי הַמְעַגֵּל הֲוָה. [3]כִּי מִצְטְרִיךְ עָלְמָא לְמִיטְרָא, הָווּ מְשַׁדְּרֵי רַבָּנַן יָנוּקֵי דְּבֵי רַב לְגַבֵּיהּ, [4]וְנָקְטֵי לֵיהּ בְּשִׁיפּוּלֵי גְלִימֵיהּ [5]וַאֲמַרוּ לֵיהּ: "אַבָּא, אַבָּא, הַב לָן מִיטְרָא!" [6]אָמַר לִפְנֵי הַקָּדוֹשׁ בָּרוּךְ הוּא: "רִבּוֹנוֹ שֶׁל עוֹלָם, עֲשֵׂה בִּשְׁבִיל אֵלּוּ שֶׁאֵין מַכִּירִין בֵּין אַבָּא דְּיָהֵיב מִיטְרָא לְאַבָּא דְּלָא יָהֵיב מִיטְרָא". [7]וְאַמַּאי קָרֵי לֵיהּ חָנָן הַנֶּחְבָּא? [8]מִפְּנֵי שֶׁהָיָה מַחְבִּיא עַצְמוֹ בְּבֵית הַכִּסֵּא.

LITERAL TRANSLATION

[1]I asked for mercy that they should die, but she asked for mercy that they should repent, and they repented."

[2]Ḥanan HaNeḥba was the son of the daughter of Ḥoni HaMe'aggel. [3]When the world was in need of rain, the Rabbis would send schoolchildren to him, [4]and they grasped him by the hem of his cloak [5]and said to him: "Father, Father, give us rain!" [6]He said before the Holy One, blessed be He: "Master of the Universe, act for the sake of these who cannot distinguish between the Father who gives rain and a father who does not give rain." [7]And why did they call him Ḥanan HaNeḥba (הַנֶּחְבָּא)? [8]Because he used to hide (מַחְבִּיא) himself in the lavatory.

RASHI

ינוקי דבי רב — להמריך לבו, ויתכוין בתפלתו. בשיפולי — בשולי בגדיו. אבא אבא — כך רגילים לקרותו, כיתום שאמר: אבי אבי. שאין מכירין — בין חוני לאבא, כסבורין עלי שאני אביהן. הכי גרסינן: שהיה מחבא ולא גרסינן שהיה מחבא בבית הכסא — כי הוה בעי רחמי אמיא היה מחבא עצמו מרוב ענוה, ומאן דגרס בית הכסא — כלומר: מתחבא בבגדיו כשהוא נכנס להסך את רגליו מרוב צניעות.

SAGES

חָנָן הַנֶּחְבָּא **Ḥanan HaNeḥba.** This Sage is mentioned only here. The sources relate that when the Sages wished to appoint him as a communal leader, he hid in the lavatory so as not to be found.

NOTES

וְהִיא בָּעֲיָא רַחֲמֵי דְּלִיהַדְרוּ **But she asked for mercy that they should repent.** Elsewhere (*Berakhot* 10a), the Gemara relates a similar story about Rabbi Meir and his wife, Beruryah. When certain outlaws persisted in antagonizing Rabbi Meir, he turned to God and prayed for their death. But his wife Beruryah chided him, arguing that the Bible — Psalms 104:35: "Sins [the word חַטָּאִים being interpreted as 'sins' rather than as 'sinners'] will be consumed out of the earth" — teaches us that God does not desire the destruction of sinners, but only of sin. Rabbi Meir then prayed that they should repent of their evil ways, and they did indeed repent.

שֶׁהָיָה מַחְבִּיא עַצְמוֹ בְּבֵית הַכִּסֵּא **Because he used to hide himself in the lavatory.** *Rashi* and others have the reading: "Because he used to hide himself," omitting the last two words found in the standard text of the Talmud. Several explanations of this passage have been offered. *Rabbenu Ḥananel* cites a Geonic tradition according to which the Sages wished to appoint Ḥanan to a position of communal leadership, but Ḥanan refused to accept the appointment and hid himself thereafter from public view. *Rabbenu Gershom* and *Rashi* explain that when Ḥanan entreated God for rain, he offered his prayers in private for reasons of modesty, so that he would not be given personal credit for bringing the drought to an end.

The standard reading, "Because he used to hide himself in the lavatory," also lends itself to a number of explanations. *Rashi* suggests that when Ḥanan entered the lavatory he would conduct himself most modestly, keeping himself covered as much as possible. The Geonim suggest that when the Rabbis came to ask him to pray for rain, he hid himself in the lavatory to avoid the honor that would be bestowed upon him if his prayers were accepted. *Maharsha* adds that this is the reason why the Rabbis sent him the schoolchildren, for they would seek him out even in the lavatory.

SAGES

רַבִּי מָנִי Rabbi Mani. He was the son of Rabbi Yonah and was one of the most important Palestinian Amoraim of the fifth generation. Rabbi Mani was a disciple of his father, but he also learned Torah from the other Sages of the previous generation, such as Rabbi Yose and Rabbi Hizkiyyah. Rabbi Mani lived in Sepphoris, where he was the rabbi of the city and the head of its yeshivah. He lived a very long time and was one of the last important Sages of Eretz Israel, since after his death persecutions increased and it became necessary to complete the Jerusalem Talmud in haste. Rabbi Mani trained many students who transmit teachings in his name. He is quoted frequently in the Jerusalem Talmud but relatively seldom in the Babylonian Talmud.

LANGUAGE

גְּוָאלְקִי My sack. This word derives from the Persian *guval,* meaning "a sack," apparently parallel to the Middle Persian *guvalak.* The word passed from Persian into Aramaic and also into Arabic.

LANGUAGE (RASHI)

טשק״א* From the Old French *tasche,* which means "a sack" or "a bag."

TRANSLATION AND COMMENTARY

אָמַר לֵיהּ [1]The Gemara continues its discussion of righteous people who offered special prayers for rain. **Rabbi Zerika said to Rav Safra: Come and see the difference between the imperious** men **of Eretz Israel and the pious** men **of Babylonia,** and you will realize that the former are much greater than the latter, for the pious of Babylonia entreat for rain in public, while the imperious men of Eretz Israel do so in private. [2]As for **the pious of Babylonia,** such as **Rav Huna and Rav Ḥisda, when** they saw that **the world was in need of rain,** [3]**they said: "Let us assemble together and petition** God **for mercy.** [4]**Perhaps the Holy One, blessed be He, will be appeased** by our prayers **and will bring** us **rain,** and the calamity threatening us will be averted." Thus we see that the Babylonian Sages let it be widely known that they were planning to pray for rain. [5]But **the imperious men of Eretz Israel,** men **like Rabbi Yonah the father of Rabbi Mani,** conducted themselves in an entirely different manner. [6]**When** Rabbi Yonah saw that **the world was** in dire **need of rain, he entered his house and said to** the members of his household: [7]**"Give me my sack, and I will go** to the marketplace and buy myself some **grain,** even though it will cost **a zuz** on account of the extended drought." [8]He did not reveal his true intentions even to his own family, for **as soon as he went out** of the house, **he went and stood in a low place** to cry out to God for rain, [9]**as it is written** (Psalms 130:1): **"Out of the depths I have cried to You, O Lord,"** from which it is derived that one should stand in a low place when praying. [10]**He stood in a place that was hidden** from public view, **covered himself with sackcloth, and petitioned** God **for mercy.** His prayers were answered **and rain came.** [11]**When he returned home,** the members of his household **said to him: "Did you bring the grain** that you wanted to buy?" [12]Rabbi Yonah **said to them:** "By the time I reached the market, it had already started to rain. [13]So **I said** to myself that it would not be sensible to buy grain now when the prices are high. **Since it has now rained, there will be relief in the world,** and the price of grain will come down." Thus we see that the Sages of Eretz Israel prayed on behalf of the community without anyone, not even their own families, knowing what they were doing.

וְתוּ [14]**And** it was reported **furthermore** about Rabbi Yonah that **Rabbi Mani his son was** once **being distressed by members of the House of the Nasi,** the head of the Jewish community in Eretz Israel.

[1]אָמַר לֵיהּ רַבִּי זְרִיקָא לְרַב סָפְרָא: תָּא חֲזִי מַה בֵּין תַּקִּיפֵי דְּאַרְעָא דְּיִשְׂרָאֵל לַחֲסִידֵי דְּבָבֶל. [2]חֲסִידֵי דְּבָבֶל רַב הוּנָא וְרַב חִסְדָּא. כִּי הֲוָה מִצְטְרִיךְ עָלְמָא לְמִיטְרָא, [3]אָמְרִי: "נִיכְנִיף הֲדָדֵי וְנִיבָּעֵי רַחֲמֵי. [4]אֶפְשָׁר דְּמִירַצֵּי הַקָּדוֹשׁ בָּרוּךְ הוּא דְּיֵיתֵי מִיטְרָא". [5]תַּקִּיפֵי דְּאַרְעָא דְּיִשְׂרָאֵל, כְּגוֹן רַבִּי יוֹנָה אֲבוּהּ דְּרַבִּי מָנִי, [6]כִּי הֲוָה מִצְטְרִיךְ עָלְמָא לְמִיטְרָא, הֲוָה עָיֵיל לְבֵיתֵיהּ, וַאֲמַר לְהוּ: [7]"הֲבוּ לִי גְּוָאלְקִי, וְאֵיזִיל וְאַיְיתֵי לִי בְּזוּזָא עִיבּוּרָא". [8]כִּי הֲוָה נָפֵיק לְבָרָא, אָזֵיל וְקָאֵי בְּדוּכְתָּא עֲמִיקְתָּא, [9]דִּכְתִיב: "מִמַּעֲמַקִּים קְרָאתִיךָ, ה'". [10]וְקָאֵי בְּדוּכְתָּא צְנִיעָא וּמְכַסֵּי בְּשַׂקָּא, וּבָעֵי רַחֲמֵי, וְאָתֵי מִיטְרָא. [11]כִּי הֲוָה אָתֵי לְבֵיתֵיהּ, אָמְרִי לֵיהּ: "אַיְיתֵי מָר עִיבּוּרָא?" [12]אֲמַר לְהוּ: [13]"אָמִינָא, הוֹאִיל וַאֲתָא מִיטְרָא הָשְׁתָּא, רְוַוח עָלְמָא". [14]וְתוּ, רַבִּי מָנִי בְּרֵיהּ הֲווּ קָא מְצַעֲרִי לֵיהּ דְּבֵי נְשִׂיאָה.

LITERAL TRANSLATION

[1]Rabbi Zerika said to Rav Safra: Come [and] see what is [the difference] between the imperious of Eretz Israel and the pious of Babylonia. [2]The pious of Babylonia were Rav Huna and Rav Ḥisda. When the world was in need of rain, [3]they said: "Let us assemble together and petition for mercy. [4]Perhaps the Holy One, blessed be He, will be appeased so that He will bring rain." [5]The imperious of Eretz Israel, such as Rabbi Yonah the father of Rabbi Mani, [6]when the world was in need of rain, he entered his house, and said to them: [7]"Give me my sack, and I will go and bring myself grain for a zuz." [8]When he went outside, he went and stood in a low place, [9]as it is written: "Out of the depths I have cried to You, O Lord." [10]And he stood in a hidden place and covered himself with sackcloth, and he asked for mercy, and rain came. [11]When he came to his house, they said to him: "Did you bring grain, Sir?" [12]He said to them: [13]"I said: Since rain has now come, the world is relieved." [14]And furthermore, Rabbi Mani his son was being distressed by [members of] the House of the Nasi.

RASHI

רב הונא ורב חסדא — חסידי דבבל מפרסמין את הדבר, ושל ארץ ישראל צנועין ולא מודיעין שבא המטר בשבילם. **תא ליכניף אהדדי** — אלמא: משום חד מינייהו לא אתי מיטרא. **תקיפי דארץ ישראל רבי יונה** — וקא חזינן דמחמתיה אתי מיטרא. **גואלקא** — *טשק״א בלעז. **ואייתי בזוזא עיבורא** — דגן, משום כפנא, שאפילו לבני ביתו לא היה מודיע. **אייתי לן מר מעיבורא** — דבעית למיזבן. **רווחא עלמא** — דליהוי שובע, ואהכי לא זבני ביוקרא דהשתא.

יִשְׁתַּטַּח עַל קִבְרָא דַּאֲבוּהּ, אֲמַר לֵיהּ: ״אַבָּא, אַבָּא, הָנֵי מְצַעֲרוּ לִי״. [2]יוֹמָא חַד הָווּ קָא חָלְפֵי הָתָם, אִינְקוּט כַּרְעָא דְּסוּסָוָותַיְיהוּ, [3]עַד דְּקַבִּילוּ עֲלַיְיהוּ דְּלָא קָא מְצַעֲרוּ לֵיהּ.
[4]וְתוּ, רַבִּי מָנִי הֲוָה שְׁכִיחַ קַמֵּיהּ דְּרַבִּי יִצְחָק בֶּן אֶלְיָשִׁיב. [5]אֲמַר לֵיהּ: ״עֲתִירֵי דְּבֵי חָמִי קָא מְצַעֲרוּ לִי״. [6]אֲמַר: ״לִיעֲנוּ״, וְאִיעֲנוּ. [7]אֲמַר: ״קָא דָּחֲקוּ לִי״. [8]אֲמַר: ״לִיעַתְּרוּ״, וְאִיעַתְּרוּ. [9]אֲמַר: ״לָא מִיקַּבְּלִי עֲלַי אֱינָשֵׁי בֵּיתִי״. [10]אֲמַר לֵיהּ: ״מַה שְּׁמָהּ״? ״חַנָּה״. [11]״תִּתְיַיפִּי חַנָּה״, וְנִתְיַיפַּת. [12]אֲמַר לֵיהּ: ״קָא מִגַּנְדְּרָא עֲלַי״. [13]אֲמַר לֵיהּ: ״אִי הָכִי, תַּחֲזוֹר חַנָּה לְשַׁחֲרוּרִיתָהּ״, [14]וְהָדְרָה חַנָּה לְשַׁחֲרוּרִיתָהּ.
[15]הָנְהוּ תְּרֵי תַּלְמִידֵי דַּהֲווּ קַמֵּיהּ דְּרַבִּי יִצְחָק בֶּן אֶלְיָשִׁיב אֲמַרוּ לֵיהּ: [16]״נִיבָּעֵי מָר רַחֲמֵי עֲלַן

LITERAL TRANSLATION

[1]He prostrated himself the grave of his father, [and] said to him: "Father, Father, these [men] are causing me distress." [2]One day they were passing by there, [and] the legs of their horses were caught, [3]until they accepted upon themselves that they would not distress him.

[4]And furthermore, Rabbi Mani was often found before Rabbi Yitzhak ben Elyashiv, [5][and] said to him: "The rich [members] of the house of my father-in-law are causing me distress." [6]He said: "Let them become poor," and they became poor. [7]He said: "They are pressing me [for support]." [8]He said: "Let them become rich," and they became rich. He said: "My wife (lit., 'the household') is not acceptable to me." [9]He said to him: "What is her name?" [10]"Hannah." "Let Hannah become beautiful," [11]and she became beautiful. [12]He said to him: "She has become presumptuous toward me." [13]He said to him: "If so, let Hannah return to her plainness (lit., 'blackness')," [14]and Hannah returned to her plainness.

[15]Two students who were before Rabbi Yitzhak ben Elyashiv said to him: [16]"Ask for mercy, Sir, on our behalf

TRANSLATION AND COMMENTARY

[1]Rabbi Mani went and **prostrated himself on the grave of his father, and said to him: "Father, Father,** certain members of the Home of the Nasi **are causing me distress.** Please intercede on my behalf, that I may find some peace." [2]**One day** those people who had been tormenting Rabbi Mani **were passing by** Rabbi Yonah's grave, **when** suddenly **the legs of their horses were rooted to the ground** in the vicinity of the grave. [3]The horses were unable to move from there **until** the men **took it upon themselves not to distress** Rabbi Mani.

וְתוּ [4]**And furthermore, Rabbi Mani was often found before Rabbi Yitzhak ben Elyashiv,** who was also a noted miracle-worker, [5]**and** once Rabbi Mani **said to him: "The wealthy members of my father-in-law's** family **are causing me distress."** [6]Rabbi Yitzhak **said: "Let them become poor,** so that they will be unable to torment you," **and indeed** soon afterwards his wife's once mighty and powerful relatives **became poor.** [7]Some time later, Rabbi Mani returned to Rabbi Yitzhak ben Elyashiv and **said** to him: "Now that my wife's relatives have become poor, **they are pressing me for** financial **support."** [8]Rabbi Yitzhak then **proclaimed: "Let them become rich** again," **and** indeed **they** soon regained their former assets and **were** once again **rich.** [9]Rabbi Mani complained on another occasion to Rabbi Yitzhak ben Elyashiv about his wife and her family and **said** to him: **"My wife is not acceptable to me,** for she is so unattractive." [10]Rabbi Yitzhak **asked him: "What is** your wife's **name?"** Rabbi Mani **answered:** "My wife is called **Hannah."** [11]Rabbi Yitzhak then declared: **"Let Hannah become beautiful," and she** soon became beautiful. But this did not put an end to Rabbi Mani's complaints. [12]**He said** to Rabbi Yitzhak ben Elyashiv: "Ever since my wife's appearance improved, **she has been acting haughtily toward me."** [13]Rabbi Yitzhak then **said to him: "If that is so, let Hannah return to her former plainness,"** [14]**and Hannah** soon lost her recently found beauty and **returned to her** former plainness.

הָנְהוּ תְּרֵי תַּלְמִידֵי [15]The Gemara now relates another anecdote regarding Rabbi Yitzhak ben Elyashiv. **Two students who were** often found **before Rabbi Yitzhak ben Elyashiv** once **said to him:** [16]"Please, **Sir, ask for mercy on our behalf that we may become very wise!"**

RASHI

הוו קא חלפי – דבי נשיאה. **התם** – עלויה מערתא דרבי יונה. **אינקוט** – נדבקו בקרקע שעל גבי מערה, ולא היו יכולין לזוז ממקומן. **עתירי דבי חמי** – עשירים של בית חמי. **ליענו** – יהיו עניים. **קא דחקי לי** – ליתן להן פרנסה. **לא מקבלי עלי אינשי ביתי** – אין אשתי מקובלת עלי, שאינה יפה. **מגנדרא** – מתגדלת עלי מתוך גבהות יופיה, מגנדרא – מלשון ״מקום הניחו לי אבותי להתגדר בו״ (חולין ז,א).

SAGES

רַבִּי יִצְחָק בֶּן אֶלְיָשִׁיב Rabbi Yitzhak ben Elyashiv. A Palestinian Amora of the fourth generation, Rabbi Yitzhak ben Elyashiv was famous for his piety and miraculous deeds. His teachings are cited in both the Babylonian Talmud and the Jerusalem Talmud.

SAGES

רַבִּי יוֹסֵי בַּר אָבִין Rabbi Yose bar Avin. A Palestinian Amora of the fourth and fifth generations, Rabbi Yose bar Avin may have been the son of Ravin (Rabbi Avin), who was a disciple of Rabbi Yoḥanan. Rabbi Yose bar Avin was a colleague of Rabbi Yose bar Zevida, and discussions between them are quoted in various places in the Talmud. Rabbi Yose bar Avin lived during the time of the persecutions in Eretz Israel and spent some time in Babylonia, where he met the Sages of his generation. He transmits teachings in their name and in the name of their teachers. His teachings, both Halakhic and Aggadic, are found in both Talmuds.

רַבִּי יוֹסֵי מִן יוּקְרַת Rabbi Yose of Yukrat. A Palestinian Amora of the third or fourth generation, he is mentioned only here, and no teachings are cited in his name. He came from the village of Yukrat, which is probably the village of Ikrit in Upper Galilee.

TRANSLATION AND COMMENTARY

[1] **He said to them:** "Prayers of that sort **were** once **with me, but I sent them away.** I was once willing to present God with such petitions, and I was also confident that my prayers would be answered. But I took it upon myself to refrain from troubling God with requests to alter people's personal destinies."

רַבִּי יוֹסֵי בַּר אָבִין [2] It was related that **Rabbi Yose bar Avin was** a Rabbinic student who **used to sit before Rabbi Yose of Yukrat.** [3] However, at one point **he left his** teacher **and came** to study **before Rav Ashi,** but he did not introduce himself to his new teacher. [24A] [4] **One day** Rabbi Yose bar Avin **heard** Rav Ashi **recite** the following ruling: [5] **"Shmuel said: If someone removes a fish from the sea on Shabbat,** having already caught it before Shabbat began, then **once an area** of the fish's body **the size of a sela has become dry, he is liable** for violating the prohibition against killing an animal on Shabbat." Removing a fish from water and keeping it out of the water until it is dead certainly falls under this category. Shmuel taught that even if a person throws the fish back into the water while it is still moving about convulsively, if he has already kept it out of the water long enough for an area of its body the size of a sela to become dry, he is liable for killing the creature on Shabbat, for the fish will certainly die after having been out of the water for so long. [6] Rabbi Yose bar Avin **said to** Rav Ashi: [7] **"But say, Sir:** This ruling applies only if the fish's body has become dry **between its fins.** But if a different part of the fish's body becomes dry, the fish may still live if thrown back into the water." [8] Not recognizing the new face in his yeshivah, Rav Ashi **said to** Rabbi Yose bar Avin: **"Do you not**

דְּנִיחְכְּמִים טוּבָא!״ [1] אֲמַר לְהוּ: ״עִמִּי הָיְתָה, וּשְׁלַחְתִּיהָ״. [2] רַבִּי יוֹסֵי בַּר אָבִין הֲוָה שְׁכִיחַ קַמֵּיהּ דְּרַבִּי יוֹסֵי דְּמִן יוּקְרַת. [3] שְׁבַקֵיהּ וַאֲתָא לְקַמֵּיהּ דְּרַב אַשִׁי. [24A] [4] יוֹמָא חַד שְׁמָעֵיהּ דְּקָא גָּרֵיס: [5] ״אָמַר שְׁמוּאֵל: הַשּׁוֹלֶה דָּג מִן הַיָּם בְּשַׁבָּת, כֵּיוָן שֶׁיָּבַשׁ בּוֹ כְּסֶלַע, חַיָּיב״. [6] אֲמַר לֵיהּ: [7] ״וְלֵימָא מָר: וּבֵין סְנַפִּירָיו״. [8] אֲמַר לֵיהּ: ״וְלָא

LITERAL TRANSLATION

that we may become very wise!" [1] He said to them: "It was with me, but I sent it away."

[2] Rabbi Yose bar Avin used [to sit] before Rabbi Yose of Yukrat. [3] He left him and came before Rav Ashi. [24A] [4] One day he heard him recite: [5] "Shmuel said: [If] someone removes a fish from the sea on Shabbat, once [an area] the size of a sela has become dry, he is liable." [6] He said to him: [7] "But say, Sir: And between its fins." [8] He said to him: "Do you, Sir, not

RASHI

עמי היתה ושלחתיה — דבר זה היה בידי, שכל מה שאני מבקש היו נותנין לי, ועכשיו אין תפלתי מקובלת כל כך. **דמן דיוקרת** — מקום. **יומא חד שמעיה** — רב אשי לרבי יוסי בר אבין, לישנא אחרינא: יומא חד שמעיה רבי יוסי בר אבין לרב אשי דקא גריס: אמר שמואל השולה דג מן הים בשבת כיון דיבש בו כסלע, אף על פי שהוא מפרכס לאחר כן, ובעוד שהוא מפרכס השליכו במים — חייב משום נטילת נשמה, שהיא אב מלאכה, דתנן (שבת עג,א) השוחטו כו׳. אמר ליה רבי יוסי: ובין סנפיריו, דודאי לא חי. וכשאין מחוסר צידה עסקינן, כגון שצדו בתוך הסל והניחו במים לחיות, כדרך שעושין הדייגין. **אמר ליה רב אשי** — ולא סבר לה מר דהאי ״ובין סנפיריו״ רבי יוסי בר אבין אמרה, כלומר, מאי טעמא לא אמרת ליה משמיה, שכל האומר דבר בשם אומרו מביא גאולה לעולם. **סנפיריו** — שפורת בהן.

NOTES

עִמִּי הָיְתָה, וּשְׁלַחְתִּיהָ It was with me, but I sent it away. According to *Rashi,* Rabbi Yitzḥak ben Elyashiv explained to the two Rabbinic students that he had lost the power to have all his prayers answered. But the expression, "I sent it away," suggests that Rabbi Yitzḥak did not want to put forward requests like those of the two students (see *Maharsha*). Thus our commentary follows *Rabbenu Gershom,* who explains that Rabbi Yitzḥak decided not to trouble God with petitions of that kind anymore. *Sfat Emet* suggests that Rabbi Yitzḥak only decided not to pray for a person to be endowed with special wisdom, because he recognized the potential danger of such a request.

הַשּׁוֹלֶה דָּג מִן הַיָּם If someone removes a fish from the sea. The Rishonim disagree concerning the prohibition being violated here. Our commentary follows *Rashi, Tosafot,* and others, who explain that Shmuel rules that if a person removes a fish from the sea on Shabbat and keeps it out of the water long enough for an area of the fish's body the size of a sela to become dry, he is liable for violating the prohibition against taking the life of a living thing on Shabbat. He is not liable for violating the prohibition against killing an animal on Shabbat, for we are dealing here with a case where the fish was caught before Shabbat, and then placed in a net in water. *Rabbenu Elyakim* maintains that he is liable for violating the prohibition against catching an animal on Shabbat, but that he is not liable for violating the prohibition against killing an animal on Shabbat, apparently because he did not kill the fish directly. According to *Rabbenu Gershom,* he is liable for transgressing both prohibitions.

HALAKHAH

הַשּׁוֹלֶה דָּג מִן הַיָּם If someone removes a fish from the sea. "If someone removes a fish from water on Shabbat, and leaves it out of the water until it dies, he is liable for killing an animal. Even if the fish has not yet actually died, but an area of the fish's body between its fins the size of a sela has become dry, he is liable, for the fish will certainly die." (*Rambam, Sefer Zemannim, Hilkhot Shabbat* 11:1.)

TRANSLATION AND COMMENTARY

maintain, Sir, that Rabbi Yose the son of Rabbi Avin introduced that qualification of Shmuel's ruling? You should have cited that qualification in his name, for the Mishnah teaches [*Avot* 6:6]: 'Whoever quotes something in the name of the person who said it brings redemption to the world.'" [1]Rabbi Yose bar Avin **said:** "There was no need for me to cite the author of that qualification of Shmuel's ruling, for **I am he,** Rabbi Yose bar Avin." [2]Rav Ashi **said to him:** "But **did you not** always **sit** as a student **before Rabbi Yose of Yukrat?"** [3]Rabbi Yose bar Avin **answered: "Yes."** [4]Rav Ashi **asked him: "What,** then, **is the reason that you left** the academy of Rabbi Yose of Yukrat **and came here** to study with me?" [5]Rabbi Yose bar Avin **answered:** "A number of incidents occurred which demonstrated that Rabbi Yose of Yukrat is **a person who has no mercy on his** own **son or daughter.** [6]**How,** then, **will he have mercy on me?** I left Rabbi Yose of Yukrat because I was afraid that he might one day become angry with me and punish me in the way he punished his own son and daughter."

בְּרֵיהּ מַאי הִיא [7]The Gemara asks: **What was** the incident involving Rabbi Yose of Yukrat and **his son?** [8]The Gemara explains: **One day** Rabbi Yose of Yukrat **hired workers to work in his field. It became late, but** Rabbi Yose **did not** come to **bring** the workers the **food** to which they were entitled. [9]So the workers **said to** Rabbi Yose's **son** who was with them in the field: **"We are starving!"** [10]The workers **were** all **sitting under a fig tree,** but there were no figs on the tree yet. [11]The son of Rabbi Yose of Yukrat turned to the tree and **said: "Fig tree, fig tree! Yield your fruit,** so that **father's workers** may have something to **eat."** [12]In response, the tree **yielded** its **fruit, and** the **workers ate.** [13]**In the meantime, his father,** Rabbi Yose, **came, and said to** his **workers:** [14]**"Do not be angry with me** for being so late with your food. [15]**The reason that I am late is that I have been engaged in** the performance of a certain **good deed, and until now I have been traveling** from place to place to complete that matter and also to bring you the food to which you are entitled." [16]Accepting his apology, the workers **said to** Rabbi Yose: **May the Merciful One satisfy you** just **as your son has satisfied us** and provided us with food!" [17]Rabbi Yose **asked them:** "But **from where** did my son procure food?" [18]**They answered: "Such-and-such happened,"** and they related to Rabbi Yose how his son had asked the fig tree to yield fruit out of season. [19]Rabbi Yose of Yukrat was enraged with his son and **said to him: "My son,** since **you have put your Creator**

סָבַר לָהּ מָר דְּהַהִיא רַבִּי יוֹסֵי בֶּן רַבִּי אָבִין אֲמָרָהּ?" [1]אֲמַר לֵיהּ: "אֲנָא נִיהוּ". [2]אֲמַר לֵיהּ: "וְלָאו קַמֵּיהּ דְּרַבִּי יוֹסֵי דְּמִן יוּקְרַת הֲוָה שְׁכִיחַ מָר?" [3]אֲמַר לֵיהּ: "הֵין". [4]אֲמַר לֵיהּ: "וּמַאי טַעְמָא שַׁבְקֵיהּ מָר וַאֲתָא הָכָא?" [5]אֲמַר לֵיהּ: "גַּבְרָא דְּעַל בְּרֵיהּ וְעַל בְּרַתֵּיהּ לָא חָס, [6]עֲלַי דִּידִי הֵיכִי חָיֵיס?"

[7]בְּרֵיהּ מַאי הִיא? [8]יוֹמָא חַד הֲווּ אַגְרֵי לֵיהּ אֲגִירֵי בְּדַבְרָא. נְגַהּ לְהוּ, וְלָא אַיְיתֵי לְהוּ רִיפְתָּא. [9]אָמְרוּ לֵיהּ לִבְרֵיהּ: "כָּפֵינַן!" [10]הֲווּ יָתְבִי תּוּתֵי תְּאֵינְתָּא. [11]אֲמַר: "תְּאֵנָה, תְּאֵנָה! הוֹצִיאִי פֵּירוֹתַיִךְ, וְיֹאכְלוּ פּוֹעֲלֵי אַבָּא". [12]אַפִּיקוּ, וַאֲכַלוּ. [13]אַדְּהָכִי וְהָכִי אֲתָא אֲבוּהּ, אֲמַר לְהוּ: [14]"לָא תִּינְקְטוּ בְּדַעְתַּיְיכוּ, [15]דְּהַאי דְּנַגְהֲנָא אַמִּצְוָה טַרְחְנָא, וְעַד הַשְׁתָּא הוּא דְּסַגַּאי". [16]אָמְרוּ לֵיהּ: רַחֲמָנָא לִישְׂבְּעָךְ, כִּי הֵיכִי דְּאַשְׂבְּעָן בְּרָךְ!" [17]אֲמַר לְהוּ: "מֵהֵיכָא?" [18]אֲמַרוּ: "הָכִי וְהָכִי הֲוָה מַעֲשֶׂה". [19]אָמַר לוֹ: "בְּנִי, אַתָּה הִטְרַחְתָּ אֶת קוֹנָךְ

LITERAL TRANSLATION

maintain that Rabbi Yose the son of Rabbi Avin said that?" [1]He said: "I am he." [2]He said to him: "Was it not before Rabbi Yose of Yukrat that you, Sir, used to [sit]?" [3]He said to him: "Yes." [4]He said to him: "And what is the reason that you left him and came here?" [5]He said: "A person who has no mercy on his son or his daughter, [6]how will he have mercy on me?"

[7]What was [the incident regarding] his son? [8]One day workers were hired by him [to work] in the field. It became late, and he did not bring them bread. [9]They said to his son: "We are starving!" [10]They were sitting under a fig tree. [11]He said: "Fig tree, fig tree! Yield your fruit, so that father's workers may eat." [12]It yielded [fruit], and they ate. [13]In the meantime his father came, [and] said to them: [14]"Do not feel resentment against me (lit., 'do not seize in your minds'), [15]for [the reason] that I am late [is that] I was engaged in a good deed, and until now I have been traveling." [16]They said to him: "May the Merciful One satisfy you, as your son has satisfied us!" [17]He said to them: "From where?" [18]They said: "Such-and-such happened." [19]He said to him: "My son, you have put your Creator to the trouble

RASHI

לא תנקטו לי בדעתייכו – לא תחשדוני שלא הבאתי לכם מזונות עד עכשיו. **דסגאי** – שטרחתי ואיחרתי.

TRANSLATION AND COMMENTARY

to the trouble of causing the fig tree to yield fruit out of its normal **season,** [1]**you will die before your time."** And Rabbi Yose's son did indeed die young.

בְּרַתֵּיהּ מַאי הִיא [2]The Gemara now asks: **What was** the incident involving Rabbi Yose of Yukrat and **his daughter?** [3]The Gemara explains: He **had a daughter who was** extremely **beautiful.** [4]**One day** Rabbi Yose **noticed** that **someone was making a hole in the hedge** surrounding his property so that he could **gaze at** his daughter. [5]Rabbi Yose **said to him: "What is this?"** [6]The man **answered: "Master, if I have not been privileged to take** your daughter **in marriage, shall I not be privileged** even **to catch a glimpse** of **her?"** [7]Rabbi Yose turned to his daughter and **said to her: "Daughter, your** unusual beauty **is causing people distress.** [8]It would be better if you were to **return to dust, so that people will not be caused to sin on account of you."** And Rabbi Yose's daughter died shortly afterwards.

הֲוְיָא לֵיהּ [9]It was further related that Rabbi Yose of Yukrat **had a certain ass** that he would hire out to others. [10]**People would hire** the ass **each day,** and in the evening they would send the animal home with the money for its hire on its back, [11]and it would return on its own to its owner's house. [12]But if by chance **they added or subtracted** money, the animal **would not go** until the correct amount of money was placed on its back. [13]**One day** it happened that the people who hired the animal **forgot a pair of sandals on its** back, [14]**and it would not move until they took them off it, and then it went off** by itself to its owner's house.

אֶלְעָזָר אִישׁ בִּירְתָּא [15]The Gemara now describes a miracle that was performed on behalf of another righteous man, **Elazar of** the town of **Birta. Whenever the charity collectors would see** Elazar coming down the street, **they would hide from him,** [16]**for whatever** money Elazar happened to **have** with him, no matter how much, **he would give them,** and the charity collectors did not want to take all his money. [17]**One day**

לְהוֹצִיא תְּאֵנָה פֵּירוֹתֶיהָ שֶׁלֹּא בִּזְמַנָּהּ; [1]יֵאָסֵף שֶׁלֹּא בִּזְמַנּוֹ״.
[2]בְּרַתֵּיהּ מַאי הִיא? [3]הֲוְיָא לֵיהּ בְּרַתָּא בַּעֲלַת יוֹפִי. [4]יוֹמָא חַד חָזְיָא לְהַהוּא גַּבְרָא כַּרְיָא בְּהוּצָא וְקָא חָזֵי לָהּ. [5]אָמַר לוֹ: ״מַאי הַאי?״ [6]אֲמַר לֵיהּ: ״רַבִּי, אִם לְלוֹקְחָהּ לֹא זָכִיתִי, לִרְאוֹתָהּ לֹא אֶזְכֶּה?״ [7]אָמַר לָהּ: ״בִּתִּי, קָא מְצַעַרְתְּ לְהוּ לִבְרִיָּיתָא. [8]שׁוּבִי לַעֲפָרֵיךְ, וְאַל יִכָּשְׁלוּ בִּיךְ בְּנֵי אָדָם״.
[9]הֲוְיָא לֵיהּ הַהוּא חֲמָרָא, [10]כִּדְהָווּ אָגְרִי לָהּ כָּל יוֹמָא, לְאוּרְתָּא הָווּ מְשַׁדְּרִי לָהּ אַגְרָהּ אַגַּבָּהּ, [11]וְאָתְיָא לְבֵי מָרָהּ. [12]וְאִי טָפוּ לָהּ אוֹ בָּצְרִי לָהּ, לֹא אָתְיָא. [13]יוֹמָא חַד אִינְשׁוּ זוּגָא דְּסַנְדָּלֵי עֲלָהּ, [14]וְלָא אָזְלָה עַד דְּשָׁקְלוּנְהוּ מִינָּהּ, וַהֲדַר אָזְלָה.
[15]אֶלְעָזָר אִישׁ בִּירְתָּא כַּד הָווּ חָזוּ לֵיהּ גַּבָּאֵי צְדָקָה, הָווּ טָשׁוּ מִינֵּיהּ, [16]דְּכָל מַאי דַּהֲוָה גַּבֵּיהּ יָהֵיב לְהוּ. [17]יוֹמָא חַד הֲוָה

LITERAL TRANSLATION

of causing a fig tree to yield its fruit out of its season; [1]you (lit., 'he') will die before your (lit., 'his') time."

[2]What was [the incident regarding] his daughter?

[3]He had a daughter who was beautiful. [4]One day he saw a certain person making a hole in the hedge and gazing at her. [5]He said to him: "What is this?" [6]He said to him: "Master, if I have not been privileged to take her [in marriage], shall I not be privileged to see her?" [7]He said to her: "My daughter, you are causing people distress. [8]Return to your dust, and let people not be caused to sin on account of you."

[9]He had a certain ass. [10]When they would hire it each day, in the evening they would send its hire on its back, [11]and it would go to the house of its owner. [12]But if they would add or subtract, it would not go. [13]One day they forgot a pair of sandals on it, [14]and it would not go until they took them from it, and then it went.

[15]When the charity collectors would see Elazar of Birta, they would hide from him, [16]for whatever he had he would give to them. [17]One day he went

RASHI

דהוה כריא בהוצא – סותר גדר העצים, כדי להסתכל דרך הנקב. **אמר ליה רבי יוסי מאי האי** – מה אתה מעיין כאן. **אינשו** = שכחו.

SAGES

אֶלְעָזָר אִישׁ בִּירְתָּא Elazar of Birta. In most versions of our text he is called Elazar Ish Kfar Bartuta (Elazar of the village of Bartuta), and he is mentioned several times in the Mishnah and in the Tosefta by his full name: Rabbi Elazar Ben Yehudah Ish Bartuta.

He was a Tanna of the third generation and was a student of Rabbi Yehoshua and a colleague of Rabbi Akiva and Rabbi Yishmael. We possess little information about Elazar's life, but the Rishonim linked the story of his righteousness here with his famous saying in *Ethics of the Fathers* (3:7): Give Him what is His, for you and what is yours are His.

NOTES

דְּכָל מַאי דַּהֲוָה גַּבֵּיהּ יָהֵיב לְהוּ For whatever he had he would give to them. The Aḥaronim ask: Elsewhere (*Ketubot* 50a), we learned that an enactment was made in Usha that even if a person wishes to be liberal in his contributions to charity, he should not give away more than one-fifth of his assets, lest he himself become financially dependent upon the charity of others. Why, then, did Elazar of Birta give away all that he had to charity? Some note that there is no difficulty according to *Rambam,* who writes in his *Commentary to the Mishnah* (*Pe'ah* 1:1) that a person is not required to donate to the poor more than one-fifth of his assets, but he is permitted to do so as an act of piety (though in *Sefer Hafla'ah, Hilkhot Arakhin* 8:13, *Rambam* writes that giving away more than one-fifth of one's assets is an act of folly, rather than an act of piety). *Gevurat Ari* suggests that the Usha enactment was the subject of a

TRANSLATION AND COMMENTARY

Elazar **went to the market to buy** things for **his daughter's dowry,** taking with him a substantial sum of money. [1]**The charity collectors saw him** coming **and** tried to **hide from him.** [2]But Elazar **went and ran after them,** determined to contribute to the poor. [3]He caught up with them and **said: "I adjure you,** please tell me **in what** good deed **you are** currently **engaged.** For what cause have you set up a collection?" [4]The charity collectors **said to him:** "We are collecting funds so that **an orphan boy and an orphan girl** can marry." [5]Elazar **said to them:** "I swear **by the Temple service!** [6]Those orphans **take precedence** even **over my own daughter,** for there is nobody to see to it that they have all that they need for marriage." [7]So **he took all** the money **he had with him,** which he had set aside for the purchase of his daughter's dowry, **and gave it to** the charity collectors. [8]Elazar **had** only **one zuz left, with which he bought himself** a small amount of **wheat, and he went and cast it into his granary.** [9]Elazar's **wife came and said to her daughter: "What has your father brought** you in preparation for your wedding?" [10]The daughter **said to her** mother: **"Whatever he has brought, he cast into the granary."** [11]Elazar's wife **went to open the door of the granary, and she saw that the granary was filled** to the top **with wheat,** [12]so much so that wheat **was coming out through the door socket, and the door could not be opened on account of the wheat.** In reward for his compassion for the orphans, Elazar of Birta's granary was miraculously filled with grain. [13]Elazar's **daughter went** immediately **to the Academy** to tell her father what had happened. [14]**She said to him: "Come and see what** the Almighty **who loves you** has done for you." [15]Her father **said to her:** "I swear **by the Temple service!** [16]The wheat that came into the world through a miracle is forbidden to you as if it had been consecrated to the Temple service, and **you** have a **share** in that grain **only** as **one of the poor of Israel."**

LITERAL TRANSLATION

to the market to buy a dowry for his daughter. [1]The charity collectors saw him [and] hid from him. [2]He went and ran after them. [3]He said to them: "I adjure you, in what are you engaged?" [4]They said to him: "With an orphan boy and an orphan girl." [5]He said to them: "By [the Temple] service! [6]They take precedence over my daughter." [7]He took everything that he had and gave it to them. [8]He had one zuz left, [with which] he bought himself wheat, and he went up [and] cast it into the granary. [9]His wife came, [and] said to her daughter: "What has your father brought?" [10]She said to her: "Whatever he brought, he cast into the granary." [11]She went to open the door of the granary, [and] she saw that the granary was filled with wheat, [12]and it was coming out through the socket of the door, and the door would not open on account of the wheat. [13]His daughter went to the Academy, [14][and] said to him: "Come and see what He who loves you has done for you!" [15]He said to her: "By [the Temple] service! [16]They are to you as consecrated, and you have [a share] in them only as one of the poor of Israel."

סָלֵיק לְשׁוּקָא לְמִיזְבַּן נְדוּנְיָא לִבְרַתֵּיהּ. [1]חָזְיוּהוּ גַּבָּאֵי צְדָקָה טָשׁוּ מִינֵּיהּ. [2]אֲזַל וּרְהַט בַּתְרַיְיהוּ. [3]אֲמַר לְהוּ: "אַשְׁבַּעְתִּיכוּ, בְּמַאי עָסְקִיתוּ?" [4]אֲמָרוּ לֵיהּ: "בְּיָתוֹם וִיתוֹמָה". [5]אֲמַר לְהֶן: "הָעֲבוֹדָה! [6]שֶׁהֵן קוֹדְמִין לְבִתִּי". [7]שְׁקַל כָּל דַּהֲוָה בַּהֲדֵיהּ וִיהַב לְהוּ. [8]פַּשׁ לֵיהּ חַד זוּזָא, זְבַן לֵיהּ חִיטֵּי, וְאַסֵּיק שַׁדְיֵיהּ בְּאַכְלְבָא. [9]אֲתַאי דְּבֵיתְהוּ, אֲמָרָה לָהּ לִבְרַתֵּיהּ: "מַאי אַיְיתִי אֲבוּךְ?" [10]אֲמָרָה לָהּ: "כָּל מַה דְּאַיְיתִי, בְּאַכְלְבָא שְׁדִיתֵיהּ". [11]אָתְיָא לְמִיפְתַּח בָּבָא דְּאַכְלְבָא, חֲזַת אַכְלְבָא דִּמְלְיָא חִיטֵּי, [12]וְקָא נָפְקָא בְּצִינוֹרָא דְּדַשָּׁא, וְלָא מִיפְּתַח בָּבָא מֵחִיטֵּי. [13]אָזְלָא בְּרַתֵּיהּ לְבֵי מִדְרְשָׁא, [14]אֲמָרָה לֵיהּ: "בֹּא וּרְאֵה מַה עָשָׂה לְךָ אוֹהַבְךָ!" [15]אֲמַר לָהּ: "הָעֲבוֹדָה! [16]הֲרֵי הֵן הֶקְדֵּשׁ עָלַיִךְ, וְאֵין לָךְ בָּהֶן אֶלָּא כְּאֶחָד מֵעֲנִיֵּי יִשְׂרָאֵל".

RASHI

טשו מפניו — היו מתחבאים. העבודה — שבועה. ביתום ויתומה — לזווג זה לזו. אכלבא — אוצר של חטים. אוהבך — הקדוש ברוך הוא. אלא כאחד מעניי ישראל — משום דמעשה נסים הוא, ואסור לאדם להנות ממעשה נסים. כדאמר לעיל (כ,ב): ואם עושין לו נס — מנכין לו מזכיותיו.

BACKGROUND

נְדוּנְיָא Dowry. This word is apparently related to the Biblical Hebrew **נֵדֶן**, meaning "gift" (cf. Ezekiel 16:33), which is synonymous with מֹהַר, meaning "dowry," and denotes the property that a bride brings with her when she marries.

צִינוֹרָא דְּדַשָּׁא The socket of the door. This term probably refers to a socket in the threshold of a house into which the projecting flange on the door was inserted. To make it easier for the door to be removed and replaced, a slit was dug next to the socket, in which small objects could be placed.

NOTES

Tannaitic dispute, and that Elazar of Birta follows the opinion of the Tanna who maintains that a person may give away more than one-fifth of his assets to charity, provided that he keeps some minimal amount for himself.

כְּאֶחָד מֵעֲנִיֵּי יִשְׂרָאֵל As one of the poor of Israel. *Rashi* and others explain that Elazar of Birta did not want his daughter to purchase her dowry with the grain because he did not want to derive benefit from something that was created by a miracle. But this leads to a certain difficulty, for if he did not want to derive benefit from the miraculously created grain, he should not have allowed her to take even a small portion of it! *Iyyun Ya'akov* suggests that Elazar of Birta did not want his daughter to purchase her dowry with the grain because he did not wish

[1]רַבִּי יְהוּדָה נְשִׂיאָה גְּזַר תַּעֲנִיתָא. [2]בְּעֵי רַחֲמֵי וְלָא אֲתָא מִיטְרָא. [3]אֲמַר: "כַּמָּה אִיכָּא מִשְּׁמוּאֵל הָרָמָתִי לִיהוּדָה בֶּן גַּמְלִיאֵל! [4]אוֹי לוֹ לַדּוֹר שֶׁכֵּן נִתְקַע! [5]אוֹי לוֹ לְמִי שֶׁעָלְתָה בְּיָמָיו כָּךְ!" [6]חֲלַשׁ דַּעְתֵּיהּ, וַאֲתָא מִיטְרָא.

[7]דְּבֵי נְשִׂיאָה גְּזַר תַּעֲנִיתָא, וְלָא אוֹדְעִינְהוּ לְרַבִּי יוֹחָנָן וּלְרֵישׁ לָקִישׁ. [8]לְצַפְרָא אוֹדְעִינְהוּ. [9]אֲמַר לֵיהּ רֵישׁ לָקִישׁ לְרַבִּי יוֹחָנָן: [10]"הָא לָא קַבֵּילְנָא עֲלַן מֵאוּרְתָּא!" [11]אֲמַר לֵיהּ: "אֲנַן בָּתְרַיְיהוּ גָּרְרִינַן".

[12]דְּבֵי נְשִׂיאָה גְּזַר תַּעֲנִיתָא, וְלָא אֲתָא מִיטְרָא. [13]תָּנָא לְהוּ אוֹשַׁעְיָא זְעֵירָא דְּמִן חַבְרַיָּיא:

LITERAL TRANSLATION

[1]Rabbi Yehudah Nesi'ah decreed a fast. [2]He petitioned for mercy but rain did not come. [3]He said: "How much is there between Samuel the Ramatite and Yehudah ben Gamliel! [4]Woe to the generation that has been placed in such [a position]! [5]Woe to him in whose days this has occurred!" [6]He became distressed, and rain came.

[7][Someone] of the House of the Nasi decreed a fast, but they did not inform Rabbi Yoḥanan or Resh Lakish. [8]In the morning they informed them. [9]Resh Lakish said to Rabbi Yoḥanan: [10]"Surely we did not accept it upon ourselves from the evening!" [11]He said to him: "We are dragged after them."

[12][Someone] of the House of the Nasi decreed a fast, but the rain did not come. [13]Oshaya the youngest [member] of the group taught them:

TRANSLATION AND COMMENTARY

רַבִּי יְהוּדָה נְשִׂיאָה [1]The Gemara continues by relating further anecdotes regarding fasts proclaimed in times of drought. **Rabbi Yehudah Nesi'ah,** the son of Rabban Gamliel the son of Rabbi Yehudah HaNasi, once **decreed a fast** because of a drought. [2]**He petitioned** God **for mercy, but** his prayers went unanswered and the **rain did not come.** [3]**He lamented** to himself: **"What** a difference **there is between** the Prophet **Samuel the Ramatite and** myself **Yehudah ben Gamliel!** Samuel prayed alone for rain during the summer months, and his prayers were immediately answered, as the verse says [I Samuel 12:17]: 'Is it not the wheat harvest today? I will call to the Lord, and He shall send thunder and rain,' and the next verse [v.18] continues: 'So Samuel called to the Lord, and the Lord sent thunder and rain that day.' By contrast, I proclaimed a fast upon the entire community because the winter rains are late in coming, but not a drop of rain has yet fallen. [4]**Woe to the generation that has been placed in such a position** and has such impotent leaders! [5]**Woe to him in whose days this has occurred!"** [6]Rabbi Yehudah Nesi'ah **became** greatly **distressed, and rain** finally **came.**

דְּבֵי נְשִׂיאָה [7]It was also related that **in the House of the Nasi** a public **fast was** once **decreed** in a time of drought, **but** Rabbi Yoḥanan and Resh Lakish, two of the outstanding Rabbinic scholars of the generation, **were not informed** about the fast beforehand. [8]It was only **on the morning** of the fast that **Rabbi Yoḥanan and Resh Lakish were informed** that a public fast had been declared for that day. [9]**Resh Lakish said to Rabbi Yoḥanan:** "Are we obligated to observe this fast? [10]**Surely we did not accept** the fast **upon ourselves** yesterday **evening.** Unless a person accepts a fast during the previous day, it is not regarded as a fast [see above, 12a]!" [11]Rabbi Yoḥanan **said to** Resh Lakish: **"We are dragged after them.** The House of the Nasi is authorized to proclaim a public fast which is binding on the entire community. When a public fast is proclaimed by the communal leadership, it is regarded as if each and every individual has committed himself to fast."

דְּבֵי נְשִׂיאָה [12]It was further related that **in the House of the Nasi a** public **fast was** once **decreed** when the rain was late, **but** even this did not help and **the rain** still **did not come.** [13]**Oshaya,** who was known as **the youngest member of the group** of Sages, **taught** his colleagues a Baraita, which stated: "If the Great Sanhedrin hands down an erroneous Halakhic decision which results in the unwitting violation of a prohibition against idolatry by the community as a whole, a special communal sin-offering must be brought.

RASHI

רבי יהודה נשיאה — היה בנו של רבן גמליאל בר רבי. **לשמואל הרמתי** — שיורדין גשמים בשבילו, דכתיב "הלא קציר חטים היום". ועכשיו באין כל ישראל והטילו על רבי יהודה בן גמליאל דלוות, וליכא דמשגח ביה. **שנתקע** — תקוע. **והא לא קבלינן מאתמול** — בהדייהו. **גרירין** — (גרירינן) גרורין ומשוכין אנו אחריהן, וכמי שקבלנו עלינו. **זעירא דמן חבריא** — לעיר שבישיבה. והאי דקרי ליה הכי — משום דאושעיא אחרינא הוה התם.

NOTES

to receive a reward for his righteous behavior in this world, as it would diminish the reward he was to receive in the World-to-Come. But once he dedicated the grain to charity, his daughter, being poor herself, had a right to a portion of it just like any other poor person.

SAGES

רַבִּי יְהוּדָה נְשִׂיאָה **Rabbi Yehudah Nesi'ah.** He was the son of Rabban Gamliel, the son of Rabbi Yehudah HaNasi, and he was called "Nesi'ah" to distinguish him from his eminent grandfather, the editor of the Mishnah. Rabbi Yehudah Nesi'ah was among the foremost Palestinian Amoraim, and the greatest disciples of Rabbi Yehudah HaNasi were his colleagues, including Rabbi Yoḥanan and Resh Lakish. The court of Rabbi Yehudah Nesi'ah introduced various ordinances and was regarded as the greatest Torah center in the Jewish world, to the degree that even the great Amora Rav revised his opinions in conformity with that court.

Rabbi Yehudah Nesi'ah served for many years as Nasi, and seems to have been the last Nasi who was a great Torah scholar and head of the Sanhedrin. His place as Nasi, though not as head of the Sanhedrin, was taken by his son, Rabban Gamliel.

אוֹשַׁעְיָא זְעֵירָא דְּמִן חַבְרַיָּיא **Oshaya, the youngest member of the group.** This Sage is mentioned several times in the Talmud and it is not clear whether he is the third generation Amora, Rav Oshaya of Babylonia. The meaning of his appellation is also not entirely clear. Was he called "Oshaya Ze'ira" to distinguish him from another Rav Oshaya, and is Ḥavraya a place, or does his appellation mean that he was the youngest of a group of Sages?

TRANSLATION AND COMMENTARY

[1]Regarding this sacrifice, the verse states [Numbers 15:2]): **'Then it shall be, if from the eyes of the congregation it shall be committed in error,** then all the congregation shall offer one young bullock for a burnt-offering, for a sweet savor to the Lord, with its meal-offering, and its drink-offering, according to the ordinance, and one kid of the goats for a sin-offering.' Now this verse refers to the community's leaders as 'the eyes of the congregation.' In what sense are the leaders the eyes of the congregation? [2]**This may be compared to a bride who is** still **in her father's home** and has not been examined by her bridegroom or his family. [3]**As long as** the bride's **eyes are beautiful, the rest of her body does not require an examination,** for surely the rest of her body is equally unblemished. [4]But **if her eyes are tearful, her entire body requires a** careful **examination.** So, too, in the case of a community's leaders who are the 'eyes of the congregation.' If the community's leaders are found lacking, the community will surely be found similarly wanting of good deeds." The thrust of Oshaya's comment was clear — that if there was no rain, something must be wrong with the heads of the community, who are the "eyes of the congregation." [5]Outraged by the insult, the **servants** of the Nasi **came and placed a scarf around** Oshaya's **neck, causing him** great **distress.** [6]Oshaya's **townsmen said to** the servants of the Nasi: **"Let him be, for he also causes us distress** with his words of rebuke and admonition. [7]But **since we have seen that all his words are** said **for the sake of Heaven** so that we should repent and mend our ways, [8]**we never say anything to him, but** rather **we let him be** and allow him to continue preaching. [9]**You too** should **let him be,** for he surely means well."

רַבִּי [10]The Gemara now continues with a story concerning **Rabbi** Yehudah HaNasi, who once **decreed a** communal **fast** in a time of drought, **but the rain** still **did not come.** Seeing that Rabbi Yehudah HaNasi's prayers were of no avail, [11]**Ilfa went down before him** to lead the communal prayer **(and some say** that it was **Rabbi Ilfai** who assumed the role of prayer leader). [12]As soon as **he recited** in his repetition of the Amidah the words: **"Who causes the wind to blow," the wind** began to **blow.** [13]And then, when he continued: **"Who causes the rain to fall," the rain came** and brought an end to the drought. Understanding that the rain must have fallen on account of Ilfa's special merit, [14]Rabbi Yehudah HaNasi **said to him:** "What are

[1]״׳וְהָיָה, אִם מֵעֵינֵי הָעֵדָה נֶעֶשְׂתָה לִשְׁגָגָה׳. [2]מָשָׁל לְכַלָּה שֶׁהִיא בְּבֵית אָבִיהָ. [3]כָּל זְמַן שֶׁעֵינֶיהָ יָפוֹת, אֵין כָּל גּוּפָהּ צְרִיכָה בְּדִיקָה. [4]עֵינֶיהָ טְרוּטוֹת, כָּל גּוּפָהּ צְרִיכָה בְּדִיקָה״. [5]אָתוּ עֲבָדֵיהּ וְרָמוּ לֵיהּ סוּדָרָא בְּצַוָּארֵיהּ, וְקָא מְצַעֲרוּ לֵיהּ. [6]אֲמַרוּ לְהוּ בְּנֵי מָאתֵיהּ: ״שְׁבַקֵיהּ, דְּהָא נַמִי מְצַעֵר לָן. [7]כֵּיוָן דְּחָזֵינַן דְּכָל מִילֵּיהּ לְשׁוּם שָׁמַיִם, [8]לָא אָמְרִי לֵיהּ מִידֵּי וְשָׁבְקִינַן לֵיהּ. [9]אַתּוּן נַמִי שְׁבַקוּהוּ״.

[10]רַבִּי גְּזַר תַּעֲנִיתָא, וְלָא אֲתָא מִיטְרָא. [11]נָחֵית קַמֵּיהּ אִילְפָא, (וְאָמְרִי לָהּ רַבִּי אִילְפַי). [12]אֲמַר: ״מַשִּׁיב הָרוּחַ״, וּנְשַׁב זִיקָא. [13]״מוֹרִיד הַגֶּשֶׁם״, וַאֲתָא מִיטְרָא. [14]אֲמַר לֵיהּ: ״מַאי

LITERAL TRANSLATION

[1]"'Then it shall be, if from the eyes of the congregation it shall be committed in error.' [2]This may be compared to a bride who is in her father's home. [3]As long as her eyes are beautiful, her entire body does not require an examination. [4][If] her eyes are tearful, her entire body requires an examination." [5]His servants came and placed a scarf around his neck, and they caused him distress. [6]His townsmen said to them: "Let him be, for he also causes us distress. [7]Since we have seen that all his words are for the sake of Heaven, [8]we say nothing to him and we let him be. [9]You too let him be."

[10]Rabbi decreed a fast, but the rain did not come. [11]Ilfa (and some say [it was] Rabbi Ilfai) went down before him. [12]He said: "Who causes the wind to blow," and the wind blew. [13]"Who causes the rain to fall," and rain came. [14]He said to him: "What

RASHI

מעיני העדה — זקנים, מאירי עיני העם. **בזמן שעיניה יפות אין כל גופה וכו׳** — דודאי כל גופה יפה. **אין עיניה יפות כו׳** — הואיל והנהו דבי נשיאה דהוו "עיני העדה" רשעים — דלת העם אין צריכין לבדוק מה מעשיהם, לכך לא משגחו בהו מן שמים. **אתו עבדי דריש גלותא וקא מצערו ליה** — לאושעיא. **אמרו ליה בני מתא** — לעבדי דבי נשיאה. **מצער לן** — מחרף ומגדף אותנו. **נחית קמיה** — לפני התיבה. **נשא** — כמו נשב.

LANGUAGE

טְרוּטוֹת Tearful. The source of this word may possibly be the Greek δηρός, *diros*, meaning "long" or "too long." Another possibility is that it comes from the Latin *teres, teritis,* meaning "oval," "something elongated with rounded ends." In this context it would then mean eyes that are very narrow.

NOTES

דְּהָא נַמִי מְצַעֵר לָן For he also causes us distress. *Rabbenu Elyakim* explains the argument as follows: Surely, when Oshaya said that if a bride's eyes are tearful, her entire body requires a careful examination, he insulted not only the Nasi (the bride's eyes), but also the rest of the community (the bride's body). Just as the rest of the community was ready to indulge Oshaya, for it was known that he meant well, so too should the Nasi's men allow him to continue preaching.

TRANSLATION AND COMMENTARY

the good **deeds** that you have performed, on account of which your prayers were so quickly answered?" [1]Ilfa **said to him: "I live in a remote** and **impoverished place where there is no wine** readily available over which to recite **kiddush and havadalah,** the blessings recited at the beginning and the end of Shabbat and Festivals. [2]But I always **make a** special **effort** to ensure that **wine is brought** so that I can recite **kiddush and havdalah,** [3]**and cause** the members of the community at large **to fulfill their obligation.** It is apparently in reward for my efforts in this matter that my prayers for rain have been answered."

רַב אִיקְלַע [4]It was related that **Rav happened to come to a certain place** that was experiencing a prolonged drought. [5]**He decreed a** communal **fast, but the rain** still **did not come.** [6]After Rav's prayers proved to be ineffective, another **prayer leader went down before him** to lead the communal prayer. [7]As soon as **he said** the words: **"Who causes the wind to blow," the wind** suddenly **blew.** [8]And when **he said: "Who causes the rain to fall," the rain** began to **come** down. [9]Rav was curious to know more about the prayer leader, so he said to him: "What are the righteous deeds that you have performed, on account of which your prayers received such a prompt response?" [10]The prayer leader **asked him: "I am** just **a teacher of young children. I teach the children of the poor just as** I teach **the children of the rich,** making no distinction between them. [11]I accept a fee for my work, but **whoever is unable to pay, I do not take any** money **from him.** [12]Moreover, **I have a fishpond,** so that **whoever is lazy** in class or lacks interest in the subject matter, [13]**I bribe him by** allowing him to leave the classroom and take **some** fish. [14]I then **set him straight and mollify him until he** is ready to **come** back **and continue his studies."**

רַב נַחְמָן [15]**Rav Naḥman** once **decreed a** communal **fast** upon his community which was suffering from drought, and **petitioned** God **for mercy.** [16]But Rav Naḥman's prayers were not answered, and **the rain did not come.** [17]Disappointed with himself, Rav Naḥman **cried out** in despair: **"Take Naḥman, and throw him** down **from the wall to the ground.** Depose me from my position of leadership, for my intercession on behalf of the community in its hour of need has proved to be ineffective." [18]Rav Naḥman **was** greatly **distressed, and rain** finally **came.**

רַבָּה [19]The Gemara now relates that **Rabbah** also **decreed a** communal **fast** on account of drought. [20]**He**

עוֹבָדָךְ?״ [1]אֲמַר לֵיהּ: ״דָּיֵירְנָא בְּקוּסְטָא דְּחִיקָא דְּלֵית בֵּיהּ חַמְרָא לְקִידּוּשָׁא וְאַבְדַּלְתָּא. [2]טָרַחְנָא וְאָתֵינָא חַמְרָא לְקִידּוּשָׁא וְאַבְדַּלְתָּא, [3]וּמַפֵּיקְנָא לְהוּ יְדֵי חוֹבָתַיְיהוּ״.

[4]רַב אִיקְלַע לְהַהוּא אַתְרָא. [5]גְּזַר תַּעֲנִיתָא, וְלָא אֲתָא מִיטְרָא. [6]נָחֵית קַמֵּיהּ שְׁלִיחָא דְּצִבּוּרָא. [7]אֲמַר: ״מַשִּׁיב הָרוּחַ״, וּנְשַׁב זִיקָא. [8]אֲמַר: ״מוֹרִיד הַגֶּשֶׁם״, וַאֲתָא מִיטְרָא. [9]אֲמַר לֵיהּ: ״מַאי עוֹבָדָךְ?״ [10]אֲמַר לֵיהּ: ״מִיקְרֵי דַּרְדְּקֵי אֲנָא, וּמַקְרֵינָא לִבְנֵי עֲנִיֵּי כִּבְנֵי עַתִּירֵי. [11]וְכָל דְּלָא אֶפְשָׁר לֵיהּ, לָא שָׁקְלִינָא מִינֵּיהּ מִידֵּי. [12]וְאִית לִי פִּירָא דְּכַוְורֵי, וְכָל מַאן דְּפָשַׁע, [13]מְשַׁחֲדִינָא לֵיהּ מִינַּיְיהוּ, [14]וּמְסַדְּרִינַן לֵיהּ, וּמְפַיְּיסִינַן לֵיהּ, עַד דְּאָתֵי וְקָרֵי״.

[15]רַב נַחְמָן גְּזַר תַּעֲנִיתָא. בְּעָא רַחֲמֵי, [16]וְלָא אֲתָא מִיטְרָא. [17]אֲמַר: ״שַׁקְלוּהּ לְנַחְמָן, חֲבוֹטוֹ מִן גּוּדָא לְאַרְעָא״. [18]חֲלַשׁ דַּעְתֵּיהּ, וַאֲתָא מִיטְרָא.

[19]רַבָּה גְּזַר תַּעֲנִיתָא. [20]בָּעֵי

LITERAL TRANSLATION

do you do (lit., 'what is your deed')?" [1]He said to him: "I live in a remote poor place in which there is no wine for kiddush and havdalah. [2]I make an effort and bring wine for kiddush and havdalah, [3]and fulfill their obligation for them."

[4]Rav happened to come to a certain place. [5]He decreed a fast, but the rain did not come. [6]The prayer leader went down before him. [7]He said: "Who causes the wind to blow," and the wind blew. [8]He said: "Who causes the rain to fall," and rain came. [9]He said to him: "What do you do?" [10]He said to him: "I am a teacher of young children, and I teach the children of the poor just like the children of the rich. [11]And whoever is unable [to pay], I do not take anything from him. [12]And I have a fishpond, and whoever is lazy, [13]I bribe him with them, [14]and I prepare for him, and I mollify him, until he comes and studies."

[15]Rav Naḥman decreed a fast. He petitioned for mercy, [16]but the rain did not come. [17]He said: "Take Naḥman, [and] throw him from the wall to the ground." [18]He was distressed, and rain came.

[19]Rabbah decreed a fast. [20]He petitioned

RASHI

בקוסטא דחיקא – בכפר דחוק, שיש בו עניות ביותר. **פירא דכוורי** = מחילות של דגים. **כל מאן דפשע** – דלא בעי מיקרי משחדינא ליה כו׳. **ומסדרינא ליה ומפייסינא ליה** – מתקנן כסדר.

TRANSLATION AND COMMENTARY

too **petitioned** God **for mercy,** [1]**but** his prayers were also not answered, and **the rain** still **did not come.** [2]His townsmen **said to him: "But surely when Rav Yehudah,** your teacher and predecessor as head of the Academy at Pumbedita, **would decree a fast, the rain would come!** Why, then, do your prayers remain unanswered?" [3]Rabbah **answered them: "What shall I do?** [4]**If** you are suggesting that my prayers have not been answered **on account** of the level of my Torah **study, we are** surely **better than** the previous generation, [5]**for in the years of Rav Yehudah the entire** curriculum of Torah **study** adopted in his academy [24B] **was** restricted **to the order of *Nezikin*,** the fourth of the six major sections of the Talmud, [6]**whereas** today **we** regularly **study** all **six orders.** [7]**And,** moreover, **when Rav Yehudah** himself **reached** the Mishnah **in** tractate *Teharot* (2:1) on the subject of ***Uktzin*** (stems of plants) which states: [8]**'If a woman was pickling vegetables in a pot,' and some say** when he reached the Mishnah in tractate *Uktzin* (2:1) which states: [9]**'Olives** that **were pickled in their leaves are ritually pure,'** [10]**he** would **say: 'I see here** matters that are as difficult for me to understand as all the **arguments** raised by my teachers **Rav and Shmuel!'** [11]**And** today **we teach** tractate ***Uktzin*** as a matter of course **in** as many as **thirteen academies** in the city! [12]**But nevertheless** whenever **Rav Yehudah** declared a public fast, **as soon as he removed his first shoe** [wearing shoes on a stringent public fast is forbidden], even before he took off the second shoe, **rain would** begin to **fall.**

רַחֲמֵי, [1]וְלָא אֲתָא מִיטְרָא. [2]אֲמַרוּ לֵיהּ: ״וְהָא רַב יְהוּדָה כִּי הֲוָה גְּזַר תַּעֲנִיתָא, אֲתָא מִיטְרָא!״ [3]אֲמַר לְהוּ: ״מַאי אַעֲבֵיד? [4]אִי מִשּׁוּם תְּנוּיֵי, אֲנַן עֲדִיפִינַן מִינַּיְיהוּ, [5]דְּבִשְׁנֵי דְרַב יְהוּדָה כָּל תְּנוּיֵי [24B] בִּנְזִיקִין הֲוָה, [6]וַאֲנַן קָא מַתְנִינַן בְּשִׁיתָא סִדְרִין. [7]וְכִי הֲוָה מָטֵי רַב יְהוּדָה בְּעוּקְצִין: [8]׳הָאִשָּׁה שֶׁכּוֹבֶשֶׁת יָרָק בִּקְדֵירָה׳, וְאָמְרִי לָהּ: [9]׳זֵיתִים שֶׁכְּבָשָׁן בִּטְרָפֵיהֶן טְהוֹרִין׳, [10]אָמַר: ׳הֲוָיוֹת דְּרַב וּשְׁמוּאֵל קָא חָזֵינָא הָכָא!׳ [11]וַאֲנַן קָא מַתְנִינַן בְּעוּקְצִין תְּלֵיסַר מְתִיבָתָא. [12]וְאִילּוּ רַב יְהוּדָה כִּי הֲוָה שָׁלֵיף חַד מְסָאנָא, אָתֵי מִיטְרָא,

LITERAL TRANSLATION

for mercy, [1]but the rain did not come. [2]They said to him: "But surely when Rav Yehudah would decree a fast, the rain would come!" [3]He said to them: "What shall I do? [4]If on account of study, we are better than they, [5]for in the years of Rav Yehudah all [their] study [24B] was in [the order of] *Nezikin*, [6]but we teach the six orders. [7]And when Rav Yehudah reached in *Uktzin*: [8]'[If] a woman was pickling vegetables in a pot,' and some say: [9]'Olives that were pickled with their leaves are ritually pure,' [10]he said: 'I see arguments of Rav and Shmuel here!' [11]And we teach *Uktzin* [in] thirteen academies! [12]But nevertheless when Rav Yehudah took off one shoe, rain came,

RASHI

הכי גרסינן: **בנזיקין הוה** — למודם לא היה גדול אלא בסדר נזיקין. **שכובשת ירק בקדירה** — במסכת [טהרות] היא, בפרק שני (משנה א) גבי ידות מיירי. דקיימא לן (עוקצין פרק ראשון משנה א): כל ידות האוכלין, אם נגעה טומאה בהן — נטמא גם האוכל הצריך לידות, דיד מכנים ומוציא. כדאמרינן ב״העור והרוטב״ (חולין קיח,א): מכל האוכל — לרבות הידות. וקתני התם: אשה שהיא כובשת ירק, דידות שלהן טהורין, דכשהיא עוצרת אותם — הידות משתברות, ואי אפשר ליטול הירקות בידות שלהן, שנשמט ונפסק האוכל מן היד, מחמת כבישה. **כובשת** = *שול״ץ בלעז, עוצרת שיצא המשקה שלהן ויבשו. דרך אשה בכך כובשת ירק ממים, שישתמרו לזמן מרובה. **טהורין** — העלין והקלחין. **ואמרי לה** — כי מטא לאידך בפרק שני (דעוקצין משנה א) ״זיתים שכבשן בטרפיהן״, כתרגומו עלה = טרפא (בראשית ח), עלין שלהן דהיינו ידות. **טהורין** — הידות להביא טומאה לאוכל, דתו לא חזי למהוי בית יד. **הוויות דרב ושמואל** — עומק גדול, ולא הוה נהירא ליה. **תליסר מתיבתא** — שלש עשרה ישיבות איכא בהן מתא דגמרי מסכת עוקצין. **כי הוה שליף חד מסאנא** — משום עינוי.

BACKGROUND

בִּנְזִיקִין Was in the order of *Nezikin*. From what follows it is clear that this does not mean they studied only the order of *Nezikin* ("Damages"), but rather that the main thrust of their study and their greatness in Torah knowledge was based on the order of *Nezikin*, since it deals with matters that are part of everyday life. In contrast, the order of *Teharot* ("Ritual Purity") is much harder, because it is mostly concerned with matters that are no longer practiced, especially outside Eretz Israel. Hence it was little studied, and there is no Talmud for that order, aside from tractate *Niddah*. Rabbah, on the other hand, studied every area of the Torah, and his expertise was particularly great in the laws of ritual purity.

LANGUAGE (RASHI)

שול״ץ* From the Old French *solz*, which means "a mixture of vegetables."

NOTES

הָאִשָּׁה שֶׁכּוֹבֶשֶׁת If a woman was pickling. The issue under discussion in both Mishnayot is the subject of "handles of food." Ordinarily, only the edible portions of food can contract ritual impurity, but not the inedible portions, such as seed coverings or stems. In some cases, however, the inedible part of the food is used to hold on to the edible part. In such cases, the inedible part is called a "handle of food," and it, too, can contract ritual impurity. Sometimes these handles may even increase the food's volume to the minimum size liable to contract ritual impurity. The leaves of olives and of vegetables are generally regarded as handles that are subject to ritual impurity. If, however, the olives or the vegetables are pickled, the leaves are no longer firm enough to serve as handles for the food, and so they are no longer liable to ritual impurity. The subject of handles of foods is discussed primarily in the tractate *Uktzin*.

תְּלֵיסַר מְתִיבָתָא Thirteen academies. Elsewhere (*Berakhot* 20a), *Rashi* offers an alternative explanation, according to which Rabbah argues that in his day thirteen versions of tractate *Uktzin* were being studied — the version found in the Mishnah, as well as the different versions found in the collections of Baraitot transmitted by Rabbi Ḥiyya, Rabbi Oshaya, Bar Kappara, and others.

SAGES

רַב כָּהֲנָא בְּרֵיהּ דְּרַב נְחוּנְיָא **Rav Kahana the son of Rav Neḥunya.** This Sage is mentioned only here, and no teachings are transmitted in his name.

BACKGROUND

כּוּסְפָּא **A container.** Some scholars suggest that this word is derived from the Greek κάψα, *kapsa*, or its Latin cognate *capsa*, with the letters inverted, meaning "a vessel" or "a box." The Aramaic word *kuspa* can also be explained from other passages in the Talmud as the material that remains after the juice and moisture have been removed from fruit or seeds. Here this would refer to the residue from dates after liquor has been made from them.

TRANSLATION AND COMMENTARY

[1]**And we cry out** in prayer **all day** long, **and** still **there is no one who pays** any **attention to us!** [2]And if you are suggesting that my prayers have not been answered **on account of** some improper **deed** on my part, **if there is anyone who saw** me doing **something** wrong, **let him speak!** You see, then, that the fault is not mine. [3]**But what can the leaders of the generation do, when their generation is not deserving** of divine aid?"

רַב יְהוּדָה [4]The Gemara now reports an incident illustrating the power of Rav Yehudah's prayers. **Rav Yehudah** once **saw two people who were treating bread wastefully.** [5]Rav Yehudah **said** to himself: "Surely **it may be inferred from this** display of irreverence **that there is plenty in the world,** if people treat bread so disrespectfully." [6]**He looked angrily** upon the world, **and** soon **there was famine** across the land. [7]**The Rabbis said to Rav Kahana the son of Rav Neḥunya,** Rav Yehudah's **attendant:** [8]**"You, Sir, who are often found before** Rav Yehudah, **persuade him to leave** his house **by the door that is nearest the market,** so that he can see the effects of the famine that he has brought upon the world." [9]Rav Yehudah's attendant arranged for him to go out to the market, [10]where Rav Yehudah **saw** that **a crowd** had formed. [11]**He asked them: "What is** the purpose of **this** gathering?" [12]**They answered: "People are standing by a container of dates which are being sold** after all their juice has been pressed out." [13]Rav Yehudah **said** to himself: "Surely **it may be inferred from this** behavior **that there is** great **famine in the world."** [14]Immediately **he said to his attendant: "Take off my shoes,** for I wish to observe a fast, so that the famine may come to an end." [15]**He took off one shoe, and the rain** already began to **fall.** [16]**When** Rav Yehudah **was about to take off the other shoe,** the Prophet **Elijah came and said to him:** [17]**"The Holy One, blessed be He, says: 'If you take off the other shoe, I will destroy the world,** so that you suffer no further distress.'" [18]**Rav**

[1]וַאֲנַן קָא צָוְוחִינַן כּוּלֵּי יוֹמָא, וְלֵיכָּא דְּאַשְׁגַּח בַּן! [2]אִי מִשּׁוּם עוּבְדָא, אִי אִיכָּא דַּחֲזָא מִידִי, לֵימָא! [3]אֲבָל מָה יַעֲשׂוּ גְּדוֹלֵי הַדּוֹר, שֶׁאֵין דּוֹרָן דּוֹמֶה יָפֶה?" [4]רַב יְהוּדָה חֲזָא הָנְהוּ בֵּי תְּרֵי דְּהָווּ קָא פָּרְצִי בְּרִיפְתָּא, [5]אֲמַר: "שְׁמַע מִינָּהּ אִיכָּא שַׂבְעָא בְּעָלְמָא". [6]יְהַיב עֵינֵיהּ, הֲוָה כַּפְנָא. [7]אֲמַרוּ לֵיהּ רַבָּנַן לְרַב כָּהֲנָא בְּרֵיהּ דְּרַב נְחוּנְיָא שַׁמָּעֵיהּ: [8]"מָר, דִּשְׁכִיחַ קַמֵּיהּ, נִיעַשְׂיֵיהּ דְּלֵיפּוּק בְּפִתְחָא דִּסְמוּךְ לְשׁוּקָא". [9]עַשְׂיֵיהּ וּנְפַק לְשׁוּקָא. [10]חֲזָא כְּנוּפְיָא. [11]אֲמַר לְהוּ: "מַאי הַאי?" [12]אֲמַרוּ לֵיהּ: "אַכּוּסְפָּא דְּתַמְרֵי קָיְימֵי דְּקָא מִזְדַּבַּן". [13]אֲמַר: "שְׁמַע מִינָּהּ כַּפְנָא בְּעָלְמָא". [14]אֲמַר לֵיהּ לְשַׁמָּעֵיהּ: "שְׁלוֹף לִי מְסָאנַיי". [15]שְׁלַף לֵיהּ חַד מְסָאנָא, וַאֲתָא מִיטְרָא. [16]כִּי מְטָא לְמִישְׁלַף אַחֲרִינָא, אֲתָא אֵלִיָּהוּ וְאָמַר לֵיהּ: [17]"אָמַר הַקָּדוֹשׁ בָּרוּךְ הוּא: 'אִי שָׁלְפַתְּ אַחֲרִינָא, מַחֲרִיבְנָא לְעָלְמָא'". [18]אֲמַר רַב

LITERAL TRANSLATION

[1]and we cry out all day, and there is no one who pays attention to us! [2]If [this is] on account of deeds, if there is someone who saw something, let him speak! [3]But what can the leaders of the generation do, when their generation does not seem worthy?"

[4]Rav Yehudah saw two people who were treating bread wastefully, [5][and] he said: "Conclude from this [that] there is plenty in the world." [6]He looked angrily (lit., "he gave his eyes"), [and] there was famine. [7]The Rabbis said to Rav Kahana the son of Rav Neḥunya, his attendant: [8]"You, Sir, who are found often before him, cause him to go out through the door that is near the market." [9]He caused him [to do so] and he went out to the market. [10]He saw a crowd. [11]He said to them: "What is this?" [12]They said to him: "They are standing by a container of dates that is being sold." [13]He said: "Conclude from this [that] there is famine in the world." [14]He said to his attendant: "Take off my shoes for me." [15]He took off one shoe for him, and rain came. [16]When he was about to take off the other [shoe], Elijah came and said to him: [17]"The Holy One, blessed be He, said: 'If you take off the other [shoe], I will destroy the world.'" [18]Rav

RASHI

דחזא מידי — חס ושלום בעוודי ביש. **פרצי בריפתא** — זורקים אותם זה לזה. **ניעשייה** — יעשנו שילא לחוץ. **אכוספא דתמרי** — על כלי מלא תמרים, או פסולת של תמרים.

NOTES

נִיעַשְׂיֵיהּ דְּלֵיפּוּק **Cause him to go out.** Even though the Rabbis could have reported to Rav Yehudah about the famine, they wanted him to see for himself what was happening in the marketplace. When Rav Yehudah saw the effects of the famine, the Rabbis thought, he would surely petition God for mercy and ask that the famine come to an end (*Maharsha*).

מַחֲרִיבְנָא לְעָלְמָא **I will destroy the world.** Elsewhere this expression is used to express God's readiness to destroy the world so that a certain righteous man will not have to

TRANSLATION AND COMMENTARY

Mari the son of the daughter of Shmuel said: "At the time **I was standing on the bank of the Pappa River,** [1]**and I saw angels appearing as sailors who brought sand and loaded** it onto **boats, and it became fine flour.** [2]**Everyone came to buy** the flour, but I refused to allow the flour to be sold. [3]**I explained** to the potential buyers, saying: **'Do not buy this flour, for it is the product of miracles,** and we must avoid deriving material benefit from miracles.' [4]**The next day boats filled with wheat from Parzina came,** and the famine was brought to an end."

רָבָא אִיקְלַע [5]It was further related that **Rava** once **happened to come to** the town of **Hagrunya,** where there was a drought. [6]Rava **decreed a** public **fast** to petition God for mercy, **but the rain** still **did not come.** [7]At the end of the day, Rava **said to** the townspeople: **"Continue your fast overnight."** [8]**The next day he** gathered the townspeople together again, and **said to them: "Whoever had a dream** last night, **let him relate it** to us." [9]**Rabbi Elazar of Hagrunya said to them:** [10]"The following sentence **was read to me in my dream: 'Good greetings to a good master from a good Lord who in His goodness does good to His people.'"** Rava understood the dream as a message from Heaven that God was ready to end the drought, [11]and so **he said: "It may be inferred from this dream that it is** now **a favorable time to petition** God **for mercy."** [12]Rava immediately **petitioned** God **for mercy, and rain** soon began to **fall.**

הַהוּא גַּבְרָא [13]The Gemara continues with a story concerning **a certain man who had been sentenced to lashes in the court of Rava because he had had sexual intercourse with a non-Jewish woman.** [14]**Rava** ordered that the sinner be **flogged,** but the man was unable to bear his punishment **and died** as a result of the flogging. [15]**The matter became known in the House of King Shavor,** the Persian monarch,

מָרִי בְּרָהּ דְּבַת שְׁמוּאֵל: ״אֲנָא הֲוָה קָאֵימְנָא אַגּוּדָא דִּנְהַר פַּפָּא, [1]חֲזַאי לְמַלְאָכֵי דְּאִידַּמּוּ לְמַלָּחֵי דְּקָא מַיְיתֵי חָלָא וּמָלוּנְהוּ לְאַרְבֵּי, וַהֲוָה קִמְחָא דִּסְמִידָא. [2]אָתוּ כּוּלֵּי עָלְמָא לְמִיזְבַּן. [3]אֲמִינָא לְהוּ: ׳מֵהָא לָא תִּיזְבְּנוּן, דְּמַעֲשֵׂה נִסִּים הוּא׳. [4]לְמָחָר אָתְיָין אַרְבֵּי דְּחִיטֵּי דְּפָרְזִינָא״.

[5]רָבָא אִיקְלַע לְהַגְרוּנְיָא. [6]גְּזַר תַּעֲנִיתָא, וְלָא אֲתָא מִיטְרָא. [7]אֲמַר לְהוּ: ״בִּיתוּ כּוּלֵּי עָלְמָא בְּתַעֲנִיתַיְיכוּ״. [8]לְמָחָר אֲמַר לְהוּ: ״מִי אִיכָּא דַּחֲזָא חֶילְמָא, לֵימָא״. [9]אֲמַר לְהוּ רַבִּי אֶלְעָזָר מֵהַגְרוּנְיָא: [10]״לְדִידִי אַקְרִיוּן בְּחֶלְמִי: ׳שְׁלָם טַב לְרַב טַב מֵרִיבּוֹן טַב דְּמִטּוּבֵיהּ מֵטִיב לְעַמֵּיהּ׳״. [11]אֲמַר: ״שְׁמַע מִינָּהּ עֵת רָצוֹן הִיא מִבָּעֵי רַחֲמֵי״. [12]בָּעֵי רַחֲמֵי, וְאָתֵי מִיטְרָא.

[13]הַהוּא גַּבְרָא דְּאִיחַיַּיב נַגְדָּא בְּבֵי דִּינָא דְּרָבָא מִשּׁוּם דְּבְעַל נָכְרִית. [14]נַגְדֵּיהּ רָבָא וּמִית. [15]אִשְׁתַּמַּע מִילְּתָא בֵּי שָׁבוֹר

LITERAL TRANSLATION

Mari the son of the daughter of Shmuel said: "I was standing on the bank of the Pappa River, [1][and] I saw angels who looked like sailors bringing sand and loading boats, and it became fine flour. [2]Everyone (lit., 'the whole world') came to buy. [3]I said to them: 'Do not buy from this, for it is the product of miracles. [4]The next day boats of wheat from Parzina came."

[5]Rava happened to come to Hagrunya. [6]He decreed a fast, but rain did not come. [7]He said to them: "Continue your fast, all of you, overnight." [8]The next day he said to them: "Whoever saw a dream, let him tell [it]." [9]Rabbi Elazar of Hagrunya said to them: [10]"They read to me in my dream: 'Good greetings to a good master from a good Lord who in His goodness does good to His people.'" [11]He said: "Conclude from this [that] it is a favorable time to petition for mercy." [12]He petitioned for mercy, and rain came.

[13][There was] a certain man who had been sentenced to lashes in the court of Rava because he had had sexual intercourse with a non-Jewish woman. [14]Rava caused him to be flogged and he died. [15]The matter was heard in the House of King Shavor,

RASHI

קאימנא אנהר פפא — ההוא יומא דעבד רב יהודה הכי. **חלא** — חול. **דסמידא** = סולת, והן עצמן מוכרין אותו. **אמר להו מעשה נסים כו׳** — וכמה דאפשר להתרחק ממעשה נסים — יותר טוב ונכון. **דפרזינא** — מקום. **אקרון** = הקרוני, הייתי קורא בחלומי. **נגדא - מלקות.**

SAGES

רַב מָרִי בְּרָהּ דְּבַת שְׁמוּאֵל Rav Mari the son of the daughter of Shmuel. A fourth-generation Babylonian Amora, Rav Mari's father was a non-Jew named Issur who married (or had relations with) Rachel, the daughter of the Amora Shmuel. Later, however, this Issur converted to Judaism. But since Issur converted while Rav Mari's mother was pregnant with him, Rav Mari is generally mentioned without a patronymic, and is instead called "Rav Mari the son of Raḥel." Rav Mari was a pious Torah scholar, and he cited the teachings of various scholars. He had business connections with Rava, with whom he was friendly. Rava also appointed him to serve as one of the leaders of the Jewish community in Babylonia. Rav Mari had two sons, Mar Zutra (see *Bava Metzia,* Part III, p. 171) and Rav Ada Sava, who were also Sages.

רַבִּי אֶלְעָזָר מֵהַגְרוּנְיָא Rabbi Elazar of Hagrunya. A Babylonian Amora of the fifth generation, Rabbi Elazar was a student of Rava. Stories about him and his Torah teachings are mentioned in several places in the Babylonian Talmud.

NOTES

suffer from its continued existence. Here the meaning of the expression is not so clear. *Maharsha* (see also *Rabbenu Elyakim*) suggests that God threatened to destroy the world because of Rav Yehudah's repeated requests, first to bring famine, and later to bring plenty to the world. If Rav Yehudah was not satisfied with the rain that had already begun to fall as soon as he took off his first shoe, God would destroy the world by inundating it with excessive rain.

PEOPLE

אִיפְרָא הוּרְמִיז Ifra Hurmiz. She was a Persian queen, the mother of Shapur II (309-379 C.E.). Since Shapur was crowned when he was born, his mother had great influence on him for many years. Ifra Hurmiz is mentioned several times in the Talmud as an admirer of Judaism and of the Sages, even giving money to some of the Sages to distribute as charity and in the performance of good deeds.

TRANSLATION AND COMMENTARY

and at first **he wished to punish Rava** for imposing a punishment that had led to the offender's death, although Rava had not been authorized by the royal house to impose capital punishment. [1] **Ifra Hurmiz, the mother of King Shavor, said to her son,** the king: [2] **"Do not** even contemplate punishing Rava or **enter into a confrontation with the Jews, for whatever they ask of their Master** in Heaven, **He gives them."** [3] King Shavor **said to** his mother: **"What is** it **that** that God grants them?" [4] Ifra Hurmiz explained to her son: **"They petition** Him **for mercy** whenever there is a shortage of rain, **and** the **rain** begins to **fall** shortly thereafter." [5] The king **said to** his mother: "That is only **because it is** then **the** proper **time for the rain** to fall. [6] **Rather,** if you wish to prove that God answers the prayers of the Jews, **let them petition** Him **for mercy now, in the summer, and let the rain come."** [7] Ifra Hurmiz then **sent** a message **to Rava,** saying: **"Direct your attention** to Heaven, **and petition** God **for mercy, so that rain will fall** now, even though it is the middle of the summer." [8] Rava immediately **petitioned** God **for** rain, but his prayers were not answered and rain did not fall. [9] Rava then said before God: "Master of the Universe! [10] The Psalmist says [Psalms 44:2]: **'We have heard with our ears, O God, our fathers have told us, what work You did in their days, in days of old.'** [11] **But with our** own **eyes we have not seen** any of your wonders. Send us rain now, so that we too may witness your miracles." [12] As soon as he finished his prayer, a heavy **rain** began to **fall, until** the water rushing through **the gutters of Meḥoza overflowed and poured into the Tigris** River. [13] Rava's **father came and appeared to him in a dream, and said to him:** [14] **"Is there anyone who puts Heaven to so much trouble,** asking for rain during the dry summer months?" [15] Rava's father then **said to him: "Change the place** where you sleep tonight." [16] Rava heeded his father's advice and **changed the place** where he slept that night.

מַלְכָּא, בְּעָא לְצַעוּרֵי לְרָבָא. [1] אֲמַרָה לֵיהּ אִיפְרָא הוּרְמִיז, אִימֵּיהּ דְּשָׁבוֹר מַלְכָּא, לִבְרָהּ: [2] "לָא לֶיהֱוֵי לָךְ עֵסֶק דְּבָרִים בַּהֲדֵי יְהוּדָאֵי, דְּכָל מַאן דְּבָעֲיָין מִמָּרַיְיהוּ, יָהֵיב לְהוּ". [3] אֲמַר לָהּ: "מַאי הִיא?" [4] "בָּעֲיַן רַחֲמֵי וְאָתֵי מִיטְרָא". [5] אֲמַר לָהּ: "הַהוּא מִשּׁוּם דְּזִימְנָא דְּמִיטְרָא הוּא. [6] אֶלָּא לִבָּעוּ רַחֲמֵי הָאִידָּנָא, בִּתְקוּפַת תַּמּוּז, וְלֵיתֵי מִיטְרָא". [7] שְׁלָחָה לֵיהּ לְרָבָא: "כַּוֵּין דַּעְתָּךְ, וּבְעֵי רַחֲמֵי דְּלֵיתֵי מִיטְרָא". [8] בָּעֵי רַחֲמֵי, וְלָא אָתֵי מִיטְרָא. [9] אָמַר לְפָנָיו: "רִבּוֹנוֹ שֶׁל עוֹלָם! [10] 'אֱלֹהִים, בְּאָזְנֵינוּ שָׁמַעְנוּ, אֲבוֹתֵינוּ סִפְּרוּ לָנוּ, פֹּעַל פָּעַלְתָּ בִימֵיהֶם, בִּימֵי קֶדֶם', [11] וְאָנוּ בְּעֵינֵינוּ לֹא רָאִינוּ". [12] אֲתָא מִיטְרָא עַד דִּשְׁפוּךְ מַרְזְבֵי דִמְחוֹזָא לְדִיגְלַת. [13] אֲתָא אֲבוּהּ אִיתְחֲזִי לֵיהּ בְּחֶלְמֵיהּ, וַאֲמַר לֵיהּ: [14] "מִי אִיכָּא דְּמִיטְרַח קַמֵּי שְׁמַיָּא כּוּלֵּי הַאי?" [15] אֲמַר לֵיהּ: "שַׁנֵּי דּוּכְתִּיךְ". [16] שַׁנֵּי דּוּכְתֵּיהּ.

LITERAL TRANSLATION

[and] he wished to cause Rava distress. [1] Ifra Hurmiz, the mother of King Shavor, said to her son: [2] "Do not have a confrontation with the Jews, for whatever they ask of their Master, He gives them." [3] He said to her: "What is that?" [4] "They petition for mercy and rain comes." [5] He said to her: "That is because it is the time for rain. [6] Rather, let them petition for mercy now, in the summer (lit., 'the season of Tammuz'), and let rain come." [7] She sent to Rava: "Direct your attention, and petition for mercy that rain should come." [8] He petitioned for rain, but rain did not come. [9] He said before Him: "Master of the Universe! [10] 'We have heard with our ears, O God, our fathers have told us, what work You did in their days, in days of old,' [11] but we with our eyes have not seen [anything]." [12] Rain came until the gutters of Meḥoza poured into the Tigris. [13] His father came [and] appeared to him in a dream, [and] said to him: [14] "Is there anyone who puts Heaven to so much trouble?" [15] He said to him: "Change your place." [16] He changed his place.

RASHI

איפרא הורמיז — כך שמה, איפרא — חן יופי שדים היה לה. **מאי היא** — מאי עביד להו. **אמרה ליה** — דכל אימת דבעי מיטרא. **זימנא דמיטרא הוא** — ואפילו לא בעו — נמי אתי מיטרא. **שלחה ליה לרבא** — דרמשא ליה לרבא. **אבותינו ספרו לנו פועל פעלת בימיהם בימי קדם** — שהיית מפליא להם נסים. **עד דשפיך מרזבי דציפורי** — שקילחו מים מן המרזיבות, עד ששוטפין בחוצות ויורדין ושופכין. **לדיגלת** — לנהר חדקל. **אשני מטתך** — אל תשכב במטתך הלילה.

NOTES

שַׁנֵּי דּוּכְתִּיךְ Change your place. The destructive forces unleashed by God are restricted in activity to a particular place. Thus a person against whom a divine decree has been issued is safe from harm if he moves to a different place (see *Maharsha*).

TRANSLATION AND COMMENTARY

[1]**The next morning he discovered that,** during the night, **his bed had been slashed by knives,** and that it was only because he had slept elsewhere that his life had been saved.

רַב פַּפָּא [2]It was further related that **Rav Pappa** once **decreed a** public **fast** on account of drought, **but rain did not fall.** [3]Rav Pappa did not fast well, and **his heart became weak** from hunger. Unable to continue his fast, Rav Pappa **swallowed a bowl of cereal.** Having regained his strength, [4]he **petitioned** God **for mercy, but rain** still **did not come.** [5]**Rav Naḥman bar Ushpazti** mockingly **said to him:** "Perhaps **if you swallow another bowl of cereal,** your prayers will be answered, and **rain will fall."** Rav Naḥman purposely sought to embarrass Rav Pappa, in the hope that God would hear Rav Pappa's prayers when He saw his suffering. [6]Indeed, Rav Pappa **was** greatly **embarrassed and distressed** by Rav Naḥman's comment, **and it** soon **began to rain.**

רַבִּי חֲנִינָא בֶּן דּוֹסָא [7]The Gemara now cites another anecdote relating to prayers for rain. **Rabbi Ḥanina ben Dosa was** once **walking along a road when it began to rain.** [8]**He said to** God: **"Master of the Universe!** [9]Is it right that **the entire world should be at ease and** only **Ḥanina**, who happens to be out on the road in the rain, **should be in distress?"** [10]Immediately **the rain stopped** falling. Rabbi Ḥanina ben Dosa continued his journey and [11]**when he arrived at his house, he said** to God: **"Master of the Universe!** [12]Is it right that **the entire world should be in distress** and in need of rain, [13]**and** only **Ḥanina,** who does not need the rain because he has no fields of his own, **should be** resting in his home **at ease?"** [14]Immediately **the rain** began to **fall.**

[1]לְמָחָר אַשְׁכְּחֵיהּ דִּמְרַשַּׁם פּוּרְיֵיהּ בְּסַכִּינֵי.
[2]רַב פַּפָּא גְּזַר תַּעֲנִיתָא, וְלָא אֲתָא מִיטְרָא. [3]חֲלַשׁ לִיבֵּיהּ, שְׂרַף פִּינְכָּא דְּדַיְיסָא, [4]וּבָעֵי רַחֲמֵי, וְלָא אֲתָא מִיטְרָא. [5]אֲמַר לֵיהּ רַב נַחְמָן בַּר אוּשְׁפַּזְתִּי: "אִי שָׂרֵיף מָר פִּינְכָּא אַחֲרִיתִי דְּדַיְיסָא, אָתֵי מִיטְרָא". [6]אִיכְסִיף וַחֲלַשׁ דַּעְתֵּיהּ, וַאֲתָא מִיטְרָא.
[7]רַבִּי חֲנִינָא בֶּן דּוֹסָא הֲוָה קָא אָזֵיל בְּאוֹרְחָא אֲתָא מִיטְרָא. [8]אָמַר לְפָנָיו: "רִבּוֹנוֹ שֶׁל עוֹלָם! [9]כָּל הָעוֹלָם כּוּלּוֹ בְּנַחַת, וַחֲנִינָא בְּצַעַר"? [10]פָּסַק מִיטְרָא. [11]כִּי מְטָא לְבֵיתֵיהּ, אָמַר לְפָנָיו: "רִבּוֹנוֹ שֶׁל עוֹלָם! [12]כָּל הָעוֹלָם כּוּלּוֹ בְּצַעַר, [13]וַחֲנִינָא בְּנַחַת"? [14]אֲתָא מִיטְרָא.

LITERAL TRANSLATION

[1]The next day he found that his bed had been slashed by knives.
[2]Rav Pappa decreed a fast, but rain did not come. [3]His heart became weak, he swallowed a bowl of cereal, [4]and petitioned for mercy, but rain did not come. [5]Rav Naḥman bar Ushpazti said to him: "If, Sir, you swallow another bowl of cereal, rain will come." [6]He was embarrassed and distressed, and rain came.
[7]Rabbi Ḥanina ben Dosa was walking along a road [when] rain came. [8]He said before Him: "Master of the Universe! [9]The whole world is at ease, and Ḥanina is in distress?" [10]The rain stopped. [11]When he came to his house, he said before Him: "Master of the Universe! [12]The whole world is in distress, [13]and Ḥanina is at ease?" [14]Rain came.

RASHI

בסכיני — שרצו שדים להורגו, וחתכו את מטתו. והיינו דאמרינן בשחיטת חולין בפרק "הזרוע" (קלג, א) וליקריוה לרבא? רבא נזוף היה. לא מצינו לו נזיפה בכל התלמוד אלא בזה המעשה, כשביקש הגשמים בתמוז שלא לצורך. הכי גרסינן — **רב פפא גזר תעניתא** חלש לביה טעים מידי בעא רחמי ולא אתא מיטרא. **אי שריף מר חדא פינכא דדייסא** — מלשון "שורפה חיה" (עבודה זרה כט,ב). פינכא — מלא כף, כמו מלחיך פינכי (פסחים מט,א). דייסא = *טריי"ס בלעז. ולחוכא קאמר ליה הכי, משום דטעים ברישא והדר בעא רחמי. **רבי חנינא בן דוסא** — תנא הוא. **כל העולם כולו בצער** — שמבקשין מים לשדותיהן. **בנחת** — שאני יושב בביתי, ואיני צריך לגשמים, לפי שאין לי שדות.

LANGUAGE

שָׂרַף Swallowed. This verb means "to suck" or "to sip" something. It is related to the Arabic root meaning "to drink."

פִּינְכָּא Bowl. This word is possibly derived from the Greek πίναξ, *pinax*, which means, among other things, "a large bowl."

LANGUAGE (RASHI)

טריי"ס* From the Old French *trejes,* which means "crushed or pounded grains."

SAGES

רַב נַחְמָן בַּר אוּשְׁפַּזְתִּי Rav Naḥman bar Ushpazti. There is an alternative reading, רַב נַחְמָן בַּר אוּשְׁפַּרְתִּי — "Rav Naḥman bar Ushparti." According to *Arukh,* Ushparti was the name of Rav Pappa's mother. Thus Rav Naḥman was his half-brother on his mother's side, and it is therefore understandable that he would permit himself to speak to Rav Pappa so disparagingly. No Torah teachings are mentioned in his name.

רַבִּי חֲנִינָא בֶּן דּוֹסָא Rabbi Ḥanina ben Dosa. A Tanna who lived at the end of the Second Temple period. Rabbi Ḥanina ben Dosa was a disciple and colleague of Rabban Yoḥanan ben Zakkai. Even while still a student he was known for his righteousness, and for his powers as a בַּעַל מַעֲשִׂים — lit., "master of deeds," that is, a miracle-worker. Only very few of his Torah teachings have been preserved, mainly in the area of Aggadah, and he is known for the many stories told of his piety, righteousness, and asceticism. For generations he served as a model of the perfectly righteous man.

NOTES

אִי שָׂרֵיף מָר פִּינְכָּא אַחֲרִיתִי If, Sir, you swallow another bowl. Rav Pappa was justified in breaking his fast, for a person who takes ill while fasting is permitted to eat. But Rav Naḥman reproached Rav Pappa for breaking his fast before praying for rain, because he felt that Rav Pappa should not have eaten until after he had prayed (*Rashi*). *Maharsha* suggests that Rav Naḥman mocked Rav Pappa for swallowing a whole bowl of cereal. Rav Pappa should have taken the food in small quantities, thus violating the fast as little as possible.

וַחֲנִינָא בְּנַחַת And Ḥanina is at ease. Our commentary follows *Rashi*, who explains that Rabbi Ḥanina was not troubled with the absence of rain, because he himself did not own any fields. But *Shittah* points out that even those who do not own their own fields should be distressed when there is a shortage of rain, for they too will feel the results of the drought when the food shortage raises prices. Rather, Rabbi Ḥanina was not troubled when it did not rain, because he was accustomed to maintaining himself on a *kav* of carobs per week (as will be explained below), and so the drought had little effect on him.

LITERAL TRANSLATION

[1]Rav Yosef said: What good was the prayer of the High Priest with respect to Rabbi Ḥanina ben Dosa? [2]For we have learned: "He would offer a short prayer in the outer room." [3]What would he pray? [4]Ravin bar Adda and Rava bar Adda both said in the name of Rav Yehudah: [5]"May it be Your will, O Lord, our God, that this year be rainy and hot." [6]Is heat an advantage? [7]On the contrary, it is a disadvantage! [8]Rather: "If it is hot, let it be rainy and moist with dew." [9]"And let the prayer of travelers not enter before You." [10]Rav Aḥa the son of Rava concluded in the name of Rav Yehudah: [11]"Let rulership not pass from the House of Judah, [12]and let Your people Israel not have to be supported by one another, nor by another people."
[13]Rav Yehudah said in the name of Rav:

[1]אָמַר רַב יוֹסֵף: מַאי אַהֲנְיָא לֵיהּ צְלוֹתָא דְּכֹהֵן גָּדוֹל לְגַבֵּי רַבִּי חֲנִינָא בֶּן דּוֹסָא? [2]דִּתְנַן: "הָיָה מִתְפַּלֵּל תְּפִלָּה קְצָרָה בַּבַּיִת הַחִיצוֹן". [3]מַאי מְצַלֵּי? [4]רָבִין בַּר אַדָּא וְרָבָא בַּר אַדָּא דְּאָמְרִי תַּרְוַיְיהוּ מִשְּׁמֵיהּ דְּרַב יְהוּדָה: [5]"יְהִי רָצוֹן מִלְּפָנֶיךָ, ה' אֱלֹהֵינוּ, שֶׁתְּהֵא הַשָּׁנָה הַזּוֹ גְּשׁוּמָה וּשְׁחוּנָה". [6]שְׁחוּנָה מַעַלְיָיתָא הִיא? [7]אַדְּרַבָּה, גְּרִיעוּתָא הִיא! [8]אֶלָּא: "אִם שְׁחוּנָה, תְּהֵא גְּשׁוּמָה וּטְלוּלָה". [9]"וְאַל יִכָּנֵס לְפָנֶיךָ תְּפִלַּת עוֹבְרֵי דְרָכִים". [10]רַב אַחָא בְּרֵיהּ דְּרָבָא מְסַיֵּים מִשְּׁמֵיהּ דְּרַב יְהוּדָה: [11]"לֹא יַעֲדֵי עָבֵיד שׁוּלְטָן מִדְּבֵית יְהוּדָה, [12]וְאַל יְהוּ עַמְּךָ יִשְׂרָאֵל צְרִיכִין לְהִתְפַּרְנֵס זֶה מִזֶּה, וְלֹא לְעַם אַחֵר".
[13]אָמַר רַב יְהוּדָה אָמַר רַב:

TRANSLATION AND COMMENTARY

אָמַר רַב יוֹסֵף [1]Commenting on this story, **Rav Yosef said: What good was the prayer of the High Priest,** which he offered after he left the Holy of Holies on Yom Kippur, **with respect to Rabbi Ḥanina ben Dosa,** for we have seen that Rabbi Ḥanina ben Dosa had the power to cancel the High Priest's prayer? [2]**For we have learned** in the Mishnah (*Yoma* 52b): "After the High Priest left the Holy of Holies on Yom Kippur, **he would offer a short prayer in the outer room** of the Sanctuary.'" [3]The Gemara asks: **What would** the High Priest **pray?** [4]**Ravin bar Adda and Rava bar Adda both said in the name of Rav Yehudah:** The High Priest would say: [5]**"May it be Your will, O Lord, our God, that this year be rainy and hot."** [6]The Gemara questions this formulation: **Is a hot year** so **advantageous** that the High Priest would request it before God on the holiest day of the year, Yom Kippur? [7]**On the contrary,** a hot year **is** highly **detrimental** to a successful crop! [8]**Rather,** the High Priest would say as follows: **"If** the coming year **is** to be extremely **hot,** then **let** the year first **be rainy and moist with dew."** [9]The High Priest would also put forward a second request: **"And let the prayers of travelers not enter before You."** Do not hearken to the prayers of travelers asking that it stop raining, for the benefit derived from the rain by the community as a whole must take precedence over the comfort of those who travel the roads. [10]**Rav Aḥa the son of Rava** reported **in the name of Rav Yehudah** that the High Priest's prayer **concluded** as follows: [11]**"Let rulership not pass from the House of Judah** [see Genesis 49:10], but rather let leadership over the Jewish community both in Eretz Israel and abroad remain in the hands of the descendants of the House of David. [12]**And let Your people Israel not have to be supported** through charity given to **one by another, or,** even worse, **by another people."** Even though the High Priest would pray to God not to heed the prayers of travelers who ask that it not rain, God indeed answered such a prayer when it was offered by Rabbi Ḥanina ben Dosa.

אָמַר רַב יְהוּדָה [13]Having mentioned Rabbi Ḥanina ben Dosa, the Gemara now continues with a series of stories about that righteous Sage: **Rav Yehudah said in the name of Rav: Each and every day**

SAGES

רָבִין בַּר אַדָּא וְרָבָא בַּר אַדָּא **Ravin bar Adda and Rava bar Adda.** These Sages were brothers, Babylonian Amoraim of the third generation. They were disciples of Rav Yehudah, and they report teachings in his name and in that of his teacher, Rav. They are often quoted together, but they are also mentioned separately in various places in the Babylonian Talmud.

רַב אַחָא בְּרֵיהּ דְּרָבָא **Rav Aḥa the son of Rava.** A Babylonian Amora of the sixth generation (not related to the famous Amora, Rava), Rav Aḥa the son of Rava was a colleague of Rav Ashi and of Ravina. Like them, he was a disciple of Rav Kahana. Rav Aḥa the son of Rava is cited frequently in the Talmud in discussion with Rav Ashi and Ravina. Wherever the Talmud states that "Rav Aḥa" disagrees with Ravina, the commentators assume that it is Rav Aḥa the son of Rava.

RASHI

מאי אהניא ליה צלותיה דכהן גדול – כשהיה מתפלל תפלה קצרה ביום הכפורים שהיה אומר: אל יכנס לפניך תפלת עוברי דרכים, דרבי חנינא מבטל ליה לצלותיה דכהן גדול. שאף על פי כן שמע הקדוש ברוך הוא תפלתו ופסיק מיטרא. **שחונה** = חמה, כמו "חמותי ראיתי אור" (ישעיהו מד), תירגם יונתן בן עוזיאל: שחינת. **אם שחונה תהא גשומה** – כשהיא חמה צריכה הארץ לגשמים מאד ותדיר.

HALAKHAH

צְלוֹתָא דְּכֹהֵן גָּדוֹל **The prayer of the High Priest.** "After he left the Holy of Holies on Yom Kippur, the High Priest would offer a short prayer in the outer chamber of the Temple, saying: 'May it be Your will that if this year be hot, it will also be rainy. And do not allow rulership to pass from the House of Judah. And let not Your people Israel be in need of support. And let not the prayers of travelers enter before You." (*Rambam, Sefer Avodah, Hilkhot Avodat Yom HaKippurim* 4:1.)

TRANSLATION AND COMMENTARY

voice goes forth and says: **"The entire world is maintained because of the merits of Ḥanina** ben Dosa, **My son,** [1]**and Ḥanina** ben Dosa, **My son,** himself **manages with** a minimal amount of food, maintaining himself on **a *kav* of carobs from one Friday to the next Friday."** [2]It was related that Rabbi Ḥanina ben Dosa's **wife was accustomed to heat** up **the oven** in her house **every Friday, and to cast something into** it **that raised** a great deal of **smoke,** to give her neighbors the impression that she was busy baking. [25A] [3]She acted in this manner **out of embarrassment,** for she did not want her neighbors to know that there was no bread in her house. [4]But **she had a certain evil neighbor, who said** to herself: [5]**"Now, I know that they do not have anything** to eat. [6]**What,** then, is the meaning of **all this** smoke rising from her oven?" [7]So **she went and knocked on** her neighbor's **door** to find out what was happening in her house. [8]Rabbi Ḥanina ben Dosa's wife **was** greatly **embarrassed** when she saw her neighbor standing at her door, **and she** immediately **fled into an inner room** of the house. [9]But **a miracle was performed on her behalf, for** her neighbor **saw the oven full of bread, and the kneading basin** similarly **full of dough.** [10]The neighbor **called** out **to** Rabbi Ḥanina ben Dosa's wife: **"So-and-so! So-and-so!** [11]**Bring the shovel** for taking bread out of the oven, **for your bread is getting burnt."** [12]Rabbi Ḥanina ben Dosa's wife returned to the room with the shovel in her hand, and **said to her** neighbor: **"I went inside for that** very purpose." [13]The Gemara now cites a Baraita referring to this incident, in which **it was taught: "Indeed,** Rabbi Ḥanina ben Dosa's wife **had gone in to bring a shovel** to remove the bread from the oven, [14]**for she was accustomed to miracles**, and expected divine intervention to save her from embarrassment."

אֲמָרָה לֵיהּ דְּבֵיתְהוּ [15]It was further related that Rabbi Ḥanina ben Dosa's **wife** once **said to** her husband: "How much longer must we continue to suffer such distress and poverty?" Rabbi Ḥanina ben Dosa **responded:**

בְּכָל יוֹם וָיוֹם בַּת קוֹל יוֹצֵאת וְאוֹמֶרֶת: ״כָּל הָעוֹלָם כּוּלּוֹ נִיזּוֹן בִּשְׁבִיל חֲנִינָא בְּנִי, [1]וַחֲנִינָא בְּנִי דַּיּוֹ בְּקַב חֲרוּבִים מֵעֶרֶב שַׁבָּת לְעֶרֶב שַׁבָּת״. [2]הֲוָה רְגִילָא דְּבֵיתְהוּ לְמֵיחֲמָא תַּנּוּרָא כָּל מַעֲלֵי דְּשַׁבְּתָא וְשָׁדְיָיא אַקְטַרְתָּא, [25A] [3]מִשּׁוּם כִּיסּוּפָא. [4]הֲוָה לָהּ הָךְ שִׁיבַבְתָּא בִּישְׁתָּא, אֲמָרָה: [5]״מִכְּדִי יָדַעֲנָא דְּלֵית לְהוּ וְלָא מִידִי. [6]מַאי כּוּלֵּי הַאי?״ [7]אָזְלָא וְטָרְפָא אַבָּבָא. [8]אִיכְסְפָא וְעַיְילָא לְאִינְדְּרוֹנָא. [9]אִיתְעֲבִיד לָהּ נִסָּא דְּחָזְיָא לְתַנּוּרָא מְלֵא לַחְמָא וְאַגָּנָא מְלֵא לִישָׁא. [10]אֲמָרָה לָהּ: ״פְּלָנִיתָא, פְּלָנִיתָא! [11]אַיְיתֵי מַסָּא, דְּקָא חָרִיךְ לַחְמִיךְ״. [12]אֲמָרָה לָהּ: ״אַף אֲנָא לְהָכִי עָיְילִי״. [13]תָּנָא: ״אַף הִיא לְהָבִיא מַרְדֶּה נִכְנְסָה, [14]מִפְּנֵי שֶׁמְּלוּמֶּדֶת בְּנִסִּים״. [15]אֲמָרָה לֵיהּ דְּבֵיתְהוּ: ״עַד אֵימַת נֵיזִיל וְנִצְטַעֵר כּוּלֵּי הַאי?״ אֲמַר לָהּ: ״מַאי

LITERAL TRANSLATION

Each and every day a [heavenly] voice goes forth and says: "The whole world is maintained for the sake of Ḥanina, My son, [1]and Ḥanina, My son, suffices with a *kav* of carobs from [one] Friday to [the next] Friday." [2]His wife was accustomed to heat the oven every Friday, and to cast [in] something that raises smoke, [25A] [3]because of embarrassment. [4]She had a certain evil neighbor, [who] said: [5]"Now I know that they do not have anything. [6]What is all this?" [7]She went and knocked on the door. [8]She was embarrassed and went into an inner room. [9]A miracle was performed for her that she [the neighbor] saw the oven full of bread and the kneading basin full of dough. [10]She said to her: "So-and-so! So-and-so! [11]Bring the shovel, for your bread is burning." [12]She said to her: "I too went in for that." [13][A Tanna] taught: "She too went in to bring a shovel, [14]for she was accustomed to miracles." [15]His wife said to him: "Until when shall we continue to suffer so?" He said to her: "What

RASHI

בת קול יוצאת ואומרת כל העולם כולו — ולא גרסינן מהר חורב. **קב חרובים מערב שבת לערב שבת** — כל השבת היה ניזון בכך. חסר לחם היה, ומתגלגל היה בחרובין. **אקטרתא** — דבר שמעלה עשן כקיטור הכבשן. **משום כיסופא** — שהיו שכינותיה אופות עיסה לכבוד שבת, והיא אינה עושה כלום. **אגנא** = עריבה. **מסא** — עתר שמוליאין בו הלחם, מרדה פאלי״א בלעז ומרדה ומסא חדא מילתא היא. **תנא אף היא להביא מרדה נכנסה** — *פל״א בלעז. על שם שרודין בה פת מן התנור. שלא היתה שואלת מפני שרגילה בניסין.

NOTES

בְּכָל יוֹם וָיוֹם בַּת קוֹל **Each and every day a heavenly voice.** Elsewhere (*Ḥullin* 86a), *Rashi* explains that this heavenly voice announcing that the entire world was being maintained on account of the merits of Rabbi Ḥanina ben Dosa issued forth each and every day during the lifetime of that Sage (see also *Maharsha*). *Rabbi Ya'akov Emden* suggests that a similar heavenly voice goes forth each and every day all the time, for there is in each and every generation a certain person whose merits sustain the entire world.

BACKGROUND

קַב חֲרוּבִים A *kav* of carobs. This means that Rabbi Ḥanina ben Dosa was so poor that he did not always have bread to eat, but subsisted on small amounts of carobs, which were usually used as animal fodder. Carobs are highly nutritious, being rich in sugar and protein.

LANGUAGE

אִינְדְּרוֹנָא An inner room. This word is apparently derived from the Persian *andrun,* meaning "the contents of a room"; hence in Aramaic it means "an inner room."

LANGUAGE (RASHI)

***פאלי״א, פל״א** From the Old French *pele,* which means "spade" or "winnowing shovel."

BACKGROUND

דְּמֵיהַב יָהֲבִי That they in Heaven give. As explained in the Talmud, when God decrees something good for a person, this is an unconditional gift, and endures in any event. But here, even though a gift was given to Rabbi Ḥanina ben Dosa from Heaven, nevertheless it was taken back (*Maharsha*).

TRANSLATION AND COMMENTARY

"What do you suggest that **we do?"** [1]His wife answered: **"Petition** God **for mercy, so that you may be given some** of the bounty that is being saved for the righteous in the World-to-Come." [2]Rabbi Ḥanina ben Dosa acceded to his wife's request, and **petitioned** God **for mercy.** [3]**Something like the palm of a hand** miraculously **emerged, and** Rabbi Ḥanina ben Dosa **was given one leg of a golden table.** [4]That night his wife **saw in a dream that the righteous are destined to eat** in the World-to-Come **at a golden table with three legs,** [5]**whereas** her husband **would eat at a table with** only **two legs.** [6]After being told the dream, Rabbi Ḥanina ben Dosa **said to** his wife: "Surely this means that the table leg that I was given was taken from the table being reserved for me in the World-to-Come! **Is it your wish that everyone** else **will eat at a table that is whole,** [7]**and we** alone will eat **at a table that is defective."** [8]**She said to him: "So what shall we do** to remedy the situation? [9]Obviously, you must at once **petition** God **for mercy** and ask that the table leg **be taken from you,** so that it may be restored to the table waiting for you in the World-to-Come." [10]Rabbi Ḥanina petitioned God for mercy and the table leg was taken from him. [11]A Tanna taught a Baraita relating to this incident, which stated: "The **latter miracle** causing the table leg to be taken from Rabbi Ḥanina ben Dosa **was greater than the first miracle** causing it to be given to him in the first place." [12]The Gemara explains: **For we have a tradition that** gifts from Heaven **are** sometimes **given but are never taken back.**

חַד בֵּי שִׁמְשֵׁי [13]The Gemara now relates that **one Shabbat Eve at twilight,** after Shabbat had already begun, Rabbi Ḥanina ben Dosa **noticed that his daughter was sad.** [14]**He asked her: "My daughter, why are you sad?"** [15]**She explained to him: "I confused a utensil** filled **with vinegar with a utensil** filled **with oil,**

נַעֲבֵיד?״ [1]״בְּעֵי רַחֲמֵי דְּנֵיתְבוּ לָךְ מִידֵּי״. [2]בְּעָא רַחֲמֵי, [3]יָצְתָה כְּמִין פִּיסַּת יָד וְיָהֲבוּ לֵיהּ חַד כַּרְעָא דִּפְתוֹרָא דְּדַהֲבָא. [4]חֲזְיָא בְּחֶלְמָא עֲתִידִי צַדִּיקֵי דְּאָכְלִי אַפְּתוֹרָא דְּדַהֲבָא דְּאִית לֵיהּ תְּלָת כַּרְעֵי, [5]וְאִיהוּ אַפְּתוֹרָא דִּתְרֵי כַּרְעֵי. [6]אֲמַר לָהּ: ״נִיחָא לָךְ דְּמֵיכָל אָכְלִי כּוּלֵּי עָלְמָא אַפְּתוֹרָא דְּמִשְׁלָם, [7]וַאֲנַן אַפְּתוֹרָא דְּמִיחֲסַר?״ [8]אֲמָרָה לֵיהּ: ״וּמַאי נַעֲבֵיד? [9]בְּעֵי רַחֲמֵי דְּנִשְׁקְלִינְהוּ מִינָּךְ״. [10]בָּעֵי רַחֲמֵי וּשְׁקָלוּהוּ. [11]תָּנָא: ״גָּדוֹל הָיָה נֵס אַחֲרוֹן יוֹתֵר מִן הָרִאשׁוֹן״. [12]דִּגְמִירִי דְּמֵיהָב יָהֲבִי, מִישְׁקַל לָא שָׁקְלִי.

[13]חַד בֵּי שִׁמְשֵׁי חַזְיֵיהּ לִבְרַתֵּיהּ דַּהֲוַות עֲצִיבָא. [14]אָמַר לָהּ: ״בִּתִּי, אַמַּאי עֲצִיבַתְּ?״ [15]אֲמָרָה לֵיהּ: ״כְּלִי שֶׁל חוֹמֶץ נִתְחַלֵּף

LITERAL TRANSLATION

shall we do?" [1]"Petition for mercy that you should be given something." [2]He petitioned for mercy, [3][and] something like the palm of a hand emerged, and he was given one leg of a golden table. [4]She saw in a dream that the righteous are destined to eat at a golden table that has three legs, [5]and [that] he would eat at a table with two legs. [6]He said to her: "Is it pleasing to you that the entire world will eat at a table that is whole, [7]and we at a table that is defective?" [8]She said to him: "So what shall we do? [9]Petition for mercy that it should be taken from you." [10]He petitioned for mercy and it was taken from him. [11][A Tanna] taught: "The latter miracle was greater than the first." [12]For we have learned as a tradition that they [in Heaven] give, [but] do not take back.

[13]One Shabbat Eve at twilight he saw that his daughter was sad. [14]He said to her: "My daughter, why are you sad?" [15]She said to him: "A utensil of vinegar got mixed up with a

RASHI

חזיא — לדביתהו בחלמא. **מישקל לא שקלי** — בתר דיהבי. **כל היכא דתני בי שמשי** — היינו ערב שבת, לא שמעתי טעם. **במנא דחלא** — בכלי שיש בו החומץ, ושמתי החומץ בנר ויכבה הנר.

NOTES

אַפְּתוֹרָא דְּדַהֲבָא דְּאִית לֵיהּ תְּלָת כַּרְעֵי At a golden table that has three legs. Various explanations of this dream have been offered by the commentators. *Maharsha* suggests that the three legs of the table allude to the reward that the righteous will receive in the World-to-Come for upholding the three foundations upon which this world rests: Torah, divine worship, and acts of charity. When Rabbi Ḥanina ben Dosa asked that his financial situation in this world be improved, he was given one of the table legs as a reward for his divine worship, for his prayers. When his wife related her dream to him, Rabbi Ḥanina understood that if he received his reward in this world, his reward in the World-to-Come would be diminished, so he asked that the table leg be taken back.

מִישְׁקַל לָא שָׁקְלִי But not taken back. Some cite the Jerusalem Talmud, which explains this passage as follows: The hand of the receiver is at the bottom, and the hand of the giver is on top. Thus man, who is found in this lowly world, can receive a gift from Heaven, but he cannot ordinarily give it back (*Mikhtam*).

TRANSLATION AND COMMENTARY

[1] **and as a result I lit the Shabbat lamp** with vinegar. The small supply of oil in the lamp will very soon be used up, the light will be extinguished, and we will be forced to sit in darkness for the rest of the evening." [2] Rabbi Ḥanina **said to** his daughter: **"My daughter, why do you fret? [3] He who commanded the oil to burn will command the vinegar to burn.** If God wills it, the vinegar in the Shabbat lamp will burn like oil." [4] **A Tanna taught** a Baraita referring to this incident, which stated: "The vinegar in the lamp **burned** not only that night but **all of the** following **day** as well. [5] The lamp was still burning at the conclusion of Shabbat, **so that they used it to light the flame for the havdalah** ceremony."

רַבִּי חֲנִינָא בֶּן דּוֹסָא [6] Rabbi **Ḥanina ben Dosa had some goats.** One day, his neighbors came to complain that he was being negligent in looking after them, [7] and **said to him: "Your goats are** grazing in our fields and **causing** us considerable **damage."** But Rabbi Ḥanina ben Dosa knew that his animals were not responsible for the damage caused to his neighbors' crops, [8] and **he said** to them: **"If** my goats **are** indeed **causing** you **damage, let them be eaten by bears,** for they deserve to be destroyed. [9] **But if** they are **not** causing you any damage, **let each one** of them **bring in this evening a bear** impaled **on its horns."** [10] A miracle indeed occurred **that evening,** for **each one** of the goats **brought in a bear** impaled **on its horns.**

הֲוָה לֵיהּ [11] Rabbi Ḥanina ben Dosa **had a certain neighbor who was building a house, but** found that **the beams** to support the roof **were not** long enough to **reach** from one wall to another. [12] She **came before** Rabbi Ḥanina ben Dosa, **and said to him: "I** have **built** the walls of my **house, but** now I find that **the** roof-support **beams do not span** the width of the building!" [13] Rabbi Ḥanina ben Dosa **asked her: "What is your name?"** [14] **She said to him: "Ikku."** Resorting to word-play with the woman's name, which can also mean "if so," [15] Rabbi Ḥanina ben Dosa **recited** the following blessing: **"If so, Ikku, may your beams** miraculously lengthen so that they **reach** from wall to wall." [16] **A Tanna taught** a Baraita which reports how the story ended: "The beams miraculously lengthened so that not only did **they reach** across the woman's house, **but they** also **projected a cubit on this side** of the building **and a cubit on that side** of the building. [17] **And there are some who say** that the beams were miraculously **extended with segments** added at both ends of each beam."

לִי בִּכְלִי שֶׁל שֶׁמֶן, [1] וְהִדְלַקְתִּי מִמֶּנּוּ אוֹר לַשַּׁבָּת". [2] אָמַר לָהּ: "בִּתִּי, מַאי אִכְפַּת לָךְ? [3] מִי שֶׁאָמַר לַשֶּׁמֶן וְיִדְלוֹק הוּא יֹאמַר לַחוֹמֶץ וְיִדְלוֹק". [4] תָּנָא: "הָיָה דּוֹלֵק וְהוֹלֵךְ כָּל הַיּוֹם כּוּלּוֹ, [5] עַד שֶׁהֵבִיאוּ מִמֶּנּוּ אוּר לְהַבְדָּלָה".

[6] רַבִּי חֲנִינָא בֶּן דּוֹסָא הָווּ לֵיהּ הָנָךְ עִיזֵּי. [7] אֲמַרוּ לֵיהּ: "קָא מַפְסְדָן". [8] אֲמַר: "אִי קָא מַפְסְדָן, נֵיכְלִינְהוּ דּוּבֵּי. [9] וְאִי לָא, כָּל חֲדָא וַחֲדָא תֵּיתֵי לְאוּרְתָּא דּוּבָּא בְּקַרְנַיְיהוּ". [10] לְאוּרְתָּא אַיְיתֵי כָּל חֲדָא וַחֲדָא דּוּבָּא בְּקַרְנַיְיהוּ.

[11] הֲוָה לֵיהּ הַהִיא שִׁיבַבְתָּא דְּקָא בָּנְיָא בֵּיתָא, וְלָא מָטוּ כְּשׁוּרֵי. [12] אָתְיָא לְקַמֵּיהּ, אֲמָרָה לֵיהּ: "בָּנִיתִי בֵּיתִי וְלָא קָמָטוּ כְּשׁוּרַאי!" [13] אֲמַר לָהּ: "מַה שְּׁמֵךְ?" [14] אֲמָרָה לֵיהּ: "אִיכּוּ". [15] אֲמַר: "אִיכּוּ, נִימְטוּ כְּשׁוּרַיִךְ". [16] תָּנָא: "הִגִּיעוּ, עַד שֶׁיָּצְאוּ אַמָּה לְכָאן וְאַמָּה לְכָאן. [17] וְיֵשׁ אוֹמְרִין: סְנִיפִין עֲשָׂאוּם".

LITERAL TRANSLATION

utensil of oil, [1] and I lit from it a light for Shabbat." [2] He said to her: "My daughter, what does it matter to you? [3] He who told the oil to burn will tell the vinegar to burn." [4] [A Tanna] taught: "It went on burning the entire day, [5] until they brought from it a flame for havdalah."

[6] Rabbi Ḥanina ben Dosa had some goats. [7] They said to him: "They are causing damage." [8] He said: "If they are causing damage, let bears eat them. [9] But if not, let each one bring in this evening a bear on its horns." [10] That evening each one brought in a bear on its horns.

[11] He had a certain neighbor who built a house, but the beams did not reach. [12] She came before him, [13] [and] said to him: "I have built my house, but my beams do not reach!" [14] He said to her: "What is your name?" [15] She said to him: "Ikku." He said: "Ikku [=if so], may your beams reach." [16] [A Tanna] taught: "They reached, until they projected a cubit on this [side] and a cubit on that [side]. [17] And there are some who say: They were made [longer] in segments."

RASHI

עד שנטלו ממנו אור להבדלה — הדליק ממנו נר אחר ליהנות בו, ונר של מעשה נסים כיבה, כי היכי דעבד רב יהודה (תענית כד,ב) בחלא דהוה סמידא. **קא מפסדי לן** — שדות. **דובים** — וזאבים בשדות. **ולא מטו כשורי** — אין הקורות מגיעות מכותל לכותל. **איכו נימטו כשוריך** — יאריכו הקורות. **סניפין היו** — הקורות של חליות היו, במעשה נס נדבקו להן חתיכות קטנות לאורכן.

LANGUAGE

אִיכּוּ Ikku. This is a woman's proper name, but it also means "if so" or "therefore." Rabbi Ḥanina Ben Dosa used this play on words when he prayed for her.

סְנִיפִין Segments. The root "סנף" is close in meaning to the root "ענף" and may be related to it. It means to join one thing to another. Here it means that short pieces of wood were miraculously attached to the ends of the long beams.

BACKGROUND

עַד שֶׁיָּצְאוּ Until they projected. This was in order that the miracle would be evident. Since the house was unlike other houses, people would ask why it was different, and they would mention the miracle that occurred with regard to it.

NOTES

סְנִיפִין עֲשָׂאוּם They were made longer in segments. Our commentary follows *Rashi* and *Rabbenu Gershom,* who

TRANSLATION AND COMMENTARY

[1] Another **Baraita was taught** relating to this incident: [2] "The Sage **Plimo says: I saw that house, and its beams projected** on both sides of the building, **a cubit on this side and a cubit on that side.** [3] **And people said to me: This is the house that Rabbi Ḥanina ben Dosa roofed through** the power of **his prayer."**

וְרַבִּי חֲנִינָא בֶּן דּוֹסָא [4] Regarding Rabbi Ḥanina ben Dosa's goats, the Gemara asks: **From where did Rabbi Ḥanina ben Dosa have goats?** [5] **Surely** we said earlier that **he was** absolutely **destitute!** [6] **And furthermore, the Sages said** (*Bava Kamma* 79b): **"Sheep and goats may not be raised in Eretz Israel,** for it is difficult to prevent them from causing damage to cultivated land."

אָמַר רַב פִּנְחָס [7] **Rav Pineḥas said** in reply: This is how the goats came into Rabbi Ḥanina ben Dosa's possession, even though they did not actually belong to him. **It once happened that a certain man was passing by the entrance** to Rabbi Ḥanina's **house, and** unwittingly **left** a number of **chickens there.** [8] **Rabbi Ḥanina ben Dosa's wife found** the chickens, and took them inside until their owner could be located. When the chickens began to lay eggs, [9] Rabbi Ḥanina ben Dosa **said to her**: "Take care that you **do not eat** any **of the eggs**, since the chickens are not ours." [10] The chickens **produced many eggs and** the eggs produced many **chickens**, and all the noise and dirt **caused** Rabbi Ḥanina ben Dosa and his wife great **distress.** [11] So Rabbi Ḥanina **sold the chickens**, **and bought goats with the proceeds** of the sale, planning to keep them until the owner of the chickens came back to claim them. [12] **Once that same man who had lost his chickens passed by** Rabbi Ḥanina ben Dosa's house again, [13] **and said to the person with him: "This is where I left my chickens."** [14] **Rabbi Ḥanina overheard** their conversation, **and said to** the man: **"Can you give**

[1] תַּנְיָא: [2] ״פְּלִימוֹ אוֹמֵר: אֲנִי רָאִיתִי אוֹתוֹ הַבַּיִת, וְהָווּ קוֹרוֹתָיו יוֹצְאוֹת אַמָּה לְכָאן וְאַמָּה לְכָאן. [3] וְאָמְרוּ לִי: בַּיִת זֶה שֶׁקֵּירָה רַבִּי חֲנִינָא בֶּן דּוֹסָא בִּתְפִלָּתוֹ״.

[4] וְרַבִּי חֲנִינָא בֶּן דּוֹסָא מֵהֵיכָן הָווּ לֵיהּ עִזִּים? [5] וְהָא עָנִי הֲוֵי! [6] וְעוֹד, אָמְרוּ חֲכָמִים: ״אֵין מְגַדְּלִין בְּהֵמָה דַּקָּה בְּאֶרֶץ יִשְׂרָאֵל״.

[7] אָמַר רַב פִּנְחָס: מַעֲשֶׂה וְעָבַר אָדָם אֶחָד עַל פֶּתַח בֵּיתוֹ וְהִנִּיחַ שָׁם תַּרְנְגוֹלִין, [8] וּמְצָאָתָן אִשְׁתּוֹ שֶׁל רַבִּי חֲנִינָא בֶּן דּוֹסָא, [9] וְאָמַר לָהּ: ״אַל תֹּאכְלִי מִבֵּיצֵיהֶן״. [10] וְהִרְבּוּ בֵּיצִים וְתַרְנְגוֹלִין, וְהָיוּ מְצַעֲרִין אוֹתָם. [11] וּמְכָרָן, וְקָנָה בִּדְמֵיהֶן עִזִּים. [12] פַּעַם אַחַת עָבַר אוֹתוֹ אָדָם שֶׁאָבְדוּ מִמֶּנּוּ הַתַּרְנְגוֹלִין, [13] וְאָמַר לַחֲבֵירוֹ: ״בְּכָאן הִנַּחְתִּי הַתַּרְנְגוֹלִין שֶׁלִּי״. [14] שָׁמַע רַבִּי

LITERAL TRANSLATION

[1] It was taught: [2] "Plimo says: I saw that house, and its beams projected a cubit on this [side] and a cubit on that [side]. [3] And they said to me: This is the house that Rabbi Ḥanina ben Dosa roofed with his prayer."

[4] But from where did Rabbi Ḥanina ben Dosa have goats? [5] But surely he was poor! [6] And furthermore, the Sages said: "One may not raise sheep and goats (lit., 'small cattle') in Eretz Israel."

[7] Rav Pinḥas said: It happened that a certain man passed by the entrance to his house, and left chickens there, [8] and Rabbi Ḥanina ben Dosa's wife found them, [9] and he said to her: "Do not eat of their eggs." [10] And they produced many eggs and chickens, and they caused them distress. [11] So he sold them, and bought goats with their money. [12] Once that same man who had lost his chickens passed by, [13] and said to his fellow: "I left my chickens here." [14] Rabbi Ḥanina heard,

NOTES

explain that small pieces of wood were miraculously added to each of the beams so that they became long enough to reach from one side of the building to the other. Others (*Geonim*, *Arukh*) write that the beams became so long that the ends were cut off and used as braces connecting the upper and lower rows of beams supporting the roof.

אֵין מְגַדְּלִים בְּהֵמָה דַקָּה בְּאֶרֶץ יִשְׂרָאֵל **One may not raise sheep and goats in Eretz Israel.** The question was asked: If one may not raise sheep and goats in Eretz Israel, how could Rabbi Ḥanina ben Dosa have kept the goats in his possession, even if he was looking after them for the owner of the lost chickens?

Some commentators suggest that Rabbi Ḥanina ben Dosa raised the goats in the desert, where raising sheep and goats is permitted (*Gevurat Ari*). Others argue that the prohibition applies only to a person who wishes to raise his own herd, but the Rabbis never forbade a person to tend the sheep or the goats belonging to someone else (*Ramat Shmuel*).

HALAKHAH

בְּהֵמָה דַקָּה בְּאֶרֶץ יִשְׂרָאֵל **Sheep and goats in Eretz Israel.** "Sheep and goats may not be raised in Eretz Israel, for they graze on other people's property and cause considerable damage. One may not raise such animals even inside one's house (*Tur*). But sheep and goats may be raised in Syria and in the deserts of Eretz Israel." (*Shulḥan Arukh*, *Ḥoshen Mishpat* 409:1.)

SAGES

פְּלִימוֹ **Plimo.** The Sage Plimo was a disciple of Rabbi Yehudah HaNasi, and we find him asking his teacher questions about the Halakhah. Some of his Halakhic teachings are reported in Baraitot, and we find him in disagreement with Rabbi's colleague, Rabbi Eliezer the son of Rabbi Shimon. Many stories are told about his great piety.

LANGUAGE

פְּלִימוֹ **Plimo.** The name Plimo is apparently derived from the Greek παλαιός, *palaios*, meaning "old." Similar names were used among Jewish communities, for the purpose of bringing good fortune.

TRANSLATION AND COMMENTARY

an identifying sign and thereby prove that the chickens left here were yours?" [1]**He said: "Yes, indeed."** He **gave him an identifying sign** for the chickens **and took the goats** that Rabbi Ḥanina ben Dosa had bought with the proceeds of their sale. [2]**These were the very goats that brought in the bears** impaled **on their horns.**

רַבִּי אֶלְעָזָר בֶּן פְּדָת [3]Having described the extreme poverty of Rabbi Ḥanina ben Dosa, the Gemara now relates that **Rabbi Elazar ben Pedat,** an Amora living in Eretz Israel, **was** also **very hard-pressed** for money. [4]Once **he let himself be bled, and did not have anything** substantial **to eat** afterwards to restore his strength. [5]So **he took a clove of garlic and put it into his mouth. His heart became weak, and he fell asleep.** [6]**The Rabbis came to inquire about his** welfare, **and saw that he was weeping and laughing** in his sleep, **and that a ray of light was shining forth from his forehead.** [7]**When he woke up, they asked him: "What is the reason that you were weeping and laughing** in your sleep?" [8]**He said to them:** "I dreamt that **the Holy One, blessed be He, was sitting with me,** [9]**and I asked Him: 'How much longer will I** continue to **suffer** such poverty **in this world?'** [10]**And He said to me: 'Elazar, my son, would you prefer that I return the world to its beginning?** [11]**Perhaps** then **you will** have the fortune to **be born in an hour** that is more propitious **for sustenance!'** [12]**I said to Him:** 'You suggest doing **all this,** recreating the entire world, **and** all that You can say is that **"perhaps"** I will be reborn at a moment that is more auspicious for an easier life!' [13]And furthermore, I **said to Him:** 'Are **the years that I** have already **lived** more numerous than those that I will live in the future, or are **those that I will live** greater in number than those that I have already lived?' [14]God **said**

חֲנִינָא, אָמַר לוֹ: "יֵשׁ לְךָ בָּהֶן סִימָן?" [1]אָמַר לוֹ: "הֵן". נָתַן לוֹ סִימָן וְנָטַל אֶת הָעִיזִּין. [2]וְהֵן הֵן עִיזֵּי דְּאַיְיתוּ דּוּבֵּי בְּקַרְנַיְיהוּ.

[3]רַבִּי אֶלְעָזָר בֶּן פְּדָת דְּחִיקָא לֵיהּ מִילְּתָא טוּבָא. [4]עֲבַד מִלְּתָא, וְלָא הֲוָה לֵיהּ מִידֵּי לְמִטְעַם. [5]שְׁקַל בְּרָא דְּתוּמָא וְשַׁדְיֵיהּ בְּפוּמֵּיהּ. חֲלַשׁ לִבֵּיהּ וְנִים. [6]אֲזוּל רַבָּנַן לְשַׁיּוּלֵי בֵּיהּ, חַזְיוּהוּ דְּקָא בָּכֵי וְחָיֵיךְ, וּנְפַק צוּצִיתָא דְנוּרָא מֵאַפּוּתֵיהּ. [7]כִּי אִתְעַר, אֲמַרוּ לֵיהּ: "מַאי טַעֲמָא קָבָכֵית וְחָיְיכַתְּ?" [8]אֲמַר לְהוּ: "דַּהֲוָה יָתֵיב עִמִּי הַקָּדוֹשׁ בָּרוּךְ הוּא, [9]וַאֲמַרִי לֵיהּ: 'עַד מָתַי אֶצְטַעֵר בְּהַאי עָלְמָא?' [10]וַאֲמַר לִי: 'אֶלְעָזָר, בְּנִי, נִיחָא לָךְ דְּאַפְכֵיהּ לְעָלְמָא מֵרֵישָׁא? [11]אֶפְשָׁר דְּמִתְיַלְדַתְּ בְּשַׁעְתָּא דִּמְזוֹנֵי'. [12]אֲמַרִי לְקַמֵּיהּ: 'כּוּלֵּי הַאי, "וְאֶפְשָׁר"?' [13]אֲמַרִי לֵיהּ: 'דְּחָיֵי טְפֵי, אוֹ דְּחָיֵינָא?' [14]אָמַר

LITERAL TRANSLATION

[and] he said to him: "Do you have in them a sign [of identification]?" [1]He said: "Yes." He gave him a sign [of identification] and took the goats. [2]And these were the very goats that brought in the bears on their horns.

[3]Rabbi Elazar ben Pedat was very hard-pressed. [4]He was bled (lit., "he did something"), and he did not have anything to eat. [5]He took a clove of garlic and put it into his mouth. His heart became weak and he fell asleep. [6]The Rabbis came to ask about him, [and] saw that he was weeping and laughing, and that a ray of light was coming out from his forehead. [7]When he woke up, they said to him: "What is the reason that you were weeping and laughing?" [8]He said to them: "For the Holy One, blessed be He, was sitting with me, [9]and I said to Him: 'Until when will I suffer in this world?' [10]And He said to me: 'Elazar, my son, would it be pleasing to you that I turned the world back to its beginning? [11]Perhaps you would be born in an hour of sustenance.' [12]I said before Him: 'All this, and [only] "perhaps"?' [13]I said to Him: 'Are [the years] that I have lived more, or are [those] that I will live [more]?' [14]He said

RASHI

רבי אלעזר בן פדת – אמורא היה, והוא הנקרא "מרא דארעא דארץ ישראל" במסכת נדה (כ, ב). בעל הוראות היה, והוא שימש רבי יוחנן אחרי מות ריש לקיש, והיה דחוק ועני. **עבד מילתא** = הקיז דם. **ברא דתומא** = בן השום, צלע של שום. **חלש ליביה** = נתעלפה. **צוציתא** = ניצוץ. **מאפותיה** = ממצחו. **כולי האי ואפשר** – בתמיה: כולי האי עבדת, ואכתי הך ספיקא דלמא לא מיתרמינא בשעתא דמזוני? **דחיי נפישא או דחיינא** – ימי חיי שחייתי כבר הם רבים ממה שאני עתיד לחיות.

BACKGROUND

עֲבַד מִלְּתָא He was bled. The letting of blood was not only regarded as a cure for disease, but was regularly practiced in several places in Eretz Israel as a means of enhancing health. However, after one's blood is let, one feels weak. In order to regain their strength, people used to then eat highly nutritious foods such as meat and fat, and easily digested sweets for energy.

אֶפְשָׁר דְּמִתְיַלְדַתְּ בְּשַׁעְתָּא דִּמְזוֹנֵי Perhaps you would be born in an hour of sustenance. Our Sages say that whether people choose good or evil depends only upon themselves, and this choice is not decreed from on high. However, the characteristics of one's body and soul, as well as success, are part of the general order of things and depend upon a complex and intricate calculation of the entire structure of the world, and are not connected with an individual's good deeds.

NOTES

רַבִּי אֶלְעָזָר בֶּן פְּדָת Rabbi Elazar ben Pedat. The Geonim write that Rabbi Elazar ben Pedat's vision of the Holy One, blessed be He, was a dream, and the details may not necessarily have special significance. But *Rashba* interprets at length the particulars of Rabbi Elazar ben Pedat's vision. The righteous suffer in this world because God knows that poverty and distress will bring them spiritual benefit. God's dialogue with Rabbi Elazar explains that spiritual reward in the World-to-Come is superior to material success in this world. The thirteen rivers allude to the thirteen attributes of God (see also *Maharsha*). *Otzar HaKavod* explains the alternative reading "twelve rivers" as an allusion to the twelve tribes of Israel.

BACKGROUND

גִּירַי בָּךְ **My arrows on you.** This response expresses joy and amusement, like an adult's reaction when a child answers a question with sharp wit.

TRANSLATION AND COMMENTARY

to me in reply: 'Those years **that you** have already **lived** are more numerous than those that you still have to live.' [1]I then **said before Him: 'If so, I do not want** you to recreate the world.' [2]God then **said to me: 'As a reward for saying "I do not want** You to recreate the world for my benefit," [3]**I will give you in the World-to-Come thirteen rivers that are as large as the Euphrates and the Tigris,** flowing with **pure balsam oil in which you may enjoy yourself.'** [4]**I said before Him: 'This** is my reward, **and nothing else?'** [5]God **answered:** 'If I give you any more, **what shall I give to your** righteous **colleagues?'** [6]**I said to Him: 'Do I ask** something **of a person who does not have** anything to give? Surely Your bounty knows no limit!' [7]God then **snapped His finger on my forehead** as if in play, **and said to me: 'Elazar, my son, My arrows** I cast **upon you, My arrows** I cast upon you!'" The Rabbis who had come to visit Rabbi Elazar ben Pedat now understood his unusual conduct. Rabbi Elazar ben Pedat wept in his sleep when he heard that he had already lived out the majority of the years of his life, and he broke out in laughter when he was told that thirteen rivers of pure balsam oil awaited him in the World-to-Come. The ray of light shining forth from his forehead marked the spot where he was touched by God's finger.

רַבִּי חָמָא בַּר חֲנִינָא [8]Returning to the topic of fasts decreed in times of drought, the Gemara relates the following story. **Rabbi Ḥama bar Ḥanina** once **decreed a fast** when the rain was late, **but the rain** still **did not fall.** [9]His townsmen **said to him: "But surely Rabbi Yehoshua ben Levi decreed a fast** when the community needed rain, **and rain fell!"** [10]Rabbi Ḥama bar Ḥanina **answered them: "I am who I am,** and **that was** Rabbi Yehoshua **ben Levi!** We are not of the same stature, he is the greater man." [11]Rabbi Ḥama bar Ḥanina's

לִי: ׳דְּחָיִית׳. [1]אֲמַרִי לְקַמֵּיהּ: ׳אִם כֵּן, לָא בָּעֵינָא׳. [2]אֲמַר לִי: ׳בְּהַאי אַגְרָא דְּאָמְרַתְּ ״לָא בָּעֵינָא״, [3]יָהֵיבְנָא לָךְ לְעָלְמָא דְּאָתֵי תְּלֵיסְרֵי נַהֲרָוָותָא דְּמִשְׁחָא אֲפַרְסְמוֹן דַּכְיָין כִּפְרָת וְדִיגְלַת, דְּמִעַנְּגַת בְּהוּ׳. [4]אֲמַרִי לְקַמֵּיהּ: ׳הַאי, וְתוּ לָא?׳ [5]אֲמַר לִי: ׳וּלְחַבְרָךְ מַאי יָהֵיבְנָא?׳ [6]אֲמַרִי לֵיהּ: ׳וַאֲנָא מִגַּבְרָא דְּלֵית לֵיהּ בָּעֵינָא?׳ [7]מָחְיָין בְּאַסְקוּטְלָא אַפּוּתַאי, וַאֲמַר לִי: ׳אֶלְעָזָר, בְּרִי, גִּירַי בָּךְ, גִּירַי!׳״ [8]רַבִּי חָמָא בַּר חֲנִינָא גְּזַר תַּעֲנִיתָא, וְלָא אֲתָא מִיטְרָא. [9]אֲמַרוּ לֵיהּ: ״וְהָא רַבִּי יְהוֹשֻׁעַ בֶּן לֵוִי גְּזַר תַּעֲנִיתָא, וְאָתֵי מִיטְרָא!״ [10]אֲמַר לְהוּ: ״הָא אֲנָא, הָא בַּר לִיוַאי!״ [11]אֲמַרוּ

LITERAL TRANSLATION

to me: 'Those that you have lived.' [1]I said before Him: 'If so, I do not want.' [2]He said to me: 'As a reward for your saying "I do not want," [3]I will give you in the World-to-Come thirteen rivers of pure balsam oil [that are as large] as the Euphrates and Tigris, that you may enjoy them.' [4]I said before Him: 'This, and nothing else?' [5]He said to me: 'And to your fellow, what shall I give?' [6]I said to Him: 'But am I asking from a person who does not have?' [7]He snapped His finger on my forehead, and said to me: 'Elazar, my son, My arrows on you, My arrows!'" [8]Rabbi Ḥama bar Ḥanina decreed a fast, but rain did not come. [9]They said to him: "But surely Rabbi Yehoshua ben Levi decreed a fast, and rain came!" [10]He said to them: "This is I, that was the son of Levi!" [11]They said

RASHI

אמר דחיית — מה שכבר חיית מרובים ממה שאתה עתיד לחיות. והיינו דקא בכי כי אמר שכינה הכי, והאי דחייך — משום שלשה עשר נהרוותא לרחוץ בהן, ולטייל בהן מזה לזה. **אי הכי לא בעינא** — דתיחרביה לעלמא. **ותו לא** — וכי אין אתה נותן לי דברים אחרים. **אמר ליה ולחברך מאי קא יהבינא** — אנא מגברא דלית ליה בעינא לא גרים בספר רבי. ובספר שלי כתוב. **באסקוטלא אפותאי** — היינו צוליתא דנפק מיניה, שמדביק אצבע צרדא עם הגודל, ומכה בצפורן האצבע. **איגרו בך גירי** — כלומר: הכיתי בחילי. לחדווה בעלמא אמר כן. **הא אנא והא בר ליואי** — הוא איש אחד ואני איש אחד, הוא עדיף מינאי. **דתברי** = שוברים.

NOTES

גִּירַי בָּךְ **My arrows on you.** *Rabbenu Elyakim* understands this as a question, expressing God's dissatisfaction with Rabbi Elazar ben Pedat's repeated requests for additional rewards: "Is it your desire that I should shoot My arrows at you?" Others (*Geonim*, *Arukh*) explain it as a blessing, taking the word גִּירַי to mean "converts." God promised Rabbi Elazar ben Pedat that he would receive his reward in the future when converts would come to dwell in his shadow.

הָא אֲנָא הָא בַּר לִיוַאי **This is I, that was the son of Levi.** Our commentary follows *Rashi* and others, who understand Rabbi Ḥama bar Ḥanina as saying that he recognized Rabbi Yehoshua ben Levi as his superior. *Maharsha* explains that Rabbi Ḥama bar Ḥanina regarded himself as Rabbi Yehoshua ben Levi's equal, but that the people who fasted with him were not of the same stature as those who fasted with Rabbi Yehoshua ben Levi. It was then suggested that the entire community should observe a fast, since the merits of the community might perhaps elicit God's compassion. When that, too, was unsuccessful, Rabbi Ḥama asked the members of the community whether "the rain should come for our sake." He asked them to admit that they were not deserving of rain, and that the rain should fall for the sake of their righteous leaders. A similar story is told in the

TRANSLATION AND COMMENTARY

townsmen then **said to him: "Let us go and concentrate our minds,** and petition God for mercy. [1]**Perhaps the community will break their hearts,** and pray sincerely **that the rain should fall."** [2]The community **petitioned** God **for mercy, but** their efforts were of no avail and **rain did not fall.** [3]Rabbi Ḥama bar Ḥanina **said to them: "Is it your wish that rain should fall for our sake?"** [4]**They answered him: "Yes."** [5]**He said: "Heaven, Heaven, cover your face** with clouds, so that rain may fall!" But Heaven **did not** heed Rabbi Ḥama bar Ḥanina's command and **cover itself** with clouds. [6]Then Rabbi Ḥama bar Ḥanina **said: "How brazen is the face of Heaven** that it does not obey!" [7]Immediately the sky **covered itself** with clouds, **and rain came.**

לֵוִי [8]**Levi** once **decreed a fast** during a time of drought, **but rain did not fall.** Disturbed by God's apparent unwillingness to send rain, [9]**Levi said before Him: "Master of the Universe!** [10]**You went up and sat** on Your throne **on high, and** now **You do not show mercy to Your children!"** [11]Levi's prayers were answered and **rain** began **to fall, but** he himself was punished for his insolence and **he became lame.** [12]Drawing a conclusion from Levi's punishment, **Rabbi Elazar said: A person should never reproach God on high, for a great man** once **reproached God on high and he became lame** as a result. [13]**And who was** that great man? It was **Levi.**

וְהָא גָּרְמָא לֵיהּ [14]The Gemara asks: **But did** Levi's manner of talking to God really **cause** him to become lame? [15]**Surely** it was reported that **Levi** once **demonstrated before Rabbi** Yehudah HaNasi the proper way to perform the High Priest's act of **prostration,** and while regaining his feet, he hurt his thigh and **became lame!**

הָא וְהָא גָּרְמָא לֵיהּ [16]The Gemara answers: There is no contradiction between these two reports. Both **this and that caused** Levi **to become lame.** Levi's insolent manner in speaking to God caused him to be punished while he was demonstrating to Rabbi Yehudah HaNasi the proper way to perform the prostration.

רַבִּי חִיָּיא בַּר לוּלְיָינִי [17]The Gemara now reports that **Rabbi Ḥiyya bar Lulyani** once **heard the clouds** hovering over Eretz Israel **saying** to each other: [18]**"Let us go and bring rain to Ammon and Moab,** Israel's neighbors

לֵיהּ: "דְּנֵיתֵי וְנִיכַּוֵּין דַּעְתִּין. [1]אֶפְשָׁר דְּתָבְרִי צִיבּוּרָא לִבַּיְיהוּ, דְּאָתֵי מִיטְרָא". [2]בְּעוֹן רַחֲמֵי, וְלָא אָתֵי מִיטְרָא. [3]אֲמַר לְהוּ: "נִיחָא לְכוּ שֶׁיָּבֹא מָטָר בִּשְׁבִילֵנוּ?" [4]אָמְרוּ לֵיהּ: "הֵן". [5]אָמַר: "רָקִיעַ, רָקִיעַ, כַּסִּי פָּנֶיךָ! לָא אִיכַּסֵּי. [6]אָמַר: כַּמָּה עַזִּין פְּנֵי רָקִיעַ! [7]אִיכַּסֵּי, וַאֲתָא מִיטְרָא.

[8]לֵוִי גְּזַר תַּעֲנִיתָא, וְלָא אֲתָא מִיטְרָא. [9]אָמַר לְפָנָיו: "רִבּוֹנוֹ שֶׁל עוֹלָם! [10]עָלִיתָ וְיָשַׁבְתָּ בַּמָּרוֹם וְאֵין אַתָּה מְרַחֵם עַל בָּנֶיךָ!" [11]אֲתָא מִיטְרָא, וְאִיטְלַע. [12]אָמַר רַבִּי אֶלְעָזָר: לְעוֹלָם אַל יַטִּיחַ אָדָם דְּבָרִים כְּלַפֵּי מַעְלָה, שֶׁהֲרֵי אָדָם גָּדוֹל הִטִּיחַ דְּבָרִים כְּלַפֵּי מַעְלָה, וְאִיטְלַע! [13]וּמַנּוּ? לֵוִי.

[14]וְהָא גָּרְמָא לֵיהּ? [15]וְהָא לֵוִי אַחֲוֵי קִידָּה קַמֵּיהּ דְּרַבִּי וְאִיטְלַע!

[16]הָא וְהָא גָּרְמָא לֵיהּ.

[17]רַבִּי חִיָּיא בַּר לוּלְיָינִי שְׁמָעִינְהוּ לְהָנָךְ עֲנָנֵי דְּקָאָמְרִי: [18]"נֵיתוּ וְנִיתְבֵי מַיָּא בְּעַמּוֹן

LITERAL TRANSLATION

to him: "Let us go and concentrate our minds. [1]Perhaps the community will break their hearts, so that rain will come." [2]They petitioned for mercy, but rain did not come. [3]He said to them: "Is it pleasing to you that rain should come for our sake?" [4]They said to him: "Yes." [5]He said: "Heaven, Heaven, cover your face!" [6]It did not cover itself. He said: "How brazen is the face of Heaven!" [7]It covered itself, and rain came.

[8]Levi decreed a fast, but rain did not come. [9]He said before Him: "Master of the Universe! [10]You went up and sat on high, and You do not show mercy to Your children!" [11]Rain came, but he became lame. [12]Rabbi Elazar said: A person should never be reproachful toward [God] on high, for a great man was reproachful toward [God] on high, and he became lame. [13]And who [was that]? Levi.

[14]But did this cause him [to become lame]? [15]But surely Levi performed a prostration before Rabbi and became lame!

[16]This and that caused him [to become lame].

[17]Rabbi Ḥiyya bar Lulyani heard the clouds saying: [18]"Let us go and bring water on Ammon

RASHI

שיבא מטר בשבילנו — מקבלים אתם עליכם, ומסכימין לדעת אחד. **כמה עזין** — דלא כסין מלבורא. **לוי אחוי קידה** — נועץ שני גודליו בארץ, ושוחה ונושק את הרצפה. **הא והא גרמא ליה** — החטא גרם לו שנצלע בקידה.

NOTES

Jerusalem Talmud (*Ta'anit* 3:4), where Rabbi Ḥanina's failure to cause rain to fall is attributed to the deficiencies of the community he represented, whereas Rabbi Yehoshua ben Levi's success in causing it to rain is connected to the merits of his community.

BACKGROUND

אַחֲוֵי קִידָּה Performed a prostration. This refers to the special way in which the High Priest prostrated himself in the Temple. In performing the prostration, the High Priest would press his entire body to the floor of the Temple. Then he would rise to his full height and stand erect without bending his body. This was a difficult movement which few people could perform, involving great pressure on the hip muscles. The effort caused Levi to dislocate his knee.

SAGES

לֵוִי Levi. Levi ben Sisi was a Palestinian Sage of the transitional generation between the Tannaitic and Amoraic periods. He was an outstanding student of Rabbi Yehuda HaNasi, editor of the Mishnah. He would sit before Rabbi Yehudah HaNasi and discuss the Halakhah with his other great students. Rabbi Yehudah HaNasi held him in great esteem, and sent him to be chief judge and preacher in the town of Simonia. He said of him that he was "a man like myself." In several sources it is told that he acquired a limp while trying to show Rabbi Yehudah HaNasi how the High Priest used to prostrate himself on Yom Kippur. It is also explained that this was a punishment for having reproached the Almighty in his prayers.

Towards the end of his life, he went to Babylonia, where he renewed his close bonds with Rav, with whom he had studied under Rabbi Yehudah HaNasi, and became a close friend of Abba bar Abba, Shmuel's father. Shmuel was his student and colleague.

Rambam decided Halakhic rulings in accordance with Levi, against Rav and Shmuel, for in his opinion Levi was their superior. It is not clear whether Levi had sons or who they were. Some authorities believe that Bar Liva'i, who is mentioned in the Talmud, was his son. Others believe that Rabbi Yehoshua ben Levi, the famous Amora, was his son. But these conjectures, have not been proven.

רַבִּי חִיָּיא בַּר לוּלְיָינִי Rabbi Ḥiyya bar Lulyani. A Palestinian Amora of the fifth generation, Rabbi Ḥiyya bar

TRANSLATION AND COMMENTARY

to the east of the Jordan River." [1] Rabbi Ḥiyya bar Lulyani appealed to God and **said before Him: "Master of the Universe! Before You gave the Torah to Your people Israel, You** first **approached all the nations of the world** and offered the Torah to them, **but none** of the other nations was **willing to accept it.** Only Your people Israel agreed to accept the Torah. [2] **And now You** are ready to **give** Ammon and Moab **rain,** and deprive Your people of the rain that is due to them? [3] Order the clouds to **cast** their water **here,** over Eretz Israel!" God accepted Rabbi Ḥiyya bar Lulyani's prayer, [4] **and** the clouds stayed where they were and **cast** their water **in their place** over Eretz Israel.

דָּרַשׁ רַבִּי חִיָּיא בַּר לוּלְיָינִי [5] Having related an anecdote featuring Rabbi Ḥiyya bar Lulyani, the Gemara now cites a Midrashic exposition taught by that Sage. **Rabbi Ḥiyya bar Lulyani expounded:** [6] **What is** the meaning of the verse **that says** (Psalms 92:13): **"The righteous man will flourish like the palm tree; he will grow like a cedar in Lebanon"?** Granted that the Psalmist wishes to liken the righteous man to a tree that flourishes and grows tall. [7] But if the palm was already mentioned, why also mention the cedar, and if the cedar was already mentioned, why also mention the palm? Why is the righteous man compared to two different trees? Rabbi Ḥiyya bar Lulyani explained: [8] **If the palm** alone **had been mentioned, but the cedar had not been mentioned, I might have said: Just as the palm,** [25B] when it is cut down, **does not grow new shoots from its stump,** [9] **so too** when **a righteous man, God forbid,** is cut down, **his stump does not grow new shoots.** If the righteous man were compared only to a palm tree, I might have thought that, if he suffers a calamity, he will not overcome the difficulty. [10] **Therefore the cedar was mentioned.** Not only is the righteous man compared to a palm tree, but also to a cedar, which grows new shoots after it is cut down. Similarly, the righteous man will persevere and emerge from his difficulties with increased strength and vigor, as the verse says (Proverbs 24:16): "For a just man falls seven times, and yet rises up again." [11] And **if the cedar** alone **had been mentioned, but the palm had not been mentioned,** [12] **I might have said:** The righteous man grows like a cedar in Lebanon. **Just as the cedar does not yield fruit,** for the cedar is not a fruit-bearing tree, [13] **so too does a righteous man, God forbid, not yield**

וּמוֹאָב״. [1] אָמַר לְפָנָיו: ״רִבּוֹנוֹ שֶׁל עוֹלָם! כְּשֶׁנָּתַתָּ תּוֹרָה לְעַמְּךָ יִשְׂרָאֵל, חָזַרְתָּ עַל כָּל אוּמּוֹת הָעוֹלָם, וְלֹא קִיבְּלוּהָ. [2] וְעַכְשָׁיו אַתָּה נוֹתֵן לָהֶם מָטָר? [3] שְׁדוֹ הָכָא!״ [4] שָׁדְיוּהָ אַדּוּכְתַּיְהוּ.

[5] דָּרַשׁ רַבִּי חִיָּיא בַּר לוּלְיָינִי: [6] מַאי דִּכְתִיב: ״צַדִּיק כַּתָּמָר יִפְרָח; כְּאֶרֶז בַּלְּבָנוֹן יִשְׂגֶּה״? [7] אִם נֶאֱמַר תָּמָר, לָמָּה נֶאֱמַר אֶרֶז, וְאִם נֶאֱמַר אֶרֶז, לָמָּה נֶאֱמַר תָּמָר? [8] אִילּוּ נֶאֱמַר תָּמָר, וְלֹא נֶאֱמַר אֶרֶז, הָיִיתִי אוֹמֵר: מַה תָּמָר [25B] אֵין גִּזְעוֹ מַחֲלִיף, [9] אַף צַדִּיק, חַס וְחָלִילָה, אֵין גִּזְעוֹ מַחֲלִיף. [10] לְכָךְ נֶאֱמַר אֶרֶז. [11] אִילּוּ נֶאֱמַר אֶרֶז, וְלֹא נֶאֱמַר תָּמָר, [12] הָיִיתִי אוֹמֵר: מָה אֶרֶז אֵין עוֹשֶׂה פֵּירוֹת, [13] אַף צַדִּיק, חַס וְחָלִילָה, אֵין עוֹשֶׂה

LITERAL TRANSLATION

and Moab." [1] He said before Him: "Master of the Universe! When You gave the Torah to Your people Israel, You approached all the nations of the world, but they did not accept it. [2] And now You give them rain? [3] Let them cast it here!" [4] They cast it in their place.

[5] Rabbi Ḥiyya bar Lulyani expounded: [6] What is that which is written: "The righteous man will flourish like the palm tree; he will grow like a cedar in Lebanon"? [7] If the palm was mentioned, why was the cedar mentioned, and if the cedar was mentioned, why was the palm mentioned? [8] If the palm had been mentioned, but the cedar had not been mentioned, I would have said: Just as the palm's [25B] trunk does not renew itself, [9] so too does the trunk of a righteous man, God forbid, not renew itself. [10] Therefore the cedar was mentioned. [11] If the cedar had been mentioned, but the palm had not been mentioned, [12] I would have said: Just as the cedar does not yield fruit, [13] so too does a righteous man, God forbid, not yield

RASHI

אין גזעו מחליף — אם נפסק. אף צדיק — אין לו זכר, צדיק אין גזעו מחליף — אינו בתחיית המתים. צדיק אינו עושה פירות — אין לו שכר לעתיד.

Lulyani is mentioned mainly in the Jerusalem Talmud, and he cites the teachings of various Sages. He also had students who reported teachings in his name. The name Lulyani is an Aramaic form of the Roman name, Julianus.

BACKGROUND

אֵין גִּזְעוֹ מַחֲלִיף **Its trunk does not renew itself.** Palms are monocotyledonous trees, a family which includes many species. Unlike other trees, the palm's trunk does not grow by depositing a succession of annual rings. Thus, when a palm is cut down, it does not produce new branches from which a new tree will ultimately grow.

NOTES

אֵין גִּזְעוֹ מַחֲלִיף **Its trunk does not renew itself.** *Rashi* explains that a person who does not renew himself and grow new shoots will not rise up in the time of the resurrection, and a person who does not yield fruit will not receive any reward in the World-to-Come. *Rashbam* (*Bava Batra* 80b) writes that one who does not grow new shoots does not have a son like himself, or else he is unable to stand up again after he stumbles. One who does not yield fruit does not have a share in the World-to-Come, or else he does not enjoy the fruit of his actions. *Rabbenu Elyakim* understands that one who does not grow new shoots does not leave a son like himself, and one who does not yield fruit does not leave a Torah legacy that is accepted and studied by later generations.

פֵּירוֹת. [1]לְכָךְ נֶאֱמַר תָּמָר וְנֶאֱמַר אֶרֶז.

[2]וְאֶרֶז גִּזְעוֹ מַחֲלִיף? [3]וְהָתַנְיָא: "הַלּוֹקֵחַ אִילָן מֵחֲבֵירוֹ לָקוּץ, [4]מַגְבִּיהוֹ מִן הַקַּרְקַע טֶפַח וְקוֹצֵץ. [5]בְּסַדַּן הַשִּׁקְמָה, שְׁנֵי טְפָחִים. [6]בִּבְתוּלַת הַשִּׁקְמָה, שְׁלֹשָׁה טְפָחִים. [7]בְּקָנִים וּבִגְפָנִים, מִן הַפְּקָק וּלְמַעְלָה. [8]בִּדְקָלִים וּבַאֲרָזִים, חוֹפֵר לְמַטָּה וּמְשָׁרֵישׁ, [9]לְפִי שֶׁאֵין גִּזְעוֹ מַחֲלִיף".

[10]הָכָא בְּמַאי עָסְקִינַן? בִּשְׁאָר מִינֵי אֲרָזִים, [11]כִּדְרַבָּה בַּר הוּנָא, [12]דְּאָמַר רַבָּה בַּר הוּנָא: עֲשָׂרָה מִינֵי אֲרָזִים הֵן, [13]שֶׁנֶּאֱמַר: "אֶתֵּן בַּמִּדְבָּר אֶרֶז, שִׁטָּה, וַהֲדַס, וגו׳".

LITERAL TRANSLATION

fruit. [1]Therefore the palm was mentioned and the cedar was mentioned.

[2]But does the cedar's trunk renew itself? [3]But surely it was taught: "[If] someone bought a tree from his fellow to cut [it down], [4]he raises [his ax] from the ground a handbreadth and cuts. [5]In the case of a sycamore, two handbreadths. [6]In the case of a virgin sycamore, three handbreadths. [7]In the case of reeds and grapevines, from the knot and above. [8]In the case of palms and cedars, he digs down and uproots [them], [9]for its trunk does not renew itself."

[10]With what are we dealing here? With other species of cedars, [11]in accordance with Rabbah bar Huna, [12]for Rabbah bar Huna said: There are ten species of cedars, [13]as it is said: "I will plant in the wilderness the cedar, the shittah tree, and the myrtle, etc."

TRANSLATION AND COMMENTARY

fruit. If the righteous man were compared only to a cedar tree, I might have thought that he will not enjoy the fruits of his good deeds. [1]**Therefore both the palm and the cedar were mentioned.** Not only is the righteous man compared to the fruitless cedar, but also to the date-bearing palm tree. The righteous man will derive benefit from the fruit he produces, as the verse says (Isaiah 3:10): "Say of the righteous, that it shall be well with him: for they shall eat the fruit of their doings."

וְאֶרֶז [2]The Gemara now points to a difficulty in Rabbi Ḥiyya bar Lulyani's exposition. **Does the cedar's stump** really **grow new shoots** after it is cut down? [3]**But surely it was taught** otherwise in the following Baraita: **"If someone buys a tree from another person** so that it will be his property only with respect **to cutting the trunk for wood,** while not acquiring total ownership of the tree, he may not level the tree to the ground, [4]but **must raise his ax a handbreadth from the ground, and** cut there. Since he only bought the trunk for wood, he must leave a stump from which the tree will be able to rejuvenate itself. In most cases, this means that he must leave a handbreadth of stump, for most trees can send forth new shoots if a handbreadth of stump is left. There are, however, exceptions to this rule. [5]**In the case** where he bought the trunk **of a sycamore** which has already been trimmed, he must leave **two handbreadths** of the stump. [6]**In the case** where he bought **an untrimmed sycamore,** he must leave **three handbreadths** of the stump. [7]**In the case** where he bought **reeds or grapevines,** he may cut them off only **from the** first **knot and above.** [8]And finally, **in the case** where he bought **palms or cedars, he** may **dig down** into the ground **and uproot them** completely, [9]**for** when those trees are cut down, **their stumps do not grow new shoots."** Thus we see that not only palm trees but also cedars do not grow new shoots after they are cut down, and this contradicts the interpretation of Rabbi Ḥiyya bar Lulyani.

הָכָא בְּמַאי עָסְקִינַן [10]The Gemara answers: There is really no difficulty. When Rabbi Ḥiyya bar Lulyani said **here** that cedar stumps send forth new shoots, **he was dealing with other species of cedars,** [11]and was speaking **in accordance with Rabbah bar Huna,** who is of the opinion that various different trees are called cedars. [12]**For Rabbah bar Huna said: There are ten** different **species of cedars,** [13]**as the verse says** (Isaiah 41:19): "I will plant in the wilderness the cedar, the shittah tree, and the myrtle, and the oil tree; I will set in the desert cypress, maple, and box tree together." According to Rabbah bar Huna, all seven trees

RASHI

בתולת השקמה — נטיעה שלא נקצצה מעולם. **סדן** — שכבר הזקין, *טרונ״ק בלעז, שנקצץ וחוזר ומתעבה. והוא מלשון: סדינא בסדניה יתיב (פסחים כח,א). **שני טפחים** — שכבר גזעו מחליף. **מן הפקק** — קשר התחתון. **מיני ארזים** — שנאמר "אתן במדבר ארז שטה והדס" וגו׳ — ובציר להו תלת, ובראש השנה (כג,א) מפרש: הוסיפו עליהם אלונים אלמונים אלמוגים.

BACKGROUND

הַשִּׁקְמָה Sycamore. The sycamore tree (*ficus sycomorus*) is related to the fig, and in antiquity it was very widely cultivated in Eretz Israel. The fruit of the sycamore was eaten only when food was very scarce, and its main value was as a source of long, strong wooden beams. Sycamore wood is light and porous but resists decay. Sometimes the sycamore tree was allowed to grow and produce many beams, mainly taken from the branches. A tree that had never been trimmed was known as בְּתוּלַת שִׁקְמָה — "a virgin sycamore." After being trimmed, the trunk (סַדַּן הַשִּׁקְמָה) would again produce branches, which would be cut off when they attained sufficient size.

בִּדְקָלִים In the case of palms. In palms, unlike most other trees, the leaves and branches do not grow from buds. Hence any injury to the palm's heart or to the area where the new leaves sprout will kill the tree, for it can no longer renew itself.

עֲשָׂרָה מִינֵי אֲרָזִים There are ten species of cedars. The word "cedar" is used in Rabbinical Hebrew (and perhaps also in the Bible) both in the narrow sense of a certain type of tree, such as the cedar of Lebanon, and also as a broader term, as in the ten types of cedars, meaning any tree that does not bear fruit edible by human beings.

LANGUAGE (RASHI)

טרונ״ק* From the French *tronc*, meaning "trunk."

HALAKHAH

הַלּוֹקֵחַ אִילָן מֵחֲבֵירוֹ לָקוּץ If someone bought a tree from his fellow to cut it down. "If someone buys an olive tree to cut the trunk for wood, he must leave a stump to a height of two fists; if he buys a virgin sycamore, he must leave three handbreadths of the stump; if he buys the trunk of a sycamore that has previously been trimmed, he must leave two handbreadths of the stump; if he buys other trees, he must leave one handbreadth; if he buys the branches of reeds or grapevines, he may cut them off from the first knot and above; if he buys palms or cedars, he may dig down and uproot them completely, for their stumps do not renew themselves." (*Shulḥan Arukh, Ḥoshen Mishpat* 216:14.)

[1]תָּנוּ רַבָּנַן: ״מַעֲשֶׂה בְּרַבִּי אֱלִיעֶזֶר שֶׁגָּזַר שְׁלֹשׁ עֶשְׂרֵה תַּעֲנִיּוֹת עַל הַצִּבּוּר, [2]וְלֹא יָרְדוּ גְּשָׁמִים. [3]בָּאַחֲרוֹנָה, הִתְחִילוּ הַצִּבּוּר לָצֵאת. [4]אָמַר לָהֶם: ׳תִּקַּנְתֶּם קְבָרִים לְעַצְמְכֶם?׳ [5]גָּעוּ כָּל הָעָם בִּבְכִיָּה, וְיָרְדוּ גְּשָׁמִים. [6]שׁוּב מַעֲשֶׂה בְּרַבִּי אֱלִיעֶזֶר שֶׁיָּרַד לִפְנֵי הַתֵּיבָה וְאָמַר עֶשְׂרִים וְאַרְבַּע בְּרָכוֹת, וְלֹא נַעֲנָה. [7]יָרַד רַבִּי עֲקִיבָא אַחֲרָיו, וְאָמַר: [8]׳אָבִינוּ, מַלְכֵּנוּ, אֵין לָנוּ מֶלֶךְ אֶלָּא אָתָּה. אָבִינוּ, מַלְכֵּנוּ, לְמַעַנְךָ רַחֵם עָלֵינוּ׳, [9]וְיָרְדוּ גְּשָׁמִים. [10]הֲווּ מְרַנְּנִי רַבָּנַן. [11]יָצְתָה בַּת קוֹל וְאָמְרָה: ׳לֹא מִפְּנֵי שֶׁזֶּה גָּדוֹל מִזֶּה, [12]אֶלָּא שֶׁזֶּה מַעֲבִיר עַל מִידּוֹתָיו, [13]וְזֶה אֵינוֹ מַעֲבִיר עַל מִדּוֹתָיו׳״.

LITERAL TRANSLATION

[1]Our Rabbis taught: "It once happened that Rabbi Eliezer decreed thirteen fasts upon the community, [2]but rains did not fall. [3]On the last one, the congregation started to leave. [4]He said to them: 'Have you prepared graves for yourselves?' [5]All the people burst out crying, and rains fell. [6]It also happened that Rabbi Eliezer went down before the ark and said the twenty-four blessings but he was not answered. [7]Rabbi Akiva went down after him, and said: [8]'Our Father, our King, we have no king but You. Our Father, our King, for Your sake, have mercy upon us,' [9]and rains fell. [10]The Rabbis murmured. [11]A heavenly voice went forth and said: 'Not because this is greater than that, [12]but rather because this one is forgiving (lit., "passes over his retaliations"), [13]but that one is not forgiving.'"

TRANSLATION AND COMMENTARY

mentioned in the verse are types of cedar, in addition to which there are another three trees which also come under the same category. Among these ten different species of cedar, there are some whose stumps grow new shoots. When Rabbi Ḥiyya bar Lulyani said that cedar stumps send forth new shoots, he was referring to these species of cedar.

תָּנוּ רַבָּנַן [1]Returning to the subject of praying for rain, the Gemara now quotes a Baraita in which **our Rabbis taught: "It once happened that** there was an extended period of drought and **Rabbi Eliezer decreed thirteen fasts upon the community** (a first set of three fasts, a second set of three fasts, and a final set of seven fasts, as explained at length in the first chapter of our tractate), [2]**but** still **rain did not fall.** [3]**At the** end of **the last** fast, **the congregation started to leave** the place where they had assembled for the special fast-day service. [4]But Rabbi Eliezer called them back and **said to them: 'Have you prepared graves for yourselves?** If rain does not fall soon, you will certainly need them, for everybody will die of starvation.' Rabbi Eliezer's final remark moved the congregation to true repentance. [5]**All the people burst out crying,** and soon afterwards the **rain** began **to fall."** The Baraita cites another story concerning Rabbi Eliezer on the same subject: [6]**"It also happened that Rabbi Eliezer went down before the ark** to lead the communal prayer on a public fast-day, **and he said the twenty-four blessings** of the special Amidah prayer recited on public fasts, **but he was not answered,** and rain did not fall. [7]Rabbi Eliezer's disciple, **Rabbi Akiva,** then **went down** before the ark **after him, and recited** the following prayer: [8]**'Our Father, our King, we have no king but You. Our Father, our King, for Your sake, have mercy upon us,'** [9]**and** immediately **it started to rain.** [10]**The Rabbis** began to **murmur** among themselves, asking each other how it was possible that Rabbi Akiva's prayers were answered, whereas Rabbi Eliezer's prayers were not. [11]**A heavenly voice went forth and said:** 'It is **not because this** Sage, Rabbi Akiva, **is greater than that** Sage, Rabbi Eliezer, [12]**but rather because this** Sage, Rabbi Akiva, **is forgiving** by nature, [13]**and that** Sage, Rabbi Eliezer, **is not forgiving** by nature. Rabbi Akiva is quick to forgive those who wrong him, whereas Rabbi Eliezer is less understanding of those who mistreat him, and insists on dealing with them according to the letter of the law. God repays the two Sages measure for measure. When Rabbi Eliezer prays to God for mercy, the request is denied, but when Rabbi Akiva prays, God quickly forgives the people's transgressions and cancels the decrees that have been issued against them.'"

RASHI

מעשה ברבי אליעזר בן הורקנוס — שלש עשרה תעניות שהתענו והלכו עד שגמרו שלשה עשרה, כדתנן (תענית יב,ב): עברו אלו ולא נענו כו׳. **התחילו הצבור לצאת** — מבית הכנסת. **קברים תקנתם** — בתמיה; אין לכם אלא לכו קברו עצמכם מפני הרעב. געו = צעקו, כמו ״אם יגעה שור על בלילו״ (איוב ו), ״הלוך וגעו״ (שמואל א׳ ו).

NOTES

שֶׁזֶּה מַעֲבִיר עַל מִידּוֹתָיו **Because this one is forgiving.** Elsewhere (*Rosh HaShanah* 17a), the Gemara states that if someone is forgiving and passes over the opportunity to retaliate against others, God repays him measure for measure and all his sins are pardoned. Just as he does not seek revenge from those who treated him wrongly, so too does God forgive him for the wrongs he himself committed. A similar story is told in the Jerusalem Talmud (*Ta'anit* 3:4),

TRANSLATION AND COMMENTARY

תָּנוּ רַבָּנַן [1]We learned in the first chapter of the tractate that if the beginning of the month of Kislev has arrived and it has not yet rained, the court decrees a series of three fasts to be observed by the entire community (see above, 10a). If this first series of fasts passes, and it still does not rain, the court decrees a second series of three fasts upon the entire community. And if the second series of fasts passes, and it still does not rain, the court decrees upon the entire community an additional seven fasts (see above, 12b). From this it may be inferred that once it has begun to rain, further fasting is unnecessary. **Our Rabbis taught** a Baraita which clarifies this issue: "If the community has already begun to observe a series of fasts because it has not rained sufficiently during the winter season, [2]**how much rain must** now **fall before the community may cease fasting?** The Tannaim disagree on the matter. [3]The community may stop fasting if the rain has penetrated the soil to **the full depth of the blade of the plow,** i.e., if the rain has penetrated the soil as far down as the the maximum penetration of the plow, or three handbreadths. [4]**This is the opinion of Rabbi Meir.** [5]**But the Sages say** that a distinction must be made between different types of soil. **If the soil is** particularly **dry,** so that the rain cannot penetrate very deeply, the community may stop fasting once the rain has penetrated to a depth of **a handbreadth.** [6]If it is **average soil,** the community may not stop fasting until the rain has penetrated to a depth of **two handbreadths.** [7]If the **ground** has already been well **plowed,** so that the rain can penetrate the soil easily, the community may not stop fasting until the rain has penetrated to a depth of **three handbreadths."**

[1]תָּנוּ רַבָּנַן: [2]עַד מָתַי יְהוּ הַגְּשָׁמִים יוֹרְדִין, וְהַצִּבּוּר פּוֹסְקִין מִתַּעֲנִיתָם? [3]כִּמְלֹא בֶּרֶךְ הַמַּחֲרֵישָׁה. [4]דִּבְרֵי רַבִּי מֵאִיר. [5]וַחֲכָמִים אוֹמְרִים: בַּחֲרֵבָה, טֶפַח. [6]בְּבֵינוֹנִית, טְפָחַיִים. [7]בַּעֲבוּדָה, שְׁלֹשָׁה טְפָחִים".

LITERAL TRANSLATION

[1]Our Rabbis taught: [2]"How much rain must fall, so that the community may end their fast? [3]The full depth of the blade (lit., 'knee') of the plow. [4][These are] the words of Rabbi Meir. [5]But the Sages say: In dry [soil], a handbreadth. [6]In average [soil], two handbreadths. [7]In plowed [soil], three handbreadths."

RASHI

ויהיו הצבור פוסקין מתעניתם — דתנן (שם): עברו אלו ולא נענו בית דין גוזרין עוד כו', אבל נענו — שוב אין צריכין להתענות. והני מילי — לצבור, אבל יחיד שהיה מתענה על החולה ונתרפא, או על צרה ועברה — הרי מתענה ומשלים, כדאמרן לעיל (י,ב). כך שמעתי. **כמלא ברך המחרישה** — אם טשטשו הגשמים בעומק הקרקע כשיעור שורת מענית המחרישה. **ברך** — הוא הכלי שחורשין בו, ומבריכין אותו סמוך לקרקע כשחורשין בו, כלומר, מילא התלם שיראו המים בתלם מחרישתו, שקו"ין קולטר"א. **בחרבה** — קרקע יבישה טפח, כיון דחריבה היא, ונכנסו בה הגשמים טפח — ודאי רוב גשמים ירדו. **בעבודה** — חרושה, כגון שדה ניר הנכנסים בה גשמים הרבה — שלשה טפחים, דאפילו בגשמים מועטין נכנסין בה בטפח או בטפחיים.

BACKGROUND

בֶּרֶךְ הַמַּחֲרֵישָׁה **The "knee" of the plow.**

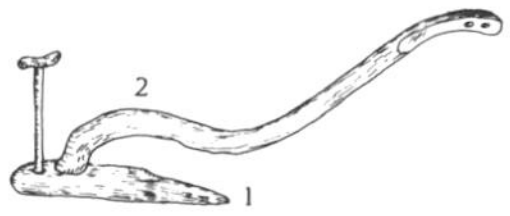

Diagram of an ancient plow

The "knee" of the plow seems to be the place where it is bent. Sometimes, when the blade of the plow plunges deep into the earth, the plow sinks in up to its "knee."

NOTES

according to which Rabbi Eliezer observed a fast, but it still did not rain, and then Rabbi Akiva observed a fast, and the rain began to fall. Rabbi Akiva accounted for the difference by means of a parable. The situation may be compared, noted Rabbi Akiva, to a king who had two daughters, one impudent and the other polite. The king wished to be rid of his impudent daughter as quickly as possible, and so he would immediately accede to any request she put forward to him. But he desired the company of his polite daughter, and so he would not answer any of her requests until after they were put forward to him repeatedly.

בֶּרֶךְ הַמַּחֲרֵישָׁה **The blade of the plow.** Most commentators agree that reference is being made here to the depth of the furrow which the plow makes in the ground, but there is disagreement as to the precise meaning of the term. *Rabbenu Ḥananel* and *Rabbenu Gershom* understand that the term *berekh* refers to the furrow itself. *Rivevan* explains that the furrow is called *berekh*, because the water gathers in it as in a pool (*berekhah*). Others explain that the *berekh* refers to the bend in the plow connecting the blade with the handle.

חֲרֵיבָה, בֵּינוֹנִית, עֲבוּדָה **Dry soil, average soil, plowed soil.** *Rabbenu Yehonatan* and others explain that dry soil is soil that has not been plowed for a long time; average soil is soil that has been plowed in previous years but not this year; and plowed soil is soil that has been plowed this year. *Mikhtam* maintains that the term "dry soil" describes the soil at the time of the first rainfall, when it is still0 extremely dry and the rain can hardly penetrate the ground at all; the term "average soil" describes the soil at the time of the second rainfall, when it is already moderately porous; and the term "plowed soil" refers to soil that has already been well plowed, so that the rainwater can penetrate it deeply.

HALAKHAH

עַד מָתַי יְהוּ הַגְּשָׁמִים יוֹרְדִין, וְהַצִּבּוּר פּוֹסְקִין מִתַּעֲנִיתָם? **How much rain must fall, so that the community may end their fast?** "If the community is fasting on account of drought, how much rain must fall so that they may end their fast? They may stop fasting if the rain has penetrated dry soil to a depth of a handbreadth, or if it has penetrated average soil to a depth of two handbreadths, or if it has penetrated plowed soil to a depth of three handbreadths, following the view of the Sages, against Rabbi Meir." (*Shulḥan Arukh, Oraḥ Ḥayyim* 575:11.)

¹תַּנְיָא: ״רַבִּי שִׁמְעוֹן בֶּן אֶלְעָזָר אוֹמֵר: ²אֵין לְךָ טֶפַח מִלְמַעְלָה שֶׁאֵין תְּהוֹם יוֹצֵא לִקְרָאתוֹ שְׁלֹשָׁה טְפָחִים״.
³וְהָא תַּנְיָא: ״טְפָחַיִים״!
⁴לָא קַשְׁיָא. כָּאן בַּעֲבוּדָה, ⁵כָּאן בְּשֶׁאֵינָהּ עֲבוּדָה.
⁶״אָמַר רַבִּי אֶלְעָזָר: כְּשֶׁמְּנַסְּכִין אֶת הַמַּיִם בֶּחָג, ⁷תְּהוֹם אוֹמֵר לַחֲבֵירוֹ: ׳אַבַּע מֵימֶיךָ, קוֹל שְׁנֵי רֵיעִים אֲנִי שׁוֹמֵעַ׳, ⁸שֶׁנֶּאֱמַר: ׳תְּהוֹם אֶל תְּהוֹם קוֹרֵא לְקוֹל צִנּוֹרֶיךָ, וגו׳׳״.
⁹אֲמַר רַבָּה: לְדִידִי חֲזֵי לִי הַאי רִידְיָא דָּמֵי לְעִיגְלָא וּפִירְסָא שִׂפְוָותֵיהּ, ¹⁰וְקַיְימָא בֵּין תְּהוֹמָא תַּתָּאָה לִתְהוֹמָא עִילָּאָה.

LITERAL TRANSLATION

1 It was taught: "Rabbi Shimon ben Elazar says: 2 There is no handbreadth from above to which the deep does not rise three handbreadths toward it." 3 But surely it was taught: "Two handbreadths"!
4 There is no difficulty. Here [it refers] to plowed [soil]; 5 here to unplowed [soil].
6 "Rabbi Elazar said: When they offer the water libation on the Festival [of Sukkot], 7 [one] deep says to the other: 'Let your water flow, [for] I hear the voice of two friends,' 8 as it is said: 'Deep calls to deep at the sound of your channels, etc.' "
9 Rabbah said: I myself saw Ridya appearing as a calf whose lips were parted, 10 and he was standing between the lower deep and the upper deep.

TRANSLATION AND COMMENTARY

תַּנְיָא 1 **It was taught** in a Baraita: **"Rabbi Shimon ben Elazar says: 2 There is no handbreadth** of rainfall **from above to which the** water of the **deep does not rise three handbreadths toward it."**

וְהָא תַּנְיָא 3 The Gemara objects: **But surely it was taught** otherwise in another Baraita, which states: "There is no handbreadth of rainfall from above to which the water of the deep does not rise **two handbreadths** toward it"!

לָא קַשְׁיָא 4 The Gemara answers: **There is** really **no difficulty. Here,** where the Baraita teaches that the water of the deep rises only two handbreadths to meet the handbreath of rainfall, it is referring to rain that fell on **plowed land** where even a small amount of rain can penetrate to the depth of a handbreadth. 5 But **here,** where the Baraita teaches that the water of the deep rises three handbreadths to meet the handbreadth of rainfall, it is referring to rain that fell on **unplowed land,** for it is only a heavier rain that can penetrate unplowed land to the depth of a handbreadth.

אָמַר רַבִּי אֶלְעָזָר 6 It was taught in a Baraita: **"Rabbi Elazar said: When the water libation is poured** over the altar **on the Festival of Sukkot, 7 one deep says to the other: 'Let your water flow, for I can hear** the voices of two of our **friends,** the regular wine libation offered every day, and the special water libation offered only on the Sukkot Festival. Since the people of Israel are faithfully fulfilling their obligation to offer the required libations, let us reward them with water flowing from the upper and lower depths.' 8 **As the verse says** [Psalms 42:8]: **'Deep calls to deep at the sound of your channels.'** The upper deep calls to the lower deep when it hears the libations flowing through the channels of the altar, and asks that they join together and let their water issue forth."

אֲמַר רַבָּה 9 **Rabbah said: I myself** once **saw Ridya,** the angel in charge of rain, **in the form of a calf whose lips were parted, 10 and he was standing between the lower deep** below ground **and the upper deep** high in

RASHI

אין לך כל טפח – כשנכנסו הגשמים בעומק הקרקע טפח – תהום עולה ומתגבר שלשה טפחים. ואף על גב דסומכא דארעא אלפא גרמידי בפרק "החליל" (סוכה נג,ב) – אפילו הכי רטיבותא מהנייא. **והתניא** – תהום יוצא לקראתו שני טפחים. **הא דקתני טפחיים ותו לא בעבודה** – דאף על גב דנכנסו טפח בקרקע פורתא הוא דנחית, ואהכי לא נפיק בהו לקבליה שלשה טפחים, אלא פורתא, טפחיים. **בשאינה עבודה** – דכי נכנסו בה טפח טפי הוא דנחית, ונפיק תהום לקיבליה שלשה טפחים. **אבע** – לשון נחל נובע. **קול שני ריעים** – ניסוך המים וניסוך היין. **תהום אל תהום קורא** – מים עליונים ומים תחתונים. **צנוריך** – אותן שני ספלים. **האי רידיא** – מלאך הממונה על הגשמים כך שמו. **דמי לעיגלא** – ולא גרסינן תלתא. **בין תהומא עילאה לתתאה** – בין הרקיע לאוקיינוס, היכא דנשקי ארעא ורקיע. **תהומא עלאה** – מים העליונים.

LANGUAGE

רִידְיָא **Ridya.** This word has been interpreted in various ways, either as derived from the Aramaic for plowing (רוּדְיָא) or from the Persian word for an abyss, *derya*, with the letters transposed. However, its meaning is not clear. The Geonim wrote that there was a voice that arose from swamps which was called *ridya* in their time.

LANGUAGE (RASHI)

קולטר״א* From the Old French *coltre*, meaning "the blade of a plow."

NOTES

כָּאן בַּעֲבוּדָה, כָּאן בְּשֶׁאֵינָהּ עֲבוּדָה **Here it refers to plowed soil, here to unplowed soil.** *Gevurat Ari* identifies the "unplowed soil" mentioned here with the "dry soil" mentioned above, which leads him to certain difficulties in reconciling the two passages. *Rashash* explains that the "unplowed soil" referred to here is the same as the "average soil" mentioned above. Thus, the ratio between the depth to which the rainwater sinks and the height to which the water of the deep rises to meet the rainwater is constant (1 to 2). When rain penetrates average soil one handbreadth, the same amount of rain penetrates plowed soil one-and-a-half handbreadths (we saw above that rain penetrates plowed soil fifty per cent more deeply [three handbreadths] than the same amount of rain penetrates average soil [two handbreadths]). And since the water of the deep rises twice as much as the rainwater penetrates, the water of the deep rises two handbreadths to meet the handbreadth of rain that falls on average soil, and it rises three handbreadths to meet the same amount of rain that falls on plowed soil (and penetrates one-and-a-half handbreadths).

דָּמֵי לְעִיגְלָא וּפִירְסָא שִׂפְוָותֵיהּ **Appearing as a calf whose**

TRANSLATION AND COMMENTARY

the sky. [1]**To the upper deep he said: "Distill your water** and let it rain." [2]And **to the lower deep he said: "Let your water flow** from below, so that it may moisten the land." [3]**As the verse says** (Song of Songs 2:12): **"The blossoms appear on the earth;** the time of the singing bird is come, and the voice of the turtledove [תּוֹר] is heard in our land." The water libation is offered once a year on the Sukkot Festival, just as the blossoms appear once a year on the earth, and the time of the songs sung on the Sukkot Festival has come. At that time the angel in charge of rain is heard in our land, instructing the upper and lower depths to let their waters flow. Rabbah understands that the word תּוֹר is not used here in its Hebrew sense as denoting the turtledove, but rather in its Aramaic sense as denoting the ox. Thus the *tor* mentioned here refers to Ridya, the angel who makes his appearance as a young ox.

הָיוּ מִתְעַנִּין [4]We learned in our Mishnah: **"If people** have undertaken to **observe a fast** on account of drought, **and rain falls for them before sunrise** on the day of the fast, and in sufficient quantities to make the fast unnecessary, **they do not** have to **complete their fast."** [5]**Our Rabbis taught** a Baraita dealing with the same issue: **"If people** have undertaken to **observe a fast** on account of drought, **and rain falls for them before sunrise** on the day of the fast, and in sufficient quantities to make the fast unnecessary, **they do not** have to **complete their fast.** [6]But if the rain falls only **after sunrise, they** must **complete their fast.** If the fast becomes superfluous only after sunrise, after the people have already begun to fast, it must be observed until completion. [7]**This is the opinion of Rabbi Meir.** [8]**Rabbi Yehudah** disagrees and **says:** If a fast has been proclaimed on account of drought, and rain falls **before noon** on the day of the fast, **the people do not** have to **complete their fast.** [9]But if the rain falls **after noon, they** must **complete their fast.** Most people take their main meal at noon, and so it is only at noon that a day begins to be regarded as a fast-day in the practical sense. If a fast was proclaimed but became unnecessary before noon, before it was actually regarded as a fast, it does not

[1]לִתְהוֹמָא עִילָּאָה אֲמַר לֵיהּ: "חֲשׁוֹר מֵימֶיךָ". [2]לִתְהוֹמָא תַּתָּאָה אֲמַר לֵיהּ: "אַבַּע מֵימֶיךָ", [3]שֶׁנֶּאֱמַר: "הַנִּצָּנִים נִרְאוּ בָאָרֶץ, וגו׳".

[4]"הָיוּ מִתְעַנִּין, וְיָרְדוּ גְּשָׁמִים קוֹדֶם הָנֵץ הַחַמָּה, כו׳". [5]תָּנוּ רַבָּנַן: "הָיוּ מִתְעַנִּין, וְיָרְדוּ לָהֶם גְּשָׁמִים קוֹדֶם הָנֵץ הַחַמָּה, לֹא יַשְׁלִימוּ. [6]לְאַחַר הָנֵץ הַחַמָּה, יַשְׁלִימוּ. [7]דִּבְרֵי רַבִּי מֵאִיר. [8]רַבִּי יְהוּדָה אוֹמֵר: קוֹדֶם חֲצוֹת, לֹא יַשְׁלִימוּ. [9]לְאַחַר חֲצוֹת, יַשְׁלִימוּ.

LITERAL TRANSLATION

[1]To the upper deep he said: "Distill your water." [2]To the lower deep he said: "Let your water flow," [3]as it is said: "The blossoms appear on the earth, etc."

[4]"[If] they were fasting, and rains fell before sunrise, etc." [5]Our Rabbis taught: "[If] they were fasting and rains fell for them before sunrise, they do not complete [their fast]. [6]After sunrise, they complete [their fast]. [7][These are] the words of Rabbi Meir. [8]Rabbi Yehudah says: Before noon, they do not complete [their fast]. [9]After noon, they complete [their fast].

RASHI

חשור מימיך – לרקיע. **אבע מימיך** – למטה בקרקע. **הנצנים נראו בארץ** – כלומר, כשמנסכין מים בחג שהניסוכין נראו בארץ, שאין באין אלא משנה לחבירתה כגון זה שאינו יוצא אלא משנה לשנה. ו"עת הזמיר הגיע" – זמירות החג, אז "קול התור" – מלאך דומה לשור, תרגום "שור" = תור, שבשעה שמנסכין מים בחג הוא אומר כן. לשון אחר: כמשמעו, הנצנים נראו והזמיר הגיע, בשוה וקול התור נשמע. **קודם הנץ החמה לא ישלימו** – דאכתי לא חל עלייהו תענית, כי נחתי גשמים. **קודם חצות** – דחצות זמן אכילה היא, מחצות ואילך חל התענית, כיון שלא סעדו בשעת סעודה.

NOTES

lips were parted. *Maharsha* explains that the angel in charge of rain appears as an ox, because the ox is the zodiacal sign of the month of Iyyar, the last month of the year during which rainfall is regarded as a blessing. *Rabbi Ya'akov Emden* suggests that the angel of rain appears as an ox because rain leaves its mark on the land just as an ox which plows the field. Both understand that the calf's parted lips symbolize a smile, for the angel of rain is happy to instruct the upper and lower depths to let their waters flow.

חֲצוֹת Noon. Our commentary follows *Rashi*, who explains that, according to Rabbi Yehudah, the fast must be observed until completion if it does not rain until after noon, for most people take their main meal at noon, and it is their refraining from that meal which determines the day as a fast-day. The Jerusalem Talmud explains that once the greater part of the day has been observed as a fast, the fast must be observed until completion.

HALAKHAH

הָיוּ מִתְעַנִּין, וְיָרְדוּ גְּשָׁמִים If they were fasting, and rains fell. "If the members of the community are fasting and it begins to rain after noon, they must prolong the fast until the end of the day. If it begins to rain before noon, they do not complete the fast, but eat and drink and celebrate the day as a holiday, and toward evening they gather together and recite the Great Hallel." (*Shulḥan Arukh, Oraḥ Ḥayyim* 575:11.)

[1]רַבִּי יוֹסֵי אוֹמֵר: קוֹדֶם תֵּשַׁע שָׁעוֹת, לֹא יַשְׁלִימוּ. [2]לְאַחַר תֵּשַׁע שָׁעוֹת, יַשְׁלִימוּ, [3]שֶׁכֵּן מָצִינוּ בְּאַחְאָב מֶלֶךְ יִשְׂרָאֵל שֶׁהִתְעַנָּה מִתֵּשַׁע שָׁעוֹת וּלְמַעְלָה, [4]שֶׁנֶּאֱמַר: ׳הֲרָאִיתָ כִּי נִכְנַע אַחְאָב, וגו׳?׳״.

[5]רַבִּי יְהוּדָה נְשִׂיאָה גְּזַר תַּעֲנִיתָא, וְיָרְדוּ לָהֶם גְּשָׁמִים לְאַחַר הָנֵץ הַחַמָּה. [6]סְבַר לְאַשְׁלוּמִינְהוּ. [7]אֲמַר לֵיהּ רַבִּי אַמִּי: ״קוֹדֶם חֲצוֹת״ [8]וְ״אַחַר חֲצוֹת״ שָׁנִינוּ.

LITERAL TRANSLATION

[1]Rabbi Yose says: Before nine hours, they do not complete [their fast]. [2]After nine hours, they complete [their fast], [3]for we find regarding Aḥab the King of Israel that he fasted from nine hours onward, [4]as it is said: 'Do you see how Ahab humbles himself, etc.?'"

[5]Rabbi Yehudah Nesi'ah decreed a fast, and rains fell for them after sunrise. [6]He thought to complete it. [7]Rabbi Ammi said to him: We have learned: "Before noon" [8]and "after noon."

TRANSLATION AND COMMENTARY

have to be observed until completion. But if the fast became unnecessary only after noon, after the day was already regarded as a fast-day, for most people had already refrained from eating their midday meal, the fast must be observed until completion. [1]**Rabbi Yose says:** If it rains **before** the end of **the ninth hour of the day** [which is in the middle of the afternoon], **the people do not** have to **complete their fast.** [2]But if it rains **after** the end of **the ninth hour of the day, they must complete their fast.** You will not bind anyone — not even among those who rise from their sleep late in the morning and put off eating for a few more hours — who has not taken his main meal of the day by the end of the ninth hour of the day. Thus, only if the people have refrained from eating until the end of the ninth hour of the day must they complete the fast, for it is only then that the day is regarded as a fast-day for everyone. [3]This is supported by what **we find regarding Ahab the King of Israel, who fasted from** the end of **the ninth hour onward, as it is said** [I Kings 21:27-29]: 'And it came to pass, when Ahab heard these words, he rent his clothes, and put sackcloth on his flesh, and fasted, and lay in sackcloth, and went softly. And the word of the Lord came to Elijah the Tishbite, [4]saying: **Do you see how Ahab humbles himself** before me?' According to tradition, Ahab did not begin his fast until the end of the ninth hour of the day. Thus we see that by the end of the ninth hour of the day, the day is surely regarded as a fast-day, which must be completed even if it rains later in the day."

רַבִּי יְהוּדָה נְשִׂיאָה [5]It was related that Rabbi Yehudah Nesi'ah once **decreed a** public **fast** on account of drought, **and it began to rain** in the morning **after sunrise** on the day of the fast. [6]Rabbi Yehudah Nesi'ah **thought that,** while the fast was now unnecessary, nevertheless since it had already been started **it should be prolonged** until the end of the day. [7]But **Rabbi Ammi said to him: We have learned** in the Mishnah that, according to Rabbi Yehudah, if it has rained **before noon,** the fast does not have to be observed until completion, [8]**but** if it rains **after noon,** the fast must be continued until the end of the day, and the law is in accordance with the viewpoint of Rabbi Yehudah. Thus there is no reason for the fast that you decreed on the community to be observed until the end of the day, for the fast became unnecessary before noon.

RASHI

ועשו יום טוב — מתוך שמחה. **הלל הגדול** — ״הודו לאלהי האלהים כי לעולם חסדו״. ומפני שנאמר בו ״נותן לחם לכל בשר״, כדאמרינן בשילהי פסחים (קיח,א). **שכן מצינו כו׳** — כלומר, שאין לך אדם בעולם שאין תענית חל עליו מתשע שעות ואילך, אפילו בני מלכים שדרכן לאכול בתשע שעות, שעד שלש שעות הן ישנים במטותיהן ושוהין ששה שעות ואוכלין. וכדאמרינן בפסחים (קז,ב): אפילו אגריפס המלך, שרגיל לאכול בתשע שעות ביום — לא יאכל עד שתחשך. שנאמר ״הראית כי נכנע אחאב מפני״, ואחאב לא חלה תעניתו עליו אלא מתשע שעות ואילך, ועד תשע שעות היה יכול לאכול, שלא גמר בדעתו להתענות. אלא שבא אליהו אותו היום שנכנס בכרם נבות היזרעאלי, ואמר ליה ״הרצחת וגם ירשת״ וגו׳, (מלכים א׳ כא) ״ילקו הכלבים״ וגו׳ (שם), וכתיב ״וילוס״ — שהתענה אותו היום.

NOTES

שֶׁכֵּן מָצִינוּ בְּאַחְאָב For we find regarding Ahab. *Rabbenu Ḥananel* notes that there is no conclusive proof from the verse that Ahab did not begin his fast until the end of the ninth hour of the day. But there is a Geonic tradition according to which Naboth's execution, Ahab's entry into Naboth's vineyard, and Elijah's prophecy all took place on the same day. Thus it was not until late afternoon — the end of the ninth hour, according to this tradition — that Ahab rent his clothes and began to fast. From the fact that Ahab began to fast only at the end of the ninth hour, yet nevertheless is regarded as having observed a fast, Rabbi Yose infers that if it does not rain until the end of the ninth hour of the day, the fast must be completed.

Rabbenu Elyakim suggests a novel explanation according to which the verse, "Do you see how Ahab humbles himself?", refers not to Ahab's repentance for his role in Naboth's execution, but rather to his repentance for his role in the episode involving the Prophet Elijah and the prophets of Baal (I Kings, chapter 18). Elijah caused the rain to fall at the time of the evening sacrifice (v. 36), after the ninth

[1]שְׁמוּאֵל הַקָּטָן גָּזַר תַּעֲנִיתָא, וְיָרְדוּ לָהֶם גְּשָׁמִים קוֹדֶם הָנֵץ הַחַמָּה. [2]כְּסְבוּרִין הָעָם לוֹמַר שִׁבְחוֹ שֶׁל צִבּוּר הוּא. [3]אָמַר לָהֶם: "אֶמְשׁוֹל לָכֶם מָשָׁל. [4]לְמָה הַדָּבָר דּוֹמֶה? [5]לְעֶבֶד שֶׁמְּבַקֵּשׁ פְּרָס מֵרַבּוֹ. [6]אָמַר לָהֶם: 'תְּנוּ לוֹ וְאַל אֶשְׁמַע קוֹלוֹ'".

[7]שׁוּב שְׁמוּאֵל הַקָּטָן גָּזַר תַּעֲנִיתָא, וְיָרְדוּ לָהֶם גְּשָׁמִים לְאַחַר שְׁקִיעַת הַחַמָּה. [8]כְּסְבוּרִים הָעָם לוֹמַר שִׁבְחוֹ שֶׁל צִבּוּר הוּא. [9]אָמַר לָהֶם שְׁמוּאֵל: 'לֹא שֶׁבַח שֶׁל צִבּוּר הוּא. [10]אֶלָּא אֶמְשׁוֹל לָכֶם מָשָׁל. [11]לְמָה הַדָּבָר דּוֹמֶה? לְעֶבֶד שֶׁמְּבַקֵּשׁ פְּרָס מֵרַבּוֹ, [12]וְאָמַר לָהֶם: 'הַמְתִּינוּ לוֹ עַד שֶׁיִּתְמַקְמֵק וְיִצְטַעֵר, וְאַחַר כָּךְ תְּנוּ לוֹ'".

LITERAL TRANSLATION

[1]Shmuel HaKatan decreed a fast, and rains fell for them before sunrise. [2]The people thought to say it was [to] the credit of the community. [3]He said to them: "I will tell you a parable: [4]To what may the matter be compared? [5]To a servant who asks a reward from his master. [6]He said to them: 'Give him and let me not hear his voice.'"

[7]Again Shmuel HaKatan decreed a fast, and rains fell for them after sunset. [8]The people thought to say it was [to] the credit of the community. [9]Shmuel said to them: "It is not [to] the credit of the community. [10]Rather, I will tell you a parable. [11]To what may the matter be compared? To a servant who asks a reward from his master, [12]and he said to them: 'Wait until he is crushed and in distress, and afterwards give him.'"

RASHI

הכי גרסינן: שמואל הקטן גזר תעניתא וירדו גשמים קודם הנץ החמה. שבח צבור הוא – שעדיין לא קראו ונענו. **למה הדבר דומה וכו׳.**

TRANSLATION AND COMMENTARY

שְׁמוּאֵל הַקָּטָן [1]It was reported that **Shmuel HaKatan** once **decreed a** communal **fast** because of drought, **and** then on the day of the proposed fast **it began to rain** early in the morning **before sunrise.** [2]**The people thought** that **it was to the credit of the community** that rain had fallen even before their special prayers for rain were offered. [3]But Shmuel HaKatan **said to them:** "It is not to your credit that it started to rain even before you began to pray. **I will tell you a parable** to illustrate what actually happened. [4]**To what may this matter be compared?** [5]It may be compared **to a servant who asks his master for a reward,** [6]and the master **says to** his attendants: **'Give** my servant what he wants, not because he is deserving, but **so that I will not have to hear his voice.'** God caused it to rain even before you began to pray, not because He thought you deserved it, but rather because He did not want to hear your prayers."

שׁוּב שְׁמוּאֵל הַקָּטָן [7]It was further related that **on another occasion Shmuel HaKatan decreed a** public **fast** because of drought, **and it began to rain after sunset,** after the fast had been completed. Remembering what Shmuel HaKatan had said following the previous fast, [8]**the people thought** that **it was to the credit of the community** that God had heard their day-long prayers. [9]But **Shmuel** HaKatan **said to them: "It was not to the credit of the community** that it did not rain until the fast was completed. [10]**Rather, I will tell you a parable** to help you understand what happened. [11]**To what may this matter be compared?** It may be compared **to a servant who asks his master for a reward,** [12]**and** the master **says to** his attendants: 'Do not grant my servant his wish right away. **Wait until he is** totally **crushed and in distress, and** only **afterwards give him** what he wants.' God did not cause rain to fall before the fast was completed, not because He found your prayers pleasing, but rather because He wanted you to suffer from hunger before He granted your desire."

NOTES

hour. He then told Ahab to go up and eat and drink (v. 41), from which it might be understood that until then Ahab had been observing a fast. But Ahab humbled himself before God, and continued his fast until the end of the day. From this it may be inferred that if a fast is proclaimed on account of drought, and it rains after the end of the ninth hour on the day of the fast, the fast must be completed.

כְּסְבוּרִין הָעָם לוֹמַר שִׁבְחוֹ שֶׁל צִבּוּר The people thought to say it was to the credit of the community. Even though it would appear from the Mishnah that rain falling on a fast-day, whether at the beginning of the day or at the day's end, is indeed a credit to the community, a pious man like Shmuel HaKatan would refrain from interpreting the rain as a sign that God was pleased with His people, and would instead take the timing of the rain as an expression of God's displeasure (*HaKotev* in *Ein Ya'akov*).

The Gemara argues that rain can only be considered as a credit to the community if, as soon as the prayer leader said: "Who causes the wind to blow," a gust of wind blew, and then when he said: "Who causes the rain to fall," rain immediately began to fall. *Keren Orah* explains this in the light of the verse (Isaiah 65:24): "Before they call, I will answer." If God is pleased with His people, He will answer their prayers immediately after they offer Him praise (i.e., "Who causes the wind to blow and the rain to fall"), even before they actually call out to Him with their requests.

BACKGROUND

אֲבִי גּוֹבָר Avi Govar. The synagogue of Avi Govar was apparently in a small town, perhaps a suburb of Meḥoza, between Meḥoza and the town of Mavrakhta. The place may have been named after the founder of this synagogue, which is mentioned several times in the Talmud, for it was visited by some of the great Amoraim over a number of generations. Thus it seems that it was an important center in the region.

TRANSLATION AND COMMENTARY

וְלִשְׁמוּאֵל הַקָּטָן [1]The Gemara asks: Shmuel HaKatan argued that if it rains before sunrise on the day of a fast, or if it rains after sunset when the fast is already over, it should be understood as an indication of God's displeasure. **Now, according to Shmuel HaKatan, how do we visualize** a case where rainfall can be considered **something to the credit of the community?**

אֲמַר [2]The Gemara answers: **If,** when the prayer leader **said: "Who causes the wind to blow,"** a gust of **wind immediately blew,** [3]and then when **he said: "Who causes the rain to fall," rain** immediately began to **fall,** that is surely a sign that God was pleased with His people's prayers, and it is to the community's credit that the rain fell.

מַעֲשֶׂה [4]Our Mishnah concluded with the following incident: **"It once happened that a fast was decreed in Lod,** and rain began to fall before noon on the day of the fast. Rabbi Tarfon told the people to go home and celebrate the day as a holiday. And indeed the people of Lod went home, and ate and drank, and celebrated the day as a holiday. In the afternoon they returned to the synagogue, and recited the Great Hallel." The Gemara asks: Why did the people first go home and eat, and only return to the synagogue later in the day to recite Hallel? [5]**Surely they should have recited Hallel before** they went home for their celebratory meal!

אַבַּיֵי וְרָבָא [6]**Abaye and Rava both said:** They did not recite Hallel immediately, because Hallel should only be recited [26A] [7]**when one's soul is satisfied and one's stomach is full.** A person cannot recite Hallel in the proper manner if he is hungry or upset. Thus the people of Lod first went home and ate and drank, in order to put themselves in the proper frame of mind to praise God.

אִינִי [8]The Gemara raises an objection: **Is it** really **true** that Hallel should be recited only when one's soul is satisfied and one's stomach is full? [9]**But surely Rav Pappa happened to come to the synagogue of Avi Govar** in the vicinity of Meḥoza, [10]**where he decreed a fast** because of drought. [11]**Rain** began to **fall before noon** on the day of the fast, and so the fast was canceled. Rav Pappa immediately [12]**recited Hallel** together with the rest of the community, **and** only **afterwards** did he send the people home to **eat and drink** in celebration of the rain!

[1]וְלִשְׁמוּאֵל הַקָּטָן, שִׁבְחוֹ שֶׁל צִבּוּר הֵיכִי דָּמֵי? [2]אָמַר: ״מַשִּׁיב הָרוּחַ״, וּנְשַׁב זִיקָא; [3]אָמַר: ״מוֹרִיד הַגֶּשֶׁם״, וַאֲתָא מִיטְרָא. [4]״מַעֲשֶׂה וְגָזְרוּ תַּעֲנִית בְּלוֹד, כו׳״. [5]וְנֵימָא הַלֵּל מֵעִיקָּרָא? [6]אַבַּיֵי וְרָבָא דְּאָמְרִי תַּרְוַיְיהוּ: לְפִי שֶׁאֵין אוֹמְרִים הַלֵּל [26A] [7]אֶלָּא עַל נֶפֶשׁ שְׂבֵעָה וְכֶרֶס מְלֵאָה. [8]אִינִי? [9]וְהָא רַב פַּפָּא אִיקְלַע לְבֵי כְּנִישְׁתָּא דַּאֲבִי גּוֹבָר, [10]וְגָזַר תַּעֲנִית, [11]וְיָרְדוּ לָהֶם גְּשָׁמִים עַד חֲצוֹת, [12]וְאָמַר הַלֵּל, וְאַחַר כָּךְ אָכְלוּ וְשָׁתוּ!

LITERAL TRANSLATION

[1]And according to Shmuel HaKatan, how do we visualize [something to] the credit of the community?

[2][If] he said: "Who causes the wind to blow," and the wind blew; [3][if] he said: "Who causes the rain to fall," and rain came.

[4]"It once happened that they decreed a fast in Lod, etc." [5]But let them recite Hallel from the outset!

[6]Abaye and Rava both said: Because we do not recite Hallel [26A] [7]except on a satisfied soul and a full stomach.

[8]Is that so? [9]But surely Rav Pappa happened to come to the synagogue of Avi Govar, [10]and he decreed a fast, [11]and rains fell for them before noon, [12]and he recited Hallel, and afterwards they ate and drank!

RASHI

אלא בנפש שבעה — מתוך שכתוב בו ״נותן לחם לכל בשר״ (תהלים קלו) — נאה להאמר על השבע. **דאבי גובר** — שם אדם, או מקום.

NOTES

הַלֵּל Hallel. The Tosefta (3:5) explains that the term "Great Hallel" refers to Psalm 136. Elsewhere (see *Pesaḥim* 118a; Jerusalem Talmud, *Ta'anit* 3:11), the term is understood as including additional Psalms as well, or perhaps even to the ordinary Hallel recited on all the Festivals (Psalms 113-118). *Rashi* explains that Psalm 136 was recited after the long-awaited rain, because it includes the words (v.25): "Who gives bread to all flesh, for his mercy endures forever." *Rabbenu Ḥananel* accepts the view that the Great Hallel starts with Psalm 135, and explains that that chapter was recited because it includes the words (v.7): "He causes vapors to ascend from the ends of the earth; He makes lightnings for the rain; He brings the wind out of his treasuries."

עַל נֶפֶשׁ שְׂבֵעָה On a satisfied soul. *Rashi* explains that since the Great Hallel includes the verse (Psalms 136:25): "Who gives bread to all flesh, for his mercy endures forever," it would be improper for a person who is hungry to recite it.

TRANSLATION AND COMMENTARY

שָׁאנֵי בְּנֵי מְחוֹזָא [1]The Gemara answers: Indeed, Hallel should only be recited on a full stomach. But the case of **the people of Meḥoza was different, for drunkenness was common among them.** Had Rav Pappa sent the congregation home to eat and drink, it is likely that they would have become drunk, so that afterwards they would not have been able to recite Hallel with the proper decorum. Thus Rav Pappa instructed them to recite Hallel first, and only afterwards did he allow them to go home for their celebratory meal.

[1]שָׁאנֵי בְּנֵי מְחוֹזָא, דִּשְׁכִיחֵי בְּהוּ שִׁכְרוּת.

הדרן עלך סדר תעניות אלו

LITERAL TRANSLATION

[1]The people of Meḥoza are different, for drunkenness is common among them.

RASHI

דשכיח בהו — יין ושכרות, ופשעי ולא יאמרו הלל.

הדרן עלך סדר תעניות אלו

Conclusion to Chapter Three

This chapter reaches the Halakhic conclusion that it is appropriate to proclaim a public fast in response to any impending calamity threatening the community's financial well-being, its health, or its peace and security. If the threat is immediate, the fast is proclaimed as close as possible to the impending danger. Moreover, even if the community is not facing any present danger, but a situation exists which may lead to danger in the future, such as if a foreign army invaded the country not in order to attack the Jewish people but to use their territory as a corridor by which to reach another country, a fast must be proclaimed.

The general rule is that whenever a calamity threatens a specific community, the people living in that community must observe a fast, but the people living in the surrounding areas are not required to fast, but they must sound the alarm with special prayers and the sounding of the shofar. Whenever it is likely that a calamity which has struck in a specific place will spread to the surrounding areas — for example, when a community has been by an infectious disease — a fast must be proclaimed throughout the province or region. If a calamity strikes Eretz Israel, the heart of the Jewish people, a fast must be proclaimed in Jewish communities throughout the world.

The Rishonim refer to this chapter as "the chapter of the saintly," for while it contains a significant number of Halakhic discussions, most of the chapter is devoted to anecdotes describing the prayers offered by the righteous during periods of distress and how these prayers were answered. In this way the chapter serves as a spiritual guide through difficult times, both because it demonstrates that God responds to the prayers of those whose prayers are fit to be answered, and because it expands the definition of "the righteous" to whose prayers God hearkens. It becomes clear from this chapter that the truly righteous people of the world, whose prayers command a heavenly response, are not always recognized as such by their contemporaries.

Introduction to Chapter Four

בִּשְׁלֹשָׁה פְּרָקִים

"And I will turn your feasts into mourning, and all your songs into lamentation. And I wll bring up sackcloth upon all loins and baldness upon every head, and I will make it as the mourning for an only son, and its end like a bitter day." (Amos 8:10.)

"Thus says the Lord of hosts: The fast of the fourth month, and the fast of the fifth, and the fast of the seventh, and the fast of the tenth, shall become times of joy and gladness and cheerful feasts for the house of Judah; therefore love truth and peace." (Zechariah 8:19.)

Until now our tractate has discussed those public fasts that are decreed in periods of severe drought or when there is some other impending calamity. Having no fixed dates, these fasts are proclaimed whenever catastrophe looms over the community. There are, however, certain public fasts that have a fixed date in the calendar. The fixed fast days discussed in this chapter fall into two very different categories. The chapter opens with a discussion regarding the fasts that were observed in the Temple period by the members of the *ma'amad*, the group of Israelites who represented the entire people in Jerusalem when the communal sacrifices were offered, and assembled for special prayer services in their home communities. The purpose of fasts observed by the members of the *ma'amad* was not so much to offer prayers relating to the specific events of the day, but rather to offer general prayers for continued stability, health, and success. This chapter deals with these fasts, the special prayers that accompanied them, and the relationship between the fasts and the various festivals celebrated in the course of the year.

The chapter continues with a discussion of fixed fasts of a completely different kind — the commemorative fasts enacted after the destruction of the First Temple, and reestablished after the destruction of the Second Temple. Referred to here are the four fasts instituted to commemorate national calamities in the past — in particular, the destruction of the Temple, in the wake of which additional catastrophes struck the Jewish people. The clarification of the laws pertaining to these days, which are not only days of fasting, but also (the Ninth of Av, in particular) days of national mourning, constitutes the primary subject matter of this chapter. The practices relating to certain days of the year which were celebrated as semi-holidays during the period of the Temple are also explained.

TRANSLATION AND COMMENTARY

MISHNAH בִּשְׁלֹשָׁה פְּרָקִים בַּשָּׁנָה [1]Our Mishnah opens with a discussion of the Priestly Blessing recited on public fasts. Every day the priests bless the congregation, using the Priestly Blessing (Numbers 6:24-26), which is inserted into the last blessing of the repetition of the Amidah prayer recited by the prayer leader. The priests face the congregation and pronounce the blessing while raising their hands according to a traditional rite. Ordinarily, the Priestly Blessing is recited once a day, during the morning service. On Shabbat and Festivals it is also recited during the musaf service. **On three occasions during the year the priests raise their hands** and recite the Priestly Blessing **four times a day (in the morning service, in the musaf service, in the afternoon service, and in the service of the closing of the gates** known as neilah, which is recited shortly before sunset); [2]**On** the public **fast-days** proclaimed during times of drought or other calamities, **at the** special prayer services conducted each day by the members of **the *ma'amad*** whose turn it was to serve that week (as will be explained below), **and on Yom Kippur.**

אֵלּוּ הֵן מַעֲמָדוֹת [3]The Mishnah now clarifies the matter of the *ma'amadot*. **These are the *ma'amadot*: The verse** referring to the daily sacrifice of two lambs, one in the morning and one in the afternoon, **says** (Numbers 28:2): **"Command the Children of Israel,** and say to them: **My offering, My bread for My sacrifices** made by fire, for a sweet savor to Me, you shall observe to offer to Me in their due season." The introduction to the verse, "Command the Children of Israel," as well as the plural verb "you shall observe [תִּשְׁמְרוּ]," teach that the daily sacrifice is a communal offering that must be purchased with the half-shekels donated to the

בִּשְׁלֹשָׁה

[1]פְּרָקִים בַּשָּׁנָה כֹּהֲנִים נוֹשְׂאִין אֶת כַּפֵּיהֶן אַרְבַּע פְּעָמִים בַּיּוֹם, בַּשַּׁחֲרִית, בַּמּוּסָף, בַּמִּנְחָה, וּבִנְעִילַת שְׁעָרִים: [2]בַּתַּעֲנִיּוֹת, וּבַמַּעֲמָדוֹת, וּבְיוֹם הַכִּפּוּרִים. [3]אֵלּוּ הֵן מַעֲמָדוֹת: לְפִי שֶׁנֶּאֱמַר: "צַו אֶת בְּנֵי יִשְׂרָאֵל... אֶת קָרְבָּנִי, לַחְמִי".

LITERAL TRANSLATION

MISHNAH [1]On three occasions in the year the priests raise their hands [in blessing] four times in the day, in the morning service, in the musaf service, in the afternoon service, and in [the service of] the closing of the gates: [2]On fast-days, on *ma'amadot*, and on Yom Kippur.

[3]These are the *ma'amadot*: For it is said: "Command the Children of Israel... My offering, My bread."

RASHI

משנה **בשלשה פרקים במוסף** — מפרש בגמרא. **נעילת שערים** — מפורש בברכות ירושלמי בפרק "תפלת השחר" אימתי נעילה: יש אומרים נעילת שערי מקדש, ויש אומרים נעילת שערי שמים, שנועלים אותן לעת ערב בגמר תפלה. ונוהגין היו להתפלל תפלת נעילה בכל תעניתם, כדרך שמתפללין ביום הכפורים. **אלו הן מעמדות** — המתענין מתפללין בעריהם שיתקבל ברצון קרבן אחיהם כדלקמן. **לפי שנאמר צו את בני ישראל וגו'** — שהתמיד בא מן השקלים של כל ישראל, ואי אפשר שיהו כל ישראל עומדין על גבי קרבנם, ומינו מעמדות להיות במקומם.

NOTES

וּבִנְעִילַת שְׁעָרִים And in the service of the closing of the gates. The Jerusalem Talmud offers two explanations of this name. Rabbi Yoḥanan suggests that the name of the service refers to the daily closing of the Temple gates, which took place toward the end of the day. Rav explains that it refers to the closing of the heavenly gates at sunset, which hides the sun from view until the following morning.

בַּתַּעֲנִיּוֹת On fast days. The Mishnah refers here to the public fast-days proclaimed in times of drought or in the face of other impending calamities, for on the fixed fasts commemorating national calamities there is no neilah service. The Rishonim disagree about whether or not the neilah service is conducted on public fasts proclaimed outside Eretz Israel (see *Ra'avad*, cited by *Ramban*; see also *Ritva*).

לְפִי שֶׁנֶּאֱמַר: "צַו" For it is said: "Command." The Mishnah seems to be arguing that, since the verse implies that the daily sacrifice is a communal offering, all Israel should be required to be present in the Temple when it is brought, but since this is a practical impossibility, the *ma'amad* system was established so that representatives of the people would always be present in the Temple when the daily sacrifices were offered. Some commentators suggest that the verse itself alludes to the *ma'amadot*, for the end of the verse reads: תִּשְׁמְרוּ לְהַקְרִיב (lit., "you shall guard to offer"), implying that watches must be set up to stand guard around the sacrificial service and pray that it be accepted by God (*Petaḥ Einayim*; see also *Tosefot Yom Tov*, whose reading of the Mishnah includes the end of the verse).

HALAKHAH

מַעֲמָדוֹת *Ma'amadot*. "A person who brings a sacrifice is required to be present in the Temple when his sacrifice is offered. Since the communal sacrifices are the sacrifices of all Israel, but the entire community of Israel cannot be present in the Temple each time those sacrifices are offered, the early Prophets instituted that worthy and sin-fearing people be selected to represent the entire people when the communal sacrifices are offered, and to that end they divided all Israel into twenty-four *ma'amadot* corresponding to the twenty-four *mishmarot* of priests and Levites." (*Rambam, Sefer Avodah, Hilkhot Klei HaMikdash* 6:1.)

[1]וְכִי הֵיאָךְ קָרְבָּנוֹ שֶׁל אָדָם קָרֵב וְהוּא אֵינוֹ עוֹמֵד עַל גַּבָּיו? [2]הִתְקִינוּ נְבִיאִים הָרִאשׁוֹנִים עֶשְׂרִים וְאַרְבָּעָה מִשְׁמָרוֹת. [3]עַל כָּל מִשְׁמָר וּמִשְׁמָר הָיָה מַעֲמָד בִּירוּשָׁלַיִם שֶׁל כֹּהֲנִים, שֶׁל לְוִיִּם, וְשֶׁל יִשְׂרְאֵלִים. [4]הִגִּיעַ זְמַן הַמִּשְׁמָר לַעֲלוֹת, כֹּהֲנִים וּלְוִיִּם עוֹלִים לִירוּשָׁלַיִם,

LITERAL TRANSLATION

[1]But how can a person's sacrifice be offered when he is not standing by it? [2]The early Prophets instituted twenty-four *mishmarot*. [3]For each and every *mishmar* there was a *ma'amad* in Jerusalem of priests, of Levites, and of Israelites. [4][When] the time arrived for the *mishmar* to go up, the priests and the Levites would go up to Jerusalem,

TRANSLATION AND COMMENTARY

Temple treasury by the entire people each year. [1]**But** this leads to a difficulty, for **how can a person's sacrifice be offered when he is not standing next to it?** Ordinarily, a person must be present in the Temple when his sacrifice is offered. Since the daily sacrifice is a communal obligation, then each and every member of the people of Israel should be in the Temple when the daily sacrifice is brought, which is clearly impossible. How, then, can the sacrifice be offered? [2]Therefore **the early Prophets** (Samuel and David, as will be explained in the Gemara) **instituted** the practice that the priests who served in the Temple were to be divided into **twenty-four** groups, called *mishmarot* ("watches"). Each *mishmar* served for one week at a time, so that each *mishmar* performed the Temple service for two weeks each year. The Levites were similarly divided into twenty-four *mishmarot*, which replaced each other every week. Corresponding to each of the *mishmarot* was a group of Israelites, called a *ma'amad* ("post" or "division"). The entire Jewish people living in Eretz Israel was divided into twenty-four *ma'amadot*. Each time a *mishmar* went to Jerusalem to serve in the Temple, part of the corresponding *ma'amad* would go there as well, and represent the entire people when the communal sacrifices were offered, while the remainder of the *ma'amad* would remain at home, and assemble for prayer in their own towns. [3]Thus, **for each and every *mishmar*, there was a *ma'amad* in Jerusalem of priests, Levites, and Israelites** — the priests to perform the sacrificial service, the Levites to offer the musical accompaniment, and the Israelites to represent the whole people when the daily offerings were sacrificed. [4]**When the time arrived for the** members of a particular ***mishmar* to go up** to Jerusalem, all **the priests and Levites** belonging to that *mishmar* **would go up to Jerusalem** to perform the sacrificial service

RASHI

נביאים הראשונים — שמואל ודוד, בגמרא מפרש. **על כל משמר** — ארבעה ועשרים משמרות של כהנים היו, ושמואל ודוד תיקנום. ועל כל משמר היה מעמד בירושלים, שקבועין ועומדין בעיר ועומדין על קרבן אחיהם. ולבד אלו הדרים בירושלים היו מעמדות בכל עיר. שישראל נחלקו לעשרים וארבעה מעמדות כנגד ארבעה ועשרים משמרות, כדתניא ב"ברייתא של ארבעים ותשע מדות". והיינו דתנן: היה מעמד בירושלים כהנים לוים וישראלים. **כהנים ולוים** — של משמר היו עולים בירושלים, כהנים לעבודה ולוים לשיר, ומכל המעמדות היו קבועין בירושלים לעמוד על קרבן אחיהם.

NOTES

וְכִי הֵיאָךְ קָרְבָּנוֹ שֶׁל אָדָם...? But how can a person's sacrifice...? The Aharonim ask: Why should all Israel be required to be present in the Temple when the daily sacrifice is offered? Granted that a person must be present in the Temple when his individual sacrifice is offered, for the person bringing the sacrifice is required to put his hands on the head of the sacrificial animal before it is slaughtered. But the daily offering, like most communal offerings, does not require that ceremony! *Iyyun Ya'akov* suggests that, since a person bringing a sacrifice is supposed to view himself as if he himself were being offered on the altar, it stands to reason that he should be present in the Temple when that sacrifice is being offered.

הָיָה מַעֲמָד בִּירוּשָׁלַיִם שֶׁל כֹּהֲנִים, שֶׁל לְוִיִּם, וְשֶׁל יִשְׂרְאֵלִים There was a *ma'amad* in Jerusalem of priests, of Levites, and of Israelites. According to the plain sense of this line, the *ma'amadot* included priests, Levites, and Israelites, and several of *Rashi's* comments on the Mishnah and Gemara also imply this. But *Ritva* and others maintain that the *ma'amadot* were made up exclusively of Israelites. They explain this line as meaning that representatives of all three groups were found in Jerusalem when the sacrifices were offered — the priests to perform the actual sacrificial service, the Levites to provide the musical accompaniment, and the Israelites to be present when the communal sacrifices were being brought.

שֶׁל כֹּהֲנִים, שֶׁל לְוִיִּם, וְשֶׁל יִשְׂרְאֵלִים Of priests, of Levites, and of Israelites. The Rishonim ask: Granted that representatives of the people must be present in the Temple when the communal sacrifices are offered. But why must ordinary Israelites be included in the *ma'amadot*? Let the priests and Levites who must be present in the Temple in

HALAKHAH

הִגִּיעַ זְמַן הַמִּשְׁמָר לַעֲלוֹת When the time arrived for the *mishmar* to go up. "Each week the members of the *ma'amad* whose week it is to serve assemble. Those who live in or near Jerusalem enter the Temple together with the *mishmar* of priests and Levites whose week it is to perform the Temple service. Those who live further away assemble in their local synagogues. All the members of the *ma'amad* fast during their week of service from Monday until Thursday." (*Rambam, Sefer Avodah, Hilkhot Klei HaMikdash* 6:2-3.)

[1]וְיִשְׂרָאֵל שֶׁבְּאוֹתוֹ מִשְׁמָר מִתְכַּנְּסִין לְעָרֵיהֶן וְקוֹרְאִין בְּמַעֲשֵׂה בְרֵאשִׁית. [2]וְאַנְשֵׁי הַמַּעֲמָד הָיוּ מִתְעַנִּין אַרְבָּעָה יָמִים בַּשָּׁבוּעַ מִיּוֹם שֵׁנִי וְעַד יוֹם חֲמִישִׁי. [3]וְלֹא הָיוּ מִתְעַנִּין עֶרֶב שַׁבָּת, מִפְּנֵי כְבוֹד הַשַּׁבָּת, [4]וְלֹא בְּאֶחָד בַּשַּׁבָּת, כְּדֵי שֶׁלֹּא יֵצְאוּ מִמְּנוּחָה וָעוֹנֶג לִיגִיעָה וְתַעֲנִית וְיָמוּתוּ.

[5]בַּיּוֹם הָרִאשׁוֹן: ״בְּרֵאשִׁית״ וִ״יְהִי רָקִיעַ״. [6]בַּשֵּׁנִי, ״יְהִי רָקִיעַ״ וְ״יִקָּווּ הַמַּיִם״. [7]בַּשְּׁלִישִׁי, ״יִקָּווּ הַמַּיִם״ וִ״יְהִי מְאֹרֹת״. [8]בָּרְבִיעִי, ״יְהִי מְאֹרֹת״ וְ״יִשְׁרְצוּ הַמַּיִם״. [9]בַּחֲמִישִׁי,

LITERAL TRANSLATION

[1]and the Israelites of that *mishmar* would assemble in their towns and would read the story of the creation. [2]And the members of the *ma'amad* would fast four days of the week from Monday until Thursday. [3]But they would not fast on Friday, because of the honor of Shabbat, [4]and not on Sunday, so that they would not go out from rest and enjoyment to exertion and fast and would die.

[5]On Sunday [they read]: "In the beginning" and "Let there be a firmament." [6]On Monday, "Let there be a firmament" and "Let the waters be gathered." [7]On Tuesday, "Let the waters be gathered" and "Let there be lights." [8]On Wednesday, "Let there be lights" and "Let the waters swarm abundantly." [9]On Thursday,

TRANSLATION AND COMMENTARY

and to offer the musical accompaniment. [1]Some of **the Israelites** belonging to the *ma'amad* corresponding **to that *mishmar*** — those living in or near Jerusalem — would enter the Temple and would be present when the communal sacrifices were offered. The remainder of the Israelites belonging to that *ma'amad* who lived further away from Jerusalem **would** remain at home and would **assemble in** the synagogues **in their towns,** would recite special prayers, **and would read** the Torah portion describing **the story of the creation,** so as to proclaim that the continued existence of the world depends upon the Temple service. [2]**The members of the *ma'amad*** whose turn it was that week to represent the people of Israel **would fast four days of the week from Monday until Thursday,** eating only at night. [3]**But they would not fast on Friday so that** due **honor** should be accorded to **Shabbat,** for it would be disrespectful if they entered Shabbat in a state of extreme hunger. [4]They would **also not** observe a fast **on Sunday, so as not to emerge from the rest and enjoyment** of Shabbat and immediately encounter a day of **exertion and fasting,** which might cause them to become ill **and** perhaps even **die.**

בַּיּוֹם הָרִאשׁוֹן [5]The Mishnah now explains how the chapter on the creation read from the Torah by the members of the *ma'amad* was divided over the six days of the week: **On Sunday, they** would **read** the section beginning with **"In the beginning** [Genesis 1:1-5]," **and** the section beginning with **"Let there be a firmament** [vv. 6-8]." [6]**On Monday,** they would read once again the section beginning with **"Let there be a firmament," and** would continue with the section beginning with **"Let the waters** under the heaven **be gathered** [vv. 9-12]." [7]**On Tuesday,** they would read for a second time the section beginning with **"Let the waters** under the heaven **be gathered," and** then they would read the section beginning with **"Let there be lights** [vv. 14-19]." [8]**On Wednesday,** they would reread the section beginning with **"Let there be lights," and** would continue with the section beginning with **"Let the waters bring forth abundantly** [vv. 20-23]." [9]**On Thursday,** the members of

RASHI

והשאר היו מתכנסין לעריהם — ומתפללין על קרבן אחיהם שיתקבל ברצון, ומתענין ומוציאין ספר תורה ביום תעניתם. **וקורין במעשה בראשית** — ובגמרא מפרש טעמא. **ביום הראשון** — של שבוע. **קורין בראשית כו׳** — פרשה ראשונה ופרשת ״יהי רקיע״, לפי שאין בפרשת בראשית לבדה תשעה פסוקים כדי קריאת כהן לוי ישראל, וכן כולן.

NOTES

order to perform the sacrificial service also act as the representatives of the people of Israel! Some Rishonim answer that, regarding certain matters, each tribe of Israel is treated as a community unto itself, and so the members of the tribe of Levi cannot represent the entire nation on their own, but must be joined by representatives of each of the other tribes (*Tosefot Rosh,* cited by *Petaḥ Einayim*).

הָיָה מַעֲמָד בִּירוּשָׁלַיִם ... וְיִשְׂרָאֵל שֶׁבְּאוֹתוֹ מִשְׁמָר מִתְכַּנְּסִין לְעָרֵיהֶן **There was a *ma'amad* in Jerusalem...and the Israelites of that *mishmar* would assemble in their towns.** According to *Rambam* (*Hilkhot Klei HaMikdash* 6:2), those members of the *ma'amad* who lived in or near Jerusalem would go to the Temple together with the priests and the Levites, while those who lived further away would assemble in the synagogues in their home towns. *Ra'avad* (cited by *Meiri*) maintains that those members of the *ma'amad* who were able to make the journey to Jerusalem would do so, but the older members of the *ma'amad* for whom travel was difficult would assemble in their local synagogues. According to *Rid,* some members of each *ma'amad* were stationed permanently in Jerusalem. It was they who entered the Temple and represented the people of Israel when the communal sacrifices were brought. The rest of the *ma'amad* remained in their home towns and assembled in their local synagogues.

וְאַנְשֵׁי הַמַּעֲמָד **And the members of the *ma'amad*.** According to *Rambam,* the *mishmar* system embraced all the priests, but not all the Israelites were included in the

TRANSLATION AND COMMENTARY

the *ma'amad* would read again the section beginning with **"Let the waters bring forth abundantly," and** would then read the section beginning with **"Let the earth bring forth** [vv. 24-31]." [1]And finally, **on Friday,** they would read for the second time the section beginning with **"Let the earth bring forth," and** would then conclude with the section beginning with **"And the heavens and the earth were finished** [Genesis 2:1-3]." Thus the Torah portion read each day was made up of two sections. Now, since three people — usually a priest, a Levite, and an Israelite — were called each day to the reading of the Torah, and since each person called to the reading of the Torah was required to read a minimum of three verses, the following arrangement was followed: [2]**The longer section** of the two **was read by two** people, **and the shorter section** was read **by one person.** For example, on Sunday, the longer section, beginning with "In the beginning" and containing five verses, was read by two people, and the shorter section, beginning with "Let there be a firmament" and containing only three verses, was read by one person. On Monday, the shorter section, beginning with "Let there be a firmament," was read by one person, and the longer section, beginning with "Let the waters under the heavens be gathered," was read by two people. The Torah portions read during the rest of the week were divided in a similar manner. [3]The chapter on the creation was read in this manner **in the morning service and** once again in **the musaf service,** on those days when an additional service was added to the regular daily services. [4]**But in the afternoon** service the members of the *ma'amad* did not read the Torah portion from a scroll. Instead **they entered** the synagogue **and** each member **read** to himself the day's portion **by heart,** just **as the** *Shema* **is read** by every individual by heart and not from a Torah scroll. [5]**On Friday afternoon** the members of the *ma'amad* **did not enter** the synagogue or read from the Torah in any manner, in order to be free to make the preparations necessary **to accord** due **honor to Shabbat.**

כָּל יוֹם [6]The Mishnah now explains that there were certain times when the members of the *ma'amad* did not gather for their special prayers and Torah reading. **Any day** on which **Hallel** (Psalms 113-118) **was**

"יִשְׁרְצוּ הַמַּיִם" וְ"תוֹצֵא הָאָרֶץ". [1]בַּשִּׁשִּׁי, "תּוֹצֵא הָאָרֶץ" "וַיְכֻלּוּ הַשָּׁמַיִם". [2]פָּרָשָׁה גְּדוֹלָה קוֹרִין אוֹתָהּ בִּשְׁנַיִם, וְהַקְּטַנָּה בְּיָחִיד, [3]בַּשַּׁחֲרִית וּבַמּוּסָף. [4]וּבַמִּנְחָה נִכְנָסִין וְקוֹרִין עַל פִּיהֶן כְּקוֹרִין אֶת שְׁמַע. [5]עֶרֶב שַׁבָּת בַּמִּנְחָה לֹא הָיוּ נִכְנָסִין, מִפְּנֵי כְבוֹד הַשַּׁבָּת.
[6]כָּל יוֹם שֶׁיֵּשׁ בּוֹ הַלֵּל, אֵין

LITERAL TRANSLATION

"Let the waters bring forth abundantly" and "Let the earth bring forth." [1]On Friday, "Let the earth bring forth" and "And the heavens [and the earth] were finished." [2]A long section would be read by two, and a short one by a single person, [3]in the morning service and in the musaf service. [4]But in the afternoon they would enter and read by heart as they read the *Shema*. [5][On] Friday in the afternoon they would not enter, because of the honor of Shabbat.

[6]Any day on which there is Hallel, there is no

RASHI

בששי ותוצא הארץ עד ויכולו – לפי שבפרשת "תוצא הארץ" אין בה אלא שמונה פסוקים, לפיכך אומר "ויכולו". **פרשה גדולה** – שבפרשיות הללו קורין אותה בשנים, כגון פרשה ראשונה של בראשית יש בה חמשה פסוקים היו קורין אותה בשנים, כדאמרינן בגמרא "יהי רקיע" באחד, וביום השני "יהי רקיע" – באחד "יקוו" – בשנים, שיש בה חמשה פסוקים. ביום השלישי "יקוו" – באחד, שאין בה אלא חמשה פסוקים, "ויהי מאורות" – בשנים, שיש בה ששה פסוקים. **וקורין אותה על פיהן** – כל אחד בפני עצמו, ובעי בגמרא: מאי קאמר, מעיקרא קתני "פרשה קטנה כו'", דמשמע דבספר תורה קורין, והדר תנא "על פיהם", פרשה בנעילה ליכא.

NOTES

ma'amad system, for only the pious and sin-fearing among them were chosen to represent the rest of the people.

נִכְנָסִין They would enter. Although the Mishnah states only that the members of the *ma'amad* would read the Torah section dealing with the story of the creation, it is clear from other sources that they would also read the section dealing with the sacrifices. Likewise, they would recite special prayers (see below, regarding the musaf prayer) and supplications each time they entered the synagogue. Thus the term *ma'amad* refers not only to the division of Israelites who served as representatives of the entire people at the communal sacrifices, but also to their assembly in the synagogue for the special Torah readings, prayers, and supplications (*Rambam, Hilkhot Klei HaMikdash* 6:5).

HALAKHAH

פָּרָשָׁה גְּדוֹלָה קוֹרִין אוֹתָהּ בִּשְׁנַיִם A long section would be read by two. "The members of the *ma'amad* would read from the Torah from the chapter on the creation. On each day of the week they would read the sections describing what was created on that day of the week and on the following day. The longer of the two sections was read by two people, and the shorter of the two was read by one person. The Torah portion that was read from a scroll in the morning service was read once again from a scroll in the musaf service, but in the afternoon service it was recited by heart." (*Rambam, Sefer Avodah, Hilkhot Klei HaMikdash* 6:6-7.)

כָּל יוֹם שֶׁיֵּשׁ בּוֹ הַלֵּל Any day on which there is Hallel. "On the eight days of Hanukkah, when the Hallel was recited, there was no *ma'amad* in the morning service. On any day on which an additional sacrifice was brought, there

TRANSLATION AND COMMENTARY

recited but an additional sacrifice was not offered, such as on Hanukkah, **there was no *ma'amad* in the morning service,** because the recitation of Hallel takes precedence over the morning *ma'amad*. But there was a *ma'amad* during the services conducted later in the day. [1]**When an additional sacrifice** was offered, such as on Rosh Ḥodesh, **there was no *ma'amad*** in the neilah service at the close of the day, nor was there a *ma'amad* during the musaf and afternoon services conducted earlier in the day. [2]And **when a wood-offering** was brought but there was no additional sacrifice — on nine days during the year, specific families brought wood-offerings to the Temple (as will be explained below) — **there was no *ma'amad* in the afternoon service,** but there was a *ma'amad* in the neilah service. [3]**This is the viewpoint of Rabbi Akiva.** [4]But **Ben Azzai** disagreed and **said to** Rabbi Akiva: [5]**Rabbi Yehoshua taught as follows:** Any day **on which an additional sacrifice** was offered, **there was no *ma'amad* in the afternoon service,** and not in the musaf service, but there was a *ma'amad* in the neilah service. [6]And any day **on which a wood-offering** was brought, **there was no *ma'amad* in the neilah service.** [7]Bowing to the authority of Rabbi Yehoshua, **Rabbi Akiva retracted** his opinion and began **to teach as Ben Azzai** had stated.

מַעֲמָד בַּשַּׁחֲרִית. [1]קָרְבַּן מוּסָף, אֵין בַּנְּעִילָה. [2]קָרְבַּן עֵצִים, אֵין בַּמִּנְחָה. [3]דִּבְרֵי רַבִּי עֲקִיבָא. [4]אָמַר לוֹ בֶּן עַזַּאי: [5]כָּךְ הָיָה רַבִּי יְהוֹשֻׁעַ שׁוֹנֶה: קָרְבַּן מוּסָף, אֵין בַּמִּנְחָה. [6]קָרְבַּן עֵצִים, אֵין בַּנְּעִילָה. [7]חָזַר רַבִּי עֲקִיבָא לִהְיוֹת שׁוֹנֶה כְּבֶן עַזַּאי.

LITERAL TRANSLATION

ma'amad in the morning service. [1][When there is] an additional sacrifice, there is no [*ma'amad*] in the closing service. [2][When there is] a wood-offering, there is no [*ma'amad*] in the afternoon service. [3][These are] the words of Rabbi Akiva. [4]Ben Azzai said to him: [5]Thus would Rabbi Yehoshua teach: [When there is] an additional sacrifice, there is no [*ma'amad*] in the afternoon service. [6][When there is] a wood-offering, there is no [*ma'amad*] in the closing service. [7]Rabbi Akiva retracted so as to teach like Ben Azzai.

RASHI

כל יום שיש בו הלל אין בו מעמד שחרית — אותן שהיו בירושלים לא היו מתפללין על קרבן אחיהם שיש בו הלל, לפי שאין להן פנאי לעשות מעמדם שקורין את הלל, ומפני ההלל היו דוחין את המעמד. **קרבן מוסף** — יום שיש בו קרבן מוסף בירושלים אין מעמד בנעילה בירושלים, וכל שכן במנחה הסמוכה למוסף, לפי שהיו טרודין במוסף, שיש בו להקריב בהמות יותר מתמיד שהוא אחד. אין לך מוסף בלא שתי בהמות, ולא היה להם פנאי כלל, שהכהנים של מעמד טרודים במוסף וישראל שבהן היו טרודים לחטוב עצים ולשאוב מים, ודוחה אפילו מעמד דנעילה. **קרבן עצים** — בגמרא מפרש: כגון אחד מתשעה זמנים. ואותו יום שהיה בו קרבן עצים אפילו לא היה בו מוסף — היה נדחה מעמד של מנחה מפני קרבן עצים, מפני שקרבן עצים קודם למנחה ודוחה מעמד הסמוך לו [ולא] של נעילה.

NOTES

קָרְבַּן מוּסָף, אֵין בַּנְּעִילָה When there is an additional sacrifice, there is no *ma'amad* in the closing service. As will be explained below (28b), on days when there was an additional sacrifice, there was certainly no *ma'amad* in the musaf service. The Rishonim note that, at first glance, this contradicts what was stated above in the Mishnah — that the members of the *ma'amad* read the story of the creation in the morning service and then once again in the musaf service, implying that there was indeed a *ma'amad* assembly for the musaf service.

Rashi and many others explain that on those days when there was an additional sacrifice, there was no *ma'amad* in Jerusalem for the musaf service, because the members of the *ma'amad* who were in Jerusalem were involved in the sacrificial service in the Temple and did not have the time to conduct the assembly. But outside Jerusalem there was indeed a *ma'amad* in the musaf service.

Ra'avad distinguishes between the special supplications offered at the *ma'amad* assembly and the Torah reading that was conducted there. On those days when there was an additional sacrifice, no special supplications were added in the musaf service, neither in Jerusalem, nor outside it. But the story of the creation was indeed read in the musaf service even on those days, and even in Jerusalem.

Rambam (*Hilkhot Klei HaMikdash* 6:4) rules that every day of the week the members of the *ma'amad* conducted a special additional service, which was inserted between the morning and the afternoon services. During that additional service, the special Torah reading for *ma'amad* assemblies was read, as was explained above. Here the Mishnah is informing us that when an additional sacrifice was brought, there was no *ma'amad* in the neilah service, and all the more so not in the ordinary musaf service conducted on such days.

קָרְבַּן עֵצִים Wood-offering. As will be explained below (28a), in the early years of the Second Temple there was not sufficient wood to burn the sacrifices on the altar, and certain families volunteered to supply it. Later, to commem-

HALAKHAH

was no *ma'amad* in the musaf and the afternoon services, but there was a *ma'amad* in the morning and the neilah services. And on any day on which a wood-offering was brought, there was no *ma'amad* in the neilah service," following Ben Azzai. (*Rambam, Sefer Avodah, Hilkhot Klei HaMikdash* 6:8.)

SAGES

בֶּן עַזַּאי Ben Azzai. This is Shimon ben Azzai, a Tanna of the fourth generation. Although Shimon ben Azzai was never ordained as a Rabbi, which is why he is known by his name alone, and usually as "Ben Azzai," without any title, he was regarded as one of the greatest Sages. His vast wisdom was held up as an example for many generations.

He did not study Torah in his youth, but later in his life he met Rabbi Akiva's daughter, and she promised to marry him if he studied Torah. Ben Azzai went to study with Rabbi Yehoshua, but he was mainly a disciple of Rabbi Akiva, later becoming his student-colleague. He regarded Rabbi Akiva as the greatest Sage of his generation.

Ultimately he did not marry Rabbi Akiva's daughter. Because of his great desire for Torah knowledge, he devoted himself to it entirely (it is said that, after Ben Azzai's death, there were no more diligent scholars).

His Halakhic and Aggadic teachings are found in the Mishnah, in Baraitot, and in the Talmud. He seems to have taught students in his native city of Tiberias.

Ben Azzai was also interested in esoteric learning and was one of the four who "entered the grove." It is said of him that "he looked and died," and the following Biblical verse was recited in his honor: "Precious in the eyes of the Lord is the death of His saints."

[1]זְמַן עֲצֵי כֹהֲנִים וְהָעָם תִּשְׁעָה: [2]בְּאֶחָד בְּנִיסָן, בְּנֵי אָרַח בֶּן יְהוּדָה; [3]בְּעֶשְׂרִים בְּתַמּוּז, בְּנֵי דָּוִד בֶּן יְהוּדָה; [4]בַּחֲמִשָּׁה בְּאָב, בְּנֵי פַּרְעוֹשׁ בֶּן יְהוּדָה; [5]בְּשִׁבְעָה בּוֹ, בְּנֵי יוֹנָדָב בֶּן רֵכָב; [6]בַּעֲשָׂרָה בּוֹ, בְּנֵי סְנָאָה בֶּן בִּנְיָמִין; [7]בַּחֲמִשָּׁה עָשָׂר בּוֹ, בְּנֵי זַתּוּא בֶּן יְהוּדָה, וְעִמָּהֶם כֹּהֲנִים וּלְוִיִּם, וְכָל מִי שֶׁטָּעָה בְּשִׁבְטוֹ, [8]וּבְנֵי גוֹנְבֵי עֱלִי וּבְנֵי קוֹצְעֵי קְצִיעוֹת; [9]בְּעֶשְׂרִים בּוֹ, בְּנֵי פַּחַת מוֹאָב בֶּן יְהוּדָה; [10]בְּעֶשְׂרִים בֶּאֱלוּל, בְּנֵי עָדִין בֶּן יְהוּדָה; [11]בְּאֶחָד בְּטֵבֵת, שָׁבוּ בְּנֵי פַּרְעוֹשׁ שְׁנִיָּה. [12]בְּאֶחָד בְּטֵבֵת לֹא הָיָה בּוֹ מַעֲמָד,

LITERAL TRANSLATION

[1]The times for the wood of the priests and the people were nine: [2]On the first of Nisan, the descendants of Arah of the tribe of (lit., "the son of") Judah; [3]on the twentieth of Tammuz, the descendants of David of the tribe of Judah; [4]on the fifth of Av, the descendants of Parosh of the tribe of Judah; [5]on the seventh of [Av], the descendants of Jonadab the son of Rechab; [6]on the tenth of [Av], the descendants of Senaah of the tribe of Benjamin; [7]on the fifteenth of [Av], the descendants of Zattu of the tribe of Judah, and with them the priests and Levites and anyone who was uncertain of his tribe, [8]and the descendants of the pestle deceivers and the descendants of the dried-fig packers; [9]on the twentieth of [Av], the descendants of Pahat Moab of the tribe of Judah; [10]on the twentieth of Elul, the descendants of Adin of the tribe of Judah; [11]on the first of Tevet, the descendants of Parosh returned a second time. [12]On the first of Tevet there was no *ma'amad*,

TRANSLATION AND COMMENTARY

זְמַן עֲצֵי כֹהֲנִים [1]The Mishnah now lists the days on which a wood-offering was brought. **The times for the wood**-offerings **of the priests and the** rest of the **people were nine:** [2]**On the first of Nisan,** a wood-offering was brought by **the descendants of Arah of the tribe of Judah** (Ezra 2:5; Nehemiah 7:10); [3]**on the twentieth of Tammuz,** it was brought by **the descendants** of King **David of the tribe of Judah;** [4]**on the fifth of Av,** a wood-offering was brought by **the descendants of Parosh of the tribe of Judah** (Ezra 2:3; Nehemiah 7:8); [5]**on the seventh of Av,** it was brought by **the descendants of Jonadab the son of Rechab** of the family of Jethro (Jeremiah 35:6); [6]**on the tenth of Av,** a wood-offering was brought by **the descendants of Senaah of the tribe of Benjamin** (Ezra 2:35; Nehemiah 7:38); [7]**on the fifteenth of Av, the descendants of Zattu of the tribe of Judah** (Ezra 2:8; Nehemiah 7:13) brought the wood-offering, **and joining them** were **the priests and the Levites and all** the Israelites **who were uncertain of their tribe,** [8]**and the descendants of those who deceived** the authorities **with a pestle** [this appellation will be explained in the Gemara], **and the descendants of those who packed dried figs** [this too will be explained in the Gemara]; [9]**on the twentieth of Av,** the wood-offering was brought by the descendants of Pahat Moab of the tribe of Judah (Ezra 2:6; Nehemiah 7:11); [10]on the twentieth of Elul, it was brought by **the descendants of Adin of the tribe of Judah** (Ezra 2:15; Nehemiah 7:20); [11]and **on the first of Tevet, the descendants of Parosh** of the tribe of Judah **returned a second time** to bring the wood-offering, having already brought such an offering on the fifth of Av. [12]**On the first of Tevet,** which is Hanukkah, Rosh Ḥodesh, and the day on which a wood-offering was brought by the descendants of Parosh,

RASHI

כך היה רבי יהושע דורש קרבן מוסף אין במנחה — **וטעמא מפרש בגמרא. זמן עצי כהנים והעם** — **שמתנדבים עצים. תשעה** — באלו התשעה זמנים היו הכהנים והעם מתנדבים להביא עצים, והיו מקריבין קרבן אותו היום. ואפילו היו עצים הרבה למערכה — היו אלו מתנדבין, ומקריבין באלו תשעה זמנים. בני ארח בן יהודה — שכשעלו בני הגולה הם התנדבו תחילה באחד בניסן, וספק להם **עצים עד עשרים בתמוז שהתנדבו בני דוד. ארח שמואל, ומשבט יהודה היה. בני דוד — ממשפחת דוד המלך. סנאה בן בנימין, זתוא בן יהודה, בני גונבי עלי, ובני קולעי קליעות משפחה אחת הן, ובגמרא מפרש אמאי מיקרו הכי. בני עדין באחד בטבת שבו שני בני פרעוש שניה** — **ובגמרא מפרש אמאי קבעו להן אלו הזמנים.**

NOTES

orate their generosity, the days on which those families had brought wood for the altar became a festival for them. They would bring wood to be offered on the altar, and they were forbidden to fast or to recite eulogies. According to many Rishonim (see *Ritva*), the term "wood-offering" refers to the wood itself, which would be burned separately on the altar. *Rambam* (*Hilkhot Klei HaMikdash* 6:9) writes that the term "wood-offering" refers to the voluntary burnt-offerings that those families would bring to the Temple together with the wood.

וְכָל מִי שֶׁטָּעָה בְּשִׁבְטוֹ And anyone who was uncertain of his tribe. The fact that the fifteenth of Av was the day on which a large proportion of the people of Israel brought their wood-offerings was one more reason (in addition to the reasons listed below, 30b-31a) for the celebration of that day as an especially joyous holiday, as is described below in the Mishnah.

¹שֶׁהָיָה בּוֹ הַלֵּל ¹וְקָרְבַּן מוּסָף וְקָרְבַּן עֵצִים.

²חֲמִשָּׁה דְּבָרִים אֵירְעוּ אֶת אֲבוֹתֵינוּ בְּשִׁבְעָה עָשָׂר בְּתַמּוּז, ³וַחֲמִשָּׁה בְּתִשְׁעָה בְּאָב. ⁴בְּשִׁבְעָה עָשָׂר בְּתַמּוּז [26B] נִשְׁתַּבְּרוּ הַלּוּחוֹת, ⁵וּבָטֵל הַתָּמִיד, ⁶וְהוּבְקְעָה הָעִיר, ⁷וְשָׂרַף אַפּוֹסְטְמוֹס אֶת הַתּוֹרָה וְהֶעֱמִיד צֶלֶם בַּהֵיכָל. ⁸בְּתִשְׁעָה בְּאָב נִגְזַר עַל אֲבוֹתֵינוּ שֶׁלֹּא יִכָּנְסוּ לָאָרֶץ, ⁹וְחָרַב הַבַּיִת בָּרִאשׁוֹנָה וּבַשְּׁנִיָּה, ¹⁰וְנִלְכְּדָה בֵּיתָר, ¹¹וְנֶחְרְשָׁה הָעִיר.

¹²מִשֶּׁנִּכְנָס אָב, מְמַעֲטִין בְּשִׂמְחָה.

¹³שַׁבָּת שֶׁחָל תִּשְׁעָה בְּאָב לִהְיוֹת בְּתוֹכָהּ, אָסוּר מִלְסַפֵּר

LITERAL TRANSLATION

for on it there was Hallel [1]and the additional sacrifice and the wood-offering.

[2]Five things happened to our ancestors on the Seventeenth of Tammuz, [3]and five on the Ninth of Av. [4]On the Seventeenth of Tammuz [26B] the Tablets [of the Covenant] were broken, [5]and the daily sacrifice ceased, [6]and the city was breached, [7]and Apostemos burned the Torah and set up an idol in the Sanctuary. [8]On the Ninth of Av it was decreed that our ancestors would not enter the Land [of Israel], [9]and the Temple was destroyed for the first and second time, [10]and Betar was captured, [11]and the city was plowed up.

[12]When Av comes in, we reduce rejoicing.

[13]The week in which the Ninth of Av falls, it is forbidden to cut hair

TRANSLATION AND COMMENTARY

there was no ***ma'amad*** at all, **for the Hallel** that **was** recited on that day on account of Hanukkah took precedence over the *ma'amad* in the morning service, [1]and **the additional sacrifice** brought on account of Rosh Ḥodesh **and the wood-offering** brought by the descendants of Parosh took precedence over the *ma'amad* of the musaf, the afternoon, and the neilah services.

חֲמִשָּׁה דְּבָרִים [2]Until now our tractate has been concerned with the public fasts proclaimed in times of drought and other impending dangers. The Mishnah now discusses some of the fixed public fast-days instituted to commemorate certain national calamities. **Five** disastrous **things happened to our ancestors on the Seventeenth of Tammuz,** [3]**and five** disastrous **things** happened to them **on the Ninth of Av,** on account of which fixed public fasts were instituted on each of these two days. [4]**On the Seventeenth of Tammuz** [26B] **the Tablets of the Covenant were broken** by Moses after he came down from Mount Sinai and saw that the people had made the golden calf; [5]**the daily sacrifice** brought in the Temple **ceased;** [6]**the** walls of the **city** of Jerusalem **were breached;** [7]the Roman officer, **Apostemos, burned a Torah scroll and set up an idol in the Sanctuary.** [8]**On the Ninth of Av it was decreed that our ancestors** who took part in the Exodus from Egypt **would not enter the Land of Israel** but would wander in the wilderness for forty years, and only then would their children enter the Promised Land; [9]**the First and Second Temples were destroyed;** [10]the fortress of **Betar was captured** by the Romans, thus bringing the Bar Kokhba revolt to an end; [11]**and the city** of Jerusalem **was plowed up,** and then rebuilt as a pagan city which the Jews were forbidden to enter.

מִשֶּׁנִּכְנָס אָב [12]The Mishnah continues: **When** the month of **Av comes in, rejoicing is reduced.** Even though only the Ninth of Av is observed as a public fast-day, expressions of joy must be diminished from the beginning of the month on account of the various national calamities that befell the Jewish people during this month. Thus, business activity must be reduced, and the construction of buildings for a joyous purpose must be suspended. Betrothals are permitted, but marriages must be put off until after the Ninth of Av.

שַׁבָּת שֶׁחָל תִּשְׁעָה בְּאָב [13]As the Ninth of Av comes closer, additional restrictions are imposed. Thus, beginning on the Sunday of the week during which the Ninth of Av falls, it is forbidden to cut one's hair or to

RASHI

באחד בטבת — שהיה ראש חדש [וחנוכה] לא היה בו מעמד כו׳. **נשתברו הלוחות** — בגמרא מפרש. **ובטל התמיד** — לפי שגזרה המלכות גזרה מלהקריב עוד. **והועמד צלם בהיכל** — שהעמידו מנשה, כדמפורש בתרגום ירושלמי בפרשת ״השמים כסאי״ וגו׳ (ישעיהו סו). **על אבותינו** — דור המדבר ״אם יראה איש באנשים האלה הדור הרע הזה את הארץ״ וגו׳ (דברים א). **ביתר** — עיר גדולה, והיו ישראל דרין בה, במסכת גיטין, פרק ״הניזקין״ (נז,א): אשקא דריספק חרב ביתר. **שבת שחל תשעה באב כו׳** — שבוע.

LANGUAGE

אַפּוֹסְטְמוֹס Apostemos. This may be connected with the Latin name, Postumus, given to someone born after his father's death. Several Roman generals bore this name, but the time and the reason for the burning of the Torah here are unknown to us.

HALAKHAH

מִשֶּׁנִּכְנָס אָב When Av comes in. "When the month of Av comes in, rejoicing is reduced." (*Shulḥan Arukh, Oraḥ Ḥayyim* 551:1.)

שָׁבוּעַ שֶׁחָל תִּשְׁעָה בְּאָב לִהְיוֹת בְּתוֹכָהּ The week in which the Ninth of Av falls. "During the week of the Ninth of Av it is forbidden to cut one's hair or to wash laundry. *Rema* writes that the Ashkenazim are stringent about these matters from the beginning of the month of Av until after the fast of the Ninth of Av. But the Sephardi custom follows Rabbi Yosef Caro that these prohibitions need only be observed during the week of the Ninth of Av." (Ibid., 551:3.)

TRANSLATION AND COMMENTARY

wash laundry. If the Ninth of Av falls on a Friday (which was possible when the date of the new month was decided on the basis of the testimony of eyewitnesses), doing laundry or cutting one's hair is forbidden all week, [1]but **on Thursday** these activities **are permitted, so that** due **honor be accorded to Shabbat,** which begins immediately after the fast.

עֶרֶב תִּשְׁעָה בְּאָב [2]**On the eve of the Ninth of Av, a person may not eat two cooked dishes** in the same meal. [3]**He may not eat meat** at all, **nor** may he **drink wine.** [4]**Rabban Shimon ben Gamliel says:** There is no specific prohibition against eating two cooked dishes, or against eating meat or drinking wine on the eve of the Ninth of Av. But a person **must make a change** and reduce his ordinary eating habits. For example, if he is ordinarily accustomed to eat two cooked dishes during his meal, on the eve of the Ninth of Av he should eat only one kind of cooked dish. Or if he is ordinarily accustomed to eat a certain quantity of meat, on the eve of the Ninth of Av he should eat only half that quantity. [5]**Rabbi Yehudah requires** that **beds be overturned** on the Ninth of Av, so that people have to sleep on the ground, as is required of those in mourning after the death of a close relative. But the Sages did not agree with him.

אָמַר רַבָּן שִׁמְעוֹן בֶּן גַּמְלִיאֵל [6]**Rabban Shimon ben Gamliel said: There were no days as joyous for** the people of **Israel as the Fifteenth of Av and Yom Kippur,** [7]**for on** those days **the daughters of Jerusalem would** all **go out in borrowed white clothes.** Even the daughters of the rich would dress themselves in borrowed clothes, [8]**so as not to embarrass** those **who did not possess** white clothes of their own. [9]**All the clothes** that the young women would borrow **required** ritual **immersion** before being worn, for they might have contracted ritual impurity if they had previously been worn by a woman who was ritually impure. [10]**The daughters of Jerusalem would go out and** would **dance in the vineyards,** thus attracting the attention of potential suitors. [11]**And what would** the young women of distinguished lineage **say** to a young man who followed them into the vineyards in search of a wife? **"Young man!** [12]**Lift up your**

וּמִלְכַבֵּס. [1]וּבַחֲמִישִׁי מוּתָּרִין מִפְּנֵי כְבוֹד הַשַּׁבָּת.

[2]עֶרֶב תִּשְׁעָה בְּאָב, לֹא יֹאכַל אָדָם שְׁנֵי תַבְשִׁילִין. [3]לֹא יֹאכַל בָּשָׂר וְלֹא יִשְׁתֶּה יַיִן. [4]רַבָּן שִׁמְעוֹן בֶּן גַּמְלִיאֵל אוֹמֵר: יְשַׁנֶּה. [5]רַבִּי יְהוּדָה מְחַיֵּיב בִּכְפִיַּית הַמִּטָּה, וְלֹא הוֹדוּ לוֹ חֲכָמִים.

[6]אָמַר רַבָּן שִׁמְעוֹן בֶּן גַּמְלִיאֵל: לֹא הָיוּ יָמִים טוֹבִים לְיִשְׂרָאֵל כַּחֲמִשָּׁה עָשָׂר בְּאָב וּכְיוֹם הַכִּפּוּרִים, [7]שֶׁבָּהֶן בְּנוֹת יְרוּשָׁלַיִם יוֹצְאוֹת בִּכְלֵי לָבָן שְׁאוּלִין, [8]שֶׁלֹּא לְבַיֵּישׁ אֶת מִי שֶׁאֵין לוֹ. [9]כָּל הַכֵּלִים טְעוּנִין טְבִילָה. [10]וּבְנוֹת יְרוּשָׁלַיִם יוֹצְאוֹת וְחוֹלוֹת בַּכְּרָמִים. [11]וּמֶה הָיוּ אוֹמְרוֹת? "בָּחוּר! [12]שָׂא נָא

LITERAL TRANSLATION

or to wash laundry. [1]But on Thursday they are permitted in honor of Shabbat.

[2][On] the eve of the Ninth of Av, a person may not eat two cooked dishes. [3]He may not eat meat nor drink wine. [4]Rabban Shimon ben Gamliel says: One must change. [5]Rabbi Yehudah obliges the overturning of the bed, but the Sages did not agree with him.

[6]Rabban Shimon ben Gamliel said: There were no festive days for Israel like the Fifteenth of Av and Yom Kippur, [7]for on them the daughters of Jerusalem go out in borrowed white clothes, [8]so as not to embarrass one who does not have [any]. [9]All the clothes require immersion. [10]And the daughters of Jerusalem would go out and dance in the vineyards. [11]And what would they say? "Young man! [12]Lift up

RASHI

בחמישי מותרין — אם חל תשעה באב בערב שבת — מותרין לכבס בחמישי, וכשחל תשעה באב ברביעי בשבת — לא איצטריך למיתני דמותרין, כדאמרינן בגמרא: לא שנו אלא לפניו כו'. **שני תבשילין** — בשר ודגים, או בשר וביצים שעליו, או דג וביצה שעליו. כדאמר בפרק "ערבי פסחים" (פסחים קיד,ב). **ישנה** — בגמרא מפרש. **כפיית המטה** — על פניה, ולא יישן עליה. **שאולין** — שכולן שואלות זו מזו, אפילו עשירות, כדי שלא לבייש כו'. **טעונין טבילה** — קודם שילבשום, לפי שאין כל אחת בקיאה בחברתה, שמא נדה היתה. **וחולות** — כמו "לחול במחולות" (שופטים כא).

NOTES

וּמֶה הָיוּ אוֹמְרוֹת And what would they say. Following the Baraita cited at the very end of the tractate (below, 31a), *Rambam* (in his *Commentary to the Mishnah*) divides the statements attributed here to the young women dancing in the vineyards between two sets of speakers. The attractive women would say: "Young man! Lift up your eyes and see what you are choosing for yourself." The women who were unattractive, but of distinguished lineage, would say: "Do not set your eyes on beauty. Set your eyes on lineage."

HALAKHAH

עֶרֶב תִּשְׁעָה בְּאָב On the eve of the Ninth of Av. "On the day before the Ninth of Av, a person may not eat meat or drink wine during the last meal before fasting, if that meal is taken after midday (even according to those authorities who say that meat and wine are permitted during the Nine Days). During that meal one may also not eat two cooked dishes." (*Shulḥan Arukh, Oraḥ Ḥayyim* 552:1.)

עֵינֶיךָ וּרְאֵה מָה אַתָּה בּוֹרֵר לָךְ. [1]אַל תִּתֵּן עֵינֶיךָ בַּנּוֹי. תֵּן עֵינֶיךָ בַּמִּשְׁפָּחָה״. [2]״שֶׁקֶר הַחֵן, וְהֶבֶל הַיֹּפִי, אִשָּׁה יִרְאַת ה׳ הִיא תִתְהַלָּל״. [3]וְאוֹמֵר: ״תְּנוּ לָהּ מִפְּרִי יָדֶיהָ, וִיהַלְלוּהָ בַשְּׁעָרִים מַעֲשֶׂיהָ״.

[4]וְכֵן הוּא אוֹמֵר: ״צְאֶינָה וּרְאֶינָה, בְּנוֹת צִיּוֹן, בַּמֶּלֶךְ שְׁלֹמֹה בַּעֲטָרָה שֶׁעִטְּרָה לוֹ אִמּוֹ בְּיוֹם חֲתֻנָּתוֹ, וּבְיוֹם שִׂמְחַת לִבּוֹ״. [5]״בְּיוֹם חֲתֻנָּתוֹ״ – זֶה מַתַּן תּוֹרָה. [6]״וּבְיוֹם שִׂמְחַת לִבּוֹ״ – זֶה בִּנְיַן בֵּית הַמִּקְדָּשׁ, [7]שֶׁיִּבָּנֶה בִּמְהֵרָה בְּיָמֵינוּ.

גמרא [8]״בִּשְׁלֹשָׁה פְּרָקִים בַּשָּׁנָה כֹּהֲנִים נוֹשְׂאִין אֶת כַּפֵּיהֶם, כו׳״. [9]תַּעֲנִיּוֹת וּמַעֲמָדוֹת מִי אִיכָּא מוּסָף?

LITERAL TRANSLATION

your eyes and see what you are choosing for yourself. [1]Do not set your eyes on beauty. Set your eyes on family." [2]"Grace is deceitful, and beauty is vain, but a woman who fears the Lord, she shall be praised." [3]And it says: "Give her of the fruit of her hands, and let her deeds praise her in the gates."

[4]And similarly it says: "Go forth, O daughters of Zion, and behold King Solomon with the crown with which his mother crowned him on the day of his wedding, and on the day of the gladness of his heart." [5]"On the day of his wedding" — this [refers to] the giving of the Torah. [6]"And on the day of the gladness of his heart" — this [refers to] the building of the Temple, [7]may it be rebuilt speedily in our days.

GEMARA [8]"On three occasions in the year the priests raise their hands [in blessing], etc." [9][On] fast-days and *ma'amadot* is there a musaf service?

RASHI

במלך שלמה — במלך שהשלום שלו. **אמו** — כנסת ישראל. **זה מתן תורה** — יום הכפורים. שניתנו בו לוחות האחרונות.

TRANSLATION AND COMMENTARY

are choosing for yourself. [1]**Do not set your eyes on** a woman's **beauty,** but rather **on** her **lineage."** [2]For the verse says (Proverbs 31:30): **"Grace is deceitful, and beauty is vain, but a woman who fears the Lord, she shall be praised."** [3]**And the** next **verse** (v. 31) **says** regarding a praiseworthy woman: **"Give her of the fruit of her hands, and let her deeds praise her in the gates."**

וְכֵן הוּא אוֹמֵר [4]The Mishnah concludes with a verse which is interpreted as describing Yom Kippur as a day of joy. **And similarly the verse says** (Song of Songs 3:11): **"Go forth, O daughters of Zion, and behold King Solomon with the crown with which his mother crowned him on the day of his wedding, and on the day of the gladness of his heart."** This verse, which according to its plain sense refers to King Solomon (שְׁלֹמֹה), is understood here as referring to the King of Peace (שָׁלוֹם) — God Himself. Thus the verse says: Behold the Holy One, blessed be He, with the crown with which His mother — the people of Israel — crowned Him on the day of His wedding, and on the day of the gladness of His heart. [5]The expression **"on the day of His wedding" refers to** the day on which **the Torah was given** to the people of Israel, creating a bond like that of marriage between God and His people. And this day was Yom Kippur, when the second set of the Tablets of the Covenant were given to Moses at Sinai. [6]The expression, **"and on the day of the gladness of His heart," refers to** the rejoicing accompanying **the building of the** First **Temple,** which was dedicated in the days of Solomon on Yom Kippur. Having mentioned the Temple, the Mishnah concludes with the following prayer: [7]**May** the Temple **be rebuilt speedily in our days.**

GEMARA בִּשְׁלֹשָׁה פְּרָקִים בַּשָּׁנָה [8]We learned in the Mishnah: **"On three occasions during the year the priests raise their hands** and recite the Priestly Blessing four times a day — in the morning service, in the musaf service, in the afternoon service, and in the neilah service." The Gemara asks: How is it possible that on all three occasions listed in the Mishnah the priests recite the Priestly Blessing four times a day? Granted that on Yom Kippur all four of these services are conducted. [9]But **on** public **fast-days and at the *ma'amad***

NOTES

בְּיוֹם חֲתֻנָּתוֹ **On the day of his wedding.** The verse from the Song of Songs is cited here together with its homiletical interpretation in order to teach us that the young women's dances on the Fifteenth of Av and on Yom Kippur allude to matters of greater spiritual significance, for even the Revelation of the Torah at Sinai is described by Scripture as a wedding celebration. As for the connection between Yom Kippur and the events desribed here, the Rishonim demonstrate that the second set of the Tablets of the Covenant were given to Moses at Sinai on Yom Kippur (see below, 30b). The connection between the building of the Temple and Yom Kippur is less clear. Some commentators suggest that there is in fact no connection, and that the building of the Temple is mentioned here only as part of the homiletical interpretation of the continuation of the verse. *Kol Bo* and *Melekhet Shlomo* argue that on the day after he received the second tablets — the day after Yom Kippur — Moses informed the Israelites that they were to begin the construction of the Tabernacle in the desert. Our commentary follows *Rashi* (on *Rif*) and *Ovadyah Bertinoro*, who explain that the dedication of the First Temple in the days of King Solomon took place on Yom Kippur (see *Mo'ed Katan* 9a).

תַּעֲנִיּוֹת וּמַעֲמָדוֹת מִי אִיכָּא מוּסָף **On fast-days and *ma'amadot* is there a musaf service?** It follows from our Gemara that

[1]חַסּוּרֵי מִיחַסְּרָא וְהָכִי קָתָנֵי: ״בִּשְׁלֹשָׁה פְּרָקִים כֹּהֲנִים נוֹשְׂאִין אֶת כַּפֵּיהֶן כָּל זְמַן שֶׁמִּתְפַּלְּלִין, [2]וְיֵשׁ מֵהֶן אַרְבָּעָה פְּעָמִים בְּיוֹם, שַׁחֲרִית, וּמוּסָף, מִנְחָה, וּנְעִילַת שְׁעָרִים. [3]וְאֵלּוּ הֵן שְׁלֹשָׁה פְּרָקִים: תַּעֲנִיּוֹת, וּמַעֲמָדוֹת, וְיוֹם הַכִּפּוּרִים״.

[4]אָמַר רַב נַחְמָן אָמַר רַבָּה בַּר אֲבוּהּ: זוֹ דִּבְרֵי רַבִּי מֵאִיר, [5]אֲבָל חֲכָמִים אוֹמְרִים: שַׁחֲרִית וּמוּסָף יֵשׁ בָּהֶן נְשִׂיאַת כַּפַּיִם; [6]מִנְחָה וּנְעִילָה אֵין בָּהֶן נְשִׂיאַת כַּפַּיִם.

[7]מַאן חֲכָמִים?

[8]רַבִּי יְהוּדָה הִיא, דְּתַנְיָא: ״שַׁחֲרִית וּמוּסָף, מִנְחָה וּנְעִילָה - כּוּלָּן יֵשׁ בָּהֶן נְשִׂיאַת כַּפַּיִם. [9]דִּבְרֵי רַבִּי מֵאִיר. [10]רַבִּי יְהוּדָה אוֹמֵר: שַׁחֲרִית וּמוּסָף יֵשׁ בָּהֶן

LITERAL TRANSLATION

[1][The Mishnah] is defective, and it teaches as follows: "On three occasions the priests raise their hands each time they pray, [2]and sometimes [even] four times a day, [in] the morning service, and the musaf service, the afternoon service, and [the service of] the closing of the gates. [3]And these are the three occasions: Fast days, and the *ma'amadot*, and Yom Kippur."

[4]Rav Naḥman said in the name of Rabbah bar Avuha: These are the words of Rabbi Meir, [5]but the Sages say: The morning service and the musaf service have the Priestly Blessing (lit., "the raising of the hands"); [6]the afternoon service and the closing service do not have the Priestly Blessing.

[7]Who are the Sages?

[8]It is Rabbi Yehudah, for it was taught: "The morning service and the musaf service, the afternoon service and the closing service — all of them have the Priestly Blessing. [9][These are] the words of Rabbi Meir. [10]Rabbi Yehudah says: The morning service and the musaf service have

TRANSLATION AND COMMENTARY

assemblies **is there** in fact **a musaf service?** Surely the musaf service is recited only when an extra public sacrifice is offered in the Temple — on Shabbat, Rosh Ḥodesh and Festivals!

חַסּוּרֵי מִיחַסְּרָא [1]The Gemara explains: The text of **the Mishnah is defective** — a sentence is missing from it — **and it should read as follows: "On three occasions** during the year **the priests raise their hands** and recite the Priestly Blessing **each time they pray.** [2]**And** among these three **there is one occasion when** the Priestly Blessing is recited **four times** during **the day, in the morning service,** in **the musaf service,** in **the afternoon service, and** in **the neilah** service. [3]**And these are the three occasions** when the priests recite the Priestly Blessing each time they pray: On public **fast-days and at the *ma'amad*** assemblies, **and** on **Yom Kippur."**

אָמַר רַב נַחְמָן [4]The Gemara now explains that the Mishnah's ruling is the subject of a Tannaitic controversy. **Rav Naḥman said in the name of Rabbah bar Avuha:** The Mishnah's ruling reflects **the viewpoint of Rabbi Meir,** [5]**but the Sages** disagree **and say:** In **the morning and musaf** services the Priestly Blessing is recited, [6]but in the afternoon and neilah services, the Priestly Blessing is not recited.

מַאן חֲכָמִים [7]The Gemara asks: Who are the Sages who disagree with Rabbi Meir?

רַבִּי יְהוּדָה הִיא [8]The Gemara answers: **It is** the opinion of **Rabbi Yehudah, as was taught** in the following Baraita: **"The morning service and the musaf service, the afternoon service and the neilah service** — in **all of them the Priestly Blessing** is recited. [9]**This is the viewpoint of Rabbi Meir.** [10]**Rabbi Yehudah** disagrees and

RASHI

גמרא כל זמן שמתפללין — דהיינו שחרית ומנחה ונעילה. יש מהן ארבעה פעמים ביום — יום הכפורים, שיש בו מוסף.

NOTES

the additional service takes place on Yom Kippur, but not on public fast-days or at the *ma'amad* assemblies. But according to *Rambam* (*Commentary to the Mishnah* 4:1, 4:4; *Hilkhot Klei HaMikdash* 6:4), a special additional service was inserted between the morning and afternoon services conducted at the *ma'amad* assemblies, during the course of which the Priestly Blessing was recited and the story of the creation was read from the Torah. Either *Rambam* had a different reading of our Gemara, according to which the Gemara asked only about fast days, or he understood that the Gemara objected to the Mishnah's formulation from which it may be inferred that the special additional service is *always* conducted at the *ma'amad* assemblies, when in fact the special additional service is not recited on days when an additional sacrifice is offered, as is implied in our Mishnah (*Kesef Mishneh*). Most Rishonim reject *Rambam*'s position (but see *Sfat Emet*, who argues that the Mishnah and the Gemara can best be reconciled according to *Rambam*'s view).

According to *Ba'al HaMa'or* (*Sefer HaMa'or*, beginning of tractate *Berakhot*), a special additional service took place on public fast-days, into which the additional blessings discussed in the second chapter of this tractate were inserted. Support for this position is brought from a passage in *Megillah* (22a), which mentions "an additional prayer" recited on public fasts, as well as from a passage in the Jerusalem Talmud (*Berakhot* 1:5). *Ritva* and *Ran* reject this position on the basis of our Gemara.

TRANSLATION AND COMMENTARY

says: In **the morning and musaf services the Priestly Blessing** is recited, [1]but in **the afternoon and neilah services, the Priestly Blessing is not** recited. [2]**Rabbi Yose** disagrees with both the other Sages and **says:** In **the neilah service the Priestly Blessing** is recited, [3]but in **the afternoon service the Priestly Blessing is not** recited."

בְּמַאי קָמִיפַּלְגִי [4]The Gemara asks: **About what do** these Tannaim **disagree?** What is the theoretical basis of their dispute?

רַבִּי מֵאִיר סָבַר [5]The Gemara answers: **Rabbi Meir maintains that the reason why the priests do not spread their hands on ordinary days** to bless the people **in the afternoon service** is **on account of** possible **drunkenness.** The afternoon service is recited after most people have eaten their main meal, which often includes wine and strong drink. Since a priest is forbidden to say the Priestly Blessing while drunk, the Rabbis decreed that the Priestly Blessing should not be recited in the afternoon service, lest a priest recite it while under the influence of drink. Such a decree is warranted on ordinary days, when there is concern that the priests may be intoxicated. [6]But on fast-days and at the *ma'amad* assemblies (in which people also fast) **there is no** concern about **drunkenness.** Therefore the Rabbis did not decree that the Priestly Blessing should be omitted in the afternoon or neilah services conducted on these special occasions. This is the viewpoint of Rabbi Meir. [7]**Rabbi Yehudah maintains** that **the Rabbis did not decree** that the Priestly Blessing should be omitted on fast-days and at the *ma'amad* assemblies in **the morning and musaf services,** [8]because those services are conducted at a time **when** even **on ordinary days drunkenness is not common.** [9]But **the Rabbis did decree** that the Priestly Blessing should not be recited on fast-days and at the *ma'amad* assemblies in **the afternoon and neilah services,** because those services are conducted at a time **when on ordinary days drunkenness is common.** The Rabbis were concerned that if the Priestly Blessing were recited in the afternoon and neilah services on those occasions, the priests might come to recite their blessing in the afternoon service even on ordinary days, when they could be drunk. [10]**Rabbi Yose maintains** that a distinction should be drawn between the afternoon service and the neilah service: [11]**The Rabbis did** in fact **decree** that the Priestly Blessing should not be recited on fast-days and at the *ma'amad* assemblies in **the afternoon service,** because the afternoon service **is** conducted **every day,** both on ordinary days as well as on fast-days. The Rabbis were afraid that if the priests were to recite the Priestly Blessing in the afternoon service on fast-days and at the *ma'amad* assemblies, they might come to recite it in the afternoon service on ordinary days, when they might be drunk. [12]But **the Rabbis did not issue a decree** that the Priestly Blessing should be omitted on fast-days and at the *ma'amad* assemblies in **the neilah service, because** the neilah service **is not** conducted

נְשִׂיאַת כַּפַּיִם; [1]מִנְחָה וּנְעִילָה אֵין בָּהֶן נְשִׂיאַת כַּפַּיִם. [2]רַבִּי יוֹסֵי אוֹמֵר: נְעִילָה יֵשׁ בָּהּ נְשִׂיאַת כַּפַּיִם; [3]מִנְחָה אֵין בָּהּ נְשִׂיאַת כַּפַּיִם".

[4]בְּמַאי קָמִיפַּלְגִי?

[5]רַבִּי מֵאִיר סָבַר: כָּל יוֹמָא טַעֲמָא מַאי לָא פָּרְשִׂי כָּהֲנֵי יְדַיְיהוּ בְּמִנְחָתָא מִשּׁוּם שִׁכְרוּת. [6]הָאִידָּנָא לֵיכָּא שִׁכְרוּת. [7]רַבִּי יְהוּדָה סָבַר: שַׁחֲרִית וּמוּסָף, [8]דְּכָל יוֹמָא לָא שְׁכִיחַ שִׁכְרוּת, לָא גָּזְרוּ בְּהוּ רַבָּנַן. מִנְחָה וּנְעִילָה, [9]דְּכָל יוֹמָא שְׁכִיחָא שִׁכְרוּת, גָּזְרוּ בְּהוּ רַבָּנַן. [10]רַבִּי יוֹסֵי סָבַר: [11]מִנְחָה, דְּאִיתָהּ בְּכָל יוֹמָא, גָּזְרוּ בָּהּ רַבָּנַן. [12]נְעִילָה, דְּלֵיתָהּ בְּכָל יוֹמָא, לָא גָּזְרוּ בָּהּ רַבָּנַן.

LITERAL TRANSLATION

the Priestly Blessing; [1]the afternoon service and the closing service do not have the Priestly Blessing. [2]Rabbi Yose says: The closing service has the Priestly Blessing; [3]the afternoon service does not have the Priestly Blessing."

[4]About what do they disagree?

[5]Rabbi Meir maintains: Every day the reason why the priests do not spread their hands in the afternoon service is on account of drunkenness. [6]Now there is no drunkenness. [7]Rabbi Yehudah maintains: [As for] the morning service and the musaf service, [8]when every day drunkenness is not common, the Rabbis did not decree regarding them. [9][As for] the afternoon service and the closing service, when every day drunkenness is common, the Rabbis did decree regarding them. [10]Rabbi Yose maintains: [11][As for] the afternoon service which takes place every day, the Rabbis decreed regarding it. [12][As for] the closing service, which does not take place every day, the Rabbis did not decree regarding it.

RASHI

כל יומא מאי טעמא לא פרשי כהני ידייהו במנחה — דכל יומא שכיחא ביה שכרות, שכבר סעד, וזימנין דמשכא סעודתיה ומשתכר, ופריש ידיה בהדי חמריה. וכהן שתוי יין אסור לישא את כפיו, שנאמר "יין ושכר אל תשת בבואכם" וגו' (ויקרא י), ונשיאת כפים מעין עבודה, כדלקמן. **האידנא** — בתעניות ובמעמדות לא שכיחא שכרות, ובמעמדות נמי מתענין כדלקמן (כז,ב). **גזרינן** — תענית אטו שאר ימים. **נעילה דליתה בבכל יומא** — אלא ביום התענית.

BACKGROUND

מִשּׁוּם שִׁכְרוּת On account of drunkenness. Sometimes the afternoon service would be recited after a copious meal. Wine was served at such meals, so there were grounds for apprehension that the priests might be drunk at the time of the service. Though they would be not so inebriated that they would be forbidden to pray at all, reciting the Priestly Blessing is a kind of priestly Temple service, regarding which there is a particular Torah prohibition against performing it while drunk. Hence people were scrupulous to have the priests remain completely sober while reciting the blessing.

TRANSLATION AND COMMENTARY

every day, and therefore there is no concern that reciting the Priestly Blessing at the neilah service conducted on those special occasions will lead the priests to recite the Priestly Blessing on ordinary days while they are drunk.

אָמַר רַב יְהוּדָה [1]**Rav Yehudah said in the name of Rav: The Halakhah is in accordance with** the viewpoint of **Rabbi Meir** that the Priestly Blessing is recited in the afternoon and neilah services conducted on fast-days and at the *ma'amad* assemblies. [2]**And Rabbi Yoḥanan said: The people act in accordance with** the viewpoint of **Rabbi Meir.** [3]**And Rava said: The** common **custom is** to act **in accordance with** the viewpoint of **Rabbi Meir.**

מַאן דְּאָמַר [4]The Gemara now explains the difference between these three formulations: **According to** Rav, **who said that the Halakhah is in accordance with** the viewpoint of **Rabbi Meir,** [5]the Halakhah was concluded decisively in his favor, and therefore the Rabbis may **expound this ruling in the public lectures** they deliver. [6]**According to** Rava, **who said that the** common **custom** is to act in accordance with the viewpoint of Rabbi Meir, [7]the Rabbis **do not expound** the ruling in their public lectures. [8]**But** if someone comes and asks how to act, the Rabbis must indeed **rule** in accordance with the viewpoint of Rabbi Meir. [9]And according to Rabbi Yoḥanan, who said that the people **act** in accordance with the viewpoint of Rabbi Meir, the Rabbis **must not rule** in accordance with Rabbi Meir's opinion, because this practice was never recognized as a binding custom. [10]**But if** someone **acts** in accordance with the viewpoint of Rabbi Meir, **the act is valid, and he is not corrected.**

וְרַב נַחְמָן אָמַר [11]**Rav Naḥman** disagreed with the three Amoraim cited above and **said: The Halakhah is in accordance with** the viewpoint of **Rabbi Yose** that in the neilah service conducted on fast-days and at the *ma'amad* assemblies the Priestly Blessing is recited, but not in the afternoon service conducted on those occasions.

וַהֲלָכָה כְּרַבִּי יוֹסֵי [12]The Gemara concludes with a decision on the matter: **And the Halakhah is in accordance with** the viewpoint of **Rabbi Yose.**

וְהָאִידָּנָא [13]The Gemara now asks about the common practice that is in conflict with this decision. If the Halakhah is in accordance with the viewpoint of Rabbi Yose, **what is the reason that nowadays the priests spread their hands** to bless the people **in the afternoon service** conducted **on fast-days?**

[1]אָמַר רַב יְהוּדָה אָמַר רַב: הֲלָכָה כְּרַבִּי מֵאִיר. [2]וְרַבִּי יוֹחָנָן אָמַר: נָהֲגוּ הָעָם כְּרַבִּי מֵאִיר. [3]וְרָבָא אָמַר: מִנְהָג כְּרַבִּי מֵאִיר.

[4]מַאן דְּאָמַר הֲלָכָה כְּרַבִּי מֵאִיר, [5]דָּרְשִׁינַן לַהּ בְּפִירְקָא. [6]מַאן דְּאָמַר מִנְהָג, [7]מִידְרַשׁ לָא דָּרְשִׁינַן, [8]אוֹרוּיֵי מוֹרֵינַן. [9]וּמַאן דְּאָמַר נָהֲגוּ, אוֹרוּיֵי לָא מוֹרֵינַן, [10]וְאִי עָבֵיד, עָבֵיד, וְלָא מְהַדְּרִינַן לֵיהּ.

[11]וְרַב נַחְמָן אָמַר: הֲלָכָה כְּרַבִּי יוֹסֵי.

[12]וַהֲלָכָה כְּרַבִּי יוֹסֵי.

[13]וְהָאִידָּנָא מַאי טַעְמָא פָּרְשִׂי כָּהֲנֵי יְדַיְיהוּ בְּמִנְחָתָא דְּתַעֲנִיתָא?

LITERAL TRANSLATION

[1]Rav Yehudah said in the name of Rav: The Halakhah is in accordance with Rabbi Meir. [2]And Rabbi Yoḥanan said: The people acted in accordance with Rabbi Meir. [3]And Rava said: The custom is in accordance with Rabbi Meir.

[4][According to] the one who said [that] the Halakhah is in accordance with Rabbi Meir, [5]we expound it at the public session. [6][According to] the one who said [that] it is the custom, [7]we do not expound it, [8]but we rule [in accordance with it]. [9]And [according to] the one who said [that] they acted [so], we do not rule [in accordance with it], [10]but if he acted, he acted, and we do not make him go back.

[11]And Rav Naḥman said: The Halakhah is in accordance with Rabbi Yose.

[12]And the Halakhah is in accordance with Rabbi Yose.

[13]And nowadays what is the reason that the priests spread their hands in the afternoon service of a fast day?

RASHI

דדרשינן בפירקא — הלכה כרבי מאיר, דבעינן דליקוס כוותיה עלמא. **אורויי אורינן** — כרבי מאיר — אי אתו לקמן, אבל בפירקא — לא דרשינן, דלא פסיטא ליה כולי האי דתיהוי הלכה כרבי מאיר. ומאן דאמר נהגו — משמע: הן נהגו מאליהן, אבל אינו עיקר. ו״מנהג״ משמע — תורת מנהג יש בדבר, ומנהג כשר הוא. **ורב נחמן אמר הלכה כרבי יוסי והלכה כרבי יוסי** — גמרא קא פסיק ומהדר סתמא, ומוקי לה הלכה כרבי יוסי. **ואהכי קא פריך ואלא האידנא כו׳.**

BACKGROUND

פִּירְקָא The public session. This is the term for public sermons given by a Sage in which he taught people how to act according to the Halakhah. These sermons were usually given before a Festival, and their contents would be related to that Festival. Since they were intended for the general public, and not only for Torah scholars, these sermons were different in character from the regular lessons taught by the Sages in the Academy. As a matter of courtesy other scholars would not challenge the Sage delivering the public sermon, a practice not observed during regular sessions.

NOTES

פָּרְשִׂי כָּהֲנֵי יְדַיְיהוּ בְּמִנְחָתָא דְּתַעֲנִיתָא The priests spread their hands in the afternoon service of a fast-day. The

HALAKHAH

פָּרְשִׂי כָּהֲנֵי יְדַיְיהוּ בְּמִנְחָתָא דְּתַעֲנִיתָא The priests spread their hands in the afternoon service of a fast-day. "On

LITERAL TRANSLATION

[1] Since they spread [their hands] close to sunset, it is like the closing service.

[2] At all events [it is the opinion] of all of them that one who is drunk is forbidden [to recite] the Priestly Blessing. [3] From where are these things [derived]?

[4] Rabbi Yehoshua ben Levi said in the name of Bar Kappara: Why is the section of the priest who blesses next to the section of the Nazirite? [5] To teach: Just as a Nazirite is forbidden wine, so too is a priest who blesses forbidden wine.

[1] כֵּיוָן דִּבְסָמוּךְ לִשְׁקִיעַת הַחַמָּה קָא פָּרְשִׂי, כִּתְפִילַּת נְעִילָה דָּמְיָא.

[2] דְּכוּלֵּי עָלְמָא מִיהַת שִׁכּוֹר אָסוּר בִּנְשִׂיאַת כַּפַּיִם. [3] מְנָהָנֵי מִילֵּי?

[4] אָמַר רַבִּי יְהוֹשֻׁעַ בֶּן לֵוִי מִשּׁוּם בַּר קַפָּרָא: לָמָּה נִסְמְכָה פָּרָשַׁת כֹּהֵן מְבָרֵךְ לְפָרָשַׁת נָזִיר? [5] לוֹמַר: מַה נָּזִיר אָסוּר בְּיַיִן, אַף כֹּהֵן מְבָרֵךְ אָסוּר בְּיַיִן.

TRANSLATION AND COMMENTARY

כֵּיוָן דִּבְסָמוּךְ [1] The Gemara answers: **Since** it has become customary to conduct the afternoon service late in the day on fast-days, the priests **spread their hands** to bless the people when it is already **close to sunset,** and the afternoon service **is** treated **like the neilah service.** Just as the Rabbis did not issue a decree that the Priestly Blessing should not be recited in the ne'ilah service on fasts-days, because there is no parallel service conducted on ordinary days, so too there is no reason nowadays to exclude the Priestly Blessing from the afternoon service conducted on fast-days. Nowadays the afternoon service is conducted on fast-days close to sunset, whereas on ordinary days the service is conducted earlier in the day, thus there is no concern that the priests may come to recite the Priestly Blessing in the afternoon service on ordinary days.

דְּכוּלֵּי עָלְמָא [2] Although the Tannaim disagree as to whether the Priestly Blessing is recited on fast-days in the afternoon and neilah services when there is no concern regarding drunkenness, **at all events all agree that someone who is drunk is forbidden to recite the Priestly Blessing.** [3] The Gemara asks: **From what** Biblical source **is this derived?**

אָמַר רַבִּי יְהוֹשֻׁעַ בֶּן לֵוִי [4] In reply **Rabbi Yehoshua ben Levi said in the name of Bar Kappara: Why does the** Torah **section dealing with the priest who recites the Priestly Blessing** (Numbers 6:22-27) **follow** immediately after the Torah **section dealing with the Nazirite** (Numbers 6:1-21)? Is there any internal connection between the two issues? He answers: The one section follows immediately after the other in order **to teach** us that one of the regulations governing a Nazirite applies equally to a priest who recites the Priestly Blessing: [5] **Just as a Nazirite is forbidden** to drink **wine, so too is a priest who recites the Priestly Blessing forbidden** to drink **wine.**

RASHI

כיון דסמוך לשקיעת החמה וכו' — שמאחרין עד שקיעת החמה, ומתפללין כל שעה, ואינן הולכין לבית הכנסת משש שעות ומחצה ולמעלה כמו שהיו עושין לאותן הימים. **כתפלת נעילה דמיא** — דהשתא ליכא למיגזר משום מנחה דכל יומא, דמנחתא כי הא ליתא בכל יומא. **שכור מיהא אסור בנשיאת כפים** — דאפילו רבי מאיר לא קאמר אלא משום דהאידנא לאו שכרות הוא. **פרשת כהן מברך** — "כה תברכו את בני ישראל אמור להם" (במדבר ו).

NOTES

Rishonim disagree about whether the Priestly Blessing is recited in the afternoon service even on Yom Kippur and on the other fast-days on which the neilah service takes place, or whether it is recited only on those fast-days on which the neilah service does not take place. Most Rishonim (*Tosafot, Rambam, Ra'avad*, and others) maintain that the Priestly Blessing is not recited in the afternoon service on Yom Kippur and other fasts, for on those days the afternoon service is conducted earlier in the day and not at the time of the neilah service, and there is therefore concern that the priests may come to recite the Priestly Blessing in the afternoon service on ordinary days, when they might actually be drunk. (*Rambam* agrees, however, that if a priest goes up before the congregation to recite the Priestly Blessing in the afternoon service of Yom Kippur, he is not ordered to go down.) But *She'iltot, Rabbenu Gershom, Ramban*, and others argue that, since the Gemara makes no such distinction, the Priestly Blessing is recited in the afternoon service of Yom Kippur and the other fasts when the afternoon service is followed immediately by neilah. The sources point to differences in practice regarding this matter between the communities in Eretz Israel and those in Babylonia, as well as to differences in practice in Babylonia itself.

HALAKHAH

a day on which the neilah service is conducted, such as Yom Kippur, the priests recite the Priestly Blessing in the morning service, in the Musaf service, and in the neilah service, but not in the afternoon service, following Rabbi Yose. But on a fast-day on which the neilah service is not conducted, the Priestly Blessing is recited in the afternoon service, as is explained in the Gemara." (*Shulḥan Arukh, Oraḥ Ḥayyim* 129:1.)

שִׁכּוֹר אָסוּר בִּנְשִׂיאַת כַּפַּיִם One who is drunk is forbidden to recite the Priestly Blessing. "A priest who has drunk a *revi'it* of wine is forbidden to recite the Priestly Blessing." (Ibid., 128:38.)

SAGES

אֲבוּהּ דְּרַבִּי זֵירָא The father of Rabbi Zera. This Sage was a Babylonian Amora of the second generation. Because of the greatness of his famous son, the father of Rabbi Zera was not known by his own name, though according to one tradition it was Isi. Although he was a tax-collector for the monarchy, he performed this work fairly and even went beyond the letter of the law to be fair. Therefore he was not regarded as one of the royal tax-collectors who were disqualified as witnesses because they abused the power invested in them. Some of his teachings are mentioned in the Babylonian Talmud.

אוֹשַׁעְיָא בַּר זַבְדָּא Oshaya bar Zavda. His name is mentioned only here. Judging by the context, it would appear that he belonged to the first generation of Amoraim.

TRANSLATION AND COMMENTARY

מַתְקִיף לָהּ [1]**The father of Rabbi Zera objected to this** derivation of the Halakhah forbidding someone who is drunk from reciting the Priestly Blessing (**and some say** that it was **Oshaya bar Zavda** who raised the objection): If we extend the Halakhah stated with respect to a Nazirite and apply it to a priest who recites the Priestly Blessing, we should not limit the comparison to the prohibition against wine. It should be equally valid to argue as follows: [2]**Just as a Nazirite is forbidden** to eat **grape kernels** — the Nazirite is forbidden to eat or drink anything derived from the vine, as the verse says (Numbers 6:4): "All the days of his separation he shall eat nothing that is made of the grapevine, from the kernels to the husk" — **so too should a priest who recites the Priestly Blessing be forbidden** to eat **grape kernels!**

אָמַר רַבִּי יִצְחָק [3]**Rabbi Yitzḥak said:** That a priest who recites the Priestly Blessing is permitted to eat anything derived from the vine other than wine is derived from another **verse** which **says** (Deuteronomy 10:8): "At that time the Lord separated the tribe of Levi, to bear the Ark of the Covenant of the Lord, [4]to stand before the Lord **to serve Him and to bless in His name."** This verse mentions the priest who serves in the Temple together with the priest who blesses the people of Israel, implying that what the Halakhah stated with respect to the former may be applied to the latter. [5]**Just as** a priest **who serves** in the Temple **is permitted** to eat **grape kernels** and anything else derived from the vine other than wine — for only a priest who is intoxicated is forbidden to perform the Temple service, as the verse says (Leviticus 10:9): "Do not drink wine or strong drink, neither you nor your sons with you, when you enter the Tent of Meeting, lest you die" — [6]**so too is a priest who recites the** Priestly Blessing **permitted grape kernels** and anything else derived from the vine other than wine.

[27B] אִי [7]The Gemara raises an objection: If we extend the law stated with respect to a priest who performs the Temple service and apply it to a priest who recites the Priestly Blessing, then the following argument can also be made: **Just as** a priest **who serves** in the Temple **must be** free of physical blemish, for a priest **who has a** physical **defect** is **not** fit to serve in the Temple, as the verse says (Leviticus 21:17): "Speak to Aaron, saying: Whoever he be of your seed in their generations that has any blemish, let him not approach to offer the bread of his God," [8]**so too must a priest who recites the Priestly Blessing be** free of physical blemish, for a priest **who has a** physical **defect** is **not** fit to bless the people!

הָא אִיתְקַשׁ לְנָזִיר [9]The Gemara answers: **Surely** a priest who recites the Priestly Blessing **was compared** not only to a priest who performs the Temple service, but also **to a Nazirite?** Thus it may be argued that just as a physical defect does not render a person unfit to be a Nazirite, so too a physical defect does not render a priest unfit to recite the Priestly Blessing.

וּמַאי חָזֵית [10]The Gemara asks: **But what led you to draw comparisons in favor of leniency?** A priest who recites the Priestly Blessing was compared both to a Nazirite and to a priest who performs the Temple service. Both of these analogies resulted in a leniency being applied to a priest who recites the Priestly

[1]מַתְקִיף לָהּ אֲבוּהּ דְּרַבִּי זֵירָא, וְאָמְרִי לָהּ אוֹשַׁעְיָא בַּר זַבְדָּא: [2]אִי מַה נָּזִיר אָסוּר בְּחַרְצָן, אַף כֹּהֵן מְבָרֵךְ אָסוּר בְּחַרְצָן! [3]אָמַר רַבִּי יִצְחָק: אֲמַר קְרָא: [4]״לְשָׁרְתוֹ וּלְבָרֵךְ בִּשְׁמוֹ״. [5]מַה מְּשָׁרֵת מוּתָּר בְּחַרְצָן, [6]אַף כֹּהֵן מְבָרֵךְ מוּתָּר בְּחַרְצָן.

[27A] [7]אִי מַה מְּשָׁרֵת בַּעַל מוּם לֹא, [8]אַף כֹּהֵן מְבָרֵךְ בַּעַל מוּם לֹא!

[9]הָא אִיתְקַשׁ לְנָזִיר!

[10]וּמַאי חָזֵית דְּמַקַּשְׁתְּ לְקוּלָּא?

LITERAL TRANSLATION

[1]The father of Rabbi Zera objected to this, and some say [it was] Oshaya bar Zavda: [2]Just as a Nazirite is forbidden [grape] kernels, so too should a priest who blesses be forbidden [grape] kernels!

[3]Rabbi Yitzḥak said: The verse says: [4]"To serve Him and to bless in His Name." [5]Just as one who serves is permitted [grape] kernels, [6]so too is a priest who blesses permitted [grape] kernels.

[27A] [7]Just as one who serves [must] not [be] one who has a defect, [8]so too a priest who blesses [must] not [be] one who has a defect!

[9]Surely he was compared to a Nazirite!

[10]And what did you see that you compared in favor of leniency?

RASHI

מה משרת כו׳ – עובד עבודה, דלא מיתסר אלא שתויי יין ממש, דכתיב "יין ושכר אל תשת" וגו׳, הא בחרצן – מותר.

HALAKHAH

בַּעַל מוּם Who has a defect. "A priest who has a physical defect on his face or hand may not recite the Priestly Blessing, lest the people stare at his defect and not pay attention to the blessing. If the local populace is already accustomed to seeing the priest's defect, or if the priests recite the blessing with their prayer shawls drawn forward to cover their heads and their hands, even a priest with a defect on his face or hand may recite the blessing." (*Shulḥan Arukh, Oraḥ Ḥayyim* 128:30-31.)

LITERAL TRANSLATION

[1]Compare in favor of stringency!

[2]They are [merely] a support for the Rabbis, [3]and in favor of leniency.

[4]"These are the *ma'amadot*: [5]For it is said: 'Command the Children of Israel, etc.'" [6]What is he saying?

[7]He says thus: "These are the *ma'amadot*. [8]And what is the reason that they instituted the *ma'amadot*? [9]For it is said: 'Command the Children of Israel, and say to them: My offering, My bread for My sacrifices made by fire.' [10]But how can a person's sacrifice be offered when he is not standing next to it? [11]The early Prophets instituted twenty-four

[1]אַקִּישׁ לְחוּמְרָא! [2]אַסְמַכְתָּא נִינְהוּ מִדְּרַבָּנַן, [3]וּלְקוּלָּא. [4]"אֵלּוּ הֵן מַעֲמָדוֹת: [5]לְפִי שֶׁנֶּאֱמַר 'צַו אֶת בְּנֵי יִשְׂרָאֵל' כו'". [6]מַאי קָאָמַר? [7]הָכִי קָאָמַר: "אֵלּוּ הֵן מַעֲמָדוֹת. [8]וּמָה טַּעַם תִּיקְנוּ מַעֲמָדוֹת? [9]לְפִי שֶׁנֶּאֱמַר: 'צַו אֶת בְּנֵי יִשְׂרָאֵל וְאָמַרְתָּ אֲלֵיהֶם: אֶת קָרְבָּנִי, לַחְמִי לְאִשַּׁי'. [10]וְהֵיאָךְ קָרְבָּנוֹ שֶׁל אָדָם קָרֵב וְהוּא אֵינוֹ עוֹמֵד עַל גַּבָּיו? [11]הִתְקִינוּ נְבִיאִים הָרִאשׁוֹנִים עֶשְׂרִים וְאַרְבָּעָה

RASHI

מאי קאמר — דקא בעי מאי ניהו מעמדות, ומייתי קרא "את קרבני לחמי לאשי" וגו'. **הכי קאמר אלו הן מעמדות** — דלקמן, וטעמא מאי תקון מעמדות — לפי שנאמר "צו את בני ישראל ואמרת אליהם את קרבני לחמי לאשי" וגו'.

TRANSLATION AND COMMENTARY

Blessing: Just as a Nazirite may have a physical defect, so too may a priest who recites the Priestly Blessing have a physical defect. And just as a priest who performs the Temple service is permitted grape kernels, so too is a priest who recites the Priestly Blessing permitted grape kernels. Why did you prefer to draw comparisons in favor of leniency? [1]It would have been just as legitimate to **draw comparisons in favor of stringency!** Thus it would follow that just as a Nazirite is forbidden grape kernels, so too a priest who recites the Priestly Blessing is forbidden grape kernels. And just as a priest who performs the Temple service must not have any physical defect, so too a priest who blesses the people must not have any physical defect!

אַסְמַכְתָּא [2]The Gemara answers: The Biblical verses cited here are not actually the sources for the laws mentioned here. **They are** merely **supports** for these laws, **which are Rabbinic** in origin. [3]Therefore the comparisons are drawn only **in favor of leniency** and not in favor of stringency.

אֵלּוּ הֵן מַעֲמָדוֹת [4]We learned in the Mishnah: **"These are the *ma'amadot*. The verse** referring to the daily sacrifice **says** [Numbers 28:2]: [5]**'Command the Children of Israel, etc.'"** [6]The Gemara asks: **What does** the Tanna of the Mishnah mean to **say?** How is the verse cited here connected to the institution of the *ma'amadot*?

הָכִי קָאָמַר [7]The Gemara answers: **This** is what the Tanna meant to **say: "These are the *ma'amadot*.** [8]**And what is the reason that the *ma'amadot* were enacted?** [9]**The verse** referring to the daily sacrifice **says: 'Command the Children of Israel, and say to them: My offering, My bread for My sacrifices made by a fire,** for a sweet savor to Me, you shall observe to offer to Me in their due season.' This verse teaches that the daily sacrifice is a communal offering brought by the entire people of Israel. [10]**But** this leads to a certain difficulty, for **how can a person's sacrifice be offered when he is not standing next to it?** Ordinarily, a person must be present in the Temple when his sacrifice is offered. Since the daily sacrifice is a communal obligation, it should be necessary for each and every member of the people of Israel to be in the Temple when the daily sacrifice is brought. [11]Since that is clearly impossible, **the early Prophets enacted** that the priests who served in the Temple were to be divided into **twenty-four *mishmarot*,** each *mishmar* serving in the Temple one week at a time. The Levites were similarly divided into twenty-four *mishmarot*, which replaced each other every week. Corresponding to each of the *mishmarot* was a group of Israelites, called

NOTES

אַסְמַכְתָּא נִינְהוּ מִדְּרַבָּנַן **They are merely a support for the Rabbis.** Some commentators explain that both analogies — that between a priest who recites the Priestly Blessing and a Nazirite, as well as that between a priest who recites the Priestly Blessing and a priest who performs the Temple service — are merely supports for laws that are Rabbinic in origin. *Ra'avad* argues that, according to the Gemara's conclusion, the analogy between a priest who recites the Priestly Blessing and a priest who performs the Temple service is a completely valid analogy by Torah law. Therefore it is by Torah law that a priest may not recite the Priestly Blessing if he is drunk, but he is permitted to do so if he only ate grape kernels. However, the analogy between a priest who recites the Priestly Blessing and a Nazirite is a mere support for a Rabbinic decree, and therefore that analogy is drawn in favor of leniency, teaching that a priest with a physical defect is permitted to recite the Priestly Blessing. *Rabbenu Ḥananel* and *Rambam* (*Hilkhot Tefillah* 15:3-4) appear to agree that the comparison between the Priestly Blessing and the sacrificial service is a completely valid comparison.

מִשְׁמָרוֹת. [1]עַל כָּל מִשְׁמָר וּמִשְׁמָר הָיָה מַעֲמָד בִּירוּשָׁלַיִם שֶׁל כֹּהֲנִים וְשֶׁל לְוִיִּם, וְשֶׁל יִשְׂרְאֵלִים. [2]הִגִּיעַ זְמַן מִשְׁמָר לַעֲלוֹת, כֹּהֲנִים וּלְוִיִּם עוֹלִין לִירוּשָׁלַיִם״.

[3]תָּנוּ רַבָּנַן: ״עֶשְׂרִים וְאַרְבָּעָה מִשְׁמָרוֹת בְּאֶרֶץ יִשְׂרָאֵל, וּשְׁתֵּים עֶשְׂרֵה בִּירִיחוֹ״.

[4]שְׁתֵּים עֶשְׂרֵה בִּירִיחוֹ?! [5]נְפִישָׁן לְהוּ טוּבָא!

[6]אֶלָּא: ״שְׁתֵּים עֶשְׂרֵה מֵהֶן בִּירִיחוֹ. [7]הִגִּיעַ זְמַן הַמִּשְׁמָר לַעֲלוֹת, [8]חֲצִי הַמִּשְׁמָר הָיָה עוֹלֶה מֵאֶרֶץ יִשְׂרָאֵל לִירוּשָׁלַיִם, [9]וַחֲצִי הַמִּשְׁמָר הָיָה עוֹלֶה מִירִיחוֹ [10]כְּדֵי

LITERAL TRANSLATION

mishmarot. [1]For each and every *mishmar* there was a *ma'amad* in Jerusalem of priests, and of Levites, and of Israelites. [2][When] the time arrived for the *mishmar* to go up, the priests and the Levites would go up to Jerusalem."

[3]Our Rabbis taught: "There are twenty-four *mishmarot* in Eretz Israel, and twelve in Jericho."

[4]Twelve in Jericho?! [5][Then] they are far too many!

[6]Rather: "Twelve of them in Jericho. [7][When] the time arrived for the *mishmar* to go up, [8]half of the *mishmar* would go up from Eretz Israel to Jerusalem, [9]and half of the *mishmar* would go up from Jericho [10]in order

TRANSLATION AND COMMENTARY

a *ma'amad*. Each time a *mishmar* went to Jerusalem to serve in the Temple, part of the corresponding *ma'amad* would go there as well and represent the entire people when the communal sacrifices were offered, while the rest of the *ma'amad* would remain at home and assemble for prayer in their own towns. [1]Thus, **for each and every *mishmar*, there was a *ma'amad* in Jerusalem of priests, Levites and Israelites** — the priests to perform the sacrificial service, the Levites to offer the musical accompaniment, and the Israelites to represent the whole people when the daily offerings were sacrificed. [2]**When the time arrived for the** members of a particular ***mishmar* to go up** to Jerusalem, all **the priests and the Levites** belonging to that *mishmar* **would go up to Jerusalem** to perform the sacrificial service and to offer the musical accompaniment. A number of the Israelites belonging to the *ma'amad* corresponding to that *mishmar* would join the priests and the Levites in the Temple and would be present when the communal sacrifices were being offered. The remainder of the Israelites belonging to that *ma'amad* would remain at home and assemble in synagogues, recite special prayers, and read the Torah portion describing the story of the creation."

תָּנוּ רַבָּנַן [3]Our Rabbis taught a Baraita, which stated: "There were twenty-four *mishmarot* in Eretz Israel, and twelve in Jericho."

שְׁתֵּים עֶשְׂרֵה בִּירִיחוֹ [4]The Gemara interrupts its presentation of the Baraita and asks in astonishment: Were there **twelve** additional *mishmarot* **in Jericho?!** [5]If so, there must have been **far too many** *mishmarot*, for if there were twelve *mishmarot* in Jericho in addition to the twenty-four *mishmarot* in the rest of Eretz Israel, there must have been thirty-six *mishmarot* altogether!

אֶלָּא [6]The Gemara answers: **Rather,** this is what the Baraita meant to say: "There were twenty-four *mishmarot* in Eretz Israel, and **twelve** of those twenty-four **were in Jericho."** The Baraita now explains what this means: "How so? Surely, Jericho could not have provided half of the *mishmarot*! [7]Rather, **when the time arrived for** the members of a particular ***mishmar* to go up** to Jerusalem for their week of service in the Temple, the *mishmar* would divide into two. [8]**Half** the members of **the *mishmar* would go up from Eretz Israel to Jerusalem** to perform the Temple service, [9]**and half** of the members of **the *mishmar* would go up to Jericho,** which is not very far from Jerusalem, [10]**in order to provide water and food** from there **for their**

BACKGROUND

הַמִּשְׁמָרוֹת The *mishmarot*. The twenty-four priestly *mishmarot* were apparently concentrated in special places in Eretz Israel. Just as there were special priestly cities at the time of the first division of the land, the tradition was apparently maintained that the priests should live in special places. Even after the destruction of the Temple, it seems that the priests went into exile family by family, and that each family of priests lived in a different settlement in Galilee.

RASHI

הכי גרסינן: תנו רבנן עשרים וארבעה משמרות היו בארץ ישראל ושנים עשר ביריחו שנים עשר ביריחו בתמיה נפישי להו טובא! אלא אימא: ושנים עשר מהן ביריחו — ברישא משמע לבד העשרים וארבעה שבעיירות ארץ ישראל היו שנים עשר ביריחו, דהוו להו שלושים וששה. ושנים עשר מהן, משמע שמאותן העשרים וארבעה היו שנים עשר ביריחו. הכי גרסינן: **הגיע זמן המשמר חצי המשמר עולה לירושלים וחצי המשמר עולה ליריחו כדי**

NOTES

וַחֲצִי הַמִּשְׁמָר הָיָה עוֹלֶה מִירִיחוֹ And half of the *mishmar* would go up from Jericho. *Meiri* writes that when the time came for the members of a particular *mishmar* to go up to Jerusalem for their week of service in the Temple, half of the group would go up to Jerusalem to perform the Temple service, while half would go to Jericho in order to obtain water and food for their brothers in Jerusalem. After three days, those who had been in Jericho would go to Jerusalem and perform the Temple service, and those who had been in Jerusalem would go to Jericho and obtain food and water for those who were then in Jerusalem.

TRANSLATION AND COMMENTARY

brothers in Jerusalem. All twenty-four *mishmarot* acted similarly, sending half of their members to Jerusalem and half to Jericho. Thus, half of each of the twenty-four *mishmarot*, which equalled twelve full *mishmarot,* were based in Jericho."

אָמַר רַב יְהוּדָה אָמַר שְׁמוּאֵל [1]**Rav Yehudah said in the name of Shmuel: Priests, Levites, and Israelites are indispensable for the sacrifice.** All must be present when a communal sacrifice is brought — the priests to perform the actual sacrificial service, the Levites to provide the musical accompaniment, and the Israelites to represent the entire people when their sacrifice is offered.

בְּמַתְנִיתָא תָּנָא [2]**In a Baraita** the same law **was taught** with a slight variation: [3]**"Rabbi Shimon ben Elazar says: Priests, Levites,** Israelites, **and musical instruments are indispensable for the sacrifice."**

בְּמַאי קָמִיפַּלְגִי [4]The Gemara asks: **About what do** Shmuel and Rabbi Shimon ben Elazar **disagree?** What is the theoretical basis of their dispute?

מָר סָבַר [5]The Gemara answers: **One Sage** — Shmuel — **maintains: The essential musical accompaniment** to the sacrificial services which must be provided by the Levites **was vocal.** The essence of their music was the choral singing of selected chapters of Psalms and other Biblical texts. The instrumental music they provided was intended merely to accompany the singing. [6]**And the other Sage** — Rabbi Shimon ben Elazar — **maintains: The essential musical accompaniment** to the sacrificial services provided by the Levites **was instrumental.** Thus not only the Levites but the musical instruments as well were indispensable for a communal offering.

אָמַר רַב חָמָא בַּר גּוּרְיָא [7]The Gemara now cites a number of conflicting traditions regarding the origin of the *mishmar* system. **Rav Ḥama bar Gurya said in the name of Rav:** [8]**Moses** originally **instituted for Israel**

שֶׁיְּסַפְּקוּ מַיִם וּמָזוֹן לַאֲחֵיהֶם שֶׁבִּירוּשָׁלַיִם."

[1]אָמַר רַב יְהוּדָה אָמַר שְׁמוּאֵל: כֹּהֲנִים וּלְוִיִּם וְיִשְׂרְאֵלִים מְעַכְּבִין אֶת הַקָּרְבָּן.

[2]בְּמַתְנִיתָא תָּנָא: [3]"רַבִּי שִׁמְעוֹן בֶּן אֶלְעָזָר: כֹּהֲנִים, וּלְוִיִּם וּכְלֵי שִׁיר מְעַכְּבִין אֶת הַקָּרְבָּן".

[4]בְּמַאי קָמִיפַּלְגִי?

[5]מָר סָבַר: עִיקַּר שִׁירָה בַּפֶּה.

[6]וּמָר סָבַר: עִיקַּר שִׁירָה בִּכְלִי.

[7]אָמַר רַב חָמָא בַּר גּוּרְיָא אָמַר רַב: [8]מֹשֶׁה תִּיקֵּן לָהֶם לְיִשְׂרָאֵל שְׁמוֹנָה מִשְׁמָרוֹת,

LITERAL TRANSLATION

to provide water and food for their brothers in Jerusalem."

[1]Rav Yehudah said in the name of Shmuel: Priests, and Levites, and Israelites are indispensable for the sacrifice.

[2]In a Baraita it was taught: [3]"Rabbi Shimon ben Elazar [says]: Priests, and Levites, and musical instruments are indispensable for the sacrifice."

[4]About what do they disagree?

[5]One Master maintains: The essence of the song is vocal (lit., "with the mouth"). [6]And one Master maintains: The essence of the song is instrumental (lit., "with an instrument").

[7]Rav Ḥama bar Gurya said in the name of Rav: [8]Moses instituted for Israel eight *mishmarot,*

RASHI

שיספקו מים ומזון לאחיהם שבירושלים — כלומר כילד היו שניס עשר ביריחו? כשהגיע זמן המשמר לעלות לירושלים בשבת, מתחלקים אנשי המשמר, חליין הולכין לירושלים לעבודה וחליין הולכין ליריחו הסמוכה לירושלים, ומתקנין שם מים ומזון לאחיהם וכן עושין כל העשרים וארבעה משמרות, נמלא שנים עשר ביריחו. לשון אחר נהירא לי. **מעכבין את הקרבן** — אם אין מעמד מכולן בירושלים, כדתנן (תענית כו,א): על כל משמר היה מעמד בירושלים. של כהנים לוים וישראלים, כיון דכולהו בעלים בעינן דליהוי כמוהו על גבי עבודה. **וכלי שיר מעכבין את הקרבן** — פלוגתא בשילהי מסכת סוכה (נ,ב), ובערכין (יא,א) מפורשת. **עיקר שירה בפה** — וכלי לבסומי קלא בעלמא, וכיון דאיכא לוים — לא מעכב משום כלי שיר. **עיקר שירה בבלי** — אבוב, וכן בפרק "החליל" (שם).

SAGES

רַב חָמָא בַּר גּוּרְיָא Rav Ḥama bar Gurya. A Babylonian Amora of the second generation, Rav Ḥama bar Gurya was one of the greatest of Rav's closest disciples, and he is often mentioned as transmitting Rav's teachings. Rav's younger disciples, such as Rav Meḥasya and Rav Ḥisda, learned Rav's teachings from Rav Ḥama bar Gurya. Despite his close association with Rav, he also greatly respected the teachings of Shmuel and studied Torah from him, perhaps after Rav's death. Rava bar Rav Huna, who was Rav's student-colleague, called Rav Ḥama bar Gurya "our teachers who are expert in the Halakhah." Gurya bar Ḥama, who is mentioned in the Talmud, may have been his son.

NOTES

מֹשֶׁה תִּקֵּן לָהֶם לְיִשְׂרָאֵל Moses instituted for Israel. According to the straightforward sense of our Gemara, the *mishmar* system originated as an enactment of the Prophets, the different traditions disagreeing only about the precise details of how the system developed. *Rambam* (*Sefer HaMitzvot,* Positive Commandment 36; see also *Hilkhot Klei HaMikdash* 4:3-4) writes, however, that the division of the priesthood into *mishmarot* is a Torah obligation. The Biblical source for the obligation is the verse (Deuteronomy 18:8): "They shall have like portions to eat, besides that which comes of the sale of his patrimony," which *Sifrei* interprets to mean: With the exception of that which the priestly forefathers sold to each other, saying: You have your week, and I have my week. (See also *Onkelos*'s translation of the verse.) *Ritva* argues that it stands to reason that the *mishmar* system is Biblically ordained, for had there been no assigned times for the priests to serve in the Temple, with each priest deciding for himself when

HALAKHAH

עִיקַּר שִׁירָה The essence of the song. "The musical accompaniment offered by the Levites to the sacrificial services in the Temple was essentially vocal. In addition to the choral singing, there was also instrumental music played by Levites and Israelites." (*Rambam, Sefer Avodah, Hilkhot Klei HaMikdash* 3:3.)

[1]אַרְבָּעָה מֵאֶלְעָזָר וְאַרְבָּעָה מֵאִיתָמָר. [2]בָּא שְׁמוּאֵל וְהֶעֱמִידָן עַל שֵׁשׁ עֶשְׂרֵה. [3]בָּא דָּוִד וְהֶעֱמִידָן עַל עֶשְׂרִים וְאַרְבָּעָה, [4]שֶׁנֶּאֱמַר: ״בִּשְׁנַת הָאַרְבָּעִים לְמַלְכוּת דָּוִיד נִדְרָשׁוּ, וַיִּמָּצֵא בָהֶם גִּבּוֹרֵי חַיִל בְּיַעְזֵיר גִּלְעָד״.

[5]מֵיתִיבֵי: ״מֹשֶׁה תִּיקֵּן לָהֶם לְיִשְׂרָאֵל שְׁמוֹנָה מִשְׁמָרוֹת, אַרְבָּעָה מֵאֶלְעָזָר וְאַרְבָּעָה מֵאִיתָמָר. [6]וּבָא דָּוִד וּשְׁמוּאֵל וְהֶעֱמִידָן עַל עֶשְׂרִים וְאַרְבַּע, [7]שֶׁנֶּאֱמַר: ׳הֵמָּה יִסַּד דָּוִיד וּשְׁמוּאֵל הָרֹאֶה בֶּאֱמוּנָתָם׳״!

[8]הָכִי קָאָמַר: ״מִיסוֹדוֹ שֶׁל דָּוִד וּשְׁמוּאֵל הָרָמָתִי הֶעֱמִידוּם עַל עֶשְׂרִים וְאַרְבַּע״.

LITERAL TRANSLATION

[1]four from Eleazar and four from Ithamar. [2]Samuel came and established them at sixteen. [3]David came and established them at twenty-four, [4]as it is said: "In the fortieth year of the reign of David they were sought for, and there were found among them mighty men of valor at Jazer of Gilead."

[5]They raised an objection: "Moses instituted for Israel eight *mishmarot*, four from Eleazar and four from Ithamar. [6]And David and Samuel came and established them at twenty-four, as it is said: [7]'Whom David and Samuel the seer did ordain in their set office.'"

[8]He says thus: "By the institution of David and Samuel the Ramatite they established them at twenty-four."

TRANSLATION AND COMMENTARY

eight priestly ***mishmarot,*** [1]**four from** the descendants of **Eleazar,** the son of Aaron, **and four from** the descendants of **Ithamar,** the second of Aaron's surviving sons. [2]Later the Prophet **Samuel came** and added another eight *mishmarot,* **establishing** the total number at **sixteen.** [3]And finally King **David came** and added yet another eight *mishmarot,* **establishing** the total number **at twenty-four,** [4]**as it is said** in the verse that concludes the listing of the twenty-four priestly and Levitical *mishmarot* (I Chronicles 26:31): **"In the fortieth year of the reign of David they were sought for, and there were found among them mighty men of valor at Jazer of Gilead."**

מֵיתִיבֵי [5]**An objection was raised** from a Baraita which reports a slightly different version of the origin of the *mishmarot*: "At first **Moses instituted for Israel eight** priestly ***mishmarot,* four from** the descendants of **Eleazar and four from** the descendants of **Ithamar.** [6]**And** later King **David and** the Prophet **Samuel came** and added another sixteen *mishmarot,* **establishing** the total number at **twenty-four,** [7]**as the verse says** [I Chronicles 9:22]: 'These were reckoned by their genealogy in their settlements, **whom David and Samuel the seer did ordain in their** set office,' which is understood as referring to the priestly and Levitical *mishmarot.*" This Baraita implies that David and Samuel acted together in expanding the number of *mishmarot* from eight to twenty-four, whereas Rav Ḥama bar Gurya said that it was a two-stage process, Samuel first adding eight *mishmarot* to the original eight established by Moses, and David later adding another eight.

הָכִי קָאָמַר [8]The Gemara answers: **This is what** the Tanna of the Baraita meant to **say: "By the institution of David and Samuel the Ramatite they established** the number of *mishmarot* **at twenty-four.** David and Samuel were together responsible for increasing the number of *mishmarot,* Samuel first adding eight and then David adding another eight.

RASHI

ארבעה מאלעזר — מבניו של אלעזר, שעשה מהן ארבעה משמרות. וגמרא גמר לה. **המה יסד דוד ושמואל הרואה באמונתם** — ותיובתא דרב חמא, דאמר: שמואל העמידם על ששה עשר, ודוד העמידן על עשרים וארבעה. דהא שמעינן מינה דתרווייהו בהדי הדדי תקנינהו. **מיסודו של שמואל הרמתי** — שהעמידן על ששה עשר, בא דוד והעמידן על עשרים וארבעה. אית ספרים שכתוב בהן: מיסודו של שמואל ודוד העמידום על עשרים וארבעה, כלומר: שניהם הועילו בדבר, ושמואל העמידם על ששה עשר ודוד על עשרים וארבע.

NOTES

to serve, there would surely have been times when no priests were present for the Temple service. The number of *mishmarot* was not fixed by Torah law but by the various enactments issued by Moses, Samuel, and David, the number growing in accordance with the changing needs. *Ramban* (in his critique of *Rambam's Sefer HaMitzvot*) concludes that the *mishmar* system does not have a Scriptural basis. It originated either as an enactment of the Prophets or as a law of Moses from Sinai — a law which was taught to Moses orally at the same time as he received the written Torah at Sinai.

שֶׁנֶּאֱמַר: ״בִּשְׁנַת הָאַרְבָּעִים״ As it is said: "In the fortieth year." This verse is cited in order to teach us that it was King David (and not the Prophet Samuel) who expanded the *mishmar* system so that the total number of *mishmarot* stood at twenty-four, for by the fortieth year of David's reign Samuel was already dead (*Meiri, Maharsha*).

HALAKHAH

מֹשֶׁה תִּקֵּן לָהֶם לְיִשְׂרָאֵל Moses instituted for Israel. "Moses divided the priesthood into eight *mishmarot,* four of the descendants of Eleazar and four of the descendants of Ithamar. And so it continued until the days of Samuel. In the days of Samuel, he and King David divided the priesthood into twenty-four *mishmarot.*" (*Rambam, Sefer Avodah, Hilkhot Klei HaMikdash* 4:3.)

TRANSLATION AND COMMENTARY

תַּנְיָא אִידָךְ [1]The Gemara continues with another version of the origin of the *mishmarot*: **It was taught in another Baraita: "Moses** originally **instituted for Israel sixteen *mishmarot*, eight from** the descendants of **Eleazar and eight from** the descendants of **Ithamar.** [2]**And** centuries later, **when** it was found that **there were** many **more descendants of Eleazar than descendants of Ithamar,** King David **divided** each of the *mishmarot* consisting of the descendants of Eleazar into two, thereby adding another eight *mishmarot* **and establishing** the total number of *mishmarot* at **twenty-four,** [3]**as the verse says** [I Chronicles 24:4]: **'And there were more chief men found of the descendants of Eleazar than of the descendants of Ithamar, and they were divided thus.** [4]**Among the descendants of Eleazar there were sixteen heads of fathers' houses, and among the descendants of Ithamar there were eight for the houses of their fathers.'** [5]**And** another **verse says** [I Chronicles 24:6]: **'One father's house was taken for Eleazar, but what had been taken for Ithamar was taken.'** Each father's house of Eleazar took another so that there were now two, but each father's house that had been originally established for Ithamar remained established for Ithamar."

מַאי "וְאוֹמֵר" [6]The Gemara asks: **Why** was it necessary for the Baraita to say: **"And** another **verse says"**? Is not the first verse cited by the Baraita sufficient to prove its point?

וְכִי תֵּימָא [7]The Gemara explains: **If** the Baraita had cited only the first verse, **you might have said that, just as the descendants of Eleazar became many, so too did the descendants of Ithamar become many,** [8]**for the eight** *mishmarot* of the descendants of Ithamar which are mentioned in the verse may **originally have been four.** The verse teaches that, after King David reorganized the *mishmarot*, there were were sixteen *mishmarot* consisting of the descendants of Eleazar and eight consisting of the descendants of Ithamar. But it does not state how many *mishmarot* of each branch of the priesthood there were before the changes instituted by David. Perhaps there had originally been four *mishmarot* from the descendants of Eleazar and four from the descendants of Ithamar, as was argued by Rav Ḥama bar Gurya. And then, when the priests increased in number, the Eleazar branch of the priesthood having increased in greater numbers than the branch of Ithamar, David reorganized the *mishmar* system, establishing sixteen *mishmarot* of the descendants of Eleazar and eight of the descendants of Ithamar. In order to avoid our drawing that erroneous conclusion the Baraita cited a second verse, saying: [9]**Come and hear: "One father's house**

[1]תַּנְיָא אִידָךְ: "מֹשֶׁה תִּיקֵּן לָהֶם לְיִשְׂרָאֵל שֵׁשׁ עֶשְׂרֵה מִשְׁמָרוֹת, שְׁמוֹנֶה מֵאֶלְעָזָר וּשְׁמוֹנֶה מֵאִיתָמָר. [2]וּכְשֶׁרַבּוּ בְּנֵי אֶלְעָזָר עַל בְּנֵי אִיתָמָר, חִלְּקוּם וְהֶעֱמִידוּם עַל עֶשְׂרִים וְאַרְבַּע, [3]שֶׁנֶּאֱמַר: 'וַיִּמָּצְאוּ בְנֵי אֶלְעָזָר רַבִּים לְרָאשֵׁי הַגְּבָרִים מִן בְּנֵי אִיתָמָר, וַיַּחְלְקוּם. [4]לִבְנֵי אֶלְעָזָר רָאשִׁים לְבֵית אָבוֹת שִׁשָּׁה עָשָׂר וְלִבְנֵי אִיתָמָר לְבֵית אֲבוֹתָם שְׁמוֹנָה'. [5]וְאוֹמֵר: 'בֵּית אָב אֶחָד אָחֻז לְאֶלְעָזָר, וְאָחֻז אָחֻז לְאִיתָמָר'".
[6]מַאי "וְאוֹמֵר"?
[7]וְכִי תֵּימָא כִּי הֵיכִי דִּנְפִישִׁי בְּנֵי אֶלְעָזָר, הָכָא נַמִי דִּנְפִישִׁי בְּנֵי אִיתָמָר, [8]שְׁמוֹנָה מֵעִיקָּרָא אַרְבָּעָה הָווּ, [9]תָּא שְׁמַע: "בֵּית

LITERAL TRANSLATION

[1]It was taught in another [Baraita]: "Moses instituted for Israel sixteen *mishmarot*, eight from Eleazar and eight from Ithamar. [2]And when the descendants of Eleazar were more numerous than the descendants of Ithamar, they divided them and established them at twenty-four, [3]as it is said: 'And there were more chief men found of the descendants of Eleazar than of the descendants of Ithamar, and they were divided [thus]. [4]Among the descendants of Eleazar there were sixteen heads of fathers' houses, and among the descendants of Ithamar there were eight for the houses of their fathers.' [5]And it says: 'One father's house was taken for Eleazar, but what had been taken for Ithamar was taken.'" [6]What is "And it says"?
[7]For if you say [that] just as the descendants of Eleazar became many, so too did the descendants of Ithamar become many, [8][for] the eight were originally four, [9]come [and] hear: "One father's house

RASHI

וימצאו בני אלעזר רבים לראשי הגברים מבני איתמר ויחלקו בני אלעזר ראשים לבית אבותם ששה עשר ולבני איתמר ראשים לבית אבותם שמונה ואומר בית אב אחד אחוז לאלעזר ואחוז אחוז לאיתמר — "וימצאו בני אלעזר רבים לראשי הגברים" כלומר, ראשי הגברים של בני אלעזר היו רבים מאיתמר. והאי "וימצאו" — משמע דקודם לכן היו קבועים, ועכשיו הוסיפו עליהן, ויחלקום לששה עשר בית אב, "אחד אחוז" שהיה מתחילה לאלעזר דהיינו שמונה, אחוז אחד בגורל דהיינו נמי שמונה, והוו להו ששה עשר. **ואחוז אחוז לאיתמר** — מה שהיה מתחילה אחוז לאיתמר אחוזים עתה כבתחילה, שלא הרבו עליהם שום בית אב. **מאי ואומר** — וכי תימא מעיקרא הוו ארבעה לאלעזר וארבעה לאיתמר. **וכי היכי דנפישי בני אלעזר הכי נמי נפישי בני איתמר** — ומיהו, בני אלעזר נפישי טפי דהא לאיתמר לא אוקמינהו אלא על שמונה, ולאלעזר על ששה עשר.

אָב אֶחָד אָחֻז לְאֶלְעָזָר, וְאָחֻז אָחֻז לְאִיתָמָר״.
[1]תְּיוּבְתָּא דְּרַב חָמָא בַּר גּוּרְיָא!
[2]אָמַר לָךְ רַב חָמָא בַּר גּוּרְיָא: תַּנָּאֵי הִיא, [3]וַאֲנָא דַּאֲמַרִי כִּי הַאי תַּנָּא דְּאָמַר שְׁמוֹנָה.
[4]תָּנוּ רַבָּנַן: ״אַרְבָּעָה מִשְׁמָרוֹת עָלוּ מִן הַגּוֹלָה, [5]וְאֵלּוּ הֵן: יְדַעְיָה, חָרִים, פַּשְׁחוּר, וְאִימֵּר. [6]עָמְדוּ נְבִיאִים שֶׁבֵּינֵיהֶם [27B] וְחִלְּקוּם וְהֶעֱמִידוּם עַל עֶשְׂרִים וְאַרְבָּעָה. [7]בְּלָלוּם וּנְתָנוּם בְּקַלְפֵּי. [8]בָּא יְדַעְיָה וְנָטַל חֶלְקוֹ וְחֵלֶק חֲבֵרָיו — שֵׁשׁ. [9]בָּא חָרִים וְנָטַל חֶלְקוֹ וְחֵלֶק חֲבֵרָיו — שֵׁשׁ. [10]וְכֵן פַּשְׁחוּר, וְכֵן אִימֵּר. [11]וְכֵן הִתְנוּ נְבִיאִים שֶׁבֵּינֵיהֶם שֶׁאֲפִילּוּ יְהוֹיָרִיב

LITERAL TRANSLATION

was taken for Eleazar, but what had been taken for Ithamar was taken."

[1]This is a refutation of Rav Ḥama bar Gurya!

[2]Rav Ḥama bar Gurya can say to you: It is [a dispute between] Tannaim, [3]and I ruled (lit., "said") in accordance with that Tanna who said eight.

[4]Our Rabbis taught: "Four *mishmarot* went up from the exile, [5]and they are these: Jedaiah, Harim, Pashhur, and Immer. [6]The Prophets among them arose [27B] and divided them and established them at twenty-four. [7]They mixed them and put them in a ballot box. [8]Jedaiah came and drew his lot and the lot of his fellows — six. [9]Harim came and drew his lot and the lot of his fellows — six. [10]And likewise Pashhur, and likewise Immer. [11]And the Prophets among them stipulated that even if Jehoiarib

RASHI

תא שמע ואחוז אחוז לאיתמר — אלמא כדקיימי קיימי, ושמע מינה דמשה תיקן להם ששה עשר, שמונה מזה ושמונה מזה, וקשיא לרב חמא דאמר ארבעה וארבעה. והא דכתב לעיל ובשנת הארבעים וגו׳ המה יסד — במה שהוסיפו עליהן עד עשרים וארבעה משמעי, [אבל] משה תיקן להם ששה עשר משמרות. **תנאי היא** — דהא איכא תנא דלעיל דקתני משה תיקן להן שמונה משמרות משניהן, ואנא קאימנא כוותיה. **עלו מן הגולה** — בבית שני. והשאר לא עלו, שהרבה מישראל נשתיירו, ולא רצו לעלות. **פשחור ואימר** — ומבעיא לי, דפשחור לא כתיב גבי עשרים וארבע משמרות (דברי הימים א כד). **וחלקום** — לעשרים וארבעה, וכתבו כנוי של כל אחד ואחד בחלק. **בללום ונתנום בקלפי** — כתבו על עשרים וארבע חתיכות קלף ראשי משמרות שחלקו מאותן ארבעה. **בא ידעיה** — משמרה של ידעיה, בא אחד מהן ונוטל חלקו וחלק חמש חתיכות קלף דהוו להו שש, ומי שהיה עולה בידו ראשון היה לשבת ראשונה שבסדר, שהיו עולין בידו זו אחר זו — כך היו עובדין בשבתותיהן זו אחר זו. **וכך התנו** — שאפילו יהויריב שהיה במקדש ראשון ראשון למשמרות, עולה מן הגולה.

TRANSLATION AND COMMENTARY

was taken for Eleazar, but what had been taken for Ithamar was taken." This implies that each of the *mishmarot* which had originally been instituted for Ithamar remained in place, but no others were added. Thus it follows that there had originally been eight *mishmarot* from the descendants of Eleazar and eight from the descendants of Ithamar. Later King David added another eight *mishmarot* of the descendants of Eleazar, setting the total number of *mishmarot* at twenty-four.

תְּיוּבְתָּא [1]The Gemara now argues that **this** Baraita, which states that Moses originally instituted sixteen priestly *mishmarot,* is surely **a refutation of** the viewpoint of **Rav Ḥama bar Gurya,** who said that at the beginning there were only eight *mishmarot*!

אָמַר לָךְ [2]The Gemara answers: **Rav Ḥama bar Gurya can say to you** that the the origin of the *mishmar* system **is** the subject of **a dispute between Tannaim** — for the Tanna of the first Baraita taught that Moses had instituted only eight *mishmarot*, whereas the Tanna of the second Baraita taught that he had established sixteen *mishmarot* — [3]**and I ruled in accordance with** the viewpoint of **that Tanna who said** that Moses had originally instituted **eight** *mishmarot.*

תָּנוּ רַבָּנַן [4]**Our Rabbis taught** a Baraita which describes the restoration of the *mishmar* system after the Babylonian exile: "Only **four** *mishmarot* **returned from the** Babylonian **exile** in the days of Ezra. The twenty others remained in Babylonia together with the great majority of the people of Israel. [5]**And these are** the *mishmarot* which returned: The descendants of **Jedaiah,** the descendants of **Harim,** the descendants of **Pashhur, and** the descendants of **Immer** [Ezra 2:36-39]. [6]**The Prophets among them** — Haggai, Zechariah, and Malachi — **arose** [27B] **and divided** each of the four returning *mishmarot* into six, thereby **establishing** the total number of *mishmarot* **at twenty-four.** [7]Then **they** wrote down the names of each of the twenty-four *mishmarot* on separate pieces of paper, **mixed them** up, **and put them** all **in a ballot box.** [8]A representative of the *mishmar* of the descendants of **Jedaiah came and drew his lot and the lot of the** five **other** *mishmarot* which had been formed from the *mishmar* of Jedaiah, making a total of **six.** [9]After the representative of the *mishmar* of Jedaiah had drawn the six lots, a representative of the *mishmar* of **Harim came and drew his lot and the lot of the** five **other** *mishmarot* which had been formed from the *mishmar* of Harim, making a total of **six.** [10]**And likewise** a representative of the *mishmar* of **Pashhur** came and drew six lots, **and likewise** a representative of the *mishmar* of **Immer** did the same. Each of the twenty-four *mishmarot* performed their week of Temple service in the order that their lots had been drawn. [11]**Furthermore, the Prophets among them stipulated that even**

LANGUAGE

קַלְפֵּי Ballot box. The source of this word is the Greek κάλπις, *kalpis,* or κάλπη, *kalpi,* meaning an urn, a box. It also has the narrower meaning of a box used for ballots, drawing lots, and the like.

NOTES

עָלוּ מִן הַגּוֹלָה Went up from the exile. *Rashi* asks: Only three of these families — Jedaiah, Harim, and Immer —

TRANSLATION AND COMMENTARY

if the descendants of **Jehoiarib, who had headed the** *mishmarot* during the First Temple period [see I Chronicles 24:7], [1]**were** later **to return** to Eretz Israel from Babylonia, the *mishmar* of **Jedaiah would not be demoted from its place** as the then head of the *mishmarot*, [2]**but Jedaiah would be the chief and Jehoiarib would be subordinate to him."** The *mishmar* of Jehoiarib forfeited its position as head of the *mishmarot* when it failed to return from Babylonia in the days of Ezra. Thus it was stipulated that if Jehoiarib were later to return, the six *mishmarot* that had been formed from the *mishmar* of Jedaiah would be reorganized into five, and the *mishmar* of Jehoiarib would take its place in the Temple rotation after the five *mishmarot* of Jedaiah.

וְיִשְׂרָאֵל שֶׁבְּאוֹתוֹ מִשְׁמָר [3]We learned in the Mishnah: "Those **Israelites** associated with **the *mishmar*** who did not go to Jerusalem with it **would** remain at home and **assemble in** the synagogues **in their towns.** They recited special prayers, **and read the Torah portion describing the story of the creation."** [4]The Gemara asks: **From where do we derive** the fact that it is the chapter on the creation that is read at the *ma'amad* assemblies?

אָמַר רַבִּי יַעֲקֹב בַּר אַחָא [5]**Rabbi Ya'akov bar Aḥa said in the name of Rav Assi: Were it not for the *ma'amadot*** and the communal sacrifices that are offered in their presence, the people of Israel would surely pass from the world in punishment for their sins. And once the people of Israel were gone, [6]**Heaven and Earth** and all of creation **would** also **no longer exist,** for they exist only on account of the merits of Israel. Reading the Torah portion describing the creation at the *ma'amad* assemblies serves as a reminder that the continued existence of the world depends upon the Temple service. [7]The connection between the continued existence of the universe and the sacrificial service in the Temple is learned from **the verse** that **says** (Genesis 15:8): **"And he** [Abraham] **said: Lord God, by what shall I know that I shall inherit it?"** [8]This is what **Abraham said:**

רֹאשׁ מִשְׁמֶרֶת עוֹלֶה, [1]לֹא יִדָּחֶה יְדַעְיָה מִמְּקוֹמוֹ, [2]אֶלָּא יְדַעְיָה עִיקָּר וִיהוֹיָרִיב טָפֵל לוֹ". [3]"וְיִשְׂרָאֵל שֶׁבְּאוֹתוֹ מִשְׁמָר מִתְכַּנְּסִין בְּעָרֵיהֶן וְקוֹרִין בְּמַעֲשֵׂה בְּרֵאשִׁית". [4]מְנָהָנֵי מִילֵּי?

[5]אָמַר רַבִּי יַעֲקֹב בַּר אַחָא אָמַר רַב אַסִי: אִלְמָלֵא מַעֲמָדוֹת, [6]לֹא נִתְקַיְּימוּ שָׁמַיִם וָאָרֶץ, [7]שֶׁנֶּאֱמַר: "וַיֹּאמַר: ה' אֱלֹהִים, בַּמָּה אֵדַע כִּי אִירָשֶׁנָּה?" [8]אָמַר

LITERAL TRANSLATION

the head of the *mishmar* were to go up, [1]Jedaiah would not be demoted from his place, [2]but Jedaiah would be the chief and Jehoiarib would be subordinate to him."

[3]"And the Israelites of that *mishmar* would assemble in their towns and would read the story of the creation." [4]From where are these things [derived]? [5]Rabbi Ya'akov bar Aḥa said in the name of Rav Assi: Were it not for the *ma'amadot*, [6]Heaven and Earth would not exist, [7]as it is said: "And he said: Lord God, by what shall I know that I shall inherit it?" [8]Abraham said:

RASHI

לא ידחה ידעיה — הואיל ומתחלה לא עלה יהויריב, אלא כל משמרות הנעשות מידעיה קודמות לעבודה ליהויריב, ויהויריב בא ועובד אחריהן במקום משמר אחר, וששה דידעיה עושין אותן חמשה שלא להרבות במשמרות. **אמר רב אסי לפי שאלמלא מעמדות** — עיסקי קרבנות שישראל עושין, הן היו כלים בחטאן, ומשהן כלין — שמים וארץ העומדים בזכותן אין מתקיימין כו׳.

NOTES

appear in the list of priestly divisions recorded in I Chronicles 24:7-18. The family of Pashhur is included among the priestly families that returned from the Babylonian exile in the days of Ezra (Ezra 2:37), but nowhere is it mentioned as a separate priestly division. *Maharsha* suggests that the *mishmar* of Pashhur was composed of the descendants of Pashhur the son of Immer, a priest of importance mentioned in Jeremiah, chapter 20. After his descendants multiplied greatly, the clan of Pashhur separated themselves from the rest of the *mishmar* of Immer, and set up their own *mishmar* (see also *Rid*). *Sfat Emet* identifies this Pashhur with Pashhur the son of Malchiah (mentioned in Jeremiah 38:1, Nehemiah 11:12, and I Chronicles 9:12), and so the *mishmar* of Pashhur is descended from the *mishmar* of Malchiah.

שֶׁאֲפִילּוּ יְהוֹיָרִיב That even if Jehoiarib. Our commentary follows Rashi, who explains that if the descendants of Jehoiarib were to return to Eretz Israel, they would not regain their position as heads of the *mishmarot*, but would take their place after the five *mishmarot* originating from Jedaiah. But according to the simple reading of the Gemara in *Arakhin* 12b (and *Rashi's* comment on that passage), it would appear that if the descendants of Jehoiarib were to return, they would not constitute an independent *mishmar,* but would become subordinate to one of the *mishmarot* formed from the descendants of Jedaiah (*Rid* and others). A number of sources, however, suggest that the descendants of Jehoiarib did indeed constitute an independent *mishmar* during the Second Temple period. *Maharsha* points out that at least two other *mishmarot* of the First Temple period — Bilgah and Jeshebiab — were active as independent *mishmarot* during the Second Temple period.

לֹא נִתְקַיְּימוּ שָׁמַיִם וָאָרֶץ Heaven and Earth would not exist. The parallel passage found in *Megillah* 31b uses a different verse to prove that the continued existence of the world depends on the *ma'amadot* and the communal sacrifices that are sacrificed in their presence. The verse (Jeremiah 33:25) states: "Thus says the Lord: If not for My covenant day and night, I would not have appointed the ordinances of heaven and earth." This teaches that, were it not for the daily sacrifices brought in the morning and toward evening, Heaven and Earth would cease to exist. In our passage the connection between the continued existence of the universe

BACKGROUND

סֵדֶר קָרְבָּנוֹת The order of the sacrifices. Even after the Jews were exiled from Eretz Israel and could no longer gather in *ma'amad* assemblies, many of them nevertheless continued to recite daily a series of Biblical verses similar to those recited at the original *ma'amadot*. This order is found in many prayer books and is known as סֵדֶר מַעֲמָדוֹת (the order of the *ma'amadot*). It contains verses from the Torah, the Prophets, and the Writings, and some passages concerning the Temple and its structure from the Mishnah and the Gemara. This order used to be recited daily after the morning prayers.

TRANSLATION AND COMMENTARY

"Master of the Universe! [1]**In case,** God forbid, **Israel sins before You, will You do to them as You did to the generation of the flood** [see Genesis 6:5-13] **and the generation of the dispersion** [the builders of the Tower of Babel; see Genesis 11:1-9]?" [2]God **said to him: "No,** I will never destroy the people of Israel, or punish them the way I punished those earlier generations." [3]Abraham then **said before Him: "Master of the Universe! Inform me, with what shall I inherit it?** Explain to me how my descendants, the people of Israel, will atone for their sins. [4]God **answered him: "Take me a heifer of three years old, and a goat of three years old,** and a ram of three years old, and a turtledove, and a young pigeon [Genesis 15:9]. If Israel sins, let them bring Me an offering, and their transgressions will be forgiven." [5]Abraham **said before Him: "Master of the Universe! This is well when the Temple is in existence** and sacrifices can be brought to atone for the sins of Israel. [6]But **when the Temple is not in existence** and sacrifices cannot be brought, **what will become of them?** What will save Israel from divine punishment?" [7]God **answered** him: "I have already established for them the order of the sacrifices as is recorded in the Torah. [8]After the Temple is destroyed, when **they read before Me** the Torah portions describing the sacrifices they are no longer able to bring, **I will count it for them as if they had** actually **offered** those sacrifices **before Me, and I will pardon them for all their transgressions."** Since the sacrificial service and the reading of the Torah portions describing that service assure the continued existence of the people of Israel, and since Heaven and Earth exist only on account of the merits of Israel, the story of the creation is read at the *ma'amad* assemblies to teach us that the continued existence of the world depends on the Temple service.

תָּנוּ רַבָּנַן [9]**Our Rabbis taught** a Baraita, which stated: **"The members of the *mishmar*** who were not actually involved in the sacrificial service **would pray that the sacrifices** brought **by their** priestly **brethren would be accepted favorably** by God. [10]**The members of the *ma'amad*** who remained at home **would assemble in** their

אַבְרָהָם: "רִבּוֹנוֹ שֶׁל עוֹלָם! [1]שֶׁמָּא יִשְׂרָאֵל חוֹטְאִין לְפָנֶיךָ, אַתָּה עוֹשֶׂה לָהֶם כְּדוֹר הַמַּבּוּל וּכְדוֹר הַפַּלָּגָה?" [2]אֲמַר לֵיהּ: "לָאו". [3]אָמַר לְפָנָיו: "רִבּוֹנוֹ שֶׁל עוֹלָם! הוֹדִיעֵנִי, בַּמָּה אִירָשֶׁנָּה?" [4]אֲמַר לֵיהּ: "קְחָה לִי עֶגְלָה מְשֻׁלֶּשֶׁת וְעֵז מְשֻׁלֶּשֶׁת, וגו'". [5]אָמַר לְפָנָיו: "רִבּוֹנוֹ שֶׁל עוֹלָם! תֵּינַח בִּזְמַן שֶׁבֵּית הַמִּקְדָּשׁ קַיָּים. [6]בִּזְמַן שֶׁאֵין בֵּית הַמִּקְדָּשׁ קַיָּים מַה תְּהֵא עֲלֵיהֶם?" [7]אָמַר לוֹ: "כְּבָר תִּקַּנְתִּי לָהֶם סֵדֶר קָרְבָּנוֹת. [8]בִּזְמַן שֶׁקּוֹרְאִין בָּהֶן לְפָנַי, מַעֲלֶה אֲנִי עֲלֵיהֶם כְּאִילּוּ הִקְרִיבוּם לְפָנַי, וַאֲנִי מוֹחֵל לָהֶם עַל כָּל עֲוֹנוֹתֵיהֶם".
[9]תָּנוּ רַבָּנַן: "אַנְשֵׁי מִשְׁמָר הָיוּ מִתְפַּלְּלִין עַל קָרְבַּן אֲחֵיהֶם שֶׁיִּתְקַבֵּל בְּרָצוֹן. [10]וְאַנְשֵׁי מַעֲמָד מִתְכַּנְּסִין לְבֵית הַכְּנֶסֶת וְיוֹשְׁבִין

LITERAL TRANSLATION

"Master of the Universe! [1]In case Israel sins before You, will You do to them as [You did to] the generation of the flood and the generation of the dispersion?" [2]He said to him: "No." [3]He said before Him: "Master of the Universe! Inform me, with what shall I inherit it?" [4]He said to him: "Take Me a heifer of three years old, and a goat of three years old, etc." [5]He said before Him: "Master of the Universe! This is well at a time when the Temple is in existence. [6]At a time when the Temple is not in existence, what will become of them?" [7]He said to him: "I have already established for them the order of the sacrifices. [8]When they read them before Me, I will count it for them as if they had offered them before Me, and I will pardon them for all their transgressions."
[9]Our Rabbis taught: "The members of the *mishmar* would pray that the sacrifice of their brothers would be accepted favorably. [10]And the members of the *ma'amad* would assemble in the synagogue and would observe (lit., 'sit')

RASHI

כאנשי דור המבול – שמאחר שהן כלין אין העולם מתקיים, והואיל שעל עיסקי קרבן העולם עומד, לכך קורין אנשי מעמד בעריהן במעשה בראשית. כבר תקנתי להם כו' – כל זמן שקורין בהן כו' מהיכא יליף לה להאי. גמגום. תנו רבנן אנשי משמר **מתפללין על קרבן אחיהן – תמידים שבכל יום. אנשי משמר – אותן עשרים וארבעה שהיו בעריהן.**

NOTES

and the sacrificial service in the Temple is derived from the conversation between Abraham and God, which teaches that the sacrifices guarantee the continued existence of the people of Israel and indirectly the continued existence of the world, which exists only on account of Israel's merits. According to this interpretation of the conversation, Abraham did not ask for a sign that his descendants would inherit the Land of Israel, but rather for a means of atonement, so that his descendants would continue to exist and the land would remain theirs forever (*Maharsha*).

אַנְשֵׁי מִשְׁמָר הָיוּ מִתְפַּלְּלִין The members of the *mishmar* would pray. Each *mishmar* was divided into six (or seven) sub-groups called *batei av* (בָּתֵּי אָב), each of which performed the Temple service for one day during the week. While one *bet av* performed the actual service, the remaining *batei av* offered prayers that the sacrifices would be accepted by God (*Rabbenu Gershom, Rabbenu Elyakim*).

אַרְבַּע תַּעֲנִיּוֹת: [1]בַּשֵּׁנִי בְּשַׁבָּת, בַּשְּׁלִישִׁי, בָּרְבִיעִי, וּבַחֲמִישִׁי. [2]בַּשֵּׁנִי, עַל יוֹרְדֵי הַיָּם. [3]בַּשְּׁלִישִׁי, עַל הוֹלְכֵי מִדְבָּרוֹת. [4]בָּרְבִיעִי, עַל אַסְכָּרָא שֶׁלֹּא תִּיפּוֹל עַל הַתִּינוֹקוֹת. [5]בַּחֲמִישִׁי, עַל עוּבָּרוֹת וּמֵינִיקוֹת. [6]עוּבָּרוֹת, שֶׁלֹּא יַפִּילוּ. [7]מֵינִיקוֹת, שֶׁיֵּנִיקוּ אֶת בְּנֵיהֶם. [8]וּבְעֶרֶב שַׁבָּת לֹא הָיוּ מִתְעַנִּין מִפְּנֵי כְּבוֹד הַשַּׁבָּת, [9]קַל וָחוֹמֶר בַּשַּׁבָּת עַצְמָהּ״.

[10]בְּאֶחָד בְּשַׁבָּת מַאי טַעֲמָא לָא? [11]אָמַר רַבִּי יוֹחָנָן: מִפְּנֵי

LITERAL TRANSLATION

four fasts: [1]On Monday, on Tuesday, on Wednesday, and on Thursday. [2]On Monday, for those who sail on the sea. [3]On Tuesday, for those who travel in the deserts. [4]On Wednesday, that diphtheria not fall on the children. [5]On Thursday, for pregnant and nursing women. [6]Pregnant women, so that they not miscarry. [7]Nursing women, that they nurse their children. [8]And on Friday they would not fast because of the honor of Shabbat, [9][and] how much more so [not] on Shabbat itself."

[10]What is the reason that [they did] not [fast] on Sunday?

[11]Rabbi Yoḥanan said: Because

TRANSLATION AND COMMENTARY

synagogues and would observe four consecutive **fasts** during the course of the week: [1]**On Monday, on Tuesday, on Wednesday, and on Thursday.** [2]**On Monday,** they would fast **on behalf of those who sail the seas.** Monday is the appropriate day to fast and pray on behalf of those who travel the seas, for it was on the second day of the creation that God said [Genesis 1:6]: 'Let there be a firmament in the midst of the waters, and let it divide water from water.' [3]**On Tuesday,** the members of the *ma'amad* would fast **on behalf of those who travel across the deserts,** because it was on the third day of the creation that God said [Genesis 1:9]: 'Let the waters under the heavens be gathered together to one place, and let the dry land appear.' [4]**On Wednesday,** they would fast **so that** the disease of **diphtheria should not fall on the children.** On the fourth day of the creation, God said [Genesis 1:14]: 'Let there be lights in the firmament of heaven to divide the day from the night.' The defective spelling of the Hebrew word for 'lights' [מְאֹרֹת] allows the word to be understood as meaning 'curses' [מְאֵרֹת], thereby suggesting that the fourth day of the week is especially susceptible to curses, such as the disease of diphtheria. [5]**On Thursday,** the members of the *ma'amad* would fast **on behalf of pregnant and nursing women,** for it was on the fifth day of the creation that the first living creatures came into being, as the verse says [Genesis 1:20]: 'Let the waters bring forth abundantly moving creatures that have life.' [6]They would fast on behalf of **pregnant women,** and would pray **that they** would **not miscarry,** [7]and on behalf of **nursing women, that they** would have sufficient milk to **nurse their children** properly. [8]**But on Friday** the members of the *ma'amad* **would not fast, because of the honor to be accorded to Shabbat,** for it would be disrespectful if they entered Shabbat hungry. [9]**And how much more so would** the members of the *ma'amad* **not** fast **on Shabbat itself,** for fasting on Shabbat is forbidden."

בְּאֶחָד בְּשַׁבָּת [10]The Gemara asks: **What is the reason why** the members of the *ma'amad* **did not fast on Sunday?**

אָמַר רַבִּי יוֹחָנָן [11]Three answers were given to this question: (1) **Rabbi Yoḥanan said:** They did not fast on

RASHI

בשני על יורדי הים — דכתיב ביה (בראשית א) ״יהי רקיע בתוך המים״ וצריך להזכיר ולרצות על הדבר. **בשלישי על הולכי מדברות** — דכתיב ״ותראה היבשה״ — תהי ראויה יבשה להולכיה, שלא יוזקו מפני חיות רעות. **ברביעי על האסכרא** — שבו נתלו המאורות, וכתיב ביה (שם) ״יהי מאורות״ — מארת כתיב. **ועל עוברות כו׳** — דכתיב ביה (שם) ״ישרצו המים שרץ נפש חיה״.

NOTES

אַרְבַּע תַּעֲנִיּוֹת Four fasts. *Maharsha* suggests that the groups on behalf of whom the members of the *ma'amad* fast correspond to those groups that are obligated to give thank-offerings and say special prayers when they are delivered from distress (alluded to in Psalm 107): Seafarers, desert travelers, the sick after they have been healed, and those who have been released from prison (a newborn child may be compared to someone who has been released from confinement). The Jerusalem Talmud infers from this Baraita that the same fast may not be proclaimed for more than one impending calamity, but rather that each possible calamity requires a separate fast. The Jerusalem Talmud (see also *Rabbenu Ḥananel*) cites a Baraita which teaches that the members of the Great Sanhedrin would also divide themselves into sub-groups, each one fasting one day of the week together with the members of the *ma'amad*.

בָּרְבִיעִי, עַל אַסְכָּרָא... On Wednesday, that diphtheria... *Rashi* follows the Jerusalem Talmud, which explains that the defective spelling of the Hebrew word for "lights" (מְאֹרֹת), which were created on the fourth day of the week, teaches that Wednesdays are especially susceptible to curses (מְאֵרוֹת), and this is why the members of the *ma'amad* would fast on Wednesdays in order to prevent the disease of diphtheria from striking children. *Riaf* adds that the moon was diminished in size on Wednesday, becoming the "lesser light." Thus children are especially prone to illness on that day. *Rashi* in *Ein Ya'akov* suggests another explanation: Since diphtheria is a divine punishment for the spreading of evil gossip, children are especially likely to be attacked by the disease on a Wednesday, for it was on that day when the first gossip was spoken: the moon spoke evil of the sun, as a result of which it was diminished in size.

LITERAL TRANSLATION

of the Christians. [1] Rabbi Shmuel bar Nahmani said: Because it is the third [day] after the creation [of man]. [2] Resh Lakish said: Because of the additional soul. [3] For Resh Lakish said: An additional soul is given to man on Friday. [4] At the conclusion of Shabbat they take it away from him, [5] as it is said: "He rested and was refreshed" — [6] once he has rested, alas, the soul is lost.

[7] "On Sunday [they read]: 'In the beginning,' [8] and 'Let there be a firmament.'" [9] [A Tanna] taught:

הַנּוֹצְרִים. [1] רַבִּי שְׁמוּאֵל בַּר נַחְמָנִי אָמַר: מִפְּנֵי שֶׁהוּא שְׁלִישִׁי לִיצִירָה. [2] רֵישׁ לָקִישׁ אָמַר: מִפְּנֵי נְשָׁמָה יְתֵירָה. [3] דְּאָמַר רֵישׁ לָקִישׁ: נְשָׁמָה יְתֵירָה נִיתְּנָה בּוֹ בְּאָדָם בְּעֶרֶב שַׁבָּת. [4] בְּמוֹצָאֵי שַׁבָּת נוֹטְלִין אוֹתָהּ מִמֶּנּוּ, [5] שֶׁנֶּאֱמַר: "שָׁבַת וַיִּנָּפַשׁ" — [6] כֵּיוָן שֶׁשָּׁבַת, וַי, אָבְדָה נֶפֶשׁ.

[7] "בַּיּוֹם הָרִאשׁוֹן: 'בְּרֵאשִׁית', [8] וִ'יְהִי רָקִיעַ'". [9] תָּנָא:

RASHI

מפני הנוצרים — שעושים אותו יום טוב שלהם. **שלישי ליצירה** — דאדם נברא ביום ששי, ובכל יום שלישי הוי חלוש, כדכתיב (שם לד) "ויהי ביום השלישי בהיותם כואבים". **נשמה יתירה** — שנוטלין אותה ממנו, והוי חלש. **נשמה יתירה** — שמרחיבים דעתו לאכילה ושתיה. **כיון ששבת** — שנח ושמר את השבת. **ווי אבדה נפש** — "וינפש" דורש בנוטריקון: ווי נפש.

TRANSLATION AND COMMENTARY

Sunday **because the Christians** observed the day as a holiday, and observing a regular fast on the Christian holiday might arouse feelings of hostility between the two faiths. (2) [1] **Rabbi Shmuel bar Nahmani said:** The members of the *ma'amad* did not fast on Sunday **because** Sunday **is the third day after the creation** of man, Adam having been created by God on a Friday. On the third day after a person has suffered an injury or an illness, he is in a particularly weakened state, as is taught by the verse describing the condition of the people of Shechem following their circumcision (Genesis 34:25): "And it came to pass on the third day, when they were in pain." Adam's creation was a similarly traumatic experience, so that he was particularly weak on the Sunday following his coming into existence. Adam's weakness on the first day of the week was passed on to all future generations of humanity, hence it would have been inappropriate for the members of the *ma'amad* to fast on that day. (3) [2] **Resh Lakish said:** The members of the *ma'amad* did not fast on Sunday **because** they were still recovering from the departure **of the additional soul** that is bestowed on those who observe Shabbat. [3] **For Resh Lakish said: An additional soul is given to man on Friday** and remains with him for the duration of Shabbat. [4] **At the conclusion of Shabbat** that additional soul **is taken away from him,** leaving him weakened and sad. [5] An allusion to this removal of the additional soul at the end of Shabbat is found in **the verse** that **says** (Exodus 31:17): "And on the seventh day **He rested and was refreshed."** The word שָׁבַת — "He rested" — which, according to the plain sense, refers to God, is understood here as referring to the person who rests on Shabbat. The word וַיִּנָּפַשׁ — "and was refreshed" — is interpreted as an abbreviated form of the two words וַי נֶפֶשׁ — "alas, soul." [6] After a person finishes **resting** on Shabbat, **alas, the** additional **soul** with which he was endowed for the previous twenty-four hours **is** gone and is **lost.** Thus the members of the *ma'amad* did not begin to fast until Monday, for on Sunday they were still weak as a result of the departure of the additional soul at the conclusion of Shabbat.

בַּיּוֹם הָרִאשׁוֹן [7] We learned in the Mishnah: **"On Sunday,** the members of the *ma'amad* would read the Torah section beginning with **'In the beginning** [Genesis 1:1-5],' [8] **and** would then continue with the section beginning **'Let there be a firmament** [vv. 6-8].'" The Mishnah then lists the Torah sections read on each of the other days, and concludes that the longer of the two sections was read by two people, and the shorter was read by one person. [9] This ruling is illustrated in a Baraita, in which **it was taught:** "On Sunday, the

BACKGROUND

נְשָׁמָה יְתֵירָה **The additional soul.** *Rashi* explains this expression as meaning an enlarged soul, since on Shabbat people not only rest their bodies but also their souls, and on the strength of this they can forget all of their troubles and worries and take pleasure in the Sabbath day. Other commentators explain that נְשָׁמָה יְתֵירָה refers to an additional soul, a new one that comes to a person on the Sabbath, giving him the power to rise to a higher level of understanding and cognition. This is how the term is explained in the *Zohar*.

NOTES

מִפְּנֵי הַנּוֹצְרִים **Because of the Christians.** Our commentary follows *Rabbenu Gershom* and others who explain that, according to Rabbi Yohanan, the members of the *ma'amad* did not fast on Sunday because the day was observed by Christians as a holiday, and there was concern that the Christians would react in a hostile way if the Jews observed a fast on their holiday (see also *Tractate Soferim* 17:4).

Maharsha maintains that the members of the *ma'amad* did not fast on Sunday because whenever they fasted they would also refrain from work, and they did not want anybody to think that they were refraining from work in deference to the Christian holiday observed on that day.

Some suggest that the word נוֹצְרִים not be read as *notzrim*, meaning "Christians," but rather as *notzarim*, "creatures." Thus Rabbi Yohanan was offering essentially the same explanation as that of Rabbi Shmuel bar Nahmani — that the members of the *ma'amad* did not fast on Sunday because Sunday is the third day after the creation of man. *Meiri* offers the surprising suggestion that the word *notzrim* here is a reference to the Babylonians (following Jeremiah 4:16: "*Notzrim* are coming from a distant country" [see *Rabbi David Kimhi's* commentary, ad loc.]). Since the Babylonians celebrated Sunday as a holiday, the Rabbis did not enact that the members of the *ma'amad* should fast on that day.

TRANSLATION AND COMMENTARY

section beginning with **'In the beginning'** and containing five verses **was read by two** people, [1]and the section beginning with **'Let there be a firmament'** and containing three verses was read **by one** person." [2]The Gemara objects: **Granted that** the section beginning **"Let there be a firmament" can be read by one** person, [3]for that section **is composed of three verses,** the minimum number of verses to be read by each person called to the Torah. [4]**But** as for the section beginning with **"In the beginning," what is the reason why it is read by two** people? [5]Surely this section **contains** only **five verses, and it has been taught** in a Baraita: [6]**"One who is called to read the Torah must not read less than three verses"!** How can two people read a section containing only five verses in such a way that each reads a minimum of three verses?

רַב אָמַר [7]The Amoraim disagreed about how a section containing five verses is to be divided between the two people called to read it. **Rav said:** The first of the two reads the first three verses of the section, and then the second of the two **goes back** and reads the third verse a second time, and continues with the final two verses of the section. [8]**But Shmuel said:** The first of the two reads the first two verses of the section and then **divides** the third verse into two, and reads only the first half, so that he reads altogether two-and-a-half verses. The second of the two then reads the second half of the third verse, and continues with the final two verses of the section, so that he too reads two-and-a-half verses altogether.

וְרַב [9]The Gemara now seeks to clarify each of these two positions: **As for Rav, who said** that the second person **goes back** and reads again the last verse read by the first person, [10]**what is the reason why he did not agree** with Shmuel that the first person **divides** the third verse into two?

קָסָבַר [11]The Gemara explains: Rav **maintains** that **any verse which Moses did not divide** into two, [12]**we may not divide.** The division of the Biblical text into verses is part of an accepted tradition handed down orally since the giving of the Torah to Moses at Sinai. A verse must be read in its entirety, as it was given to Moses. Thus the first reader cannot read only the first half of the verse.

וּשְׁמוּאֵל אָמַר [13]The Gemara now analyzes the viewpoint of **Shmuel,** who **said** that one may divide a single **verse** into two. [14]The Gemara immediately raises an objection: **But** is it true that **a verse may be divided** into two? [15]**Surely Rabbi Hanina the Bible teacher said:** I had great trouble convincing

”׳בְּרֵאשִׁית׳ בִּשְׁנַיִם. [1]׳יְהִי רָקִיעַ׳ בְּאֶחָד”. [2]בִּשְׁלָמָא ”יְהִי רָקִיעַ” בְּאֶחָד, [3]תְּלָתָא פְּסוּקֵי הָווּ. [4]אֶלָּא ”בְּרֵאשִׁית” בִּשְׁנַיִם מַאי טַעֲמָא? [5]חֲמִישָּׁה פְּסוּקֵי הָוְיָין, וְתַנְיָא: [6]”הַקּוֹרֵא בַּתּוֹרָה אַל יִפְחוֹת מִשְּׁלשָׁה פְּסוּקִים”!

[7]רַב אָמַר: דּוֹלֵג. [8]וּשְׁמוּאֵל אָמַר: פּוֹסֵק.

[9]וְרַב, דְּאָמַר דּוֹלֵג, [10]מַאי טַעֲמָא לָא אָמַר: פּוֹסֵק?

[11]קָסָבַר: כָּל פְּסוּקָא דְּלָא פְּסָקֵיהּ מֹשֶׁה, [12]אֲנַן לָא פָּסְקִינַן לֵיהּ.

[13]”וּשְׁמוּאֵל אָמַר: פּוֹסֵק”. [14]וּמִי פָּסְקִינַן? [15]וְהָאָמַר רַבִּי חֲנִינָא קָרָא: צַעַר גָּדוֹל הָיָה לִי אֵצֶל

LITERAL TRANSLATION

"'In the beginning' [is read] by two; [1]'Let there be a firmament' [is read] by one." [2]Granted that "Let there be a firmament" [is read] by one, [3]there are three verses. [4]But what is the reason [why] "In the beginning" [is read] by two? [5]There are five verses, and it is taught: [6]"One who reads the Torah must not read less than three verses"!

[7]Rav said: He goes back. [8]But Shmuel said: He divides [the verse].

[9]As for Rav, who said [that] he goes back, [10]what is the reason [why] he did not say: He divides [it]?

[11]He maintains: Any verse which Moses did not divide, [12]we may not divide.

[13]"And Shmuel said: He divides [the verse]." [14]But do we divide [a verse]? [15]But surely Rabbi Hanina the Bible teacher said: I had great trouble with

RASHI

בראשית בשנים — כהן ולוי קורין ביום תענית בראשית. **תלתא פסוקי הווי** — וסגיא בהו לחד גברא. **רב אמר דולג** — הראשון קורא שלשה פסוקים, והשני מתחיל בפסוק שסיים בו הראשון, והשנים עמו — הרי שלשה. ומשום אין משיירין בפרשה פחות משלשה פסוקים ליכא, משום דלא אפשר. **פוסק** — מפסיק הפסוק לשנים, ראשון קורא שני פסוקים וחצי, ולוי משלים חצי אותו הפסוק שקרא הכהן עם שנים הנותרים. **רבי חנינא קרא** — שהיה בעל מקרא, ויודעה בגירסא ובקי בטעמיה. **צער גדול** — הרבה טרחתי וחזרתי עליו שיתיר לי לפסוק הפסוק לשנים לצורך תינוקות שלומדים לפני, שאין יכולין לקרות פסוק כולו.

BACKGROUND

אַל יִפְחוֹת מִשְּׁלשָׁה פְּסוּקִים Must not read less than three verses. The reason for this appears to be so that everyone who reads the Torah will read something of significance. In the Talmud the principle is enunciated that something which is done three times is thereby reinforced and given extra power.

HALAKHAH

דּוֹלֵג He goes back. "On occasions when the Torah reading cannot be divided in such a way that each person reads a separate section consisting of three verses, such as on Rosh Hodesh, one of the readers may read again a verse that has already been read by the previous reader," following Rav. (*Shulhan Arukh, Orah Hayyim* 423:2.)

רַבִּי חֲנִינָא הַגָּדוֹל, ¹וְלֹא הִתִּיר לִי לִפְסוֹק אֶלָּא לְתִינוֹקוֹת שֶׁל בֵּית רַבָּן, הוֹאִיל וּלְהִתְלַמֵּד עֲשׂוּיִן.
²וּשְׁמוּאֵל: הָתָם טַעֲמָא מַאי מִשּׁוּם דְּלָא אֶפְשָׁר. ³הָכָא נַמִי לָא אֶפְשָׁר.
⁴״וּשְׁמוּאֵל אָמַר: פּוֹסֵק״. ⁵מַאי טַעֲמָא לָא אֲמַר: דּוֹלֵג?
⁶גְּזֵירָה מִשּׁוּם הַנִּכְנָסִין, ⁷וּגְזֵרָה מִשּׁוּם הַיּוֹצְאִין.
⁸מֵיתִיבִי: ״פָּרָשָׁה שֶׁל שִׁשָּׁה פְּסוּקִים קוֹרִין אוֹתָהּ בִּשְׁנַיִם, ⁹וְשֶׁל חֲמִשָּׁה בְּיָחִיד. ¹⁰וְאִם הָרִאשׁוֹן קוֹרֵא שְׁלֹשָׁה, הַשֵּׁנִי קוֹרֵא שְׁנַיִם מִפָּרָשָׁה זוֹ, וְאֶחָד מִפָּרָשָׁה אַחֶרֶת. ¹¹וְיֵשׁ אוֹמְרִים: ¹²שְׁלֹשָׁה, לְפִי שֶׁאֵין מַתְחִילִין בְּפָרָשָׁה פָּחוֹת מִשְּׁלֹשָׁה

LITERAL TRANSLATION

Rabbi Ḥanina the Great, [1]but he only allowed me to divide [verses] for schoolchildren, since they are [thus] made [easier] to be taught.

[2]And Shmuel [can say]: There the reason why is because it is impossible. [3]Here too it is impossible.

[4]"And Shmuel said: He divides [the verse]." [5]What is the reason [why] he did not say: He goes back?

[6][It is] a decree on account of those entering, [7]and [it is] a decree on account of those leaving.

[8]They raised an objection: "A section of six verses is read by two, [9]and [a section] of five [verses is read] by a single person. [10]And if the first reads three [verses], the second reads two [verses] from this section, and one from a different section. [11]And there are some who say: [12]Three, because we do not begin a section [by reading] less than three

TRANSLATION AND COMMENTARY

Rabbi Ḥanina the Great to give permission in this matter, [1]**and** in the end **he only allowed me to divide** long verses into two **for** the benefit of **schoolchildren, since they are thus made easier to be taught.** Surely, then, it follows that in all other situations a verse may not be divided in any way other than the way in which it was divided by Moses!

וּשְׁמוּאֵל [2]The Gemara answers: **Shmuel can counter** this argument as follows: **There,** in the case of the schoolchildren, **the reason** why Rabbi Ḥanina the Great permitted Rabbi Ḥanina the Bible teacher to divide a verse into two **was because it was impossible** for him to teach in any other manner. [3]**Here, too,** with respect to the Torah reading at the *ma'amad* assemblies, **it is impossible** for the Torah reading to be conducted in any other manner, and the only way to divide a five-verse section between two people in a way that will allow each person to read three verses is to divide the middle verse.

וּשְׁמוּאֵל אָמַר [4]The Gemara now asks: As for **Shmuel,** who **said** that the first reader **divides** the third verse of the section into two and reads only the first half, leaving the second half of the verse for the next reader, [5]what is the reason why he did not agree with Rav that the second person goes back and reads again the last verse read by the first person?

גְּזֵירָה מִשּׁוּם הַנִּכְנָסִין [6]The Gemara explains: This arrangement was not adopted because **a decree was enacted on account of those entering** during the middle of the Torah reading, [7]**and on account of those leaving** at that time. If someone enters a synagogue during the middle of the Torah reading, after the first reader has already concluded his portion, and he hears the second reader starting from the third verse of a section, he may come to the erroneous conclusion that the first person read only the first two verses, and that a person who is called to the Torah is permitted to read only two verses. Similarly, if someone leaves the synagogue during the middle of the Torah reading, after the first reader has read three verses, leaving only two verses in that section for the next reader, he may think that the second reader will in fact read only two verses and that this is permitted. Thus it was impossible to adopt the solution that the second person reads the second verse a second time, because it may lead to an erroneous conclusion.

מֵיתִיבִי [8]**An objection was raised** from a Baraita dealing with the rules governing Torah reading, which stated: **"A** Torah **section** consisting **of six verses may be read by two** different people, for each can read three verses. [9]**But a section** consisting **of** only **five verses should be read by a single person,** for each person called to the Torah must read a minimum of three verses. [10]**If one** person **reads** the first **three verses** of a five-verse Torah section, **the second** reader **should read** the next **two verses of that section and** then **one** more verse **from the next section.** [11]**But there are some who** disagree with this ruling and **say:** [12]The second reader must read at least **three** verses from the next section, **for** the rule is that **we do not** read **less than three verses**

RASHI

הכי נמי לא אפשר – גבי ספר תורה. ודילוג אי אפשר, משום הנכנסין והיוצאין, אם שני דולג ומתחיל בפסוק שסיים בו הראשון, בני אדם הנכנסין שלא שמעו קריאת הראשון סבורין לומר שלא קרא הראשון אלא שני פסוקים ונפיק מיניה תורבא. וכשהראשון קורא שלשה פסוקים ואינו משייר אלא שנים איכא גזרת יוצאין, דסברי האי שני דסגיא ליה בשני פסוקים. **מיתיבי פרשה של ששה פסוקים** – אשאר ימות השנה קאי. **ויש אומרים שלשה** – מפרשה אחריתי.

SAGES

רַבִּי חֲנִינָא קָרָא Rabbi Ḥanina the Bible teacher. A Palestinian Amora of the second generation, this Rabbi Ḥanina was a disciple of Rabbi Ḥanina bar Ḥama (Rabbi Ḥanina the Great) and of Rabbi Yannai. Rabbi Ḥanina seems to have been not only a teacher of young children (סוֹפֵר), but also an expert in Bible, which is why he is called קָרָא. He is mentioned in the Talmud and the Midrash in discussion with his two teachers, both on matters relating to his work and also on other Halakhic questions.

רַבִּי חֲנִינָא הַגָּדוֹל Rabbi Ḥanina the Great. This refers to Rabbi Ḥanina bar Ḥama, who, since he was one of the outstanding Sages of his generation, is called, "the Great." In the Jerusalem Talmud he is known as "Rabbi Ḥanina Rabba," which has the same meaning. This epithet is generally used when Rabbi Ḥanina is mentioned at the same time as another Sage of that name, such as Rabbi Ḥanina Kara, and a distinction must be made between them.

Rabbi Ḥanina was a first-generation Amora from Eretz Israel. He originally came from Babylonia, although he immigrated to Eretz Israel at a relatively early age and studied there with Rabbi Yehudah HaNasi, who was very fond of him (and indeed remarked that he was "not a human being, but an angel"). Rabbi Ḥanina also studied with Rabbi Yehudah's most distinguished students, in particular with Rabbi Ḥiyya. On his deathbed, Rabbi Yehudah HaNasi designated Rabbi Ḥanina as the new head of his yeshivah, although the latter, in his great modesty, refused to accept the position as long as his older colleague, Rabbi Efes, was still alive.

Rabbi Ḥanina lived in Sepphoris, where he earned a living as a honey dealer, from which he became wealthy and established a large academy. He was renowned for his acuity, as well as for his righteousness and piety.

Numerous Halakhic and Aggadic teachings of Rabbi Ḥanina appear in the Babylonian and the Jerusalem Talmud. He lived to a great

פְּסוּקִין״. [1]לְמַאן דְּאָמַר דּוֹלֵג, [2]לִידְלוֹג, [3]וּלְמַאן דְּאָמַר פּוֹסֵק, [4]לִיפְסוֹק!

[5]שָׁאנֵי הָתָם [28A] דְּאִית לֵיהּ רַוְוחָא.

[6]״פָּרָשָׁה גְּדוֹלָה קוֹרִין אוֹתָהּ בִּשְׁנַיִם בַּשַּׁחֲרִית וּבַמּוּסָף. [7]וּבַמִּנְחָה קוֹרִין עַל פִּיהֶן, כו׳״. [8]אִיבַּעְיָא לְהוּ: הֵיכִי קָאָמַר? [9]בַּשַּׁחֲרִית וּבַמּוּסָף קוֹרִין אוֹתָהּ

LITERAL TRANSLATION

verses." [1]According to the one who said [that] he goes back, [2]let him go back, [3]and according to the one who said [that he] divides [the verse], [4]let him divide it!

[5]It is different there [28B] because he has room.

[6]"A long section would be read by two in the morning service and in the musaf service. [7]But in the afternoon service they would read by heart, etc." [8]It was asked of them: What does he mean (lit., "how does he say")? [9]In the morning service and in the musaf service they would read it from

TRANSLATION AND COMMENTARY

at the beginning of a section. A person may not stop the Torah reading in the middle of a section at a point less than three verses into the section, lest those who enter the synagogue at that point think that he has read only those first one or two verses." Now, says the Gemara, this Baraita is difficult according to both Rav and Shmuel. [1]**According to** Rav, **who said** that the second person **may go back** and reread the last verse read by the first person, why does the Baraita rule that a section consisting of five verses should be read by a single person? [2]**Let** one person read three verses and then let the second person **go back** and reread the third verse! [3]**And according to** Shmuel, **who said** that the readers **divide** the third verse of the section into two, why does the Baraita rule the way it does? [4]**Let** the first person **divide** the third verse into two, read the first half himself, and leave the second half for the next person!

שָׁאנֵי הָתָם [5]The Gemara answers this objection: **It is different there,** [28B] **because** the second person **has the option** of reading one verse or more from the next section. Both Rav and Shmuel agree that if a Torah section has only five verses, the second person should read one verse or more from the next section rather than repeat a verse or divide a verse into two. But with respect to the *ma'amad* assemblies, the second person cannot read from the next section, for there is a fixed Torah portion which must be read each day. In such a case, Rav and Shmuel disagree about how a five-verse section should be divided. Rav maintains that one of the verses should be read twice, once by each of the two readers, and Shmuel maintains that one of the verses should be divided into two, with each person reading half the verse.

פָּרָשָׁה גְּדוֹלָה [6]The Mishnah continues: **"The longer** of the two **sections was read by two** people, and the shorter of the two was read by one person. The chapter on the creation was read in this manner — by three people who were called to read from a Torah scroll — **in the morning service** conducted by the *ma'amad* assemblies **and** once again **in the musaf service.** [7]**But in the afternoon service** the members of the *ma'amad* did not read the Torah portion from a scroll. Instead **they** entered the synagogues and each person **read** to himself the day's portion **by heart,** just as the *Shema* is recited by every individual by heart and not from a Torah scroll." [8]**The following problem arose** in discussion among the Sages: **What did** the Tanna of the Mishnah mean to **say?** Is the Mishnah meant to be understood as it was just cited: [9]**In the morning service and** in the **musaf service** the members of the *ma'amad* **read** a portion of the chapter on the creation **from**

RASHI

הכי גרסינן: **למאן דאמר דולג לידלוג למאן דאמר פוסק ליפסוק** — כלומר, פרשה של חמשה פסוקין אמאי קורא שני שלשה פסוקין בפרשה אחרת? לידלוג או ליפסוק. **דאית ליה רווחא** — שיכול לקרות מפרשה אחרת. אבל הכא לית ליה רווחא, דהא לא מצי למיקרי אלא "בראשית" "ויהי רקיע".

age, and had many students over an extended period, among them Rabbi Yehoshua ben Levi, who was a student-colleague of his, and Rabbi Yoḥanan, who studied with him for many years. His son was the Amora Rabbi Ḥama the son of Rabbi Ḥanina.

BACKGROUND

קוֹרִין עַל פִּיהֶן They would read by heart. The problem underlying this discussion is the Halakhah that the written Torah may not be recited by heart but must be read from a scroll. On the other hand, the Sages permitted the reciting of certain passages by heart, because they were known by everyone and recited in public (like the *Shema*, which comes from the written Torah). The question was whether recital by heart of Torah passages should be limited or extended.

NOTES

וּלְמַאן דְּאָמַר פּוֹסֵק לִיפְסוֹק And according to the one who said that he divides the verse, let him divide it. Our commentary follows the reading found in the standard text, according to which the Gemara raises an objection to both Rav and Shmuel. *Rashi* explains here that both of their positions are contradicted by the clause of the Baraita which states that a five-verse section should be read by a single person, for according to both of them it should be possible for the section to be read by two people — according to Rav, the third verse can be read twice, and according to Shmuel, that verse can be divided. In the parallel passage found in *Megillah* 22a, *Rashi* deletes the words: "And according to the one who said that he divides the verse, let him divide it." There *Rashi* explains that the difficulty is being raised from the last part of the Baraita, which states that if the first person read three verses from the five-verse section, the second person should read the next two verses of that section and one verse (or three verses) from the next section. That clause is difficult according to Rav, who maintains that it should be possible for the second reader to reread the third verse and then continue with the next two verses. But there is no difficulty according to Shmuel, for the first reader has already read the third verse, and so it is no longer possible to divide that verse between the two readers (see also *Tosafot, Rashba,* and *Ritva* on *Megillah*).

TRANSLATION AND COMMENTARY

a Torah scroll, [1]but in the afternoon service each person reads the day's portion to himself by heart in the same manner that a person reads the Shema? [2]Or perhaps the Mishnah is to be understood as follows: In the morning service the members of the ma'amad read a portion of the chapter on the creation from a Torah scroll, [3]but in the musaf service and in the afternoon service each person reads the day's portion to himself by heart just as a person reads the Shema?

תָּא שְׁמַע [4]The Gemara answers: Come and hear what we have learned in the following Baraita in which it was taught: [5]"In the morning and the musaf services the members of the ma'amad would enter their local synagogues and read the day's Torah portion from a scroll in the same manner that the Torah is read throughout the year. [6]But in the afternoon service a single individual reads by heart the day's portion on behalf of the rest of the assembly. [7]Rabbi Yose said: But is a single individual permitted to read words of the Torah by heart for the rest of the community? [8]Rather, we must say that all the members of the ma'amad would enter the synagogues and each individual would read the day's portion to himself by heart just as a person reads the Shema." It is clear from this Baraita that the musaf service was similar to the morning service in that the Torah portion was read from a scroll, and it was only in the afternoon service that the Torah portion was read by heart.

כָּל יוֹם [9]We learned in our Mishnah: "Any day on which Hallel was recited but an additional sacrifice was not offered, there was no ma'amad in the morning service. Any day on which an additional sacrifice was offered, there was no ma'amad in the neilah service. And any day on which a wood-offering was brought, there was no ma'amad in the afternoon service. This is the viewpoint of Rabbi Akiva. But Ben Azzai said: Any day on which an additional sacrifice was offered, there was no ma'amad in the afternoon service. And any day on which there was a wood-offering, there was no ma'amad in the neilah service. Rabbi Akiva retracted his opinion and taught as Ben Azzai had stated." [10]The Gemara asks about the viewpoint of Ben Azzai: What is the difference between the neilah service and the afternoon service, that the wood-offering takes precedence over the ma'amad of the former but does not take precedence over the ma'amad of the latter?

LITERAL TRANSLATION

the scroll, [1]but in the afternoon service they would read it by heart as they read the Shema? [2]Or perhaps he teaches thus: In the morning service they would read it from the scroll, [3]but in the musaf service and in the afternoon service they would read it by heart as they read the Shema? [4]Come [and] hear, for it was taught: [5]"In the morning service and in the musaf service they would enter the synagogue and would read in the manner that they read all year. [6]But in the afternoon service an individual would read it by heart. [7]Rabbi Yose said: But can an individual read words of the Torah by heart for the community? [8]Rather, all would enter and would read it by heart as they read the Shema." [9]"Any day on which there is Hallel, there is no ma'amad, etc." [10]What is the difference between this and that?

בַּסֵּפֶר, [1]וּבַמִּנְחָה קוֹרִין אוֹתָהּ עַל פֶּה כְּקוֹרִין אֶת שְׁמַע? [2]אוֹ דִּלְמָא הָכִי קָתָנֵי: בַּשַּׁחֲרִית קוֹרִין אוֹתָהּ בַּסֵּפֶר, [3]וּבַמּוּסָף וּבַמִּנְחָה קוֹרִין אוֹתָהּ עַל פֶּה כְּקוֹרִין אֶת שְׁמַע? [4]תָּא שְׁמַע, דְּתַנְיָא: [5]"בַּשַּׁחֲרִית וּבַמּוּסָף נִכְנָסִין לְבֵית הַכְּנֶסֶת וְקוֹרִין כְּדֶרֶךְ שֶׁקּוֹרִין כָּל הַשָּׁנָה. [6]וּבַמִּנְחָה יָחִיד קוֹרֵא אוֹתָהּ עַל פֶּה. [7]אָמַר רַבִּי יוֹסֵי: וְכִי יָחִיד יָכוֹל לִקְרוֹת דִּבְרֵי תּוֹרָה עַל פֶּה בַּצִּבּוּר? [8]אֶלָּא: כּוּלָּן נִכְנָסִין וְקוֹרִין אוֹתָהּ עַל פֶּה כְּקוֹרִין אֶת שְׁמַע". [9]"כָּל יוֹם שֶׁיֵּשׁ בּוֹ הַלֵּל, אֵין בּוֹ מַעֲמָד, כו'". [10]מַה הֶפְרֵשׁ בֵּין זֶה לָזֶה?

RASHI

מה הפרש בין זה לזה — מאי שנא דקרבן עלים דחי מעמד דנעילה, ומעמד דמנחה לא דחי?

NOTES

מַה הֶפְרֵשׁ בֵּין זֶה לָזֶה What is the difference between this and that. The Rishonim offer several explanations of this passage. Our commentary follows Rashi, who explains that the Gemara is seeking to understand why, according to Ben Azzai, the wood-offering takes precedence over the ma'amad of the neilah service but not over the ma'amad of the afternoon service. The Gemara answers that the wood-offering does not take precedence over the ma'amad of the afternoon service, because there is an allusion to that service in the Torah itself, but it does take precedence over the ma'amad

HALAKHAH

בַּשַּׁחֲרִית וּבַמּוּסָף נִכְנָסִין לְבֵית הַכְּנֶסֶת In the morning service and in the musaf service they would enter the synagogue. "The Torah portion that was read from a scroll in the morning service conducted by the ma'amad assembly was read once again from a scroll in the musaf service, but in the afternoon service it was read by heart." (Rambam, Sefer Avodah, Hilkhot Klei HaMikdash 6:7.)

[1] הַלָּלוּ דִּבְרֵי תוֹרָה, [2] וְהַלָּלוּ דִּבְרֵי סוֹפְרִים.
[3] ״זְמַן עֲצֵי כֹהֲנִים וְהָעָם, כו׳״.
[4] תָּנוּ רַבָּנַן: ״לָמָּה הוּצְרְכוּ לוֹמַר זְמַן עֲצֵי כֹהֲנִים וְהָעָם?
[5] אָמְרוּ: כְּשֶׁעָלוּ בְּנֵי הַגּוֹלָה,
[6] לֹא מָצְאוּ עֵצִים בַּלִּשְׁכָּה,
[7] וְעָמְדוּ אֵלּוּ וְהִתְנַדְּבוּ מִשֶּׁלָּהֶם.
[8] וְכָךְ הִתְנוּ נְבִיאִים שֶׁבֵּינֵיהֶן שֶׁאֲפִילּוּ לִשְׁכָּה מְלֵאָה עֵצִים,
[9] יִהְיוּ אֵלּוּ מִתְנַדְּבִין מִשֶּׁלָּהֶן,

LITERAL TRANSLATION

[1] These are words of the Torah, [2] and these are words of the Rabbis.

[3] "The times for the wood of the priests and the people, etc." [4] Our Rabbis taught: "Why was it necessary to state the time for the wood of the priests and the people? [5] They said: When the people of the exile went up, [6] they did not find wood in the chamber, [7] and [so] these [families] arose and donated of their own. [8] And thus the Prophets among them stipulated that even if the chamber were full of wood, [9] these [families] would donate of their own,

RASHI

הללו דברי תורה – מנחה, כדאמרינן בברכות (כו,ב): יצחק אבינו תיקן תפלת מנחה, שנאמר "ויצא יצחק לשוח בשדה לפנות ערב" ודנעילה מדברי סופרים – וצריכין חיזוק לא גרסינן הכא. **עמדו אלו** – זמן דקתני במתניתין – אהכי הוצרכו למנות, משום ההיא תקנה דעבוד להו הנך נביאים כי היכי דלא לידחינהו מאתרייהו.

TRANSLATION AND COMMENTARY

הַלָּלוּ דִּבְרֵי תוֹרָה [1] The Gemara explains: The institution of the afternoon service **is hinted at in the Torah,** for the verse says (Genesis 24:63): "And Isaac went out to meditate in the field at the evening time," which the Rabbis understand as an allusion to Isaac's enactment of the afternoon service. [2] But the neilah service **is a Rabbinic enactment** not based on any Biblical precedent. Thus the celebration associated with the wood-offering, which is also only of Rabbinic origin, takes precedence over the *ma'amad* of the neilah service, but does not take precedence over the *ma'amad* of the afternoon service.

זְמַן עֲצֵי כֹהֲנִים [3] Our Mishnah continues: **"The times for the wood offerings of the priests and the** rest of **people** were nine," and it then gives a list of nine dates. [4] **Our Rabbis taught** a Baraita which explains the origins of these wood-offerings: **"Why was it necessary to list the times for the wood-offerings of the priests and the** rest of the **people?** [5] The Sages **said: When the people** who had been dispersed in the **exile went up** from Babylonia to Jerusalem at the beginning of the Second Temple period, [6] **they did not find** enough **wood in the** Temple **chamber** to burn the sacrifices on the altar. [7] **And so** the members of **certain families arose and donated their own** wood to the Temple, so that the sacrificial service could continue without interruption. To commemorate their generosity, [8] **the Prophets among them stipulated that, even if the** Temple **chamber were full of wood,** [9] the descendants of **these families would donate** wood **of their own** to the Temple on specified days of the year,

NOTES

of the neilah service, because there is no reference, however slight, to that service in the Bible

Tosafot understands the Gemara's question as follows: According to Ben Azzai, what is the difference between the additional sacrifice and the wood-offering, that the former takes precedence over the *ma'amad* of the afternoon service, but the latter does not? The Gemara answers that the additional sacrifice is a Torah obligation, and this is why it takes precedence over the *ma'amad* of the afternoon service, to which there is no more than an allusion in the Torah. But the wood-offering is not a Torah obligation, and this is why it takes precedence only over the *ma'amad* of the neilah service, which is also only of Rabbinic origin.

According to *Rambam* (*Commentary to the Mishnah*), the Gemara is asking what the difference is between the days on which Hallel is recited but there is no additional sacrifice, and the days on which Hallel is recited and there is also an additional sacrifice — so that on the former there is no *ma'amad* even in the morning service, whereas on the latter the *ma'amad* is excluded only from the musaf service and the afternoon or neilah service. The Gemara answers that the days on which Hallel is recited but there is no additional sacrifice, such as Hanukkah, are regarded as Festivals only by Rabbinic enactment, and are thus in need of reinforcement. Therefore on Hanukkah the *ma'amad* is excluded from the morning service. But the days on which there is an additional sacrifice are regarded as Festivals by Torah law, and so no reinforcement is required. Therefore on these days the *ma'amad* is excluded only from the musaf service and from one of the other services conducted during the day. *Rambam* apparently had the following reading, which *Rashi* rejected: "These are words of the Torah, and these are words of the Rabbis. Words of the Rabbis need reinforcement, but words of the Torah do not need reinforcement."

Rabbenu Elyakim had the same reading, but he understood the Gemara's question differently: What is the difference between the wood-offering and the *ma'amad* assembly, that the former takes precedence over the latter and not vice versa? The Gemara answers that the *ma'amad* assemblies are a matter of Torah law and therefore do not require reinforcement, but the wood-offerings are Rabbinic enactments and therefore do require reinforcement.

Rabbenu Gershom also had the same reading, but he understood the Gemara's question as follows: What is the difference between the additional sacrifice and the wood-offering, that the former takes precedence only over the *ma'amad* of the afternoon service, whereas the latter also takes precedence over the *ma'amad* of the neilah service? The Gemara answers that the additional sacrifice is a matter of Torah law, and therefore does not require reinforcement, but the wood-offering is only a Rabbinic enactment and therefore does require reinforcement.

לָמָּה הוּצְרְכוּ לוֹמַר זְמַן עֲצֵי כֹהֲנִים וְהָעָם **Why was it necessary**

BACKGROUND

מַלְכוּת הָרְשָׁעָה The wicked kingdom. Although the term, "the wicked kingdom," usually refers to Rome, it seems probable that the story related here took place during the Hellenistic period and refers to the persecutions of the Jews before the Hasmonean uprising. This is also the formula that appears in *Megillat Ta'anit*.

LANGUAGE

פְּרוֹזְדָאוֹת Guards. This word is probably derived from the Latin *praesidia*, meaning "watches."

LITERAL TRANSLATION

[1]as it is said: 'And we cast the lots among the priests, the Levites, and the people, for the wood-offering, to bring it into the house of our God, according to our fathers' house, at appointed times, year by year, to burn upon the altar of the Lord our God, as it is written in the Torah.'" [2]"And with them the priests and Levites and anyone who, etc." [3]Our Rabbis taught: "Who were the descendants of the pestle deceivers and the descendants of the dried-fig packers? [4]They said: Once the wicked kingdom decreed persecution on Israel that they should not bring wood for the pile [on the altar] and that they should not bring first-fruits to Jerusalem, [5]and they placed guards on the roads in the same way as Jeroboam the son of Nebat placed [them] so that Israel should not go up on pilgrimage. [6]What did

[1]שֶׁנֶּאֱמַר: ׳וְהַגּוֹרָלוֹת הִפַּלְנוּ עַל קָרְבַּן הָעֵצִים הַכֹּהֲנִים, הַלְוִיִּם, וְהָעָם, לְהָבִיא לְבֵית אֱלֹהֵינוּ, לְבֵית אֲבוֹתֵינוּ, לְעִתִּים מְזֻמָּנִים שָׁנָה בְשָׁנָה, לְבַעֵר עַל מִזְבַּח ה׳ אֱלֹהֵינוּ, כַּכָּתוּב בַּתּוֹרָה׳״. [2]״וְעִמָּהֶם כֹּהֲנִים וּלְוִיִּם וְכָל מִי, כו׳״. [3]תָּנוּ רַבָּנַן: ״מָה הָיוּ בְּנֵי גּוֹנְבֵי עֱלִי וּבְנֵי קוֹצְעֵי קְצִיעוֹת? [4]אָמְרוּ: פַּעַם אַחַת גָּזְרָה מַלְכוּת הָרְשָׁעָה שְׁמָד עַל יִשְׂרָאֵל שֶׁלֹּא יָבִיאוּ עֵצִים לַמַּעֲרָכָה וְשֶׁלֹּא יָבִיאוּ בִּכּוּרִים לִירוּשָׁלַיִם, [5]וְהוֹשִׁיבוּ פְּרוֹזְדָאוֹת עַל הַדְּרָכִים כְּדֶרֶךְ שֶׁהוֹשִׁיב יָרָבְעָם בֶּן נְבָט שֶׁלֹּא יַעֲלוּ יִשְׂרָאֵל לָרֶגֶל. [6]מֶה עָשׂוּ

RASHI

פרוזדאות — שומרים.

TRANSLATION AND COMMENTARY

[1]**as the verse says** [Nehemiah 10:35]: **'And we cast lots among the priests, the Levites, and the people, for the wood-offering, to bring it into the house of our God, according to our fathers' house, at appointed times year by year, to burn upon the altar of the Lord our God, as it is written in the Torah.'"** Even though in later years these individual donations were no longer necessary, the descendants of the families whose generosity was so vital in the early days of the Second Temple continued to bring wood-offerings on the nine days mentioned in our Mishnah.

וְעִמָּהֶם כֹּהֲנִים וּלְוִיִּם [2]Among the dates on which the wood-offering was brought is the fifteenth of Av, about which the Mishnah stated: "On the fifteenth of Av, the descendants of Zattu of the tribe of Judah brought the wood-offering, **and joining them** were **the priests and the Levites and all** the Israelites **who** were uncertain of their tribe, and the descendants of those who deceived the authorities with a pestle, and the descendants of those who packed dried figs into cakes." In order to clarify these unusual expressions, [3]a Baraita is cited in which **our Rabbis taught: "Who were the descendants of those who deceived** the authorities **with a pestle and the descendants of those who packed dried figs** into cakes? [4]The Sages **said:** It **once** happened that **the wicked kingdom** of Greece **issued a decree of religious persecution against** the people of **Israel, forbidding them to bring wood for the pile on** the altar. Furthermore, the Greek authorities decreed that the Jews **must not bring** their first-fruits **to** Jerusalem. In Temple times, the first-fruits of the new harvest were brought to Jerusalem in a basket, placed before the altar in the Temple, and then given to the priests after a prayer of gratitude had been recited. The first-fruits were brought to Jerusalem in a public procession, which is vividly described in the Mishnah [*Bikkurim* 3:2-9]. Not only did the Greeks prohibit bringing first-fruits to Jerusalem, [5]but **they** also **placed guards on the road** in order to enforce their decree, **just as Jeroboam the son of Nebat,** the first King of Israel, **had placed** guards on the roads **so that** the people of **Israel should not go up** to Jerusalem **for the Pilgrim Festivals** of Pesaḥ, Shavuot, and Sukkot [see I Kings 12:28]. [6]**What did the** families

NOTES

מָה הָיוּ בְּנֵי גּוֹנְבֵי עֱלִי Who were the descendants of the pestle deceivers? The Baraita's question is based on the fact that the wood-offerings were enacted to commemorate the generosity of those families who donated wood for the altar when the Second Temple was first built, and the pestle deceivers did not contribute wood in those early years. The Baraita explains that the pestle deceivers were given their own day on which to bring wood-offerings because of the special efforts they made to ensure that the first-fruits would reach Jerusalem and that the sacrificial service would continue without interruption (*Rabbenu Elyakim*).

to state the time for the wood of the priests and the people? *Rabbenu Ḥananel* and others have the reading: "Why was it necessary for the times of the wood of the priests and the people to be counted?" According to this reading the Baraita is asking: Why did the Mishnah need to mention that there are nine dates on which the wood-offering is brought? Let it just list the dates, and we can count them up on our own! The Baraita answers that the Mishnah itself enumerates the dates in order to emphasize their importance, for those dates were assigned to the descendants of the families that donated wood for the altar in the early days of the Second Temple.

כְּשֵׁרִין וְיִרְאֵי חֵטְא שֶׁבְּאוֹתוֹ הַדּוֹר? [1]הֵבִיאוּ סַלֵּי בִכּוּרִים וְחִיפּוּם בִּקְצִיעוֹת, [2]וּנְטָלוּם וָעֱלִי עַל כִּתְפֵיהֶן. [3]וְכֵיוָן שֶׁהִגִּיעוּ אֵצֶל פְּרוֹזְדָאוֹת, אָמְרוּ לָהֶם: [4]׳לְהֵיכָן אַתֶּם הוֹלְכִין?׳ [5]אוֹמְרִין לָהֶם: ׳לַעֲשׂוֹת שְׁנֵי עִגּוּלֵי דְבֵילָה בַּמַּכְתֶּשֶׁת שֶׁלְּפָנֵינוּ וּבָעֱלִי שֶׁעַל כְּתֵפֵינוּ׳. [6]כֵּיוָן שֶׁעָבְרוּ מֵהֶן, עִיטְּרוּם בְּסַלִּים וֶהֱבִיאוּם לִירוּשָׁלַיִם״. [7]תָּנָא: ״הֵן הֵן בְּנֵי סַלְמַאי הַנְּתוֹפָתִי״. [8]תָּנוּ רַבָּנַן: ״מַה הֵן בְּנֵי סַלְמַאי הַנְּתוֹפָתִי? [9]אָמְרוּ: פַּעַם אַחַת גָּזְרָה מַלְכוּת הָרְשָׁעָה שְׁמָד עַל יִשְׂרָאֵל שֶׁלֹּא יָבִיאוּ עֵצִים לַמַּעֲרָכָה, [10]וְהוֹשִׁיבוּ פְּרוֹזְדָאוֹת עַל הַדְּרָכִים כְּדֶרֶךְ שֶׁהוֹשִׁיב יָרָבְעָם

LITERAL TRANSLATION

the righteous and the sin-fearing of that generation do? [1]They brought baskets of first-fruits and covered them with dried figs, [2]and they took them and a pestle on their shoulders. [3]And when they reached the guards, they said to them: [4]'Where are you going?' [5]They would say to them: 'To make two round cakes of pressed figs with the mortar that is before us and with the pestle that is on our shoulders.' [6]Once they had passed them, they decorated them in the baskets and brought them to Jerusalem."

[7][A Tanna] taught: "A similar thing [was done by] the descendants of Salmai of Netofah." [8]Our Rabbis taught: "Who are the descendants of Salmai of Netofah? [9]They said: Once the wicked kingdom decreed persecution on Israel that they should not bring wood for the pile [on the altar], [10]and they placed guards on the roads in the same way as Jeroboam

TRANSLATION AND COMMENTARY

of **righteous and sin-fearing people of that generation do** to circumvent the decree? [1]**They brought baskets of first-fruits and covered them with dried figs** which were ready to be pressed into cakes (and were ineligible to be brought as first-fruits). [2]**They** then **took** the baskets **and a pestle** and carried them **on their shoulders** on their journey in the direction of Jerusalem. [3]**When they reached the guards** blocking the road to Jerusalem, the guards **said to them:** [4]**'Where are you going?'** [5]**They** explained **to** the guards: 'We are planning **to make two** large, **round cakes of pressed figs with the mortar that is** located down the road in the town **before us, using the pestle that** we are carrying **on our shoulders.'** [6]**As soon as they had** safely **passed** the roadblock, **they** removed the dried figs, **decorated** the first-fruits **in the baskets** as was required, **and brought them to Jerusalem."** From that time these families were referred to as "those who deceived the authorities with a pestle and those who packed dried figs into cakes."

תָּנָא [7]**A Tanna taught: "A similar thing was done by the descendants of Salmai of Netofah."** [8]The Gemara explains this name by citing a Baraita in which **our Rabbis taught: "Who were the descendants of Salmai of Netofah?** [9]The Sages **said:** It once happened that **the wicked kingdom** of Greece **issued a decree of religious persecution against** the people of **Israel, forbidding them to bring wood** to the Temple **for the pile on the altar.** [10]In addition, the Greek

RASHI

בכורים — אדם נכנס לתוך שדהו ורואה אשכול שביכר, תאנה שביכרה קושר עליה גמי ועושה אותה בכורים. **בקציעות** — תאנים יבשים, כותשין אותן ועושין מהן עגולין. **הכי גרסינן: והעלי על כתפיהן** — (בוכיא) [בוכנא]. **במכתשת שלפנינו** — שהוא במקום אחר לפנינו בסמוך. וזהו ״גונבי עלי״ — על שם שמתגנבין מן הפרוזדאות על עסקי עלי. **הן הן בני סלמאי הנתופתי** — כעין מעשה זה עשו.

NOTES

הֵן הֵן בְּנֵי סַלְמַאי הַנְּתוֹפָתִי A similar thing was done by the descendants of Salmai of Netofah. *Rabbi Ovadyah of Bertinoro* understands this expression as meaning that those very families who are referred to in the Mishnah as "the descendants of those who deceived the authorities with a pestle and those who pressed dried figs into cakes" were also known as the descendants of Salmai of Netofah because of another courageous act they performed. From *Rashi* and others (followed by our translation and commentary) it would seem that the expression refers to other people who were the heroes of the second story, and that the Baraita wishes merely to compare the efforts of the two groups of people to circumvent the decrees enacted to interfere with the Temple service.

הַנְּתוֹפָתִי Of Netofah. The story told by the Baraita does not account for the name הַנְּתוֹפָתִי as it appears in the standard Talmud texts. The Jerusalem Talmud, as well as certain manuscripts of the Babylonian Talmud and the Tosefta, has the reading הַנְּתוֹצָתִי, which can be understood as referring to the dismantling (נתץ = "to tear down") of the ladders, the wood of which was then brought to the altar. But the most plausible reading is הַנְּטוֹפָתִי, the whole Baraita then being understood as a homiletical interpretation of the verse (I Chronicles 2:54): "The sons of Salma: Beth-Lehem, and the Netophathites [בְּנֵי שַׂלְמָא בֵּית לֶחֶם וּנְטוֹפָתִי]." Indeed, the Targum to that verse interprets the names by citing the two artifices that were employed to circumvent the decrees against bringing first-fruits and wood to the Temple. There the name Netofah is expounded to mean that the acts performed by those people were as good as balm (נְטוֹפָה).

BACKGROUND

עִגּוּלֵי דְבֵילָה Round cakes of pressed figs. Figs (קְצִיעוֹת) were dried in the sun, and then the dried figs (דְּבֵילָה) were crushed together in round vessels, forming the large and heavy cakes of dried figs known as עִגּוּלֵי דְבֵילָה.

בֶּן נְבָט עַל הַדְּרָכִים שֶׁלֹּא יַעֲלוּ יִשְׂרָאֵל לָרֶגֶל. [1]מֶה עָשׂוּ יִרְאֵי חֵטְא שֶׁבְּאוֹתוֹ הַדּוֹר? [2]הֵבִיאוּ גְּזִירֵיהֶן וְעָשׂוּ סוּלָּמוֹת, וְהִנִּיחוּ עַל כִּתְפֵיהֶם וְהָלְכוּ לָהֶם. [3]כֵּיוָן שֶׁהִגִּיעוּ אֶצְלָן, אָמְרוּ לָהֶם: [4]'לְהֵיכָן אַתֶּם הוֹלְכִין?' [5]אָמְרוּ לָהֶם: 'לְהָבִיא גּוֹזָלוֹת מִשּׁוֹבָךְ שֶׁלְּפָנֵינוּ, וּבַסּוּלָּמוֹת שֶׁעַל כְּתֵפֵינוּ'. [6]כֵּיוָן שֶׁעָבְרוּ מֵהֶן, פֵּירְקוּם וֶהֱבִיאוּם, וְהֶעֱלוּם לִירוּשָׁלַיִם. [7]וַעֲלֵיהֶם וְעַל כַּיּוֹצֵא בָּהֶם הוּא אוֹמֵר: [8]'זֵכֶר צַדִּיק לִבְרָכָה', [9]וְעַל יָרָבְעָם בֶּן נְבָט וַחֲבֵרָיו נֶאֱמַר: 'וְשֵׁם רְשָׁעִים יִרְקָב'".

[10]"בְּעֶשְׂרִים בּוֹ, בְּנֵי פַּחַת מוֹאָב בֶּן יְהוּדָה". [11]תָּנָא: "בְּנֵי פַּחַת מוֹאָב בֶּן יְהוּדָה הֵן הֵן בְּנֵי דָוִד בֶּן יְהוּדָה. [12]דִּבְרֵי רַבִּי מֵאִיר. [13]רַבִּי יוֹסֵי אוֹמֵר: הֵן הֵן בְּנֵי יוֹאָב בֶּן צְרוּיָה".

[14]"בְּעֶשְׂרִים בֶּאֱלוּל, בְּנֵי עָדִין בֶּן יְהוּדָה, וכו'". [15]תָּנוּ רַבָּנַן: "בְּנֵי

LITERAL TRANSLATION

the son of Nebat placed [them] so that Israel should not go up on pilgrimage. [1]What did the sin-fearing of that generation do? [2]They brought their pieces [of wood] and made ladders, and they placed [them] on their shoulders and went off. [3]When they reached them, they said to them: [4]'Where are you going?' [5]They said to them: 'To bring doves from the dovecote that is before us, and with the ladders that are on our shoulders.' [6]Once they had passed them, they dismantled them and brought them, and they took them up to Jerusalem. [7]And about them and about those like them it says: [8]'The memory of the righteous is for a blessing.' [9]And about Jeroboam the son of Nebat and his fellows it is said: 'But the name of the wicked shall rot.'"

[10]"On the twentieth of [Av], the descendants of Pahat Moav of the tribe of Judah." [11][A Tanna] taught: "The descendants of Pahat Moav of the tribe of Judah are the descendants of David of the tribe of Judah. [12][These are] the words of Rabbi Meir. [13]Rabbi Yose says: They are the descendants of Joab the son of Zeruiah."

[14]"On the twentieth of Elul, the descendants of Adin of the tribe of Judah, etc." [15]Our Rabbis taught: "The descendants

TRANSLATION AND COMMENTARY

authorities **placed guards on the roads** in order to enforce their decree, **just as Jeroboam the son of Nebat had placed** guards on the roads **so that** the people of **Israel should not go up** to Jerusalem **on the Pilgrim Festivals** of Pesah, Shavuot, and Sukkot. [1]**What did the** the families of **sin-fearing people of that generation do?** [2]**They brought their pieces of wood and made ladders** out of them, **and they placed** those ladders **on their shoulders and went off** in the direction of Jerusalem. [3]**When they reached** the guards blocking the road to Jerusalem, they were stopped and the guards **said to them:** [4]**'Where are you going?'** [5]**They explained to** the guards: 'We are intending **to take down the doves from the dovecotes that are** located down the road in the town **before us, and** for that purpose we have brought **these ladders** that we **are** carrying **on our shoulders.'** [6]**As soon as they had** safely **passed** the roadblock, **they dismantled** the ladders, **took** the pieces of wood, **and brought them up to** the Temple in **Jerusalem.** From that time the members of these families were referred to as 'the descendants of Salmai [סַלְמַאי] of Netofah,' on account of the artifice involving the ladders [סוּלָּם in Hebrew] which they used to outwit the Greek authorities. [7]**And** it is **about these** families, whose courageous efforts ensured that the sacrificial services would continue without interruption, **and others like them,** that **the verse says** [Proverbs 10:7]: [8]**'The memory of the righteous is for a blessing.'** [9]**And** it is **about** the wicked King of Israel, **Jeroboam the son of Nebat, and those like him,** that the same **verse** continues: **'But the name of the wicked shall rot.'"**

בְּעֶשְׂרִים בּוֹ [10]We learned in the Mishnah: **"On the twentieth of Av,** the wood-offering was brought by **the descendants of Pahat Moab of the tribe of Judah."** [11]**A Tanna taught** a Baraita which stated: **"The descendants of Pahat Moab of the tribe of Judah are the descendants of** King **David,** who was **of the tribe of Judah.** The descendants of David were known as the descendants of Pahat Moab on account of Ruth the Moabitess, from whom the Davidic family is descended. [12]**This is the opinion of Rabbi Meir.** [13]**Rabbi Yose said:** The descendants of Pahat Moab **are the descendants of Joab the son of Zeruiah,** King David's commander-in-chief. Joab's descendants were so named because Joab was also descended from Ruth the Moabitess, for Zeruiah, the mother of Joab, was a sister of David [I Chronicles 2:16]."

בְּעֶשְׂרִים בֶּאֱלוּל [14]The Mishnah continues: **"On the twentieth of Elul,** the wood-offering was brought by **the descendants of Adin of the tribe of Judah."** [15]**Our Rabbis taught** the following Baraita: **"The descendants**

RASHI

הן הן בני דוד בן יהודה — דוד מלך ישראל. ואהכי קרו ליה "פחת מואב" — שבא מרות המואביה. **יואב בן צרויה** — שבא מרות המואביה. כי צרויה אם יואב אחות דוד היתה, שנאמר (דברי הימים א ב). "ואחיותיהם צרויה ואביגיל".

עָדִין בֶּן יְהוּדָה הֵן הֵן בְּנֵי דָוִד בֶּן יְהוּדָה. [1]דִּבְרֵי רַבִּי יְהוּדָה. [2]רַבִּי יוֹסֵי אוֹמֵר: הֵן הֵן בְּנֵי יוֹאָב בֶּן צְרוּיָה״.

[3]״בְּאֶחָד בְּטֵבֵת, שָׁבוּ בְּנֵי פַּרְעוֹשׁ שְׁנִיָּה, כו׳״. [4]מַנִּי מַתְנִיתִין? [5]לָא רַבִּי מֵאִיר, [6]וְלָא רַבִּי יְהוּדָה, [7]וְלָא רַבִּי יוֹסֵי. [8]אִי רַבִּי מֵאִיר, לִיתְנֵי שָׁבוּ בְּנֵי דָוִד בֶּן יְהוּדָה שְׁנִיָּה. [9]אִי רַבִּי יְהוּדָה, לִיתְנֵי שָׁבוּ בְּנֵי דָוִד בֶּן יְהוּדָה שְׁנִיָּה. [10]אִי רַבִּי יוֹסֵי, לִיתְנֵי שָׁבוּ בְּנֵי יוֹאָב בֶּן צְרוּיָה שְׁנִיָּה!

[11]לְעוֹלָם רַבִּי יוֹסֵי, [12]וּתְרֵי תַּנָּאֵי אַלִּיבָּא דְּרַבִּי יוֹסֵי.

LITERAL TRANSLATION

of Adin of the tribe of Judah are the descendants of David of the tribe of Judah. [1][These are] the words of Rabbi Yehudah. [2]Rabbi Yose says: They are the descendants of Joab the son of Zeruiah."

[3]"On the first of Tevet, the descendants of Parosh returned a second time, etc." [4][According to] whose [view] is our Mishnah? [5]It is not Rabbi Meir, [6]and it is not Rabbi Yehudah, [7]and it is not Rabbi Yose. [8]If Rabbi Meir, let it teach [that] the descendants of David of the tribe of Judah returned a second time. [9]If Rabbi Yehudah, let it teach [that] the descendants of David of the tribe of Judah returned a second time. [10]If Rabbi Yose, let it teach [that] the descendants of Joab the son of Zeruiah returned a second time!

[11]In fact it is Rabbi Yose, [12]and there are two Tannaim according to Rabbi Yose.

TRANSLATION AND COMMENTARY

of Adin of the tribe of Judah are the descendants of King **David of the tribe of Judah.** The descendants of the Davidic family were known as the descendants of Adin, because the list of David's warriors [II Samuel 23:8] is headed by Adino the Eznite, who is identified elsewhere with David himself. [1]**This is the opinion of Rabbi Yehudah.** [2]**Rabbi Yose said:** The descendants of Adin **are the descendants of Joab the son of Zeruiah,** King David's commander-in-chief, because Adino the Eznite, chief among David's warriors, was Joab, and is not to be identified with David himself."

בְּאֶחָד בְּטֵבֵת [3]We learned in the Mishnah: **"On the first of Tevet, the descendants of Parosh** of the tribe of Judah **returned a second time** to bring the wood-offering, having already brought such an offering on the fifth of Av." [4]The Gemara asks: **According to whose view was our Mishnah** taught? [5]**It cannot have been** taught in accordance with the viewpoint of **Rabbi Meir,** who identified the descendants of Pahat Moab with the descendants of David, [6]**nor** in accordance with the viewpoint of **Rabbi Yehudah,** who identified the descendants of Adin with the descendants of David, [7]**nor** in accordance with the viewpoint of **Rabbi Yose,** who identified both the descendants of Pahat Moab and the descendants of Adin with the descendants of Joab. [8]For **if** the Mishnah had been in accordance with the viewpoint of **Rabbi Meir, it should have taught that the descendants of** King **David of the tribe of Judah returned a second time.** Just as the Mishnah said that the descendants of Parosh returned a second time, it should have stated that King David's descendants returned a second time on the twentieth of Av. A similar argument can be made with respect to Rabbi Judah, [9]for **if** the Mishnah had been taught in accordance with the viewpoint of **Rabbi Yehudah, it should have taught that the descendants of** King **David of the tribe of Judah returned a second time.** Since the Mishnah has already taught that on the twentieth of Tammuz the wood-offering was brought by the descendants of King David, then if the descendants of Adin were in fact the descendants of King David, the Mishnah should have stated that King David's descendants returned a second time on the twentieth of Elul. The same can be said about Rabbi Yose, [10]for **if** the Mishnah had been taught in accordance with the viewpoint of Rabbi Yose, **it should have taught that the descendants of Joab the son of Zeruiah returned a second time.** If both the descendants of Pahat Moab and the descendants of Adin were the descendants of Joab the son of Zeruiah, the Mishnah should have stated that Joab's descendants returned a second time on the twentieth of Elul, having already brought a wood-offering on the twentieth of Av!

לְעוֹלָם רַבִּי יוֹסֵי [11]The Gemara answers: **In fact** the Mishnah was taught in accordance with the viewpoint of **Rabbi Yose,** [12]**and there are two Tannaim** who disagree **about** the viewpoint of **Rabbi Yose.** According to

RASHI

בני עדין הן הן בני דוד — להכי קרי ליה בספר שמואל (ב כג): ״עדינו העצני״, שבשעה שעוסק בתורה — מעדן עצמו כתולעת, וכשיוצא למלחמה — מתקשה כעץ. **הן הן בני יואב בן צרויה** — פלוגתא היא (במסכת חגיגה), חד אמר: עדינו העצני זה דוד, וחד אמר: זה יואב. **ליתני שבו בני דוד שניה** — דהא קאמר רבי מאיר פחת מואב היינו דוד. **ולרבי יהודה** — בני עדין היינו דוד. ובמתניתין קתני בהדיא ״בני דוד״ והדר קתני ״בני פחת מואב״, דלרבי מאיר ולרבי יהודה בני עדין — היינו דוד, ״שבו שניה״ מיבעי ליה. **ולרבי יוסי** — דאמר פחת מואב ועדין היינו יואב, ״שבו שניה״ מיבעי ליה. **לעולם רבי יוסי ותרי תנאי אליבא דרבי יוסי** —

NOTES

לְעוֹלָם רַבִּי יוֹסֵי In fact it is Rabbi Yose. *Tosafot* asks: Why does the Gemara answer that the Mishnah was taught in accordance with the viewpoint of Rabbi Yose, and that two Tannaim reported different versions of this viewpoint? The

TRANSLATION AND COMMENTARY

one Tanna, Rabbi Yose maintains that the descendants of Pahat Moab were the descendants of Joab. But that Tanna did not say that Rabbi Yose maintains that the descendants of Adin were the descendants of Joab. Thus he did not say that the descendants of Joab the son of Zeruiah returned a second time. According to the second Tanna, Rabbi Yose maintains that the descendants of Adin were the descendants of Joab. But that Tanna did not say that Rabbi Yose maintains that the descendants of Pahat Moab were the descendants of Joab. Thus he did not say that the descendants of Joab the son of Zeruiah returned a second time.

בְּאֶחָד בְּטֵבֶת ¹We learned in the Mishnah: **"On the first of Tevet,** which is Hanukkah, Rosh Hodesh, and the day on which a wood offering was brought by the descendants of Parosh, **there was no** *ma'amad* at all." ²**Mar Keshisha the son of Rav Hisda said to Rav Ashi:** [28B] We learned in the Mishnah that on a day when Hallel was recited but no additional sacrifice was offered, there was no *ma'amad* in the morning service. And on a day when an additional sacrifice was offered, there was no *ma'amad* in the neilah service. We may infer that, on days when an additional sacrifice was offered, there was a *ma'amad* in the musaf service. ³**In what** way **is Hallel different that it takes precedence over its own** *ma'amad,* the *ma'amad* connected to the service during which Hallel itself is recited, ⁴**whereas the additional sacrifice does not take precedence over its own** *ma'amad,* the *ma'amad* conducted in the musaf service?

אָמַר לֵיה רַב אַשִׁי ⁵**Rav Ashi said to him: Since** the additional sacrifice **takes precedence over a** *ma'amad* **which is not its own,** the *ma'amad* conducted in the neilah service, ⁶**how much more so should it take precedence over its own** *ma'amad,* the *ma'amad* conducted in the musaf service! The Mishnah needed only to teach us that, on those days when an additional sacrifice was offered, there was no *ma'amad* in the neilah service, for it is obvious that on those same days there was no *ma'amad* in the musaf service.

LITERAL TRANSLATION

¹"On the first of Tevet there was no *ma'amad,* etc." ²Mar Keshisha the son of Rav Hisda said to Rav Ashi: [28B] ³In what is Hallel different that it takes precedence over its own [*ma'amad*], ⁴and in what is the additional sacrifice different that it does not take precedence over its own [*ma'amad*]? ⁵Rav Ashi said to him: Now that it takes precedence over [a *ma'amad*] which is not its own, ⁶how much more so [should it take precedence over] its own!

¹"בְּאֶחָד בְּטֵבֶת לֹא הָיָה בּוֹ מַעֲמָד, כו׳". ²אָמַר לֵיה מָר קָשִׁישָׁא בְּרֵיה דְּרַב חִסְדָּא לְרַב אַשִׁי: [28B] ³מַאי שְׁנָא הַלֵּל דְּדָחֵי דִּידֵיה, ⁴וּמַאי שְׁנָא מוּסָף דְּלָא דָּחֵי דִּידֵיה? ⁵אָמַר לֵיה רַב אַשִׁי: הַשְׁתָּא דְּלָאו דִּידֵיה דָּחֵי, ⁶דִּידֵיה לֹא כָּל שֶׁכֵּן!

RASHI

דְּמַאן דְּאָמַר בְּנֵי עָדִין בֶּן יְהוּדָה הַיְינוּ בְּנֵי יוֹאָב — לֹא סָבַר לֵיה דְּנֵי פַחַת מוֹאָב הַיְינוּ יוֹאָב, וְלָהֲכִי לֹא קָתָנֵי "שָׁבוּ בְּנֵי יוֹאָב שְׁנִיָּה". וְלֹא סְבִירָא לֵיה נָמֵי דְּהָן הֵן בְּנֵי דָוִד — דְּאִם כֵּן "שָׁבוּ בְּנֵי דָוִד שְׁנִיָּה" מִיבָּעֵי לֵיה לְמִיתָנֵי, אֶלָּא מִשְׁפָּחָה אַחֶרֶת הֵן. וּמַאן דְּאָמַר בְּנֵי פַחַת מוֹאָב הַיְינוּ בְּנֵי יוֹאָב — לֹא סְבִירָא לֵיה דְּנֵי עָדִין הַיְינוּ יוֹאָב, אֶלָּא מִשְׁפָּחָה אַחֶרֶת הֵן. מַאי שְׁנָא הַלֵּל דְּדָחֵי דִּידֵיה — מַעֲמָד דְּשַׁחֲרִית. וּמַאי שְׁנָא מוּסָף דְּלָא דָּחֵי דִּידֵיה — דְּקָתָנֵי: יֵשׁ שָׁם בּוֹ מוּסָף אֵין בּוֹ מִנְחָה, וְלֹא קָתָנֵי: אֵין בּוֹ מוּסָף, דְּלָא דְּמֵי דִידֵיה אֶלָּא דְּמִנְחָה.

NOTES

Gemara should have answered that the Mishnah was taught in accordance with the viewpoint of Rabbi Meir (for there is a general rule that an anonymous Mishnah follows the viewpoint of Rabbi Meir), and that two Tannaim reported different versions of his view. *Tosafot* answers that the Gemara prefers to explain our Mishnah in accordance with the viewpoint of Rabbi Yose, because, as is stated elsewhere (*Gittin* 67a), "Rabbi Yose, his depth is with him"; in other words, Rabbi Yose has good reason for what he says.

Maharsha explains that had the Gemara said that there are two versions of Rabbi Meir's viewpoint, the Baraita reflecting one of those viewpoints would have been in conflict with the Mishnah that reflects the other. The Gemara prefers to say that the Mishnah follows the viewpoint of Rabbi Yose, because in that way the two Baraitot reflecting the two versions of Rabbi Yose's viewpoint can be reconciled with the Mishnah.

מַאי שְׁנָא הַלֵּל דְּדָחֵי דִּידֵיה **In what is Hallel different that it takes precedence over its own.** A number of fundamental questions, regarding the cancellation of the *ma'amad* assemblies on days of special joy, arise in connection with this passage. First, there is the question of the reading of our Mishnah. According to the standard texts and most Rishonim, Rabbi Akiva first maintained that when there was an additional sacrifice, there was no *ma'amad* in the neilah service, and when there was a wood-offering, there was no *ma'amad* in the afternoon service. Later, Rabbi Akiva reversed his position in accordance with Ben Azzai's viewpoint. But according to the Geonim and some Rishonim, Rabbi Akiva's earlier and later positions were just the opposite. The Gemara here assumes that when there was a wood-offering, there was no *ma'amad* in the afternoon service, a position that can be reconciled with Rabbi Akiva's later position only according to the reading of the Geonim.

The Rishonim disagree on why Hallel, the additional sacrifice, and the wood-offering take precedence over the various *ma'amad* assemblies. According to *Rashi, Tosafot,* and others, the *ma'amad* assemblies were canceled because

אֲמַר לֵיהּ: הָכִי קָאָמִינָא לָךְ: [1]
לָא לִידְחֵי אֶלָּא דִּידֵיהּ! [2]
אֲמַר לֵיהּ: אִיכָּא רַבִּי יוֹסֵי דְּקָאֵי כְּוָותָךְ. [3]
דְּתַנְיָא: ״רַבִּי יוֹסֵי אוֹמֵר: [4]
כָּל יוֹם שֶׁיֵּשׁ בּוֹ מוּסָף, יֵשׁ בּוֹ מַעֲמָד״. [5]
מַעֲמָד דְּמַאי? [6]
אִילֵימָא מַעֲמָד דְּשַׁחֲרִית, הָא תַּנָּא קַמָּא נַמִי הָכִי קָאָמַר. [7]
אֶלָּא מַעֲמָד דְּמוּסָף. [8]
דִּידֵיהּ נַמִי לָא דָּחֵי? [9]
אֶלָּא דְּמִנְחָה. [10]
קָרְבַּן עֵצִים דָּחֵי! [11]
אֶלָּא לָאו דִּנְעִילָה. [12]
שְׁמַע מִינָּהּ: דִּידֵיהּ דָּחֵי; [13]
דְּלָאו דִּידֵיהּ לָא דָּחֵי. [14]
שְׁמַע מִינָּהּ. [15]

LITERAL TRANSLATION

[1] He said to him: This is what I say to you: [2] Let it not take precedence except over its own!

[3] He said to him: There is Rabbi Yose who agrees with you. [4] For it was taught: "Rabbi Yose says: [5] Any day on which there is an additional sacrifice, there is a *ma'amad*." [6] Which *ma'amad*? [7] If we say the *ma'amad* of the morning service, surely the first Tanna also said so. [8] Rather, [he must mean] the *ma'amad* of the musaf service. [9] Does it not take precedence even over its own [*ma'amad*]? [10] Rather, that of the afternoon service. [11] [But] the wood-offering takes precedence over it! [12] Rather, is it not that of the neilah service. [13] Infer from this: It takes precedence over its own [*ma'amad*]; [14] it does not take precedence over [a *ma'amad*] that is not its own. [15] Infer from this.

RASHI

הכי קאמינא — הכי קא בעינא למימר. אלא דידיה — דמוסף. הכי גרסינן: רבי יוסי אומר כל יום שיש בו מוסף יש בו מעמד — ותנא קמא פליג, דאמר: יום שיש בו מוסף אין בו נעילה, ואתא רבי יוסי למימר דיש בו מעמד, אף על פי שיש בו מוסף. אלא לאו דנעילה הוא — דאמר רבי יוסי דיש בו מעמד, ואין מוסף דוחה אותו.

TRANSLATION AND COMMENTARY

אֲמַר לֵיהּ [1] Mar Keshisha the son of Rav Ḥisda **said to** Rav Ashi: **This** is what **I meant to ask you:** Why is it that, on those days on which an additional sacrifice was brought, the *ma'amad* conducted in the neilah service was also suspended? [2] **Let** the additional sacrifice **take precedence only over its own** *ma'amad*, the *ma'amad* conducted in the musaf service!

אֲמַר לֵיהּ [3] Rav Ashi **said to him:** The Tanna **Rabbi Yose agrees with you,** [4] **for it was taught** in a Baraita: **"Rabbi Yose** disagrees with the Tanna of our Mishnah and **says:** [5] **Any day on which there was an additional sacrifice, there was a** ***ma'amad*****."** Let us clarify what Rabbi Yose means. [6] **Which** ***ma'amad*** was there on those days on which there was an additional sacrifice? [7] **If we say** that Rabbi Yose is referring to **the** ***ma'amad*** **of the morning service, surely the first Tanna also said** that there was a *ma'amad* in the morning service on days when an additional sacrifice was offered, because the additional sacrifice does not take precedence over the *ma'amad* in the morning service. [8] **Rather,** Rabbi Yose **must mean the** ***ma'amad*** **of the musaf service.** [9] But this, too, is difficult, for can Rabbi Yose maintain that the additional sacrifice **does not take precedence even over its own** ***ma'amad*****?** [10] **Rather,** Rabbi Yose **must mean** the *ma'amad* **of the afternoon service.** [11] **But** this, too, is difficult, for if **the wood-offering takes precedence over** the *ma'amad* of the afternoon service, then the additional sacrifice certainly takes precedence over it! [12] **Rather,** Rabbi Yose must mean that, on days when there was an additional sacrifice, there was a *ma'amad* **in the neilah service.** [13] Thus we can **infer from this** that, according to Rabbi Yose, the additional sacrifice **takes precedence over its own** *ma'amad*, the *ma'amad* of the musaf service, [14] but **it does not take precedence over a** ***ma'amad*** **that is not its own,** the *ma'amad* of the neilah service. [15] The Gemara summarizes its conclusion: We can indeed **infer from this** that Rabbi Yose maintains that the additional sacrifice takes precedence over its own *ma'amad*, but not over a *ma'amad* that is not its own.

NOTES

there was no time to conduct them on the days when Hallel was recited, or an additional sacrifice or wood-offering was brought. For example, on days when Hallel was recited, there was no time to conduct the *ma'amad* assembly in the morning service, and similarly with respect to the additional sacrifice and the wood-offering and the *ma'amad* assemblies which those sacrifices cancel. The Rishonim ask: Why should the additional sacrifice offered in Jerusalem cancel the *ma'amad* assemblies conducted throughout Eretz Israel? Moreover, why should the wood-offerings brought by specific families interfere with the assemblies conducted by the members of the *ma'amad*? *Ritva* and others argue that the additional sacrifice canceled the *ma'amad* assembly only for those members of the *ma'amad* who were present in the Temple for the sacrificial service. Similarly, *Ra'avad* maintains that the wood-offering canceled the *ma'amad* assembly only for members of the family who brought the offering. The Geonim offer an entirely different reason for the cancelation of the *ma'amad* assemblies: The *ma'amad* assemblies were canceled in order to grant distinction to those days on which Hallel was recited, or an additional sacrifice or wood-offering was brought. In honor of Hallel, the additional sacrifice, and the wood-offering, the *ma'amad* assemblies were canceled even outside Jerusalem. According to *Rid*, the *ma'amad* assemblies were canceled only outside Jerusalem, because only outside Jerusalem were such assemblies conducted.

The Rishonim also disagree about what precisely was canceled — the Torah reading, the special supplications, or the entire assembly.

TRANSLATION AND COMMENTARY

וְלִיתְנֵי נַמִי [1]The Mishnah stated that on the first of Tevet there was no *ma'amad* at all, because there was Hallel on account of Ḥanukkah, an additional sacrifice on account of **Rosh Ḥodesh**, and a wood-offering brought by the descendants of Parosh. In the light of this, the Gemara objects: **But** the Mishnah **should also have taught** that **on the first of Nisan there was no *ma'amad*** at all, [2]**because on** that day, too, **there was Hallel** on account of Rosh Ḥodesh, **an additional sacrifice** on account of Rosh Ḥodesh, **and a wood-offering** brought by the descendants of Arah!

אֲמַר רָבָא [3]**Rava said** in reply: The fact that the Mishnah does not state that there was no *ma'amad* at all on the first of Nisan **implies that the Hallel** that is recited **on Rosh Ḥodesh is not** an obligation **imposed by Torah law,** and therefore it does not take precedence over the *ma'amad* in the morning service. The recitation of Hallel on Rosh Ḥodesh is considered to be a custom. [4]This also follows from what **Rabbi Yoḥanan said in the name of Rabbi Shimon ben Yehotzadak: There are eighteen days during the year on which an individual recites the full Hallel** (Psalms 113-118), for on those days there is a personal obligation on every individual to recite the Hallel. [5]**They are as follows: The eight days of the Festival of Sukkot** (the first day of the Festival, the six intermediate days, and the festive day concluding the Festival), **the eight days of Ḥanukkah, the first festive day of Pesaḥ, and the festive day of Shavuot.** [6]This applies only in Eretz Israel; but **in the Diaspora,** where a second day of each of the festive days of the Festivals is observed, **there are twenty-one days** on which the Hallel is recited. [7]**And they are as follows: The nine days of the Festival of Sukkot** (the first two festive days of the festival, the five intermediate days, and the two final festive days), **the eight days of Ḥanukkah, the first two days of Pesaḥ, and the two festive days of Shavuot.** It follows from Rabbi Yoḥanan's statement that one does not recite Hallel on Rosh Ḥodesh.

[1]וְלִיתְנֵי נַמִי: בְּאֶחָד בְּנִיסָן לֹא הָיָה בּוֹ מַעֲמָד, [2]מִפְּנֵי שֶׁיֵּשׁ בּוֹ הַלֵּל וְקָרְבַּן מוּסָף וְקָרְבַּן עֵצִים! [3]אֲמַר רָבָא: זֹאת אוֹמֶרֶת הַלֵּילָא דִּבְרֵישׁ יַרְחָא לָאו דְּאוֹרַיְיתָא. [4]דְּאָמַר רַבִּי יוֹחָנָן מִשּׁוּם רַבִּי שִׁמְעוֹן בֶּן יְהוֹצָדָק: שְׁמוֹנָה עָשָׂר יוֹם בַּשָּׁנָה יָחִיד גּוֹמֵר בָּהֶן אֶת הַלֵּל, [5]וְאֵלּוּ הֵן: שְׁמוֹנַת יְמֵי הֶחָג, וּשְׁמוֹנַת יְמֵי חֲנוּכָּה, וְיוֹם טוֹב הָרִאשׁוֹן שֶׁל פֶּסַח, וְיוֹם טוֹב שֶׁל עֲצֶרֶת. [6]וּבַגּוֹלָה, עֶשְׂרִים וְאֶחָד יוֹם, [7]וְאֵלּוּ הֵן: תִּשְׁעַת יְמֵי הֶחָג, וּשְׁמוֹנַת יְמֵי חֲנוּכָּה, וּשְׁנֵי יָמִים הָרִאשׁוֹנִים שֶׁל פֶּסַח, וּשְׁנֵי יָמִים טוֹבִים שֶׁל עֲצֶרֶת.

LITERAL TRANSLATION

[1]But let it also teach: On the first of Nisan there was no *ma'amad*, [2]for on it there was Hallel and the additional sacrifice and the wood-offering!

[3]Rava said: This implies (lit., "says") [that] the Hallel of Rosh Ḥodesh is not instituted by Torah law. [4]For Rabbi Yoḥanan said in the name of Rabbi Shimon ben Yehotzadak: There are eighteen days in the year on which an individual completes the Hallel, [5]and these are they: The eight days of the Festival [of Sukkot], and the eight days of Ḥanukkah, and the first festive day of Pesaḥ, and the festive day of Shavuot. [6]And in the Diaspora, there are twenty-one days, [7]and these are they: The nine days of the Festival [of Sukkot], and the eight days of Ḥanukkah, and the first two days of Pesaḥ, and the two festive days of Shavuot.

RASHI

באחד בניסן – דאית ביה הלל דראש חדש. **קרבן עצים** – (קרבן מוסף) דבני ארח בן יהודה. **זאת אומרת** – מדלא קתני נמי: באחד בניסן – אלמא הלל דראש חדש לא דחי ליה למעמד, שמע מינה דלאו דאורייתא הוא, אלא מנהגא כדלקמן.

SAGES

רַבִּי שִׁמְעוֹן בֶּן יְהוֹצָדָק Rabbi Shimon ben Yehotzadak. A first generation Palestinian Amora. Rabbi Shimon ben Yehotzadak was a teacher of Rabbi Yoḥanan. Most of his teachings — some of which were given the status of Baraitot — are transmitted by Rabbi Yoḥanan. He was a priest and died in Lod (Lydda).

BACKGROUND

שְׁמוֹנָה עָשָׂר יוֹם בַּשָּׁנָה There are eighteen days in the year. This list of dates proves that Hallel is recited on festive and joyous days, and also when thanks are offered to God for His redemption. Hallel is not recited on Rosh HaShanah or on Yom Kippur, although these are festivals designated by the Torah, for they are days of judgment. Further, full Hallel is not recited on the intermediate days or on the final holiday of Pesaḥ, for these days are regarded only as the end of a seven-day holiday, and not as holy days on their own account. Hallel is also not recited on Purim, for one of two reasons — either because that miracle did not lead to the full liberation of the Jewish people but only to their temporary rescue, or because the miracle occurred outside Eretz Israel.

NOTES

הַלֵּילָא דִּבְרֵישׁ יַרְחָא לָאו דְּאוֹרַיְיתָא The Hallel of Rosh Ḥodesh is not instituted by Torah law. The Gemara does not wish to imply that the celebration of Hanukkah is an obligation imposed by Torah law. Rather, the Gemara must be understood as follows: The recitation of Hallel on Hanukkah is a Torah obligation, for there is an obligation to recite Hallel whenever the people of Israel are miraculously delivered from an impending calamity (see *Pesaḥim* 117a), and the miracle of Hanukkah surely warrants Hallel. But the recitation of Hallel on Rosh Ḥodesh is only a custom, for Rosh Ḥodesh is not regarded as a festival, nor does it commemorate a miracle performed for Israel (*Rabbenu Yehonatan*).

HALAKHAH

שְׁמוֹנָה עָשָׂר יוֹם בַּשָּׁנָה There are eighteen days in the year. "There are eighteen days during the year on which there is an obligation to recite the entire Hallel: the eight days of Sukkot, the eight days of Ḥanukkah, the first day of Pesaḥ, and the day of Shavuot. In the Diaspora, where a second day of each of the festive days of the Festivals is observed, Hallel is recited on twenty-one days during the year: the nine days of Sukkot, the eight days of Ḥanukkah, the first two days of Pesaḥ, and the two days of Shavuot." (*Rambam, Sefer Zemannim, Hilkhot Ḥanukkah* 3:6-7.)

הַלֵּילָא בְּרֵישׁ יַרְחָא The Hallel of Rosh Ḥodesh. "On Rosh Ḥodesh, Hallel is recited in an abridged version, whether it

LITERAL TRANSLATION

[1] Rav happened to come to Babylonia. [2] He saw that they recited Hallel on Rosh Ḥodesh. He thought to stop them. [3] When he saw that they were omitting (lit., "skipping") [parts], he said: [4] Infer from this: The custom of their fathers is in their hands.

[5] [A Tanna] taught: "An individual should not begin, [6] but if he began, he completes [it]."

[7] "Five things happened to our ancestors on the Seventeenth of Tammuz, etc." [8] "The tablets were broken." [9] From where [do we know this]?

[1] רַב אִיקְלַע לְבָבֶל, חָזֵינְהוּ דְּקָא קָרוּ הַלֵּילָא בְּרֵישׁ יַרְחָא. [2] סְבַר לְאַפְסוּקִינְהוּ. [3] כֵּיוָן דַחֲזָא דְּקָא מְדַלְּגֵי דַּלּוּגֵי, אֲמַר: [4] שְׁמַע מִינָּהּ: מִנְהַג אֲבוֹתֵיהֶם בִּידֵיהֶם.

[5] תָּנָא: "יָחִיד לֹא יַתְחִיל, [6] וְאִם הִתְחִיל, גּוֹמֵר".

[7] "חֲמִשָּׁה דְּבָרִים אֵירְעוּ אֶת אֲבוֹתֵינוּ בְּשִׁבְעָה עָשָׂר בְּתַמּוּז, וכו׳". [8] "נִשְׁתַּבְּרוּ הַלּוּחוֹת". [9] מְנָלַן?

TRANSLATION AND COMMENTARY

רַב אִיקְלַע לְבָבֶל [1] The Gemara now relates that **Rav** once **happened to come to Babylonia,** where **he saw that** people **were reciting Hallel on Rosh Ḥodesh.** [2] Unfamiliar with their practice, Rav **thought to stop them,** for Rosh Ḥodesh is not included among the days on which Hallel is recited. [3] **When** Rav **saw that** the people **were omitting parts** of Hallel, leaving out Psalms 115:1-11 and 116:1-11 and reciting only an abridged version, **he said:** [4] We can **infer from this** that the Babylonian Jews **have a custom** handed down to them **from their ancestors** to recite Hallel on Rosh Ḥodesh. By reciting the Hallel in an abridged version they demonstrate that they understand that the recitation of Hallel on Rosh Ḥodesh is only a custom.

תָּנָא [5] **A Tanna taught** a Baraita which stated: **"An individual should not begin** to recite Hallel on Rosh Ḥodesh, [6] **but if he has begun, he should complete it."**

חֲמִשָּׁה דְּבָרִים [7] We learned in our Mishnah: **"Five** disastrous **things happened to our ancestors on the Seventeenth of Tammuz,** and five disastrous things happened to them on the Ninth of Av." The Mishnah then begins to list the calamities that befell the Jewish people on these two days: [8] "On the Seventeenth of Tammuz, **the** two **Tablets** of the Covenant **were broken** by Moses after he saw that the people had made the golden calf." [9] The Gemara asks: **From where do we know** that the Tablets of the Covenant were shattered on the Seventeenth of Tammuz?

RASHI

מנהג אבותיהם בידיהן — אבל הלל דחנוכה, כגון באחד בטבת — ודאי דמי, דכיון דנביאים תיקנוהו שיהו אומרים אותו על כל פרק ופרק ועל כל צרה שלא תבא עליהן, כשנגאלין יהו אומרין אותו על גאולתן — כדאורייתא דמי. **יחיד** — כלומר, אפילו יחיד גומר בהן את ההלל. שכל אחד ואחד חייב לגמור בו את ההלל. במסכת ערכין מפורש מאי שנא דגומר כל ימי החג, ובפסח לא גומר אלא יום ראשון — משום דחג הסוכות חלוק בקרבנותיו, וכל אחד ואחד כחג בפני עצמו דמי. **ובגולה** — שעושין שני ימים טובים משום ספיקא. **דמדלגי דלוגי** — כגון אנן, דמדלגין "לא לנו ה׳ לא לנו" ונתחיל מן "ה׳ זכרנו יברך". **לא יתחיל** — אינו צריך להתחיל בראש חדש.

BACKGROUND

מִנְהַג אֲבוֹתֵיהֶם בִּידֵיהֶם The custom of their fathers is in their hands. This is why Hallel is read in abbreviated form (חֲצִי הַלֵּל) on the intermediate days and final holiday of Pesaḥ (which is two days in the Diaspora). In some places the abbreviated Hallel is recited with blessings, but in other places the blessings are not recited.

NOTES

רַב אִיקְלַע לְבָבֶל Rav happened to come to Babylonia. According to the plain sense of this story, Rav was unfamiliar with the custom of reciting Hallel on Rosh Ḥodesh, because that custom was practiced only in Babylonia, but not in Eretz Israel where Rav came from. Some suggest that it became customary in Babylonia to recite Hallel on Rosh Ḥodesh in order to distinguish between that day and ordinary days. But in Eretz Israel it was not necessary to take any steps to stress the unique aspects of the day, for it was in Eretz Israel that Rosh Ḥodesh was proclaimed, and it was there that the additional sacrifice was offered during the days of the Temple (*Hashlamah, Meiri*). Others explain that it was customary to recite Hallel on Rosh Ḥodesh even in Eretz Israel, but that different sections of Hallel were omitted there. When Rav went to Babylonia and saw that the people were reciting Hallel on Rosh Ḥodesh without making the omissions that were familiar to him, he thought that they were reciting the complete Hallel, and so he felt he ought to stop them. But when he saw that the Babylonians also left out certain sections of Hallel, he withdrew his objection, for he saw that they too understood that the recitation of Hallel on Rosh Ḥodesh was not ordained by Torah law or by Rabbinic enactment, but only by custom.

יָחִיד לֹא יַתְחִיל An individual should not begin. The Rishonim disagree about how to understand this Baraita. Some maintain that the Baraita teaches that even in a place where it is customary to recite Hallel on Rosh Ḥodesh, it

HALAKHAH

is recited by an individual or by the congregation. Some authorities maintain that when this Hallel is recited by the congregation, it is preceded and followed by blessings, and that no blessings are said when it is recited by an individual (following *Rif*). Others maintain that there are no blessings even when this Hallel is recited by the congregation (following *Rambam,* whose viewpoint is accepted in most Sephardi communities). *Rema* notes that the custom among Ashkenazim follows the opinion (of *Rosh and Rabbenu Tam*) that blessings precede and follow Hallel, even when it is recited by an individual." (*Shulḥan Arukh, Oraḥ Ḥayyim* 422:2.)

TRANSLATION AND COMMENTARY

דְּתַנְיָא [1]The Gemara explains: **It was taught** in a Baraita: **"On the sixth of the month** of Sivan **the Ten Commandments were given to Israel.** [2]**Rabbi Yose** disagrees and **says:** It was **on the seventh** of Sivan." [3]**According to** the anonymous first Tanna **who said** that it was **on the sixth** of Sivan that the Ten Commandments **were given, they were given on the sixth, and** the next day — **on the seventh — Moses went up** Mount Sinai. [4]And **according to** Rabbi Yose, **who said** that it was **on the seventh** of Sivan that the Ten Commandments were given, **they were given on the seventh, and** on the very same day — **on the seventh — Moses went up** Mount Sinai to receive the two Tablets of the Covenant. [5]**For the verse says** (Exodus 24:16): "And the glory of the Lord rested upon Mount Sinai, and the cloud covered it for six days; **and He called to Moses on the seventh day** out of the midst of the cloud." [6]**And** two verses later **it says** (v. 18): **"And Moses went into the midst of the cloud, and he went up into the mountain, and Moses was on the mountain forty days and forty nights."** Thus we see that Moses went up the mountain on the seventh of Sivan. Since he remained on the mountain for forty days, it follows that he came down from the mountain on the seventeenth of Tammuz. How so? He was on the mountain from the seventh of Sivan until the end of that month, [7]**twenty-four days during Sivan, and** he remained there for the first **sixteen days of Tammuz,** thereby **completing the forty days.** [8]**On the seventeenth of Tammuz he went down** from the mountain with the two Tablets of the Covenant in his hands, **approached** the camp, saw that the people were dancing around the golden calf, **and broke the tablets** into pieces, [9]**as the verse says** (Exodus 32:19): **"And it came to pass, as soon as he came near to the camp, he saw the calf** and the dancing; and Moses' anger burned, **and he cast the tablets out of his hands, and broke them beneath the mountain."**

[1]דְּתַנְיָא: ״בְּשִׁשָּׁה לַחֹדֶשׁ נִיתְּנוּ עֲשֶׂרֶת הַדִּבְּרוֹת לְיִשְׂרָאֵל. [2]רַבִּי יוֹסֵי אוֹמֵר: בְּשִׁבְעָה בּוֹ״. [3]מַאן דְּאָמַר בְּשִׁשָּׁה נִיתְּנוּ, בְּשִׁשָּׁה נִיתְּנוּ וּבְשִׁבְעָה עָלָה מֹשֶׁה. [4]מַאן דְּאָמַר בְּשִׁבְעָה, בְּשִׁבְעָה נִיתְּנוּ וּבְשִׁבְעָה עָלָה מֹשֶׁה, [5]דִּכְתִיב: ״וַיִּקְרָא אֶל מֹשֶׁה בַּיּוֹם הַשְּׁבִיעִי״. [6]וּכְתִיב: ״וַיָּבֹא מֹשֶׁה בְּתוֹךְ הֶעָנָן וַיַּעַל אֶל הָהָר, וַיְהִי מֹשֶׁה בָּהָר אַרְבָּעִים יוֹם וְאַרְבָּעִים לָיְלָה״. [7]עֶשְׂרִים וְאַרְבָּעָה דְּסִיוָן וְשִׁיתְּסַר דְּתַמּוּז מְלוֹ לְהוּ אַרְבְּעִין. [8]בְּשִׁיבְסַר בְּתַמּוּז נָחֵית, אֲתָא, וּתְבַרִינְהוּ לַלּוּחוֹת. [9]וּכְתִיב: ״וַיְהִי כַּאֲשֶׁר קָרַב אֶל הַמַּחֲנֶה, וַיַּרְא אֶת הָעֵגֶל... וַיַּשְׁלֵךְ מִיָּדָיו אֶת הַלֻּחֹת, וַיְשַׁבֵּר אֹתָם תַּחַת הָהָר״.

LITERAL TRANSLATION

[1]For it was taught: "On the sixth of the month the Ten Commandments were given to Israel. [2]Rabbi Yose says: On the seventh." [3][According to] the one who said [that] they were given on the sixth, they were given on the sixth and on the seventh Moses went up. [4][According to] the one who said on the seventh, they were given on the seventh and on the seventh Moses went up, [5]as it is written: "And He called to Moses on the seventh day." [6]And it is written: "And Moses went into the midst of the cloud and he went up into the mountain, and Moses was on the mountain forty days and forty nights." [7]Twenty-four [days] of Sivan and sixteen [days] of Tammuz complete the forty [days]. [8]On the seventeenth of Tammuz he went down, came, and broke the tablets. [9]And it is written: "And it came to pass, as soon as he came near to the camp, he saw the calf... and he cast the tablets out of his hands, and broke them beneath the mountain."

RASHI

רבי יוסי אומר בשבעה — וטעמייהו מקרא במסכת שבת בפרק ״רבי עקיבא״. **בשבעה עלה משה** — לקבל הלוחות. כלומר, ודאי ליכא מאן דפליג עלה דמתניתין דקתני דבשבעה עשר בתמוז נשתברו הלוחות — מכלל דכולהו סבירא להו דבשבעה עלה, ולאו מקרא נפקא לן דבשבעה עלה, דהאי דכתיב ״וישכון כבוד ה׳ על הר סיני ויכסהו הענן ששת ימים ויקרא אל משה ביום השביעי״ — איכא מאן דדריש ליה במסכת יומא כי אחר מתן תורה הוה. משבעה בסיון עד שבעה עשר בתמוז איכא ארבעים יום: עשרים וארבעה דסיון שהוא מלא, וששה עשר דתמוז — הרי ארבעים יום שעמד משה בהר.

NOTES

is only recited in the course of congregational worship. An individual should not recite Hallel on Rosh Ḥodesh. But if he has already recited the blessing, he should complete the Hallel — in other words, read Hallel in its abridged form — so that the blessing should not have been recited in vain (*Geonim*).

Rif and many other Rishonim maintain that in places where it is customary to recite Hallel on Rosh Ḥodesh, it may be recited even by an individual. The Baraita teaches that an individual should not recite Hallel on Rosh Ḥodesh with a blessing, but if he began to recite Hallel with a blessing he should complete his recitation of Hallel (according to some, with the concluding blessing, and according to others, without it).

Rabbenu Tam explains that there is no difference whatsoever between an individual and the congregation regarding Hallel recited on Rosh Ḥodesh, for even an individual recites Hallel with a blessing. The Baraita refers here not

TRANSLATION AND COMMENTARY

בָּטֵל הַתָּמִיד [1]The Mishnah continues: "On the Seventeenth of Tammuz **the daily sacrifice** brought in the Temple **was suspended."** [2]The Gemara explains: This is known **by tradition.**

הוּבְקְעָה הָעִיר [3]We learned in the Mishnah: "On the Seventeenth of Tammuz, the walls of **the city** of Jerusalem **were breached."** The Gemara asks: [4]**Was it** really **on the Seventeenth** of Tammuz that the walls of Jerusalem were breached? [5]**But surely the verse says** (Jeremiah 52:6): **"And in the fourth month, on the ninth day of the month, the famine was severe in the city,** and there was no bread for the people of the land." [6]**And the next verse says** (v. 7): **"And the city was breached,** and all the men of war fled." Thus the verse clearly states that the breach in the walls of Jerusalem occurred on the ninth of Tammuz, and not on the seventeenth of the month, as taught in our Mishnah!

אֲמַר רָבָא [7]**Rava said** in reply: **There is no difficulty** in reconciling this contradiction. [8]**Here** in the Bible the verse refers to the breach in the walls of Jerusalem **in** the time of **the First** Temple, which occurred on the ninth of Tammuz. By contrast, [9]**here** in our Mishnah the reference is to the breach in the walls of Jerusalem **in** the time of **the Second** Temple, which occurred on the seventeenth. [10]**For it was taught** in a Baraita: **"In** the period of **the First Temple, the walls of the city** of Jerusalem **were breached on the ninth of Tammuz;** [11]**in** the period of **the Second** Temple, they were breached **on the seventeenth** of that month."

שָׂרַף אַפּוֹסְטְמוֹס [12]The Mishnah continues: "On the Seventeenth of Tammuz the Roman officer, **Apostemos, burned a Torah scroll."** [13]The Gemara explains: This is known **by tradition.**

הֶעֱמִיד צֶלֶם בַּהֵיכָל [14]The Mishnah concludes the list of calamities that occurred on the Seventeenth of Tammuz with the following: "On the Seventeenth of Tammuz **an idol was set up in the Sanctuary."**

[1]״בָּטֵל הַתָּמִיד״. [2]גְּמָרָא.
[3]״הוּבְקְעָה הָעִיר״. [4]בְּשִׁבְעָה עָשָׂר הֲוָה? [5]וְהָכְתִיב: ״בַּחֹדֶשׁ הָרְבִיעִי, בְּתִשְׁעָה לַחֹדֶשׁ, וַיֶּחֱזַק הָרָעָב בָּעִיר״. [6]וּכְתִיב בַּתְרֵיהּ: ״וַתִּבָּקַע הָעִיר, וגו׳״!
[7]אֲמַר רָבָא: לָא קַשְׁיָא. [8]כָּאן בָּרִאשׁוֹנָה; [9]כָּאן בַּשְּׁנִיָּה. [10]דְּתַנְיָא: ״בָּרִאשׁוֹנָה, הוּבְקְעָה הָעִיר בְּתִשְׁעָה בְּתַמּוּז; [11]בַּשְּׁנִיָּה, בְּשִׁבְעָה עָשָׂר בּוֹ״.
[12]״שָׂרַף אַפּוֹסְטְמוֹס אֶת הַתּוֹרָה״. [13]גְּמָרָא.
[14]״הֶעֱמִיד צֶלֶם בַּהֵיכָל״.

LITERAL TRANSLATION

[1]"The daily sacrifice was suspended." [2][This is] tradition.

[3]"The city was breached." [4]Was it on the seventeenth? [5]But surely it is written: "In the fourth month, on the ninth day of the month, the famine was severe in the city." [6]And it is written after it: "And the city was breached, etc."!

[7]Rava said: There is no difficulty. [8]Here [it refers] to the First [Temple]; [9]here [it refers] to the Second [Temple]. [10]For it was taught: "In the first, the city was breached on the ninth of Tammuz; [11]in the second, on the seventeenth."

[12]"Apostemos burned the Torah scroll." [13][This is] a tradition.

[14]"He set up an idol in the Sanctuary."

RASHI

גמרא — כך קיבלנו מאבותינו.

BACKGROUND

כָּאן בָּרִאשׁוֹנָה; כָּאן בַּשְּׁנִיָּה Here it refers to the First Temple; here it refers to the Second Temple. Fast-days commemorating the destruction of the Temple were instituted after the destruction of the First Temple, as is explained in Zechariah (8:19). But the specific days of the fasts are not mentioned, only the months in which they fell. These fast-days were rescinded during the Second Temple period, but were reinstituted after the destruction of the Second Temple. Because mourning for the Second Temple was closer in time, the fast-days were determined according to events that occurred at the time of the destruction of that Temple.

NOTES

to the Hallel recited on Rosh Ḥodesh, but to the Hallel recited by an individual in commemoration of a private miracle performed on his behalf. Such an individual should not recite Hallel with a blessing, but if he began with a blessing, he should complete the Hallel with a blessing.

בָּטֵל הַתָּמִיד The daily sacrifice was suspended. Opinions differ about the calamity mentioned here. The Jerusalem Talmud implies that the Seventeeth of Tammuz marks the suspension of the daily sacrifice during the period of the Second Temple. *Rambam* writes (*Hilkhot Ta'aniyyot* 5:2) that the Seventeenth of Tammuz commemorates the suspension of the daily sacrifice during the time of the First Temple. According to *Rashi*, the daily sacrifice was suspended because of a decree banning the sacrifice, which was issued by the ruling foreign authorities. *Rabbenu Yehonatan* writes that the sacrifice was suspended because the animals needed for the rite were no longer available on account of the siege of Jerusalem.

הוּבְקְעָה הָעִיר The city was breached. The Babylonian Talmud reconciles the Mishnah with the verse in Jeremiah by explaining that the Scriptural source refers to the breach in the walls of Jerusalem during the First Temple period, which took place on the ninth of Tammuz, whereas the Mishnah refers to the breach in the walls of the city during the Second Temple period, which occurred on the seventeenth of Tammuz. According to the Jerusalem Talmud, however, the breach in the walls of Jerusalem during the First Temple period also took place on the seventeenth of Tammuz, but because of the many calamities that overwhelmed the people of Israel at the time, errors entered into the calculation of the calendar, and it was mistakenly believed that the breach took place on the ninth of the month. *Maharsha* explains at length that the mistake arose when it became impossible to announce the beginning of the new month on the basis of the testimony of witnesses who had seen the new moon, and the calculations of the calendar were then made in accordance with the solar rather than the lunar calendar.

הֶעֱמִיד צֶלֶם בַּהֵיכָל He set up an idol in the Sanctuary. The Jerusalem Talmud records a disagreement about this

¹מְנָלַן?
²דִּכְתִיב: ״וּמֵעֵת הוּסַר הַתָּמִיד, וְלָתֵת שִׁקּוּץ שֹׁמֵם״.
³וְחַד הֲוָה? ⁴וְהָכְתִיב: ״וְעַל כְּנַף שִׁקּוּצִים מְשֹׁמֵם״!
⁵אֲמַר רָבָא: תְּרֵי הֲווּ, וְנָפַל חַד עַל חַבְרֵיהּ וּתְבָרֵיהּ לֵיהּ לִידֵיהּ,
⁶וְאִשְׁתַּכַּח דַּהֲוָה כְּתִיב: [29A] ⁷״אַנְתְּ צָבֵית לַחֲרוּבֵי בֵּיתָא;
⁸יָדָךְ אַשְׁלֵימַתְּ לֵיהּ״.
⁹״בְּתִשְׁעָה בְּאָב נִגְזַר עַל אֲבוֹתֵינוּ שֶׁלֹּא יִכָּנְסוּ לָאָרֶץ״.
¹⁰מְנָלַן?
¹¹דִּכְתִיב: ״וַיְהִי בַּחֹדֶשׁ הָרִאשׁוֹן בַּשָּׁנָה הַשֵּׁנִית, בְּאֶחָד לַחֹדֶשׁ, הוּקַם הַמִּשְׁכָּן״. ¹²וְאָמַר מָר: שָׁנָה רִאשׁוֹנָה עָשָׂה מֹשֶׁה אֶת הַמִּשְׁכָּן, שְׁנִיָּה הֵקִים מֹשֶׁה אֶת הַמִּשְׁכָּן וְשָׁלַח מְרַגְּלִים.

LITERAL TRANSLATION

¹From where [do we know this]? ²For it is written: "And from the time that the daily sacrifice shall be taken away, and the abomination that makes desolate is set up."

³But was there [only] one? ⁴But surely it is written: "And upon the wing of abominations shall come one who makes desolate"!

⁵Rava said: There were two, but one fell on its fellow and broke its hand, ⁶and it was found that it was written: [29A] ⁷"You wanted to destroy the house; ⁸I have completed your hand."

⁹"On the Ninth of Av it was decreed that our ancestors would not enter the land [of Israel]." ¹⁰From where do we [know this]?

¹¹For it is written: "And it came to pass in the first month in the second year, on the first day of the month, that the Tabernacle was erected." ¹²And the Master said: The first year Moses made the Tabernacle, the second [year] Moses erected the Tabernacle and sent the spies.

TRANSLATION AND COMMENTARY

¹The Gemara asks: **From where do we know this?**

דִּכְתִיב ²The Gemara explains: This is derived **from the verse** which **says** (Daniel 12:11): **"And from the time that the daily sacrifice shall be taken away, and the abomination that makes desolate is set up,** there shall be one thousand two hundred and ninety days." This verse implies that on the very same day that the daily sacrifice was suspended, on the Seventeenth of Tammuz, an abomination was set up in the Temple.

וְחַד הֲוָה ³The Gemara asks: **But was there only one** idol set up in the Temple? ⁴**Surely the verse says** (Daniel 9:27): **"And upon the wing of abominations shall come one who makes desolate"!** The plural "abominations" implies that more than one idol was set up in the Temple!

אֲמַר רָבָא ⁵**Rava said** in reply: In fact **two idols were** set up in the Temple, **but one** of the idols **fell on the other and broke its hand.** Thus the earlier verse in Daniel speaks of "abominations," whereas the later verse speaks of a single abomination, the broken idol no longer being counted. ⁶An inscription **was found** on the broken idol **which read** as follows: [29A] ⁷**"You wanted to destroy** God's **Temple** by leading His people astray. ⁸Here I have added to your power by giving you my hand to assist you in your mission."

בְּתִשְׁעָה בְּאָב ⁹The Mishnah continues with a list of the calamities that befell the Jewish people on the Ninth of Av. The list begins: **"On the Ninth of Av it was decreed that our ancestors** who left Egypt **would not enter the Land of Israel** but would wander in the wilderness for forty years." ¹⁰The Gemara asks: **From where do we know** that **this** decree was issued on the Ninth of Av?

דִּכְתִיב ¹¹The Gemara explains: **The verse says** (Exodus 40:17): **"And it came to pass in the first month in the second year, on the first day of the month, that the Tabernacle was erected."** ¹²**And** in connection with this **a Sage said:** During **the first year** after the Israelites left Egypt **Moses made the Tabernacle,** and during **the second year,** on the first of Nisan, **Moses erected the Tabernacle, and** about three months later, on the twenty-ninth of Sivan [as will be explained below], he **sent** out **the spies** to spy out the Land of Israel.

RASHI

ומעת הוסר התמיד לתת שקוץ שומם וגו' — דבעת שהוסר ונתבטל התמיד — באותו היום נתן שקוץ שומם, דהיינו הועמד צלם בהיכל. הכי גרסינן: **והא כתיב על כנף שקוצים** — כלומר הא כתיב קרא אחרינא, דכתיב ביה "שקוצים" דמשמע תרי. **תרי הוו** — שהעמידן מנשה בהיכל. **ונפל חד על חבריה וקטעיה לידיה** — והנקטע לא קא חשיב, והיינו דכתיב "שקוץ" אחד. **אשתכח דכתיב** — על ההוא צלם הכי. **אנת צבית לאחרובי ביתיה וידך אשלימת ליה** — הצלם אומר לחבירו: אתה רצית להחריב ביתו של מקום, שהטית ישראל אחריך — ואני עשיתי בך נקמה ושילמתי לך ידי. לשון אחר: אנת צבית לאחרובי ביתא וידך [אושלית] לי. לשון שאילת [כלים], כלומר: ועלה בידי.

NOTES

matter. Some read הָעֳמַד צֶלֶם — "an idol was set up" — and explain that the Mishnah refers to the idol set up in the First Temple by Manasseh, King of Judah. *Gevurat Ari* considers the difficulty concerning the order of the events listed in the Mishnah which arises according to this interpretation. Others read הֶעֱמִיד צֶלֶם — "he set up an idol" — and explain that the Mishnah refers to the idol set up in the Second Temple by the Roman officer, Apostemos, who also burned the Torah scroll on the same day.

אַנְתְּ צָבֵית You wanted. There are numerous readings and interpretations of this cryptic inscription found on the idol. Some understand that the inscription was found on the broken idol, while others suggest that it was found on the idol that remained whole.

[1]וּכְתִיב: ״וַיְהִי בַּשָּׁנָה הַשֵּׁנִית, בַּחֹדֶשׁ הַשֵּׁנִי בְּעֶשְׂרִים בַּחֹדֶשׁ, נַעֲלָה הֶעָנָן מֵעַל מִשְׁכַּן הָעֵדֻת״. [2]וּכְתִיב: ״וַיִּסְעוּ מֵהַר ה׳ דֶּרֶךְ שְׁלֹשֶׁת יָמִים״. [3]אָמַר רַבִּי חָמָא בַּר חֲנִינָא: אוֹתוֹ הַיּוֹם סָרוּ מֵאַחֲרֵי ה׳. [4]וּכְתִיב: ״וְהָאסַפְסֻף אֲשֶׁר בְּקִרְבּוֹ הִתְאַוּוּ תַּאֲוָה, וַיָּשֻׁבוּ וַיִּבְכּוּ גַּם בְּנֵי יִשְׂרָאֵל, וגו׳״. [5]וּכְתִיב: ״עַד חֹדֶשׁ יָמִים, וגו׳״, [6]דְּהָווּ לְהוּ עֶשְׂרִין וְתַרְתֵּין בְּסִיוָן. [7]וּכְתִיב: ״וַתִּסָּגֵר מִרְיָם שִׁבְעַת יָמִים״, [8]דְּהָווּ לְהוּ עֶשְׂרִין וְתִשְׁעָה בְּסִיוָן. [9]וּכְתִיב: ״שְׁלַח לְךָ אֲנָשִׁים״. [10]וְתַנְיָא: ״בְּעֶשְׂרִים וְתִשְׁעָה בְּסִיוָן שָׁלַח מֹשֶׁה מְרַגְּלִים״. [11]וּכְתִיב: ״וַיָּשֻׁבוּ מִתּוּר הָאָרֶץ מִקֵּץ אַרְבָּעִים יוֹם״.

LITERAL TRANSLATION

[1]And it is written: "And it came to pass in the second year, on the twentieth day of the second month, that the cloud was taken up from off the Tabernacle of the Testimony." [2]And it is written: "And they traveled from the mountain of the Lord a journey of three days." [3]Rabbi Ḥama bar Ḥanina said: That day they turned away from God, [4]and it is written: "And the mixed multitude that was among them felt a desire, and the Children of Israel also wept again, etc." [5]And it is written: "Until a whole month, etc.," [6]so that it was the twenty-second of Sivan. [7]And it is written: "And Miriam was shut out for seven days," [8]so that it was the twenty-ninth of Sivan. [9]And it is written: "Send men." [10]And it was taught: "On the twenty-ninth of Sivan Moses sent the spies." [11]And it is written: "And they returned from searching the land at the end of forty days."

TRANSLATION AND COMMENTARY

[1]**And the verse says** (Numbers 10: 11-12): **"And it came to pass in the second year, on the twentieth day of the second month** [Iyyar], **that the cloud was taken up from off the tabernacle of the Testimony.** And the children of Israel took their journeys out of the wilderness of Sinai, and the cloud rested in the wilderness of Paran." [2]**And a later verse says** (Numbers 10:33): **"And they traveled from the mountain of the Lord a journey of three days,"** which takes us to the twenty-third of Iyyar. [3]And **Rabbi Ḥama bar Ḥanina said: That** very **day they turned away from God.** They hastily departed from Mount Sinai, and once again complained. [4]**For** a few verses later **it says** (Numbers 11:4): **"And the mixed multitude that was among them felt a desire, and the Children of Israel also wept again,** and said: Who will give us meat to eat?" [5]**And** further on **it says** (Numbers 11:18-20). "Therefore the Lord will give you meat, and you will eat. Not one day will you eat... **but a whole month,** until it comes out of your nostrils, and it will be loathsome to you." [6]**Thus** the plague with which God smote the people who lusted for meat **lasted until the twenty-second of Sivan.** The Israelites then journeyed to Hazeroth, where Miriam spoke ill about Moses and was stricken with leprosy. [7]Regarding that event, **the verse says** (Numbers 12:15): **"And Miriam was shut out** from the camp **for seven days,** and the people did not journey until Miriam was brought in again." [8]**Thus** the Israelites remained in Hazeroth until **the twenty-ninth of Sivan,** on which day they moved on into the wilderness of Paran. [9]**And** immediately afterwards **the verse says** (Numbers 13:2): **"Send men,** that they may spy out the land of Canaan." [10]This calculation **was taught** in a Baraita, which states: **"On the twenty-ninth of Sivan Moses sent** out **the spies** to spy out the Land of Israel." [11]**And** a later **verse says** (Numbers 13:25): **"And they returned from searching the land at the end of forty days,"** which brings us to the eighth of Av.

RASHI

ואמר רבי חמא בר חנינא אותו היום וכו׳ — מהר, לשון מַהֵר, עכשיו.

כשתטול תשעה עשר ימים מחדש אייר קודם עליית הענן פשו להו עשרה, והנהו עשרה היו בין דרך שלשת ימים ושבעה דהסגרת מרים, וחדש של עשרים ותשעה ימים שאכלו בשר — הוה שלשים ותשעה. והשתא אשתכח דמשה שלח מרגלים בעשרים ותשעה דסיון.

NOTES

אוֹתוֹ הַיּוֹם סָרוּ **That day they turned away.** It would appear from the plain reading of our Gemara that Rabbi Ḥama bar Ḥanina's comment, that the Israelites "turned away from God" as soon as they departed from Mount Sinai, is based on the juxtaposition of the Israelites' departure and the mixed multitude's complaints about the lack of meat (see *Meiri,* and *Rashi* on *Shabbat* 116a). Here, however, *Rashi* writes that Rabbi Ḥama bar Ḥanina's comment is based on a play on words: With a slight alteration of the vocalization, the verse "And they departed from the mountain [מֵהַר] of the Lord," can be understood to mean: "And they departed hastily [מַהֵר] from the Lord." According to the Midrash, the Israelites departed from Mount Sinai the way school- children run away from their master. *Yalkut* adds that Moses instructed the Israelites to advance one day's journey, but they went on a three-day journey, as if to distance themselves from the mountain of the Lord.

עַד חֹדֶשׁ יָמִים **Until a whole month.** The Rishonim explain these calculations in several ways, disagreeing about whether the three days of travel are included in the count, whether a part of a day is counted as a day, and whether the months were full or defective (see *Tosafot, Tosefot Rid,* and *Maharsha*).

BACKGROUND

תַּמּוּז דְּהַהִיא שַׁתָּא Tammuz of that year. The length of the month in the Jewish calendar is determined by the cycle of the moon. In practice it varies and can be either twenty-nine or thirty days. This is both because of the need for eyewitnesses to the new moon, which can sometimes be late, when the new moon appears during daylight hours, and sometimes because of irregularities in the moon's orbit. Today the calendar is fixed, and according to our calendar the month of Tammuz always has twenty-nine days, but this was not the case when Rosh Ḥodesh was determined by eyewitnesses and the decision of a court. Since we do not have a clear tradition regarding the first year of the Exodus from Egypt, there are different approaches among the Sages regarding the months and the days of the week on which various events occurred.

TRANSLATION AND COMMENTARY

הָנֵי אַרְבָּעִים יוֹם [1]The Gemara interjects: If the spies were sent out on the twenty-ninth of Sivan and returned on the eighth of Av, surely they were away for only **thirty-nine days** — two days of Sivan, twenty-nine days of Tammuz, and eight days of Av!

אָמַר אַבַּיֵי [2]**Abaye said:** The month of **Tammuz that year was declared full,** and was designated as a month of thirty days. Thus the spies were away for forty days — two days of Sivan, thirty days of Tammuz, and eight days of Av. An allusion to the addition of another day to the month of Tammuz that year may be found in **the** following **verse,** [3]which **says** (Lamentations 1:15): **"He has called an appointed time against me to crush my young men"** — an additional festive day ("appointed time") was added to the month of Tammuz, so that the decree against the young men would be issued on the ninth of Av.

וּכְתִיב [4]The Gemara continues its calculation: **The verse** that describes the people's reaction to the report of the spies **says** (Numbers 14:1): **"And all the congregation lifted up their voice and cried, and the people wept that night."** [5]Rabbah said in the name of Rabbi Yoḥanan: That night of weeping was the night of the ninth of Av. [6]When the sound of their weeping reached Heaven, **the Holy One, blessed be He, said to them: "You wept** tonight **for no cause,** for I promised to bring you safely to the Land of Israel, and you had no reason to doubt Me. [7]**But I will establish for you a** valid reason for **weeping** on this day **in future generations."** It was then that God decreed that the Temple would be destroyed on the Ninth of Av, the day on which the people of Israel wept for no reason in the wilderness.

חָרַב הַבַּיִת בָּרִאשׁוֹנָה [8]The Mishnah's list of disastrous events which occurred on the Ninth of Av continues: "On the Ninth of Av **the First Temple was destroyed."** [9]The Gemara explains the basis of this statement: **The verse says** (II Kings 25:8-9): **"And in the fifth month** [Av], **on the seventh day of the month, which was the nineteenth year of King Nebuchadnezzar King of Babylon, Nebuzaradan, captain of the guard, a servant of the King of Babylon, came to Jerusalem. And he burnt the house of the Lord,** and the king's house, and all the houses of Jerusalem, and every house of a great man he burnt with fire." [10]**And** elsewhere **the verse says** (Jeremiah 52:12-13): **"And in the fifth month, on the tenth day of the month, which was the nineteenth year of King Nebuchadnezzar, King of Babylon, Nebuzaradan, captain of the guard, who served the**

[1]הָנֵי אַרְבָּעִים יוֹם נְכֵי חַד הָווּ! [2]אָמַר אַבַּיֵי: תַּמּוּז דְּהַהִיא שַׁתָּא מַלּוּיֵי מַלְיוּהּ, [3]דִּכְתִיב: "קָרָא עָלַי מוֹעֵד לִשְׁבֹּר בַּחוּרָי". [4]וּכְתִיב: "וַתִּשָּׂא כָּל הָעֵדָה וַיִּתְּנוּ אֶת קוֹלָם, וַיִּבְכּוּ הָעָם בַּלַּיְלָה הַהוּא". [5]אָמַר רַבָּה אָמַר רַבִּי יוֹחָנָן: אוֹתוֹ לַיְלָה לֵיל תִּשְׁעָה בְּאָב הָיָה. [6]אָמַר לָהֶם הַקָּדוֹשׁ בָּרוּךְ הוּא: "אַתֶּם בְּכִיתֶם בְּכִיָּה שֶׁל חִנָּם, [7]וַאֲנִי קוֹבֵעַ לָכֶם בְּכִיָּה לְדוֹרוֹת". [8]"חָרַב הַבַּיִת בָּרִאשׁוֹנָה". [9]דִּכְתִיב: "וּבַחֹדֶשׁ הַחֲמִישִׁי, בְּשִׁבְעָה לַחֹדֶשׁ, הִיא שְׁנַת תְּשַׁע עֶשְׂרֵה שָׁנָה לַמֶּלֶךְ נְבֻכַדְנֶאצַּר, מֶלֶךְ בָּבֶל, בָּא נְבוּזַרְאֲדָן, רַב טַבָּחִים, עֶבֶד מֶלֶךְ בָּבֶל, יְרוּשָׁלָם. וַיִּשְׂרֹף אֶת בֵּית ה׳, וגו׳". [10]וּכְתִיב: "וּבַחֹדֶשׁ הַחֲמִישִׁי, בֶּעָשׂוֹר לַחֹדֶשׁ, הִיא שְׁנַת תְּשַׁע עֶשְׂרֵה שָׁנָה לַמֶּלֶךְ נְבוּכַדְנֶאצַּר, מֶלֶךְ בָּבֶל, בָּא נְבוּזַרְאֲדָן, רַב טַבָּחִים,

LITERAL TRANSLATION

[1]These are forty days less one! [2]Abaye said: Tammuz of that year they declared full, [3]for it is written: "He has called an appointed time against me to crush my young men." [4]And it is written: "And all the congregation lifted up their voice and cried, and the people wept on that night." [5]Rabbah said in the name of Rabbi Yoḥanan: That night was the night of the ninth of Av. [6]The Holy One, blessed be He, said to them: "You wept a weeping for no cause, [7]but I will establish for you a weeping for generations." [8]"The Temple was destroyed for the first time." [9]For it is written: "And in the fifth month, on the seventh day of the month, which was the nineteenth year of King Nebuchadnezzar, King of Babylon, Nebuzaradan, captain of the guard, a servant of the king of Babylon, came to Jerusalem. And he burnt the house of the Lord, etc." [10]And it is written: "And in the fifth month, on the tenth day of the month, which was the nineteenth year of King Nebuchadnezzar king of Babylon, Nebuzaradan, captain of the guard,

RASHI

הני ארבעים נכי חד — שנים מסיון ועשרים ותשעה מתמוז — הוה שלשים ואחד, ושמונה מאב — הוה שלשים ותשעה.

NOTES

קָרָא עָלַי מוֹעֵד He has called an appointed time against me. Some commentators understand the proof as follows: Every month that contains a festival (מוֹעֵד) is a full month of thirty days. Thus the verse, "He has called an appointed time against me," may be interpreted to mean that the month was declared full, as if it were a month containing a festival (*Rabbenu Elyakim* and others).

עָמַד לִפְנֵי מֶלֶךְ בָּבֶל, בִּירוּשָׁלַם, וגו׳". [1]וְתַנְיָא: "אִי אֶפְשָׁר לוֹמַר בְּשִׁבְעָה, שֶׁהֲרֵי כְּבָר נֶאֱמַר בֶּעָשׂוֹר. [2]וְאִי אֶפְשָׁר לוֹמַר בֶּעָשׂוֹר, שֶׁהֲרֵי כְּבָר נֶאֱמַר בְּשִׁבְעָה. [3]הָא כֵּיצַד? [4]בְּשִׁבְעָה נִכְנְסוּ נׇכְרִים לַהֵיכָל, וְאָכְלוּ וְקִלְקְלוּ בּוֹ שְׁבִיעִי שְׁמִינִי, וּתְשִׁיעִי סָמוּךְ לַחֲשֵׁיכָה הִצִּיתוּ בּוֹ אֶת הָאוּר, וְהָיָה דּוֹלֵק וְהוֹלֵךְ כָּל הַיּוֹם כּוּלּוֹ, [5]שֶׁנֶּאֱמַר: 'אוֹי לָנוּ, כִּי פָנָה הַיּוֹם, כִּי יִנָּטוּ צִלְלֵי עָרֶב'". [6]וְהַיְינוּ דְּאָמַר רַבִּי יוֹחָנָן: אִלְמָלֵי הָיִיתִי בְּאוֹתוֹ הַדּוֹר, לֹא קְבַעְתִּיו אֶלָּא בַּעֲשִׂירִי, [7]מִפְּנֵי שֶׁרוּבּוֹ שֶׁל הֵיכָל בּוֹ נִשְׂרַף.

[8]וְרַבָּנַן?

[9]אַתְחַלְתָּא דְּפוּרְעָנוּתָא עֲדִיפָא.

[10]"וּבַשְּׁנִיָּה". מְנָלַן?

[11]דְּתַנְיָא: "מְגַלְגְּלִין זְכוּת לְיוֹם זַכַּאי, וְחוֹבָה לְיוֹם חַיָּיב.

LITERAL TRANSLATION

who served the King of Babylon, came into Jerusalem, etc." [1]And it was taught: "It is not possible to say on the seventh, for it has already said on the tenth. [2]And it is not possible to say on the tenth, for it has already said on the seventh. [3]So how was it? [4]On the seventh the heathens entered the Sanctuary, and they ate and fornicated in it [on] the seventh [and the] eighth, and [on] the ninth close to nightfall they set fire to it, and it continued to burn the entire day, [5]as it is said: 'Woe unto us, for the day has declined, for the shadows of the evening are lengthening.'" [6]And this is what Rabbi Yoḥanan said: Had I been in that generation, I would only have established it on the tenth, [7]because most of the Sanctuary was burnt then.

[8]And the Rabbis?

[9]The beginning of the punishment takes precedence.

[10]"And second time." From where do we [know this]?

[11]For it was taught: "A good thing is assigned to a good day, and a bad thing to a bad day.

TRANSLATION AND COMMENTARY

King of Babylon, came into Jerusalem. And he burned the house of the Lord, and the king's house; and all the houses of Jerusalem, and every house of the great he burned with fire." [1]**And it was taught** in a Baraita: **"It is not possible to say** that the Temple was destroyed **on the seventh** of Av, as is stated in the Book of Kings, **for it has already been said** in the Book of Jeremiah that it was destroyed **on the tenth** of that month. [2]**And it is** also **not possible to say** that the Temple was destroyed **on the tenth** of Av, as is stated in the Book of Jeremiah, **for it has already been said** in the Book of Kings that it was destroyed **on the seventh** of that month. [3]**So how is it** that these dates can be reconciled? [4]**On the seventh** of Av, **the heathens entered the Temple, and** for the next two days, **on the seventh and the eighth, they ate and fornicated inside** the Temple. Then late **on the** day of **the ninth, close to nightfall, they set** the Temple **on fire, and it continued to burn the entire** next **day,** on the tenth. Thus the verse in Kings which speaks of the seventh of Av refers to Nebuzaradan's entry into the Temple, whereas the verse in Jeremiah which speaks of the tenth of Av refers to the total destruction of the Temple. [5]That the Temple was set on fire late in the day is alluded to in **the verse** that **says** (Lamentations 6:4): **'Woe unto us, for the day has declined, for the shadows of the evening are lengthening.'** This refers to the actual destruction of the Temple, which began close to nightfall on the ninth of Av." [6]Referring to the Baraita's chronology of the Temple's destruction, the Gemara notes that **this is what Rabbi Yoḥanan** meant when he **said: Had I been** alive **in the generation** of the destruction of the First Temple, **I would only have established** the fast commemorating that event **on the tenth** of Av, [7]**because** the Temple was set on fire late in the day on the ninth of Av, and **most of the Temple was burnt** on the tenth.

וְרַבָּנַן [8]The Gemara asks: **And** what is the viewpoint of **the Rabbis,** who fixed the ninth rather than the tenth of Av as the day marking the destruction of the Temple?

אַתְחַלְתָּא דְּפוּרְעָנוּתָא עֲדִיפָא [9]The Gemara explains: The Rabbis maintained that **it is preferable** to mark **the beginning of the** disaster.

וּבַשְּׁנִיָּה [10]We learned in the Mishnah: "On the Ninth of Av **the Second** Temple was destroyed." The Gemara asks: **From where do we know** that the Second Temple was destroyed on the exact anniversary of the destruction of the First Temple?

דְּתַנְיָא [11]The Gemara answers: **It was taught** in a Baraita: **"A good thing is assigned to a good day,** a day on which other joyous events took place in the past, **and a bad thing** is assigned to a bad day, the anniversary

NOTES

לֹא קְבַעְתִּיו אֶלָּא בַּעֲשִׂירִי **I would only have established it on the tenth.** *Gevurat Ari* discusses at length whether Rabbi Yoḥanan's statement refers only to the fast established in the aftermath of the destruction of the First Temple, or also to the fast enacted following the destruction of the Second Temple. He also discusses the practical ramifications of the fast commemorating the First Temple's destruction, bearing in mind that the fast observed today relates to the destruction of the Second Temple.

TRANSLATION AND COMMENTARY

of some other calamity. [1]The Sages **said: When the Temple was destroyed for the first time** at the hands of Nebuzaradan, **that day was the ninth of Av, and it was the day following Shabbat, and it was the year following the Sabbatical Year,** i.e., the first year of the seven-year Sabbatical cycle, [2]**and it was** the week during which **the *mishmar* of Jehoiarib** was serving in the Temple, **and** at that very hour **the Levites were singing the songs** of praise that accompany the sacrificial service **as they stood on their platform** in the Temple Courtyard. [3]**And what song were** the Levites **singing** when the Babylonian forces set the Temple on fire? [4]They were singing the verse [Psalm 94:23]: **'And He brought upon them their own iniquity, and He will cut them off in their own wickedness.'** [5]**And** the Levites **did not** even **have time** to complete the last few words of the verse and **say: 'The Lord our God will cut them off,' before the heathens burst in and captured them. And similarly** when the Temple was destroyed **a second time** at the hands of Titus, the destruction occurred on the very same day, on the ninth of Av."

נִלְכְּדָה בֵּיתָר [6]The Mishnah's list continues: "On the Ninth of Av the fortress of **Betar was captured** by the Romans, thus bringing the Bar Kokhba revolt to an end." The Gemara explains: This fact is known **by tradition.**

נֶחֶרְשָׁה הָעִיר [7]We learned in the Mishnah: "On the Ninth of Av **the city** of Jerusalem **was plowed up,** and then rebuilt as a pagan city which the Jews were forbidden to enter." [8]**It was taught** in a Baraita: **"After the wicked** Roman commander **Turnus Rufus plowed up the Temple, a decree of execution was issued against** the Nasi, **Rabban Gamliel,** who was the head of the Academy of Yavneh a generation after the destruction of the Second Temple. [9]**A certain** Roman **general** who knew about the decree **came** to warn Rabban Gamliel. **He stood in the Academy and declared:** [10]**'The man with the nose is being sought, the man with the nose is being sought,'** hoping that Rabban Gamliel would understand that he was trying to convey the message that the most prominent man of the generation — the man who stands out just as the nose protrudes from the face — was being sought by the Roman authorities. [11]**Rabban Gamliel heard** what the general said, understood the hint, and **went into hiding.**

[1]אָמְרוּ: כְּשֶׁחָרַב בֵּית הַמִּקְדָּשׁ בָּרִאשׁוֹנָה אוֹתוֹ הַיּוֹם תִּשְׁעָה בְּאָב הָיָה, וּמוֹצָאֵי שַׁבָּת הָיָה, וּמוֹצָאֵי שְׁבִיעִית הָיְתָה, [2]וּמִשְׁמַרְתָּהּ שֶׁל יְהוֹיָרִיב הָיְתָה, וְהַלְוִיִּם הָיוּ אוֹמְרִים שִׁירָה וְעוֹמְדִין עַל דּוּכָנָם. [3]וּמָה שִׁירָה הָיוּ אוֹמְרִים? [4]״וַיָּשֶׁב עֲלֵיהֶם אֶת אוֹנָם, וּבְרָעָתָם יַצְמִיתֵם״. [5]וְלֹא הִסְפִּיקוּ לוֹמַר: ״יַצְמִיתֵם ה׳ אֱלֹהֵינוּ״, עַד שֶׁבָּאוּ נָכְרִים וּכְבָשׁוּם. וְכֵן בַּשְּׁנִיָּה״. [6]״נִלְכְּדָה בֵּיתָר״. גְּמָרָא. [7]״נֶחֶרְשָׁה הָעִיר״. [8]תַּנְיָא: ״כְּשֶׁחָרַשׁ טוּרְנוּסְרוּפוּס הָרָשָׁע אֶת הַהֵיכָל, נִגְזְרָה גְּזֵרָה עַל רַבָּן גַּמְלִיאֵל לַהֲרִיגָה. [9]בָּא אוֹתוֹ הֶגְמוֹן וְעָמַד בְּבֵית הַמִּדְרָשׁ, וְאָמַר: [10]׳בַּעַל הַחוֹטֶם מִתְבַּקֵּשׁ, בַּעַל הַחוֹטֶם מִתְבַּקֵּשׁ׳. [11]שָׁמַע רַבָּן גַּמְלִיאֵל. אֲזַל טָשָׁא מִינַּיְיהוּ.

LITERAL TRANSLATION

[1]They said: When the Temple was destroyed the first time, that day was the ninth of Av, and it was the day following Shabbat, and it was the year following the Sabbatical Year, [2]and it was the *mishmar* of Jehoiarib, and the Levites were saying the song and standing on their platform. [3]And what song were they saying? [4]'And He brought upon them their own iniquity, and He will cut them off in their own wickedness.' [5]And they did not have time to say: 'The Lord our God will cut them off,' before the heathens came and captured them. And similarly the second time."

[6]"Betar was captured." [This is] a tradition.

[7]"The city was plowed up." [8]It was taught: "When Turnus Rufus the wicked plowed up the Temple, a decree was decreed against Rabban Gamliel for execution. [9]A certain general came and stood in the Academy, and said: [10]'The man with the nose is being sought, the man with the nose is being sought.' [11]Rabban Gamliel heard. He went [and] hid from them.

RASHI

וחובה על ידי חייב — היינו תשעה באב, דרגילין להיות בו רעות. הכי גרסינן — מגלגלין זכות על ידי זכאי. מוצאי שבת — יום ראשון. מוצאי שביעית — שמינית. **דוכן** — מקום עשוי כעין אילטבא, ועליו לוים עומדין לשורר. **וישב עליהם את אונם וברעתם יצמיתם ה' אלהינו** — במזמור "אל נקמות ה'" והוא שיר של יום רביעי. והאי דאמרי ליה ביום ראשון — איליא בעלמא הוה דנפל בפומייהו, כדאמרינן בערכין (יב,א). פירוש איליא — קינה, שכן תרגום יונתן בן עוזיאל "שא קינה" (יחזקאל כח) — טול איליא. וכמו "אלי כבתולה חגורת שק על בעל נעוריה" (יואל א) שפירושו: קונני וכו׳. **נחרשה העיר** — כדכתיב (מיכה ג) "ציון שדה תחרש", שנחרשה כולה ונעשית כשדה חרושה. **בעל החוטם** — בעל קומה וצורה, לשון אחר: גדול הדור. **מתבקש** — ליהרג, ברמז אמר ליה, שלא יכירו בו אנשי המלך. **טשא** = נחבא, כמו "טשו במערתא" (שבת לג,ב). **אזל** — האדון אצל רבן גמליאל בצנעא.

BACKGROUND

וּמָה שִׁירָה הָיוּ אוֹמְרִים And what song were they singing? *Rashi* notes that this Psalm is the "Psalm of the day" for Wednesday, the Psalm that accompanied the daily sacrifice and that is still recited in synagogues during morning services, whereas the day when the Temple was destroyed was Sunday. However, reference is not to the Psalm of the day but to the Psalm they happened to be reciting then. Moreover, it is likely that, for several weeks prior to this, they had been unable to offer the daily sacrifice because of the famine, and when a sacrificial animal happened to become available, they offered it, without maintaining all of the regular rituals.

טוּרְנוּסְרוּפוּס Turnus Rufus. This was the name given by the Talmud to Tineius Rufus, the Roman governor of Judea at the time of the Bar Kokhba revolt, who took part in its brutal repression. The Talmud calls him טוּרְנוּסְרוּפוּס, meaning "the cruel tyrant" (from the Greek τύραννος, *tyrannos*). The Talmud also describes arguments he held with Rabbi Akiva, stating that it was he who later condemned Rabbi Akiva to be tortured to death. As mentioned here, he also commanded that the Temple Mount be plowed up, to symbolize its utter destruction.

נִגְזְרָה גְּזֵרָה עַל רַבָּן גַּמְלִיאֵל **A decree was decreed against Rabban Gamliel.** Chronologically this refers to the end of the Bar Kokhba revolt in 135 C.E. After a savage war involving a large number of losses, the Romans instituted many severe decrees against the Jews. Although members of the House of the Nasi were apparently not actively involved in the revolt, in the eyes of the authorities they were regarded as the leaders of the Jews, and political responsibility for what was happening in the country was laid at their door. For that reason the Nasi, Rabban Shimon ben Gamliel the First, was executed after the destruction of the Temple in 70 C.E.

בַּעַל הַחוֹטֶם The man with the nose. *Rashi* and others

TRANSLATION AND COMMENTARY

[1]The Roman general then **went to** Rabban Gamliel **in secret, and said to him: 'If I save you** from death, **will you bring me to the World-to-Come?'** [2]Rabban Gamliel **said to him: 'Yes.'** Not entirely convinced, [3]the Roman general **said to him: 'Swear to me.'** [4]Rabban Gamliel **swore to** the general that he would be rewarded with entry to the World-to-Come for rescuing him. The Roman general then **went up to the roof, fell** to the ground, **and died.** [5]The decree of execution which had been issued against Rabban Gamliel was immediately canceled, for the Romans **had a tradition that when** they **issued a decree and one of** the advisors who advocated the decree **died, they would cancel the decree,** fearing that the advisor's death was a sign that it had been unwise. [6]**A heavenly voice** then **went forth and proclaimed: 'The** Roman **general** who saved Rabban Gamliel **is** indeed **designated for life in the World-to-Come.'"**

תָּנוּ רַבָּנַן [7]The Gemara continues with a Baraita, in which **our Rabbis taught: "When the Temple was being destroyed for the first time, groups of young priests gathered together with the Temple keys in their hands.** [8]**They went up to the roof of the Temple,** which had already been set on fire, **and said before God:** [9]**'Master of the Universe! Since we have not been worthy of being faithful treasurers** of the Temple, **let the** Temple **keys be handed over to You.'** [10]The young priests then **threw** the keys **upwards, and something like the palm of a hand came forth to receive** the keys. [11]Relieved of their responsibilities, the young priests then **jumped** from the roof of the Temple **and fell** directly **into the fire** that by then had spread to the entire building. [12]And concerning them the Prophet Isaiah lamented [Isaiah 22:1-2]: 'The burden of the Valley of Vision. [13]What ails you now, that you have all gone up to the roofs? You that were full of uproar, a tumultuous **city, a joyous city, your slain are not slain** with the sword, nor dead in war.' The Prophet Isaiah speaks here of the young priests who went up to the roof of the Temple after it had already been overrun by the enemy. These priests were not killed in battle, but met their deaths when they jumped into the flames raging beneath them. [14]**So too regarding the Holy One, blessed be He, the verse says** [Isaiah 22:5]: 'For it is a day of trouble, and of trampling, and of confusion for the Lord God of hosts in the Valley of Vision,

[1]אֲזַל לְגַבֵּיהּ בְּצִנְעָא. אֲמַר לֵיהּ: ׳אִי מַצֵילְנָא לָךְ, מַיְיתִית לִי לְעָלְמָא דְּאָתֵי?׳ [2]אֲמַר לֵיהּ: ׳הֵן׳. [3]אֲמַר לֵיהּ: ׳אִשְׁתַּבַּע לִי׳. [4]אִשְׁתַּבַּע לֵיהּ. סְלֵיק לְאִיגְּרָא, נָפֵיל, וּמִית. [5]וּגְמִירִי, דְּכִי גָּזְרִי גְּזֵירְתָא וּמִית חַד מִינַּיְיהוּ, מְבַטְּלִי לִגְזֵרַתַיְיהוּ. [6]יָצְתָה בַּת קוֹל וְאָמְרָה: ׳אוֹתוֹ הֶגְמוֹן מְזוּמָּן לְחַיֵּי הָעוֹלָם הַבָּא׳״.
[7]תָּנוּ רַבָּנַן: ״מִשֶּׁחָרַב הַבַּיִת בָּרִאשׁוֹנָה, נִתְקַבְּצוּ כִּיתּוֹת כִּיתּוֹת שֶׁל פִּרְחֵי כְהוּנָּה וּמַפְתְּחוֹת הַהֵיכָל בְּיָדָן. [8]וְעָלוּ לְגַג הַהֵיכָל וְאָמְרוּ לְפָנָיו: [9]׳רִבּוֹנוֹ שֶׁל עוֹלָם! הוֹאִיל וְלֹא זָכִינוּ לִהְיוֹת גִּזְבָּרִין נֶאֱמָנִים, יִהְיוּ מַפְתְּחוֹת מְסוּרוֹת לְךָ׳. [10]וּזְרָקוּם כְּלַפֵּי מַעְלָה, וְיָצְתָה כְּעֵין פִּיסַּת יָד וְקִיבְּלָתָן מֵהֶם. [11]וְהֵם קָפְצוּ וְנָפְלוּ לְתוֹךְ הָאוּר. [12]וַעֲלֵיהֶן קוֹנֵן יְשַׁעְיָהוּ הַנָּבִיא: ׳מַשָּׂא גֵּיא חִזָּיוֹן. [13]מַה לָּךְ אֵפוֹא, כִּי עָלִית כֻּלָּךְ לַגַּגּוֹת? תְּשֻׁאוֹת מְלֵאָה, עִיר הוֹמִיָּה, קִרְיָה עַלִּיזָה, חֲלָלַיִךְ לֹא חַלְלֵי חֶרֶב, וְלֹא מֵתֵי מִלְחָמָה׳. [14]אַף בְּהַקָּדוֹשׁ בָּרוּךְ הוּא נֶאֱמַר:

LITERAL TRANSLATION

[1]He went to him secretly. He said to him: 'If I save you, will you bring me to the World-to-Come?' [2]He said to him: 'Yes.' [3]He said to him: 'Swear to me.' [4]He swore to him. He went up to the roof, fell, and died. [5]And there is a tradition that when they decree a decree and one of them dies, they cancel their decree. [6]A [heavenly] voice went forth and said: 'That general is designated for life in the World-to-Come.'"

[7]Our Rabbis taught: "After the Temple was destroyed for the first time, groups of young priests gathered together with the keys of the Sanctuary in their hands. [8]And they went up to the roof of the Sanctuary, and said before Him: [9]'Master of the Universe! Since we have not merited to be faithful treasurers, let the keys be handed over to You.' [10]And they threw them upwards, and something like the palm of a hand came forth and received them from them. [11]And they jumped and fell into the fire. [12]And concerning them the Prophet Isaiah laments: 'The burden of the Valley of Vision. [13]What ails you now, that you have all gone up to the roofs? You that were full of uproar, a tumultuous city, a joyous city, your slain are not slain with the sword, nor dead in war.' [14]So too regarding the Holy One, blessed be He, it is stated:

interpret this expression literally — a man with a big nose means someone especially prominent in his generation. Others, however, maintain that it is a play on words, and that the man with the nose is *Nasotus* in Latin, which is an allusion to the Hebrew *Nasi* (an elevated man, a prince or president), indicating that they were seeking the head of the Sanhedrin.

RASHI

ומית חד מינייהו — מן היועצין, וכסבורין שאירע להן על שהרעו לגזור. **גיא חזיון** — ירושלים, שהכל מסתכלין שם.

TRANSLATION AND COMMENTARY

a breaking down of walls and a shouting to the mountain.' God Himself shouted out and lamented when the walls of His Temple were broken down and the Temple Mount was made desolate."

מִשֶּׁנִּכְנָס אָב [1]We learned in the Mishnah: **"When** the month of **Av comes in, rejoicing is reduced.** Even though only the Ninth of Av is observed as a public fast-day commemorating the destruction of the two Temples and the various other national calamities that occurred on that day, expressions of joy must be diminished from the beginning of the month." [2]**Rav Yehudah the son of Rav Shmuel bar Shilat said in the name of Rav: Just as when** the month of **Av comes in, rejoicing is reduced,** [3]**so too when** the month of Adar **comes in, rejoicing is increased.** Just as the calamities that occurred on the Ninth of Av cast an air of gloom over the month, so too the miracle of Purim, which was performed on the fourteenth and fifteenth of Adar, invests the whole month with a joyful character.

[29B] אָמַר רַב פַּפָּא [4]**Rav Pappa said:** Since a good thing is brought about on a good day, and a bad thing is brought about on a bad day, it is **therefore** advisable that if **a Jew has litigation** pending **with a non-Jew,** he **should avoid him during** the month of **Av,** [5]**when** the Jew's **luck is bad, and he should make himself available** for the court proceedings **during** the month of **Adar, when his luck is good.** If a Jew is forced to sue a non-Jew in a non-Jewish court, or to respond there to a suit brought against him by a non-Jew, it is recommended that he do so during the month of Adar, which is a time of good fortune for the Jewish people, and not during the month of Av, when numerous calamities befell it.

לָתֵת לָכֶם אַחֲרִית וְתִקְוָה [6]Having cited a ruling reported by Rav Yehudah the son of Rav Shmuel bar Shilat in the name of Rav, the Gemara now offers another statement with a similar chain of tradition. Scripture says (Jeremiah 29:10-11): "For thus says the Lord, that after seventy years are accomplished in Babylon I will take heed of you, and I will perform My good word toward you, to cause you to return to this place. For I know the thoughts that I think toward you, says the Lord, thoughts of peace, and not of evil, **to give you a**

'מְקַרְקַר קִר וְשׁוֹעַ אֶל הָהָר'". [1]"מִשֶּׁנִּכְנָס אָב, מְמַעֲטִין בְּשִׂמְחָה, וכו'". [2]אָמַר רַב יְהוּדָה בְּרֵיהּ דְּרַב שְׁמוּאֵל בַּר שִׁילַת מִשְּׁמֵיהּ דְּרַב: כְּשֵׁם שֶׁמִּשֶּׁנִּכְנָס אָב מְמַעֲטִין בְּשִׂמְחָה, [3]כָּךְ מִשֶּׁנִּכְנָס אֲדָר מַרְבִּין בְּשִׂמְחָה.

[29B] [4]אָמַר רַב פַּפָּא: הִלְכָּךְ בַּר יִשְׂרָאֵל דְּאִית לֵיהּ דִּינָא בַּהֲדֵי נָכְרִי לִישְׁתַּמֵּיט מִינֵּיהּ בְּאָב, [5]דְּרִיעַ מַזָּלֵיהּ, וְלִימְצִי נַפְשֵׁיהּ בַּאֲדָר, דְּבָרִיא מַזָּלֵיהּ. [6]"לָתֵת לָכֶם אַחֲרִית וְתִקְוָה".

LITERAL TRANSLATION

'A breaking down of walls and a shouting to the mountain.'"

[1]"When Av comes in, we reduce rejoicing, etc." [2]Rav Yehudah the son of Rav Shmuel bar Shilat said in the name of Rav: Just as when Av comes in we reduce rejoicing, [3]so too when Adar comes in we increase rejoicing.

[29B] [4]Rav Pappa said: Therefore a Jew who has litigation with a non-Jew should avoid him during Av, [5]when his luck is bad, and he should present himself during Adar, when his luck is good.

[6]"To give you a future and a hope."

RASHI

ניזיל בהדיה — בערכאות שלהן. **ונתתי לכם אחרית ותקוה** — איידי דאיירי רב יהודה לעיל, נקיט ואזיל. **דקלים** — להתפרנס מהן, שיש מהן בבבל הרבה, כדאמרינן בפרק קמא (ט,ב): עולא איקלע לבבל חזא מלא צנא דתמרי כו'.

NOTES

מִשֶּׁנִּכְנָס אֲדָר מַרְבִּין בְּשִׂמְחָה **When Adar comes in we increase rejoicing.** *Rashi* and most Rishonim explain that the joyful character of the month of Adar stems from the miracle of Purim, which was performed on behalf of the Jewish people during that month. *Sfat Emet* suggests that, just as expressions of gladness are restricted from the beginning of the month of Av as a reminder of the destruction of the Temple, which took place in that month, so too is rejoicing increased from the beginning of the month of Adar, because it was then that they began to collect the shekalim for the Temple and the sacrificial service.

HALAKHAH

מִשֶּׁנִּכְנָס אָב, מְמַעֲטִין בְּשִׂמְחָה **When Av comes in, we reduce rejoicing.** "When the month of Av comes in, expressions of rejoicing are reduced. Thus, there is a reduction of business activity and a halt to the construction of buildings which are erected for a joyous purpose. For this reason, there are those who refrain from eating meat and drinking wine from the first of Av. This is the custom of Ashkenazim." (*Shulḥan Arukh, Oraḥ Ḥayyim* 551:1,9.)

בַּר יִשְׂרָאֵל דְּאִית לֵיהּ דִּינָא **A Jew who has litigation with a non-Jew.** "A Jew who has litigation pending with a non-Jew should try to avoid court proceedings during the month of Av (or at least until after the Ninth of Av; *Korban Netanel*), following Rav Pappa." (Ibid., 551:1.)

TRANSLATION AND COMMENTARY

future and a hope." [1]**Rav Yehudah the son of Shmuel bar Shelat said in the name of Rav:** The "future" and the "hope" mentioned here **are** allusions to **palm trees and linen garments.** During their captivity, they would maintain themselves on the profits from their orchards of palm trees and would clothe themselves in linen garments.

וַיֹּאמֶר [2]The Gemara now cites another exposition of a Biblical verse, reported with the same chain of tradition. When Jacob received the blessing from his father Isaac, Isaac asked Jacob to come near and to kiss him (Genesis 27:27), and the verse continues: **"And he said: See, the smell of my son is like the smell of a field which the Lord has blessed."** [3]**Rav Yehudah the son of Rav Shmuel bar Shilat said in the name of Rav:** Isaac meant to say that his son's smell was **like the smell of a field of apples.**

שַׁבָּת [4]Our Mishnah continues: "Beginning on the Sunday of **the week during which the Ninth of Av falls, it is forbidden to cut one's hair or to wash laundry."** The Amoraim disagree about the scope of the Mishnah's ruling. [5]**Rav Naḥman said:** The Sages **only taught that it is forbidden to wash laundry** during the week of the Ninth of Av if the person wishes **to wear the** clean **clothing** before the Ninth of Av, [6]**but** if he wishes to **wash laundry** during the week of the Ninth of Av **and to set** the clean clothing **aside** until after the Ninth of Av, he **is permitted** to do so. [7]**But Rav Sheshet said: Even** if a person wishes **to wash laundry** during the week of the Ninth of Av **and to set** the clean clothing **aside** to be worn after the Ninth of Av, it **is forbidden** to do so, for by occupying himself with his laundry, the person demonstrates that he has diverted his attention from the calamities that befell the Jewish people on the Ninth of Av.

אָמַר רַב שֵׁשֶׁת [8]**Rav Sheshet added: Know my opinion is true** — that laundering clothing is forbidden during the week preceding the Ninth of Av, even if the clean garments are not to be worn until after the Ninth of Av — [9]**for the launderers** employed **in the house of Rav were** absolutely **idle** during the week of the Ninth of Av.

מְתִיב רַב הַמְנוּנָא [10]**Rav Hamnuna raised an objection** against the ruling of Rav Naḥman from our Mishnah, which stated: "If the Ninth of Av falls on a Friday, doing laundry is forbidden all week, but **on Thursday**

[1]אָמַר רַב יְהוּדָה בְּרֵיהּ דְּרַב שְׁמוּאֵל בַּר שִׁילַת מִשְּׁמֵיהּ דְּרַב: אֵלּוּ דְּקָלִים וּכְלֵי פִשְׁתָּן. [2]״וַיֹּאמֶר: רְאֵה, רֵיחַ בְּנִי כְּרֵיחַ שָׂדֶה אֲשֶׁר בֵּרְכוֹ ה׳״. [3]אָמַר רַב יְהוּדָה בְּרֵיהּ דְּרַב שְׁמוּאֵל בַּר שִׁילַת מִשְּׁמֵיהּ דְּרַב: כְּרֵיחַ שָׂדֶה שֶׁל תַּפּוּחִים.

[4]״שַׁבָּת שֶׁחָל תִּשְׁעָה בְּאָב לִהְיוֹת בְּתוֹכָהּ, אֲסוּרִין לְסַפֵּר וּלְכַבֵּס״. [5]אָמַר רַב נַחְמָן: לֹא שָׁנוּ אֶלָּא לְכַבֵּס וְלִלְבּוֹשׁ, [6]אֲבָל לְכַבֵּס וּלְהַנִּיחַ מוּתָּר. [7]וְרַב שֵׁשֶׁת אָמַר: אֲפִילּוּ לְכַבֵּס וּלְהַנִּיחַ אָסוּר.

[8]אָמַר רַב שֵׁשֶׁת: תֵּדַע, [9]דְּבַטְלִי קַצְּרֵי דְּבֵי רַב.

[10]מְתִיב רַב הַמְנוּנָא: ״בַּחֲמִישִׁי

LITERAL TRANSLATION

[1]Rav Yehudah the son of Shmuel bar Shilat said in the name of Rav: These are palm trees and linen garments.

[2]"And he said: See, the smell of my son is like the smell of a field which the Lord has blessed." [3]Rav Yehudah the son of Rav Shmuel bar Shilat said in the name of Rav: Like the smell of a field of apples.

[4]"The week in which the Ninth of Av falls, it is forbidden to cut hair or to wash laundry." [5]Rav Naḥman said: They only taught [that it is forbidden] to wash laundry and to wear [the clothes], [6]but to wash laundry and to set [it] aside is permitted. [7]But Rav Sheshet said: Even to wash laundry and to set [it] aside is forbidden.

[8]Rav Sheshet said: Know [that this is true], [9]for the launderers in the house of Rav were idle.

[10]Rav Hamnuna raised an objection: "On Thursday

RASHI

ניזול בהדיה — בערכאות שלהן. **ונתתי לכם אחרית ותקוה** — איידי דאיירי רב יהודה לעיל, נקיט ואזיל. **דקלים** — להתפרנס מהן, שיש מהן בבבל הרבה, כדאמרינן בפרק קמא (ט,ב): עולא איקלע לבבל חזא מלא צנא דתמרי כו׳.

BACKGROUND

דְּקָלִים וּכְלֵי פִשְׁתָּן Palm trees and linen garments. These two items seem to have been chosen because they can be bought without a large investment and can be used for a long time without large expenditure. Palm trees do not demand a great deal of attention, and in a country like Babylonia they usually have enough water and do not need to be irrigated. They also give nourishing fruit for a long time. Similarly, linen garments, always useful, were manufactured and sold by the Jews of Babylonia.

שָׂדֶה שֶׁל תַּפּוּחִים A field of apples. *Tosafot* was surprised by this comparison. The Sages based it on the local variety of apple (סוּבָּרִי), which turns yellow when it ripens and whose fruit is sweet and juicy. This variety has a strong and pleasant fragrance.

LANGUAGE (RASHI)

פורלו״ר (correct reading: פול״ר). From the Old French *foler,* meaning "a launderer."

NOTES

דְּקָלִים וּכְלֵי פִשְׁתָּן Palm trees and linen garments. *Rashi* explains that palm trees served as the people of Israel's "future and hope" during their seventy-year period of exile in Babylonia, because they supported themselves from the fruit of these palms. Indeed, several Talmudic sources indicate that palm trees served as an important source of income for Babylonian Jewry. *Maharsha* explains that palm trees and linen garments are singled out here as the "future and hope" of the Jewish people during its exile because both last an especially long time.

דְּבַטְלִי קַצְּרֵי דְּבֵי רַב The launderers in the house of Rav were idle. According to a Geonic source, the term בֵּי רַב, which usually refers to a Talmudic academy (lit., "the House of the Master"), should be understood here as a reference to the House of the Exilarch (lit., "the House of the great one").

מוּתָּרִים מִפְּנֵי כְּבוֹד הַשַּׁבָּת״. [1]לְמַאי? [2]אִילֵימָא לְכַבֵּס וְלִלְבּוֹשׁ, [3]מַאי כְּבוֹד שַׁבָּת אִיכָּא? [4]אֶלָּא, לְהַנִּיחַ. [5]וּבַחֲמִישִׁי הוּא דְּשָׁרֵי, [6]אֲבָל הַשַּׁבָּת כּוּלָּהּ אָסוּר!

[7]לְעוֹלָם, לְכַבֵּס וְלִלְבּוֹשׁ, [8]וּכְשֶׁאֵין לוֹ אֶלָּא חָלוּק אֶחָד. [9]דְּאָמַר רַב אַסִּי אָמַר רַבִּי יוֹחָנָן: מִי שֶׁאֵין לוֹ אֶלָּא חָלוּק אֶחָד מוּתָּר לְכַבְּסוֹ בְּחוּלוֹ שֶׁל מוֹעֵד.

[10]אִיתְּמַר נַמִי: אָמַר רַבִּי בִּנְיָמִין אָמַר רַבִּי אֶלְעָזָר: [11]לֹא שָׁנוּ אֶלָּא לְכַבֵּס וְלִלְבּוֹשׁ, [12]אֲבָל לְהַנִּיחַ מוּתָּר.

LITERAL TRANSLATION

they are permitted in honor of Shabbat." [1]For what? [2]If we say to wash laundry and to wear [the clothes], [3]what honor of Shabbat is there? [4]Rather, [it must mean] to set [the clothes] aside. [5]And it is on Thursday that it is permitted, [6]but the entire week it is forbidden!

[7]In fact, [it means] to wash laundry and to wear [the clothes], [8]and [only] where he has only one shirt. [9]For Rav Assi said in the name of Rabbi Yoḥanan: He who has only one shirt is permitted to launder it on the intermediate days of a Festival.

[10]It was also stated: Rabbi Binyamin said in the name of Rabbi Elazar: [11]They only taught [that it is forbidden] to wash laundry and wear [the clothes], [12]but to set [the clothes] aside is permitted.

TRANSLATION AND COMMENTARY

doing laundry **is permitted, so that** due **honor be accorded to Shabbat."** [1]**What** exactly is permitted on Thursday? [2]**If we say** that it is permitted **to wash laundry** on the Thursday of that week **and to wear the** clean **clothing** immediately, [3]**how is honor accorded to Shabbat** by wearing clean clothing on Thursday? [4]**Rather,** the Mishnah **must mean** that if the Ninth of Av falls on a Friday, it is permitted to do laundry on the Thursday of that week and **to set the** clean **garments aside** for Shabbat. [5]**And** the Mishnah states clearly that **it is** only **on Thursday that** doing laundry and setting the clean clothing aside until after the Ninth of Av **is permitted,** [6]**implying that** during **the rest of the week** doing laundry **is forbidden,** even if the clean garments are set aside to be worn only after the Ninth of Av. This implication contradicts the ruling of Rav Naḥman!

לְעוֹלָם [7]The Gemara rejects this argument: **In fact,** the Mishnah **means** to say that if the Ninth of Av falls on a Friday, it is permitted **to wash laundry** on the Thursday of that week **and to wear the** clean **clothing** on that day, even before the Ninth of Av. For if someone wishes to do laundry and to set the clean clothing aside until after the Ninth of Av, he is permitted to do so even on the other days of the week, as was argued by Rav Naḥman. And as for how wearing clean clothing on Thursday adds to the honor of Shabbat, [8]the Mishnah can be interpreted as referring to a person **who has only one shirt.** A person who has only one garment may wash his clothing on the Thursday before the Ninth of Av, otherwise he will not have anything clean to wear on Shabbat. [9]**For Rav Assi said in the name of Rabbi Yoḥanan: A person who has only one shirt is permitted to launder it on the intermediate days of a Festival**, even though it is ordinarily forbidden to do laundry on such days. The Rabbis decreed that laundry must not be done on any of the days between the first and the last days of Pesaḥ and Sukkot, lest a person intentionally postpone laundering his clothing until the intermediate days of the Festival and enter the holiday with soiled garments. But if a person has only one garment, he may wash it even on the intermediate days of a Festival. Just as a special allowance is granted to such a person on the intermediate days of a Festival, so too is a special allowance granted with respect to the prohibition against doing laundry during the week of the Ninth of Av.

אִיתְּמַר נַמִי [10]**It was also stated** that Rav Naḥman's viewpoint had been put forward by an earlier Amora, for **Rabbi Binyamin said in the name of Rabbi Elazar:** [11]The Sages **only taught** that it is forbidden **to wash laundry** during the week of the Ninth of Av if the person wishes **to wear the** clean **clothing** before the Ninth of Av, [12]**but** if he wishes **to** do the laundry and **to set the** clean **clothing aside** until after the Ninth of Av, he **is permitted** to do so.

RASHI

אילימא לכבס וללבוש — מיד בחמישי, מאי כבוד שבת איכא? **אלא** — לאו לכבס ולהניח עד השבת. **לעולם לכבס וללבוש** — מיד בחמישי. **ובמי שאין לו אלא חלוק אחד** — דאין לו להחליף. ומאי "מפני כבוד השבת", דאי לא מכבס השתא בחמישי — תו לא מצי לכבס ליה. **חולו של מועד** — שאין לו אלא חלוק אחד, דלא סגיא דלא מכבס מפני הכנימה. ואפילו כיבס לפני המועד — מותר לכבסה במועד.

LANGUAGE

חָלוּק Shirt. The precise meaning of this word is an undergarment that people wore next to the skin. Usually such shirts were made of linen in the form of a long tunic.

HALAKHAH

מִי שֶׁאֵין לוֹ אֶלָּא חָלוּק אֶחָד He who has only one shirt. "A person who has only one garment is permitted to launder it on the intermediate days of a Festival." (*Shulḥan Arukh, Oraḥ Ḥayyim* 534:1.)

LITERAL TRANSLATION

[1]They raised an objection: [2]"It is forbidden to wash laundry before the Ninth of Av, even to set [it] aside until after the Ninth of Av. [3]And our [fine] laundering is like their [plain] washing. [4]But linen garments do not have [fine] laundering." [5]It is a refutation.

[6]Rav Yitzḥak bar Giyyore sent in the name of Rabbi Yoḥanan: Although they said [that] linen garments

[1]מֵיתִיבִי: [2]"אָסוּר לְכַבֵּס לִפְנֵי תִשְׁעָה בְּאָב, אֲפִילּוּ לְהַנִּיחַ לְאַחַר תִּשְׁעָה בְּאָב. [3]וְגִיהוּץ שֶׁלָּנוּ כְּכִיבּוּס שֶׁלָּהֶן. [4]וּכְלֵי פִשְׁתָּן אֵין בָּהֶם מִשּׁוּם גִּהוּץ". [5]תְּיוּבְתָּא.

[6]שְׁלַח רַב יִצְחָק בַּר גִּיּוֹרֵי מִשְּׁמֵיהּ דְּרַבִּי יוֹחָנָן: אַף עַל פִּי שֶׁאָמְרוּ כְּלֵי פִשְׁתָּן אֵין בָּהֶם

RASHI

וגיהוץ שלנו — אינו יפה אלא ככיבוס שלהן, ואסור לגהץ לפני תשעה באב אפילו להניח לאחר תשעה באב, אבל כיבוס שלנו — מותר. **כלי פשתן אין בהן** — ליאסר משום גיהוץ, אלא בכלי מילת, *לושקי״י בלעז.

TRANSLATION AND COMMENTARY

מֵיתִיבִי [1]**An objection was raised** against this position from a Baraita, which stated: [2]**"It is forbidden to wash laundry** during the week **before the Ninth of Av, even** if the person plans **to set** the clean clothing **aside** and not wear it **until after the Ninth of Av.** Doing laundry is forbidden during that week only if it achieves a certain level of cleanness. [3]Plain washing does not achieve the same level of cleanness here in Babylonia as it does in Eretz Israel. It is only **our fine laundry work,** accomplished by scrubbing garments with abrasive stones, which achieves a level of cleanness **comparable** to that attained by **their plain washing.** Thus plain washing is forbidden during the week of the Ninth of Av in Eretz Israel but not in Babylonia. In Babylonia, only fine laundry work is forbidden during that week, even if the clean clothing is to be set aside and not worn until after the Ninth of Av. [4]**But,** in any event, **linen garments do not** attain a high level of cleanness even if they undergo the process of **fine laundry work** practiced in Babylonia. Thus, regarding linen garments, even fine laundry work is permitted during the week of the Ninth of Av." The Baraita states explicitly that laundry may not be done during the week of the Ninth of Av, even if the clothing is not to be worn until after the Ninth of Av, and this surely contradicts the rulings of Rav Naḥman and Rabbi Elazar!

תְּיוּבְתָּא [5]The Gemara concludes: This Baraita **is** indeed **a** conclusive **refutation** of the viewpoints of Rav Naḥman and Rabbi Elazar.

שְׁלַח [6]**Rav Yitzḥak bar Giyyore sent** the following ruling **in the name of Rabbi Yoḥanan: Although** the Sages **said that linen garments do not** attain a high level of cleanness even if they undergo the process

LANGUAGE

גִּיהוּץ **Laundering.** In ancient times, at the end of the laundering process, garments were given a finishing wash in water containing detergents, and they were scrubbed with soft stones. In Eretz Israel the water was more suitable for laundering, and better detergents were available, so that the first laundering in Eretz Israel produced garments as clean as did the more complex laundering process in Babylonia. However, linen garments were not finished in this way, and finishing was not so significant with respect to linen. For certain types of dirt do not cling to it and are not absorbed as with woolen garments. Hence, even if linen garments were given a finishing wash, it would not improve the results very much.

LANGUAGE (RASHI)

לושקי״י* From the Old French *lischier,* meaning "to iron clothes."

NOTES

גִּיהוּץ שֶׁלָּנוּ כְּכִיבּוּס שֶׁלָּהֶן **And our fine laundering is like their plain washing.** The Rishonim deal at length with the different aspects of washing clothes mentioned here in the Gemara. Our commentary follows *Rashi, Ra'avad,* and others, who explain that when the Gemara says that "our fine laundering is like their plain washing," it means that whereas plain washing is forbidden during the week of the Ninth of Av in Eretz Israel, such washing is permitted during that period in Babylonia, for only fine laundry work is forbidden there. As for the difference between Eretz Israel and Babylonia, most explain that the water in Eretz Israel or the process of laundering practiced there was superior to the water or laundering process found in Babylonia. Thus the level of cleanness achieved in Eretz Israel through simple washing could be achieved in Babylonia only through fine laundry work, i.e., by scrubbing the garments with abrasive stones. (The Rishonim disagree about whether plain washing is permitted in all communities outside Eretz Israel, or only in Babylonia; see Halakhah.) *Arukh* suggests that plain washing in Eretz Israel achieved the same level of cleanness as the fine laundry work in Babylonia because the garments in Eretz Israel were made of thinner fabrics, which were easier to launder.

Hashlamah, Mikhtam and others interpret the statement, "our fine laundering is like their plain washing," differently: The fine laundry work which we do now, after the initial washing process, is like the plain washing that was done by earlier generations. Just as their plain washing was forbidden during the week of the Ninth of Av, the fine laundry work we do now is also forbidden. Thus the text is not teaching that plain washing is permitted anywhere during the week of the Ninth of Av. Instead, it is teaching that our fine laundry work is forbidden during the week of the Ninth of Av, even if it is applied to clothing that underwent plain washing the week before.

כְּלֵי פִשְׁתָּן אֵין בָּהֶם מִשּׁוּם גִּהוּץ **But linen garments do not have fine laundering.** *Ritva* explains that regarding linen garments, even fine laundry work is permitted during the week of the Ninth of Av, because linen garments do not emerge from the fine laundering process looking like new

HALAKHAH

אָסוּר לְכַבֵּס לִפְנֵי תִשְׁעָה בְּאָב **One is forbidden to wash laundry before the Ninth of Av.** "During the week of the Ninth of Av, it is forbidden to cut hair or to wash laundry. Laundry is forbidden that week, even if the person does not intend to wear the clean clothing until after the Ninth of Av, and even if he has only one garment. Similarly, it is forbidden to wear freshly washed clothing or to use freshly washed linen, even if they were laundered before the week of the Ninth of Av." (*Shulḥan Arukh, Oraḥ Ḥayyim* 551:3.)

גִּהוּץ וְכִיבּוּס **Fine laundering and plain washing.** "Our plain washing is permitted during the week of the Ninth of Av,

TRANSLATION AND COMMENTARY

of **fine laundry work** practiced in Babylonia, [1]**it is still forbidden to wear** linen garments that have undergone that process **during the week of the Ninth of Av.**

אָמַר רַב [2]There is a disagreement among the early Amoraim about the prohibitions that apply during the week of the Ninth of Av. **Rav said:** The prohibitions against laundering clothing and cutting hair during the week of the Ninth of Av **apply only before** the Ninth of Av, [3]**but after** the Ninth of Av these activities are **permitted.** [4]**But Shmuel said: Even after** the Ninth of Av, laundering clothing and cutting hair **are forbidden** until the end of the week.

מֵיתִיבִי [5]**An objection was raised** against the viewpoint of Shmuel from a Baraita, which states: "During **the week in which the Ninth of Av falls, it is forbidden to cut hair or to wash laundry,** [6]**but on Thursday** doing laundry **is permitted, so that** due **honor be accorded to Shabbat.** [7]**How so? If** the Ninth of Av **falls on Sunday,** [8]**it is permitted to wash laundry** during **the entire** preceding **week,** for that is not the week during which the Ninth of Av falls. [9]If the Ninth of Av falls **on Monday, Tuesday, Wednesday or Thursday,** then on the days **before** the Ninth of Av **it is forbidden** to do laundry or to cut hair, but on the days after the Ninth of Av these activities **are permitted.** [10]If the Ninth of Av **falls on Friday,** laundry is forbidden most of the week, but it is permitted to wash laundry on Thursday, so that due honor be accorded to Shabbat.

מִשּׁוּם גִּהוּץ, [1]אֲבָל אָסוּר לְלוֹבְשָׁן בְּשַׁבָּת שֶׁחָל תִּשְׁעָה בְּאָב לִהְיוֹת בְּתוֹכָהּ.
[2]אָמַר רַב: לֹא שָׁנוּ אֶלָּא לְפָנָיו, [3]אֲבָל לְאַחֲרָיו מוּתָּר. [4]וּשְׁמוּאֵל אָמַר: אֲפִילּוּ לְאַחֲרָיו נַמִּי אָסוּר.
[5]מֵיתִיבִי: ״שַׁבָּת שֶׁחָל תִּשְׁעָה בְּאָב לִהְיוֹת בְּתוֹכָהּ אָסוּר לְסַפֵּר וּלְכַבֵּס. [6]וּבַחֲמִישִׁי מוּתָּרִין מִפְּנֵי כְבוֹד הַשַּׁבָּת. [7]כֵּיצַד? חָל לִהְיוֹת בְּאֶחָד בְּשַׁבָּת, [8]מוּתָּר לְכַבֵּס כָּל הַשַּׁבָּת כּוּלָּהּ. [9]בְּשֵׁנִי, בִּשְׁלִישִׁי, בִּרְבִיעִי, וּבַחֲמִישִׁי, לְפָנָיו אָסוּר, לְאַחֲרָיו מוּתָּר. [10]חָל לִהְיוֹת בְּעֶרֶב שַׁבָּת, מוּתָּר לְכַבֵּס בַּחֲמִישִׁי, מִפְּנֵי כְבוֹד הַשַּׁבָּת.

LITERAL TRANSLATION

do not have [fine] laundering, [1]nevertheless it is forbidden to wear them in the week in which the Ninth of Av falls.

[2]Rav said: They only taught before it, [3]but afterwards it is permitted. [4]But Shmuel said: Even afterwards it is forbidden.

[5]They raised an objection: "The week in which the Ninth of Av falls, it is forbidden to cut hair or to wash laundry. [6]But on Thursday they are permitted in honor of Shabbat. [7]How so? [If] it falls on Sunday, [8]it is permitted to wash laundry the entire week. [9]On Monday, on Tuesday, on Wednesday, or on Thursday, before it it is forbidden, afterwards it is permitted. [10][If] it falls on Friday, it is permitted to wash laundry on Thursday in honor of Shabbat.

RASHI

לא שנו – שאסור ללובשו בשבוע שחל תשעה באב להיות בתוכה אלא בימים שלפני תשעה באב, שאם חל ביום רביעי – אסור ללובשו ראשון ושני ושלישי. **אבל לאחריו** – חמישי וששי ושביעי מותר. **חל להיות באחד בשבת מותר לכבס כל השבת כולה** – דהיינו לאחריו. **חל להיות בשני או בשלישי וברביעי ובחמישי כו׳.**

NOTES

as do woolen garments. *Hashlamah* writes that linen garments that have been washed by plain washing before the week of the Ninth of Av may undergo fine laundry work during the week of the Ninth of Av, provided that they are not to be worn until after the Ninth of Av. But they may not undergo fine laundry work during the week of the Ninth of Av if they are to be worn immediately.

חָל לִהְיוֹת בְּעֶרֶב שַׁבָּת **If it falls on Friday.** *Rabbenu Yehonatan* notes that this law was applicable only when Rosh Ḥodesh was established on the basis of the testimony of witnesses who sighted a sliver of the new moon, for only then was it possible for the Ninth of Av to fall on a Friday. Nowadays a fixed calendar is in use, according to which the Ninth of Av can never fall on a Friday.

HALAKHAH

but our fine laundry work is forbidden. Regarding linen garments, even our fine laundry work is permitted. But it is customary to forbid all laundry work during the week of the Ninth of Av, even plain washing and even linen garments, for the following reasons: Some authorities maintain that the plain washing of all countries with the exception of Babylonia is forbidden like the plain washing of Eretz Israel. Other authorities maintain that the plain washing mentioned in the Gemara refers to washing with water alone, and the fine laundry work refers to washing with water and soap. Thus all of our washing is forbidden, for all our laundry is done with soap (*Nimmukei Yosef*). *Rema* writes that it is the Ashkenazi custom to refrain from all laundry work from the first of the month of Av. But someone who has only one garment is permitted to wash it before the week of the Ninth of Av (*Mishnah Berurah*)." (*Shulḥan Arukh, Oraḥ Ḥayyim* 551:3.)

לְאַחֲרָיו מוּתָּר **Afterwards it is permitted.** "After the fast of the Ninth of Av is over, cutting one's hair and doing one's laundry are permitted immediately, following Rav. *Mishnah Berurah* notes that it is customary to refrain from engaging in these activities until midday on the tenth of Av." (Ibid., 551:4.)

[1]וְאִם לֹא כִּבֵּס בַּחֲמִישִׁי בְּשַׁבָּת, מוּתָּר לְכַבֵּס בְּעֶרֶב שַׁבָּת מִן הַמִּנְחָה וּלְמַעְלָה״.
[2]לָיֵיט עֲלָהּ אַבַּיֵי, וְאִיתֵימָא רַב אַחָא בַּר יַעֲקֹב, אַהָא.
[3]״חָל לִהְיוֹת בְּשֵׁנִי וּבַחֲמִישִׁי, קוֹרִין שְׁלֹשָׁה וּמַפְטִיר אֶחָד. [4]בִּשְׁלִישִׁי וּבִרְבִיעִי, קוֹרֵא אֶחָד וּמַפְטִיר אֶחָד. [5]רַבִּי יוֹסֵי אוֹמֵר: לְעוֹלָם קוֹרִין שְׁלֹשָׁה וּמַפְטִיר אֶחָד״. [6]תְּיוּבְתָּא דִּשְׁמוּאֵל!
[7]אָמַר לָךְ שְׁמוּאֵל: תַּנָּאֵי הִיא. [8]דְּתַנְיָא: ״תִּשְׁעָה בְּאָב שֶׁחָל לִהְיוֹת בְּשַׁבָּת, וְכֵן עֶרֶב תִּשְׁעָה בְּאָב שֶׁחָל לִהְיוֹת בְּשַׁבָּת, [9]אוֹכֵל וְשׁוֹתֶה כָּל צָרְכּוֹ, וּמַעֲלֶה עַל שׁוּלְחָנוֹ אֲפִילּוּ

LITERAL TRANSLATION

[1]And if he did not wash laundry on Thursday, he is permitted to wash laundry on Friday from [the time of] the afternoon service and onward."

[2]Abaye, and some say [that it was] Rav Aḥa bar Ya'akov, cursed for this.

[3]"[If] it falls on Monday or on Thursday, three read and one recites the Haftarah. [4]On Tuesday or on Wednesday, one reads and one recites the Haftarah. [5]Rabbi Yose says: In all cases three read and one recites the Haftarah." [6][This is] a refutation of Shmuel!

[7]Shmuel can say to you: It is [a dispute between] Tannaim. [8]For it was taught: "[If] the Ninth of Av falls on Shabbat, and similarly [if] the eve of the Ninth of Av falls on Shabbat, [9][a person] may eat and drink whatever he needs, and he may serve [food] on his table

TRANSLATION AND COMMENTARY

[1]**And if** the Ninth of Av falls on Friday and for some reason **a person did not wash** his **laundry on Thursday, he is permitted to do** his **laundry on Friday,** even though it is the Ninth of Av, provided that he begins **from the time of the afternoon service and onward."**

לָיֵיט עֲלָהּ אַבַּיֵי [2]The Gemara interrupts its presentation of the Baraita with the following note: Even though the Baraita permits it, **Abaye (and some say that it was Rav Aḥa bar Ya'akov) cursed** those who acted in **this** manner and did their laundry on the afternoon of the Ninth of Av which fell on a Friday.

חָל לִהְיוֹת בְּשֵׁנִי וּבַחֲמִישִׁי [3]The Gemara now resumes its citation of the Baraita: **"If the** Ninth of Av **falls on Monday or Thursday, three** people are called to **read** from the Torah, just as three people are called to read from the Torah on an ordinary Monday or Thursday, **and one** of those three **recites the Haftarah,** the portion from the Books of the Prophets which is read after the Torah reading. [4]If the Ninth of Av falls **on Tuesday or Wednesday, one** person is called to **read** from the Torah, **and that same** person **recites the Haftarah.** [5]**Rabbi Yose says: In all cases** — on whatever day of the week the Ninth of Av falls — **three** people are called to **read** from the Torah, **and one** of those three **recites the Haftarah."** [6]This Baraita serves as **a refutation** of the viewpoint **of Shmuel,** for it states explicitly that the prohibitions associated with the week of the Ninth of Av apply only on the days before the Ninth of Av, but after the Ninth of Av all the prohibited activities are once again permitted!

אָמַר לָךְ שְׁמוּאֵל [7]The Gemara rebuts this objection: **Shmuel can say to you** that the matter **is** the subject of **a dispute between Tannaim.** [8]**For it was taught** in a Baraita: **"If the Ninth of Av falls on Shabbat, and similarly if** the Ninth of Av falls on Sunday, so that **the eve of the Ninth of Av falls on Shabbat,** [9]**a person may eat and drink** on that Shabbat whatever he needs, and he may serve on his table a meal of the most lavish kind, **like the feast given**

RASHI

לייט עלה אביי ואיתימא רב אחא בר יעקב אהא — המכבס בתשעה באב, אפילו מן המנחה ולמעלה. ואדקאי בברייתא מפסיק לה למילתא, וקאמר: לייט עלה אביי כו׳. **חל להיות בשני כו׳** — סיפא דהיא ברייתא גופה היא. **ומפטיר** — מאותן שלשה אחרון מפטיר, מתוך שאין מוסיפין בחול יותר משלשה אנשים ולא בראש חדש על ארבעה, שאין לנו להוסיף אלא בשבת וביום טוב, כדמפרש במגילה (כא,א). ולפיכך קורין שלשה, דזמן ספר תורה הוא, ובלאו הכי הוו קרו שלשה, שהוא מתקנת עזרא לקרות בשני ובחמישי כהן ולוי וישראל. **קורא אחד ומפטיר אחד** — אחד קורא והוא עצמו המפטיר, קתני מיהת: לאחריו מותר, תיובתא דשמואל. **וכן ערב תשעה באב שחל להיות בשבת** — אינו מפסיק סעודתו, ואינו ממעט בתבשילין, אלא אוכל כל צרכו ומעלה על שולחנו אפילו כסעודת שלמה בשעתו, דפלוגתא היא במסכת גיטין בפרק [״מי שאחזו״] (סח,ב), דאיכא למאן דאמר: מלך והדיוט ומלך, ואיכא למאן דאמר: מלך והדיוט, כלומר, כשנטרד — שוב לא חזר למלכותו. לפיכך הוצרך לומר ״בשעתו״ — בשעת מלכו ותקפו, שהיה אוכל הוא ושריו ששים כור סולת כו׳.

HALAKHAH

קוֹרִין שְׁלֹשָׁה וּמַפְטִיר אֶחָד **Three read and one recites the Haftarah.** "On the Ninth of Av, three people are called up to read from the Torah, both in the morning and in the afternoon service, and the third person recites the Haftarah." (*Tur, Oraḥ Ḥayyim* 559.)

תִּשְׁעָה בְּאָב שֶׁחָל לִהְיוֹת בְּשַׁבָּת **If the Ninth of Av falls on Shabbat.** "If the Ninth of Av falls on Sunday or if it falls on Shabbat and is deferred until Sunday, one may eat meat and drink wine during the last meal before the fast, and one may even partake of a lavish meal, it being unnecessary to make any changes on account of the impending fast." (*Shulḥan Arukh, Oraḥ Ḥayyim* 552:10.)

BACKGROUND

כִּסְעוּדַּת שְׁלֹמֹה בְּשַׁעְתּוֹ Like the feast of Solomon in his time. According to *Rashi* this alludes to a story told in the Gemara about King Solomon: In the middle or toward the end of his reign, Solomon was exiled from his throne and lived almost as a beggar. Therefore the Gemara emphasizes the word בְּשַׁעְתּוֹ — "in his time" — here, meaning the time when he actually reigned. The Bible (1 Kings 5:2-3) describes the banquets that Solomon held for his courtiers every day.

TRANSLATION AND COMMENTARY

by King **Solomon in his time,** because the restrictions imposed on the Ninth of Av and on the eve of the Ninth of Av do not apply on Shabbat. [1] **It is forbidden to cut hair or to wash laundry from Rosh Hodesh until** after **the fast** of the Ninth of Av. [2] **This is the viewpoint of Rabbi Meir.** [3] **Rabbi Yehudah** disagrees and **says:** During **the entire month** of Av these activities **are forbidden.** [4] **Rabban Shimon ben Gamliel** adopts a third position and **says:** These activities **are forbidden only during the week** of the Ninth of Av." [5] **And** similarly **it was taught in another Baraita: "A person must observe** certain rites of **mourning** and must refrain from cutting his hair or doing laundry **from Rosh Hodesh until** after **the fast** of the Ninth of Av. [6] **This is the viewpoint of Rabbi Meir.** [7] **Rabbi Yehudah** disagrees and **says:** During **the entire month** of Av these activities **are forbidden.** [8] **Rabban Shimon ben Gamliel says:** These activities **are forbidden only during the week** of the Ninth of Av." Thus Shmuel can argue that he is following the Tannaitic opinion that laundering clothing and cutting hair are still forbidden until the end of the week of the Ninth of Av, whereas the anonymous Baraita quoted above may follow the Tannaitic opinion that those activities are forbidden only until the Ninth of Av.

כִּסְעוּדַּת שְׁלֹמֹה בְּשַׁעְתּוֹ. [1] וְאָסוּר לְסַפֵּר וּלְכַבֵּס מֵרֹאשׁ חֹדֶשׁ וְעַד הַתַּעֲנִית. [2] דִּבְרֵי רַבִּי מֵאִיר. [3] רַבִּי יְהוּדָה אוֹמֵר: כָּל הַחֹדֶשׁ כּוּלּוֹ אָסוּר. [4] רַבָּן שִׁמְעוֹן בֶּן גַּמְלִיאֵל אוֹמֵר: אֵינוֹ אָסוּר אֶלָּא אוֹתָהּ שַׁבָּת בִּלְבַד". [5] וְתַנְיָא אִידָךְ: "וְנוֹהֵג אֵבֶל מֵרֹאשׁ חֹדֶשׁ וְעַד הַתַּעֲנִית. [6] דִּבְרֵי רַבִּי מֵאִיר. [7] רַבִּי יְהוּדָה אוֹמֵר: כָּל הַחֹדֶשׁ כּוּלּוֹ אָסוּר. [8] רַבָּן שִׁמְעוֹן בֶּן גַּמְלִיאֵל אוֹמֵר: אֵינוֹ אָסוּר אֶלָּא אוֹתָהּ שַׁבָּת בִּלְבַד".

[9] אָמַר רַבִּי יוֹחָנָן: וּשְׁלָשְׁתָּן מִקְרָא אֶחָד דָּרְשׁוּ, [10] דִּכְתִיב: "וְהִשְׁבַּתִּי כָּל מְשׂוֹשָׂהּ, חַגָּהּ, חָדְשָׁהּ, וְשַׁבַּתָּהּ". [11] מַאן דְּאָמַר מֵרֹאשׁ חֹדֶשׁ וְעַד הַתַּעֲנִית [30A] מֵ"חַגָּהּ". [12] וּמַאן דְּאָמַר כּוּלּוֹ

LITERAL TRANSLATION

like the feast of Solomon in his time. [1] And it is forbidden to cut hair or to wash laundry from Rosh Hodesh until the fast. [2] [These are] the words of Rabbi Meir. [3] Rabbi Yehudah says: The entire month it is forbidden. [4] Rabban Shimon ben Gamliel says: It is forbidden only [in] that week alone." [5] And it was taught in another [Baraita]: "And he observes mourning from Rosh Hodesh until the fast. [6] [These are] the words of Rabbi Meir. [7] Rabbi Yehudah says: The entire month it is forbidden. [8] Rabban Shimon ben Gamliel says: It is forbidden only [in] that week alone."

[9] Rabbi Yohanan said: And the three of them expounded the same verse, [10] for it is written: "And I will bring all her mirth to an end, her feast-days, her months, and her Sabbaths." [11] The one who says from Rosh Hodesh until the fast [30A] [derives this] from "her feast-days." [12] And the one who says the entire [month]

RASHI

ועד התענית — אלמא דסבירא ליה לרבי מאיר לפניו אסור לאחריו מותר ורבי יהודה ורבן (גמליאל) [שמעון בן גמליאל] סבירא להו דאפילו לאחריו נמי אסור. **מחגה** — כלומר, יליף טעמא מן "חגה" דהיינו ראש חדש שנקרא חג, כדאמרינן לעיל (כט, ט): "קרא עלי מועד".

אָמַר רַבִּי יוֹחָנָן [9] Concerning this Tannaitic dispute, **Rabbi Yohanan said: The three** Tannaim who disagree about the prohibitions against cutting hair and doing laundry all **expounded the same verse,** each arriving at a different conclusion. [10] **For the verse says** (Hosea 2:13): **"And I will bring all her mirth to an end, her feast-days, her months, and her Sabbaths,** and all her appointed times." This verse alludes to the period of mourning that will be observed in commemoration of the destruction of the Temple, and speaks about feast-days, months, and Sabbaths. [11] Rabbi Meir, **who said** that laundry and haircuts are forbidden **from Rosh Hodesh until** after **the fast** of the Ninth of Av, [30A] **derives this** ruling **from** the expression **"her feast-days,"** which according to Rabbi Meir refers to Rosh Hodesh. [12] **And** Rabbi Yehudah, **who said** that these activities

NOTES

וְאָסוּר לְסַפֵּר וּלְכַבֵּס מֵרֹאשׁ חֹדֶשׁ וְעַד הַתַּעֲנִית And it is forbidden to cut hair or to wash laundry from Rosh Hodesh until the fast. The dispute regarding the prohibitions against doing laundry and cutting hair continued well beyond the Tannaitic period. The Jerusalem Talmud notes that different customs were followed in the various centers of Jewry in Eretz Israel — Tiberias, Sepphoris, and the cities of the South. Even though the Babylonian Talmud decides that the law is in accordance with the lenient aspects of the views of Rabban Shimon ben Gamliel and Rabbi Meir, many communities adopted some of the stringencies of the various Tannaitic positions.

מֵ"חַגָּהּ" From "her feast-days." Our commentary follows *Rashi,* who explains that Rosh Hodesh itself comes under the category of a feast-day, and thus the verse teaches us that the mourning rites commemorating the destruction of the Temple begin on Rosh Hodesh of Av. Other authorities suggest that the verse is informing us that the Ninth of Av

אָסוּר מֵ״חָדְשָׁהּ״. [1] וּמַאן דְּאָמַר כָּל הַשַּׁבָּת כּוּלָּהּ אָסוּר מִ״שַּׁבַּתָּהּ״.

[2] אָמַר רָבָא: הֲלָכָה כְּרַבָּן שִׁמְעוֹן בֶּן גַּמְלִיאֵל. [3] וְאָמַר רָבָא: הֲלָכָה כְּרַבִּי מֵאִיר. [4] וְתַרְוַיְיהוּ לְקוּלָּא, [5] וּצְרִיכָא. [6] דְּאִי אַשְׁמוּעִינַן הֲלָכָה כְּרַבִּי מֵאִיר, [7] הֲוָה אָמִינָא: אֲפִילּוּ מֵרֹאשׁ חֹדֶשׁ. [8] קָמַשְׁמַע לָן: הֲלָכָה כְּרַבָּן שִׁמְעוֹן בֶּן גַּמְלִיאֵל. [9] וְאִי אַשְׁמוּעִינַן הֲלָכָה כְּרַבָּן שִׁמְעוֹן בֶּן גַּמְלִיאֵל, [10] הֲוָה אָמִינָא: אֲפִילּוּ לְאַחֲרָיו. [11] קָמַשְׁמַע לָן: הֲלָכָה כְּרַבִּי מֵאִיר.

[12] ״עֶרֶב תִּשְׁעָה בְּאָב, לֹא יֹאכַל אָדָם שְׁנֵי תַבְשִׁילִין, כו׳״.

LITERAL TRANSLATION

it is forbidden [derives this] from "her months." [1] And the one who says the entire week it is forbidden [derives this] from "her Sabbaths."

[2] Rava said: The Halakhah is in accordance with Rabban Shimon ben Gamliel. [3] And Rava said: The Halakhah is in accordance with Rabbi Meir.

[4] And both of them are for leniency, [5] and it was necessary [to state both]. [6] For if he had informed us [that] the Halakhah is in accordance with Rabbi Meir, [7] I might have said: Even from Rosh Ḥodesh. [8] [Therefore] he informs us: The Halakhah is in accordance with Rabban Shimon ben Gamliel. [9] And if he had informed us [that] the Halakhah is in accordance with Rabban Shimon ben Gamliel, [10] I might have said: Even afterwards. [11] [Therefore] he informs us: The Halakhah is in accordance with Rabbi Meir.

[12] "[On] the eve of the Ninth of Av, a person may not eat two cooked dishes, etc."

TRANSLATION AND COMMENTARY

are forbidden during **the entire month** of Av, **derives this** from the words **"her months."** [1] **And** Rabban Shimon ben Gamliel, **who said** that these activities **are forbidden** during **the entire week** of the Ninth of Av, **derives this from** the expression **"her Sabbaths."**

אָמַר רָבָא [2] The Gemara now cites two rulings issued by the same authority regarding this Tannaitic dispute. **Rava said: The Halakhah is in accordance with Rabban Shimon ben Gamliel,** who said that laundry and haircuts are forbidden during the week of the Ninth of Av. [3] **And Rava** also **said: The Halakhah is in accordance with Rabbi Meir,** who said that these activities are forbidden from Rosh Ḥodesh Av until after the fast of the Ninth of Av.

וְתַרְוַיְיהוּ לְקוּלָּא [4] The Gemara now explains that there is no contradiction between these two rulings. Rava is saying that the Halakhah is in accordance with **both of them** — Rabban Shimon ben Gamliel and Rabbi Meir — **with respect to the lenient aspect** of each of their positions. The Halakhah follows Rabban Shimon ben Gamliel in that only during the week of the Ninth of Av are laundry and haircuts forbidden, but not before. And the Halakhah follows Rabbi Meir in that these activities are forbidden only on the days before the Ninth of Av, but are permitted afterwards. [5] The Gemara adds: **And it was necessary** for Rava **to issue both** rulings. [6] **For if** Rav **had** only **informed us that the Halakhah is in accordance with** the viewpoint of **Rabbi Meir,** [7] **I might** mistakenly **have said** that laundry and haircuts are forbidden **even from Rosh Ḥodesh** Av, for, according to Rabbi Meir, these prohibitions begin from the first day of the month. [8] **Therefore** it was necesessary for Rava to **inform us** that **the Halakhah is** also **in accordance with** the viewpoint of **Rabban Shimon ben Gamliel** that laundry and haircuts are forbidden only during the week of the Ninth of Av, but not before. [9] **And if** Rava **had** only **informed us that the Halakhah is in accordance with** the viewpoint of **Rabban Shimon ben Gamliel,** [10] **I might** mistakenly **have said** that laundry and haircuts are forbidden during the week of the Ninth of Av **even after** the Ninth of Av, for according to Rabban Shimon ben Gamliel these prohibitions apply during the entire week, both before and after the fast of the Ninth of Av. [11] **Therefore** it was necessary for Rava to **inform us** that the Halakhah is also **in accordance with** the viewpoint of **Rabbi Meir** that laundry and haircuts are not forbidden on the days following the Ninth of Av.

עֶרֶב תִּשְׁעָה בְּאָב [12] We learned in our Mishnah: "On the eve of the Ninth of Av, a person may not eat two

RASHI

הלכה כרבי מאיר — דלפניו אסור ולאחריו מותר. **הלכה כרבן שמעון בן גמליאל** — דאין איסור נוהג אלא באותה שבת. **תרוייהו לקולא** — כדמפרש ואזיל, דבלפניו מוקי הלכה כרבי מאיר — דלפניו ולא לאחריו, ובאותה שבת — אבל קודם אותה שבת אפילו לפניו מותר.

NOTES

is treated as if it were the final day of the "feast" of Sukkot, which is celebrated for eight days. From this it follows that some of the mourning rites must be observed during the eight days preceding the Ninth of Av.

לֹא יֹאכַל אָדָם שְׁנֵי תַבְשִׁילִין **A person may not eat two cooked dishes.** The Rishonim discuss at length the definition of "cooked dishes" in connection with this prohibition, for this concept is found in several areas of

BACKGROUND

מִשֵּׁשׁ שָׁעוֹת וּלְמַעְלָה From six hours and onward. In Talmudic times the day was divided into twelve equal "hours" from sunrise to sunset. These are known today as שָׁעוֹת זְמַנִּיּוֹת, "provisional hours," for they grow longer and shorter in proportion to the length of the day. The hours are counted exactly from sunrise, so that the sixth hour is precisely the astronomic meridian.

סְעוּדָה הַמַּפְסִיק בָּהּ The meal in which he ceases eating. Special rulings apply to this meal, because it is eaten close to the beginning of the fast, whereas earlier meals are regarded as ordinary ones. Practices associated with the impending fast are followed at the final meal before major fasts. The one before Yom Kippur is festive, whereas the one before the Ninth of Av is mournful, in preparation for this day of mourning.

TRANSLATION AND COMMENTARY

cooked dishes in the same meal." [1] **Rav Yehudah said:** The Mishnah's ruling **applies only from** the end of **the sixth hour** of the day **and onward,** i.e., after midday. [2] **But before the sixth hour,** eating two cooked dishes **is permitted.**

וְאָמַר רַב יְהוּדָה [3] The Gemara continues: **Rav Yehudah** also **said:** The Mishnah's ruling **applies only to the meal in which he ceases** eating, the last meal he eats before the fast. [4] **But during a meal in which he does not cease** to eat — a meal which the person does not expect to be his last meal before the beginning of the fast — eating two cooked dishes **is permitted.**

וְתַרְוַיְיהוּ לְקוּלָּא [5] The Gemara adds: Rabbi Yehudah's **two** rulings are to be understood together, **so that the lenient aspect** of each is followed. A person may not eat two cooked dishes after midday on the eve of the Ninth of Av, if he intends that meal to be his last before the fast. But in a meal eaten in the morning, or in a meal which is not intended to be the last of the day, two cooked dishes may indeed be eaten. [6] **And it was necessary** for Rav Yehudah **to issue both** rulings. [7] **For if** Rav Yehudah **had** only **informed us** that the prohibition against eating two cooked dishes is restricted **to the meal in which a person ceases eating,** [8] **I might** mistakenly **have said** that the prohibition applies **even** to a meal eaten **before the sixth hour** of the day, provided that it is intended to be the last meal before the fast. [9] Therefore it was necessary for Rav Yehudah to **inform us** that the prohibition applies only to a meal eaten **from the sixth hour** of the day **onward.** [10] **And if** Rav Yehudah **had** only **informed us** that the prohibition against eating two cooked dishes is restricted to a meal eaten **from the sixth hour** of the day **onward,** [11] **I might** mistakenly **have said** that the prohibition applies **even to a meal in which the person does not** intend to **cease eating,** provided that it is eaten during the afternoon. [12] **Therefore** it was necessary for Rav Yehudah to **inform us** that the prohibition applies only **to a meal in which the person ceases eating.**

[1] אָמַר רַב יְהוּדָה: לֹא שָׁנוּ אֶלָּא מִשֵּׁשׁ שָׁעוֹת וּלְמַעְלָה, [2] אֲבָל מִשֵּׁשׁ שָׁעוֹת וּלְמַטָּה מוּתָּר.

[3] וְאָמַר רַב יְהוּדָה: לֹא שָׁנוּ אֶלָּא בִּסְעוּדָה הַמַּפְסִיק בָּהּ, [4] אֲבָל בִּסְעוּדָה שֶׁאֵינוֹ מַפְסִיק בָּהּ, מוּתָּר.

[5] וְתַרְוַיְיהוּ לְקוּלָּא, [6] וּצְרִיכָא. [7] דְּאִי אַשְׁמְעִינַן בִּסְעוּדָה הַמַּפְסִיק בָּהּ, [8] הֲוָה אָמִינָא: אֲפִילּוּ מִשֵּׁשׁ שָׁעוֹת וּלְמַטָּה. [9] קָמַשְׁמַע לָן: מִשֵּׁשׁ שָׁעוֹת וּלְמַעְלָה. [10] וְאִי אַשְׁמְעִינַן מִשֵּׁשׁ שָׁעוֹת וּלְמַעְלָה, [11] הֲוָה אָמִינָא: אֲפִילּוּ בִּסְעוּדָה שֶׁאֵינוֹ מַפְסִיק בָּהּ. [12] קָמַשְׁמַע לָן בִּסְעוּדָה הַמַּפְסִיק בָּהּ.

LITERAL TRANSLATION

[1] Rav Yehudah said: They only taught from six hours and onward, [2] but from six hours and before it is permitted.

[3] And Rav Yehudah said: They only taught [this] regarding the meal in which he ceases [eating], [4] but regarding a meal in which he does not cease [eating], it is permitted.

[5] And both of them are for leniency, [6] and it was necessary [to state both]. [7] For if he had informed us regarding the meal in which he ceases [eating], [8] I might have said: Even from six hours and before. [9] [Therefore] he informs us: From six hours and onward. [10] And if he had informed us from six hours and onward, [11] I might have said: Even regarding a meal in which he does not cease eating. [12] [Therefore] he informs us regarding a meal in which he ceases [eating].

RASHI

משש שעות ולמטה — כלפי השחר.
המפסיק בה — דשוב אינו אוכל עוד מאותה סעודה ואילך.

NOTES

Halakhah, but the definition is not always the same. Some argue that whatever is regarded as a cooked dish in connection with the laws of *eruvin* or is regarded as a cooked dish in the context of the Pesaḥ Seder is also regarded as a cooked dish in the context of the prohibition imposed on the eve of the Ninth of Av (*Rashi,* above, 26b; *Ran,* in the name of the *Geonim*). Others maintain that the prohibition here depends on the importance of the dish and the enjoyment derived from it. Thus whatever is prepared in one pot is regarded as a single cooked dish, and whatever is prepared in two pots is regarded as two cooked dishes (*Ramban, Ritva*). The Rishonim also disagree as to whether cooked food that could have been eaten raw is excluded from the prohibition discussed in our Gemara, just as it is excluded from the prohibition against eating foods that were cooked by a non-Jew (see *Tosafot, Ritva,* and others).

HALAKHAH

בִּסְעוּדָה הַמַּפְסִיק בָּהּ Regarding the meal in which he ceases eating. "On the eve of the Ninth of Av, it is forbidden to eat meat or to drink wine during the last meal a person eats before fasting, if that meal is taken after midday. During that meal it is also forbidden to eat two cooked dishes. It is even customary to refrain from eating salted meat, fowl, and fish, and from drinking wine that has not yet fermented properly. If the same type of dish was cooked in two separate pots, the food is regarded as two cooked dishes. It is proper to act stringently and to refrain from eating two foods cooked in the same pot, unless those two foods are regularly cooked in the same

TRANSLATION AND COMMENTARY

תַּנְיָא כְּלִישָּׁנָא קַמָּא [1]The Gemara notes: A Baraita **was taught in accordance with the first version** of Rav Yehudah's qualification of the Mishnah's ruling, [2]**and** a Baraita **was** also **taught in accordance with the second version** of Rav Yehudah's qualification of the Mishnah.

תַּנְיָא כְּלִישָּׁנָא בַּתְרָא [3]The Gemara now cites the two Baraitot: The following Baraita **was taught in accordance with the second version** of Rav Yehudah's qualification of the Mishnah's ruling: [4]**"Regarding someone who dines on the eve of the Ninth of Av, if he** still **intends to eat another meal** before beginning his fast, **he is permitted to eat meat and to drink wine** during his meal. He may also partake of two cooked dishes. [5]**But if** he does **not** intend to eat another meal before beginning his fast, **he is forbidden to eat meat or to drink wine** or to eat two cooked dishes."

תַּנְיָא כְּלִישָּׁנָא קַמָּא [6]The following Baraita **was taught in accordance with the first version** of Rav Yehudah's qualification of the Mishnah's ruling: **"On the eve of the Ninth of Av, a person may not eat two cooked dishes.** [7]**He may not eat meat, nor may he drink wine.** [8]**Rabban Shimon ben Gamliel says:** There are no specific prohibitions, but a person **must make a change** from his ordinary eating habits. **Rabbi Yehudah says:** [9]**How does he make** such **a change?** [10]**If he was** ordinarily **accustomed to eat two cooked dishes** during his meal, on the eve of the Ninth of Av **he should eat** only **one kind** of cooked dish. [11]**If he was accustomed to dine in** the company of **ten** other **people,** on the eve of the Ninth of Av **he should dine in** the company of only **five** other people. [12]**If he was** ordinarily **accustomed to drink ten cups** of wine, on the eve of the Ninth of Av **he should drink** only **five cups** of wine. [13]**When do these** regulations **apply?** [14]They apply only to a meal eaten after midday, **from the sixth hour** of the day **onward.** [15]**But** if a person takes a meal in the morning, **before the sixth hour** of the day, both according to the anonymous first Tanna of the Baraita and according to Rabban Shimon ben Gamliel, **he is permitted** to eat whatever he wishes and in his usual manner."

[1]תַּנְיָא כְּלִישָּׁנָא קַמָּא, [2]תַּנְיָא כְּלִישָּׁנָא בַּתְרָא.
[3]תַּנְיָא כְּלִישָּׁנָא בַּתְרָא: [4]"הַסּוֹעֵד עֶרֶב תִּשְׁעָה בְּאָב, אִם עָתִיד לִסְעוֹד סְעוּדָה אַחֶרֶת, מוּתָּר לֶאֱכוֹל בָּשָׂר וְלִשְׁתּוֹת יַיִן. [5]וְאִם לָאו, אָסוּר לֶאֱכוֹל בָּשָׂר וְלִשְׁתּוֹת יַיִן".
[6]תַּנְיָא כְּלִישָּׁנָא קַמָּא: "עֶרֶב תִּשְׁעָה בְּאָב, לֹא יֹאכַל אָדָם שְׁנֵי תַבְשִׁילִין. [7]לֹא יֹאכַל בָּשָׂר וְלֹא יִשְׁתֶּה יַיִן. [8]רַבָּן שִׁמְעוֹן בֶּן גַּמְלִיאֵל אוֹמֵר: יְשַׁנֶּה. [9]אָמַר רַבִּי יְהוּדָה: כֵּיצַד מְשַׁנֶּה? [10]אִם הָיָה רָגִיל לֶאֱכוֹל שְׁנֵי תַבְשִׁילִין, יֹאכַל מִין אֶחָד, [11]וְאִם הָיָה רָגִיל לִסְעוֹד בַּעֲשָׂרָה בְּנֵי אָדָם, סוֹעֵד בַּחֲמִשָּׁה. [12]הָיָה רָגִיל לִשְׁתּוֹת עֲשָׂרָה כּוֹסוֹת, שׁוֹתֶה חֲמִשָּׁה כּוֹסוֹת. [13]בַּמֶּה דְּבָרִים אֲמוּרִים? [14]מִשֵּׁשׁ שָׁעוֹת וּלְמַעְלָה, [15]אֲבָל מִשֵּׁשׁ שָׁעוֹת וּלְמַטָּה מוּתָּר".

LITERAL TRANSLATION

[1]It was taught in accordance with the first version, [2][and] it was taught in accordance with the last version.

[3]It was taught in accordance with the last version: [4]"[Regarding] someone who dines [on] the eve of the Ninth of Av, if he intends to eat another meal, he is permitted to eat meat and to drink wine. [5]But if not, he is forbidden to eat meat or to drink wine."

[6]It was taught in accordance with the first version: "[On] the eve of the Ninth of Av, a person may not eat two cooked dishes. [7]He may not eat meat and he may not drink wine. [8]Rabban Shimon ben Gamliel says: He must change. [9]Rabbi Yehudah says: How does he change? [10]If he was accustomed to eat two cooked dishes, he should eat one kind, [11]and if he was accustomed to dine with ten people, he should dine with five. [12]If he was accustomed to drink ten cups, he should drink five cups. [13]In what [case] are these things said? [14]From six hours and onward, [15]but from six hours and before, he is permitted."

RASHI

הכי גרסינן — כיצד ישנה אמר רב יהודה אם הוא רגיל כו׳.
בעשרה — שהיו סועדין עמו לכבודו.

BACKGROUND

אִם הָיָה רָגִיל לֶאֱכוֹל If he was accustomed to eat. The quantity of food a person may eat at this meal is not limited, but the way in which it is eaten is emphasized. All these rulings are meant to make the meal as minimally festive as possible, limiting the number of dishes, the number of participants, and those elements that have a joyous aspect and ease one's heart.

NOTES

יְשַׁנֶּה He must change. It would appear from the two Baraitot quoted here that the change is limited to a reduction in the number of cooked dishes or the amount of wine drunk, or a reduction in the number of people in whose company a person eats. *Rashash* suggests that the Baraita should read: "If he was accustomed to eat two cooked dishes, he should eat a *different* kind [מִין אַחֵר rather than מִין אֶחָד]." In addition to reducing the amount of food a person eats and the number of people with whom he dines, a person should make a change in his ordinary eating habits and eat a different type of food.

HALAKHAH

pot. Food that was cooked but could have been eaten raw is regarded as a cooked dish in this context. *Rema* adds that, regarding this prohibition, there is no difference between boiling and roasting." (*Shulhan Arukh, Orah Hayyim* 552:1-3.)

¹תַּנְיָא אִידָךְ: ״עֶרֶב תִּשְׁעָה בְּאָב, לֹא יֹאכַל אָדָם שְׁנֵי תַבְשִׁילִין. לֹא יֹאכַל בָּשָׂר וְלֹא יִשְׁתֶּה יַיִן. ²דִּבְרֵי רַבִּי מֵאִיר. ³וַחֲכָמִים אוֹמְרִים: יְשַׁנֶּה, וּמְמַעֵט בְּבָשָׂר וּבְיַיִן. ⁴כֵּיצַד מְמַעֵט? ⁵אִם הָיָה רָגִיל לֶאֱכוֹל לִיטְרָא בָּשָׂר, יֹאכַל חֲצִי לִיטְרָא. ⁶הָיָה רָגִיל לִשְׁתּוֹת לוֹג יַיִן, יִשְׁתֶּה חֲצִי לוֹג יַיִן. ⁷וְאִם אֵינוֹ רָגִיל כָּל עִיקָּר, אָסוּר. ⁸רַבָּן שִׁמְעוֹן בֶּן גַּמְלִיאֵל אוֹמֵר: אִם הָיָה רָגִיל לֶאֱכוֹל צְנוֹן אוֹ מָלִיחַ אַחַר סְעוּדָתוֹ, הָרְשׁוּת בְּיָדוֹ״.

⁹תַּנְיָא אִידָךְ: ״כָּל שֶׁהוּא מִשּׁוּם תִּשְׁעָה בְּאָב, אָסוּר לֶאֱכוֹל בָּשָׂר וְאָסוּר לִשְׁתּוֹת יַיִן, וְאָסוּר לִרְחוֹץ. ¹⁰כָּל שֶׁאֵינוֹ

LITERAL TRANSLATION

[1] It was taught in another [Baraita]: "[On] the eve of the Ninth of Av, a person may not eat two cooked dishes. He may not eat meat and he may not drink wine. [2] [These are] the words of Rabbi Meir. [3] And the Sages say: He must change, and reduce the meat and the wine. [4] How does he reduce? [5] If he was accustomed to eat a pound of meat, he should eat half a pound. [6] If he was accustomed to drink a *log* of wine, he should drink half a *log*. [7] And if he was not accustomed at all, he is forbidden. [8] Rabban Shimon ben Gamliel says: If he was accustomed to eat radishes or a salted dessert after his meal, he is permitted to do so (lit., 'the permission is in his hand')."

[9] It was taught in another [Baraita]: "Whatever is because of the Ninth of Av, it is forbidden to eat meat and it is forbidden to drink wine, and it is forbidden to bathe. [10] Whatever is not

TRANSLATION AND COMMENTARY

תַּנְיָא אִידָךְ [1] **It was taught in another,** related **Baraita: "On the eve of the Ninth of Av, a person may not eat two cooked dishes. He may not eat meat, nor may he drink wine. [2] This is the viewpoint of Rabbi Meir. [3] But the Sages say:** There are no specific prohibitions, but a person **must make a change** from his ordinary eating habits **and reduce the** amount of **meat** he eats **and** the amount of **wine** he drinks. [4] **How does** a person **reduce** his consumption of meat and wine? [5] **If he was** ordinarily **accustomed to eat a pound of meat,** on the eve of the Ninth of Av **he should eat** only **half a pound.** [6] **If he was** ordinarily **accustomed to drink a *log* of wine,** on the eve of the Ninth of Av **he should drink** only **half a *log*.** [7] **And if** ordinarily **he was not accustomed** to eat meat or to drink wine **at all, he is forbidden** to do so on the eve of the Ninth of Av. [8] **Rabban Shimon ben Gamliel says: If** a person **was** ordinarily **accustomed to eat radishes or a salted dessert after his meal, he is permitted to do so** on the eve of the Ninth of Av."

תַּנְיָא אִידָךְ [9] The Gemara now cites **another Baraita in which it was taught:** "When a person eats his last **meal in anticipation of** the fast of **the Ninth of Av, he is forbidden to eat meat or to drink wine,** and he is **forbidden to wash** himself, even his hands and his face, during the meal or afterwards. [10] When he is **not** eating

RASHI

וחכמים אומרים ישנה — א״שני תבשילין״ קיימי, בשר ויין ימעט. **מליח** — דג או בשר מליח, דאין בו טעם כל כך אחר ששהה שלשה ימים במלח, כדלקמן, כשלמים והנותר מבשר זבח השלמים וגו׳, טפי לא אשכחן דמקרי בשר. **כל שהוא משום תשעה באב** — כגון סעודה המפסיק בה.

NOTES

אָסוּר לִרְחוֹץ **And it is forbidden to bathe.** Our translation and commentary follows the standard text of the Talmud, but the text found in many manuscripts, as well as in the parallel Baraita found in the Tosefta, reads: "Whatever is not because of the Ninth of Av, it is permitted to eat meat and to drink wine, and it is *permitted* to bathe. Rabbi Yishmael the son of Rabbi Yose says in the name of his father: As long as it is permitted to eat [the word *meat* being omitted], it is permitted to bathe."

Our commentary follows *Ramban* and others who explain that the expression "Whatever is because of the Ninth of Av" refers to the last meal eaten before that fast, and the expression "Whatever is not because of the Ninth of Av" refers to a meal eaten earlier in the day. *Ra'avad* maintains that the second expression refers to the last meal eaten before other public fast days, even those that begin at night like the Ninth of Av. *Rashi* cites both explanations.

According to *Ramban,* the first Tanna maintains that once a person begins to eat his last meal before the fast of the Ninth of Av, he is forbidden to eat meat or to drink wine, and he is already forbidden to wash himself. Washing is forbidden, for the benefit derived from washing lasts for a significant period of time, and he appears to be washing in order to benefit from his washing on the Ninth of Av itself. But he is still permitted to wear shoes and engage in the other activities that are forbidden on the Ninth of Av. But during a meal eaten earlier in the day, he is permitted to eat meat and to drink wine, and he may also wash himself. Rabbi Yishmael the son of Rabbi Yose disagrees with the first Tanna's first ruling. Even if he has finished his last meal before the fast, nevertheless, as long as he is still permitted to eat, i.e., until sunset, he is permitted to wash.

According to *Ra'avad,* the first Tanna maintains that, once a person has completed his last meal before the fast of the Ninth of Av, at which he is forbidden to eat meat or to drink wine, he is forbidden to eat, because he is viewed as having taken it upon himself to stop eating, and he is likewise forbidden to wash. But regarding the last meal before other fasts, at which he is permitted meat and wine, even if he may not eat anymore, he is still permitted to wash. Rabbi Yishmael the son of Rabbi Yose disagrees and says that, even after he has completed his last meal before the Ninth of Av, as long as he would have been permitted to eat had he not stopped eating, i.e., until sunset, he is permitted to wash.

TRANSLATION AND COMMENTARY

his last **meal in anticipation of** the fast of **the Ninth of Av,** and he still intends to eat another meal before beginning to fast, **he is permitted to eat meat and to drink wine** during the meal, **but he is** already **forbidden to wash** himself. This is the viewpoint of the anonymous first Tanna of the Baraita. But [1]**Rabbi Yishmael the son of Rabbi Yose** disagreed and **said in the name of his father: As long as** a person **is permitted to eat meat, he is** still **permitted to wash** himself."

תָּנוּ רַבָּנַן [2]**Our Rabbis taught** the following Baraita: **"All the restrictions that apply to a mourner** upon the passing of a close relative **apply** to everybody **on the Ninth of Av,** which is the day of national mourning. [3]Thus on the Ninth of Av **it is forbidden to eat and drink, to anoint** one's body with oil or to apply to it any kind of ointment or lotion, **to wear** leather **shoes, or** to engage in **sexual relations.** It is also forbidden to engage in the study of Torah, for Torah study is a source of joy and pleasure. [4]Thus **it is forbidden to read** from the **Torah, the Prophets, and the Writings.** A person may also not **study the Mishnah, the Talmud,** and **the Midrash,** or **Halakhot and Aggadot.** [5]**But** a person **may read a** Biblical **section that he is not accustomed**

מִשּׁוּם תִּשְׁעָה בְּאָב, מוּתָּר לֶאֱכוֹל בָּשָׂר וְלִשְׁתּוֹת יַיִן, וְאָסוּר לִרְחוֹץ. [1]רַבִּי יִשְׁמָעֵאל בְּרַבִּי יוֹסֵי אוֹמֵר מִשּׁוּם אָבִיו: כָּל שָׁעָה שֶׁמּוּתָּר לֶאֱכוֹל בָּשָׂר מוּתָּר לִרְחוֹץ״.

[2]תָּנוּ רַבָּנַן: ״כָּל מִצְוֹת הַנּוֹהֲגוֹת בְּאָבֵל נוֹהֲגוֹת בְּתִשְׁעָה בְּאָב: [3]אָסוּר בַּאֲכִילָה וּבִשְׁתִיָּה, וּבְסִיכָה, וּבִנְעִילַת הַסַּנְדָּל, וּבְתַשְׁמִישׁ הַמִּטָּה. [4]וְאָסוּר לִקְרוֹת בַּתּוֹרָה, בַּנְּבִיאִים, וּבַכְּתוּבִים, וְלִשְׁנוֹת בַּמִּשְׁנָה, בַּתַּלְמוּד, וּבַמִּדְרָשׁ, וּבַהֲלָכוֹת וּבָאַגָּדוֹת. [5]אֲבָל קוֹרֵא הוּא בְּמָקוֹם שֶׁאֵינוֹ רָגִיל

LITERAL TRANSLATION

because of the Ninth of Av, it is permitted to eat meat and to drink wine, but it is forbidden to bathe. [1]Rabbi Yishmael the son of Rabbi Yose says in the name of his father: As long as it is permitted to eat meat it is permitted to bathe."

[2]Our Rabbis taught: "All the restrictions that apply to a mourner apply on the Ninth of Av: [3]One is forbidden [to engage] in eating and in drinking, in anointing, and in wearing shoes, and in sexual relations. [4]And it is forbidden to read the Torah, the Prophets, and the Writings, and to study the Mishnah, the Talmud, and the Midrash, the Halakhot and Aggadot. [5]But he may read a section that he is not accustomed

RASHI

כל שאינו משום תשעה באב — כגון סעודה המפסיק בה בתענית צבור, אי נמי סעודה שאינו מפסיק בה. הכי גרסינן: **רבי ישמעאל ברבי יוסי אומר משום אביו כל שעה שמותר לאכול מותר לרחוץ** — ולא גרסינן נ״ו, כלומר, אפילו בשעת סעודה המפסיק מותר לרחוץ, הואיל ומותר לאכול. **אסור באכילה ובשתיה** — הני אין נוהגין באבל, דקא חשיב נמי איסורים שנוהגין בו לבד מהני דנהיגי באבל: רחילה סיכה ונעילה כו׳. **ואסור לקרות בתורה כו׳** — דכתיב בהו ״משמחי לב״. **במקום שאינו רגיל לקרות** — דכיון דלא ידע — אית ליה צערא.

BACKGROUND

וְאָסוּר לִקְרוֹת בַּתּוֹרָה And it is forbidden to read the Torah. The prohibition against studying Torah has a double source. First, as stated explicitly in the Gemara, the very study of Torah is a religious duty that gives one pleasure. Second, immersion in an intellectual pursuit makes the student forget that he is in mourning, for he is drawn to the subject he is studying. In order not to forget that one is in mourning, one should not engage in matters that may distract one's mind.

NOTES

כָּל מִצְוֹת הַנּוֹהֲגוֹת בְּאָבֵל All the restrictions that apply to a mourner. One practical ramification of this principle that is not mentioned in this Baraita relates to the issue of wearing tefillin on the Ninth of Av. According to some Rishonim, just as a mourner does not wear tefillin on the first day of mourning, nobody wears tefillin on the Ninth of Av (*Ra'avad*). Others argue that only the restrictions that apply for the entire seven days of mourning also apply on the Ninth of Av, and therefore tefillin must be worn on the Ninth of Av. Moreover, the mourning observed on the Ninth of Av does not cancel the Torah obligation to wear tefillin (*Ramban, Ritva,* and others). In actual practice the customs vary. Most Sephardim wear tefillin on the Ninth of Av in the regular manner. Most Ashkenazim wear tefillin only after midday, when certain leniencies regarding the mourning restrictions are allowed.

בְּמָקוֹם שֶׁאֵינוֹ רָגִיל A section that he is not accustomed. *Rashi* explains that the first Tanna of the Baraita permits a person to study a Biblical or Talmudic section with which he is not familiar, for such study causes him distress when he comes to a passage that he does not understand. *Rivan* explains that such study is permitted because the person experiences distress when he is forced to make a special effort to understand difficult passages.

HALAKHAH

כָּל מִצְוֹת הַנּוֹהֲגוֹת בְּאָבֵל נוֹהֲגוֹת בְּתִשְׁעָה בְּאָב All the restrictions that apply to a mourner apply on the Ninth of Av. "On the Ninth of Av a person is forbidden to wash himself, to anoint himself with oil, to wear leather shoes, or to engage in sexual relations. He is forbidden to read from the Torah, the Prophets, or the Writings. He may not study Mishnah, Talmud, Midrash, Halakhot or Aggadot. Even schoolchildren must abstain from their studies. But a person is permitted to read from the Book of Job and from the Book of Lamentations, and from the prophecies of evil in the Book of Jeremiah, and he may study the Midrash on the Book of Lamentations and the Talmudic sections dealing with the destruction of the Temple. Some authorities prohibit a person from even thinking about the Torah sections he is forbidden to read and study. But a person is permitted to read the Torah sections that have been incorporated into the daily liturgy (though it is customary to read some of those sections only after midday)." (*Shulḥan Arukh, Oraḥ Ḥayyim* 554:1-4.)

BACKGROUND

וּבַדְּבָרִים הָרָעִים שֶׁבְּיִרְמְיָהוּ And the bad things in Jeremiah. The Book of Jeremiah contains many prophecies of doom and descriptions of destruction. These are the "bad things" which it is permitted to study on the Ninth of Av. However, Jeremiah also contains prophecies of consolation, the good things. These should not be studied in a time of mourning, because they ease one's heart.

TRANSLATION AND COMMENTARY

to read, and he may study a Talmudic **section that he is not accustomed to study.** Since he is not familiar with that particular section, he will encounter difficulties and will not derive pleasure from his studies. [1]**He may** also **read** from the Book of **Lamentations, and** from the Book of **Job, and** from **the prophecies of evil in** the Book of **Jeremiah,** for the subject matter of these parts of the Bible is appropriate to the mood of the day, and reading from them will not bring a person any joy. [2]**Schoolchildren,** too, **must** also **be made to abstain** from their studies on the Ninth of Av, [3]**for** Torah study brings them joy, as **the verse says** [Psalms 19:9]: **'The statutes of the Lord are right, rejoicing the heart.'** [4]**Rabbi Yehudah** disagrees with one of the above rulings and **says:** On the Ninth of Av, a person **may not even read** a Biblical **section that he is not accustomed to read, nor may he study a** Talmudic **section that he is not accustomed to study,** for a person derives pleasure from his Torah studies, even when he studies sections of Torah that are unfamiliar to him. [5]**But he may read** from the Book of **Job, and** from the Book of **Lamentations, and from the prophecies of evil in the Book of Jeremiah.** [6]**Schoolchildren, too, must be made to abstain from their studies on the Ninth of Av,** [7]**for the verse says: 'The statutes of the Lord are right, rejoicing the heart.'"**

לִקְרוֹת, וְשׁוֹנֶה בְּמָקוֹם שֶׁאֵינוֹ רָגִיל לִשְׁנוֹת. [1]וְקוֹרֵא בְּקִינוֹת, בְּאִיּוֹב, וּבַדְּבָרִים הָרָעִים שֶׁבְּיִרְמְיָה. [2]וְתִינוֹקוֹת שֶׁל בֵּית רַבָּן בְּטֵלִין, [3]מִשּׁוּם שֶׁנֶּאֱמַר: ׳פִּקּוּדֵי ה׳ יְשָׁרִים, מְשַׂמְּחֵי לֵב׳. [4]רַבִּי יְהוּדָה אוֹמֵר: אַף אֵינוֹ קוֹרֵא בְּמָקוֹם שֶׁאֵינוֹ רָגִיל לִקְרוֹת, וְאֵינוֹ שׁוֹנֶה בְּמָקוֹם שֶׁאֵינוֹ רָגִיל לִשְׁנוֹת. [5]אֲבָל קוֹרֵא הוּא בְּאִיּוֹב, וּבְקִינוֹת, וּבַדְּבָרִים הָרָעִים שֶׁבְּיִרְמְיָהוּ. [6]וְתִינוֹקוֹת שֶׁל בֵּית רַבָּן בְּטֵלִים בּוֹ, [7]מִשּׁוּם שֶׁנֶּאֱמַר: ׳פִּקּוּדֵי ה׳ יְשָׁרִים, מְשַׂמְּחֵי לֵב׳״.
[8]״לֹא יֹאכַל בָּשָׂר וְלֹא יִשְׁתֶּה יַיִן״. [9]תָּנָא: ״אֲבָל אוֹכֵל הוּא בָּשָׂר מָלִיחַ וְשׁוֹתֶה יַיִן מִגִּתּוֹ״.
[10]בָּשָׂר מָלִיחַ עַד כַּמָּה?
[11]אָמַר רַב חִינְנָא בַּר כָּהֲנָא מִשְּׁמֵיהּ דִּשְׁמוּאֵל: כָּל זְמַן

LITERAL TRANSLATION

to read, and he may study a section that he is not accustomed to study. [1]And he may read Lamentations, and Job, and the bad things in Jeremiah. [2]And schoolchildren must be idle, [3]because it is said: 'The statutes of the Lord are right, rejoicing the heart.' [4]Rabbi Yehudah says: He may not even read a section that he is not accustomed to read, nor may he study a section that he is not accustomed to study. [5]But he may read Job, and Lamentations, and the bad things in Jeremiah. [6]And schoolchildren must be idle on it, [7]because it is said: 'The statutes of the Lord are right, rejoicing the heart.'"

[8]"He may not eat meat nor drink wine." [9][A Tanna] taught: "But he may eat salted meat and he may drink wine from his vat."

[10]For how long is salted meat [regarded as ordinary meat]?

[11]Rav Ḥinena bar Kahana said in the name of Shmuel: As long

RASHI

עד כמה — הוי בשר גמור, דלא הוי בשר מליח — כל זמן שהוא כשלמים, שלא שהה במלחו אלא שני ימים ולילה אחד, כזמן אכילת שלמים. ולהכי נקט כשלמים, דזמן אכילת שלמים אשכחן דאקרי בשר, דכתיב (ויקרא ז) ״והנותר מבשר זבח השלמים״ וגו׳. טפי לא אשכחן דמקרי בשר, שהטעם נפסל אחרי שנים ושלשה ימים. **יין מגתו** — חדש ומתוק, ואינו טוב כיין ישן, ומשלשל ומזיק.

לֹא יֹאכַל בָּשָׂר [8]We learned in our Mishnah: "During the last meal a person eats before beginning the fast of the Ninth of Av, **he may not eat meat nor may he drink wine."** [9]**A Tanna taught** a Baraita which qualifies this ruling: "He may neither eat meat nor drink wine, **but he may eat** heavily **salted meat and he may drink from his vat wine** that has not yet had time to ferment properly, for heavily salted meat and partially fermented wine do not give a person pleasure."

בָּשָׂר מָלִיחַ [10]The Gemara now seeks to clarify this matter: The Baraita stated that heavily **salted meat** may be eaten in the last meal before the fast of the Ninth of Av. **For how long is meat** that has been heavily **salted regarded as ordinary meat** that may not be eaten at the last meal before the Ninth of Av?

אָמַר רַב חִינְנָא בַּר כָּהֲנָא [11]**Rav Ḥinena bar Kahana said in the name of Shmuel: As long as it is like** the meat of **peace-offerings**. The portions of a peace-offering which are permitted to be eaten may be eaten on

HALAKHAH

בָּשָׂר מָלִיחַ וְיַיִן מִגִּתּוֹ Salted meat and wine from his vat. "During the last meal eaten before the Ninth of Av it is customary to refrain from eating heavily salted meat and from drinking wine that has not yet fermented properly (even though these foods are permitted by Talmudic law)." (*Shulḥan Arukh, Oraḥ Ḥayyim* 552:2.)

שֶׁהוּא כִּשְׁלָמִים.
[1]וְיַיִן מִגִּתּוֹ עַד כַּמָּה?
[2]כָּל זְמַן שֶׁהוּא תּוֹסֵס.
[3]תָּנָא: "יַיִן תּוֹסֵס אֵין בּוֹ מִשּׁוּם גִּילּוּי. [4]וְכַמָּה תְּסִיסָתוֹ? שְׁלֹשָׁה יָמִים".
[5]אָמַר רַב יְהוּדָה אָמַר רַב: כָּךְ הָיָה מִנְהָגוֹ שֶׁל רַבִּי יְהוּדָה בְּרַבִּי אִילְעַאי: [6]עֶרֶב תִּשְׁעָה בְּאָב מְבִיאִין לוֹ פַּת חֲרֵבָה בְּמֶלַח, וְיוֹשֵׁב [30B] [7]בֵּין תַּנּוּר לַכִּירַיִים, וְאוֹכֵל, וְשׁוֹתֶה עָלֶיהָ

LITERAL TRANSLATION

as it is like peace-offerings.

[1]And for how long is wine [regarded as] from his vat?

[2]As long as it is fermenting.

[3][A Tanna] taught: "Regarding fermenting wine there is no [concern about] exposure. [4]And how long is its fermentation? Three days."

[5]Rav Yehudah said in the name of Rav: Thus was the practice of Rabbi Yehudah the son of Rabbi Il'ai: [6][On] the eve of the Ninth of Av they would bring him stale bread with salt, nd he would sit [30B] between the oven and the stove, [7]and he would eat, and he would drink with it

RASHI

תוסס = רותח. **אין בו משום גילוי** — שאין נחש שותהו, כי יכרת מרתיחתו. **בין תנור לכיריים** — מקום מנוול שבבית.

TRANSLATION AND COMMENTARY

the day the animal is sacrificed, on the following day, and during the intervening night. Unless two days and the intervening night have passed since the time the meat was salted, the meat is regarded as ordinary meat and may not be eaten during the last meal before the Ninth of Av. But once that time has passed, the meat is regarded as heavily salted and may be eaten even during the last meal before the fast.

וְיַיִן מִגִּתּוֹ [1]The Baraita also taught that **wine** taken straight **from** a person's **vat** may be drunk in the course of the last meal before the fast of the Ninth of Av. The Gemara asks: **For how long** may wine remain in the vat and still be permitted at the last meal before the fast of the Ninth of Av?

כָּל זְמַן [2]The Gemara answers: **As long as** the wine **is** still **fermenting.**

תָּנָא [3]**A Tanna taught** the following Baraita: **"Regarding wine that is** still **fermenting, there is no concern about** the prohibition imposed on **exposed liquids."** If wine, water, or other liquids are left exposed and unattended, there is concern that a poisonous snake may drink from these liquids and deposit its vemon in them. The Rabbis therefore enacted a decree forbidding the drinking of exposed liquids. But no prohibition was imposed on wine that is still fermenting in the vat, for snakes do not drink from fermenting wine. [4]The Baraita continues: **"How long does** it take for wine to **ferment? Three days** from the time that the grapes were trodden in the press."

אָמַר רַב יְהוּדָה [5]**Rav Yehudah said in the name of Rav: This was the practice of Rabbi Yehudah the son of Rabbi Il'ai:** [6]As evening approached **on the day before the Ninth of Av,** Rabbi Yehudah the son of Rabbi Il'ai **would be brought stale bread with salt, and he would sit** [30B] on the floor in the most undignified place in the house, **between the oven and the stove,** [7]**and he would eat** his bread, **and he would drink with it**

BACKGROUND

יַיִן תּוֹסֵס **Fermenting wine.** After the grapes have been pressed and yeast has been added, the wine begins to ferment. The fermentation lasts from three to four days, during which the temperature of the wine rises to 40 degrees centigrade. A beverage is usually not left exposed, lest a snake drink some of it and poison the rest with venom. But the heat caused by the fermentation process deters a snake from drinking fermenting wine.

תַּנּוּר **Oven.** Ovens were mainly used for baking or for preparing food requiring particularly high temperatures. For ordinary cooking just a stove was used. The place between the oven and the stove was used to prepare food, and would usually be littered with scraps of firewood and ashes, making it the least pleasant place in the house. Rabbi Yehudah would sit specifically in that place to emphasize his grief over the destruction of the Temple.

NOTES

כָּל זְמַן שֶׁהוּא כִּשְׁלָמִים **As long as it is like peace-offerings.** There are two readings to this passage: "As long as it is like peace-offerings," and "As long as it is *not* like peace-offerings." There is no practical difference between these two readings, for all agree that peace-offerings may be eaten for two days and the intervening night, and that meat that has been heavily salted for that period of time no longer tastes like ordinary meat. According to the first reading, the Gemara explains how long heavily salted meat is regarded as ordinary meat, so that it is included in the prohibition against eating meat during the last meal before the fast of the Ninth of Av, while according to the alternative reading, the Gemara explains when heavily salted meat ceases to be treated as ordinary meat, so that it is excluded from the prohibition.

HALAKHAH

יַיִן תּוֹסֵס אֵין בּוֹ מִשּׁוּם גִּילּוּי **Regarding fermenting wine there is no concern about exposure.** "Regarding wine that is still fermenting there is no concern about the prohibition imposed on exposed liquids. Wine is regarded as fermenting for three days from the time that the grapes are trodden in the press." (*Rambam, Sefer Nezikin, Hilkhot Rotze'aḥ U'Shmirat Nefesh* 11:8.)

כָּךְ הָיָה מִנְהָגוֹ שֶׁל רַבִּי יְהוּדָה **Thus was the practice of Rabbi Yehudah.** "If a person is able to do so, during the last meal he eats before the Ninth of Av he should restrict himself to bread with salt and a cup of water. *Rema* adds that some dip their bread in ashes. Some have the custom of eating a dish of lentils cooked with eggs, a dish often served to mourners. *Rema* writes that some are accustomed to eat hard-boiled eggs, another food eaten by mourners." (*Shulḥan Arukh, Oraḥ Ḥayyim* 552:5-6.)

קִיתוֹן שֶׁל מַיִם, [1]וְדוֹמֶה כְּמִי שֶׁמֵּתוֹ מוּטָּל לְפָנָיו.
[2]תְּנַן הָתָם: "מָקוֹם שֶׁנָּהֲגוּ לַעֲשׂוֹת מְלָאכָה בְּתִשְׁעָה בְּאָב, עוֹשִׂין. [3]מָקוֹם שֶׁנָּהֲגוּ שֶׁלֹּא לַעֲשׂוֹת, אֵין עוֹשִׂין. [4]וּבְכָל מָקוֹם תַּלְמִידֵי חֲכָמִים בְּטֵלִים. [5]רַבָּן שִׁמְעוֹן בֶּן גַּמְלִיאֵל אוֹמֵר: לְעוֹלָם יַעֲשֶׂה כָּל אָדָם עַצְמוֹ כְּתַלְמִיד חָכָם".
[6]תַּנְיָא נַמִּי הָכִי: [7]"רַבָּן שִׁמְעוֹן בֶּן גַּמְלִיאֵל אוֹמֵר: [8]לְעוֹלָם יַעֲשֶׂה אָדָם עַצְמוֹ כְּתַלְמִיד חָכָם, כְּדֵי שֶׁיִּתְעַנֶּה".
[9]תַּנְיָא אִידָךְ: [10]"רַבָּן שִׁמְעוֹן בֶּן גַּמְלִיאֵל אוֹמֵר: כָּל הָאוֹכֵל

LITERAL TRANSLATION

a ladle of water, [1]and he would resemble someone whose deceased [relative] was lying before him.

[2]We have learned elsewhere: "[In] a place where it is customary to work on the Ninth of Av, they may work. [3][In] a place where it is customary not to work, they may not work. [4]And in every place Rabbinic scholars must be idle. [5]Rabban Shimon ben Gamliel says: Every person should always conduct himself like a Rabbinic scholar."

[6]It was also taught thus: [7]"Rabban Shimon ben Gamliel says: [8]A person should always conduct himself like a Rabbinic scholar, in order to afflict himself."

[9]It was taught in another [Baraita]: [10]"Rabban Shimon ben Gamliel says: Whoever eats

TRANSLATION AND COMMENTARY

a ladle of water. [1]Thus **he would resemble someone whose deceased relative was lying before him** awaiting burial.

תְּנַן הָתָם [2]**We have learned elsewhere** in the Mishnah (*Pesaḥim* 54b): **"In a place where it is customary** for people **to work on the Ninth of Av, one may** indeed **work,** for the Rabbis did not impose a prohibition against working on the Ninth of Av. [3]But **in a place where it is customary** for people **to refrain from working, one may not work,** for it is not permitted to deviate from a local stringency, even if, according to the Halakhah, the activity is permitted. [4]**And everywhere,** even where people are accustomed to work, **Rabbinic scholars must abstain** from working. [5]**Rabban Shimon ben Gamliel says:** Even in places where it is customary for people to work on the Ninth of Av, it is proper that **every person should always conduct himself as if he were a Rabbinic scholar** and refrain from working."

תַּנְיָא נַמִּי הָכִי [6]**The same** thing **was also taught** in the following Baraita, which stated: [7]**"Rabban Shimon ben Gamliel says:** Even in places where people are accustomed to work on the Ninth of Av, [8]it is proper that **a person should always conduct himself as if he were a Rabbinic scholar** and refrain from working, **so that he will feel the affliction** of the day with greater force."

תַּנְיָא אִידָךְ [9]The Gemara now cites **another Baraita** in which **it was taught:** [10]**"Rabban Shimon ben Gamliel**

LANGUAGE

קִיתוֹן **Ladle.** This word is derived from the Greek κώθων, *kothon*, meaning "a vessel used for drinking," "a large cup."

BACKGROUND

לְעוֹלָם יַעֲשֶׂה אָדָם עַצְמוֹ כְּתַלְמִיד חָכָם A person should always conduct himself like a Rabbinic scholar. This ruling was issued in connection with the general principle expressed above in this tractate (10b), that ordinarily a man who is not a Rabbinic scholar must not behave according to the rules followed by Rabbinic scholars, for this would appear to be inappropriate arrogance. However, when the customs of Rabbinic scholars entail grief and affliction, this general principle is not insisted upon, and everyone is permitted to be stringent with himself.

NOTES

וְדוֹמֶה כְּמִי שֶׁמֵּתוֹ מוּטָּל לְפָנָיו **And he would resemble someone whose deceased relative was lying before him.** Rabbi Yehudah the son of Rabbi Il'ai wished to demonstrate that he did not view the Ninth of Av as the commemoration of an event that had taken place in the distant past, but rather as a day of mourning for a recent loss, as if a deceased relative was lying before him awaiting burial (*Maharsha*).

כְּדֵי שֶׁיִּתְעַנֶּה **In order to afflict himself.** *Rabbi Zvi Ḥayyot* notes that the clause "in order to afflict himself" explains why a person is permitted to act as if he were a Rabbinic scholar and refrain from working on the Ninth of Av. For elsewhere (above, 10b) Rabban Shimon ben Gamliel maintains that a student may not act like a full scholar in a matter that is a source of praise, but only in a matter that is a source of pain. Thus Rabban Shimon ben Gamliel teaches that a person should always act as if he were a Rabbinic scholar in order to afflict himself. In other words, he is permitted to act that way because refraining from work on the Ninth of Av is for him a source of affliction. *Mikhtam* offers two explanations for the affliction mentioned here: A person should refrain from working on the Ninth of Av, so that he not become involved in his work and fail to feel the affliction of the day. Alternatively, a person should refrain from working, in order to preserve his strength and be able to observe the fast until its end.

HALAKHAH

מָקוֹם שֶׁנָּהֲגוּ לַעֲשׂוֹת מְלָאכָה **In a place where it is customary to work.** "In a place where it is customary for people to work on the Ninth of Av, working is permitted. But in a place where it is customary for people to refrain from working, working is forbidden. In all places, Rabbinic scholars must abstain from working. Any person who wishes to act as if he were a Rabbinic scholar and refrain from working is permitted to do so. Even in a place where it is customary to refrain from working, work may be performed for a Jew by a non-Jew. *Rema* adds that it is customary to refrain from working only until midday. Until midday it is customary not to engage in any type of work which requires a significant amount of time to complete, even if it does not require professional expertise. But work which does not require a significant amount of time to complete, such as lighting a candle or tying a knot, is permitted even before midday." (*Shulḥan Arukh, Oraḥ Ḥayyim* 554:22.)

וְשׁוֹתֶה בְּתִשְׁעָה בְּאָב כְּאִילּוּ[1] אוֹכֵל וְשׁוֹתֶה בְּיוֹם הַכִּיפּוּרִים. רַבִּי עֲקִיבָא אוֹמֵר: כָּל הָעוֹשֶׂה[2] מְלָאכָה בְּתִשְׁעָה בְּאָב אֵינוֹ רוֹאֶה סִימַן בְּרָכָה לְעוֹלָם. וַחֲכָמִים אוֹמְרִים: כָּל הָעוֹשֶׂה[3] מְלָאכָה בְּתִשְׁעָה בְּאָב וְאֵינוֹ מִתְאַבֵּל עַל יְרוּשָׁלַיִם אֵינוֹ רוֹאֶה בְּשִׂמְחָתָהּ, שֶׁנֶּאֱמַר:[4] ׳שִׂמְחוּ אֶת יְרוּשָׁלַיִם, וְגִילוּ בָהּ, כָּל אֹהֲבֶיהָ: שִׂישׂוּ אִתָּהּ מָשׂוֹשׂ, כָּל הַמִּתְאַבְּלִים עָלֶיהָ׳. מִכָּאן[5] אָמְרוּ: כָּל הַמִּתְאַבֵּל עַל יְרוּשָׁלַיִם זוֹכֶה וְרוֹאֶה בְּשִׂמְחָתָהּ, וְשֶׁאֵינוֹ מִתְאַבֵּל עַל יְרוּשָׁלַיִם אֵינוֹ רוֹאֶה בְּשִׂמְחָתָהּ״.

תַּנְיָא נַמִּי הָכִי:[6] ״כָּל הָאוֹכֵל בָּשָׂר וְשׁוֹתֶה יַיִן בְּתִשְׁעָה בְּאָב, עָלָיו הַכָּתוּב אוֹמֵר: ׳וַתְּהִי[7] עֲוֹנוֹתָם עַל עַצְמוֹתָם׳״.

״רַבִּי יְהוּדָה מְחַיֵּיב בִּכְפִיַּית[8]

LITERAL TRANSLATION

[1] or drinks on the Ninth of Av [is regarded] as if he ate or drank on Yom Kippur. [2] Rabbi Akiva says: Whoever works on the Ninth of Av will never see a sign of blessing. [3] And the Sages say: Whoever works on the Ninth of Av and does not mourn for Jerusalem will not witness her joy, [4] as it is said: 'Rejoice with Jerusalem, and be glad with her, all you that love her: rejoice for joy with her, all you that mourn for her.' [5] From here they said: Whoever mourns for Jerusalem will merit to witness her joy, and he who does not mourn for Jerusalem will not witness her joy."

[6] It was also taught thus: "Whoever eats meat or drinks wine on the Ninth of Av, regarding him the verse says: [7] 'But their iniquities shall be upon their bones.'"

[8] "Rabbi Yehudah requires the overturning

TRANSLATION AND COMMENTARY

says: Whoever eats [1] **or drinks on the Ninth of Av is regarded as if he ate or drank on Yom Kippur,** even though the prohibitions applying to the Ninth of Av are Rabbinic decrees, whereas the prohibitions applying to Yom Kippur are Torah laws. [2] **Rabbi Akiva says:** Even though the Rabbis did not impose a prohibition against working on the Ninth of Av, **whoever engages in work on the Ninth of Av will never see a blessing** from that work. [3] **And the Sages say: Whoever works on the Ninth of Av and fails to mourn for Jerusalem will not merit to witness** the rebuilt Jerusalem **in her** future **joy,** [4] **as the verse says** [Isaiah 66:10]: **'Rejoice with Jerusalem, and be glad with her, all you that love her: rejoice for joy with her, all you that mourn for her.'** Isaiah is describing the future celebration of those who once mourned for the destroyed Jerusalem. [5] **From here** the Sages **said: Whoever mourns for Jerusalem will merit to witness** the rebuilt Jerusalem **in her** future **joy, and whoever fails to mourn for Jerusalem will not** merit to **witness her** future **joy."**

תַּנְיָא נַמִּי הָכִי [6] The same idea **was also taught** in the following Baraita: **"Whoever eats meat or drinks wine** during the last meal he eats **on** the eve of **the Ninth of Av, regarding him the verse says** [Ezekiel 32:27]: [7] **'But their iniquities shall be upon their bones.'"** He who does not mourn deeply for Jerusalem will be excluded from the resurrection that will accompany the rebuilding of the Temple, so that even his bones will be punished for his iniquity.

רַבִּי יְהוּדָה [8] We learned in our Mishnah: **"Rabbi Yehudah requires** that **beds be overturned** on the Ninth of Av, so that people will sleep on the floor, as is required of those observing mourning after the death of

RASHI

אינו רואה סימן ברכה — מאותה מלאכה. **כל האוכל בשר ושותה יין בתשעה באב עליו הכתוב אומר ותהי עונותם על עצמותם** — בתשעה באב, כלומר בסעודה המפסיק בה.

BACKGROUND

כְּאִילּוּ אוֹכֵל וְשׁוֹתֶה בְּיוֹם הַכִּיפּוּרִים As if he ate or drank on Yom Kippur. The comparison between the Ninth of Av and Yom Kippur relates only to the length of the fast and to the additional prohibitions associated with it. However, the fast of Yom Kippur is extremely important and is explicitly ordained in the Torah, and there is severe punishment at the hands of Heaven for anyone who does not observe it. By contrast, the fast of the Ninth of Av was ordained by the Rabbis. Despite the gravity of the day, Yom Kippur is a holiday, a day of joy and atonement for sin, whereas the Ninth of Av is a day of mourning and grief.

כְּפִיַּית הַמִּטָּה The overturning of the bed. In Mishnaic and Talmudic times it was customary to overturn one's bed in times of mourning. The legs of the bed would face upward, and people would lie on its underside. This practice emphasized that in a time of grief all the ordinary arrangements of life are reversed, and nothing persists and remains in place.
This practice was abandoned over the generations because beds in later times could not be overturned in this manner. And the Gemara states that beds that cannot be turned over in such a way that one can lie on their underside need not be overturned.

NOTES

״וַתְּהִי עֲוֹנוֹתָם עַל עַצְמוֹתָם״ "But their iniquities shall be upon their bones." Our commentary follows *Ritva,* who explains that this verse teaches us that if a person does not mourn properly for Jerusalem, punishment for his iniquity will be inflicted on his bones, and they will not take part in the resurrection that will accompany the rebuilding of the Temple. This resurrection is promised to those who mourn for Jerusalem and who patiently await salvation. *Maharsha* explains the verse as teaching that the iniquity of eating meat and drinking wine on the eve of the Ninth of Av will leave an imprint on a person's bones even after he is dead and his flesh has turned to dust.

HALAKHAH

כָּל הָעוֹשֶׂה מְלָאכָה בְּתִשְׁעָה בְּאָב Whoever works on the Ninth of Av. "Whoever engages in work (even after midday; *Magen Avraham*) on the Ninth of Av will not see a blessing from that work." (*Shulḥan Arukh, Oraḥ Ḥayyim* 554:24.)

כָּל הָאוֹכֵל בָּשָׂר וְשׁוֹתֶה יַיִן בְּתִשְׁעָה בְּאָב Whoever eats meat or drinks wine on the Ninth of Av. "Whoever eats or drinks on the Ninth of Av (even those who are permitted for health reasons to do so) will not witness the future joy of Jerusalem. Whoever mourns deeply for Jerusalem will merit to see Jerusalem in her future joy. Whoever eats meat or drinks wine during the last meal eaten on the eve of the Ninth of Av, regarding him Scripture says: 'But their iniquities shall be upon their bones.'" (Ibid., 554:25.)

BACKGROUND

בִּשְׁלָמָא יוֹם הַכִּפּוּרִים Granted Yom Kippur. The Gemara emphasizes here that, although Yom Kippur is a fast- day, it is actually a day of joy, both intrinsically, because of the pardoning of transgressions and the purification from sin, and also because it commemorates a joyful event, the giving of the second Tablets of the Covenant to the Israelites. This explains why festive practices were observed on that day, including the dances of the young women.

TRANSLATION AND COMMENTARY

a close relative. [1]**But the Sages did not agree with him."** [2]**It was taught** in a Baraita: "The Sages **said to Rabbi Yehudah:** [3]**According to your opinion** that beds must be overturned on the Ninth of Av, **what will become of pregnant and nursing women** who are surely unable to sleep on the floor? [4]Rabbi Yehudah **said to** his colleagues: When I said that beds must be overturned on the Ninth of Av, **I, too, spoke only about those who are able** to sleep on the floor."

תַּנְיָא נַמִי הָכִי [5]**The same** thing **was also taught** in the following Baraita: **"Rabbi Yehudah agrees with the Sages regarding someone who is unable** to sleep on the floor, and accepts that such a person is not required to overturn his bed. [6]**And the Sages agree with Rabbi Yehudah regarding someone who is able** to sleep on the floor, and accept that such a person is required to overturn his bed."

מַאי בֵּינַיְיהוּ [7]The Gemara asks: If Rabbi Yehudah agrees with the Sages regarding someone who is unable to sleep on the ground, and the Sages agree with Rabbi Yehudah regarding someone who is able to sleep on the ground, what is the practical difference between their opinions?

אִיכָּא בֵּינַיְיהוּ [8]The Gemara explains: **There is a difference between them** regarding **other beds** in the house, upon which the person has no intention of sleeping. According to Rabbi Yehudah, someone who is able to sleep on the floor is required to overturn all the beds in the house on the Ninth of Av, even those that are not in use. But according to the Sages, even if a person is able to sleep on the floor, he is required to overturn only the bed where he himself would have slept. [9]**For** a Baraita **was taught** in accordance with the viewpoint of Rabbi Yehudah: **"When** the Sages **said** that a mourner is required **to overturn his bed,** they meant that **he must overturn not only his own bed, but all the beds** in the house."

אֲמַר רָבָא [10]**Rava said: The Halakhah is in accordance with** the viewpoint of **the Tanna of our Mishnah,** who stated that **the Sages did not agree at all with** Rabbi Yehudah, not even about someone who is able to sleep on the floor, and all are permitted to sleep in their own beds on the Ninth of Av

אָמַר רַבָּן שִׁמְעוֹן בֶּן גַּמְלִיאֵל [11]We learned in the Mishnah: **"Rabban Shimon ben Gamliel said: There were no days as joyous for** the people of **Israel as the Fifteenth of Av and Yom Kippur."** [12]The Gemara asks: **Granted** that **Yom Kippur** is a time of joy, **because it is** the day on which **pardon and forgiveness** are granted for the sins and transgressions committed during the previous year, **and it is the day on which the second** set of the **Tablets** of the Covenant were given to Moses at Sinai, indicating that the people of Israel had once again

הַמִּטָּה, [1]וְלֹא הוֹדוּ לוֹ חֲכָמִים״.
[2]תַּנְיָא: ״אָמְרוּ לוֹ לְרַבִּי יְהוּדָה:
[3]לִדְבָרֶיךָ, עוּבָּרוֹת וּמֵנִיקוֹת מַה
תְּהֵא עֲלֵיהֶן? [4]אָמַר לָהֶם: אַף
אֲנִי לֹא אָמַרְתִּי אֶלָּא בְּיָכוֹל״.
[5]תַּנְיָא נַמִי הָכִי: ״מוֹדֶה רַבִּי
יְהוּדָה לַחֲכָמִים בְּשֶׁאֵינוֹ יָכוֹל.
[6]וּמוֹדִים חֲכָמִים לְרַבִּי יְהוּדָה
בְּיָכוֹל״.
[7]מַאי בֵּינַיְיהוּ?
[8]אִיכָּא בֵּינַיְיהוּ שְׁאָר מִטּוֹת,
[9]כִּדְתַנְיָא: ״כְּשֶׁאָמְרוּ לִכְפּוֹת
הַמִּטָּה, לֹא מִטָּתוֹ בִּלְבַד הוּא
כּוֹפֶה, אֶלָּא כָּל הַמִּטּוֹת כּוּלָּן
הוּא כּוֹפֶה״.
[10]אֲמַר רָבָא: הִלְכְתָא כְּתַנָּא
דִּידָן, וְלֹא הוֹדוּ לוֹ חֲכָמִים כָּל
עִיקָּר.
[11]״אָמַר רַבָּן שִׁמְעוֹן בֶּן
גַּמְלִיאֵל: לֹא הָיוּ יָמִים טוֹבִים
לְיִשְׂרָאֵל כַּחֲמִשָּׁה עָשָׂר בְּאָב
וּכְיוֹם הַכִּפּוּרִים״. [12]בִּשְׁלָמָא יוֹם
הַכִּפּוּרִים, מִשּׁוּם דְּאִית בֵּיהּ
סְלִיחָה וּמְחִילָה, יוֹם שֶׁנִּיתְּנוּ בּוֹ

LITERAL TRANSLATION

of the bed, [1]but the Sages did not agree with him." [2]It was taught: "They said to Rabbi Yehudah: [3]According to your words, what will become of pregnant and nursing women? [4]He said to them: I too only spoke about someone who is able."

[5]It was also taught thus: "Rabbi Yehudah agrees with the Sages regarding someone who is not able. [6]And the Sages agree with Rabbi Yehudah regarding someone who is able."

[7]What is [the difference] between them?

[8]There is [a difference] between them [regarding] other beds, [9]as it was taught: "When they said to overturn the bed, not only does he overturn his own bed, but he overturns all the beds."

[10]Rava said: The Halakhah is in accordance with our Tanna, and the Sages did not agree with him at all.

[11]"Rabban Shimon ben Gamliel said: There were no days as joyous for Israel as the Fifteenth of Av and Yom Kippur." [12]Granted Yom Kippur, because it contains pardon and forgiveness, [and it is] the day on which

RASHI

עוברות ומניקות — שאינן יכולות לישן על גבי קרקע. **ביכול** — שאפשר לו.

מאי בינייהו — כיון דזה מודה לו ביכול, וזה מודה לו בשאינו יכול. **שאר מטות** — שבבית, שאינו שוכב בהן, רבי יהודה דמחייב במתניתין בכפיית המטה — קמחייב נמי ביכול בשאר מטות, ורבנן סברי: מטתו כופה ולא שאר מטות, וכדתניא גבי אבל.

לוּחוֹת הָאַחֲרוֹנוֹת. [1]אֶלָּא חֲמִשָּׁה עָשָׂר בְּאָב מַאי הִיא? [2]אָמַר רַב יְהוּדָה אָמַר שְׁמוּאֵל: יוֹם שֶׁהוּתְּרוּ שְׁבָטִים לָבוֹא זֶה בָּזֶה.

[3]מַאי דְּרוּשׁ?

[4]״זֶה הַדָּבָר אֲשֶׁר צִוָּה ה׳ לִבְנוֹת צְלָפְחָד, וגו׳״. [5]דָּבָר זֶה לֹא יְהֵא נוֹהֵג אֶלָּא בְּדוֹר זֶה.

LITERAL TRANSLATION

the latter tablets were given. [1]But what is [the special joy of] the Fifteenth of Av?

[2]Rav Yehudah said in the name of Shmuel: [It was] the day on which the tribes were permitted to intermarry.

[3]What did they expound?

[4]"This is the thing that the Lord commanded concerning the daughters of Zelophehad, etc." [5]This thing will apply only in this generation.

TRANSLATION AND COMMENTARY

found favor in the eyes of God. The first set of tablets were broken on the seventeenth of Tammuz, as was explained earlier. The next day Moses burned the golden calf and ground it into powder. He then ascended the mountain a second time. He spent forty days in prayer on the mountain, and for a further forty days he remained there and prepared himself to receive the Tablets of the Covenant. Altogether, he spent eighty days on the mountain: the last twelve days of Tammuz, thirty days of Av, twenty-nine days of Elul, and the first nine days of Tishri. Thus it was on the tenth of Tishri, Yom Kippur, that Moses received the second set of tablets and descended the mountain. This explains why Yom Kippur is a day of joy. [1]**But what is the special joy of the Fifteenth of Av?**

אָמַר רַב יְהוּדָה [2]The Gemara answers this question by mentioning six fortunate events that occurred on the fifteenth of Av: (1) **Rav Yehudah said in the name of Shmuel:** The fifteenth of Av **was the day on which the** members of the various **tribes** of Israel **were permitted to intermarry.** The Torah says (Numbers 36:8-9): "And every daughter, who possesses an inheritance in any tribe of the children of Israel, shall marry one of the family of the tribe of her father, so that every man of the children of Israel may enjoy the inheritance of his fathers. Neither shall the inheritance remove from one tribe to another tribe; but every one of the tribes of the children of Israel shall keep himself to his own inheritance." A daughter succeeding to her father's estate was enjoined to marry a member of her father's tribe, so that the estate would not pass to another tribe upon her death. One year, on the fifteenth of Av, the Rabbis ruled that thenceforth the members of the various tribes of Israel were permitted to intermarry as they wished.

מַאי דְּרוּשׁ [3]The Gemara asks: In **what** way **did they expound** the verses so as to cancel the Biblical regulation?

זֶה הַדָּבָר [4]The Gemara answers: The verse says (Numbers 36:6): **"This is the thing that the Lord commanded concerning the daughters of Zelophehad,** saying, Let them marry whom they think best; only within the family of the tribe of their father shall they marry." When the Torah prohibited a daughter who succeeded to her father's estate from marrying out of her tribe, it emphasized that the prohibition was issued as a result of the plight of the daughters of Zelophehad. [5]The Rabbis inferred that **this** regulation **was applicable only to that** particular **generation,** the generation of the daughters of Zelophehad which conquered and divided up the Land of Israel. The day on which the barrier between the various tribes of Israel was removed by the reinterpretation of this verse became a day of rejoicing for future generations.

RASHI

שניתנו בו לוחות אחרונות — שבשבעה עשר בתמוז ירד משה מן ההר תחלה ושיבר את הלוחות, ובשמונה עשר טחן את העגל, ודן את הפושעים, ועלה למרום, נשתהה שם שמונים יום, ארבעים יום עמד בתפלה, דכתיב (דברים ט) ״ואתנפל לפני ה׳ ארבעים יום וארבעים לילה״, וארבעים יום עמד כבראשונה. חשוב משבעה עשר בתמוז עד יום הכפורים — והוו להו שמונים יום: שנים עשרה שנשתיירו מתמוז דהוא חסר, ושלשים דאב, ותשעה ועשרים דאלול — הרי אחד ושבעים, ותשעה דתשרי — הרי שמונים יום. וליל יום השלים כנגד לילו של שבעה עשר תמוז דלא הוה בחושבניה, דהא נפק ליה כבר בשעה שעלה — השתא הוי להו שמונים שלמין, לילה ויום. ובוקר יום כפור ירד, שהוא עשרה בתשרי, ואותו היום נקבע ליום כפור — להודיע שמחל וניחם על הרעה אשר דבר לעשות לעמו, ועל כן נקבע יום כפור בעשרה בתשרי, כך שמעתי.

NOTES

יוֹם שֶׁנִּיתְּנוּ בּוֹ לוּחוֹת הָאַחֲרוֹנוֹת **The day on which the latter tablets were given.** According to *Rashi,* the day after Moses broke the first set of tablets, the eighteenth of Tammuz, he once again ascended the mountain, and spent forty days in prayer and then another forty days preparing to receive the second set of tablets. The eighty days ended on Yom Kippur, the day on which Moses received the second set of tablets and descended from the mountain. *Gevurat Ari* discusses whether Moses spent the first forty-day period on the mountain or in the Israelites' camp. According to *Pirkei DeRabbi Eliezer,* Moses spent the first forty days in the camp, and on the first of Elul he ascended the mountain a second time, remaining there until the tenth of Tishri. This is the source of the custom of reciting special prayers from the first of Elul until Yom Kippur.

יוֹם שֶׁהוּתְּרוּ שְׁבָטִים **The day on which the tribes were**

¹אָמַר רַב יוֹסֵף אָמַר רַב נַחְמָן: יוֹם שֶׁהוּתַּר שֵׁבֶט בִּנְיָמִין לָבוֹא בַּקָּהָל, ²שֶׁנֶּאֱמַר: "וְאִישׁ יִשְׂרָאֵל נִשְׁבַּע בַּמִּצְפָּה, לֵאמֹר: אִישׁ מִמֶּנּוּ לֹא יִתֵּן בִּתּוֹ לְבִנְיָמִן לְאִשָּׁה".

³מַאי דְּרוּשׁ?

⁴אָמַר רַב: "מִמֶּנּוּ", ⁵וְלֹא מִבָּנֵינוּ.

⁶אָמַר רַבָּה בַּר בַּר חָנָה אָמַר רַבִּי יוֹחָנָן: ⁷יוֹם שֶׁכָּלוּ בּוֹ מֵתֵי מִדְבָּר. ⁸דְּאָמַר מָר: עַד שֶׁלֹּא כָּלוּ מֵתֵי מִדְבָּר, לֹא הָיָה דִּבּוּר

LITERAL TRANSLATION

¹Rav Yosef said in the name of Rav Naḥman: [It was] the day on which the tribe of Benjamin was permitted to marry into (lit., "to enter") the congregation, ²as it is said: "And the men of Israel had sworn in Mitzpah, saying: No man from us shall give his daughter to Benjamin as a wife."

³What did they expound?

⁴Rav said: "From us," ⁵but not from our children.

⁶Rabbah bar Bar Ḥanah said in the name of Rabbi Yoḥanan: ⁷[It was] the day on which the dead of the wilderness ceased. ⁸For a Master said: As long as the dead of the wilderness had not ceased, there was no [divine] speaking

RASHI

שהותרו שבטים לבא זה בזה — דרחמנא אמר "וכל בת יורשת נחלה" וגו' (במדבר לו) וכתיב (שם) "ולא תסוב נחלה ממטה למטה אחר כי איש בנחלתו ידבקו בני ישראל" ועמדו והתירו דבר זה בחמשה עשר באב. **זה הדבר אשר צוה ה' לבנות צלפחד וגו'** — "זה" מיעוט הוא. כלומר, לא יהיה דבר זה נוהג אלא בדור זה, בדור של בנות צלפחד. **לבא בקהל** — לישא נשים, לפי שנשבעו ישראל מלהינשא להם, כדכתיב בשופטים (כא). **ממנו** — מיעוט הוא, דכתיב "איש ממנו לא יתן בתו לבנימין" — לא גזרו אלא מהם (ממנו), אבל מבניהם לא גזרו. **שכלו מתי מדבר** — דתניא: כל ארבעים שנה שהיו במדבר בכל ערב תשעה באב היה הכרוז יוצא ואומר: צאו לחפור, והיה כל אחד ואחד יוצא וחופר לו קבר, וישן בו, שמא ימות קודם שיחפור, ולמחר הכרוז יוצא וקורא: יבדלו חיים מן המתים,

TRANSLATION AND COMMENTARY

אָמַר רַב יוֹסֵף (2) ¹**Rav Yosef said in the name of Rav Naḥman** : The fifteenth of Av **was the day on which** the members of **the tribe of Benjamin were permitted** once again **to marry into the congregation** of Israel. At the conclusion of the intertribal war which followed the incident of the concubine in Gibeah (see Judges 19-21), the rest of Israel took an oath not to give their daughters in marriage to members of the tribe of Benjamin, ²**as the verse says** (Judges 21:1): **"And the men of Israel had sworn in Mitzpah, saying: No man from us shall give his daughter to Benjamin as a wife."** Subsequently, on the fifteenth of Av, a dispensation was granted which allowed the Benjaminites to be readmitted into the community.

מַאי דְּרוּשׁ ³The Gemara asks: In **what** way **did they expound** the verse so as to allow marriage with the tribe of Benjamin?

אָמַר רַב ⁴**Rav said** in reply: A careful examination of the text of the vow reveals that the Israelites vowed that "no man **from us**" shall give his daughter to Benjamin as a wife. They swore that they themselves would not give their daughters in marriage to the Benjaminites, ⁵**but** they did **not** state that **their children** would also be bound by this oath. The day on which the Benjaminites were readmitted into the community of Israel was fixed as a minor holiday to be celebrated by future generations.

אָמַר רַבָּה בַּר בַּר חָנָה (3) ⁶Rabbah bar Bar Ḥanah said in the name of Rabbi Yoḥanan: ⁷The fifteenth of Av was the day on which the deaths of the Israelites in the wilderness ceased (see Numbers 14:32-34). Following the sin of the spies who were sent to explore the Land of Israel, God decreed that the Israelites must wander in the wilderness for forty years, and that all those who were twenty years and older when they left Egypt would perish in the wilderness. On the fifteenth of Av of the fortieth year, it became clear that the punishment had come to an end, and that all those who were to die had already perished. After the last members of that generation had died, God once again began to speak to Moses. ⁸**For** a certain **Sage** said: **As long as the death of** the Israelites in **the wilderness** of Sinai **had not ceased, God did not speak**

NOTES

permitted. *Rashbam* (*Bava Batra* 121a) explains that on the fifteenth of Av one year the last member of the generation that had entered Eretz Israel died, so that thenceforth there were no longer any restrictions barring the tribes of Israel from intermarrying. *Gevurat Ari* explains that it was on the fifteenth of Av that the Rabbis expounded the verse to permit the different tribes to intermarry.

יוֹם שֶׁכָּלוּ בּוֹ מֵתֵי מִדְבָּר The day on which the dead of the wilderness ceased. *Rashi, Tosafot,* and others cite a Midrash according to which every year on the eighth of Av a herald proclaimed in the camp of the Israelites: "Let each person dig his grave." Each person dug his grave, and spent the night in it. The next day a second herald proclaimed: "Let the living separate themselves from the dead." Whoever was still alive would rise up from his grave. Every year about fifteen thousand Israelites died. But on the ninth of Av of the fortieth year everybody who had lain in his grave rose up again in the morning. At first they thought that they had miscalculated, and that it was not yet the ninth of Av. Thus they lay in their graves every night for a week. When the fifteenth of Av arrived, the full moon that shone that night convinced them that the ninth of Av had passed,

עִם מֹשֶׁה, [1]שֶׁנֶּאֱמַר: ״וַיְהִי, כַּאֲשֶׁר תַּמּוּ כָּל אַנְשֵׁי הַמִּלְחָמָה לָמוּת..., וַיְדַבֵּר ה׳ אֵלַי״. [2]אֵלַי הָיָה הַדִּבּוּר.

[3]עוּלָּא אָמַר: יוֹם שֶׁבִּיטֵּל הוֹשֵׁעַ בֶּן אֵלָה פְּרוֹסְדִיּוֹת שֶׁהוֹשִׁיב יָרָבְעָם בֶּן נְבָט עַל הַדְּרָכִים, שֶׁלֹּא יַעֲלוּ יִשְׂרָאֵל לָרֶגֶל, [4]וְאָמַר: [31A] [5]לְאֵיזֶה שֶׁיִּרְצוּ יַעֲלוּ.

[6]רַב מַתְנָה אָמַר: יוֹם שֶׁנִּתְּנוּ הֲרוּגֵי בֵיתָר לִקְבוּרָה.

LITERAL TRANSLATION

to Moses, [1]as it is said: "And it came to pass, when all the men of war were consumed and dead [from among the people], that the Lord spoke to me." [2]To me was the speaking.

[3]Ulla said: [It was] the day on which Hoshea the son of Elah removed the guards whom Jeroboam the son of Nebat had placed on the roads, so that Israel should not go up on pilgrimage, [4]and he said: [31A] [5]They may go up to whichever they wish.

[6]Rav Matenah said: [It was] the day on which those killed at Betar were allowed to be buried.

TRANSLATION AND COMMENTARY

to Moses, [1]**as the verse says** (Deuteronomy 2:16-17): **"And it came to pass, when all the men of war were consumed and dead from among the people, that the Lord spoke to me."** [2]Only after the last members of that generation had died **did** God once again **speak to Moses,** but not before. In commemoration of the end of the punishment and to celebrate the resumption of God's direct communication with Moses, the fifteenth of Av was established as a minor holiday to be observed by later generations.

עוּלָּא אָמַר (4) [3]**Ulla said:** The fifteenth of Av **was the day on which** the last King of the Kingdom of Israel, **Hoshea the son of Elah, removed the guards whom** the first King of Israel, **Jeroboam the son of Nebat, had placed on the roads in order to prevent** the people of **Israel from going up** to Jerusalem **for the Pilgrim Festivals** of Pesaḥ, Shavuot, and Sukkot (see I Kings 12:28; II Kings 18:4). Although Hoshea removed the checkposts that had barred the people from reaching Jerusalem, he was nevertheless a wicked king, for after he cleared the roads, [4]**he said:** [31A] [5]The people **may go up** on pilgrimage **to whichever** place **they wish.** Those who wish to go to the Temple in Jerusalem may do so, and those who wish to go to the sanctuaries established by Jeroboam in Bet El and in Dan may do so. The removal of the guards blocking the road to Jerusalem was sufficient reason to establish the fifteenth of Av as a minor holiday.

רַב מַתְנָה אָמַר (5) [6]**Rav Matenah said:** The fifteenth of Av **was the day on which** the soldiers of Bar Kokhba's army who were **killed at Betar were allowed to be buried.** As was mentioned in our Mishnah, Betar,

RASHI

וכל שהיה בו נפש חיים — היה עומד ויוצא. וכל שנה היו עושין כן, ובשנת ארבעים שנה עשו, ולמחר עמדו כולן חיים, וכיון שראו כך תמהו ואמרו: שמא טעינו בחשבון החדש, חזרו ושכבו בקבריהן בלילות עד ליל חמשה עשר. וכיון שראו שנתמלאה הלבנה בחמשה עשר, ולא מת אחד מהם — ידעו שחשבון חדש מכוון, וכבר ארבעים שנה של גזרה נשלמו, קבעו אותו הדור לאותו היום יום טוב. **דאמר מר כו׳** — לפיכך יום טוב הוא. **לא היה הדבור עם משה** — ביחוד וחיבה, דכתיב ״וידבר ה׳ אלי לאמר״ — אלי נתייחד הדיבור. ואף על גב דמקמי הכי כתיבי קראי בהו ״וידבר״. איכא דאמרי: לא היה פה אל פה, אלא בחזיון לילה. גמגום. **לאיזה שירצה יעלו** — הושע בן אלה רשע היה, דכתיב (מלכים ב׳ יז) ״ויעש הרע בעיני ה׳ רק לא כמלכי ישראל״, והיינו דקאמר ״רק״ — שבטל את הפרוסדאות, ואמר: לאיזה שירצו יעלו. **הרוגי ביתר** — בפרק ״הניזקין״ (גיטין נז,א).

NOTES

and all those who were destined to die had already perished. (The Rishonim disagree as to whether all those who were supposed to die indeed perished in the wilderness, or whether those who were supposed to die during the fortieth year were pardoned.) In commemoration of the end of the punishment, the fifteenth of Av was established as a minor holiday for later generations. *Tosafot* (*Bava Batra* 121a) explains that the holiday was instituted in commemoration of the resumption of God's direct communication with Moses, which took place when the generation of the wilderness stopped dying. The regular number of Israelites died on the ninth of Av of the fortieth year, and a seven-day mourning period was then observed. At the conclusion of that period of mourning, on the fifteenth of Av, God's direct communication with Moses resumed and a holiday was celebrated.

אֵלַי הָיָה הַדִּבּוּר To me was the speaking. Though God did in fact speak to Moses during the Israelites' journey through the wilderness (see Deuteronomy 2:2), it was only after the last members of the generation of the wilderness had died that the divine revelation took the form of *dibbur*, a more direct form of communication than *amirah* (see *Rashi, Meiri, Rabbenu Beḥaye* on Deuteronomy 2:16-17).

לְאֵיזֶה שֶׁיִּרְצוּ יַעֲלוּ They may go up to whichever they wish. Hoshea was an evil king, as *Rashi* notes, for the verse states (II Kings 17:2): "And he [Hoshea the son of Elah] did what was evil in the sight of the Lord, but not like the kings of Israel who were before him." Hoshea was not as evil as the kings before him, because he removed the guards whom Jeroboam had placed on the roads in order to prevent the people of Israel from going to Jerusalem. But he was evil nevertheless, because he let the people choose whether to go to Jerusalem or to attend the idolatrous sanctuaries that had been established in Bet El and in Dan. The Jerusalem Talmud explains that Hoshea was punished for presenting the people of Israel with this choice, for during his reign Shalmaneser, King of Assyria, put an end to the Israelite Kingdom.

יוֹם שֶׁנִּתְּנוּ הֲרוּגֵי בֵיתָר לִקְבוּרָה The day on which those killed at Betar were allowed to be buried. *Gevurat Ari*

[1]וְאָמַר רַב מַתְנָה: אוֹתוֹ יוֹם שֶׁנִּתְּנוּ הֲרוּגֵי בֵיתָר לִקְבוּרָה [2]תִּקְּנוּ בְּיַבְנֶה "הַטּוֹב וְהַמֵּטִיב". [3]"הַטּוֹב" — שֶׁלֹּא הִסְרִיחוּ. [4]"וְהַמֵּטִיב" — שֶׁנִּתְּנוּ לִקְבוּרָה. [5]רַבָּה וְרַב יוֹסֵף דְּאָמְרִי תַּרְוַיְיהוּ: יוֹם שֶׁפָּסְקוּ מִלִּכְרוֹת עֵצִים לַמַּעֲרָכָה, [6]דְּתַנְיָא: "רַבִּי אֱלִיעֶזֶר הַגָּדוֹל אוֹמֵר: [7]מֵחֲמִשָּׁה עָשָׂר בְּאָב וְאֵילָךְ תָּשַׁשׁ כּוֹחָהּ שֶׁל חַמָּה, וְלֹא הָיוּ כּוֹרְתִין עֵצִים לַמַּעֲרָכָה, [8]לְפִי שֶׁאֵינָן יְבֵשִׁין".

LITERAL TRANSLATION

[1]And Rav Matenah said: [On] that day on which those killed at Betar were allowed to be buried [2]they instituted in Yavneh [the blessing] "Who is good and who does good." [3]"Who is good" — because they did not decompose. [4]"And who does good" — because they were allowed to be buried.

[5]Rabbah and Rav Yosef both said: [It was] the day on which they stopped chopping down trees for the pile of wood [on the altar], [6]for it was taught: "Rabbi Eliezer the Great says: [7]From the fifteenth of Av onward the strength of the sun weakens, and they would not chop down trees for the pile of wood [on the altar], [8]because they would not dry."

RASHI

מלכרות — לפי שהן לחין, ומאותו הזמן אין כח בחמה לייבשן. וחיישינן מפני התולעת, לפי שעץ שיש בו תולעת פסול למערכה, כדאמרינן (מדות פרק ב משנה ה).

TRANSLATION AND COMMENTARY

the last stronghold of the Bar Kokhba revolt, fell on the Ninth of Av. The Roman authorities did not allow the survivors to bring the fallen to burial until years later on the fifteenth of Av.

וְאָמַר רַב מַתְנָה [1]On the same subject, **Rav Matenah** also **said: On the day on which** the soldiers of Bar Kokhba's army who were **killed at Betar were allowed to be buried,** [2]the Rabbis **in** the Academy at **Yavneh instituted the blessing,** "Blessed are You, O Lord, our God, King of the Universe, **who is good and who does good,"** the fourth blessing of the Grace after Meals. To the original structure of the prayer containing three blessings — for sustenance, for the Land of Israel, and for the rebuilding of Jerusalem — the Rabbis of Yavneh added a fourth blessing in gratitude to God that the dead of Betar were brought to burial. [3]The first expression, **"who is good,"** was enacted in gratitude for the miracle **that** the corpses of the unburied dead **did not decompose**. [4]The second expression, **"and who does good,"** was instituted in gratitude for the miracle **that** the Roman authorities ultimately **allowed** the dead soldiers **to be buried.**

רַבָּה וְרַב יוֹסֵף דְּאָמְרִי תַּרְוַיְיהוּ (6) [5]**Rabbah and Rav Yosef both said:** The fifteenth of Av **was the day on which** each year **they stopped chopping down trees for the pile of wood** that was burned **on the altar.** This day was celebrated as a holiday because their obligation to supply firewood had been fulfilled, [6]**as was taught** in the following Baraita: **"Rabbi Eliezer the Great says:** [7]**From the fifteenth of Av onward the strength of the sun's** rays **grows weaker,** and this is why from that day onward **they would not chop down** any more **trees for the pile of wood** that was burned **on the altar,** [8]because the freshly cut logs would not dry adequately, and damp wood is unfit for the sacrificial services, there being concern that it may be infested with worms."

NOTES

asks: Surely the fifteenth of Av was celebrated as a holiday during the Second Temple period, for the Baraita cited below describes how the daughters of the High Priest, his deputy and the priest anointed for war would borrow clothing from each other on that day, and these priestly functions ceased with the destruction of the Temple. How, then, could the holiday celebrated on the fifteenth of Av have been instituted to commemorate a joyous event that took place after the Temple was destroyed?

Gevurat Ari suggests that the Baraita describing how the young women borrowed clothes from each other refers to the celebration that accompanied Yom Kippur, whereas the holiday celebrated on the fifteenth of Av was in fact instituted after the destruction of the Temple. Alternatively, it may be suggested that the holiday was indeed instituted in the time of the Second Temple, and Rav Matenah teaches us that because a number of joyous events had already occurred on the fifteenth of Av, another joyous event took place on that same date. Moreover, he explains why the day is observed as a semi-holiday even today.

HALAKHAH

תִּקְּנוּ בְּיַבְנֶה "הַטּוֹב וְהַמֵּטִיב" They instituted in Yavneh the blessing "Who is good and who does good." "The fourth blessing of the Grace after Meals, 'Who is good and who does good,' was enacted by the Sages of the Mishnah in Yavneh after those who died at Betar were brought to burial." (*Rambam, Sefer Ahavah, Hilkhot Berakhot* 2:1.)

חֲמִשָּׁה עָשָׂר בְּאָב The fifteenth of Av. "It is the custom on the fifteenth of Av not to recite the supplicatory prayers that follow the Amidah." (*Shulḥan Arukh, Oraḥ Ḥayyim* 131:6.)

LITERAL TRANSLATION

[1] Rav Menashya said: And they called it the day of the breaking of the saw.

[2] From now onward he who adds will add, [3] and he who does not add will be gathered.

[4] What is [meant by] "will be gathered"?

[5] Rav Yosef said: His mother will bury him.

[6] "For on them the daughters of Jerusalem, etc." [7] Our Rabbis taught: [8] "The daughter of the king borrows from the daughter of the High Priest, the daughter of the High Priest from the daughter of the deputy, and the daughter of the deputy from the daughter of the [priest] anointed for war, and the daughter of the [priest] anointed for war from the daughter of an ordinary priest, and all Israel borrow from each other, [9] so that she who does not have should not be embarrassed."

[10] "All the clothes require immersion."

[1] אָמַר רַב מְנַשְּׁיָא: וְקָרוּ לֵיהּ יוֹם תְּבַר מַגָּל.

[2] מִכָּאן וְאֵילָךְ דְּמוֹסִיף יוֹסִיף, [3] וּדְלָא מוֹסִיף יֶאֱסַף.

[4] מַאי ״יֶאֱסַף״?

[5] אָמַר רַב יוֹסֵף: תִּקְבְּרֵיהּ אִימֵּיהּ.

[6] ״שֶׁבָּהֶן בְּנוֹת יְרוּשָׁלַיִם, כו׳״.

[7] תָּנוּ רַבָּנַן: [8] ״בַּת מֶלֶךְ שׁוֹאֶלֶת מִבַּת כֹּהֵן גָּדוֹל, בַּת כֹּהֵן גָּדוֹל מִבַּת סְגָן, וּבַת סְגָן מִבַּת מְשׁוּחַ מִלְחָמָה, וּבַת מְשׁוּחַ מִלְחָמָה מִבַּת כֹּהֵן הֶדְיוֹט, וְכָל יִשְׂרָאֵל שׁוֹאֲלִין זֶה מִזֶּה, [9] כְּדֵי שֶׁלֹּא יִתְבַּיֵּישׁ אֶת מִי שֶׁאֵין לוֹ״.

[10] ״כָּל הַכֵּלִים טְעוּנִין טְבִילָה״.

TRANSLATION AND COMMENTARY

אָמַר רַב מְנַשְּׁיָא [1] **Rav Menashya said:** The fifteenth of Av **was called the day of** the **breaking** of **the saw,** for on that day the felling of trees for the Temple was discontinued.

מִכָּאן וְאֵילָךְ [2] The Gemara adds: **From** the fifteenth of Av **onward,** as the nights begin to grow longer, **he who adds** to the time he engages in the study of Torah at night **adds** years to his life, as the verse says (Proverbs 3:2): "For length of days, and long life, and peace, shall they add to you." [3] **And he who does not add** to the time he spends studying Torah at night **will be gathered.**

מַאי ״יֶאֱסַף״ [4] The Gemara asks: **What is meant by** the expression **"will be gathered"?**

אָמַר רַב יוֹסֵף [5] **Rav Yosef said:** If someone does not spend adequate time studying Torah, **his mother will bury him,** for he will be "gathered unto his people" prematurely (see Genesis 49:33). A person who neglects his Torah studies shows that he does not wish for a long life, and so he dies early.

שֶׁבָּהֶן בְּנוֹת יְרוּשָׁלַיִם [6] We learned in the Mishnah: "There were no days as joyous for the people of Israel as the Fifteenth of Av and Yom Kippur, **for on** those days **the daughters of Jerusalem** would all go out in borrowed white clothes and would dance in the vineyards." [7] **Our Rabbis taught** the following Baraita, which describes the celebration in greater detail: "All the daughters of Jerusalem would dress themselves in borrowed white clothes — even the daughters of the rich who had enough clothing of their own. [8] **The daughter of the king would borrow** a white garment **from the daughter of the High Priest, the daughter of the High Priest** would borrow **from the daughter of the** High Priest's **deputy, the daughter of the** High Priest's **deputy** would borrow **from the daughter of the priest anointed for war** [the priest who before the people set out to war was appointed to perform certain duties in connection with the war and who was governed by some of the regulations applying to a High Priest], **the daughter of the priest anointed for war** would borrow **from the daughter of an ordinary priest, and all** the daughters of ordinary **Israelites** would borrow white garments **from** each other. [9] **All would dress themselves in borrowed clothes so as not to** embarrass those who do not have any."

כָּל הַכֵּלִים טְעוּנִין טְבִילָה [10] The Mishnah continues: "**All the clothes** which the young women would borrow **required** ritual **immersion** before being worn, lest they had previously been worn by a woman who was

RASHI

יום תבר מגל — שבירת הגרזן, שפסק החוטב מלחטוב עצים. **מכאן ואילך** — מחמשה עשר באב ואילך, דמוסיף לילות על הימים לעסוק בתורה — יוסיף חיים על חייו. **דלא יוסיף** — לעסוק בתורה בלילות. **תקבריה אימיה** — כלומר: ימות בלא עתו. **בת מלך** — אף על פי שהיה לה — שואלת מבת כהן גדול כו׳, שלא לבייש את השואלת מתוך שאין לה. **מבת כהן גדול** — שהוא קרוב וסמוך למלכות. **סגן** — כהן חשוב, ממונה תחת כהן גדול להיות תחתיו ביום הכפורים, אם יארע פסול בכהן גדול ביום הכפורים — ישמש זה הסגן תחתיו. **משוח מלחמה** — הוא הכהן המכריז במלחמה ״מי האיש הירא ורך הלבב״ וגו׳ (דברים כ).

NOTES

בַּת מֶלֶךְ שׁוֹאֶלֶת מִבַּת כֹּהֵן גָּדוֹל The daughter of the king borrows from the daughter of the High Priest. Ordinarily, a person borrows from a person who enjoys a higher economic and social status than he does. But here, the Rabbis arranged that the daughter of a person of higher status should borrow from the daughter of a person of lower status, so that nobody would be embarrassed to borrow and everybody would be dressed in similar clothing (*Sfat Emet*).

טְעוּנִין טְבִילָה Require immersion. Most Rishonim explain that the clothes that the young women borrowed from each other required ritual immersion because the clothes might

BACKGROUND

בַּת מֶלֶךְ The daughter of the king. This hierarchy, presented in descending order of importance, is the official hierarchy of Israel. In tractate *Horayot* there is a fuller list of the holders of various offices according to their importance and the honor that must be given to every one of them.

LANGUAGE

סְגָן Deputy. The Deputy High Priest was responsible for the internal organization of the Temple. He had another very important task, for on Yom Kippur (when most of the Temple service was performed by the High Priest), if the High Priest was unable to fulfill his function, the Deputy High Priest would do so.

CONCEPTS

מְשׁוּחַ מִלְחָמָה The priest anointed for war. Before the Jews set out to war, a special priest was appointed to perform certain duties in connection with the war. This priest, who was anointed with שֶׁמֶן הַמִּשְׁחָה — "the anointing oil" — was called the מְשׁוּחַ מִלְחָמָה. He was responsible for reminding those exempt from fighting to return home, and for encouraging the other soldiers to go out and fight, as stated in the Torah (Deuteronomy 20:2ff). The אוּרִים וְתוּמִּים — "oracular stones" — in the breastplate that he wore would be consulted before the army went out to battle. The same prohibitions that apply to a High Priest applied to the מְשׁוּחַ מִלְחָמָה, although he did not bring the sacrifices brought by a High Priest, and his special status was not inherited by his sons. The institution of מְשׁוּחַ מִלְחָמָה ceased to exist as far back as the beginning of the Second Temple period.

¹אָמַר רַבִּי אֶלְעָזָר: אֲפִילּוּ מְקוּפָּלִין וּמוּנָּחִין בְּקוּפְסָא.
²״בְּנוֹת יִשְׂרָאֵל יוֹצְאוֹת וְחוֹלוֹת בַּכְּרָמִים״. ³תָּנָא: ״מִי שֶׁאֵין לוֹ אִשָּׁה נִפְנֶה לְשָׁם״.
⁴״מְיוּחָסוֹת שֶׁבָּהֶן הָיוּ אוֹמְרוֹת: ׳בָּחוּר, וכו׳׳״. ⁵תָּנוּ רַבָּנַן: ״יְפֵיפִיּוֹת שֶׁבָּהֶן מֶה הָיוּ אוֹמְרוֹת? ⁶׳תְּנוּ עֵינֵיכֶם לְיוֹפִי, שֶׁאֵין הָאִשָּׁה אֶלָּא לְיוֹפִי׳. ⁷מְיוּחָסוֹת שֶׁבָּהֶן מֶה הָיוּ אוֹמְרוֹת? ⁸׳תְּנוּ עֵינֵיכֶם לַמִּשְׁפָּחָה, לְפִי שֶׁאֵין הָאִשָּׁה אֶלָּא לְבָנִים׳. ⁹מְכוֹעָרוֹת שֶׁבָּהֶם מֶה הָיוּ אוֹמְרוֹת? ¹⁰׳קְחוּ מִקַּחֲכֶם לְשׁוּם שָׁמַיִם, וּבִלְבַד שֶׁתְּעַטְּרוּנוּ בִּזְהוּבִים׳״.

TRANSLATION AND COMMENTARY

ritually impure." [1]**Rabbi Elazar says: Even** if the **clothes were folded and lying in a box,** they had to undergo ritual immersion before being worn.

בְּנוֹת יִשְׂרָאֵל [2]We learned in the Mishnah: "On the Fifteenth of Av, **the daughters of Israel would go out** in borrowed clothes **and dance in the vineyards."** [3]**A Tanna taught** a Baraita, which stated: "Any man **who did not have a wife would enter** the vineyards and choose a bride from among the young women he saw dancing there, and if she and her family agreed, they would be betrothed."

מְיוּחָסוֹת שֶׁבָּהֶן [4]The Mishnah continues: **"Those of distinguished lineage among** the daughters of Israel **would say** to a young man who followed them into the vineyards in search of a wife: **'Young man!** Lift up your eyes and see what you are choosing for yourself. Do not set your eyes on a woman's beauty, but rather on her lineage.'" [5]**Our Rabbis taught** the following Baraita: **"What would the beautiful among** the daughters of Israel **say** to the young men? [6]**'Set your eyes on beauty, for a wife is only** to be chosen **for** her **beauty.'** [7]**What would those of distinguished lineage among** the young women **say** to their potential suitors? [8]**'Set your eyes on family, for a wife is only for children,** and a woman of distinguished lineage will bring into the world children of similar distinction.' [9]What would the **ugly among** the young women **say**? 'Do not be seduced by a woman's beauty. [10]Acquire your purchase for the sake of Heaven, but only provided that** after the marriage **you adorn us with golden** jewels, to make us more attractive.'"

LITERAL TRANSLATION

[1]Rabbi Elazar says: Even [clothes] that are folded and lying in a box.

[2]"The daughters of Israel would go out and dance in the vineyards." [3][A Tanna] taught: "He who did not have a wife turned to there."

[4]"Those of distinguished lineage among them would say: 'Young man, etc.'" [5]Our Rabbis taught: "What would the beautiful among them say? [6]'Set your eyes on beauty, for a wife is only for beauty.' [7]What would those of distinguished lineage among them say? [8]'Set your eyes on family, for a wife is only for children.' [9]What would the ugly among them say? [10]'Acquire your purchase for the sake of Heaven, but only provided that you adorn us with golden jewels.'"

RASHI

אפילו מקופלין ומונחין בקופסא — *אישקוריי״ן. **צריכין טבילה** — כולן, שלא לבייש את שצריכה טבילה. **שאין אשה אלא לבנים** — אם בניך יהיו מיוחסין הכל קופצין עליהם, בין זכרים בין נקבות. **על מנת שתעטרונו בזהובים** — שאחרי הנישואין תתנו לנו תכשיטין. ומילתא בעלמא הוא דאמרי, כלומר: ובלבד שתתנו לנו מלבושים נאים.

LANGUAGE (RASHI)

אישקוריי״ן* From the Old French *escrin*, which means "a cupboard" or "a box."

NOTES

have contracted ritual impurity by being worn by a woman who was ritually impure. Even clothes that had been folded away in boxes required ritual immersion, so as not to embarrass those women who were indeed ritually impure and whose clothes needed to be immersed, and so as not to create a situation in which the more meticulous about ritual impurity would refrain from borrowing clothes from those who were less meticulous (*Rashi, Rid, Rabbenu Yehonatan*). The Jerusalem Talmud (cited by *Ra'avad* and others) explains this regulation differently: The Rabbis enacted that all clothes must undergo ritual immersion so that the young women would be more willing to lend them out. Once the garments had been taken out of storage for immersion (*Ritva*), and once they had become wet (*Mikhtam*), even those young women who would otherwise have preferred not to lend out their clothes would be ready to exchange their clothes with the others.

בְּנוֹת יִשְׂרָאֵל יוֹצְאוֹת וְחוֹלוֹת The daughters of Israel would go out and dance. The Geonim explain that this practice commemorates the readmission of the Benjaminites into the community of Israel, for they too were told to lie in wait in the vineyards, and to select wives for themselves from among the daughters of Shiloh who came out to dance (Judges 21:20-23).

The Rishonim ask: How is it possible that the Rabbis sanctioned this practice, encouraging young men to go out to the vineyards and take wives for themselves from among the young women dancing there? *Rabbenu Yehonatan* says that the men would only betroth the young women after receiving permission from the girls' parents. *Mikhtam* explains that this practice was organized primarily for those young women for whom it was difficult to find fitting partners. It was considered preferable that they find husbands that way than that they remain unmarried.

שֶׁתְּעַטְּרוּנוּ בִּזְהוּבִים That you adorn us with golden jewels. *Rabbi Ya'akov Emden* suggests that this should be understood in the light of the Mishnaic statement (*Nedarim* 66a): "The daughters of Israel are beautiful; it is only poverty that makes them ugly." With the proper treatment even the ugly among them can be made to appear attractive. According

TRANSLATION AND COMMENTARY

אָמַר עוּלָּא בִּירָאָה [1]The discussion now turns from the annual dancing of the young women in the vineyards on the fifteenth of Av to the future dancing of the righteous in the Garden of Eden: **Ulla of Birya said in the name of Rabbi Elazar: In the future** world, **the Holy One, blessed be He, will arrange a** dancing **circle for the righteous, and He will sit among them in the Garden of Eden and** will reveal Himself in such a way that **each** of the righteous **will** be able to **point to Him with his finger** and say, "Behold, this is our God," [2]**as the verse says** (Isaiah 25:9): **"And it shall be said on that day: Behold, this is our God; we have waited for Him that He should save us. [3]This is the Lord; we have waited for Him. We will be glad and rejoice in His salvation."**

[1]אָמַר עוּלָּא בִּירָאָה אָמַר רַבִּי אֶלְעָזָר: עָתִיד הַקָּדוֹשׁ בָּרוּךְ הוּא לַעֲשׂוֹת מָחוֹל לַצַּדִּיקִים, וְהוּא יוֹשֵׁב בֵּינֵיהֶם בְּגַן עֵדֶן, וְכָל אֶחָד וְאֶחָד מַרְאֶה בְּאֶצְבָּעוֹ, [2]שֶׁנֶּאֱמַר: "וְאָמַר בַּיּוֹם הַהוּא: הִנֵּה, אֱלֹהֵינוּ זֶה; קִוִּינוּ לוֹ וְיוֹשִׁיעֵנוּ. [3]זֶה ה׳; קִוִּינוּ לוֹ. נָגִילָה וְנִשְׂמְחָה בִּישׁוּעָתוֹ".

הדרן עלך בשלשה פרקים וסליקא לה מסכת תענית

LITERAL TRANSLATION

[1]Ulla of Birya said in the name of Rabbi Elazar: In the future, the Holy One, blessed be He, will arrange a circle for the righteous, and He will sit among them in the Garden of Eden, and each and every one will point [to Him] with his finger, [2]as it is said: "And it shall be said on that day: Behold, this is our God; we have waited for Him that He should save us. [3]This is the Lord; we have waited for Him. We will be glad and rejoice in His salvation."

RASHI

מחול – סביב, לשון "מחול הכרם" (כלאים, פרק רביעי משנה א). **מראה באצבעו** – ואומר: זה ה׳ קוינו לו ויושיענו, זה ה׳ קוינו לו נגילה ונשמחה בישועתו.

הדרן עלך בשלשה פרקים וסליקא לה מסכת תענית

BACKGROUND

מָחוֹל לַצַּדִּיקִים A circle for the righteous. The conceptual connection between the dancing of the maidens of Jerusalem and the metaphysical dancing of the righteous in the World-to-Come is a direct continuation of the conclusion of the Mishnah, which gives the expression "his wedding day" a more extended and exalted meaning. The conclusion of the tractate gives the dancing of the maidens an allegorical meaning — it is likened to the status of Saints ("the daughters of Jerusalem," according to allegorical interpretations) who achieve total spiritual devotion ("marriage") to the Creator.

NOTES

to a variant reading, "that you are adorned with golden jewels," the unattractive young women told their potential suitors that those who selected wives for the sake of Heaven would be rewarded with wealth and honor.

מָחוֹל לַצַּדִּיקִים A circle for the righteous. *Rabbenu Beḥaye* (*Commentary* to Exodus 25:31) explains that the dancing circle symbolizes something that has no beginning or end. Thus the righteous are promised endless spiritual reward in the World-to-Come. *Alshikh* adds that at that time all the righteous will attain prophetic powers, so that each will be able to use his finger to point to God's revelation. At that time the secrets of the Torah will be revealed to the righteous (*Kaftor VaFeraḥ*). The entire matter is alluded to in the verse (Jeremiah 31:12). "Then shall the virgin rejoice in the dance, both young men and old together, for I will turn their mourning to joy, and will comfort them, and make them rejoice from their sorrow." This verse alludes to the spiritual revelations that will take place in the future, and associates the dancing of the young women on their days of joy with the dancing of the righteous in the World-to-Come (*Maharal*).

Conclusion to Chapter Four

The common denominator connecting the *ma'amad* assemblies with the wood-offerings was that both institutions were designed to allow the entire people of Israel to participate in various ways in the Temple service. Though the essential aspects of the sacrificial service in the Temple were performed by the priests, the entire people (or special representatives of it) were given certain opportunities to participate in the Temple ritual. In the course of the discussion relating to the regulations governing the *ma'amad* assemblies and the days on which wood-offerings were brought, the rule was laid down that on days of joy — whether Biblically-ordained Festivals, or days on which Hallel was recited, or days on which a wood-offering was brought — the special services conducted at the *ma'amad* assemblies were reduced, and the festive aspects of these days were emphasized.

The second topic discussed at length in our chapter relates to the fixed public fast days. The national calamities commemorated by the various public fasts were explained in detail. Special attention was given to the laws relating to the Ninth of Av, the major day of mourning for the destruction of the Temple. Not only was the day established as a public fast, but it was treated like the great public fasts observed during times of extended drought. Thus, the fast must be observed from sunset to sunset, and not only eating but also various other pleasurable activities are forbidden. In addition, a person is obliged to observe on that day all the mourning rites that apply in the case of the death of a close relative. Some of these mourning rites must be observed even before the Ninth of Av, during the week of the fast, or even from the beginning of the month.

In order to end the chapter (as well as the tractate) on a happier note, the chapter concluded with a description of the joyous celebrations that took place on Yom Kippur and on the fifteenth of Av.

List of Sources

Aggadot Bereshit, collection of Aggadot from the Talmud with commentary, by an author whose name is not known.

Aharonim, lit., "the last," meaning Rabbinical authorities from the time of the publication of Rabbi Yosef Caro's code of Halakhah, *Shulḥan Arukh* (1555).

Ahavat Eitan, novellae on Aggadot in the Talmud, by Rabbi Avraham Maskileison, Byelorussia (1788-1848).

Alshikh, Rabbi Moshe, Bible commentator, Safed, Israel, 16th century.

Arba'ah Turim, code of Halakhah by Rabbi Ya'akov ben Asher, b. Germany, active in Spain (c. 1270-1343).

Arukh, first Talmudic dictionary, by Rabbi Natan of Rome, 11th century.

Arukh HaShulḥan, commentary on *Shulḥan Arukh*, by Rabbi Yeḥiel Mikhel Epstein, Byelorussia (1829-1908).

Ba'al HaMa'or, Rabbi Zeraḥyah ben Yitzḥak HaLevi, Spain, 12th century. *HaMa'or*, Halakhic commentary on *Hilkhot HaRif.*

Ba'er Hetev, commentary on *Shulḥan Arukh*, by Rabbi Zeḥaryah Mendel of Belz, Poland (18th century).

Bah (Bayit Ḥadash), commentary on *Arba'ah Turim*, by Rabbi Yoel Sirkes, Poland (1561-1640).

Bereshit Rabbah, Midrash on the Book of Genesis.

Bertinoro, Rabbi Ovadyah, 15th century Italian commentator on the Mishnah.

Bet Yosef, Halakhic commentary on *Arba'ah Turim*, by Rabbi Yosef Caro (1488-1575), which is the basis of his authoritative Halakhic code, the *Shulḥan Arukh.*

Darkhei Moshe, commentary on *Tur*, by Rabbi Moshe ben Yisrael Isserles, Poland (1525-1572).

Derash Moshe, novellae on *Ein Ya'akov*, by Rabbi Moshe ben Yitzḥak, Moravia, 16th century.

Derishah and *Perishah*, commentaries on *Tur*, by Rabbi Yehoshua Falk Katz, Poland (c. 1555-1614).

Dikkdukei Soferim, a collection of variant readings on tractates of the Talmud, by Rabbi Raphael Natan Nata Rabbinovicz, Russia (1835 1888).

Divrei Shlomo, glosses on the Talmud, by Rabbi Zalman Rivlin, Poland, 19th century.

Ein Ya'akov, collection of Aggadot from the Babylonian Talmud by Rabbi Ya'akov ben Shlomo Ḥabib, Spain and Salonika (c. 1445-1515).

Eliyah Rabbah, commentary on *Shulḥan Arukh, Orah Ḥayyim*, by Rabbi Eliyahu Shapira, Prague (1660-1712).

Eshel Avraham, novellae on the Talmud, by Rabbi Avraham Ya'akov Neimark, Israel (20th century).

Eshkol, Halakhic compondium, by Rabbi Avraham ben Yitzḥak of Narbonne, France (c. 1110-1179).

Even HaEzer, section of *Shulḥan Arukh* dealing with marriage, divorce, and related topics.

Geonim, heads of the academies of Sura and Pumbedita in Babylonia from the late 6th century to the mid-11th century.

Gevurat Ari, novellae on the Talmud, by Rabbi Aryeh Leib ben Asher, Lithuania, 18th century.

Gilyon HaShas, glosses on the Talmud, by Rabbi Akiva Eger, Posen, Germany (1761-1837).

Gra, Rabbi Eliyahu ben Shlomo Zalman (1720-1797), the Gaon of Vilna. Novellae on the Talmud and *Shulḥan Arukh.*

HaKotev, commentary on *Ein Ya'akov*, by Rabbi Ya'akov ben Shlomo Ḥabib (author of *Ein Ya'akov*), Spain and Salonika (c. 1445-1515).

Hashlamah, see *Sefer HaHashlamah.*

Ḥokhmat Manoaḥ, commentary on the Talmud, by Rabbi Manoaḥ ben Shemaryah, Poland, 16th century.

Iyyun Ya'akov, commentary on *Ein Ya'akov*, by Rabbi Ya'akov bar Yosef Riesher, Prague, Poland and France (d. 1773)

Kaftor VaFeraḥ, novellae on Aggadah, by Rabbi Ya'akov ben Yitzḥak Luzzato, Safed, Israel, 16th century.

Keren Orah, novellae on the Talmud, by Rabbi Yitzḥak Karlin, Poland, 19th century.

Kesef Mishneh, commentary on Mishneh Torah, by Rabbi Yosef Caro, author of *Shulḥan Arukh.*

Lamentations Rabbah, Aggadic Midrash on the Book of Lamentations.

Leḥem Mishneh, commentary on *Mishneh Torah,* by Rabbi Avraham di Boton, Salonika (1560-1609).

Levush, abbreviation of *Levush Mordekhai,* Halakhic code by Rabbi Mordekhai Yafe, Poland (1530-1612).

Magen Avraham, commentary on *Shulḥan Arukh, Oraḥ Ḥayyim,* by Rabbi Avraham HaLevi Gombiner, Poland (d. 1683).

Maggid Mishneh, commentary on *Mishneh Torah,* by Rabbi Vidal de Tolosa, Spain, 14th century.

Maharal, Rabbi Yehudah Loew ben Betzalel of Prague (1525-1631). Novellae on the Talmud.

Maharsha, Rabbi Shmuel Eliezer ben Yehudah HaLevi Edels, Poland (1555-1631). Novellae on the Talmud.

Maḥatzit HaShekel, commentary on *Magen Avraham,* by Rabbi Shmuel HaLevi, Poland, 18th century.

Meiri, commentary on the Talmud (called *Bet HaBeḥirah*), by Rabbi Menaḥem ben Shlomo, Provence (1249-1316).

Melekhet Shlomo, commentary on the Mishnah, by Rabbi Shlomo Adeni, Yemen and Eretz Israel (1567-1626).

Midrash Shoḥer Tov, Aggadic Midrash on the Book of Psalms.

Mikhtam, Halakhic treatise, by Rabbi David ben Levi, Narbonne, France, 13th-14th century.

Mishnah Berurah, commentary on *Shulḥan Arukh, Oraḥ Ḥayyim,* by Rabbi Yisrael Meir HaKohen, Poland (1837-1933).

Mordekhai, compendium of Halakhic decisions, by Rabbi Mordekhai ben Hillel HaKohen, Germany (1240?-1298).

Nefesh HaḤayyim, treatise on ethics and Kabbalah, by Rabbi Ḥayyim of Volozhin, Lithuania (1749-1821).

Nezer HaKodesh, commentary on *Midrash Rabbah,* by Rabbi Yeḥiel Mikhal ben Uzziel, Vienna (d. 1730).

Nimmukei Yosef, commentary on *Hilkhot Rif,* by Rabbi Yosef Ḥaviva, Spain, early 15th century.

Oraḥ Ḥayyim, section of *Shulḥan Arukh* dealing with daily religious observances, prayers, and the laws of the Sabbath and Festivals.

Otzar HaKavod, commentary on Aggadah in the Talmud, by Rabbi Todros Abulafiya, Spain (1234-c. 1304).

Perishah, see *Derishah.*

Pesikta DeRav Kahana, Aggadic Midrash.

Petaḥ Enayim, novellae on the Talmud, by Rabbi Ḥayyim Yosef David Azulai, Israel and Italy (1724-1807).

Pirkei DeRabbi Eliezer, Aggadic Midrash on the Torah.

Pri Ḥadash, novellae on *Shulḥan Arukh,* by Rabbi Ḥizkiyah Da Silva, Livorno, Italy and Eretz Israel (1659-1698).

Pri Megadim, super-commentary to commentaries on *Shulḥan Arukh,* by Rabbi Yosef Te'omim, Lvov, Ukraine, and Germany (1727-1793).

Ra'avad, Rabbi Avraham ben David, commentator and Halakhic authority. Wrote comments on *Mishneh Torah*. Provence (c. 1125-1198?).

Rabbenu Efraim, Efraim Ibn Avi Alragan, Halakhist, North Africa, late 11th-early 12th century.

Rabbenu Elyakim, German Talmudist, 11th century.

Rabbenu Gershom, commentator and Halakhic authority, France (960-1040).

Rabbenu Ḥananel (ben Ḥushiel), commentator on Talmud, North Africa (990-1055).

Rabbenu Meshullam, French Tosafist, 12th century.

Rabbenu Tam, commentator on Talmud, Tosafist, France (1100-1171).

Rabbenu Yehonatan, Yehonatan ben David HaKohen of Lunel, Provence, Talmudic scholar (c. 1135-after 1210).

Rabbi Akiva Eger, Talmudist and Halakhic authority, Posen, Germany (1761-1837).

Rabbi David Kimḥi (Radak), grammarian and Bible commentator, Narbonne, Provence (1160?-1235?).

Rabbi Tzvi Ḥayyot, (Chajes), Galician Rabbi, 19th century.

Rabbi Ya'akov Emden,, Talmudist and Halakhic authority, Germany (1697-1776).

Rabbi Ya'akov of Orleans, French Tosafist, died London, 1189.

Ramat Shmuel, novellae on the Talmud, by Rabbi Shmuel HaLevi, 16th century.

Rambam, Rabbi Moshe ben Maimon, Rabbi and philosopher, known also as Maimonides. Author of *Mishneh Torah*, Spain and Egypt (1135-1204).

Ramban, Rabbi Moshe ben Naḥman, commentator on Bible and Talmud, known also as Naḥmanides, Spain and Eretz Israel (1194-1270).

Ran, Rabbi Nissim ben Reuven Gerondi, Spanish Talmudist (1310?-1375?).

Rash, Rabbenu Shimshon of Sens. Commentary on the Mishnah on the Order of *Zeraim.* France and Eretz Israel (died c. 1230).

Rashash, Rabbi Shmuel ben Yosef Shtrashun, Lithuanian Talmudic scholar (1794-1872).

Rashba, Rabbi Shlomo ben Avraham Adret, Spanish Rabbi famous for his commentaries on the Talmud and his responsa (c. 1235-c. 1314).

Rashbam, Rabbi Shmuel ben Meir, commentator on the Talmud, France (1085-1158).

Rashi, Rabbi Shlomo ben Yitzḥak, the paramount commentator on the Bible and the Talmud, France (1040-1105).

Rav Amram Gaon, Amram ben Sheshna, Gaon of Sura (died c. 875).

Rav Hai Gaon, Babylonian Rabbi, head of Pumbedita Yeshivah, 10th century.

Rema, Rabbi Moshe ben Yisrael Isserles, Halakhic authority, Cracow, Poland (1525-1572).

Ri, Rabbi Yitzḥak ben Shmuel of Dampierre, Tosafist, France (died c. 1185).

Ri of Lunel, see *Rabbenu Yehonatan*.

Riaf, Rabbi Yoshiyah ben Yosef Pinto, Eretz Israel and Syria (1565-1648). Commentary on *Ein Ya'akov.*

Rid, see *Tosefot Rid*.

Rif, Rabbi Yitzḥak Alfasi, Halakhist, author of *Hilkhot HaRif,* North Africa (1013-1103).

Rishon LeTzion, novellae on the Talmud, by Rabbi Ḥayyim Ibn Attar, Italy and Eretz Israel (1696-1743).

Rishonim, lit., "the first," meaning Rabbinical authorities active between the end of the Geonic period (mid-11th century) and the publication of the *Shulḥan Arukh* (1555).

Ritva, novellae and commentary on the Talmud, by Rabbi Yom Tov ben Avraham Ishbili, Spain (c. 1250-1330).

Rivash, Rabbi Yitzḥak ben Sheshet, Spain and North Africa (1326-1408). Novellae on the Talmud mentioned in *Shittah Mekubbetzet.*

Rosh, Rabbi Asher ben Yeḥiel, also known as Asheri, commentator and Halakhist, Germany and Spain (c. 1250-1327).

Rosh Yosef, novellae on the Talmud, by Rabbi Yosef ben Ya'akov of Pinczow, Lithuania, 17th century.

Sefer HaHashlamah, supplement to *Hilkhot HaRif,* by Rabbi Meshullam ben Moshe, Provence, early 13th century.

Sefer HaMa'or (see *Ba'al HaMa'or*)

Sefer HaMeorot, commentary on *Ta'anit,* by Rabbi Meir ben Shimon HaMe'ili, Narbonne, France, 13th century.

Sfat Emet, novellae on the Talmud, by Rabbi Yehudah Leib Alter, Poland, 19th century.

Sha'ar HaGemul, treatise on resurrection and reward and punishment, by *Ramban.* See *Ramban.*

Sha'arei Teshuvah, commentary and responsa on *Shulḥan Arukh,* by Rabbi Ḥayyim Mordekhai Margoliyot, Poland, 18th-19th century.)

Shakh (Sifte Kohen), commentary on *Shulḥan Arukh* by Rabbi Shabbetai ben Meir HaKohen, Lithuania (1621-1662).

Sheiltot, by Aḥa (Aḥai) of Pumbedita Yeshivah (650-702). One of the first books of Halakhah arranged by subjects.

Shelah (Shenei Luḥot HaBrit), an extensive work on Halakhah, ethics and Kabbalah, by Rabbi Yeshayahu ben Avraham HaLevi Horowitz. Prague, Poland and Eretz Israel (c. 1565-1630).

Shittah, commentary on tractate *Ta'anit,* attributed to Rabbenu Ḥayyim ben Rabbi Shmuel ben David of Toledo, Spain, 13th-14th century.

Shulḥan Arukh, code of Halakhah by Rabbi Yosef Caro, b. Spain, active in Eretz Israel (1488-1575).

Smag (Sefer Mitzvot Gadol), an extensive work on the positive and negative commandments by Rabbi Moshe ben Ya'akov of Coucy, 13th century.

Talmid HaRamban, commentary on *Hilkhot HaRif* on tractate *Ta'anit,* by a student of *Ramban,* 13th century.

Targum Onkelos, Aramaic translation of the Five Books of Moses, attributed to the proselyte Onkelos, Eretz Israel, 2nd century C.E.

Taz, abbreviation for *Turei Zahav.* See *Turei Zahav.*

Teshuvot HaRamban, responsa literature, by *Ramban* (see *Ramban*).

Tiferet Israel, commentary on the Mishnah, by Rabbi Yisrael Lipshitz, Germany (1782-1860).

Torat Ḥayyim, novellae on the Talmud, by Rabbi Avraham Ḥayyim Shor, Galicia (d.1632).

Tosafot, collection of commentaries and novellae on the Talmud, expanding on Rashi's commentary, by the French-German Tosafists (12th-13th centuries).

Tosefot Rid, commentary on the Talmud by Rabbi Yeshayahu ben Mali di Trani, Italian Halakhist (c. 1200-before 1260).

Tosefot Rosh, an edition based on *Tosefot Sens* by the *Rosh,* Rabbi Asher ben Yeḥiel, Germany-Spain (c. 1250-1327).

Tosefot Yom Tov, commentary on the Mishnah by Rabbi Yom Tov Lipman HaLevi Heller, Prague and Poland (1579-1654).

Tur, abbreviation of *Arba'ah Turim*, Halakhic code by Rabbi Ya'akov ben Asher, b. Germany, active in Spain (c. 1270-1343).

Yalkut (see *Yalkut Shimoni*)

Yalkut Shimoni, Aggadic Midrash on the Bible.

Ya'akov Castro, Rabbinic authority, Egypt and Eretz Israel (1525-1610).

Yoreh De'ah, section of *Shulḥan Arukh* dealing with dietary laws, interest, ritual purity, and mourning.

About the Type

This book was set in Leawood, a contemporary typeface designed by Leslie Usherwood. His staff completed the design upon Usherwood's death in 1984. It is a friendly, inviting face that goes particularly well with sans serif type.